Lecture Notes in Computer Science 13864

Founding Editors

Gerhard Goos
Juris Hartmanis

Editorial Board Members

The series Lecture Notes in Computer Science (LNCS), including its subseries Lecture Notes in Artificial Intelligence (LNAI) and Lecture Notes in Bioinformatics (LNBI), has established itself as a medium for the publication of new developments in computer science and information technology research, teaching, and education.

LNCS enjoys close cooperation with the computer science R & D community, the series counts many renowned academics among its volume editors and paper authors, and collaborates with prestigious societies. Its mission is to serve this international community by providing an invaluable service, mainly focused on the publication of conference and workshop proceedings and postproceedings. LNCS commenced publication in 1973.

Ching-Hsien Hsu · Mengwei Xu · Hung Cao ·
Hojjat Baghban · A. B. M. Shawkat Ali
Editors

Big Data Intelligence and Computing

International Conference, DataCom 2022
Denarau Island, Fiji, December 8–10, 2022
Proceedings

Editors
Ching-Hsien Hsu (iD)
Asia University
Taichung, Taiwan

Hung Cao
University of New Brunswick
Fredericton, NB, Canada

A. B. M. Shawkat Ali
University of Fiji
Samabula, Fiji

Mengwei Xu
Beijing University of Posts
and Telecommunications
Beijing, China

Hojjat Baghban (iD)
Asia University
Taichung, Taiwan

ISSN 0302-9743   ISSN 1611-3349 (electronic)
Lecture Notes in Computer Science
ISBN 978-981-99-2232-1   ISBN 978-981-99-2233-8 (eBook)
https://doi.org/10.1007/978-981-99-2233-8

This Springer imprint is published by the registered company Springer Nature Singapore Pte Ltd.
The registered company address is: 152 Beach Road, #21-01/04 Gateway East, Singapore 189721, Singapore

Preface

Big data is a rapidly expanding research area spanning the fields of computer science and information management and has become a ubiquitous term in understanding and solving complex problems in different disciplinary fields such as engineering, applied mathematics, medicine, computational biology, healthcare, social networks, finance, business, government, education, transportation, and telecommunications. Big data analytics solutions, distributed computation paradigms, on-demand services, autonomic systems, and pervasive applications and services are all expected to benefit from the development of future computing. This volume contains the proceedings of the 2022 International Conference on Big Data Intelligence and Computing (DataCom 2022), which was held at the Sheraton Fiji Golf, Denarau Island, Fiji on December 8–10, 2022. DataCom 2022 was collocated with two symposia, 1. Space-Air-Ground Computing for Big Data Applications, and 2. Future Computing Paradigm for Big Data Analysis.

This year, we received a total of 88 submissions from 20 countries and regions. All papers were rigorously and independently peer-reviewed by the Technical Program Committee members. After a thorough review process, in which each paper was evaluated by at least three reviewers, 30 papers were selected as regular papers (acceptance rate 34.1%) and 10 papers were recommended as short papers for presentation and publication. We believe that the program and this volume present novel and interesting ideas.

The organization of conferences requires a lot of hard work and dedication from many people. DataCom 2022 would not have been possible without the exceptional commitment of many expert volunteers. We would like to take this opportunity to extend our sincere thanks to all the authors, keynote speakers, Technical Program Committee members, and reviewers. Special thanks go to the entire local Organizing Committee for their help in making the conference a success. We would also like to express our gratitude to all the organizations that supported our efforts to bring the conference to fruition. We are grateful to Springer for publishing the proceedings.

Last, but not least, we hope that the participants enjoyed the technical program during this prestigious conference and discovered a lot of unique cultural flavors in Fiji to make their stay unforgettable.

December 2022

Ching-Hsien Hsu
Mengwei Xu
Hung Cao
Hojjat Baghban
A. B. M. Shawkat Ali

Organization

2022 International Conference on Big Data Intelligence and Computing (DataCom 2022)

General Chairs

A. B. M. Shawkat Ali	University of Fiji, Fiji
Robert Ching-Hsien Hsu	Asia University, Taiwan
Shangguang Wang	Beijing University of Posts and Telecommunications, China

Program Chairs

Weizhe Zhang	Harbin Institute of Technology, China
Jemal Abawajy	Deakin University, Australia
Sanjay Mathrani	Massey University, New Zealand
Hung Cao	University of New Brunswick, Canada

Program Co-chairs

Brij B. Gupta	Staffordshire University, UK
M. G. M. Khan	University of the South Pacific, Fiji
Feng Xia	Federation University, Australia

Workshop Chair

Anal Kumar	Fiji National University, Fiji

Publication Chairs

Neeraj Sharma	University of Fiji, Fiji

Publicity Chairs

Hojjat Baghban	Asia University, Taiwan
Kunal Kumar	University of Fiji, Fiji
Surya Prakash	Indian Institute of Technology Indore, India
Mengwei Xu	Beijing University of Posts and Telecommunications, China

Advisory Committee

Anna Kobusinska	Poznan University of Technology, Poland
Beniamino Di Martino	Second University of Naples, Italy
Christophe Cérin	Université Paris 13, France
Grace Lin	Asia University, Taiwan
Cho-Li Wang	University of Hong Kong, China
Jinsong Wu	University of Chile, Chile
Rajiv Ranjan	Newcastle University, UK
Song Guo	Hong Kong Polytechnic University, China
Vincent S. Tseng	National Yang Ming Chiao Tung University, Taiwan
Wenguang Cehn	Tsinghua University, China
Xiaolin Li	University of Florida, USA
Yeh-Ching Chung	Chinese University of Hong Kong, China

Steering Committee

Sanjay Ranka	University of Florida, USA
Robert Ching-Hsien Hsu	Asia University, Taiwan
Shangguang Wang	Beijing University of Posts and Telecommunications, China
Manish Parashar	Rutgers University, USA
Hai Jin	HUST, China
Jie Li	University of Tsukuba, Japan
Yuanyuan Yang	Stony Brook University, USA

Technical Program Committee

Dragan Peraković	University of Zagreb, Croatia
Alberto Huertas	University of Murcia (UMU), Spain

Imran Razzak	Deakin University, Australia
Andrea Bruno	University of Salerno, Italy
Nadia Nedjah	State University of Rio de Janeiro, Brazil
Konstantinos Psannis	University of Macedonia, Greece
Yining Liu	Guilin University of Electronic Technology, China
Ammar Almomani	Al- Balqa Applied University, Jordan
Balwinder Raj	National Institute of Technology Jalandhar, India
Francisco José García-Peñalvo	University of Salamanca, Spain
Arcangelo Castiglione	University of Salerno, Italy
Anupama Mishra	Swami Rama Himalayan University, India
Jinsong Wu	University of Chile, Chile
Shingo Yamaguchi	Yamaguchi University, Japan
Manish Kumar Goyal	Indian Institute of Technology Indore, India
Xiaochun Cheng	Middlesex University London, UK
Andrew Ip	University of Saskatchewan, Canada
Michael Sheng	Macquarie University, Australia
Anagha Jamthe	University of Texas at Austin, USA
Virendra Bhavsar	University of New Brunswick, Canada
Justin Zhang	University of North Florida, USA
Chinthaka Premachandra	Shibaura Institute of Technology, Japan
Mohammed Ali	University of Manchester, UK
Aniket Mahanti	University of Auckland, New Zealand
T. Perumal	Universiti Putra Malaysia (UPM), Malaysia
Rajhans Mishra	Indian Institute of Management Indore, India
Srivathsan Srinivasagopalan	AT&T, USA
Sugam Sharma	Iowa State University, USA
Suresh Veluru	United Technologies Research Centre Ireland, Ltd., Ireland
Manoj Gupta	SMVDU Katra, India
Francesco Palmieri	University of Salerno, Italy
Pethuru Raj	Reliance Jio Infocomm. Ltd (RJIL), India
S. K. Gupta	Indian Institute of Technology Delhi, India
Mouna Jouini	University of Tunis, Tunisia
Angela Amphawan	University of Malaysia, Malaysia
Phuc Do	University of Information Technology, Vietnam
Ahmed M. Manasrah	Higher Colleges of Technology, Sharjah, UAE
Ahmed A. Abd El-Latif	Menoufia University, Egypt
Sugam Sharma	eFeed-Hungers.com, USA
Zhili Zhou	Nanjing University of Information Science and Technology, China
Ing-Ray Chen	Virginia Tech, USA

Space-Air-Ground Computing

General Chairs

Monica Wachowicz	RMIT University, Australia
Bernady O. Apduhan	Kyushu Sangyo University, Japan
David Taniar	Monash University, Australia

Program Chairs

Mengwei Xu	BUPT, China
Hung Cao	University of New Brunswick, Canada

Publicity Chairs

Hojjat Baghban	Asia University, Taiwan
Xiaobin Xu	Beijing University of Technology, China
Kok-Seng Wong	VinUniversity, Vietnam
Changhee Joo	Korea University, South Korea
Yuben Qu	Shanghai Jiao Tong University, China
Wei Jin	Huizhou University, China

Steering Committee

Shangguang Wang (Chair)	Beijing University of Posts and Telecommunications, China
Ching-Hsien Hsu	Asia University, Taiwan

Technical Program Committee

Chiara Renso	ISTI Institute, National Research Council of Italy, Italy
Emanuele Carlini	ISTI Institute, National Research Council of Italy, Italy
René Richard	National Research Council, Canada
Rongxing Lu	University of New Brunswick, Canada

Xianfu Chen	VTT Technical Research Centre of Finland, Finland
Suzhi Cao	Chinese Academy of Sciences, China
Kaijun Ren	National University of Defense Technology, China
Celimuge Wu	University of Electro-Communications, Japan
Nan Zhao	Dalian University of Technology, China
Tingting Zhang	Harbin Institute of Technology, Shenzhen, China
Mohamed Mahmoud	Tennessee Technological University, USA
Dajiang Chen	University of Electronic Science and Technology of China, China
Kok-Seng Wong	VinUniversity, Vietnam
Sai Mounika Errapotu	University of Texas at El Paso, USA
Zhi Liu	Shizuoka University, Japan
Hassan Aboubakr Omar	Huawei Technologies Canada Co., Ltd., Canada
Xuanli Wu	Harbin Institute of Technology, China
Khalid Aldubaikhy	Qassim University, Saudi Arabia
Tao Huang	James Cook University, Australia
Muhammad Ismail	Tennessee Tech University, USA
Huaqing Wu	University of Waterloo, Canada
Tao Han	University of North Carolina at Charlotte, USA

Future Computing Paradigm for Big Data Analysis

General Chairs

| Christophe Cérin | Université Sorbonne Paris Nord, France |
| Keqin Li | State University of New York at New Paltz, USA |

Program Chairs

Hung-Yu Wei	National Taiwan University, Taiwan
Bingwei Liu	Aetna Inc., USA
Hung Cao	University of New Brunswick, Canada

Publication Chairs

Xiaojun Chang   Monash University Clayton Campus, Australia
Suresh Veluru   United Technologies Research Centre Ireland,
                                    Ltd., Ireland

Publicity Chairs

Hojjat Baghban   Asia University, Taiwan
Marjan Kuchaki Rafsanjani   Shahid Bahonar University of Kerman, Iran
Raffaele Pizzolante   University of Salerno, Italy

Steering Committee

Robert Hsu   Asia University, Taiwan
Christine Miyachi   Xerox Corporation, USA
Gregorio Martinez Perez   University of Murcia (UMU), Spain
Brij Gupta   National Institute of Technology Kurukshetra,
                                    India
Mazin Yousif   T-Systems International, USA

Advisory Committee

Neal Xiong   Colorado Technical University, USA
Blesson Varghese   Queen's University Belfast, UK
Xiang Yang   Swinburne Institute of Technology, Australia
Shingo Yamaguchi   Yamaguchi University, Japan
Wadee Alhalabi   KAU, Saudi Arabia
Jie Wu   Temple University, USA
Francisco José García-Peñalvo   University of Salamanca, Spain
Srivathsan Srinivasagopalan   AT&T, USA
Bahman Javadi   Western Sydney University, Australia
Irena Bojanova   NIST, USA

Web Chairs

Kwok Tai Chui   Open University of Hong Kong, China
Deepak Gupta   LoginRadius Inc., Canada

Award Chairs

Francisco José García-Peñalvo   University of Salamanca, Spain
Arcangelo Castiglione   University of Salerno, Italy

Registration/Finance Chair

Chun-Yuan Lin   Asia University, Taiwan

Technical Program Committee

Dragan Peraković   University of Zagreb, Croatia
Alberto Huertas   University of Murcia (UMU), Spain
Imran Razzak   Deakin University, Australia
Andrea Bruno   University of Salerno, Italy
Nadia Nedjah   State University of Rio de Janeiro, Brazil
Konstantinos Psannis   University of Macedonia, Greece
Yining Liu   Guilin University of Electronic Technology, China
Ammar Almomani   Al- Balqa Applied University, Jordan
Balwinder Raj   National Institute of Technology Jalandhar, India
Francisco José García-Peñalvo   University of Salamanca, Spain
Arcangelo Castiglione   University of Salerno, Italy
Anupama Mishra   Swami Rama Himalayan University, India
Jinsong Wu   University of Chile, Chile
Shingo Yamaguchi   Yamaguchi University, Japan
Manish Kumar Goyal   Indian Institute of Technology Indore, India
Xiaochun Cheng   Middlesex University London, UK
Andrew Ip   University of Saskatchewan, Canada
Michael Sheng   Macquarie University, Australia
Anagha Jamthe   University of Texas at Austin, USA
Virendra Bhavsar   University of New Brunswick, Canada
Justin Zhang   University of North Florida, USA
Chinthaka Premachandra   Shibaura Institute of Technology, Japan
Mohammed Ali   University of Manchester, UK

Contents

Big Data Analytics and Applications

Big Data Managements and Services

Miscellaneous Topic of Big Data

Big Data Algorithm and Systems

Tiansuan Constellation

Intelligent Software-Defined Microsatellite with Orbital Attention for Sustainable Development Goals

Yingxi Tang[✉]

National Remote Sensing Laboratory and Earth Big Data Laboratory, Zhicheng International Academy, Beijing 100032, China
yingxitang@buaa.edu.cn

Abstract. Space flight, which we anticipate as SpaceX does, has the potential to address the challenge of human life in the near future. The first stage towards interstellar travel is to establish a satellite network, which could deliver worldwide internet access to every location on the planet. However, satellites are not as smart as everyone thinks! Because the satellite industry faces severe problems including Cost, Speed, Vacuum environment, Energy, Computing power, Hardware stability, Software lightweight, Model optimization, Data set related, etc., these are all obstacles to upgrading the local calculation to orbital computation. And because this research category involves the scientific research secrets of various countries, many related materials are kept confidential and difficult to access publicly. Although AI researchers have enthusiasm for the application of deep learning in the field of remote sensing data, the processing speed and scale of remote sensing image information have been improved. However, the above research work belongs to ground-oriented processing, and the orbital application is still blank! The visual models currently popularly used on the ground are evaluated, and their respective computing power requirements are analyzed for possibilities in orbit.

Experiments on genuine microsatellites are hampered by the high expense of deployment and unknown risks associated with space technology. Our Tiansuan constellation, fortunately, can facilitate experimentation on real satellite networks. We introduce our brand-new integrated hybrid Orbital Deep Neural Network Model WolongPro 1.0 system based on edge computing and 2.0 research concept scheme about Spintronics, which can have human attention on disaster risk reduction. The attention of the orbital satellite can be focused on reporting early warning of perils, instead of transmitting high-resolution pictures and then analyzing them by computer or manually on the ground, to improve the recognition accuracy and predict disasters in advance, such as tornadoes and floods, etc. Our research: Intelligent software-defined microsatellite with orbital DNN attention for SDGs based on edge computing, can be applied to early warning of perils, and facilitate the Sustainable Development Goals of the United Nations Office for Disaster Risk Reduction (UNDRR).

Keywords: Orbital Edge Computing · AI in Space · Vision Transformer

C.-H. Hsu et al. (Eds.): DataCom 2022, LNCS 13864, pp. 3–21, 2023.
https://doi.org/10.1007/978-981-99-2233-8_1

1 Introduction

Global warming, water pollution, food scarcity, and resource depletion are among the development barriers that humanity is experiencing. Is it essential for humanity to go to other planets to expand its horizons? If this is the case, the satellite network will be vital at the outset of interstellar travel. At present, among the sustainable development goals of the United Nations, many of them can benefit from the development of satellite technology. Through the development of satellite technology, disaster reduction and prevention can be achieved.

Object detection with the help of a satellite is always been a tough task. Normally satellites are used for communication of signals and cover the entire earth and give us reliable information like TV signals, mobile communication, broadband, microwaves, internet, and many more [1].

To make satellites play a greater role, we need to make satellites more intelligent. For example, attention is a very common but ignored fact for humans. When a UAV flies over from the sky, human attention will often follow the UAV (as shown in Fig. 1 left). The sky naturally becomes background information in our visual system. The fundamental goal of the attention mechanism in computer vision [2] is to teach the system to focus on important information while ignoring extensive but irrelevant information. Human vision is similar, you swipe across and it is almost difficult to notice some information, but if you pay attention to the past, the details of things will form an impression in your mind. The same principle will benefit the computer Convolutional Neural Network [3], if you don't tell it you want to focus on the UAV, then the information of the whole picture is a larger proportion of the sky, so it will think that this is a photo of the sky, and not mainly UAV.

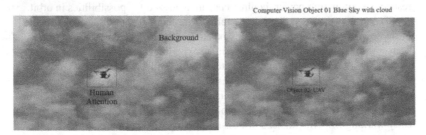

Fig. 1. Human Attention vs. Computer Vision

Why ignore irrelevant information? This can save a lot of computing power and give priority to important events, such as disasters. In this paper, on our Tiansuan constellation [4] platform, we further make the microsatellites on orbital more intelligent. We introduce the brand-new integrated hybrid Orbital Deep Neural Network Model Wolong-Pro 1.0 system, which has intelligent human attention deployed on KubeEdge [5] Edge Computing [6] framework. For example, in Fig. 2, an intelligent Tiansuan microsatellite can focus on the eye of the storm and output "A cyclone moving from the location one ", which can shorten the traditional bent-pipe satellite [6] one day processing time to one hour, then further shorten to 6–8 min. This will make the satellite not only an after-the-fact data transmission but also a pre-warning, which can reduce losses on a large scale. In this scene, time is a race against the devil.

Fig. 2. Attention to the eye of the storm

However, there are many problems to make microsatellites intelligent in the current situation, including Cost, Speed, Vacuum environment, Energy, Computing power, Hardware stability, Software lightweight, Model optimization, Data set related, etc., these are all obstacles to upgrading the local calculation to orbital computation. As Table 1 is described below, including but not comprehensively covered.

Table 1. The obstacles to upgrading the local calculation to orbital computation

No.	Problem Description	References
1	Space-rated hardware is costly	[4]
2	On-orbit satellite software updates are rare and extremely expensive	[4, 6]
3	Software development and delivery processes are slow, and the initialization of the satellite system takes several months	[6]
4	Cause the vacuum environment in space, there is cold outside but the inability to dissipate heat internally, The CPU needs to dissipate heat, but there is no air convection	[6]
5	Hardware needs to be durable, and how does software choose a lightweight system, The adaptation of computing platforms to satellites is also a difficult problem	[7]
6	Limited computing power, how to increase energy access	[6, 7]
7	Local processing of data is required for traditional satellites. How to implement on-orbit deployment if local deployment is not mainly preferred	[6]
8	AI researchers have enthusiasm for the application of deep learning in the field of remote sensing data, and the processing speed and scale of remote sensing image information have been improved step by step. However, these research works belong to ground-oriented processing, and the application of this technology in space-based remote sensing is still blank	[8]

(continued)

Table 1. (*continued*)

No.	Problem Description	References
9	Terrible ground infrastructure, could only be affordable for and operated by NASA	[6]
10	Processing delay, because the relative position between the ground station and the satellite orbit is not fixed	[6]
11	Lack of standardized remote sensing training data set. As a typical data-driven approach, deep learning relies on a large amount of well-labeled data set. Although remote sensing data is big data in total, it corresponds to specific goals and specific applications, and there is very little data that can be used to make samples for training. Too little data cannot meet the needs of deep learning now	[7, 9]
12	The on-orbit application of deep convolutional neural network technology is limited by the limited space-based computing resources. Although some breakthroughs have been made in the research of deep neural network lightweight technology and deep learning embedded computing platforms, the traditional electronic deep neural network is still difficult to exert its full capabilities under the condition of limited power consumption. There is an urgent need to develop new artificial intelligence acceleration hardware to improve computing power and reduce computing energy consumption to meet the needs of space-based remote sensing intelligence. How to improve the operation efficiency and reduce the size?	[10, 11]
13	Satellite-related information is confidential research, it's difficult to access publicly	[4]
14	Unknown risks. For example, one of the difficulties is that high-energy particles in outer space may penetrate satellites and change 0 in circuits to 1 and 1 to 0, greatly increasing the risk of miscalculation	[4]

Our solution is to build an open platform for the on-orbit test of computing in Industry-University-Research by adopting the "Tiansuan Constellation" [4] microsatellite program, through the intelligent, service-oriented, and open design of satellites, and to provide technical support for promoting the development of 6G networks, Satellite Internet and other technologies.

We choose Huawei Cloud [5] Edge Computing [6] to solve the problem of excessive on-orbit computation, and then reduce energy consumption. The test results show that, through the collaborative reasoning between the satellite and the ground station, the calculation accuracy is improved by more than 50%, the amount of data returned by the satellite can be reduced by 90%, and the satellite will enter the new era [4]. In the satellite photos, most of the information is useless, such as the need for ground details, but there are large clouds in the photos, which wastes valuable downlink traffic. The Tiansuan satellite first makes AI calculations, which will discard low-quality images that people are not interested in, and then send photos to the ground for analysis. In this way, the report generation time is shortened from the past one day to one hour. This is just the beginning of intelligent satellites. Through our orbital WolongPro 1.0 system, one hour is shortened to 6–8 min. Our intelligent software-defined microsatellite with orbital DNN attention for SDGs based on edge computing provides a comprehensive and detailed solution and will provide effective satellite technical support for disaster prevention and the realization of the United Nations SDG goals.

2   Related Work

The launch vehicle sector has had tremendous growth during the last four years (2018–2022). Due to the declining prices of satellite component manufacture and ride-sharing launch, Low Earth Orbit (LEO) satellites can offer global internet and connectivity. To provide low-latency, high-bandwidth internet, several space businesses are planning to launch LEO constellations all over the planet. As we know, with a target date of November 2021, SpaceX has now launched 1,844 Starlinks [12]. The real action has been in the extremely fast introduction of potential new vehicles in the sub-1000 kg to the LEO class [13]. First, let's take a look at the global satellite companies and organizations who focus on AI recently (Table 2).

Table 2. Summary of Satellite with AI

Country	Name	Founding Year	Project	Partner
Irish	Ubotica Technologies	2016	PhiSat-1	Intel
Australian	LatConnect 60	2019	NA	None
Hungarian	AImotive	2012	NA	C3S
Italian	AIKO	2017	MiRAGE	None
U.S	Hypergiant	2018	Chameleon	U.S. Air Force
China	Maiarstar Technology	2020	NA	None
American	Lockheed Martin (LMT)	1995	IntelligentSat	None
American	Amazon Web Services	2006	Kuiper Project	Iridium Communications

After summarizing the space race between nations, the next step, let's summarize the previous technical solutions as follows (Table 3).

In a sub conclusion, many researchers have done research (such as Intermittent, Approximate, and ONN) in the direction of saving energy and reducing electricity or not using electricity, the traditional mode of "satellite data acquisition->ground station receiving and processing" needs to quickly convert data into information and send it to end users at different levels in real-time, which can't meet the requirements of high timeliness for future high mobility and emergency monitoring applications [20]. Or have tried in the most advanced quantum computing at present, however, existing remote

Table 3. Previous technical solutions for satellite

Solutions	Description	Shortcomings	Ref.
Intermittent computation with batteryless IoT	The maturation of energy-harvesting technology and ultra-low-power computer systems has led to the advent of intermittently-powered, batteryless devices that operate entirely using energy extracted from their environment	The difficulty stems from the fact that an intermittent execution proceeds in bursts when energy is available and includes periods of inactivity when energy is not available	[14]
Approximate computing	A modern technique for the design of low-power efficient arithmetic circuits for portable error-resilient applications	Approximate computing relies on the ability of many systems and applications to tolerate some loss of quality or optimality in the computed result	[15–17]
Optical neural network (ONN)	Effectively reduce some operations of software and electronic hardware, and provides a promising method to replace artificial neural network	There is no efficient network training method. The accuracy of the all-optical neural network proposed before is far lower than that of an equivalent electronic neural network	[18]
Quantum Computing	Quantum technologies hold the potential to revolutionize the design and management of protocols for communication, observation, metrology, and sensing by developing strategies enhanced by the exploitation of features of a genuine quantum mechanical nature	Related technologies are evolving	[19]

sensing satellites can't make real-time optimization and targeted adjustment of load parameters in orbit according to the differences of observation objects, observation tasks, and observation area environments [21].

Last, but not least, about the Model, previous researchers' solution was manual intervention adjustment to simulate the ground and the real space environment. Our solution is to provide artificial intelligence in orbit and apply a hybrid lightweight model to design one integrated model that can have both low energy cost and high accuracy. And Edge Computing is adopted for deployment instead of other technologies.

2.1 Design Overview

Our remedy is the Tiansuan constellation [4], a Chinese open research platform shown in Fig. 3. Three stages make up the Tiansuan constellation, the first of which has six satellites.

To support experiments including the 6G core network system, satellite internet (also known as satellite digital networking), satellite operating system, federated learning and AI acceleration, and on-board service capability, Tiansuan aims to offer an open platform. There are three phases: the first will consist of six satellites, the second will consist of 24 satellites, and the third will consist of 300 orbiters. There are three types of satellites in the Tiansuan constellation's three phases.

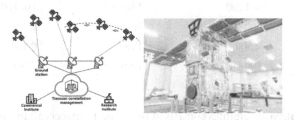

Fig. 3. Tiansuan Constellation Framework.

The first satellite of the Tianxuan constellation was launched in May 2022 The characteristics of the first stage satellites are given in Table 4 [4] Satellites in Tiansuan are manufactured according to the standard [22] The vast majority of satellites will be placed in a sun-synchronous orbit.

As seen in Fig. 3, circular stations collect data from satellites and transmit it via the Internet. One track of a satellite passes over ground stations every 6 to 8 min on average daily, only transmitting data as it does so. Most frequently in Changsha and Xinjiang, many ground stations have been set up. Additionally serving as access points to the cloud computing system are ground stations [4]. Broadband from space already exists, but it relies on geosynchronous satellites that orbit 35,000 km above the Earth. The connection speed is too slow, and it can't effectively compete with new applications on the ground network. In contrast, Elon Musk's Starlink Internet is located 550 km above the earth [12], which makes this system a potential speed advantage even compared with the fastest submarine fiber network. And our Tiansuan satellite is also located at 550 km. The satellites are classified based on their applications, orbits, mass, etc. As Table 5 shows, the classification is accepted by many organizations and study groups [23]. Tiansuan belongs to the Micro Satellite category.

Table 4. Key parameters of Tiansuan Constellation Stage 1 [4].

Number	Orbital Altitude	Mass	Battery Capacity	Spectrum	Uplink Rate	Downlink Rate	ISLs	Processors
1	500 ± 50 km	≤30 kg	118 Wh–236 Wh	X-band	0.1 Mbps–1Mbps	100 Mbps–600 Mbps	No	CPU/NPU
2	500 ± 50 km	≤30 kg	118 Wh–236 Wh	X-band	0.1 Mbps–1 Mbps	100 Mbps–600 Mbps	No	CPU/NPU
3	500 ± 50 km	≤30 kg	118 Wh–236 Wh	X-band	0.1 Mbps–1 Mbps	100 Mbps–600 Mbps	No	CPU/NPU
4	>500 km	>50 kg	>360 Wh	X, Ku, and Ka bands	≥200 Mbps	≥1 Gbps	Yes	CPU/NPU/GPU
5	>500 km	>50 kg	>360 Wh	X, Ku, and Ka bands	≥200 Mbps	≥1 Gbps	Yes	CPU/NPU/GPU
6	>500 km	>50 kg	>360 Wh	X, Ku, and Ka bands	≥200 Mbps	≥1 Gbps	Yes	CPU/NPU/GPU

Table 5. Satellite classification [23]

Class	Mass (kg)	Class	Mass (kg)
Large	> 1000	Micro	10–100
Medium	500–1000	Nano	1–10
Small	<500	Pico	0.1–1
Mini	100–500	Femto	<0.1

The constellation of satellites consists of two or more spacecraft in similar orbits with no active control to maintain a relative position. Constellations are utilized for special applications, such as Earth observations, Disaster forecasting and Damage estimation [24], Low earth orbit (LEO) based communication, etc.

2.2 Edge Computing and AI in Space

Edge computing is an emerging paradigm aiding responsiveness, reliability, and scalability of terrestrial computing and sensing networks like cellular and IoT. Edge computing places processing hardware near data sources, unlike cloud architectures that centralize data analysis [25]. Satellite communication, as an enabling technology of 6G networks, is crucial to achieving global coverage of mobile networks. Based on the platform of Tiansuan Constellation, we adopt the edge computing of KubeEdge [26], a cloud-native edge computing platform developed and open source by Huawei, and its edge cloud collaborative AI capability Sedna plays a key role in the satellite. With KubeEdge, a satellite is like a mobile phone using an App. You can install it at any time.

On December 10th, 2021, the experimental satellite equipped with the "Tiansuan" computing platform ran stably in orbit [4]. KubeEdge edge collaborative AI subproject Sedna [26], which constructs multi-model collaboration between the ground and the satellite, and the ground model incremental training usage scenario, using small models on the satellite and large models on the ground, to support the use of very few resources on the satellite to better support AI (Fig. 4).

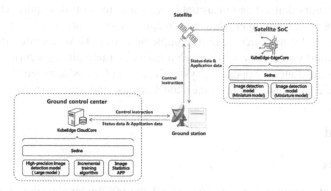

Fig. 4. Image Inference based on KubeEdge.

About 45% of LEO satellites in orbit are used for earth observation, which can be further used in various applications, such as natural disaster management [27] (e.g. forest fires, floods, etc.). As the constellation size increases, the struggle among big space-local records extent and constrained downlink potential is the bottleneck of real-time Earth observation. There are capability methods to cope with the challenge, modeling the freshness of the fascinating facts and most effective downloading hottest facts, leveraging a couple of dispensed floor stations to time table downloads effectively. Tiansuan picks the primary way.

Since real-time programs want sparkling facts for decision-making, it's miles important to make certain that the obtained facts are treasured and timely. As satellite edge computing and satellite Internet become more prevalent, onboard applications will become more common, allowing satellite-based AI approaches to emerge.

We propose establishing federated learning (FL) [28] and an AI acceleration platform based on the Tiansuan constellation [4], via which we can maintain to research and confirm the subsequent studies points: machine learning model training and acceleration capability verification using space-borne computing equipment, design and verification of AI algorithms for specific satellite application scenarios, and the establishment and verification of federated learning experimental platform based on Tiansuan constellation.

While advancing toward the idea of software-defined satellite computing, this technique avoids re-developing platform-specific applications. Previous research [29] looked at the challenges of putting typical container orchestration technologies on a satellite that is co-located with the ground station, which we refer to as inter-satellite orchestration [4, 6].

The satellite operating system should be a soft real-time and hard real-time operating system for embedded hardware, due to the absence of software and API in the standard operating system ecosystem [30]. As a result, the satellite operating system must be able to serve users defined and measurable real-time multi-task requirements, such as databases, machine learning engines, and image and video processing. However, there are several obstacles to overcome during implementation: How can you offer a method for allowing third-party software to be uploaded while maintaining security and extensibility? This necessitates the operating system's support for a wide range of technologies, including static code analysis, run-time stain analysis, and execution sandboxing.

3   Method

3.1   Datasets

As the brain of intelligent remote sensing load, the intelligent algorithm is the focus of research. In the research of intelligent algorithms based on deep learning, the ability of recognition technology needs to be continuously improved. Image segmentation, image detection, and other methods are adopted to realize the identification and processing of key information under certain constraints, identify specific targets from real-time remote sensing images, improve the accuracy and speed of target identification, and provide technical support for rapid task decision-making. Moving target imaging is affected by attitude, illumination, and other factors, and its characteristics are not the same. Therefore, moving target image recognition algorithms should have a certain anti-interference ability to the above factors [31]. Compared with several continuous large images of remote sensing data of the Earth, the satellite should concentrate on finding those parts that have changed (which often means disasters), instead of indiscriminately transmitting back all large-size images as at present. As China's advanced intelligent satellite, Tiansuan Satellite can intelligently filter out useless data such as clouds first, and give priority to important positions [4]. Remote sensing data is different from most data types. It is not only a time series data but also a huge volume because of its rich data information. Therefore, it will be of great value to put the limited computing power in the satellite cloud in a noticeable place for rapid return and early warning.

Satellite data offer great promise for improving measures related to sustainable development goals [32], such as SDG 13 Climate Action, and expanding to other targets in 2022 (such as SDG 7 affordable clean energy, etc.) [33]. There is no consistency in the scope or hazards in these lists nor in the definitions or descriptions that apply to the hazards [34]. The data division of the Disaster Reduction Center is based on land, ocean, hydrometeorology, and other disasters and environmental disasters caused by human beings. Our data set preparation based on SDGs follows these classifications as Table 6 shows.

The data set mainly comes from the data storage of the National Remote Sensing Laboratory of Zhicheng International Academy and is supplemented by Stanford SustainBench data set [36], xBD data set [37], MIT 19 kinds of satellite disaster data sets [38], and other data sets, such as Kaggle, Image Net, etc. (Fig. 5).

Table 6. Peril classification of the Family, Main Event, and Historical Number of Hits [35].

Family	Main Event
Geophysical	Earthquake (180 hits), Mass Movement, Volcanic Activity (31 hits)
Hydrological	Flood (226 hits), Landslide, Wave Action (141 hits)
Meteorological	Convective Strom, Extratropical Strom, Extreme Temperature, Fog, Tropical Cyclone (107 hits)
Climatological	Drought (143 hits), Glacial Lake Outburst, Wildfire (32 hits)
Biological	Animal Incident, Disease, Insect Infestation (5 hits)
Extraterrestrial	Impact, Space Weather

Fig. 5. Dataset Sample of Tropical Cyclone

3.2 Model Design

Artificial intelligence plays a significant role in cutting costs, reducing the design cycle time, simulation, prototyping, optimization, maintenance, manufacturing, and updating products, and is all set to drive many developments in the aerospace sector in the next 15 years [39]. Nonetheless, there is a restricted reception of AI procedures in the flying business and the principal justification for this is the absence of admittance to great information, in-wrinkled constancy on straightforward models when contrasted with complex models, and an absence of talented labor force to successfully execute it.

Humans can naturally and effectively find salient regions in complex scenes. Motivated by this observation, attention mechanisms were introduced into computer vision to imitate this aspect of the human visual system [40]. Attention was first proposed by Google as Transformer [41]. Transformer model architectures have garnered immense interest lately due to their effectiveness across a range of domains like language, vision, and reinforcement learning. Recently, a dizzying number of "X-former" models (such as MixFormer [42]) have been proposed which improve upon the original Transformer architecture, many of which make improvements around computational and memory efficiency [43]. Because of the limits of related innovations, it is much of the time important to prepare a lot of named information to get a superior and more competent model. The new rise of pre-preparing models in light of the Transformer structure has eased this issue. They are first pre-prepared through self-administered discovery that normally exploits assistant assignments (pre-preparing goals) to mine management signals from huge scope unlabeled information to prepare the model [44] (Table 7).

Table 7. Popular Model of Attention

Solutions	Description	Features	Ref.
Convolution Neural Network	CNN is a deep neural network that is most suitable when dealing with images. CNN will help to provide higher classification accuracy	Applying convolutional neural networks to large images is computationally expensive because the number of computations scales linearly with the number of image pixels	[45, 46]
Vision Transformer	An attention-based encoder-decoder architecture, not only completely changed the field of natural language processing (NLP), but also made some pioneering work in the field of computer vision (CV)	Time-consuming	[47, 48]
Visual transformer	(a) representing images as semantic visual tokens and (b) running transformers to densely model token relationships	Big size	[49]
Coordinate Attention	A novel light-weight attention mechanism for mobile networks, such as MobileNetV2, MobileNeXt, and EfficientNet with nearly no computational overhead	It is simple and can be flexibly plugged into classic mobile networks,	[50]

Wolong Prophet (WolongPro) 1.0

Named after Zhuge Liang, another name is Wolong [51], who was good at observing astrology and predicting wind direction and successfully commanded the victory of the Great Battle.

We deployed the Wolong 1.0 system on the Tiansuan satellite. As Fig. 6 shows, the functional components of the system include:

Fig. 6. WolongPro Design Structure

- Raspberry Pi Hardware Capture Remote Sensing Picture
- Input pictures after KubeEdge deployment (trained to reduce power consumption)
- Output pictures with self-attention marked with SDG (such as disaster) areas
- The marked pictures need to correspond to geographic coordinate information
- Timely return relevant information on the ground.

We compare the latest lightweight models as Table 8 illustrated. The hybridization of different machine learning methods and the integration of statistical and machine learning methods could acquire more efficient results [52]. WolongPro 1.0 is a hybrid and lightweight model based on Mobile ViT XS.

Table 8. Lightweight Model Comparison

No.	Model	Params(M)	Flops(G)	Dataset	Size	Acc (%)
1	Moblie-ViT-XS [53]	2.3	0.7	ImageNet validator	224 * 224	74.8
2	ParC-Net [54]	5		ImageNet-1k		78.6
3	LightViT-T [55]	9.4	0.7	ImageNet validator	224 * 224	78.7
4	RegNetY-800M [56]	6.3	0.8	ImageNet validator	224 * 224	76.3
5	MobileNetv2 [57]	2.6		ImageNet validator	224 * 224	69.8
6	TinyViT-5M [58]	5.4	1.3	ImageNet validator		80.7

WolongPro 2.0

Spintronics has opened a window for researchers because of their ultra-low power consumption devices. Our research plan explores the application of spintronics in artificial intelligence and computer vision and achieves high-accuracy image recognition under low energy consumption by designing spintronic chips and experiments. We plan to use Spin-NODE [59] a revolutionary tool for accurately predicting to conduct experimental simulations, and apply Spintronics AIoT chip in the Tiansuan constellation, which realizes low-power natural disaster risk recognition with orbital self-attention. This will open up new areas from basic academic research to practical applications of Spintronics artificial intelligence.

3.3 Hardware

The Tiansuan constellation also supports space experiments and in-orbit testing of new hardware devices. Raspberry Pi [60] is a microcomputer the size of a credit card, which is designed for learning computer programming education. Astro Pi is an upgrade and replacement for the original Astro Pi hardware that flew to the ISS in 2015 for the mission of ESA [61] astronaut Tim Peake. Our experiment chooses Raspberry Pi 4 integrated with Raspberry Pi Camera Module 2.

4   Experimental Results

4.1   The Comparison

The Cyclone Global Navigation Satellite System (CYGNSS) is a space-borne mission concept focused on tropical cyclone (TC) inner core process studies. CYGNSS constellation, eight observatories are positioned in low inclination (35°) low earth (500 km altitude) orbit. The average revisit time for TC sampling is predicted to be 4.0 h, and the mean revisit time will be 1.5 h [62]. Compare to that, our Tiansuan not only shows the high accuracy of identification (for example, a tornado is moving from Taiwan Province, a volcano near Tonga is erupting), and the return speed is compared in time (decrease to 6–8 min) to improve the decision-making efficiency.

4.2   Future Work

Use VR edge computing maps the satellite vision, while Quantum computing is a prediction.

Metaverse the Universe
Given the high computation costs required, e.g., to render immersive 3D worlds and run data-hungry artificial intelligence (AI) driven applications, we will design the computation challenges and cloud-edge-end computation framework-driven solutions to realize the Metaverse on resource-constrained edge devices [63] (Fig. 7).

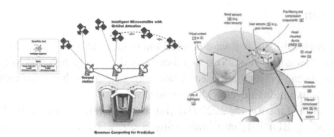

Fig. 7. Metaverse the Universe.

Quantum on Ground

Much work has been embraced in improving cutting-edge computational models to upgrade gauging throughout the long term, and much headway has been made. Determining weather conditions requires breaking down tremendous information containing several dynamic factors, like air temperature, tension, and thickness that cooperate in a non-minor way. Be that as it may, there are constraints to involving old-style PCs and even supercomputers in creating mathematical climate and environment forecast models. Additionally, the most common way of investigating climate information by conventional PCs may not be quick enough to stay aware of always changing weather patterns.

Indeed, even local weather conditions anticipating, which are quickly developing constantly, can bear benefitting from further developed estimating. Take, for instance, rainstorms, where exceptionally precise and high-level expectations by further developed information examination could limit the subsequent harm, as there could be advance notice further ahead of time about potential blackouts, and expanded readiness, permitting the nearby local area to reestablish power quicker.

Quantum figuring will effectively help weather conditions gauging on both the neighborhood scale as well as on a more excellent scale for further developed and precise admonition of outrageous climate occasions, possibly saving lives and lessening property harm every year.

Quantum computing can enhance traditional numerical strategies to reinforce monitoring and predictions of meteorological situations by coping with big quantities of records containing many variables efficaciously and quickly, by harnessing the computing electricity of qubits, and through the use of quantum-stimulated optimization algorithms. Moreover, sample recognition, important for the information on the weather, may be improved by utilizing quantum device learning we plan the destiny studies guidelines to understand the authentic imaginative and prescient of the edge-enabled Metaverse.

Spin-AI in Space

Our next major research will focus on applying ultra-low power devices based on spintronic theory to in-orbit artificial intelligence. This is because using the spin of electrons instead of their charge properties will lead to ultra-low power AI chips with low heat dissipation, minimal energy demand, and fast operation that are very suitable for use in space.

5 Conclusion

Our research: An intelligent software-defined microsatellite with orbital DNN attention for SDGs based on edge computing together with the newly debuted WolongPro 1.0 integrated system can be applied to early warning of peril, which can focus on more important events like human eyes with attention.

At 11:14 am on January 15, 2023 (Beijing time), China successfully launched 14 satellites, including BUPT 1, into orbit using a CZ 2D carrier rocket from Taiyuan Satellite Launch Center. It is reported that after the launch of the BUPT 1 satellite, the satellite was in orbit normally, the telemetry parameters were normal, and the solar wing and antenna were deployed normally. As the first main star of the Tiansuan Constellation, BUPT 1 was developed by the Beijing University of Posts and Telecommunications and Changsha Tianyi Research Institute. We deployed the whole WolongPro system on Tiansuan Constellation. The feedback time is greatly shortened to 6–8 min. This will greatly facilitate the Sustainable Development Goals of the United Nations Office for Disaster Risk Reduction (UNDRR), which will have a far-reaching impact. And let's stay tuned for the new design of WolongPro 2.0 with Spintronics.

Acknowledgments. I want to thank my mentor Shangguang Wang, a Professor from the Beijing University of Posts and Telecommunications, Head of the State Key Laboratory of Networking and Switching Technology, who appreciated AI-related instruction from Mengwei Xu and Xiao Ma from BUPT.

I am very grateful for the research discussions and assistance from Ke Zhang from National Remote Sensing Laboratory, Zhicheng International Academy. Special thanks to my instructor, Associate Prof. Le Yu, Department of Earth System Science, Tsinghua University, for long-term kindly instructions with patience.

I want to thank my mentor for Machine Learning, Mark Vogelsberger, Associate Professor from the Massachusetts Institute of Technology. Also, my mentor for Quantum Computing: Isaac Chuang, Professor, Electrical Engineering & Computer Science; Senior Associate Dean of Digital Learning, MIT.

Thanks to Tiansuan Constellation's strategic partner, Space Tianyi, Huawei Cloud & KubeEdge Community.

I am appreciating that this project was selected as the "National Talent Pool Project" (Ying Cai Ji Hua Project for middle school students' scientific and technological innovation reserve talents), which was hosted by the China Association for Science and Technology and the Ministry of Education of the People's Republic of China.

References

1. Vivek, S., Deepika, G.: Study of satellite object detection algorithms with pixel value and OTSU method algorithm. Int. J. Future Revolution Comput. Sci. Commun. Eng. 013–015 (2015). http://www.ijfrcsce.org
2. Li, L.-J., Li, F.-F.: What, where, and who? Classifying events by scene and object recognition, pp. 1–8 (2007). https://doi.org/10.1109/ICCV.2007.4408872
3. Teoh, T.T., Rong, Z.: Convolutional Neural Networks. In: Artificial Intelligence with Python. MLFMA, pp. 261–275. Springer, Singapore (2022). https://doi.org/10.1007/978-981-16-8615-3_16

4. Wang, S., Li, Q., Xu, M., Ma, X., Zhou, A., Sun, Q.: Tiansuan Constellation: An Open Research Platform. http://www.sguangwang.com/index.html?aspxerrorpath=/ (2021)
5. Wang, S., et al.: KubeEdge.AI: AI platform for edge devices. In: EAIS'19. Shenzhen, Guangdong, China (2019)
6. Denby, B., Lucia, B.: Orbital edge computing: nanosatellite constellations as a new class of computer system. In: ASPLOS'20, Lausanne, Switzerland, 16–20 Mar 2020
7. Li, W., et al.: The application of deep learning in space-based intelligent optical remote sensing. Spacecraft Recovery Remote Sens. 41(6), 56–65 (2020). (Chinese)
8. Tan, K., et al.: Research progress of the remote sensing classification combining deep learning and semi-supervised learning. J. Image Graphics 24(11), 1823–1841 (2019). (Chinese)
9. Li, Z., Wang, L., Yu, J., et al.: Remote sensing ship target detection and recognition method. Remote Sens. Inform. 35(1), 64–72 (2020)
10. Wang, Z., Li, H., Liu, Z., et al.: Satellite image change monitoring based on deep learning algorithm. Comput. Syst. Appl. 29(1), 40–48 (2020). (Chinese)
11. Zhou, M., et al.: Aircraft classification in remote sensing images using convolutional neural networks. J. Image Graphic 22(5), 0702–0708 (2017). (Chinese)
12. https://www.starlink.com
13. Niederstrasser, C.: Small launch vehicles – a 2018 state of the industry survey. In: 32nd Annual AIAA/USU Conference on Small Satellites (2018)
14. Lucia, B., Balaji, V., Colin, A., Maeng, K., Ruppel, E.: Intermittent computing: challenges and opportunities. In: 2nd Summit on Advances in Programming Languages (SNAPL 2017), Article No. 8; pp. 8:1–8:14. Dagstuhl Publishing, Germany (2017)
15. Nelson Kingsley Joel, P., Vijeyakumar, K.N.: Design of low power architecture for approximate parallel mid-point filter (2022). https://doi.org/10.21203/rs.3.rs-1191570/v1
16. Sparsh, M.: A survey of techniques for approximate computing. ACM Comput. Surv. 48, 62 (2016). https://doi.org/10.1145/28933356
17. Barua, H.B., Mondal, K.C.: Approximate computing: a survey of recent trends—bringing greenness to computing and communication. J. Inst. Eng. (India): Ser. B 100(6), 619–626 (2019). https://doi.org/10.1007/s40031-019-00418-8
18. Tyler, W.H., et al.: Training of photonic neural networks through in situ backpropagation and gradient measurement. Optica 5(7), 864–871 (2018). https://doi.org/10.1364/OPTICA.5.000 8641
19. Angelo, B., Mauro, P., et al.: Chair and deputy chair COST action QTSpace, the scientific committee. In: Policy White Papers on Quantum Technologies for Space: Strategic Report for ESA and the National Space Agenciesr. www.qtspace.eu (2017)
20. Li, X., et al.: A review of target motion information extraction from high-resolution optical satellite images. Remote Sens. Land Resour. 31(3), 1–9 (2019). (Chinese)
21. Danying, F.U., et al.: The opportunities and challenges in optical payload of micro-nano satellite. Spacecraft Recovery Remote Sens. 38(4), 64–69 (2018). (Chinese)
22. Cubesat design specification: California Polytechnic State University, rev. 13. Technical report (2014)
23. Hameed, H.: Small satellites: entrepreneurial paradise and legal nightmare. J. Space Technol. 18(1) (2018)
24. Santilli, G., et al.: CubeSat constellations for disaster management in remote areas. Acta Astronaut. 145, 11–17 (2018)
25. Denby, B., Lucia, B.: Orbital edge computing: machine inference in space. IEEE Comput. Archit. Lett. 18, 59–62 (2019)
26. https://kubeedge.io/en/
27. Barmpoutis, P., Papaioannou, P., Dimitropoulos, K., Grammalidis, N.: A review on early forest fire detection systems using optical remote sensing. Sensors 20, 6442 (2020)

28. McMahan, B., et al.: Communication-efficient learning of deep networks from decentralized data. In: Proceedings of Artificial intelligence and statistics (2017)
29. Bhosale, V., Bhardwaj, K., Gavrilovska, A.: Toward loosely coupled orchestration for the LEO satellite edge. In: Proceedings of Workshop on Hot Topics in Edge Computing (2020)
30. Stankovic, J.A., Rajkumar, R.: Real-time operating systems. Real-Time Syst. **28**, 237–253 (2004)
31. Li, Y., Liu, X., Zhang, H., et al.: Optical remote sensing image retrieval based on convolutional neural networks. Optics Precis. Eng. **26**(1), 200–207 (2018). (Chinese)
32. Lobell, D.B., et al.: Twice is nice: the benefits of two ground measures for evaluating the accuracy of satellite-based sustainability estimates. Remote Sens. **13**, 3160 (2021). https://doi.org/10.3390/rs13163160
33. Big Earth Data in Support of the SDGs, Chinese Academy of Sciences (2021)
34. Hazard Definition & Classification Review: UNDRR, Sendai Framework for Disaster Risk Reduction 2015–2030, International Science Council, Technical Report, 2020 UNITED NATIONS (2020)
35. Integrated Research on Disaster Risk: Peril Classification and Hazard Glossary (IRDR DATA Publication No. 1). Integrated Research on Disaster Risk, Beijing (2014)
36. Christopher, Y., et al.: SUSTAINBENCH: benchmarks for monitoring the sustainable development goals with machine learning. In: 35th Conference on Neural Information Processing Systems (NeurIPS 2021) Track on Datasets and Benchmarks, arXiv:2111.04724v1 8 Nov 2021 [cs.LG]
37. Ritwik, G., et al.: xBD: A Dataset for Assessing Building Damage from Satellite Imagery. arXiv:1911.09296v1[cs.CV] 21 Nov 2019
38. Ethan, W., Hassan, K.: Building Disaster Damage Assessment In Satellite Imagery With Multi-Temporal Fusion, presentation at the ICLR 2020 AI For Earth Sciences Workshop, arXiv:2004.05525v1[cs.CV] 12 Apr 2020
39. Machine Learning & Artificial Intelligence in Aerospace Industry, Whitepaper, AXISCADES. www.axiscades.com
40. Guo, M.-H., et al.: Attention mechanisms in computer vision: a survey. Comput. Visual Media **8**, 331–368 (2022). https://doi.org/10.1007/s41095-022-0271-y
41. Ashish, V., et al.: Attention is all you need. In: Advances in neural information processing systems, pp. 5998–6008 (2017)
42. Tay, Y., et al.: Efficient Transformers: A Survey. arXiv:2009.06732v3 [cs.LG] (2022)
43. Wu, S., et al.: Pale Transformer: A General Vision Transformer Backbone with Pale-Shaped Attention, 2022, www.aaai.org. arXiv:2112.14000v1 [cs.CV] (2021)
44. Chen, F., et al.: VLP: A Survey on Vision-Language Pre-training, arXiv:2202.09061v2 (2022)
45. Manohar, N., Pranav, M.A., Aksha, S., Mytravarun, T.K.: Classification of satellite images. In: Senjyu, T., Mahalle, P.N., Perumal, T., Joshi, A. (eds.) ICTIS 2020. SIST, vol. 195, pp. 703–713. Springer, Singapore (2021). https://doi.org/10.1007/978-981-15-7078-0_70
46. Pan, X., et al.: On the Integration of Self-Attention and Convolution, arXiv:2111.14556v2 (2022)
47. Dosovitskiy, A., et al.: An image is worth 16×16 words: transformers for image recognition at scale. arXiv:2010.11929v1 [cs.CV] 22 Oct 2020
48. Li, Y., Mao, H., Girshick, R., He, K.: Exploring Plain Vision Transformer Backbones for Object Detection. arXiv:2203.16527v1 (2022). https://doi.org/10.48550/arXiv.2203.16527
49. Wu, B., et al.: Visual Transformers: Token-based Image Representation and Processing for Computer Vision, arXiv:2006.03677v4 [cs.CV], 20 Nov 2020
50. Hou, Q., Zhou, D., Feng, J.: Coordinate Attention for Efficient Mobile Network Design, arXiv:2103.02907v1 [cs.CV], 4 Mar 2021
51. Luo, G.: The Legend of Three Kingdom, Baidu Encyclopedia, Baidu Baike. www.baidu.com

52. Jenice Aroma, R., Kumudha, R.: An overview of technological revolution in satellite image analysis. J. Eng. Sci. Technol. Rev. **9**(4), 1–5 (2016)
53. Sachin, M., Mohammad, R.: MobileViT: Light-weight, General-purpose, and Mobile-friendly Vision Transformer (2021), https://arxiv.org/abs/2110.02178
54. Zhang, H., et al.: ParC-Net: Position Aware Circular Convolution with Merits from ConvNets and Transformer (2022). https://doi.org/10.48550/arXiv.2203.03952
55. Tao, H., et al.: LightViT-T: Towards Light-Weight Convolution-Free Vision Transformers (2022). https://doi.org/10.48550/arXiv.2207.05557
56. Jing, X., et al.: RegNet: self-regulated network for image classification. IEEE Trans. Neural Netw. Learn. Syst., 1–6 https://doi.org/10.1109/TNNLS.2022.3158966 (2022)
57. Mark, S., et al.: MobileNetV2:Inverted Residuals and Linear Bottlenecks: Mobile Networks for Classification, Detection and Segmentation. https://arxiv.org/pdf/1801.04381.pdf (2019)
58. Wu, K., et al.: TinyViT: Fast Pretraining Distillation for Small Vision Transformers. https://arxiv.org/pdf/2207.10666.pdf
59. Chen, X., et al.: Forecasting the outcome of spintronic experiments with neural ordinary differential equations. Nat. Commun. **13**, 1016 (2022). https://doi.org/10.1038/s41467-022-28571-7
60. https://www.raspberrypi.org/
61. https://www.esa.int/
62. Christopher, S.R., et al.: The CYGNSS nanosatellite constellation hurricane mission. In: IGARSS 2012, Conference Paper, July 2012, 978-1-4673-1159-5/12 IEEE (2012). https://doi.org/10.1109/IGARSS.2012.6351600
63. Xu, M., et al.: A Full Dive into Realizing the Edge-enabled Metaverse: Visions, Enabling Technologies, and Challenges, arXiv:2203.05471v1[cs.NI] 10 Mar 2022

Adopting a Deep Learning Split-Protocol Based Predictive Maintenance Management System for Industrial Manufacturing Operations

Biswaranjan Senapati[1]($\boxtimes$) and Bharat S. Rawal[2]($\boxtimes$)

[1] Computer Science Department, Capitol Technology University, Laurel, USA
bsenapati@captechu.edu
[2] Cybersecurity Department, Benedict College, Columbia, SC, USA

Abstract. This paper presents the best computational modeling (AI/ML and Quantum Computing) methods to predict the performance optimization of predictive maintenance and management of the shop floor activities in manufacturing sites within the industrial manufacturing facility. For industrial manufacturing sites, shop floor activities play a vital role in the productivity and operational efficiencies of any industrial manufacturing site/facility. In manufacturing units, production planners and supervisors have a critical time to predict the production downtimes and predictive maintenance, and sometimes with the production line, a tiny milling bit breaks, shutting down the line. Some cases of unplanned downtime are not only costly deals but also hamper the unplanned delay and downtime for the supervisors at the production sites/factories in industrial productions. In this paper, we introduce a failure detection system that focuses only most probable failure state at maximum utilization and is delicate in incoming jobs to the backup unit while the overloaded unit will recover and resume in the very fresh state. Our proposed scheme introduces an additional parallel system component with help of split protocol and improves overall systems reliability in case of a component failure.

Keywords: SAP S/4 · SAP HANA · Cyber security · AI · ML · IoT

1 Introduction

In a general statement, in the twenty-first century, most of the industrial manufacturing facilities/units along with the operations facilities are still using paper, spreadsheets, excel sheet- based and phone calls to share information on predictive maintenance (PdM) with the plant shop floor from other departments, outside suppliers and customers to fulfill the demand and supply network [7, 8]. Very early digital adder fascinated scientist and engineers. O. Bedrij described adder system accelerates the addition process by cutting the carry-propagation time to the absolute lowest consistent with a cost-effective circuit design [1]. All these manual activities and work schedules are not easy to maintain, and they are unable to control the operations as per the planned schedule. In industrial manufacturing sites/production units, the downtime of the equipment/machines is the most

C.-H. Hsu et al. (Eds.): DataCom 2022, LNCS 13864, pp. 22–39, 2023.
https://doi.org/10.1007/978-981-99-2233-8_2

significant issue, hard to manage, and difficult to predict the downtime and maintenance hours to make them useful. In the manufacturing industry, the failure of the equipment results in downtime, i.e., it remains useless until the maintenance is conducted and it starts functioning again, which may effectively result in a decline in the productivity of the equipment, machines, and shop floor activities [2, 3]. According to a recent survey, 10% to 25% of downtime and production losses occur frequently due to predictive maintenance issues (PdM) within heavy industrial manufacturing sites, resulting in large losses and costly deals for the business. This would be important when considering a Make to Order (MTO) and Make to Stock (MTS) scenario [4]. Machine failures can bring production to a screeching halt, and it costs the industry millions of dollars to overcome the sales and operation planning in critical business scenarios [9]. However, traditional ML models need improvement and more thorough tokenization for text pre-processing [6]. A few of the computational models within AI, ML, or IoT can help in improving the overall efficiency of the industry and predict much more accurately the machine/equipment downtimes as per the available datasets [1]. The ML techniques, can assess the historical data of the equipment over a fixed period and develop some patterns of degradation of the component and machine, predicting the potential failure and scheduling the maintenance before the system collapses entirely. Predictive analytics considers both current and historical data patterns of machines/equipment and worksites in industrial plants when making forecasts about future outcomes and performance. It determines whether those patterns are likely to re-emerge, thus allowing manufacturers to adjust their resources to take advantage of probable future events, improve operational efficiencies, and avoid risk. Some industrial manufacturers are also heavily utilizing industrial IoT devices, sensors, and SAP S/4 Manufacturing Execution services, which are built on ML, AI, and Edge Computing features, to calculate PdM Factors and downtimes in work/production sites. Most of these facilities are highly dependent on predictive analytics and smart factories, which drive efficiency on the plant floor and allow companies to convert collected data into tangible, relevant actions [12]. Intelligent predictive maintenance strategies are now being adopted by most production sites to reduce the overall cost and optimize the efficient production score [9]. There are a few key strategies to developing an interactive online application, data collectors to collect the data from machines, humans/operators, and equipment, and reading the machine sensor data as input to predict the possibility of downtime of the machine because of the entire chain of neural constructions in the AI and ML Models. This will be done in a few steps as stated below.

1. Understand the current state, operations, capabilities, technology, and usability of resources and machines. Identify the current or potential gaps, including any existing equipment that does not support activities like automated data capture (ADC).
2. Making the necessary changes at the equipment/machine and factory levels to understand the maturity curve and the potential downtimes and lead times.
3. Data cleansing of the machine/equipment data records, attributes with different parameters of collected data from the devices/sensors of the tubing machine, finds the correlation to identify the pattern concerning downtime of the tubing machine.
4. Collect the datasets from the manufacturing towers to get the actual downtime vs the predictive maintenance downtime (PdM).

5. This step will need to be analyzing the data set, deriving the correlation, and identifying and training the most suitable machine learning model which can predict the system failure well in advance using the live data provided to the corresponding model.
6. The best predictive models with the help of ML, AI, and IoT models are certainly beneficial to the industrial manufacturers (production sites and facilities/supervisors/operators/managers/shop floor managers) who are on the machine and their respective managers and other stakeholders in terms of operations.
7. Predictive analytics assists manufacturers in better understanding, monitoring, and optimizing their plant floor activities by combining historical data with artificial intelligence, machine learning, and the Internet of Things [16].

To maintain a competitive edge, and support the customer/distributor demands, the manufacturers must act now to make strategic investments, and adopt of best computational tools/methods to provide the best potential model to manage the market demands and fulfillment of the customer/distributor demand. With the help of digital twins and shifting from traditional to digital, learning how to manage, and optimize data, information, skilled full resources tools (ERP, Bigdata, Clouds, AI, ML, and MDM) which can run the supply chains, and factory operation. IIoT Devices are deployed on the shop floor, and then it acts on these insights to control the PdM. During the earlier days, there are no certain best practices on PdM and the preventive maintenance of the machine in production units and operational benefits were able to manage [10].

In the early days, the production units have no interconnected and integration layer due to a lack of sensor data, industrial internet of things devices along with digital twins which were available now in all modern facilities and able to capture a huge amount of data for the future predictions of PdM scores. In smart factories and industries 4.0, the advancement of digital twins and smart equipment like sensors, IIoTs, PLCs, and other machinery could provide the data from across systems and provide the best machine learning models and industrial analytics for the machine and equipment and determine the PdM scores. Industrial manufacturing companies deal with a rising number of product variants as well as aging personnel due to demographic change and customer demand across the globe and outlier detection [28]. Due to these challenges and unprecedented customer demands and unpredictable downtimes, sales and operation planning are key challenges, and optimizations are not up to the mark as per demand vs supply. Industrial manufacturers need to develop their employees' competencies in shop floor activities, skilled development, and adoption of the manufacturing toolset to improve the production lines. In industrial manufacturing and Industries 4.0, the PdM requires data from various sensors, devices, and machines which are connected, monitored, and connected with the equipment to collect the other operational data to complete the production cycles. Mostly all these Predictive maintenance systems are capable to conduct data analysis. Also, stores the results within the production cycles at a low defect. A machine learning tool and a quantum computing tool can certainly help to understand the pattern of predictive maintenance (PdM) and be able to solve real-world problems.

The following is how the rest of the paper is structured: The introduction is covered in Sect. 1, and the related work is covered in Sect. 2. Then, Sect. 3 describes predictive maintenance and industry 4.0. Section 4 describes the strategy to adopt in predictive maintenance. Section 5 pillars of the total predictive maintenance in industries 4.0. Section 6 describes quantum computing and digital manufacturing 4.0. Section 7 talks about reliability-centered maintenance (RCM). Section 8 describes intelligent asset management (IAM) and RCM-controlled predictive maintenance. Section 9 presents system architectures and PDM in Industry 4.0. Section 10 presents AI-enabled split-migration architecture. The Sect. 11 talks about the implementation. Finally, Sect. 12 concludes the research paper.

2 Literature Reviews

Here are a few facts and research publications that are evidence and supportive of these publications. Most industrial manufacturers have a strong problem statement concerning the predictive maintenance (PDM) score as per their current business scope. Few of the recent research focused on the various Machine Learning and computational applications for Predictive Maintenance and the most effective way to understand the occurrence of a failure, recurrent events, and any critical breakdown failure as before this happens in the production sites/units. Machine downtime could be analyzed and able to perform predictive maintenance as per the Industrial productions. The computational model and Machine Learning model could help to understand the machine/equipment's/device records and process for the optimized information to predict the better predictive maintenance score in industrial operations. In production and manufacturing operation sites, the industrial information related to production data, device information, production worksheets along with Sensor, IIoT, and PLCs and DCS are stored in a database, and acquires data from plant DCS, registers, associated PLCs, chips, capacitors, and electronic registers around the network [18].

Most of the recent research publication on PdM elaborates on the benefits and utilization of the digital twins and the application of the computational model (AI, ML, QML, QAI, IIoT, and cloud applications) which offer the best way to manage the PdM Capabilities in an industrial manufacturing operation. Most industrial equipment-sensor, electronics batteries, capacitors, and electrical machines degrade with time, load, and use as per the capacity. Ideally each component of the industrial manufacturing equipment's, devices will have a certain deadline and will reach to end f its useful life. Most of these manufacturing sites used to have the schedule-based maintenance planned or time-based maintenance approach to maintaining the equipment across the plant/sites. Some of time, industrial manufacturing sites also adopt the best practices of condition-based maintenance methods which are to maintain or replace equipment/devices/sensors at exactly the right time just before its event/failure, and this is a most tedious job at the site level [11].

3 Overview of Predictive Maintenance and Industries 4.0

Industrial manufacturing is based on the equipment, machines, devices, and IIoT across the sites, and all these devices need to be zero defect and error-free. Typically, system failures are a common occurrence across all manufacturing industries and within production sites. Predictions of Predictive Maintenance (PdM) scores play a vital role in the fourth industrial revolution and are beneficial for smart factories in Industry 4.0. PdM is the best use case and driver to make a successful critical factor within manufacturing facilities to have smart factories and digital innovations in industrial manufacturing sites [26]. The ML-based predictive approach analyses the live data and tries to find the correlation between certain parameters to predict the system failure or scheduled maintenance of the equipment. ML technology helps identify the fault lines by predicting the failures at the right time and thus utilizing resources effectively. This ensures the establishment of a balance between maintenance needs and resource utilization [11].

Qiushi et al. Presented the knowledge-based predictive learning model for predictive maintenance in Industry 4.0 [13]. Deng et al. Introduced a low-cost and easy-to-implement solution, with wireless sensors that monitor gradual failures of components [14]. Additionally, with the help of Asset Intelligence Network (AIN) and Artificial Intelligence (AI) computational models, predictive maintenance could be easily managed, and enterprise predictive maintenance scores could be as high as the previously checked in the scoreboard.

Thus, the idea of preventative maintenance (PM), which emphasizes the avoidance of asset breakdowns and the contexts in which they occur, evolved. In contrast to traditional maintenance methods that rely on the life cycle of machine parts, predictive maintenance uses machine learning techniques to identify specific patterns of system failure by learning from data gathered over some time and using live data [17]. In the real world, most of the PdM and the preventive maintenance could be handled by the application of computational models, and by using the right machine learning tools/methods to predict accurately and understand the key data parameters to train the model in PdM. There are multi dimensions benefits while applying the best machine learning and AI prediction model to understand the real time application in Industrial operations. Below are a few benefits:

- Reduce downtime of the machine/equipment's/devices/IIoT
- Increase productivity/operational effectiveness of machines
- Reduce the TCO and Increase the ROI for the enterprise operations.
- Improve safety and identify the root causes of failures
- Derive the Intelligent assets management by adopting the QML, QAI, ML, and Artificial Intelligence
- Reduced unplanned downtime, and Increase production uptime in industrial manufacturing operation
- Enhance the resource productivity (including human resources and machines) and Improve product quality (Fig. 1)

4   Strategy to Adopt in Predictive Maintenance

The recent study on the manufacturing and production operations, and per the industry 4.0 best practices recommends a few key critical strategies, steps, and processes to be adopted while considering a better predictive maintenance score (PdM) Scores for the industrial manufacturing automation and optimization as part of digital twins. A few of the key critical steps which need to be followed to obtain the PdM are listed below [14].

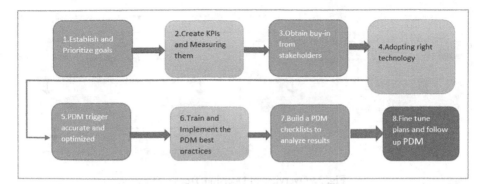

Fig. 1. Steps in Predictive Maintenance (PdM)

- Identify and prioritize goals.
- Create, track, and monitor the KPIs.
- Update the stakeholder buy-in
- Adoption of the right technology or software and Set up PdM mechanism update
- Training on the best implementation methods for preventive maintenance plans in Industrial sites.
- Develop the preventive maintenance checklist.
- Fine-tune plan based on results in Production sites.
- Smart Manufacturing Sites and Automation
- IIoT, sensors, and smart factories.

4.1 Application of Machine Learning Methods to Predict Predictive Maintenance (PdM)

Abidi et al., used various machine learning and computational model (AI, ML, QML, QAI) are used to understand the reality in accuracy while considering the predictive maintenance in the industrial operations and useful for the manufacturing facilities to get the most accurate and updated PdM score [5]. In our case, we have been using the Decision tree, based on the available data sets and data parameters, and trained the model to get the most updated score of prediction and optimized them as per our case. The decision Trees are extremely useful for the decision-making process and help to consider a decision in a complex mathematical calculation process. Computational models require collecting massive amounts of data on the failure Vector Space Model (VSM), LR, DT, and RF [5]. The below Figs. 2 and 3 represents the various machine learning models with the most accuracy in the prediction factors in PDM score for the predictive maintenance in large industrial manufacturing facilities in the USA.

In this paper, we have analyzed the collected data, understood the data from various equipment, prepared the model, and finally trained the model to get the ultimate prediction factors for the machine/device and the equipment. In our data model, we used more variables to get the most accurate predictions, which was an iterative process.

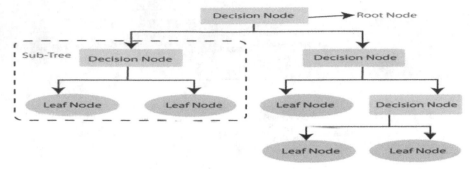

Fig. 2. Overview of Decision Trees (DT)

	Model	Accuracy	AUC	Recall	Prec.	F1	Kappa	MCC	TT (Sec)
xgboost	Extreme Gradient Boosting	0.9959	0.7732	0.8095	0.9951	0.9953	0.9385	0.9388	0.6180
lightgbm	Light Gradient Boosting Machine	0.9956	0.7711	0.7976	0.9950	0.9951	0.9342	0.9346	0.8470
catboost	CatBoost Classifier	0.9956	0.7776	0.8097	0.9949	0.9951	0.9342	0.9344	5.3500
rf	Random Forest Classifier	0.9953	0.7805	0.8049	0.9945	0.9948	0.9297	0.9299	0.1260
et	Extra Trees Classifier	0.9949	0.7809	0.7965	0.9942	0.9943	0.9232	0.9234	0.0920
lda	Linear Discriminant Analysis	0.9940	0.7804	0.7818	0.9939	0.9934	0.9094	0.9097	0.0100
gbc	Gradient Boosting Classifier	0.9932	0.7741	0.7620	0.9936	0.9932	0.9002	0.9009	1.5040
nb	Naive Bayes	0.9931	0.7827	0.7516	0.9927	0.9925	0.8961	0.8964	0.0080
dt	Decision Tree Classifier	0.9913	0.7771	0.7378	0.9922	0.9914	0.8714	0.8717	0.0210
ridge	Ridge Classifier	0.9836	0.0000	0.4907	0.9780	0.9795	0.7529	0.7547	0.0840
knn	K Neighbors Classifier	0.9720	0.6008	0.3143	0.9563	0.9621	0.3719	0.4340	0.0440
svm	SVM - Linear Kernel	0.9651	0.0000	0.1865	0.9365	0.9502	0.0530	0.0940	0.0680
ada	Ada Boost Classifier	0.9486	0.7532	0.5671	0.9812	0.9595	0.6820	0.6956	0.0910
qda	Quadratic Discriminant Analysis	0.0107	0.0000	0.1733	0.0001	0.0002	0.0000	0.0000	0.0480
lr	Logistic Regression	0.0000	0.0000	0.0000	0.0000	0.0000	0.0000	0.0000	0.8840

Fig. 3. Various Machine Learning models with % prediction rates in PdM

5 Pillars of the Total Predictive Maintenance in Industries 4.0

In a broader sense, total predictive maintenance (PdM) is the state of optimizing maintenance scores, records, and productibilities and reaching the maximum state of optimized
predictive maintenance (PdM) which is the most efficient in any production site for the
operations (Fig. 4).

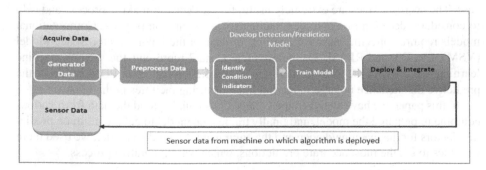

Fig. 4. Implementing the predictive algorithm model in PdM

PdM is the focus of predictive maintenance and events which can be managed through various machines, devices, and IIoT devices within the industrial operations. The ideal goal of predictive maintenance is to achieve the overall efficiency of predictive maintenance score in PdM, and it is based on the below factors.

- Non-stoppages or suboptimal production rates.
- No defects and zero defects.
- Managed unplanned downtime or reactive time losses.
- No accidents occur around the production units

The below Picture shows the most sought pillars of Total productive maintenance (TPM) in a holistic approach within the industrial manufacturing space. It also emphasizes proactive and preventative maintenance to maximize the operational efficiency of equipment/machines and devices within the production factory/units [15] (Fig. 5).

Fig. 5. Steps in Predictive Maintenance (PdM)

Within the machine learning tools, XG Boost classifier, we could be able to predict the most ROC curve along with the True positive and false negative ratios. The below graphs explain the most accurate prediction of the machine and equipment's database and the ROC of the class.

6   Quantum Computing and Digital Manufacturing 4.0

In production sites, most of them are adopting the best modern control processes, equipment, IIoT devices, Sensors, and advanced analytics along with the machine learning and automation in place to optimize their production growths and satisfy their make to order and make to stock capacity. In the digital era, Quantum computing and quantum machine learning play a vital role over the classical computers as Quantum computers run the principle of Qubits over the bytes, which is a supernatural, entanglement and optimized the most successful in the predictions of the success rates. Most of the manufacturing operational planning and executions could be much more accurate and optimized through the industrial applications of quantum computing, quantum machine learning, and quantum AI. Industries leaders are focusing on the user benefits and application benefits of quantum computing, smart factories, and the optimized prediction factors in any of the given datasets. Com- pared to classical computers and machine learning, quantum machine learning, and quantum AI would be in much demand and have a significant benefit to the industrial and operation applications in production sites. Quantum computing and applications could reduce shop floor pain, and Predictive maintenance issues, and in the event of failure of productions sites, it may also help to increase significantly industrial manufacturing and critical business operational planning in productions, capacity, business continuity, production flows, and robotics scheduling for complex products, such as industrial automobiles, are highly complex, and their simulation and optimization are very computed intensive (Fig. 6).

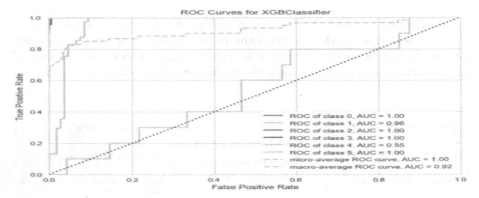

Fig. 6. ROC Curves for XGB Classifier

The quantum simulation model could help industrial manufacturers to design the productions, new features and add the new BOMs into the sopping floor capacity, and optimize the most complex industrial sensors, machines, and IIoT devices across the business units [20].

7   Reliability-Centered Maintenance (RCM)

In the industrial manufacturing space, reliability-centered maintenance (RCM) offers a wide range of service-based maintenance and ensures that all systems can run at optimal efficiency and accuracy as per the business needs. It offers best practices and adaptive models to save money, improve safety, and enhance machine performance and reliability in industrial manufacturing sites.

7.1   Benefits of the RCM Approach

The RCM-guided program to the sites provides numerous benefits to industrial manufacturers, including the prevention of machinery failures and shutdowns.

- Cost efficiency
- Improved performance:
- Enhanced safety

- Equipment longevity
- Production predictability.

The RCM-based predictive maintenance could be assessed and achieved with the following steps, and it should be applied to the Industrial applications and production units.

7.2 Key Principles of Reliability-Centered Maintenance (RCM)

Reliability centered maintenance (RCM) is to manage the electrical power distribution, the most effective way to manage the power equipment, sensors, and devices within the industrial manufacturing sites. Essentially, RCM helps to understand the best cost-effective way of managing the industrial Predictive maintenance (PdM) and the time-based maintenance (TBM) method, to use the effectiveness of industrial power distributions [21] (Figs. 7 and 8).

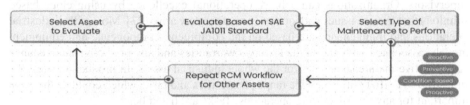

Fig. 7. Flow chart of RCM Approach

UDI	Type	Air temperature [K]	Process temperature [K]	Rotational speed [rpm]	Torque [Nm]	Tool wear [min]	Target	Failure Type		Label	Score
0	6	M	298.1	308.6	1425	41.9	11	0	No Failure	No Failure	1.0000
1	19	H	298.8	309.2	1306	54.5	50	0	No Failure	No Failure	0.9999
2	38	L	298.8	309.1	1439	39.2	104	0	No Failure	No Failure	1.0000
3	40	L	298.8	309.1	1350	52.5	111	0	No Failure	No Failure	0.9999
4	58	L	298.8	309.1	1513	40.3	160	0	No Failure	No Failure	0.9999

Fig. 8. Overview of RCM Approach

There are a few best practices and steps that need to be followed while adopting RCM (reliability-centered maintenance) in industrial production sites:

- Accept the failure events
- Failures are not the final number as it is the way to manage the rest of equipment life
- Learn to recognize the failure (type of failure and impact of the failure as per their risk parameters)
- Identify the breakdown facts on equipment's
- Identification of possible hidden failures.
- Possible Maintenance plan for the equipment and devices.

8 Intelligent Asset Management (IAM and RCM-Controlled Predictive Maintenance)

In industrial manufacturing and Industries 4.0, asset management plays a vital role and substantial demands for better outcomes, which may reduce and helps to manage the predictive maintenance at the production sites/factory locations. In the digital journey, most of the production sites, and factories are using heavily "digital devices, sensors, IIoT's and enterprise asset managers" to manage the production sites in a better way. As per the industrial manufacturing scenario, the Asset Intelligence Network (AIN) would help to manage the predictive maintenance (PdM) score and the degree of efficiency in the production sites. The strain on operators to enter equipment information decreases as this asset information grows, data quality improves, and both parties can communicate information about the asset's performance over its lifetime [22].

The AIM is the combination of the registered industrial/manufacturing devices/sensors/IIoT devices in industrial units. All this equipment's registered with the OEMs- original equipment manufacturers' calendrer and within the production site supervisors. Organizations can achieve operational excellence by using cloud-based solutions that foresee issues with operations before they arise [23]. Most of the industrial operations and maintenance are based on the equipment, components, and equipment models, associated with any of the factory's warranties and any predictive maintenance or preventive maintenance plan for the whole industrial assets. In production sites, the Industrial IoT (IIoT) offers a wide range of activities and tasks which could be the most important for any manufacturing operations. Tasks are listed below.

- Data collection on industrial manufacturing readings
- Vibrations and frequency, TPM
- Motor current, device temperature, and IAM

The predictive asset insights (PIA) within the SAP-IAM offers the assets health indicators, connectivity, and monitoring scores of any industrial manufacturing assets in the industrial manufacturing units, moreover it is built on "in-memory computing" and with the help of most computational models-AI, ML, Quantum AI, Quantum ML, and Qubits, in the Business Technology Platform (BTP) to update the best prediction and computational model to provide the best accurate and suitable Predictive maintenance management(PdM). It also offers alerts when problems are detected enabling maintenance to occur when truly needed at the factory sites and production units for any failure of the predictive maintenance suitable to industrial manufacturing applications to reduce the cost, and risks and avoid downtime compared to other maintenance strategies, like run-to-failure and preventive maintenance [25]. On the other hand, the IAM (Intelligent asset management) could be of significant use to manage the predictive maintenance and score in any of the production sites/user plants. IAM is a combination of the digital twin, Internet of Things, machine learning, and data analytics applications that are used to solve real-world problems in industrial manufacturing facilities. The potential takeaways within the IAM solutions are:

- Enterprise Asset Management (EAM): can effectively manage the life cycle of physical assets in production sites/factory areas.
- Organizations can achieve operational excellence by using cloud-based solutions that fore—see possible operational issues before they arise.
- Cost management effectively within the production sites.

8.1 Wings Within the IAM

- *Asset Intelligence Network (AIN)*
- *PDMSMS—stands for Predictive Maintenance Service.*
- *Asset Strategy and Performance Management (ASPM)* (Fig. 9)

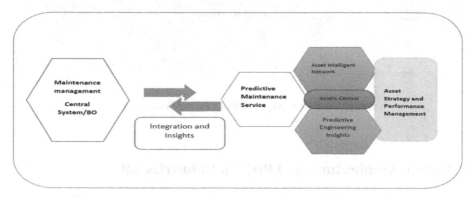

Fig. 9. IAM and digital manufacturing In Industry 4.0

8.2 Benefits that Could Be Achieved from AIN

In the paradigm of predictive maintenance (PdM), intelligent asset management (IAM), asset intelligence network (AIN), AI, ML, and quantum AI play vital roles to optimize the most valuable predictive maintenance score of the assets, machinery, and equipment's in industrial manufacturing. Most asset intelligence applications are the combination of IIoT, AI, and the digital twins which focused on the digital business transformation of any manufacturing business. Some of the key pillars within AIM are listed below:

- Connected with Products – end-to-end visibility into product-centric operations in manufacturing operations.
- Connected with Assets – an enabler to linking the production system and s, assets with manufacturing industrial operation and reduce costs and increase asset uptime.
- Connected the Fleets – the ability to offer the tracking, monitoring, analyzing, and maintaining all the moving assets wherever they are in a production site.
- Connected Infrastructure – ability to offer digital operational intelligence for better performance and capabilities.

The below diagram represents the Intelligent asset management and the best practices of the portfolio for predictive maintenance and services in industrial manufacturing operations. SAP IAM offers asset performance, reduces maintenance across the production units, and performs the dynamic asset performance and service management of the associated assets and devices, real prediction of asset maintenance could be easily possible to manage through the SAP IAM Applications in any industrial production sites (Fig. 10).

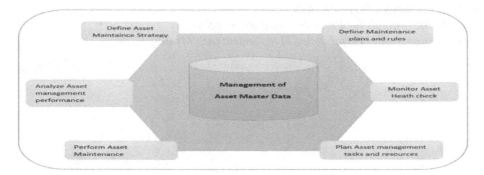

Fig. 10. SAP IAM portfolio for PdM Management

9 System Architectures and PDM in Industries 4.0

In a holistic approach within the Predictive maintenance management (PdM), a system architecture and database system play important roles and interconnective with the machinery, equipment, sensors, IIoTs, and Devices and understand the up-to-date data, conditions of machinery health checks and determine any specific conditions when the machine is going to fail or need some attention to gain the maintenance capacity to have long run operations. There are several methods, industrial practices, and technologies trends that are accelerating or KPIs to update the predictive maintenance (PdM). There are many of these critical system nodes, a few of them are listed below and updated in this paper.

Server: In industrial manufacturing, the data from various sensors, IIoTs, devices, and machines of the tubing machine is fetched continuously and stored on the company server (back offices) or any of the ERP applications for further use. Most enterprises use SQL or MongoDB databases since the volume of data generated is large in nature. This data is then later used for maintenance of the manufacturing unit. Because this project deals with a small amount of data, it makes use of the MySQL database and uploads the data to the server. Few modern industrial shop floors use digital twins (including Big Data- data warehouses, cloud computing, quantum machine learning (QML), edge computing, Internet of things (IoT), and most supercomputers like Quantum computers in place, which will be the key enabler within the system architecture and part of integration architecture of the PdM landscape.

Client: The operator at a particular manufacturing plant can get updates on the manufacturing unit, and they would get to know the sensor readings at a particular timestamp from the server, which would help to know if the unit is functioning properly or not, Hence, they can conduct the maintenance of the machine, accordingly, thus preventing the complete machine failure in any given instance.

Backend System/Office: The data fetched from the sensors are cleaned and preprocessed to extract prominent features for data analysis and finding patterns and correlations among the parameters. The cleaned data is then used to train a machine learning model, which would predict the parameter values over a period. Different models were trained on the parameters and their accuracy was calculated. The models were trained using classification and regression algorithms. An LSTM model of deep learning was also implemented to make the predictions. Most of cases, any ERP, Large data processing system could offer a wide range of back office and operational benefits to manage the predictive maintenance (PdM) in industrial manufacturing sites.

10   AI-Enabled Split-Migration Architecture

Failure Categories

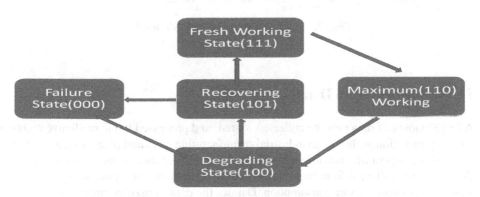

Fig. 11. Component failure state diagram

A. Sudden Failure State (000): A sudden (but noticeable) breakdown occurs while the production line is running well. This includes things like broken tools, snapped bands, melted wire, etc.
B. Intermittent Failure State (010); The "complete" machine failure is typically on the path to intermittent failures, which come and go. By their very nature, these intermittent or random failures might be challenging to pinpoint. Regular maintenance can frequently stop intermittent breakdowns.

C. Gradual Failure State (100); These are the malfunctions that become apparent over time as a machine's usefulness gradually deteriorates. Regular maintenance can frequently stop Gradual breakdowns. For this work, we assume an intermittent failure state and a gradual failure state as a degrading state (100). As shown in Figs. 11 and 12, AI will predict a maximum working state i.e., a state in which a component is heavily stressed-out state adding more loads will go into a degrading state or a failed state. As soon as AI detects or predicts an MWS (110) state it will migrate new tasks to the backup unit FSW (111) using a split-migration technique [32]. The split components [29–34], are considered parallel components so each additional component will improve the reliability of the system.

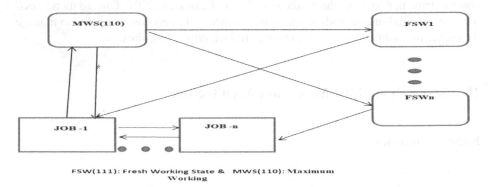

FSW(111): Fresh Working State &   MWS(110): Maximum
Working

Fig. 12. Task Delegation with Split-Protocol

11   Implementation Details

A large amount of data must be collected, stored, and processed in the predictive maintenance prediction within large industrial manufacturing sites and plants to get a better prediction of upcoming downtimes and predictive maintenance in the sites and plants. Data has been collected from the condition of the equipment; vibration; acoustic; ultrasonic; temperature; power consumption. Dataset the dataset used comprises the sensor data of the machine MNL15, of which the main factors thought are stated below [26].

- EJECTION-PCT: Excess material ejected from the machine during production.
- Error history: can be collected from the factory and plant sites from machine and equipment sites.
- EXTRUDER PRESSURE: Pressure sensor value from the extruder of the machine.
- Maintenance/repair history/Speed: Speed of the machine while manufacturing and under-standing its repair history.
- Machine operating conditions and actual values-inputs: input of raw material given to the machine.

- Equipment metadata and Heating Zone: Temperature reading of each section and equipment metadata.
- Standard feed-forward neural networks, such as CNN and RNN, do not have feedback connections. LSTMs have an advantage in this aspect over simple neural networks.
- The fields of Deep Learning and Natural Language Processing use the artificial recurrent neural network (RNN) architecture known as LSTM (Long Short-Term Memory) [24].

12 Conclusion

This model proposes a system that will predict the failure of the manufacturing unit based on parameters like temperature, and pressure and the machine parameters like speed, revolutions per min, ams/ccm input, etc. These parameters are recorded by the sensors of the tubing machine over a period, even the IIOT devices and automated sensors are capable enough to read the data from the machines, and devices from the various production units/units, and hence maintenance can be scheduled as per the requirements. This model will prove to be extremely useful in maintaining productivity and minimizing the cost of maintenance. This will reduce the time for which the unit remains idle for maintenance. The model was highly effective in predicting the time when the machine would be down based on the previous historical sensor data that it received. In our AI-enabled failure prediction model, the AI will forecast a maximum operating state or a state in which a component is severely stressed-out and will enter a degraded state or a failed state when further loads are applied.

When AI recognizes or anticipates that a component is stressed, it will shift the new task to the backup unit. This will even result in a minizine system failure. Each new component will increase the system's reliability because the split protocol components are thought of as parallel components.

References

1. Bedrij, O.J.: Carry-select adder. IRE Trans. Electron. Comput. **EC-11**(3), 340–346 (1962)
2. Salunkhe, T., Jamadar, N.I., Kivade, S.B.: Prediction of remaining useful life of mechanical components-a review. Int. J. Eng. Educ. **2**(1), 1–5 (2018)
3. Angius, A., Colledani, M., Yemane, A.: Impact of condition-based maintenance policies on the service level of multi-stage manufacturing systems. Control. Eng. Pract **76**, 65–78 (2018)
4. SAP IAM (Intelligent Asset Management) in a Capsule l SAP Blogs
5. Abidi, M.H., Alkhalefah, H., Mohammed, M.K., Umer, U., Qudeiri, J.E.: Optimal scheduling of flexible manufacturing system using improved lion-based hybrid machine learning approach. IEEE Access **8**, 96088–96114 (2020)
6. Usuga-Cadavid, J.P., Lamouri, S., Grabot, B., Fortin, A.: Using deep learning to value free-form text data for predictive maintenance. Int. J. Prod. Res. **60**(14), 4548–4575 (2022)
7. Abidi, M.H., Alkhalefah, H., Umer, U., Mohammed, M.K.: Blockchain-based secure information sharing for supply chain management: Optimization assisted data sanitization process. Int. J. Intell. Syst. **36**, 260–290 (2021)
8. Chen, X., Feng, D., Takeda, S., Kagoshima, K., Umehira, M.: Experimental validation of a new measurement metric for radio-frequency identification-based shock-sensor systems. IEEE J. Radio Freq. Identif. **2**, 206–209 (2018)

9. Gohel, H.A., Upadhyay, H., Lagos, L., Cooper, K., Sanzetenea, A.: Predictive maintenance architecture development for nuclear infrastructure using machine learning. Nucl. Eng.
Technol. **52**, 1436–1442 (2020)

10. Wen, Y., Fashiar Rahman, M., Xu, H., Bill Tseng, T.-L.: Recent advances and trends of
predictive maintenance from data-driven machine prognostics perspective. Measurement **187**,
110276 (2022). https://doi.org/10.1016/j.measurement.2021.110276

11. Zhu, F.: The application of data mining technology in the predictive maintenance for oil and
gas equipment. Acad. J. Eng. Technol. Sci. **5**(3), 45–48 (2022)

12. Coelho, D., Costa, D., Rocha, E.M., Almeida, D., Santos, J.P.: Predictive maintenance on sen-
sorized stamping presses by time series segmentation, anomaly detection, and classification
algorithms. Procedia Comput. Sci. **200**, 1184–1193 (2022)

13. Cao, Q., et al.: KSPMI: a knowledge-based system for predictive maintenance in industry
4.0. Robot. Comput.-Integr. Manuf. **74**, 102281–102281 (2022)

14. Deng, W., Guo, Y., Liu, J., Li, Y., Liu, D., Zhu, L.: A missing power data filling method based
on an improved random forest algorithm. Chin. J. Electr. Eng **5**, 33–39 (2019)

15. Vanderschueren, T., Boute, R., Verdonck, T., Bart, B., Wouter, V.: Prescriptive maintenance
with causal machine learning (2022)

16. Züfle, M., Moog, F., Lesch, V., Krupitzer, C., Kounev, S.: A machine learning-based workflow
for automatic detection of anomalies in machine tools. ISA Trans. **125**, 445–458 (2022)

17. Ren, S., Zhang, Y., Sakao, T., Liu, Y., Cai, R.: An advanced operation mode with product-
service system using lifecycle big data and deep learning. Int. J. Precis. Eng. Manuf.-Green
Technol. **9**(1), 287–303 (2022)

18. Mishra, S., Bordin, C., Taharaguchi, K., Purkayastha, A.: Predictive analytics beyond time
series: predicting series of events extracted from time series data. Wind Energy **25**, 1491–1653
(2022)

19. Márquez, A.C., de la Fuente Carmona, A., Antomarioni, S.: A process to implement an
artificial neural network and association rules techniques to improve asset performance and
energy efficiency. Energies **12**(18), 3454 (2019). https://doi.org/10.3390/en12183454

20. Gushanskiy, S., Potapov, V.: Investigation of quantum algorithms for face detection and
recognition using a quantum neural network. In: 2021 International Conference on Industrial
Engineering, Applications and Manufacturing (ICIEAM), pp. 791–796 (2021)

21. Moon, J.-F., Yoon, Y.T., Lee, S.-S., Kim, J.-C., Lee, H.-T., Park, G.-P.: Reliability-centered
maintenance model to managing power distribution system equipment. IEEE Power Eng.
Soc. Gen. Meet. (6) (2006)

22. Lin, C.Y., Hsieh, Y.M., Cheng, F.T., Huang, H.C., Adnan, M.: Time series prediction algorithm
for intelligent predictive maintenance. IEEE Robot. Autom. Lett **4**, 2807–2814 (2019)

23. Fernández-Navarro, F., Carbonero-Ruz, M., Alonso, D.B., Torres-Jiménez, M.: Global sensitivity estimates for neural network classifiers. IEEE Trans. Neural Netw. Learn. Syst **28**,
2592–2604 (2017)

24. Çınar, Z., et al.: Machine learning in predictive maintenance towards sustainable smart
manufacturing in industry 4.0. Sustainability **12**(19), 8211–8211 (2020)

25. Kane, A.P., Kore, A.S., Khandale, A.N., Nigade, S.S., Joshi, P.P.: Predictive Maintenance
using Machine Learning (2022)

26. Martens, D., Baesens, B.B., Gestel, T.V.: Rule extraction from support vector machines by
active learning. IEEE Trans. Knowl. Data Eng **21**, 178–191 (2009)

27. Singh, K., Upadhyaya, S.: Outlier detection: applications and techniques. Int. J. Comput. Sci
9, 307–323 (2012)

28. Limnios, N.: Interval reliability, corrections and developments of "reliability measures of
semi-markov systems with general state space. Methodol. Comput. Appl. Probab. **16**, 765–770
(2014)

29. Barlow, R., Hunter, L.: Optimum preventive maintenance policies. Oper. Res. **8**(1), 90–100 (1960)
30. Rawal, B., Karne, R., Wijesinha, A.L.: Splitting HTTP requests on two servers. In: The Third International Conference on Communication Systems and Networks: COMPSNETS 2011 (2011)
31. Rawal, B.S., Karne, R.K., Wijesinha, A.L.: Mini web server clusters for HTTP request splitting. In: IEEE, 13th International Conference on High Performance Computing and Communications (HPCC) (2011)
32. Rawal, B., Karne, R., Wijesinha, A.L.: A split protocol technique for web server migration. In: The 2012 International workshop on Core Network Architecture and protocols for Internet (IEEE MASS-ICNA-2012) (2012)
33. Rawal, B., Karne, R., Wijesinha, A.L.: Split protocol client server architecture. In: Seventeenth IEEE Symposium on Computers and Communication (ISCC'12) (2012)
34. Rawal, B.S., Duan, Q., Vijayakumar, P.: Dissection of the experimental outcome of split-protocol. Int. J. Adv. Intell. Paradigms **10**(1–2), 23–44 (2018)

A Digital Twin for Bus Operation in Public Urban Transportation Systems

Patricia Ruiz[1,3]([envelope]) [iD], Marcin Seredynski[2] [iD], Álvaro Torné[1],
and Bernabé Dorronsoro[1,3] [iD]

[1] School of Engineering, University of Cadiz, Cadiz, Spain
{patricia.ruiz,bernabe.dorronsoro}@uca.es
[2] E-Bus Competence Center, Schifflange, Luxembourg
marcin.seredynski@ebcc.lu
[3] Faculty of Engineering, The University of Sydney, Camperdown, Australia

Abstract. Advances in technology, jointly with technology transfer and the digital transformation is leading to a new industrial revolution where digitalization enables the improvement of production and safety as well as operational effectiveness by monitoring, diagnosing and correcting process flaws. In this work, we propose a Digital Twin (DT) of a public transportation system in Badalona (Spain) for obtaining in depth understanding of the bus dynamics. We use a genetic algorithm for finding the most suitable configurations for simulating the traffic in a city based on real data. Results show that the proposed DT accurately reproduces the real traffic, the bus schedule and that it easily adapts to possible anomalies.

Keywords: Digital twin · Urban transport · Traffic Simulation · Metaheuristics

1 Introduction

New technologies and awareness of climate change are motivating authorities to redesign their public transport (PT) systems towards more sustainable and efficient ones. Designing an efficient urban mobility system is of utmost importance. It can bring societal, economic and environmental benefits for the city, from enhancing its citizens quality of life to reducing its cost, while improving the air quality, the traffic, and reducing total energy consumption. However, it implies a number of technological challenges and important and cost-effective decision making that need a deep understanding of the city traffic dynamics.

A simulation accurately reflecting the traffic conditions in the city is an extremely useful tool to take appropriate decisions in the design of the urban mobility system. Additionally, it would be also desirable its capability to adapt to any anomalies that affect traffic conditions. Such a tool could be able to estimate the traffic state in the near future, making it possible to anticipate to any new situation that is expected to happen before it actually occurs.

C.-H. Hsu et al. (Eds.): DataCom 2022, LNCS 13864, pp. 40–52, 2023.
https://doi.org/10.1007/978-981-99-2233-8_3

Digital twins (DT) [18,22] are highly precise and realistic simulators able to accurately reproduce some physical system in real time, making use of different kinds of sensors and data to observe the current state of the system. DTs enable different innovative applications allowing evaluating the impact of any change in the system before applying it, detecting anomalies in the functioning of the system, or even predicting situations that might happen in the future. DTs are already essential tools for many companies, because they allow improving their products and processes [10]. Recent Markets research suggests that the DT market –worth US$6.9 billion in 2022– is projected to reach US$73.5 billion in value by 2027 [20].

The implementation of a DT of a bus helps to analyze its dynamic performance, capabilities, factors influencing the energy usage, monitoring the current and future state of health of the vehicle, its performance as well as the battery state of charge and state of health (if electric), among other benefits. In the context of smart cities, it provides accurate information for decision making, capabilities, limitations and potential improvements.

In this work, we propose creating a DT of an urban bus called BODIT (Bus Operation Digital Twin), that accurately reproduces the traffic in the city, allowing the detection of any lack of punctuality at the stops, and adapting itself to the new observed situation. Therefore, BODIT enables predicting the effects of any action that might be taken (at the levels of either the bus or traffic management), and facilitates decision making when facing unusual situations, as those motivated by accidents, broken down vehicles on the road, traffic lights malfunctioning, or crowds caused by social events. BODIT makes use of SUMO traffic simulator [4,13] and a Genetic Algorithm (GA) to reproduce the real traffic and the optimal configurations. In this work the metropolitan area of Badalona (Spain) is chosen as test case for validating BODIT. Data of real traffic flows as well as real data of the M6 bus schedule along 5 operating days is used.

The main contributions of this work are presented next. First, the division of the metropolitan area of Badalona into different types of attraction areas for accurately reproducing the real traffic data. Second, we integrate SUMO simulator and a genetic algorithm for obtaining a set of optimal configurations for the digital twin under different traffic situations. Third we present BODIT, able to reproduce the traffic in the city and adapt to new traffic conditions based on the information of the bus schedule.

The paper is structured as follows. Next Section reviews relevant related works. Section 3 presents the proposed methodology. The experiments accomplished and the results obtained are explained in Sects. 4 and 5, respectively. Finally, Sect. 6 concludes the paper and provides some future research lines.

2   Related Works

Michael Grieves claims that he presented the model of a digital twin for the first time in the Society of Manufacturing Engineering (SME) Management Forum in October of 2002 [18] later formalized in his white paper [17], although the name was not coined until 2010 by John Vickers in NASA [22]. However, the concept is much older and it was born in 1960 during the Apollo 13 space mission. After the explosion of the oxygen tank, simulators did not reflect the actual state of the vehicle, and they had to be adapted to match conditions of actual state of the spacecraft [1]. During the last years, the names and features of DTs have changed. For an extensive review of the evolution of digital twin, its applications and main challenges refer to [3,23].

Digital twins offer many benefits, e.g. they can reduce operational costs, apply preventive maintenance of physical process, extend the lifetime of equipment, optimize performance and sustainability, continuous refinement of models, more efficient and informed decision support system, or personalized products and services [16,23]. Thus, it is being applied in many different fields like in aerospace [5], e-health [19], meteorology [8], manufacturing and process technology [27], education [6], smart cities [12], architecture [2], transportation [15], or energy sector [30], among others.

In the context of smart cities and more specifically in transportation, the concept of DT is also being applied. In [21], a digital twin battery of an electric vehicle (EV) is proposed for monitoring its state of charge and its state of health. Authors in [29] explore the potentials of the DT technology for optimizing the efficiency and reliability of EVs. Rodriguez et al. propose in [24] a thermal digital twin of e-powertrain elements for monitoring these relevant temperatures during the system operation. In [26], Szalay presents a novel framework for automotive testing and validation that connects physical and virtual testing using a DT.

More specifically in the PT systems there are few works that use DT technology. In [7], authors set the basis and challenges for the implementation of a DT of an electric bus with the idea to analyze the technology's adaptability level, capabilities, scope, limits, and future improvements. Deng et al. introduce in [11] a DT model for demand responsive transit, i.e. a customized transport system that aggregates users' demand into clusters and then dispatches vehicles to those locations. Also a smart city processing architecture is presented and validated in [28] where a digital twin of the city is created. Specifically, a demonstration of the proactive management of the London public bus system through a DT (*DEDUCE-PT*) is presented.

3   Methodology

This section presents the methodology followed by design of BODIT. First, Sect. 3.1 presents SUMO, the realistic traffic simulator used in this work. Second, we explain in Sect. 3.2 how SUMO is configured to accurately reproduce real traffic with little information. Finally, Sect. 3.3 describes the functioning of the proposed DT.

3.1   Simulation of Urban Mobility (SUMO)

SUMO [18,22] is an accurate open source traffic simulator that works at both macroscopic and microscopic levels. It is implemented in C++, so it can perform efficient simulations on large scenarios, and it is among the most well-known traffic simulators in the literature [14].

SUMO implements a large number of micromobility models as car-following models, lane changing, intersections management, overtaking or traffic light logic. Additionally, it includes many different kinds of vehicles, all with their own physical behavior, including cars, emergency vehicles, trucks, buses or vans.

As one of the most interesting features of SUMO, it allows importing real maps in various formats, including *OpenStreetMap*[1], wich offers a rich selection of layers. Also, the traffic can be generated at the level of establishing the journeys of each individual vehicle. Finally, it can generate a variety outputs that allow fine-grained statistics.

3.2   Configuring SUMO to Reproduce Observed Traffic

SUMO has a large number of parameters to be configured. Among them, there are important ones as the number of vehicles, their type, their origin and destination, the route they follow or their departure time. The values assigned to these parameters markedly influence on the simulation, and therefore they must be carefully selected.

It is usual that the required information for an accurate simulation is not available (as the exact routes of all vehicle trips in the city), making it difficult to reproduce the real traffic in the city. In practice, available public information is given in a few locations of the whole road network of the city and at a very low level of detail. For instance, it is usual that this information is provided as the average number of vehicles per hour along several days. Additionally, in many cases there is no differentiation on the type of vehicles counted. Therefore, we propose in this work a generic methodology for fine-tuning SUMO to reproduce the traffic in the city without any information from real traffic. The only information required is the time when the bus arrives to each bus stop in its route. However, in case some information is available, it can be used in the model to enhance its accuracy.

Inspired by the proposal of Seredynski et al. [25], we consider three kinds of areas, namely residential, commercial, and industrial. In that work, authors defined the areas as circles on the map. Therefore, some areas were not covered by the circles, and some others could belong overlapped circles of different kinds. We propose in this work a more realistic approach in which these areas are defined using polygons, whose borders are streets. This new approach allows covering the whole city surface with areas that do not overlap. The information on the different types of areas is provided by *OpenStreetMap*, and those areas with more than one activity are tagged with the predominant one.

The different areas are considered to be probabilistic attraction poles, and vehicles will depart from and head for them with some probabilities. In [25], vehicles starting points were randomly chosen from aomng the residential areas. However that is not a realistic assumption: buses generally depart from industrial

---

[1] https://www.openstreetmap.org/.

areas or vehicles may return home after work/shopping. Therefore, we consider in our approach that vehicles can start their trips from any kind of area.

Once the depart and arrival probabilities are set for all areas, they can be used to generate the traces for all vehicles in our scenario. However, setting these probabilities to reflect real traffic is a difficult task, specially if we consider the high number of probabilities that are needed to be defined. A GA is used to find them. The solution of the GA indicates the optimal percentage of vehicles departing from every specific area and the probabilities of arriving to a industrial, commercial or residential area. During the generation of the vehicle traces, some data may be used to enrich the model, if available, as the traffic volume counters in some street(s), or statistics on travels among different districts in the city, information we use in this work (as described in Sect. 4.2).

In order to evaluate how realistic the simulations generated by a given configuration are, we compute the differences in time between the simulation and the real-world data of the bus arrival times at the different stops during the whole route. This is used as the fitness function, averaged on the number of stops, to be minimized by the GA. It is mathematically defined in Eq. (1), where n is the number of stops in the route and d_i is the difference between the real and estimated arrival times at stop i. With this approach, no information is needed about the traffic, further than the bus arrival times at the stops, easy to measure (or even the official scheduled times could be used).

$$minimize \quad F = \frac{1}{n} \sum_{i=1}^{n} abs(d_i) \ . \tag{1}$$

3.3   Bus Operation Digital Twin (BODIT)

The GA generates and evaluates thousands of different solutions during its execution. All unique configurations generated are stored in a database, together with the time difference obtained by the bus at every stop in those solutions. They will be used by BODIT, as explained hereinafter.

The best solution thrown by the GA corresponds to a highly accurate simulation of the real traffic in generic conditions, according to observations of several days. This configuration will be the one used by BODIT when the real bus starts its route. Therefore, BODIT immediately offers a prediction of the traffic and the bus stops arrival times for the whole route duration. Every time the bus arrives a stop, the time is compared with the one predicted by BODIT. If the real bus is over a given threshold ahead or behind the predicted schedule, BODIT adapts itself by changing the SUMO configuration to the one that better fits the new arrival time, from those in the generated database. Then, BODIT is again perfectly synchronized with the real bus from that stop. Therefore, the only data BODIT requires to adapt to any changes or anomalies that may happen affecting traffic in the city is the time when the bus arrived the last stop. This methodology is shown in Fig. 1.

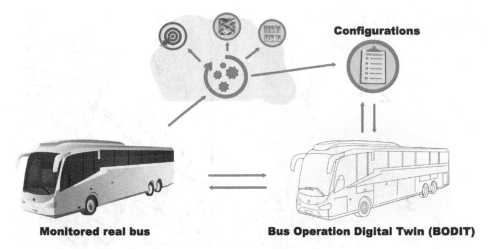

Fig. 1. The data gathered by the real bus, real traffic data, traffic simulations and optimization provide a set of accurate configurations for BODIT.

4   Experiments

In this section the scenario used and the experimental setting of the GA are presented.

4.1   Description of the Scenario

As already mentioned, in order to evaluate and validate BODIT, we focus on PT system of the metropolitan area of Badalona. Real data of buses operating in the city of Badalona is used. As a case of study, we consider the M6 bus route operation. It has 30 stops round trip that the bus performs in roughly one hour. Information about 5 days operation is used in this work. Specifically, for the GA execution, we use the median value of the time stamp of the buses arriving at each bus stop for four days, and use the fifth day to validate our model.

Real traffic data provided by the Consejería de Movilidad of Badalona town hall[2] is also used. In it, the city is divided into 5 districts and the hourly average of trips within a district and between its 5 districts is provided. It also differentiates between public and private transport dividing the former into buses and taxis. As it can be seen in Fig. 2(a), the M6 bus route only operates in suburbs of 2 of the 5 districts of Badalona, thus we will replicate the traffic in these two areas from the available real data.

As stated in Sect. 3.2, the districts are divided into three different type of areas in order to simulate the traffic flows (industrial, residential and commercial). There is also an additional classification as green area, but no traffic is related within this area (therefore is not relevant for modeling the traffic flows).

---

[2] https://www.barcelona.cat/mobilitat/en.

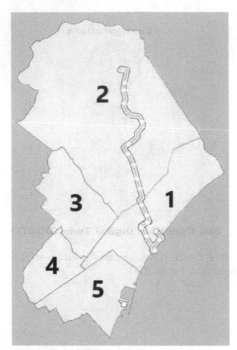 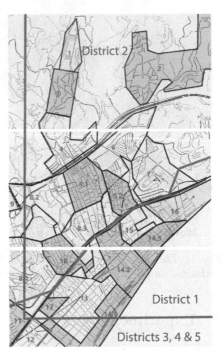

(a) M6 bus route over the two different districts of the five districts composing the Badalona metropolitan area.

(b) Division of the scenario into residential (blue), commercial (pink) and industrial (orange) zones. Green ones represent parks and green areas.

Fig. 2. M6 bus route in Badalona is the considered scenario in this work color figure online.

Figure 2(b) shows the resulting 22 different areas after the subdivision of districts 1 and 2. It can be observed that several areas were very large (e.g. area 5, 8 and 14) and were further divided into smaller ones.

Traffic is simulated in SUMO by adding vehicles all along the simulation time. From real traffic data, the number of vehicles moving every hour is known, thus a uniform distribution of this value is used. In the experiments we include different types of vehicles available in SUMO with different acceleration, speed and breaking profiles in order to have vehicle diversity.

Traffic flows are recreated by defining the routes of each simulated vehicle. In this work, we propose to randomly choose one edge from the departure area and another from the destiny area. The SUMO API TraCI method *findRoute* will find the vehicle's route if it exists. If not, a new random origin/destination pair will be chosen. The process is repeated until the route is built.

4.2 Experimental Setup

The experiments were performed on a Huawei TaiShan 2280 V2 server with 2 Kunpeng 920 CPUs of 48 cores each. It is a massively parallel server with 96

ARM computing cores, distributed into 4 NUMA nodes. Ubuntu 20.04.1 LTS Linux operating system runs on the server.

The GA used is implemented in C, and a number of scripts were implemented in Python for its interaction with SUMO, e.g., to set SUMO configuration, run it with the desired parameters, get the output of the simulation, etc. We used SUMO version v1.9.2.

One simulation of our scenario in SUMO takes over 360 s in our server, and it must be done for every individual evaluation in the GA. The fact that the GA requires performing tens of thousands of evaluations supposes an important challenge for our experiments. We therefore implemented a parallel GA, where all fitness evaluations can be performed in parallel. This way, one generation takes around 360 s instead of 360 s times the number of individuals. Because the server used in our experiments provides 96 cores, we decided to use a population of 90 individuals that are evaluated in parallel, one in each core, using OpenMP. Six cores are left free for the operating system and its processes.

The encoding of individuals is shown in Fig. 3. The length of the chromosome is established as follows. There are four genes for every area districts 1 and 2 have been divided into. The first one represents the percentage of vehicles whose starting point is the intended area. The next three genes represent the probability that the destination point of this route is a residential, a commercial or an industrial area, respectively. Traffic related to districts 3, 4 and 5 are represented together (they are outside the bus itinerary) in the last four genes.

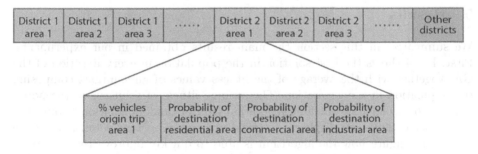

Fig. 3. Encoding of each individual in the population of the algorithm.

As it can be seen in Fig. 2(b), the map is divided into 22 different areas. Because area 11 is known to suffer from heavy traffic digesting most of the incoming traffic from areas 3, 4 and 5, we do not consider the generation of additional traffic in this area. Therefore, the chromosome is composed of 21 areas from districts 1 and 2 and another representing districts 3, 4 and 5.

The parameters of the GA are summarized in Table 1. Individuals are composed by 88 variables (representing 22 groups of 4 variables each). The population is randomly initialized just after the GA starts, and a simple amendment method is always applied before evaluating any individual during the whole optimization process in order to ensure that the three probabilities in each of the

Table 1. Parameters of the GA used.

Length of individuals	88
Population size	90
Population initialization	Random
Parents selection	Random selection
Recombination	SBX
Recombination probability	$\rho_c = 0.9$
Mutation	Random Value
Mutation probability	$\rho_m = 0.001$
Replacement	Replace if non worse
Termination condition	500 generations

22 groups of variables sum 1.0, as required by the selected representation. Both parents are selected at random in the population, and they are recombined using the well-known Simulated Binary Recombination (SBX) operator [9] with probability 0.9. The mutation operator simply replaces genes by a random double number in the interval $[0, 1]$ with 0.001 probability. Newly generated individuals replace those in the population if they are non-worse, according to their fitness values. Finally, the algorithm iterates for 500 generations.

5   Results

We summarize in this section the main results obtained in our experiments. First, Fig. 4 shows the best solution in the population in every iteration of the GA, together with the average of the fitness values of all solutions composing the population in the generation. The average fitness of solutions in the population is over 650 s for the first generation (initial random solutions), but only values below 200 s are displayed to avoid missing important details. It can be seen in the figure how the algorithm is able to quickly improve the quality of the initial solutions, and the convergence speed gets slower from generation 150 (approximately). The difference between the best and average fitness value in the population shows that there is still diversity at the end of the run, so the algorithm could be able to keep improving solutions in longer executions. However, performing 500 generations takes over 42 h computing time.

We analyzed the capacity of BODIT to reproduce real traffic in the city and adapt to anomalies by using real data from another day, not used in the training process. The results are provided in Table 2. We studied four different threshold values of 120, 90, 60, and 30 s respectively. When the gap between the simulated and real stop arrival time is over the threshold, BODIT automatically changes its traffic simulator configuration to fit the observed behavior.

In Table 2, the stops where the gap between the bus arrival timestamp and the expected time are over the threshold, thus requiring a change in the traffic configuration, is emphasized with grey background. We can see in the table that BODIT is able to accurately reproduce real traffic during the bus operation, requiring a low number of adaptations. Specifically, the number of changes in one hour and 5 min operation time is 2 for 120 and 90 s thresholds, 6 for 60 s, and 14 when the threshold is set to 30 s. We can assume that the latter case is too restrictive, given that a 30 s gap with respect to the expected time is not an important delay, and it can be caused by details as stopping on some pedestrian cross or by the time for passengers entering/leaving the bus. However, despite how high restrictive the threshold is, BODIT needs to adapt its traffic only once every 4.6 min.

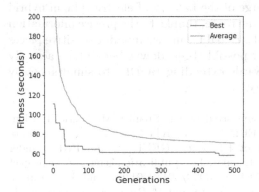

Fig. 4. Convergence plot of the best and average fitness in the population.

Table 2. Results of BODIT.

Stop	Max allowed gap 120 s	90 s	60 s	30 s	Stop	Max allowed gap 120 s	90 s	60 s	30 s
1	7	-17	42	-5	16	-26	30	-12	22
2	0	33	7	4	17	13	-7	-6	-19
3	-44	0	-1	-30	18	34	-37	-19	-8
4	3	-25	-10	-24	19	-31	21	-10	18
5	-8	4	3	25	20	54	88	47	15
6	-37	57	-16	-18	21	37	4	6	17
7	-15	-1	-58	-27	22	-20	-11	21	-2
8	48	61	42	26	23	14	6	12	1
9	-35	11	32	14	24	-36	-25	10	-10
10	71	14	7	-10	25	13	22	48	12
11	-52	20	-10	23	26	28	11	1	5
12	78	74	50	5	27	-55	-11	41	-8
13	66	24	43	30	28	39	-14	21	-28
14	36	39	16	0	29	-35	-15	-1	14
15	-19	-6	56	25	30	18	-14	-9	-26

We consider that a 120 or 90 s threshold is more suitable for our purposes. In these cases, BODIT only requires performing two traffic configuration changes to adapt to real-world observations, one in each of the trips done, exposing the high robustness and accuracy of our digital twin to reproduce real conditions.

6   Conclusion and Future Work

This work presents BODIT, an accurate digital twin for urban public transport bus system. BODIT makes use of SUMO simulator to realistically reproduce traffic in the city. For that, BODIT only needs information on the real and expected bus arrival times at every stop. Although it is not required, it also allows incorporating data from traffic (if available), to make even more realistic simulations. In our work, we make use of some rough traffic statistics provided by the town hall of Badalona (Spain), the city considered as a case of study.

The city is divided into residential, commercial and industrial areas, and a genetic algorithm (GA) is used to find the probabilities that these areas are selected as departure or arrival for every vehicle in the simulation. We have implemented a massively parallel GA that makes use of 90 computing cores simultaneously, given that it requires performing tens of thousands of SUMO runs, which take around 6 min each.

BODIT is able to adapt to any anomalies happening during the bus operation, which are not required to be explicitly notified. It detects such anomalies just by monitoring the bus arrival times at the bus stops, both in the simulation and in real world. When this gap is considered to be important enough (some thresholds are defined for that), BODIT will react by adapting its simulation to make it closer to the real traffic, by choosing an appropriate configuration from a database, created during the GA execution.

As future work, we plan to enrich BODIT with new features, making use of more data obtained from sensors in the bus. For instance, BODIT will be used to accurately predict the state of charge of the battery of electric/plugin hybrid buses at any moment until the end of the route, thanks to the precise information on the simulated bus circulation profile. BODIT can also monitor sensitive pieces and mechanisms in the bus to predict possible breakdowns before they actually happen. Finally, we are working towards extending BODIT to simultaneously consider all urban bus lines in the city.

Acknowledgements. This work was supported by the Spanish Ministerio de Ciencia, Innovación y Universidades and the ERDF (iSUN – RTI2018-100754-B-I00), Junta de Andalucía and ERDF under contract P18-2399 (GENIUS), and ERDF under project (OPTIMALE – FEDER-UCA18-108393). This publication is part of the project TED2021-131880B-I00, funded MCIN/AEI/10.13039/501100011033 and the European Union "NextGenerationEU"/PRTR. B. Dorronsoro and P. Ruiz acknowledge "ayuda de recualificación" funding by Ministerio de Universidades and the European Union-NextGenerationEU.

References

1. Allen, B.D.: Digital twins and living models at NASA. Technical report, Digital Twin Summit (2021). https://ntrs.nasa.gov/citations/20210023699
2. Alonso, R., Borras, M., Koppelaar, R.H.E.M., Lodigiani, A., Loscos, E., Yöntem, E.: SPHERE: BIM digital twin platform. Proceedings **20**(1), 1 (2019)
3. Barricelli, B.R., Casiraghi, E., Fogli, D.: A survey on digital twin: definitions, characteristics, applications, and design implications. IEEE Access **7**, 167653–167671 (2019)
4. Behrisch, M., Bieker, L., Erdmann, J., Krajzewicz, D.: SUMO - simulation of urban mobility: an overview. In: International Conference on Advances in System Simulation (2011)
5. Bellinger, N., Tuegel, E.J., Ingraffea, A.R., Eason, Thomas, G., Spottswood, S.M.: Reengineering aircraft structural life prediction using a digital twin. Int. J. Aerosp. Eng. 1687–5966 (2011)
6. Berisha-Gawlowski, A., Caruso, C., Harteis, C.: The concept of a digital twin and its potential for learning organizations. In: Ifenthaler, D., Hofhues, S., Egloffstein, M., Helbig, C. (eds.) Digital Transformation of Learning Organizations, pp. 95–114. Springer, Cham (2021). https://doi.org/10.1007/978-3-030-55878-9_6

7. Botín-Sanabria, D.M., et al.: Digital twin for a vehicle: electrobus case study. In: International Conference on Industrial Engineering and Operations Management (2021)
8. Chinesta, F., Cueto, E., Abisset-Chavanne, E., Duval, J.L., Khaldi, F.E.: Virtual, digital and hybrid twins: a new paradigm in data-based engineering and engineered data. Arch. Comp. Methods Eng. 27(1), 105–134 (2020)
9. Deb, K., Kumar, A.: Real-coded genetic algorithms with simulated binary crossover: studies on multimodal and multiobjective problems. Complex Syst. 9(6), 431–454 (1995)
10. Deloitte Insights: Digital twins bridging the physical and digital (2020). https://www2.deloitte.com/us/en/insights/focus/tech-trends/2020/digital-twin-applications-bridging-the-physical-and-digital.html
11. Deng, S., Zhong, J., Chen, S., He, Z.: Digital twin modeling for demand responsive transit, pp. 410–413. Institute of Electrical and Electronics Engineers Inc. (2021)
12. Deren, L., Wenbo, Y., Zhenfeng, S.: Smart city based on digital twins. Comput. Urban Sci. 1, 1–11 (2021)
13. DLR and contributors: SUMO homepage. https://www.eclipse.org/sumo/
14. Dorronsoro, B., Ruiz, P., Danoy, G., Pigne, Y., Bouvry, P.: Evolutionary Algorithms for Mobile Ad Hoc Networks. ACM/IEEE Society (2014)
15. Gao, Y., Qian, S., Li, Z., Wang, P., Wang, F., He, Q.: Digital twin and its application in transportation infrastructure. In: IEEE International Conference on Digital Twins and Parallel Intelligence, pp. 298–301 (2021)
16. GAVS Technologies: Digital twin concept (2017). https://www.gavstech.com/wp-content/uploads/2017/10/Digital_Twin_Concept.pdf
17. Grieves, M.: Digital twin: manufacturing excellence through virtual factory replication (2014). https://www.3ds.com/fileadmin/PRODUCTS-SERVICES/DELMIA/PDF/Whitepaper/DELMIA-APRISO-Digital-Twin-Whitepaper.pdf
18. Grieves, M.W.: Virtually intelligent product systems: digital and physical twins, pp. 175–200 (2019)
19. Laaki, H., Miche, Y., Tammi, K.: Prototyping a digital twin for real time remote control over mobile networks: application of remote surgery. IEEE Access 7, 20325–20336 (2019)
20. MARKETSANDMARKETS: Digital twin market by enterprise, application (predictive maintenance, business optimization), industry (aerospace, automotive & transportation, healthcare, infrastructure, energy & utilities) and geography - global forecast to 2027 (2022). https://www.marketsandmarkets.com/Market-Reports/digital-twin-market-225269522.html?gclid=Cj0KCQjwrs2XBhDjARIsAHVymmTo3ZZI9HhY0PuBwQMOTROTNX4XrmfNTG2yabssY5uvP7kOg4taJnEaAgm1EALw_wcB
21. Merkle, L., Pöthig, M., Schmid, F.: Estimate e-golf battery state using diagnostic data and a digital twin. Batteries 7(1), 15 (2021)
22. Piascik, R., et al.: Technology area 12: materials, structures, mechanical systems, and manufacturing road map (2010)
23. Rasheed, A., San, O., Kvamsdal, T.: Digital twin: values, challenges and enablers from a modeling perspective. IEEE Access 8, 21980–22012 (2020)
24. Rodríguez, B., Sanjurjo, E., Tranchero, M., Romano, C., González, F.: Thermal parameter and state estimation for digital twins of e-powertrain components. IEEE Access 9, 97384–97400 (2021)
25. Seredynski, M., Danoy, G., Tabatabaei, M., Bouvry, P., Pigné, Y.: Generation of realistic mobility for VANETs using genetic algorithms. In: IEEE Congress on Evolutionary Computation, pp. 1–8 (2012)

26. Szalay, Z.: Next generation x-in-the-loop validation methodology for automated vehicle systems. IEEE Access **9**, 35616–35632 (2021)
27. Tao, F., et al.: Digital twin-driven product design framework. Int. J. Prod. Res. **57**(12), 3935–3953 (2019)
28. Van Den Berghe, S.: A processing architecture for real-time predictive smart city digital twins. In: IEEE International Conference on Big Data, pp. 2867–2874 (2021)
29. Van Mierlo, J., et al.: Beyond the state of the art of electric vehicles: a fact-based paper of the current and prospective electric vehicle technologies. World Electr. Veh. J. **12**(1), 20 (2021)
30. Yu, W., Patros, P., Young, B., Klinac, E., Walmsley, T.G.: Energy digital twin technology for industrial energy management: classification, challenges and future. Renew. Sustain. Energy Rev. **161**, 112407 (2022)

Predicting Residential Property Valuation in Major Towns and Cities on Mainland Fiji

Kunal Maharaj[1]([✉]), Kunal Kumar[2], and Neeraj Sharma[1,2]

[1] Fiji National University, Lautoka, Fiji
kunal.maharaj@fnu.ac.fj
[2] University of Fiji, Lautoka, Fiji

Abstract. The real estate sector plays a pivotal role towards the economy of every nation. Transaction of properties heavily rely on the valuation price as determined by the appraisers who use many variations of techniques to determine the valuation of respective properties. This value is used by investors, sellers, intermediary agencies such as real estate agencies and financial institutions as well as government entities. However, the value determined by the appraisers is just an approximation, excluding the accuracy and error rate with respect to the actual price. This study aims to integrate the capabilities of machine learning models and algorithms towards determining valuation price. Four algorithms were selected, namely, Multiple Linear Regression, Decision Tree, Random Forest, and Artificial Neural Network, for supervised learning against training and testing of a dataset acquired from real estate agencies based on residential properties in major towns and cities on mainland Fiji. Results show that Random Forest and Artificial Neural network produce high levels of accuracy based on Mean Absolute Error (MAE), Mean Squared Error (MSE) and Root Mean Squared Error (RSME) values. The study has significantly contributed towards developing insights to developing accurate models which could enable users access to valuation of properties based on the input of property features through machine learning predictions.

Keywords: Property Valuation · Machine Learning · Multiple Linear Regression · Decision Tree · Random Forest · Artificial Neural Networks

1 Introduction

The real estate sector is a major contributor of every nation's economy with billions of dollars' worth of transactions occurring around the globe annually. The significant motivator behind such ordeal is the direct result of growth and developments which invokes the need to invest in properties. The determination of the valuation in transacting properties plays a crucial role, as investors, sellers, intermediary agencies, and financial institutions rely on the approximated current value to reach an agreement. Accuracy, however, of the determined valued price remains a concern, as the current methods of determining valuation of possessions, items and properties are done using industry experts and appraisers based on several methods and algorithms. The current

© The Author(s), under exclusive license to Springer Nature Singapore Pte Ltd. 2023
C.-H. Hsu et al. (Eds.): DataCom 2022, LNCS 13864, pp. 53–68, 2023.
https://doi.org/10.1007/978-981-99-2233-8_4

means of obtaining a respective value by appraisers are in relations to drawing comparisons between similar properties from the vicinity with careful considerations given to the attributes and features. Other factors such as expert judgements and experience of appraisers are used. The non-inclusivity of computer-based algorithms to determine such an important commodity is a concern since the attributes and features of every property presents non-linear complexities. The ability of data mining algorithms to consider these multi-collinearity dimensions, is simply beyond human capabilities, and presents us with the scope of drawing more accurate values.

Property advertising and sale often relies on online media platforms such as websites and social media. The digital age, including migration to Web 3.0 has enabled every user accessibility to such forms of marketing platforms to search and advertise properties and possessions. The transparency and integrity between advertisements and sales heavily depend on market value, which need not necessarily fall in the proximity of the value being sought after. Even property owners would need some form of comparison metric to establish a fair value before considering advertising and selling properties.

This paper aims at comparing residential property valuations predictions on mainland Fiji, achieved through machine learning algorithms including multiple linear regression (MLA), Decision Tree (DT), Random Forest (RF) and Artificial Neural Network (ANN). The algorithm which produces the highest possible accuracy with minimal errors towards predicting residential property prices will be considered for the prediction model. The motivation behind such is to enable investors and sellers alike with a platform where features of properties can be entered to retrieve predicted price based on the machine learning model.

2   Literature Review

2.1   Property Valuation Approaches

Valuation of properties plays a crucial role in carrying out investment related transactions, however, methods and models employed in determining the value are always questioned due to its inefficiency led by the error-rate and low transparency. The current models and methods employed by appraisers include sales comparison, cost approach and income approach whereby factors, such as socio-economic and environmental factors along with property features are considered to arrive to an estimated value [1]. Other traditional methods include comparative method, profit's method, and contractor's/cost method where prices are deduced either by comparing similar property sales, estimating market rates for revenue generating properties or cost to build a similar property. With massive information and data available, computer aided models can be integrated with machine learning to highly optimize the valuation models used by appraisers. Computer aided modelling has the ability to analyze and integrate fluctuating market constraints, asymmetrical information and non-linear complexities surrounding features of respective properties. The integration of machine learning algorithms to current models' provision anomaly detection and time series analysis, while also recognizing unfamiliar patterns to filter and determine factors influencing market segments providing spatial and feature-based clustering to eliminate outliers [2].

Limitations due to the non-inclusivity in the traditional valuation approach and the recognition of data analytics has many institutions from various disciplines leaning towards hedonic price modelling and automated valuation models [3]. In comparison to the traditional approaches, these models yield more accurate predictions and efficiency with respect to being cost effective and timely [4, 5]. However, hedonic models used in automated valuation modelling does not always outweigh the benefits of traditional components. Some of the limitations of these modern techniques include the possibility of omitting important features from a human perception, consideration of policies, and flaws in comparability of valuations due to different locations [6]. As such, [7] strongly suggests a hybrid valuation system which integrates both, the modern and traditional approaches as an optimum solution, whereby the use of machine learning to deduce valuation price is further annotated by appraisers, guiding the process of valuation determination by incorporating expert judgements.

2.2 Feature Selection of Properties

The real estate sector, due to its massive contribution towards economy, in every nation is abound by legislations and policies. The features which affect real estate valuation vary in every nation and can be classified under local, spatial, physical, and legal features. The relatively high number of attributes makes it difficult to incorporate all the features in price prediction. Several selection criteria are continually being conducted to refine the uninformative and insignificant variance of features.

Features attributed to properties differ based on each location and domain. As a result, features are non-standardized, making it even more critical to identify the significant features that affect property valuations for accuracy purposes. Utilizing the aid of experts and citizens and employing the various analysis approaches such as principal component analysis, analytical hierarchy process, frequency, and factor analysis, [8] identifies significant features attributed to property valuation using multiple regression method. Similarly, by utilizing particle swarm optimization on classification and regression models, [9] addresses the fluctuations in house prices with composite features, reducing the prediction error by simply eliminating the irrelevant features. [10] applies conformal predictors as a framework to supplement regression algorithms on large number of characteristics that automated valuation models uses to achieve a measure of confidence for reliability. Similarly, economic factors also play a pivotal role in determining property prices and needs to be incorporated within the feature set. Current modelling of price predictions and property valuations heavily rely on hedonic methods, whereas, other important commodities, such as economic principals, which state, that market price can only be deduced correctly when the demand and supply curve integrate accordingly [11]. By comparing the optimized parametric values of algorithms, [12] can draw critical economical patterns through XGBoost algorithm while predicting property prices in Boston.

Applying the nonconformity measure as a real-valued function, efficiency can be greatly [13]. While complex valuation models have the ability to factor in high dimensional data, other reasons to reduce the complexity of feature selections include limitations in the dataset, optimizing computational power and model composition [14, 15]. Several algorithms have been effectively employed for feature selection. Linear regression, primarily due to its popularity, multiple regression, artificial neural networks, and decision trees. ANNs [4] and Random Forest yield a high degree of accuracy in determining the feature selection from datasets comprising of complex relationships. [16] places emphasis on single respective variable analysis, missing values, and outlier data pre-processing to optimize the training dataset whereby each of these analysis employs a variety of multilevel machine learning algorithms and methods to remove skewness from dataset and achieve more accuracy.

2.3 Machine Learning Models for Property Predictions

The digital age has enabled acquisition of data in volumes and with velocity. Real estate sector is one of the many disciplines where data is generated in abundance. This allows the possibility of employing machine learning algorithms to build predictive models which can produce valuation prices with relatively minimal errors. Several studies based on various locations and domains have explored the possibility with tremendous success in depicting price modelling using dataset with refined features.

Linear regression is one of the simplest algorithms which can be used to predict the price of properties by taking into consideration a singular standard feature or independent variable. By considering past patterns, [17, 18] uses simple linear regression model to predicts residential property prices for stakeholders' future investment. Multiple linear regression algorithms can also be used for the same purpose. [19–21] has utilized several multiple regression models such as polynomial, ridge, lasso and boosting algorithms to predict property prices and drawing comparison to each of the multiple regression model. In addition to multiple regression models, while [22] examines other classification algorithms such as naïve bias, random forest, and decision trees in depth and establishing patterns in projected predictions of rent and selling price. Similarly, [23] utilizes the Bayesian approach to introduce latent variable to identify factors in the submarket which impact properties and predicts values with the assumption on the number of submarkets, modelling based on the location, house features and price within each submarket. Having established the parameters, the authors take the Bayesian average of the probabilities and use it to compare with the posterior characteristics of houses within respective submarkets.

Random forest algorithm has been proven in much research as the optimal algorithm for prices prediction mainly due to its ability to invoke multiple decision trees and stability with outliers in the dataset. Random forest produced the highest accuracy in many papers. [24] compares the results obtained between random forest, linear regression and decision trees and establishes that random forest yields minimal errors based on root mean square values.

Consequently, while identifying opportunities in the real sector, [25] employs several algorithms such as support vector, k-nearest neighbor, and neural networks, identifying predominant aspects as well as limitations on each of the models. Support vector transforms data into a high dimensional state so as not to discriminate between instances of the output. K-nearest neighbor technique is an instance of geometric classification technique which traverses the entire dataset to predict a single output whereas the neural networks identify multi-collinearity and hidden relationships distributed amongst several variables. Gradient boost models such as XGBoost, LGBM, kernel ridge and elastic net are also compared alongside support vector and random forest by [26] in predicting real estate prices, yielding highly accurate results through elastic net and gradient boosting algorithm [27, 28] establishes the regularization in dataset and employs the concept of clipping using multi-threading to obtain better house price index using XGBoost. One of the key components suggested was the need to use stacking rather than bagging data in each of the models [29] takes the motivation from the impact of economic growth to property prices and employs optimized gradient boosting model, attaining the lowest possible error of 0.01%.

The ability of neural networks for prediction cannot be ignored due to its ability to factor in hidden layers and deduce complex non-linear relationships between variables. By comparing the prediction capabilities of statistical and machine learning models over investment of assets, [30–32] observes that convolutional neural network outperforms other models including recurrent neural networks, long short-term memory, and auto-regressive integrated moving average. By using a relatively larger dataset with 1.2million records, [33] uses hybrid ANN to analyze data and predict market prices of properties, establishing an accuracy rate of 98.7951%. ANN has been proven to outperform the hedonic price models and other neural network models such as LSTM [34]. The ARIMA model was proven to outperform support vector machines as well [35]. Similarly, a complex model is built to test the cross sub-market estimations for spatially aggregated data using ANN by [36], whereas [37, 38] tests the prediction model with regularization model with hidden layers, stating the ability of artificial neural networks to outperform automated valuation models in residential property market prices. [39] combines the multilayer perception with content-based filtering to predict users' preference for properties and achieves an accuracy of 60.7% through the model, while [40] builds different networks from the dataset, to establish a refined STN model, conducting several experiments beginning with a basic deep learning model, picking out strong features from each network with a joint self-attention mechanism. This goes to prove the ability of neural networks in predictions and the scope it provides for employing machine learning in hedonic price modelling in the real estate sector.

Based on the prediction capabilities of machine learning algorithms and models, regression trees, random forest and artificial neural networks have been proven to yield high accuracies with relatively low error rates. Hence, to build an accurate model, this paper intends to identify the optimum model by comparing the results from several models including multiple linear regression, decision trees, random forest and artificial neural networks based on the dataset constructed from major towns and cities in Fiji.

3   Methodology

The goal of predicting property valuations is based on experimenting real datasets constructed from real transactions on properties, hence, a deterministic approach of postpositive philosophical worldview is employed. There is a need to identify attributes which possibly affects the outcomes of the result. The data mining models employed to predict values have been supervised to follow a definite law of certainty.

The outcome of predicting valuations requires experimenting attributes and variables from datasets using unbiased approaches and standards of validity and viability to produce numerical information, hence, the research design has been quantitative in nature.

3.1   Data Analysis

The data has been obtained from real estate agencies and the dataset has been carefully built, to eliminate redundancies and capture as many features and attributes which can possibly affect the valuation price. The initial dataset built contains 18 columns as feature attributes with 2056 number or rows. The dataset contains categorical and numerical data along with added description and missing values due to data obtained from several agencies, and the lack of a standard template or format defined by any governing entities.

3.2   Data Pre-processing

The initial dataset is built on Excel to include all the features, from which 16 features are identified for conducting the experiment. Table 1 shows the attributes from the dataset and the procedure undertaken to prepare data for processing. Each of these features have been allocated categorical or numerical data type. The conversion of ordinal data into numerical enables machine learning process to become significantly lighter, to yield better results conveniently.

A descriptive statistic for the quantitative variables within the dataset is presented in Table 2 which enables a better insight to the type of data that will be analyzed and modelled.

Table 1. Procedure employed for cleansing data during pre-processing of initial dataset

Features	Description	Variable Type	Definition/Annotation
City/Town	Town/city over the mainland	Numerical	Nadi-1, Lautoka-2, Ba-3, Suva-4, Nausori-5, Lami-6, Sigatoka-7
Sales Price	Value of the property	Numerical	Currency in Fijian Dollars
Area (Sq. Mtrs)	Size of the property	Numerical	Size of the property in square meters
Location	Area in the city the dwelling is situated	Categorical	Sub-urban location
Land Type	Type of Land on which the property is situated	Numerical	Freehold-1, iTaukei/Native-2, CrownC-3, CrownB-4
Zoning	Type of dwelling the property is situated in	Numerical	Residential-1, Commercial-2, Industrial-3, Agricultural-4
Title	Document stating proprietors	Boolean	Yes-1, No-2
Engineers Certificate	Certification of the property against natural disasters	Boolean	Yes-1, No-2
No. Bedrooms	Number of Bedrooms in the dwelling	Numerical	
HVAC	Heating, Ventilation and Air Conditioning Units	Numerical	The number of units are ignored. Yes-1, No-2
Bath	Bathrooms in the property	Numerical	
Garage	Availability of garage for parking	Boolean	
Lawn	Existence of lawn in the property	Boolean	Yes-1, No-2
Swimming Pool	Inclusivity of Swimming pool	Boolean	Yes-1, No-2
Master Beds	Number of master bedrooms in the property	Numerical	
No. Flats	Number of flats in the dwelling	Numerical	

Table 2. Descriptive statistics for the quantitative variables in the dataset for modelling.

	count	mean	std	min	25%	50%	75%	max
City	72.0	2.972222e+00	2.034714e+00	1.0	1.00	2.0	4.25	7.0
HVAC	72.0	9.444444e-01	2.306689e-01	0.0	1.00	1.0	1.00	1.0
Bedroom	72.0	3.583333e+00	4.811225e+00	1.0	2.00	3.0	3.25	43.0
Zoning	72.0	2.416667e+00	1.147563e+00	1.0	1.00	2.0	3.00	4.0
Bath	72.0	1.736111e+00	5.033145e-01	1.0	1.00	2.0	2.00	3.0
Pool	72.0	2.777778e-01	4.510464e-01	0.0	0.00	0.0	1.00	1.0
Garage	72.0	1.000000e+00	6.713451e-01	0.0	1.00	1.0	1.00	3.0
MasterBed	72.0	1.000000e+00	6.051423e-01	0.0	1.00	1.0	1.00	2.0
Lawn	72.0	7.500000e-01	4.360514e-01	0.0	0.75	1.0	1.00	1.0
Land Type	72.0	1.888889e+00	1.055576e+00	1.0	1.00	1.0	3.00	4.0
Flats	72.0	1.875000e+00	8.547712e-01	1.0	1.00	2.0	2.00	4.0
Area	72.0	1.141944e+03	8.489170e+02	108.0	797.75	914.0	1149.75	6232.0
Price	72.0	1.203597e+06	1.440703e+06	75000.0	418750.00	649500.0	1192500.00	7500000.0
EC	72.0	9.027778e-01	2.983392e-01	0.0	1.00	1.0	1.00	1.0
Title	72.0	8.194444e-01	3.873488e-01	0.0	1.00	1.0	1.00	1.0

3.3 Data Visualization

Visualization enables a greater understanding of the features and the relationships between the variables. Having pre-processed and prepared the data for modelling, the numerical values analysis is presented through the heat map in Fig. 1. The lighter colors in the heat map reflect stronger correlations between the variables as opposed to the darker colors. The heat map proves to be a useful means of establishing features correlated to the valuation price variable.

An in-depth analysis of the features was further determined by the pair plots. Outliers in the dataset is expected to significantly affect the accuracy of the model, while at the same time, these outliers cannot be ignored or eliminated from the dataset. Based on the correlations determined from the heat map, the features having stronger correlations with the price variable were independently verified and evaluated. Figure 2 shows the correlation between zoning and number of flats with respect to price.

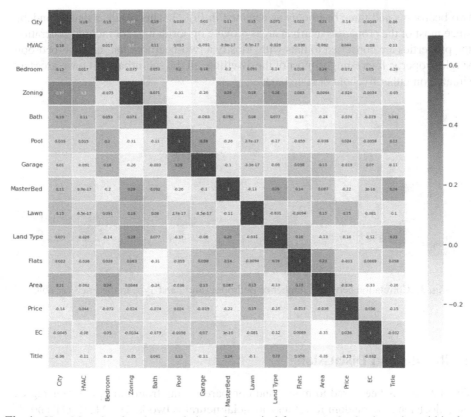

Fig. 1. Heat Map showing the correlation of numerical features and valuation price within the dataset

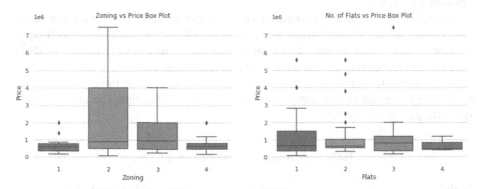

Fig. 2. Correlation between Zoning and Number of Flats to the Price variable

While a great number of properties appear in the residential and commercial zone, with either a single flat, or properties having been converted into multiple flat for income generating purposes, based on the location. Most of the properties are shown to have two bedrooms and three bedrooms as depicted in Fig. 3. This result is understandable since most of the properties in urban areas provide opportunities for income generation, the properties are converted to flats with, mostly a two-bedroom flat, or three-bedroom single property. Interestingly, most of the dwellings in the sub-urban and town areas are situated on either freehold or state land.

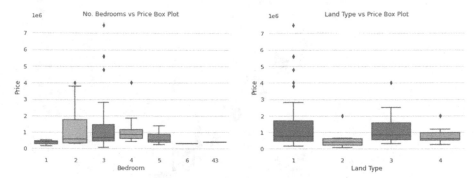

Fig. 3. Correlation between Number of Bedrooms and Land Type to the Price variable

4   Results and Discussion

The dataset has been used to model and compare results from multiple linear regression, decision tree, random forest and artificial neural network. The MLR, DT and RF algorithms were employed without normalizing the sample data. The training and modelling of data for these algorithms was done collectively, while the entire dataset was remodeled for ANN.

Normalization of data was done to ensure variables have the values contained between the interval of 0 and 1. Since normalization only matters while using multi-layer perceptron such as neural networks, normalization was done when performing ANN to compute differences between the actual and predicted values.

The values determined by the regression models are depicted in Table 3, where Random Forest regression model outperforms decision tree and Multiple Linear Regression by yielding an 89% accuracy.

Table 3. Performance of Regression Models

Model	Score	Explained Variance Score
Random Forest Regression	0.89025	0.85354
Decision Tree	0.75296	0.73561
Multiple Linear Regression	0.64778	0.52314

Training the model for ANN required using batch size. The batch used was 128, since smaller batch size would take longer processing time. The model was trained for 400 epochs, with the regressor being 15 × 5 units. Figure 4 shows the training loss per epoch which helps to depict any overfitting. No overfitting actuated in our model, evident from both the lines going down at the same time. The accuracy in the training model is achieved by the 15th epoch.

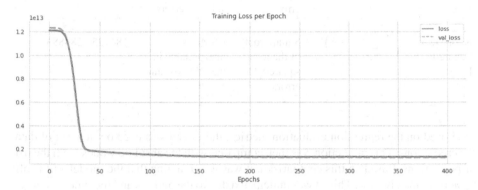

Fig. 4. Training loss per epochs

While residual sum based on iterations was relied upon for MLR, DT and RF, the mean absolute error (MAE), mean squared error (MSE) and the root mean squared error (RSME) were employed to measure the accuracy of ANN, as the models capability to correctly predict the house price heavily depend on the error values.

4.1 Evaluation on Test Data

The regression evaluation metrics chosen for normalization and error determination comprises of MAE, MSE and RSME. Table 4 depicts the value and attributes along with the formula used for each metric.

Table 4. Regression Metrics for Evaluation on Trained Model

Regression Value Metrics				
Metric	*Formula*	*Value*	*Attribute*	*Score*
Mean Absolute Error	$\frac{1}{n}\sum_{i=1}^{n}\lvert y_i - \hat{y}_i \rvert$	Mean of the absolute value of errors	Easiest to understand since it is the average error	1161933.458333333

(continued)

Table 4. (*continued*)

Regression Value Metrics

Metric	Formula	Value	Attribute	Score
Mean Squared Error	$\frac{1}{n} \sum_{i=1}^{n} (y_i - \hat{y}_i)^2$	Mean of the squared errors	Stringently accounts for large value of errors	3420103.873604843
Root Mean Squared Error	$\sqrt{\frac{1}{n} \sum_{i=1}^{n} (y_i - \hat{y}_i)^2}$	Square root of the mean squared errors	RSME is interpretable in the 'Y' axis units	1849352.284883776

Based on the regression evaluation metrics, the model was used on new set of data for predictions. This prediction was then compared with the absolute values from the list of predictions. Based on this comparison, it was worth noting that the model's fit is off by approximately 21%. This fit was anticipated due to the outliers and the type of values. To better comprehend the error, a variance regression score was utilized, where values closer to 1.0 (perfect score) are desirable. The variance score yielded a value 0.8, which is normal and accepted result. A comparison of the model score against the perfect fit is shown in Fig. 5 -along with the error yielded by the variance regressor.

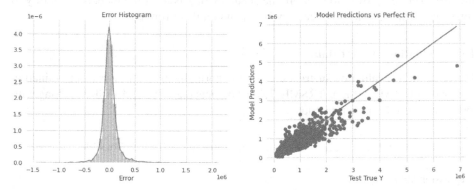

Fig. 5. Error Values and the Model Predictions Curve.

The accuracy rate of the ANN model was deduced to be 87.73%. This was done by predicting the new values and comparing the values with the prediction model, a difference in the value divided by the initial value yields the percentage error. The accuracy of the prediction model is lower than the desired level, however, the value determined by the model anticipated since ANN works better on significantly larger datasets in comparison to the dataset size utilized in this paper.

5 Conclusion

The extensive study based on previous literature and the methodology employed on the dataset including property prices in Fiji, has enabled desired results using the algorithms used. Multiple linear regression is best suited for analysis based on linear relationships between distinguished variables. It yielded a percentage accuracy of 65%, while decision tree produced an accuracy rate of 75%. Random forest algorithm utilizes multiple decision trees to derive output based on predictions, hence, it was expected to have produced better results compared to multiple linear and decision tree algorithms. Random Forest produced an accuracy rate 89%. Neural networks are optimal and best suited for complex datasets due to its ability to correlate non-colinear relationships by identifying hidden layers. The artificial neural network algorithm produced an accuracy of 88%, which is impressive given that the dataset was not as large as desired, and the simplicity derived during pre-processing between data types and relationships between variables. Finally, based on the results produced by the models, both random forest and artificial neural network algorithms can be used for making highly accurate predictions. Taking into consideration the dynamics of the data, this paper proposes the use of random forest for prediction, unless the dataset is deemed to be relatively large and complex with many variables, in which case ANN can be utilized.

6 Limitations

The dataset used in this paper to build the model for training and testing purposes has been obtained from real estate agencies' listings from the past 5 years. While recency of data is maintained, other sources of data such as that from social media has not been incorporated. The primary reason for this is the scope and the work required. Scraping data from social media sites such as Meta is no longer made possible or accessible for ethical reasons, while scraping from other advertising platforms which gives users the liberty to advertise for properties, also require additional work such as annotating the data based on categorical and numerical information, being present in unstructured and semi-structured form. Annotating such forms of data will also require special consideration be given to incorrect and misspellings as well as data being presented in mixed or multiple languages combined. Obtaining data from real estate agencies board and valuers association board proved futile, limiting data acquisition from only a few real estate agencies. The interpretation of the result also needs to accommodate the fact that the prices feature obtained from the listing does not reflect the true valuation as this sale price also has a certain, yet no fixed percentage, of additional commission that real estate agencies include to the actual selling price.

7 Future Work

The prediction capability of the models has strongly envisioned the need to develop a web-based application which provides the users with ability to input features of desired properties to obtain a valuation price for comparison purposes. The dataset will need to be extended to include data from all major locations, including all types of properties, not just residential. Based on the algorithms, a novel model will be developed which will be trained to handle non-linear complexities of certain features which are already known, for better accuracy and minimal errors.

References

1. Su, T., Li, H., An, Y.: A BIM and machine learning integration framework for automated property valuation. J. Build. Eng. **44**(44), 102636 102661 (2021)
2. Kabaivanov, S., Markovska, V.: Artificial intelligence in real estate market analysis. In: AIP Conference Proceedings, vol. 2333, no. 1, pp. 30001–30008 (2021)
3. Glumac, B., Des Rosiers, F.: Practice briefing – Automated valuation models (AVMs): their role, their advantages and their limitations. J. Property Investment Finan. **39**(5), 481–491 (2020)
4. Abidoye, R.B., Chan, A.P.C.: Improving property valuation accuracy: a comparison of hedonic pricing model and artificial neural network. Pac. Rim Prop. Res. J. **24**(1), 71–83 (2018)
5. Valier, A.: Who performs better? AVMs vs hedonic models. J. Property Investment Finan. **38**, 213–225 (2020)
6. Wang, D., Li, V.J.: Mass appraisal models of real estate in the 21st century: a systematic literature review. Sustainability **11**(24), 7006 (2019)
7. Renigier-Bilozor, M., Zobrek, S., Walacik, M., Borst, R., Grover, R., d'Amoto, M.: International acceptance of automated modern tools use must-have for sustainable real estate market development. Land Use Policy **113**, 105876 (2022)
8. Yalpir, S., Sisman, S., Akar, A.U., Unel, F.B.: Feature selection applications and model validation for mass real estate valuation systems. Land Use Policy **108**, 105539 (2021)
9. Sakri, S.B., Ali, Z.: Analysis of the dimensionality issues in house price forecasting modeling. In: Fifth International Conference of Women in Data Science at Prince Sultan University (WiDS PSU), pp. 13–19. IEEE (2022)
10. Lim, Z., Bellotti, A.: Normalized nonconformity measures for automated valuation models. Expert Syst. Appl. **180**, 115165 (2021)
11. Zhang, Q.: Housing Price Prediction Based on Multiple Linear Regression. Scientific Programming **2021**, 1–9 (2021). https://doi.org/10.1155/2021/7678931
12. Ghatnekar, A., Shanbhag, A.D.: Explainable, multi-region price prediction. In: International Conference on Electrical, Computer and Energy Technologies (ICECET), pp. 1–7. IEEE (2021)
13. Boström, H., Linusson, H., Löfström, T., Johansson, U.: Accelerating difficulty estimation for conformal regression forests. Ann. Math. Artif. Intell. **81**(1–2), 125–144 (2017)
14. Chanasit, K., Chuangsuwanich, E., Suchato, A., Punyabukkana, P.: A real estate valuation model using boosted feature selection. IEEE Access **9**, 86938–86953 (2021)
15. Wang, W.C., Chang, Y.J., Wang, H.C.: An application of the spatial autocorrelation method on the change of real estate prices in Taitung city. Int. J. Geo-Inform. **8**(6), 249 (2019)
16. Cheri, X.: Optimizations of training dataset on house price estimation. In: 2nd International Conference on Big Data Economy and Information Management (BDEIM), pp. 197–203. IEEE (2021)
17. Ghosalkar, N.N., Dhage, S.N.: Real estate value prediction using linear regression. In: Fourth International Conference on Computing Communication Control and Automation (ICCUBEA), pp. 1–5. IEEE (2018)
18. He, K., He, C.: Housing price analysis using linear regression and logistic regression: a comprehensive explanation using melbourne real estate data. In: International Conference on Computing (ICOCO), pp. 241–246. IEEE (2021)

19. Sanyal, S., Biswas, S.K., Das, D., Chakraborty, M., Purkayastha, B.: Boston house price prediction using regression models. In: International Conference on Intelligent Technologies (CONIT), pp. 1–6. IEEE (2022)
20. Madhuri, C.R., Anuradha, G., Pujitha, M.V.: House price prediction using regression techniques: a comparative study. In: International Conference on Smart Structures and Systems (ICSSS), pp. 1–5. IEEE (2019)
21. Manasa, J., Gupta, R., Narahari, N.S.: Machine learning based predicting house prices using regression techniques. In: 2nd International conference on innovative mechanisms for industry applications (ICIMIA), pp. 624–630. IEEE (2020)
22. Gampala, V., Sai, N.Y., Bhavya, T.N.S.: Real-estate price prediction system using machine learning. In: International Conference on Applied Artificial Intelligence and Computing (ICAAIC), pp. 533–538. IEEE (2022)
23. Liu, Z., et al.: A bayesian approach to residential property valuation based on built environment and house characteristics. In: IEEE international conference on big data (big data), pp. 1455–1464. IEEE (2018)
24. Yee, W.L., Bakar, N.A.A., Hassan, N.H., Zainuddin, N.M.M., Yusoff, R.C.M., Ab Rahim, N.Z.: Using machine learning to forecast residential property prices in overcoming the property overhang issue. In: International Conference on Artificial Intelligence in Engineering and Technology (IICAIET), pp. 1–6. IEEE (2021)
25. Baldominos, A., Blanco, I., Moreno, A.J., Iturrarte, R., Bernardez, O., Afonso, C.: Identifying real estate opportunities using machine learning. Appl. Sci. 8(11), 2321 (2018)
26. Dey, S.K., Urolagin, S.: Real estate price prediction using data mining techniques. In: 4th International Conference on Computing, Power and Communication Technologies (GUCON), pp. 1–4. IEEE (2021)
27. Li, Z.: Predictions of house price index based on machine learning methods. In: 2nd International Conference on Computing and Data Science (CDS), pp. 472–476. IEEE (2021)
28. Zhao, Y., Chetty, G., Tran, D.: Deep learning with XGBoost for real estate appraisal. In: IEEE symposium series on computational intelligence (SSCI), pp. 1396–1401. IEEE (2019)
29. Almaslukh, B.: A gradient boosting method for effective prediction of housing prices in complex real estate systems. In: International Conference on Technologies and Applications of Artificial Intelligence (TAAI), pp. 217–222. IEEE (2020)
30. Aithal, P.K., Acharya, U.D., Geetha, M., Sagar, R., Abraham, R.: A comparative study of deep neural network and statistical models for stock price prediction. In: 3rd International Conference for Emerging Technology (INCET), pp. 1–5. IEEE (2022)
31. Piao, Y., Chen, A., Shang, Z.: Housing price prediction based on CNN. In: 9th International Conference on Information Science and Technology (ICIST), pp. 491–495. IEEE (2019)
32. Zhan, C., Wu, Z., Liu, Y., Xie, Z., Chen, W.: Housing prices prediction with deep learning: an application for the real estate market in Taiwan. In: 18th International Conference on Industrial Informatics (INDIN), vol. 1, pp.719–724. IEEE (2020)
33. Al-Gbury, O., Kurnaz, S.: Real estate price range prediction using artificial neural network and grey wolf optimizer. In: 4th International Symposium on Multidisciplinary Studies and Innovative Technologies (ISMSIT), pp. 1–5. IEEE (2020)
34. Lee, C.: Forecasting spatially correlated targets: simultaneous prediction of housing market activity across multiple areas. Int. J. Strateg. Prop. Manag. 26(2), 119–126 (2022)
35. Wang, F., Zou, Y., Zhang, H., Shi, H.: House price prediction approach based on deep learning and ARIMA model. In: 7th International Conference on Computer Science and Network Technology (ICCSNT), pp. 303–307. IEEE (2019)
36. Horvath, S., Scoot, M., Zaddach, S., Neuner, H., Weitkamp, A.: Deriving adequate sample sizes for ANN-based modelling of real estate valuation tasks by complexity analysis. Land Use Policy 107, 105475 (2021)

37. Stubnova, M., Urbanikova, M., Hudakova, J., Papcunova, V.: Estimation of residential property market price: comparison of artificial neural networks and hedonic pricing model. Emerg. Sci. J. **4**(6), 530–538 (2020)
38. Peterson, S., Flanagan, A.: Neural network hedonic pricing models in mass real estate appraisal. J. Real Estate Res. **31**(2), 147–164 (2009)
39. Kato, N., Yamasaki, T., Aizawa, K., Ohama, T.: Users' preference prediction of real estates featuring floor plan analysis using FloorNet. In: Proceedings of the 2018 ACM Workshop on Multimedia for Real Estate Tech, pp. 7–11 (2018)
40. Wang, P.Y., Chen, C.T., Su, J.W., Wang, T.Y., Huang, S.H · Deep learning model for house price prediction using eterogeneous data analysis along with joint self-attention mechanism. IEEE Access **9**, 55244–55259 (2021)

Designing an AI-Driven Talent Intelligence Solution: Exploring Big Data to Extend the TOE Framework

Ali Faqihi[1]([✉]) and Shah J. Miah[2]([✉])

[1] Department of Business Administration, Jazan University, Jazan, KSA, Saudi Arabia
ali.faqihi@uon.edu.au
[2] Newcastle Business School, University of Newcastle, Newcastle, NSW, Australia
shah.miah@newcastle.edu.au

Abstract. AI has the potential to improve approaches to talent management enabling dynamic provisions through implementing advanced automation. This study aims to identify the new requirements for developing AI-oriented artifacts to address talent management issues. Focusing on enhancing interactions between professional assessment and planning attributes, the design artifact is an intelligent employment automation solution for career guidance that is largely dependent on a talent intelligent module and an individual's growth needs. A design science method is adopted for conducting the experimental study with structured machine learning techniques which is the primary element of a comprehensive AI solution framework informed through a proposed moderation of the technology-organization-environment (TOE) theory. Moreover, the study will recommend practical directions for an IS researcher for addressing unique talent growth requirements in the organization and automated features in talent management solutions.

Keywords: Talent Intelligence · AI · Design Artifact · Career Centre · Design Research

1 Introduction

The use of artificial intelligence (AI) in talent management has been already established as a significant research trend. Many modern technologies address the issues involved in developing such systematic automated information support solutions, but AI has been rarely applied to enhancing practices in employment management [1]. Capabilities of AI are viewed in existing cases of studies for the construction of interventions from an employment perspective, but various disruptive innovations to enhance the current frameworks of talent systems are not been holistically studied in the past recent years. The advancement of general-purpose AI technology is a paramount task in revolutionizing workforce management [2]. While creating new AI-oriented applications for employment management, a number of obstacles such as dehumanization, biased algorithms

C.-H. Hsu et al. (Eds.): DataCom 2022, LNCS 13864, pp. 69–82, 2023.
https://doi.org/10.1007/978-981-99-2233-8_5

and fairness in requirements have been identified, so it is imperative to conduct precise design research [3].

A recent industry survey identified at least 300 h technology start-ups developing AI tools for people management, with roughly 60 of these companies achieving traction in terms of clients and venture investment [4]. Furthermore, an AI-powered talent intelligence platform that aids in attracting, developing, and retaining outstanding employees, has just raised $220 million and is now valued at over $2 billion [5]. Many organizations have started with their massive investment in AI for workforce management. The HR technology startup that automates work processes in order to improve many practices such as, the job search experience, has *"quietly become a billion-dollar unicorn"* [6]. Accenture has invested strategically in the London-based startup Beamery, which provides options for their recruiting operating system and is valued at $800 million [7]. Large multinational technology organizations have already begun integrating AI into their talent acquisition systems and procedures [8] IBM calculated that the cost savings from implementing AI in HR were close to $100 million per year [9]. This implies that talent management would be an important part to AI initiatives in organization indicating research significance in the field.

Talent management is an area of HR operations in which various data about individuals' skills and experience, as well as the skills required for certain jobs, are managed; however, such huge amounts of workforce employment data are divisive in nature and huge in volume and rapidly evolving in terms of their complexity [10]. A new technological approach using AI can address the issue of managing such data by transforming them into useful insights for both managerial and operational decision-making. In this paper, we propose a new talent management AI approach that utilizes machine learning to combine different data sources for delivering more insightful predictions. The use of AI reveals issues, such as discrimination, biased algorithms, and dehumanization [5, 11]. Therefore, when designing and evaluating the AI solution, it is important to consider both the potential benefits and risks of designing such systems. In particular, decision-makers should ensure that AI systems are designed in a way that minimizes the risk of perpetuating existing biases and discriminatory [12]. Furthermore, it is important to monitor AI based solutions on an ongoing basis to ensure that they are functioning as intended morally with an attachment of human ethics and not causing any negative unintended consequences.

The remaining portion of the article is organized as below. The essential background literature is discussed in Sect. 2, which provides an overview of the solution artefact design. The methodology of the research study is broken down in depth, and the next part delves into the specifics of the design artefact, situating our contribution within the framework of earlier work that is pertinent to the topic at hand. Following the part on the discussion, which focuses on the general contributions of the study, comes the section on the conclusion.

2   Background of the Study

AI helps organizations to manage large volumes of data more effectively, as well as to identify patterns and extract insights that would be difficult to discern using traditional methods [13]. In the context of talent management, AI can be used to improve the accuracy of job candidates' assessments, as well as to identify potential employees who may be a good match for vacant positions [14]. Therefore, AI oriented management solutions have the potential to improve organizational efficiency by reducing the time and resources required to screen job applicants and identify suitable candidates.

Despite the potential benefits of AI in HR, there are also risks that need to be considered. For example, AI-based systems may offer biases and discriminatory practices [15]. When designing and evaluating AI-powered talent management solutions, it is therefore important to consider both the potential benefits and risks of using such systems. In particular, decision-makers should ensure that AI systems are designed in a way that minimizes the risk of perpetuating existing biases and discriminatory practices. When compared to various other HR procedures, talent. management is one in which the impact of AI can be seen as a driving force for substantial improvements in terms of the practices. However, if AI is to be applied in this process, we will need to effectively outline a conceptual solution model to meet its key requirements. Following Table 1 shows existing studies in the problem domain.

Table 1. Existing studies in AI for talent management

Studies related to AI applications in talent management	Used ML approaches	Key findings of the papers
Fritts & Cabrera (2021) [11]	ML concepts identification	Examines the issue of recruitment algorithms with an eye toward the under-explored concerns of HR managers
Xiao & Yi (2021)	Tensorflow platform for supervised ML	Implements the design using AI to career planning or related areas
Joshi, Goel & Kumar (2020) [31]	Support Vector Machine (SVM)	Builds AI solutions for career services
Zhao et al. (2021)	Algorithm model design	AI for addressing fairness concerns for designing recruitment systems
Beloff & White (2021)	a minimum viable product (MVP), Natural Language Processing (NLP), and explanatory knowledge derived system	AI architecture that holds AI models and a data repository for recruiting model
Shafagatova & Van Looy (2021)	Supervised ML	AI for "process-oriented appraisals and rewards"
Meng (2017)	Supervised ML	Utilizes the design routine of modular design, real-time evaluation, and standard analysis for assessing emotional stability

2.1 Ethical Implications of AI in Talent Management

Many studies have addressed the need for AI in improving workforce processes. The promise and reality of AI in workforce management are vastly different to acquire, manage and retain talent- where there are complexity, constraints of data set and fairness [3]. In order to rapidly improve talent management enabling advantages of the potential of various data sets through the application of AI tools, it is important to design information systems solution that will support shifting organizational focus from developing more ethical HR systems for better efficiencies [15]. This implies that the need of ethical AI solutions in Talent Management is essential to govern the hiring and selection process. Uncertainty in the labor market, fast-changing business strategies, and new technology in workforce operations all call for a dynamic talent management system. Numerous scientists have expressed a variety of ethical concerns regarding AI such as predictive analytics algorithms to make judgments that have a significant impact on the life chances of humans [16]. It implies the demands of developing more practical solutions that would be meeting the demands of three overlapping workforce principles: causal reasoning, randomization and experiments, and employee contributions [3].

2.2 The Application of AI in Talent Management

The fourth industrial revolution, driven by demography, technology, and globalization, has fundamentally altered employment, with far-reaching ramifications for workers. In recent years, AI has begun to be applied to the field of talent management. Talent management relates in improving process of identifying, developing, and retaining employees and their potential to contribute to an organization's success [10]. Going beyond to automate repetitive tasks such as job postings and resume screening by AI applications, it is important to identify patterns in data that can help organizations to make better decisions about talent development and retention.

The use of AI in career services is still in its early stages, but there is potential for it to be used in a variety of ways. For example, AI can be used to create predictive models that can identify which students are at risk of not getting a job after graduation [17]. A number of AI-based tools have been developed for career guidance purposes. One such tool is Job Finder, which uses machine learning to match job seekers with appropriate jobs based on their skills and preferences [18]. There is no doubt that AI has the potential to assist career counselors with some of their daily tasks. For instance, it can help in resume writing and interview preparation. Additionally, AI can be used to create a bot that helps students search for jobs and internships. The bot can also provide personalized recommendations based on the student's interests and skills. Moreover, AI can be used to develop a chatbot that can answer frequently asked questions about careers, job applications, and resumes. Based on the above discussion, we identified a requirement for developing a new AI driven talent management solution. AI Talent Intelligent will present with innovative options to integrate technology in career advice which result in enhanced cost-effectiveness, decreased total expenses, and higher cost-effectiveness, in addition to improvements in accessibility and increased access to information, assessment, and networks [19].

2.3 Career Services in Higher Education

Uses of AI in education have been around for decades. There is a growing demand for the automated process of career advice services, which is increasing the planned uses and broadening the breadth of services. Various sectors have adopted talent intelligence, such as higher educational systems, labour markets, and private and governmental sectors that offer career counselling. As the need for assistance grows, it is vital for them to use digital services to reduce the cost of resources while also making a significant contribution to career guidance [20]. Smart technology has the potential to help both guiding practitioners and future talents. The relationships between information technologies, and big data may serve as a bridge to connect human and technological factors for improving organizational performance.

The literature on AI presents a very optimistic view of its potential. For example, it is argued that AI can help harness "the power of big data" in order to better match individuals to jobs [21]. Big data has been defined as "datasets whose size is beyond the ability of commonly used software tools to capture, store, manage, and analyze [22]. The use of big data in career services is still in its early stages, but there is potential for it to be used in a variety of ways. For example, big data can be used to create predictive models that can identify which students are at risk of dropping out of college or not getting a job after graduation [23]. Big data can also be used to create "heat maps" that show which areas of the country have the highest demand for certain types of jobs [24]. Finally, big data can be used to create "recommender systems" that suggest which jobs a person might be interested in based on their skills and interests [25]. HEIs are slower than corporations to completely incorporate AI, which may have a negative impact on the opportunities experienced by students by not adequately preparing them for the professional world beyond their diplomas [26]. Therfore, EdTech has been developing over the years and Tech companies offers employment products to education institutions such as CareerHub, Simplicity, Abintegro and InPlace [27]. AI can also help students better prepare for their careers after graduation. Colleges and organizations are collaborating to boost engagement and nurture more future-focused students by utilizing "career GPS" platforms, such as MARi [28]. Career Centres are a vital aspect of higher education institutions that are continually seeking innovative methods to prepare students for the workforce [29].

Students believe that AI may assist them in identifying their strengths and limitations and, in turn, facilitating their growth [30]. They have the desire to be able to employ AI to compare their talents to the competency needs of certain sectors or professions, in addition to general working life competencies [30]. Some students may not have a clear job path after completing their college studies, and they want additional direction and counselling on selecting the proper degree course for their future career growth. AI can be used to present sophisticated in-depth career roadmaps as recommendations to students [31]. According to the same study, governments and relevant technological resources are important in AI adoption, and IT developers should simplify AI. This comprehensive theoretical framework will inspire future researchers to better understand HRM technology adoption [32].

Based on the above discussion, we identified a requirement for developing a new AI driven talent management solution that would assist users in a university career management centre. AI Talent Intelligent will present with innovative options to integrate technology in career advice which result in enhanced cost-effectiveness, decreased total expenses, and higher cost-effectiveness, in addition to improvements in accessibility and increased access to information, assessment, and networks [19]. The ongoing epidemic has resulted in an increasing demand for advisory services that may be provided remotely or digitally [33]. Career Guidance staff see AI in a supporting role to their work, balancing out the benefits and risks of incorporating technology into the guidance process [34]. Staff feel AI could replace human effort in some areas, changing their role and tasks. Students see potential in AI applications that propose studies, thesis topics, work placements and jobs based on skills, experiences, and interests.

2.4 Theories in Technological Adoption

The literature that currently exists has explored the adoption of new technologies and innovations from a variety of perspectives. The concept that is referred to as the diffusion of innovation (DoI) focuses on the process by which an invention is disseminated across a social system over the period of time via a variety of different routes [35]. In the context of user technology adoption, the technology acceptance model (TAM) takes into consideration the theorised causal links between individuals' subjective beliefs, intentions, and behaviours [36]. On the other hand, the unified theory of acceptance and use of technology (UTAUT) provides additional drivers of behaviour intention, including performance and effort expectation, social influence, and enabling factors [37]. The Adaptive Structuring Theory (AST) investigates how organisational participants adapt to the norms and resources of information technology in order to impact the results of the organization's activities. [38]. The technology-organization-environment (TOE) framework investigates the role that technical, organisational, and environmental contexts play in the decision-making process regarding cutting-edge innovations [39]. The task-technology fit model is used to figure out whether or not the capabilities of a certain piece of technology are a good match for the prerequisites of a specific job [40]. However, the primary focus of these theories is on the subjective viewpoints of individuals and specific activities (such as the dissemination of innovative ideas, the adoption of innovative technologies, the decision-making process regarding innovative adaptations, etc.), and they completely disregard the power that individuals possess. None of them address the particulars of the adoption of information technology since they were written before widespread usage of information technology, therefore none of them provide a full vision or an accurate explanation. The contemporary technology affordance approach, which was created from sociomateriality, assigns equal relevance to the social and material elements of technology [41]. However, similar to TAM, affordance in IT does not always guarantee real adoption, and as a result, its explanatory power in the heterogeneity of technology adoption in organisations is similarly limited (Fig. 1).

This study will employ an integrated framework based on the technology, organization, and environment (TOE) framework as well as on the diffusion of innovation (DOI) theory. The research investigates the significant aspects that are relevant for the adoption of AI TM artefacts in the career services of the higher education sector. The technology viewpoint of the TOE model takes into account the external as well as the internal technical resources that are necessary for the implementation of technology in an

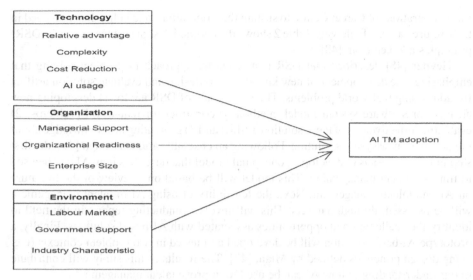

Fig. 1 Proposed Conceptual Framework

organization [42]. The technology factors discussed are reliability, security, capability, quality, relative cost advantages, and the compatibility of TM solution and technology benefits [43]. The organizational perspective puts considerable emphasis on a variety of factors, including the scope and size of the firm, the formalization and centralization of the organization, the complexity of the organizational structure, the quality of the HR available, the support of top management, and the readiness of the organisation [44].

The diffusion of innovations hypothesis (DOI) is an innovative framework that has been applied in the form of a theory to support studies that aim to elucidate the elements that contribute to the spread of innovation through the application of technology [45] The degree of organisational influence (DOI) theory examines the possibility of an organisation adopting a new technology based on the relative advantages of the new technology, as well as its observation of complexity, compatibility, and amount of advantage spent trialling and observing it [46].

3   Design Science Methodology

This study aims to design a new AI solution therefore it is essential to investigate its suitability in the design context. We plan to develop a methodological framework for the deployment of talent management AI software solutions for career services. Key components of talent management and related processes integrating talent management systems will be extracted from the latest relevant literature and validated with secondary data collected from social media or any other sources that make big training and development datasets freely available. The emerging themes of the proposed proof-of-concept prototype will also be designed and compared with existing software solutions available in the market for talent management [47]. A comprehensive talent management artefact will be prototyped, which will meet the concurrent talent requirements and support the future operations of Career Centre to sustain their operations and help talents succeed in their future careers. Following Table 2 shows the adopted design science research (DSR) principles adopted from [48].

Hevner [48] described that DSR is a scientific approach to problem-solving that emphasizes the development of new knowledge to design and evaluate solution artifact for addressing real-world problems. The main goals of DSR are to: 1) developing new artifacts or software system model, method or construct for real-world problems; 2) evaluating effectiveness of these solution artifact and 3) generating new knowledge about the design of new systems solution. Following an ensemble artefact design [49], the first step in this process is to develop a conceptual model that describes how AI can be used to improve talent management. This model will be based on a review of the literature on AI and talent management. Next, the feasibility of using AI in talent management will be assessed, through datasets. This will involve conducting reports in the field to identify the challenges and opportunities associated with AI-based solutions. Finally, a prototype AI-based solution will be developed and tested in two problem contexts (e.g. using design principles defined by Miah, [47]. The results of this study will contribute to our understanding of how AI can be used to improve talent management.

Table 2. Hevner's seven guidance in a summarized form

DSR Adopted Guideline	Its relevant to the proposed solution
Guideline 1: Design as an Artifact: Design-	Design-science research must result in a valid construct, model, technique, or instance
Guideline 2: Problem Relevance:	The objective of design-science research is to create technological response to significant business issues. Identified is a genuine issue domain that supports the specified software solution prototype
Guideline 3: Design Evaluation:	The utility, quality, and feasibility of an AI design need to be stringently shown by well-executed assessment procedures in order to satisfy the requirements. For prototype testing with industry various stakeholders, a descriptive assessment approach will be used with utilizing secondary data
Guideline 4: Research Contributions:	The models utilised for the AI artifact's features were designed by domain specialists with information gleaned from actual practice, through prototyping

(*continued*)

In this study, secondary data will be employed to accomplish the study's purpose. The study will use a mapping approach to locate and assess AI-enabled companies, corporations, and/or initiatives that have begun to look for solutions to solve the cognitive

Table 2. (*continued*)

DSR Adopted Guideline	Its relevant to the proposed solution
Guideline 5: Research Rigor:	DSR is dependent on the use of rigors procedures in the creation and assessment of the AI design artefact informing through IS theories
Guideline 6: Design as a Search Process:	The search for a functional artefact necessitates the utilisation of accessible ways to achieve desired purposes in compliance with the issue domain,
Guideline 7: Communication of Research:	DSR will help successfully communicated about the research outcome to both technical and managerial groups

and employability gaps. The steps of the search process used to produce an engaging map are outlined below:

1. The investigation of professional growth and employability frameworks.
2. The exploration of research on AI applications in TM associated with higher education.
3. Desk research on the uses of AI in recruiting and those associated with career centers.
4. The mapping of AI-using organizations within the framework for TM and employment.
5. The utilization and analysis of a few programs to develop a greater understanding of how they function.
6. Finally, the analysis of the collected data and the development of an innovative talent employability framework that leverages AI's ability to learn, identify complex patterns, and provide more accurate insights to assist students in making more informed career decisions, universities in attracting and serving students, and employers in selecting talent and accelerating the hiring process.

This study will employ an integrated framework based on the technology, organization, and environment (TOE) framework as well as on the diffusion of innovation (DOI) theory. The research investigates the significant aspects that are relevant for the adoption of AI TM artefacts in the career services of the higher education sector. The technology viewpoint of the TOE model takes into account the external as well as the internal technical resources that are necessary for the implementation of technology in an organization [42].The technology factors discussed are reliability, security, capability, quality, relative cost advantages, and the compatibility of IT solution and technology benefits [43].

4   Proposed AI Oriented TM Approach

Figure 2 shows a conceptual framework that we have drawn from the existing literature. An evolving prototype is an innovative design approach for transforming system requirements into a reasonable solution model design so that potential users may see the advantages or conceptual outcome. The understanding required to identify the problems with a present system and create an artefact solution is covered in the prototype design. Three phases are considered for the creation of the minimum viable product (MVP). These phases will include the following desired services: the talent pool, graduate personality traits assessment, career guidance chatbots, skills and knowledge building, CV screening software, mock interview screening, and jobs or opportunities matchmaking. The bots are software tools that have been created in natural language and have the ability to carry on conversations by themselves [50]. It is mostly divided into three different portions. The very first thing that must be done is to obtain information from the end-user. This can be done either vocally or by typing in natural language. The second step is to get the bot to provide output in the form of spoken words, and the third step is to process the input through the software in order to get output that is accurate and simple to comprehend. Most of the time, these counselling bots are utilized for producing predictions and questions regarding a career, such as which industry would be the best choice and which courses are the most recent. This system's principal function is to understand human speech with the assistance of natural language processing so that the results can be given to the user.

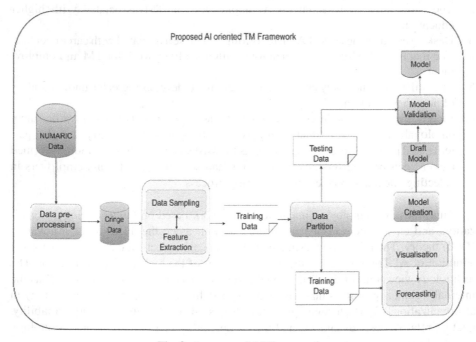

Fig. 2 A proposed AI Framework

    Following other design artifacts [51–55]. The proposed framework in Fig. 2 illustrates how the input (Numeric data) is going to convert to an AI-Driven Talent Intelligence Solution When our big data has been pre-processed (e.g., data cleansing, data integration, stop word removal), it is ready for sampling process and then be ready for separating into training and testing datasets. Figure 2 presents the proposed framework, which depicts how the output (an AI-driven talent intelligence solution) is going to be converted from the input (numerical data). When our big data has been pre-processed (for example, via data purification, data integration, stop word removal), it is ready for the sampling process, and after that, it will be ready to be separated into training and testing datasets. The generation of a draught model may be accomplished by the application of data analytics techniques such as visualization and forecasting. Following an analysis of its validity, the model will be transformed into a rigorous representation that may be put to work in forecasting, planning, and decision-making.

5 Discussion and Conclusion

Artificial intelligence (AI) is hailed as a revolutionary, all-purpose technology that will transform the workplace. In the field of HR, AI is becoming increasingly prevalent. The proposed hybrid approach to TM will utilize multiple data sources to deliver data in a larger loop. We aimed to examine the design and development of a new AI-driven TM artefact. Our project will facilitate the daily operations of universities. AI can assist professional talent managers by identifying, forecasting, and investigating talent acquisition and performance-related trends. There is a growing demand for automated career counselling processes. Various sectors have adopted talent intelligence, including higher education systems, labour markets, the private sector, and the government. Higher education requires innovative ways to prepare students for the workforce. Smart technologies have the potential to assist in mentoring both current professionals and future talent.

Our aim is to create the AI platform that can help employment centre staff identify the best candidates for open positions, as well as to provide recommendations on how to improve organizational efficiency. Our case context is a university career center. In this project, we develop an initial machine learning algorithm that is trained by the data gathered on employment centers' current staffing levels, job openings, and hiring practices. Subsequently, the AI algorithm is to test a sample employment center data to determine, if it can accurately predict which candidates are best suited for open positions. Finally, The AI algorithm as the purposeful artifact is to be evaluated to determine its effectiveness in improving employment centre organizational efficiency or in similar domain such as public healthcare [56] and higher education [57] by following design principles of conducting impactful design research [58, 59].

References

1. Vrontis, D., Christofi, M., Pereira, V., Tarba, S., Makrides, A., Trichina, E.: Artificial intelligence, robotics, advanced technologies and human resource management: a systematic review. The Int. J. Human Res. Manag. **33**(6), 1237–1266 (2022)
2. Agrawal, A., Gans, J., Goldfarb, A.: Prediction, judgment, and complexity: a theory of decision-making and artificial intelligence. In: The Economics of Artificial Intelligence: An Agenda, pp. 89–110. University of Chicago Press (2018)
3. Tambe, P., Cappelli, P., Yakubovich, V.: Artificial intelligence in human resources management: challenges and a path forward. Calif. Manage. Rev. **61**(4), 15–42 (2019)

4. Bailie, I., Butler, M.: An examination of artificial intelligence and its impact on human resources. CognitioX (ed.) (2018)
5. Charlwood, A., Guenole, N.: Can HR adapt to the paradoxes of artificial intelligence? Human Res. Manag. J. **32**, 729–742 (2022)
6. Kelly, J.: Billion-dollar unicorn and artificial intelligence career-tech startup is improving the job search experience. Forbes. Com. (2021)
7. Lunden, I.: Beamery raises $138 M at an $800 M valuation for its 'operating system for recruitment. TechCrunch, 17th June. techcrunch.com/2021/06/17/beamery-raises-138m-for-its-end-to-end-crm-for-recruitment (2021). Retrieved 3 Dec 2021
8. van den Broek, E., Sergeeva, A., Huysman, M.: When the machine meets the expert: an ethnography of developing AI for hiring. MIS Q. **45**(3), 1557–1580 (2021)
9. Guenole, N., Feinzig, S.: The business case for AI in HR. With Insights and Tips on Getting Started. Armonk: IBM Smarter Workforce Institute, IBM Corporation. https://www.ibm.com/blogs/ibm-training/building-skills-for-a-smarter-workforce/ (2018). 12 Nov 2022
10. Collings, D.G., Mellahi, K.: Strategic talent management: a review and research agenda. Hum. Res. Manag. Rev. **19**(4), 304–313 (2009)
11. Fritts, M., Cabrera, F.: AI recruitment algorithms and the dehumanization problem. Ethics Inform. Technol. **23**(4), 791–801 (2021)
12. Shrestha, Y.R., Ben-Menahem, S.M., Von Krogh, G.: Organizational decision-making structures in the age of artificial intelligence. Calif. Manag. Rev. **61**(4), 66–83 (2019)
13. Nemati, H., Steiger, D.M., Iyer, L.S., Herschel, R.T.: Knowledge warehouse: an architectural integration of knowledge management, decision support, artificial intelligence and data warehousing. Decis. Support Syst. **33**(2), 143–161 (2002)
14. Jia, Q., Guo, Y., Li, R., Li, Y., Chen, Y.: A conceptual artificial intelligence application framework in human resource management. In: Proceedings of the International Conference on Electronic Business (ICEB) Collections (2018)
15. Chamorro-Premuzic, T., Polli, F., Dattner, B.: Building ethical AI for talent management. Harvard Bus. Rev. **21** (2019)
16. Mittelstadt, B.D., Allo, P., Taddeo, M., Wachter, S., Floridi, L.: The ethics of algorithms: mapping the debate. Big Data Soc. **3**(2), 2053951716679679 (2016)
17. Mehraj, T., Baba, A.M.: Scrutinizing artificial intelligence based career guidance and counselling systems: an appraisal. Int. J. Interdisc. Res. Innovations **7**(1), 402–411 (2019)
18. Liu, R., Rong, W., Ouyang, Y., Xiong, Z.: A hierarchical similarity based job recommendation service framework for university students. Front. Comput. Sci. **11**(5), 912–922 (2017)
19. Sampson, J.P., Kettunen, J., Vuorinen, R.: The role of practitioners in helping persons make effective use of information and communication technology in career interventions. Int. J. Educ. Vocat. Guidance **20**(1), 191–208 (2020)
20. Toni, A., Vuorinen, R.: Lifelong guidance in Finland: key policies and practices. In: Career and career guidance in the Nordic countries, Brill, pp. 127–143 (2020)
21. Sydell, E., Hudy, M., Ashley, M.: Decoding Talent: How AI and Big Data Can Solve Your Company's People Puzzle. Greenleaf Book Group (2022)
22. Sagiroglu, S., Sinanc, D.: Big data: a review. In: 2013 International Conference on Collaboration Technologies and Systems (CTS), pp. 42–47. IEEE (2013)
23. Von Hippel, P.T., Hofflinger, A.: The data revolution comes to higher education: identifying students at risk of dropout in Chile. J. High. Educ. Policy Manag. **43**(1), 2–23 (2021)
24. Davenport, T.H., Ronanki, R.: Artificial intelligence for the real world. Harvard Bus. Rev. **96**(1), 108–116 (2018)
25. Siting, Z., Wenxing, H., Ning, Z., Fan, Y.: Job recommender systems: a survey. In: 2012 7th International Conference on Computer Science & Education (ICCSE), pp. 920–924. IEEE (2012)

26. Hannan, E., Liu, S.: AI: new source of competitiveness in higher education. Competitiveness Rev.: An Int. Bus. J. **33**, 265–279 (2021)
27. Knight, E., Staunton, T., Healy, M.: About University Career Services' Interaction with EdTech. Digital Transformation and Disruption of Higher Education, p. 303 (2022)
28. King, M.: The AI revolution on campus. In: EDUCAUSE Rev, pp. 10–22 (2017)
29. Dey, F., Cruzvergara, C.Y.: Evolution of career services in higher education. New Dir. Student Serv. **2014**(148), 5–18 (2014)
30. Westman, S., et al.: Artificial Intelligence for Career Guidance-Current Requirements and Prospects for the Future. IAFOR J. Educ. **9**(4), 43–62 (2021)
31. Joshi, K., Goel, A. K., Kumar, T.: Online career counsellor system based on artificial intelligence: an approach. In: 2020 7th International Conference on Smart Structures and Systems (ICSSS), pp. 1–4. IEEE (2020)
32. Pan, Y., Froese, F., Liu, N., Hu, Y., Ye, M.: The adoption of artificial intelligence in employee recruitment: the influence of contextual factors. The Int. J. Hum. Resour. Manag. **33**(6), 1125–1147 (2022)
33. Šapale, S., Iliško, D., Badjanova, J.: Sustainable career guidance during the pandemic: building pathways into a 'new normal.' Discourse Commun. Sustain. Educ. **12**(1), 140–150 (2021)
34. Westman, S., et al.: Artificial Intelligence for Career Guidance-Current Requirements and Prospects for the Future. IAFOR J. Educ. **9**(4), 43–62 (2021)
35. Chang, H.C.: A new perspective on twitter hashtag use: diffusion of innovation theory. Proc. Am. Soc. Inform. Sci. Technol. **47**(1), 1–4 (2010)
36. Davis, F.D.: Perceived usefulness, perceived ease of use, and user acceptance of information technology. MIS Q. **13**, 319–340 (1989)
37. Venkatesh, V., Morris, M.G., Davis, G.B., Davis, F.D.: User acceptance of information technology: toward a unified view. MIS Q. **27**, 425–478 (2003)
38. DeSanctis, G., Poole, M.S.: Capturing the complexity in advanced technology use: adaptive structuration theory. Organ. Sci. **5**(2), 121–147 (1994)
39. Tornatzky, L.G., Fleischer, M., Chakrabarti, A.K.: Processes of technological innovation. Lexington books (1990)
40. Goodhue, D.L., Thompson, R.L.: Task-technology fit and individual performance. MIS Q. **19**, 213–236 (1995)
41. Robey, D., Raymond, B., Anderson, C.: Theorizing information technology as a material artifact in information systems research. In: Leonardi, P.M., Nardi, B.A., Kallinikos, J. (eds.) Materiality and Organizing: Social Interaction in a Technological World, pp. 216–236. Oxford University Press, Oxford (2012). https://doi.org/10.1093/acprof:oso/978019966 4054.003.0011
42. Depietro, R., Wiarda, E., Fleischer, M.: The context for change: organization, technology and environment. The Process Technol. Innovation **199**, 151–175 (1990)
43. Al-Qirim, N.: The role of the government and e-commerce adoption in small businesses in New Zealand. Int. J. Internet Enterp. Manag. **4**(4), 293–313 (2006)
44. Mukherjee, S., Chittipaka, V.: Analysing the adoption of intelligent agent technology in food supply chain management: an empirical evidence. FIIB Bus. Rev. **11**, 438–454 (2021)
45. Rogers, E.M., Singhal, A., Quinlan, M. M.: Diffusion of innovations. In: An integrated approach to communication theory and research:, Routledge, pp. 432–448 (2014)
46. Rogers, E.M.: Diffusion of preventive innovations. Addict. Behav. **27**(6), 989–993 (2002)
47. Miah, S.J., Vu, H., Gammack, J.: A big-data analytics method for capturing visitor activities and flows: the case of an island country. Inform. Technol. Manag. **20**(4), 203–221 (2019)
48. Hevner, A.R., March, S.T., Park, J., Ram, S.: Design science in information systems research. MIS Q. **28**, 75–105 (2004)

49. Miah, S.J., Solomonides, I., Gammack, J.G.: A design-based research approach for developing data-focussed business curricula. Educ. Inform. Technol. **25**(1), 553–581 (2020)
50. Khan, R., Das, A.: Introduction to chatbots. In: Build better chatbots, pp. 1–11. Springer (2018)
51. Miah, S.J.: An ontology based design environment for rural business decision support. Griffith University Nathan, Brisbance, Australia (2008)
52. Miah, S.J., Gammack, J.: A Mashup architecture for web end-user application designs. In: 2008 2nd IEEE International Conference on Digital Ecosystems and Technologies, pp. 532–537. IEEE (2008)
53. Miah, S.J.: A new semantic knowledge sharing approach for e-government systems. In: 4th IEEE International Conference on Digital Ecosystems and Technologies, pp. 457–462. IEEE (2010)
54. Miah, S.J., Ahamed, R.: A cloud-based DSS model for driver safety and monitoring on Australian roads. Int. J. Emerg. Sci. **1**(4), 634 (2011)
55. Miah, S.J., McKay, J.: A new conceptualisation of design science research for DSS development research. In: The Proceedings of PACIS 2016, accessed from Miah, Shah Jahan and McKay, Judy, A New Conceptualisation of Design Science Research for DSS Development Research. PACIS 2016 Proceedings. https://aisel.aisnet.org/pacis2016/384 (2016)
56. Aghdam, A.R., Watson, J., Cliff, C., Miah, S.J.: Improving the theoretical understanding toward patient-driven health care innovation through online value cocreation: systematic review. J. Med. Internet Res. **22**(4), e16324 (2020)
57. Fahd, K., Miah, S.J., Ahmed, K.: Predicting student performance in a blended learning environment using learning management system interaction data. Appl. Comput. Inform. (2021) https://doi.org/10.1108/ACI-06-2021-0150
58. Shee, H.K., Miah, S.J., De Vass, T.: Impact of smart logistics on smart city sustainable performance: an empirical investigation. The Int. J. Logistics Manag. **32**(3), 821–845 (2021). https://doi.org/10.1108/IJLM-07-2020-0282
59. Miah, S.J., Vu, H.Q., Gammack, J., McGrath, M.: A big data analytics method for tourist behaviour analysis. Inform. Manag. **54**(6), 771–785 (2017)

Development of Bilingual Chatbot for University Related FAQs Using Natural Language Processing and Deep Learning

Rishal Ravikesh Chand$^{(\boxtimes)}$ and Neeraj Anand Sharma$^{(\boxtimes)}$

The University of Fiji, Saweni Campus, Lautoka, Fiji
{rishalc,neerajs}@unifiji.ac.fj

Abstract. Ever since the rise of the Covid-19 pandemic many organizations have shifted to the new online norm of digitalization. In the list of educational intuitions, the Universities are now offering online programmes to students. The admission process can be frustrating and time-consuming for both the students and the university. Students will have several queries and issues that need to be answered on the spot and clarified before the application process begins. However, chatbots are widely being used everywhere from websites to personal devices. Everyone wants flexibility and ease of access to information faster and in an accurate form, this research paper explores the fundamentals of conversational chatbots in the University system driven by system-chatterbots using neural networks. Focusing on developing a bilingual chatbot that uses Fijian (iTaukei - (Vosa Vakaviti)) and English language through the use of NLP and deep learning algorithms to respond to student FAQs efficiently using intents, a bag of words, and tokenization. This bilingual chatbot can be deployed by any University to provide 24/7 student support to strengthen student communication and ease the flow of information dissemination to its prospective and existing students with prompt responses.

Keywords: Chatbot · University System · Intents · Natural Language Processing · Deep Learning-Neural Networks

1 Introduction

Chatbots are widely being used everywhere from websites to personal devices. A software that can humanly make conversations with natural language based on input and responses. Conversational chatbot technology ultimately enables machines to naturally interact with humans via language. The ability to use language is as old as humanity [1, 2].

Many educational websites contain loads of information that is available but the users are not able to easily navigate and browse through to get the correct information that they are trying to find out. However, prospective and existing students find it difficult to access the chain of information. Moreover, English will be considered the main language for communication but visitors who do not have a proper command of English will find it difficult to chat therefore using iTaukei language can be used.

C.-H. Hsu et al. (Eds.): DataCom 2022, LNCS 13864, pp. 83–94, 2023.
https://doi.org/10.1007/978-981-99-2233-8_6

As the educational sector thrives with new changes in the teaching and learning mode, new strategies are placed to enhance the delivery mode in education. Universities provide various types of information in various forms to the public. It takes time to search for particular information and on websites at times the search feature does not contain the full sitemap of the particular website [3]. Hence, there is a need for a custom chatbot that uses conversational AI which can be implemented on a website that targets the visitors/ students and takes in input, and provides an immediate response based on the user's input. Taking the example of getting the student email login guide, where the input is student email guide and the chatbot immediately responds with the URL link, this saves time and implements a secondary vernacular language in the chatbot which caters to bilingual languages (English and Vosa Vakaviti) [4].

iTaukei language is one of the three official languages spoken in Fiji Islands. It is the first language that the natives still speak and this language has total dialects from 14 provinces [5].

The purpose of this research paper is to develop a bilingual chatbot that uses iTaukei language and English language revolving around the university-related frequently asked questions to which an existing and new prospective student can ask anything and get a prompt response back with no human interaction. This chatbot will work on a defined category of intents using a neutral network and deep learning.

This will assist universities to fast tract with any general to specific student queries in:

- Admissions
- Enrolment
- Fees
- Scholarships
- Campus
- Withdrawals
- Graduations & General Queries.

This chatbot will be completely automated and will not require any human supervision as it will respond to user input dynamically based on the intent identified it will respond immediately, also using iTaukei language will benefit Fiji nationals to converse in their language also to easily communicate and get access to information. The rest of the paper covers the background on Chatbot technologies, different types of chatbots, development, testing, and results along with Limitations and Future recommendations finally Conclusion and References.

This new proposed chatbot handles user responses in iTaukei and English language. A dataset intent was created using a subset of user-based interactions for the student query in iTaukei and English. An intent consists of the input from the user who is interacting with the chatbot, ranging from each question that can be posed by the user to the chatbot. Based on the intents from the knowledge base, that chatbot is trained using different intents classified as bag of words and tags in the model training data using natural language processing techniques–NER model to identify the user text and use it for further conversations.

2 Background

2.1 What is a Chatbot and How it Works?

A chatbot is an essential computer program also known as software that can mimic in a way how normal human conversation flow follows in natural language. Chatbots are known called digital assistants, chatterbots that can be text-based and voice-activated as it responds to user input and requests and then understands the requests, by analyzing and identifying by the intents which will match with the knowledge base and if matched with the user's request it responds back and if it fails to match then responds with an appropriate message (see Fig. 1).

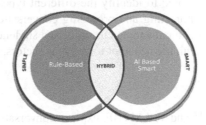

Fig. 1. Chatbot Types

Rule-based also known as linguistic based are operated on the pre-programmed user commands which are already written and stored in the chatbot, the user can only interact with the chatbot if the conditions are met then the conversation flows. Designed for single-channel operation and keyword-driven based on predetermined straightforward answers.

AI-based chatbots use artificial intelligence and a subset of other algorithms which combine various tools of machine learning, deep learning, natural language processing, and neural networks to interpret the user input and understand intents before responding to the user input [6]. AI chatbots can consist of a hybrid model approach which first learns by training the data based on intents and context, having the ability to perform and predict intelligence and sentiments, and mimic near-human behavior interaction [7]. Powered by deep learning which enables easy scalability, understanding multiple ways in which a person can ask questions without being explicitly trained on every utterance [8], smarter chatbots will understand spelling mistakes and short forms.

Input from a user   Analyze User's request   Identify intent and entities   Compose reply

Fig. 2. How AI Chatbots Work

In the above Fig. 2, it shows how a chatbot operates by taking in user requests by understanding the user input using Natural Language Processing where the chatbot analyzes the user input which could be text or voice in sentence form also known as unstructured text, then NLP starts categorizing words and comprehending from user language to machine language. The request is analyzed in real-time which uses NLP and other deep learning algorithms integrated with artificial intelligence. Once the chatbot has analyzed the user input, into structured form then it will check with the knowledge base and defined intents which consist of structured data [9].

3 Methodology

A literature review was conducted for this research paper where various journals and conference papers were explored to identify the different types of chatbot techniques used in different sectors automating and providing conversational online support for frequently asked questions and enhancing customer and student interaction. Below are a few listed related works with uses chatbot for various sectors.

3.1 Existing Studies

Sasha S, Vinod S, Sonali V, and Ved M [10], explore conversation to automation in the banking sector through the use of artificial intelligence integrated into the chatbot. AIML (the artificial intelligence markup language used to implement the A.I.L.C.E chatbot [10]. The structure follows the tags in the chatbot by matching the user responses, categories include atomic, default, and recursive. The framework follows a sequence where the user is required to submit the personal details followed by the support. Yogi Chandra and Suyanto Suyantyo [11] show how a question-answering system based on a sequence-to-sequence model can be used in an Indonesian university chatbot for the admission process. Seq2seq model used two layered-LSTM encoders to encode user input. Output BLEU scores with attention: 44.68.

Walid H, Yasmin M, Mina A, and Slim A, proposed a bilingual chatbot for university admissions, the chatbot was named Jooka [12]. An Amazon web server was deployed which hosted the JavaScript back-end code and this chatbot was deployed on social media sites incorporated with Dialog flow essentials – google cloud. Using English and Arabic as the input language. This study examined the effectiveness of the admission process in a university system which proved that chatbots are highly helpful in saving time and resources.

Further research also showed that chatbots using artificial intelligence and deep learning are effective through vigorous training and testing for a university chatbot that performed well in the Myanmar language through natural language processing. That chatbot aimed to answer university-related FAQs in the Myanmar language using AIML. The results showed that the efficiency metric with sample dialogues is effective and has shown positive Responses [13].

While there are papers suggesting the use of AIML [14] in chatbots is possible also different concepts of AI are implemented together with various chatbots [15]. However, using various deep learning algorithms and concepts like neural networks can train a new set of user input in other words iTaukei language which is not recolonized by Google Translate to date. We can use different techniques and implement various deep learning tools like stemming, and tokenization to train and handle user input in other languages to act as a chatbot in different and generic situations that responds efficiently.

4 Proposed Chatbot

In this new proposed chatbot, we have developed a bilingual chatbot for university-related frequently asked questions (FAQs) using natural language processing and deep learning which uses neural networks. Figure 3 illustrates the workflow of the proposed system which will use English and iTaukei language as part of NLP techniques. The proposed system is divided into sections:

- User input
- Input preprocessing using NLP techniques to understand the input.
- NLP preprocessing pipeline Query check intents
- Chatbot response

An overview of the chatbot is shown, where the user (prospective students, existing students, anyone with general university inquiries) inputs the request in the messaging platform in this case we have added a GUI which uses Flask App on a webpage, then the input is analyzed using natural language processing techniques such as Tokenization, Stemming and Bag of Words to breakdown and understand the user input as it uses English and iTaukei language in real-time processing, utilizing neural networks and

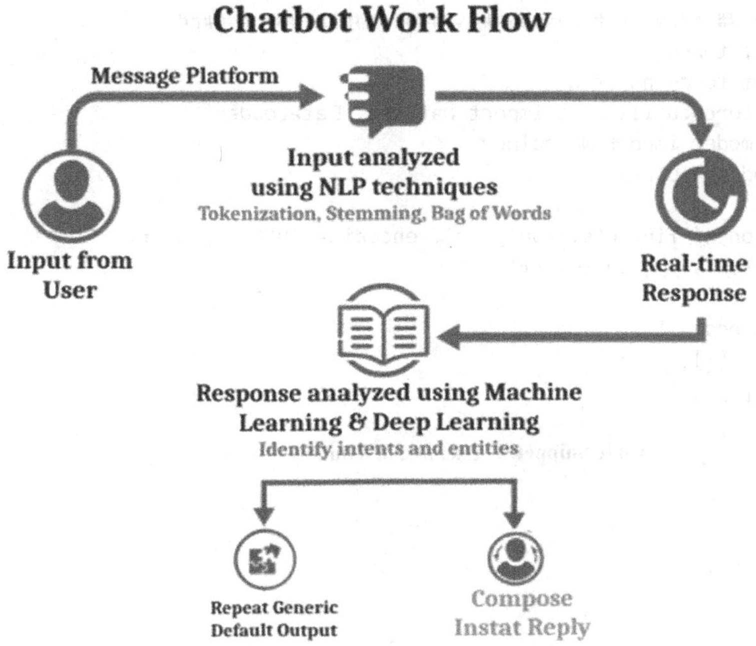

Chatbot Work Flow

Message Platform

Input analyzed using NLP techniques
Tokenization, Stemming, Bag of Words

Input from User

Real-time Response

Response analyzed using Machine Learning & Deep Learning
Identify intents and entities

Repeat Generic Default Output

Compose Instat Reply

Fig. 3. Proposed Chatbot Work Flow

deep learning the chatbot pickups intents – tags and analyzes the patterns to respond to the user instantly.

4.1 NLP Techniques Used

Intents contain elements such as tags and responses. It is a representation of a thing a user wants to do in a conversational term and what we do is we have one intent that will map to many different utterances or things a user might say, intents don't have to be narrow however, in fact, a broader intent can be a really useful way to trigger the chatbot to respond by identifying entities which is a simplification of conversation as a whole and what it means is that you can take many different utterances and map them to a single intent and then decide what you do based on that intent. Intents make modeling conversations much more tractable and reduce uncertainty in overall chatbot behavior.

The following code snippet- in the PyTorch training model uses NN (Neural Network) to sense and mimic the computer to handle input like a human brain. Intent Tags in Table 1- are used for the testing of this proposed system in a JSON 5, UTF-8 encoding below in Code 1.

```
from model import NeuralNet
from main import bag_of_words, tokenize
device = torch.device('cuda' if torch.cuda.is_available() else 'cpu')
with open('fintents.json', 'r', encoding='UTF-8') as json_data:
    fintents = json.load(json_data)

#######################################################
import torch
import torch.nn as nn
from torch.utils.data import Dataset, DataLoader
from model import NeuralNet
#encoding='UTF-8'

with open('fintents.json', 'r', encoding='UTF-8') as f:
    fintents = json.load(f)

all_words = [ ]
tags = [ ]
xy = [ ]
```

Code Snippet. 1. Example of Training Model

Custom tags and separate patterns were listed in thc tag intents JSON file which gets trigged based on user input for the university chatbot for students and the general public Tags include English and iTaukei, separate tags represent itk in short as iTaukei language with the common pattern are listed in Table 2.

Table 1. Intent Tags

Tags		
"Tag:" Greetings"	"Tag:" Greetings_itk"	"Tag:" Offerings_itk"
"Tag:" Goodbye"	"Tag:" Goodbye_itk"	"Tag:" Study_itk"
"Tag:" Personal_Greetings"	"Tag:" Personal_Greetings_itk"	"Tag:" Why_Study_itk"
"Tag:" Thanks"	"Tag:" Thanks_itk"	"Tag:" Withdrawal_itk"
"Tag:" Undergraduate_Programme"	"Tag:" Undergraduate_Programme_itk"	"Tag:" Offerings"
"Tag:" Postgraduate_Programme"	"Tag:" Postgraduate_Programme_itk"	"Tag:" Study"
"Tag:" Apply"	"Tag:" Apply_itk"	"Tag:" Why_Study"
"Tag:" Why_Apply"	"Tag:" Why_Apply_ikt"	"Tag:" Withdrawal"
"Tag:" Fees"		"Tag:" Location_itk"
		"Tag:" Fees_itk"
		"Tag:" Location"

Table 2. iTaukei Patterns.

Patterns
"patterns": [
"Bula",
"ei", "Yadra vinaka", "Mataka", "Na caka soti",
"Veikidavaki", "Veita bula", "Bula vua e dua ",
"?", "Vekei au mada", "Veivuke",
"Yalovinaka veivuke", "au gadreva na veivuke"],

Tokenization. The process of how computers can understand language, and that's words and sentences breaking down words and sentences into each character which are represented in a numeric form then encoding them whereby the computer can then understand and train neural networks. The strings are split into meaningful units for example words, punctuation characters, and numbers in Table 3 below.

Table 3. Tokenization Example

User input: Hi, How can I apply?
After Tokenization: ['Hi', ',', 'How', 'can', 'i', 'apply' , '?']
User input: Yadra vinaka!
After Tokenization: ['Yadra', 'vinaka', '!']

Stemming. Another NLP technique that generates the root form of words, reduce words to their base crude heuristic that chops off the ends of words. Stemming is essential which is part of natural language understanding as it reduces words from words identifying the common root word as shown in Table 4. It helps in understanding the words by recognizing more words from their prefixes, suffixes, and lower casing the words therefore, stemming can be used to make the chatbot system understand the user input efficiently.

Table 4. Tokenization Example

User input: ['Programme', 'Programmes', 'Programes', 'Offerings', 'Offer', 'Offered']
After Stemming: ['programm', 'programm', 'program', 'offer', 'offer', 'offer']
Common root word: programm, offer

Bag of words. As the chatbot will mostly work with text-related user input and responses bag of words is used to convert the text into vector form text preprocessing before NLP can understand and process the user input.

4.2   Chatbot Application Development on Web

Flask has been used for the backend web application server framework in python and is easily linked with the frontend GUI with JavaScript to create an HTML file. This user GUI is linked with the chatbot which is in its testing phase.

Table 5. Trained Model Outcome

Patterns	147
Tags	28
Stemmed Words	148
Epochs	Epoch [100/1000], Loss: 0.8399 Epoch [200/1000], Loss: 0.0058 Epoch [300/1000], Loss: 0.0056 Epoch [400/1000], Loss: 0.0071 Epoch [500/1000], Loss: 0.0005 Epoch [600/1000], Loss: 0.0003 Epoch [700/1000], Loss: 0.2812 Epoch [800/1000], Loss: 0.0000 Epoch [900/1000], Loss: 0.0000 Epoch [1000/1000], Loss: 0.0000 final loss: 0.0000

Currently, there are 28 tags classified with patterns and responses relating to the university FAQ. The University-based general student information is added with generic responses. The trained model results in Table 5, include 14 English based and 14 iTaukei-based tags. After training the model 147 patterns are detected with 148 unique stemmed words, and the epoch loop after each iteration of the intent's dataset is gradually decreased the final epoch is very low therefore the neural network trained shows a positive result.

5 Advantages of the Proposed System

The proposed chatbot will provide benefits to the users and the university itself, by automating the process of communication and user interaction with quick real-time responses to achieve and deliver a better user experience. The key advantages include:

5.1 24/7 Availability

The users of the University chatbot will no longer have to wait for student academic services to get back to the time-consuming emails and texts. This chatbot will be live on the implemented platform and will be running round-the-clock basis eliminating the time factor as an instant response can drive potential students in. Easy access by just a message away no matter the time as it eliminates human input and the need to wait for a response.

Many prospective students would not be able to have direct communication with the staff member or not be able to come on campus due to many factors.

5.2 Instant Response

Many incoming queries can be handled all at once, since this chatbot will be on a web browser it will simultaneously answer multiple queries instantly. It will have very minimal waiting time therefore it will maintain and hold the user's attention while responding timelessly.

5.3 Consistency

Endless patience – University customer support might experience delays, internet outages, and lose their patience but the chatbot will not. Being impatience is one of the common practices to avoid late replies, different replies based on the customer support personnel's mode chatbots will be consistent to respond to each of the queries. Chatbots will dominate in handling different sorts of queries and show patience while answering questions. At this point, a human-sourced consumer service problem can be resolved directly.

5.4 Bilingual

Since this Chatbot can also handle the iTaukei language, this will improve student communication for the local and international universities who come from the Fijian background as they can communicate in their language to find it more flexible communication.

6 Chatbot Testing

As testing shows the chatbot can sufficiently respond to the user query for satisfactory communication. This chat does not require users to select whether they want to switch to the iTaukei language, the chatbot automatically detects the input then understands the texts to identify the language required then responds instantly. As discussed earlier, the input is generated on the patterns by tokenization and stemming which are part and parcel of NLP and neural networks (see Fig. 4).

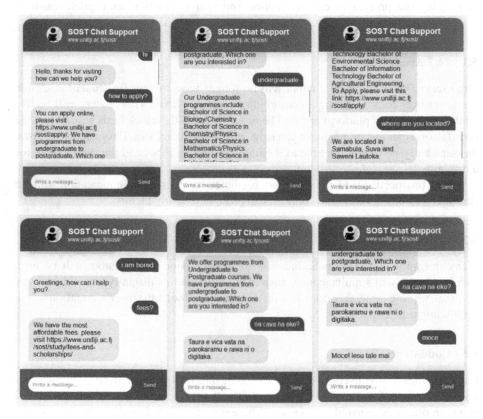

Fig. 4. Chatbot Sample Test

7 Limitations

While the chatbot is fully functional and able to respond to user input, it does require more testing, and more dataset is required to fulfill user request and respond to a more specific directed question. The bilingual chatbot uses the iTaukei language, in iTaukei, there are many different dialects in this language also which vary slightly from each other. For instance, one common example is if the input is in a form of the greeting "Bula" then the response can be "Bula Vinaka" another dialect uses "Bula re". Nevertheless, this chatbot uses the commonly spoken iTaukei with a mix of formal and informal dialogues.

In this paper the main focus is on the development of the Chatbot, using English and iTaukei language for the University related frequently asked questions by using NLP and deep learning techniques. However, more can be added in the development in terms of defining more intent tags that revolve around the university FAQ's classifying more patterns for that chatbot to detect based on user input, and implementing the Chatbot on a live platform to fully explore and test the outcomes. Future data analysis can be conducted to identify the gaps and some shortcomings of this chatbot can be explored by researchers including:

- Implementation of this chatbot can be done by integrating it on the Dialogue Flow platform which can run on live websites in the footer section [16].
- Addition of my iTaukei dialects and common tags.
- Improvement and Customization of the GUI components, adding graphics to make it more appealing and images to make it more user-friendly.
- introducing more NLP algorithms and Ai components.

8 Recommendations and Future Scope

In this paper the main focus is on the development of the Chatbot, using English and iTaukei language for the University related frequently asked questions by using NLP and deep learning techniques. However, more can be added in the development in terms of defining more intent tags that revolve around the university FAQ's classifying more patterns for that chatbot to detect based on user input, and implementing the Chatbot on a live platform to fully explore and test the outcomes. Future data analysis can be conducted to identify the gaps and some shortcomings of this chatbot can be explored by researchers including:

- Implementation of this chatbot can be done by integrating it on the Dialogue Flow platform which can run on live websites in the footer section [16].
- Addition of my iTaukei dialects and common tags.
- Improvement and Customization of the GUI components, adding graphics to make it more appealing and images to make it more user-friendly.
- introducing more NLP algorithms and Ai components.

9 Conclusion

The need for constant communication and interaction is ever growing rapidly. Chatbots have also evolved from rule-based to Ai with text, audio, and video visuals to fulfill the need for information demands as organizations are more with the technology the demand will more for these software-based solutions. Everyone needs access to the information within seconds with ease and with less human interaction. In this paper, we have proposed a Chatbot and implemented it on a webpage that includes a graphical user interface using bilingual languages - English and iTaukei.

In future work, we plan to make modifications and improvements to the current chatbot which uses NLP and ML to be migrated on Dialogue Flow which then can be live on a university website by conducting more training and testing.

References

1. Prabhuraj, R.P., Jeyabalan, S.: An intelligent behaviour shown by chatbot system for banking in vernacular languages. Int. Res. J. Eng. Technol. (IRJET). **6**(3), (2019)
2. Mudikanwi, L.T., Gotora, T.T.: Student personal assistant using machine learning (2018)
3. Dole, A., Sansare, H., Harekar, R., Athalye, S.: Intelligent chat bot for banking system. Int. J. Emerg. Trends Technol. Comput. Sci. (IJETTCS). **4**(5), October (2015)
4. Mohamed, A.S.: Chatbot powered by deep learning with neural machine translation. Int. Innovative Res. J. Eng. Technol. **4** (2018)
5. Fijian Government - iTaukei Affairs. iTaukei Institute of Language & Culture. [Online]. Available: https://www.itaukeiaffairs.gov.fj/index.php/divisions/tilc. Accessed 28 Sep 2022.
6. Wei, Y., Zhu, X., Sun, B.: Comparative studies of AIML. In: 3rd International Conference on Systems and Informatics (ICSAI) (2016)
7. Nguyen, T., Shcherbakov, M.: A neural network based vietnamese chatbot. In: International Conference on System Modeling & Advancement in Research Trends (SMART) (2018)
8. Bozic, J., Tazl, O.A., Wotawa, F.: Chatbot testing using AI planning. In: IEEE International Conference On Artificial Intelligence Testing (AITest) (2019)
9. Patel, N.P., Parikh, D.R., Patel, D.A., Patel, R.R.: AI and web-based human-like interactive university chatbot (UNIBOT). In: 3rd International conference on Electronics, Communication and Aerospace Technology (ICECA) (2019)
10. Suhel, S.F., Shukla, V.K., Vyas, S., Mishra, V.P.: Conversation to automation in banking through chatbot using artificial machine intelligence language. In: IEEE. Noida, India (2020)
11. Chandra, Y.W., Suyantoa, S.: Indonesian chatbot of university admission using a question answering system based on sequence-to-sequence model. Procedia Comput. Sci. **157**, 367–374 (2019)
12. Abdennadher, S., Abdallah, M., Mansy, Y., Hefny, W.E.: Jooka: a bilingual chatbot for university admission. World Conf. Inf. Syst. Technol. **1367**, 671–681 (2021)
13. Khin, N.N., Soe, K.M.: University chatbot using artificial intelligence markup language. In: IEEE. Yangon, Myanmar (2020)
14. Saqib, G., Faizan, K., Ghatte, N.: Intelligent chatting service using AIML. In: International Conference on Current Trends towards Converging Technologies (ICCTCT) (2018)
15. Prasad, P.V.K.V., Krishna, N.V., Jacob, T.P.: AI chatbot using web speech API and node.Js. In: International Conference on Sustainable Computing and Data Communication Systems (ICSCDS) (2022)
16. Singh, A., Ramasubramanian, K., Shivam, S.: Deployment and a continuous improvement framework. In: Building an Enterprise Chatbot, pp. 345-375. Apress Berkeley, CA (2019)

Machine Learning Algorithms Performance Investigation in Fake News Detection

Monesh Sami[1](✉) and A. B. M. Shawkat Ali[2](✉)

[1] Department of Computer Science and Information Systems, Fiji National University, Nadi, Fiji
monesh.sami@fnu.ac.fj
[2] School of Science and Technology, The University of Fiji, Lautoka, Fiji
shawkat.ali@ieee.org

Abstract. Mass media has always been one of the most enriching forms of information dissemination and sharing across the world among millions of people. It has taken the news industry by storm where traditionally, news media was transmitted using printed materials, radios and television, whereas over its existence it has become more effective and powerful with the use of the Internet. Social media is a very powerful tool in today's era that is being used to reach out to a larger audience which was not possible traditionally. This paper conducts a research on the top 6 algorithms that has been utilized for fake news detection in the recent 5 years (2017–2021). From the top 6 algorithms, the best performing algorithm was determined using the confusion matrix. The literature review shows that Naïve Bayes (NB), Decision Tree (DT), Random Forest (RF), Support Vector Machine (SVM), K-Nearest Neighbor (KNN) and Logistic Regression (LR) were the best algorithms that have been utilized for fake news detection in the recent 5 years indicating that simple algorithms had better accuracy and performed much better compared to the complicated ones. The experimental outcomes indicate that out of the top 6 algorithms, the best performing algorithm is Decision Tree with an accuracy of 99.38% whereas the least performing algorithm was K-Nearest Neighbor with an accuracy of 86.59%. The confusion matrix determines the performance of algorithms that also indicates that Decision Tree got the highest score compared to other algorithms for True Positive (7008/13470), where the algorithm correctly identified fake news. Hence proving that the best algorithm is the Decision Tree from the top 6 algorithms to identify a fake news accurately from this study.

Keywords: Algorithms · Fake News · Fake News Detection · Machine Learning · Mass Media · Performance · Social Media

1 Introduction

News is a piece of vital information in today's world where the general public has a right to know what is happening around them and in the world. There has been a significant rise in the number of internet users ever since the birth of the World Wide Web (WWW) [1]. The Internet has revolutionized the communication world like nothing ever before with the capability of broadcasting, information dissemination and interaction

C.-H. Hsu et al. (Eds.): DataCom 2022, LNCS 13864, pp. 95–110, 2023.
https://doi.org/10.1007/978-981-99-2233-8_7

among users regardless of the geographical locations [2]. Internet has opened doors to endless possibilities which were not possible or beyond feasible traditionally. The Internet has become a powerful tool in today's era where words published on the web can change people's attitudes, moods and behaviour. The broadcasting system is one the strongest medium for disseminating mass media communication, with the development of numerous innovative devices made distant communication possible with ease.

Mass media is a significant force in the modern era, providing a key chain for communication in either written, verbal or publicized to reach out to audiences across thousands of miles. Today, mass media utilizes diverse technologies that allow reachability to a large group of audience which was not possible with traditional means [3]. Internet connectivity has opened doors for various technologies that have enriched the mass media industry, where social media has taken the mass media by storm. The social media platform has elevated the connectivity of mass media among audiences to reach newer heights by providing flexibility and convenience at the audience's fingertips [4]. The fusion of social media, mass media and handheld devices produced magical outcomes by eliminating all barriers that could not connect people with mass media. Mass media has embraced social media as a platform to disseminate news and connect with large audiences across nations.

Fake news is on the hype nowadays, where the spread of distorted information is spread using public platforms like wildfire. Fake news is not a new concept that was formed due to the advancement of technology. However, its existence is for centuries [5]. Traditionally fake news dissemination was very limited however, due to the advancement of today's technologies and era, the dissemination of fake news has gradually evolved. Fake news has a strong relation with events and during an event such as elections [6] and crises like Covid-19 [7], fake news can strike either in the form of a false new post, clickbait, distorted image or videos to manipulate the human mind.

2 Traditional Media

Communication is an essential aspect of circulating information to people, mass media dissemination was traditionally limited to a few sources. The traditional media's were very popular in the past that had maintained the authenticity and credibility as news has a huge impact and effect on the message presented to its audience [8]. The traditional media is considered an evergreen news media that provides accurate and verified information which had built trust and is highly used among audiences to date. The famous and widely used traditional media of the past includes;

2.1 Printed Media

Newspapers and magazines were the most widely utilized printed media and one of the oldest forms of mass communication, yet its popularity is eternal in today's world [9]. The printed news is based on periodic publication such as daily, weekly, fortnightly or monthly, even annually. Printed media contains vast categories of news's such as sports [10], political [11, 12], businesses [13], educational [14], weather forecast [15], local and international news [16] and entertainment [17]. Newspaper was one of the most powerful media and great form of information of its time to disseminate information among people. Printed media are also considered one of the least expensive mass medias that can be obtained till date.

2.2 Radio

Radios were considered the most popular and highly consumable auditory media across the world regardless of the geographical locations. Radios enabled mass media dissemination to people at rural location where there were inaccessibility of electricity or newspapers and television signals [18]. Radios supported both electricity and battery operation which enhanced its efficiency giving a rise to more audience with the spread of information. After newspapers, radios has been the most affordable and highly consumable media for many audiences such as fishermen who are out in the sea [19] for weeks and the only source of weather and news bulletin is radio, cab drivers [20] to stay updated with the latest bulletins and illiterate audience [21] encountering hardships in reading and understanding news. Radio was practically a wireless media and way ahead of its time for news dissemination from distant locations without wires which are still utilized in the 21st century regardless of numerous innovative technologies. Even today, radios are highly consumed to transfer demise news to friends and relatives at distant locations.

2.3 Television

Television gained popularity after the massive usage of newspapers and radios which became a crucial portion of human lives that portrayed the news media with more than words, images and voice. The invention of live images and video footage drew more audiences towards graphical television interfaces [22]. This technology has naturally bought the entire nation into the audience's home, which was a noble substitute for radios and newspapers. Television enables connection to the outside world and provides a range of channels to acquire the current happening in the region and across the globe that the audience can connect to obtain information [23]. This media allowed the audience to communicate effectively in a limited time frame with greater understanding using footage compared to plain voiceover and text.

3 Modern Media

In this modern world, communication has reached newer heights with innovative technologies where mass media information can be acquired via the Internet with as simple as human touch [24]. The mass media is transitioning from traditional media to digitalized news with innovative technologies that can reach larger audiences than traditional media. Traditional mass media lacked a critical feature which was portability and connection with large audiences however, with the mixture of the Internet, social media and mobile devices, this barrier has been eliminated [25].

Social media is a very powerful tool in today's era that has gained huge popularity for news dissemination among the general public by reaching out and connecting the entire nation from a single group [26]. With the help of social media, a range of news content mechanisms can be viewed and shared among larger audiences, providing flexibility and accessibility among people [27]. Online news has been around for years ever since the existence of the internet. However, over the year social media has taken over the news industry by connecting people and mass media flawlessly. This innovative media has provided ease of interaction among the audience with the additional functionality of sharing, commenting and participating with other audiences [28]. With the power of the internet and social media, abundant data can be easily obtained from newsgroups making analysis much easier. In this age of digitalization, modern media are gradually replacing the traditional media with its features, mobility and benefits [29].

4 Research Objective

This paper proposes a study that will measure the performance of the top six algorithms that was used in the recent five years (2017–2021) to determine the best algorithm performer for fake news detection. The following research questions will be addressed in this paper;

1. What type of algorithm is best suited for fake news detection?
2. Which are the top 6 algorithms used in the recent five years for fake news detection?
3. Which algorithm performs the best out of the six chosen algorithms?

5 Methodology

A longitudinal study was proposed for this research, where both qualitative and quantitative method was utilized to meet the findings. The first phase of the study included qualitative research, which involved a literature review where a survey related to published works by other researchers was reviewed to find out which were the top six algorithms used for fake news detection in the recent five years (2016–2021). Subsequently, from the discovered algorithms, the best algorithm was determined through a quantitative method (confusion matrix).

The quantitative study was conducted in order to measure the performance to determine the best-performing algorithm.

The first stage of the research involved conducting a literature review where various databases such as IEEE Xplore, ScienceDirect, Wiley, Springer and Taylor and Francis were utilized to discover the algorithms used in the recent five years to detect fake news.

The second stage of the research involved conducting quantitative research where the top 6 algorithms discovered from the literature review undergo a performance test using a confusion matrix to determine which algorithm performs best using the same dataset.

For this phase, a set of the reliable datasets (true and fake news) was acquired from the Kaggle website. Subsequently, the dataset was prepared for analysis that involved cleaning the data thus, the model prepared can deliver accurate results. Afterwards, data transformation occurs which involved the conversion of data into a format that can be processed easily. The dataset was split into training data (70%) and testing data (30%).

The training data was used to design the model which was larger than the training data thus, the model can learn and understand patterns whereas the testing data was used to test the model that was created. The final step involved plotting a confusion matrix for each algorithm to determine which is the best performer from all the selected algorithms.

6 Literature Review

A literature review was conducted for this research paper where various journals and conference papers were explored to identify the different algorithms that were identified and utilized in the recent five years for fake news detection, to determine which is the best performing algorithm.

6.1 Naïve Bayes

Granik and Mesyura [30] propose a Naïve Bayes classifier to detect fake news on Facebook posts with an accuracy of 74%, proving artificial intelligence methods as a problem-solving tool for false information. Another similar study by Jain and Kasbe [31] on Facebook social media to detect fake news, Naïve Bayes classification model predicts whether a post on Facebook is real or fake, where AUC scores shows significant improvement with n_gram hence proving better judgment of model. Adiba et al., [32] incorporate corpora to improve the performance and accuracy with the Naïve Bayes algorithm that was able to classify authentication of news achieving an accuracy of 87% with moderate-sized corpora and 92% with enriched corpora. Agarwal and Dixit [33] proposes a model built on ensemble network portrayals of news reports, authors, and titles simultaneously to detect fake news with the help of machine learning algorithms where Naïve Bayes achieves an accuracy of 91%. A hybrid approach [34] proposes to detect false information on Twitter posts. The combination of two popular machine learning algorithms of Naïve Bayes and Support Vector Machine incorporates as the hybrid solution achieving an accuracy of 97.01%. Mugdha et al., [35] investigate fake headlines and misleading information where the author proposes a model that is able to detect whether the information is fake or accurate based on the news headlines, Gaussian Naïve Bayes algorithm achieves an accuracy of 87%.

6.2 Decision Tree

Lyu and Lo [36] propose a preliminary study to investigate the best-performing machine learning algorithm. The results indicate that the Decision Tree is the most suitable algorithm to detect fake news with an acceptable accuracy of 95%. Hoax news spreading has caused a lot of raising concerns impairing individual and groups, Irena and Setiawan [37] built a system to identify hoax news on Twitter social media for 50,610 tweet data with the help of the Decision Tree algorithm coupled with the use of weighting (TF-IDF)) and selection feature, achieving an accuracy of 72.91% with a 10.98% increase in accuracy using the n-gram feature. Poor accuracy is a limitation for fake news detection due to poor selection of features, ineffective tuning of parameters and imbalance of dataset. Hakak et al., [38] proposes an ensemble classification model for detecting fake news achieving a better accuracy with Decision Tree, Random Forest and Extra Tree Classifier. The training and testing accuracy acquires 99.8% and 44.15% on the Liar dataset whereas 100% accuracy with ISOT dataset. Another novel study by Dinesh and Rajendra [39] proposes a higher classification of fake political news by implementing a fake news detector using machine learning classifiers. The experimental results show Decision Tree outperforms Naïve Bayes with an accuracy of 99.70%.

6.3 Random Forest

A research by Islam *et al.,* [40] shows more than 200 million use Bengali as a communication language. The author proposes a web based classifier for the Bengali language to detect fake and real news using random forest with an accuracy of 85%. Faustini and Covoes [41] propose a study to detect fake news comprising only text features in German, Latin and Slavic language where Random Forest algorithm outperforms other classification algorithms. Recent studies shows the utilization of Random Forest algorithms for fake news detection in the Twitter social media where Iftene and Cusmulic [42] proves 95.93% accuracy and Azer, *et al.,* [43] proves 83.4% accuracy. Bharadwaj and Shao [44] conducts a research on fake news detection for online articles with the use of semantic feature such as bigram with random forest classifier which provides an accuracy of 95.66%, this is a hybrid approach which outperforms other features like unigrams, trigrams and quadgrams. An assemble learning approach by Al-Ash and Putri [45] uses fake Indonesian news to separate fake and real news, the performance results of random forest algorithm outperform both Support Vector Machine and Naive Bayes with a performance of 0.98 (f1-score). Amer and Siddiqui [46] research on covid-19 news with a text mining and machine learning algorithm to detect real and fake news, where Random Forest classifier outperforms decision tree with an accuracy of 94.49%.

6.4 Support Vector Machine (SVM)

Aphiwongsophon and Chongstitvatana [47] uses machines learning technique for fake news detection where Naïve Bayes, Neural Network and Support Vector Machine incorporates with normalization for data cleaning before classification of data, the results of the experiment proves SVM achieves the highest accuracy of 99.90%. On the other hand, Yazadi, *et al.,*[48] propose fake news detection with feature extraction method integrating K-means clustering achieving a better outcome and the highest precision to Decision Tree and Naïve Bayes. Poddar *et al.,* [49] focus on classification news content compared various machine learning models, hence proving that Support Vector Machine(SVM) with Term Frequency Inverse Document Format(TF-IDF) vectorizer provides the most accurate prediction for fake news detection to the other algorithms. Subsequently Shaikh and Patil [50] constructs a model using feature extraction technique as Term Frequency-Inverted Document Frequency (TF-IDF) with Support Vector Machine (SVM) as classifier achieves an accuracy of 95.05%. Jain *et al.,*[51] demonstrates a smart model using Support Vector Machine for detecting fake news achieves an accuracy of 93.6%. A computerized model [52] proposes to check the news validation from Twitter and recognizes fake messages from post, where the results confirm SVM as the best performer in Logistic Regression and Recurrent Neural Network model.

6.5 K-Nearest Neighbors (KNN)

Kesarwani *et al.,* [53] proposes a simple approach of detecting fake news on social media with the help of K-Nearest Neighbor classifier for Facebook news posts as the datasets achieves maximum accuracy of 79%. Another research by Zuliarso *et al.,* [54] proposes K-Nearest Neighbor to detect true and hoax news with 74 hoaxes website and 74 real news website, achieves an accuracy of 83.6%. Benamira *et al.,* [55] proposes a content based misinformation detection using K-Nearest Neighbor graph among articles using word embedding similarities that were accompanied by graph neural network, signifying much better performance. Another approach practices feature extraction in fake news detection by Kareem and Awan [56] utilizing Term Frequency (TF) and Term Frequency-Inverse Document Frequency (TF-IDF) with classification algorithms. K-Nearest Neighbor performs the best accuracy of 70% among the seven algorithms in this study.

6.6 Logistic Regression

Tiwari *et al.,* [57] uses feature extraction method with logistic regression to establish if news article is true or false achieving an accuracy of 71% with Term Frequency-Inverse Document Frequency (TF-IDF) feature. According to a comparison of related work by Awan *et al.,* [58] the proposed study scores the highest accuracy of 99.45% with excellent algorithms like Logistic Regression, Random Forest and Decision Tree Classifiers. Tacchini *et al.,* [59] proposes two techniques of Logistic Regression and Boolean Crowdsourcing algorithms for fake news detection on social media site consisting of 15,500 Facebook posts and 909,236 users, where the accuracy exceeds 99% for logistic regression even when the training set comprises less than a percent of the post. Pinnaparaju *et al.,* [60] proposes content analysis and user modelling to capture fake news propagators where TF-IDF text transformation method couples with Logistic Regression algorithm, achieving an accuracy of 71.5% in identifying fake news spreaders for both English and Spanish. Islam *et al.,* [61] proposes a novel solution of detecting the authenticity of news with the scheme comprising of stance detection, author credibility verification and machine learning classification where Logistic Regression algorithm ranks second highest accuracy of 87.20%. This solution performs a reliability check to determine whether the news is trustworthy of news.

7 Findings

7.1 Algorithm Category Best Suited for Fake News Detection

There are infinite number of algorithms that are out there to detect fake news till date. Machine learning algorithms are naturally categorized into classification, regression and clustering. For fake news detection problem, a classification type was best suited according to the classes for this study. The classes for this study were determined as the output variable where the news can only have two outcomes which was either a true news or a fake news. In this scenario binary classification was the finest choice determining the outcome of the news.

7.2 Top 6 Algorithms for Fake News Detection In Recent Five Years

There were numerous algorithms proposed in machine learning in the recent 5 years, however, it was proven using many studies that simple algorithms are much more efficient, effective and reliable compared to complex algorithms. From the literature review, the top 6 algorithms identified as Naïve Bayes, Decision Tree, Random Forest, Support Vector Machine, K-Nearest Neighbour and Logistics Regression were used as the most recent fake news detections. The selected algorithm was most ideal and top-notch choice due to its simplicity to fake news detection and its accuracy and performance.

7.3 Best Algorithm Performer for Fake News Detection

The research question of which algorithms perform the best is still a mystery that was achieved from the confusion matrix. A confusion matrix is a standard table that measures and defines the performance of classification algorithms with 4 diverse combinations of predicted and actual values. The confusion matrix provided real-time virtualization, summarizing the performance of each algorithm to determine the best-performed algorithm. The confusion matrix consisted of four diverse characteristics that defined the measurement metrics of the classifier as (Table 1);

Table 1. Confusion Matrix Measurement Outcome

		Actual	
		Include Fake News	Does Not Include Fake News
Predicted	Include Fake News	TP	FP
	Does Not Include Fake News	FN	TN

1) True Positive- these are news that includes fake news that were correctly identified by the algorithm
2) False Positive – these are news that are not fake, but the algorithm identifies it as fake
3) False Negative- these are when the news is fake, but the algorithm was not able to identify it as fake
4) True Negative- these are news that did not include fake news that were correctly identified by the algorithm

7.4 Naïve Bayes

Naïve Bayes algorithm builds models based on Bayes theorem that ensures quicker and effective prediction on the basis of conditional probability (Fig. 1).

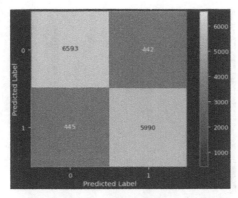

Fig. 1. Naive Bayes Confusion Matrix

7.5 Decision Tree

Decision Tree algorithm builds models based on tree structures where node represents dataset features, branches represent decision rule and lead represents the outcome results (Fig. 2).

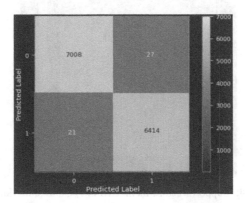

Fig. 2. Decision Tree Confusion Matrix

7.6 Random Forest

Random Forest algorithm builds models based on ensemble learning where majority votes are classified and average predicted outcome are determined from a number of decision trees (Fig. 3).

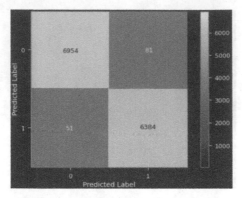

Fig. 3. Random Forest Confusion Matrix

7.7 Support Vector Machine (SVM)

Support Vector Machine (SVM) algorithm builds models based on decision boundary that determines the class to where data belongs according to data characteristics (Fig. 4).

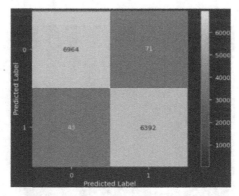

Fig. 4. Support Vector Machine (SVM) Confusion Matrix

7.8 K-Nearest Neighbor(KNN)

The k-Nearest Neighbor (KNN) algorithm builds models based on how closely the data points appear in the available categories, predicting the outcome (Fig. 5).

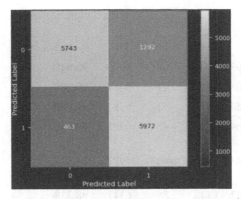

Fig. 5. K-Nearest Neighbor (KNN) Confusion Matrix

7.9 Logistic Regression

Logistic regression algorithm builds models based on predictive modelling which is used to predict categorical dependent variable using independent variables (Fig. 6).

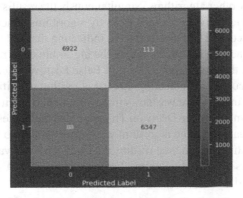

Fig. 6. Logistic Regression Confusion Matrix

7.10 Experimental Results Summary

The following table summarizes the experimental confusion matrix results for easier analysis of the four diverse characteristics that defined the measurement metrics of the classifier in this study. The total news tested in this confusion matrix was 13,470 for each algorithm.

Table 2. Confusion Matrix Summary Results

Algorithms	TP	FP	FN	TN	Accuracy in %	Performance Rank
Naïve Bayes	6593	442	445	5990	**93.04%**	5
Decision Tree	7008	27	21	6414	**99.38%**	1
Random Forest	6954	81	51	6384	**99.00%**	3
Support Vector Machine (SVM)	6964	71	43	6392	**99.04%**	2
K-Nearest Neighbor (KNN)	5743	1292	463	5972	**86.59%**	6
Logistic Regression	6922	113	88	6347	**98.33%**	4

8   Discussion

According to the confusion matrix, the Decision Tree algorithm recorded the highest score (7008), True Positive, which indicates that the algorithm correctly identified fake news compared to any other algorithms. Simultaneously the results were also illustrated errors encountered in identifying the fake news by algorithms, where the Decision Tree recorded the lowest score (21), False Negative indicating that the algorithm had incorrectly identified fake news whereas the rest of the algorithm error rate was significantly higher. Subsequently, there was another case of False Positive where the Decision Tree recorded the lowest score (27), indicating that the algorithm identified the news as fake, which was not fake. Finally, there was news that was not fake and it was correctly determined by the algorithm where the Decision Tree recorded the highest score (6414), True Negative, which indicated that the algorithm was correctly able to identify the news as not fake news. From the experimental results, the Decision Tree was the best algorithm for detecting fake news followed by Support Vector Machine (SVM) and Random Forest, which were the second best ranking algorithms.

9   Conclusion

Social media is one of the most cost-effective and powerful tools in today's era as news media reach out to a larger audience which was not possible previously with limited mass media tools. Social media is like a double-edged sword which has an infinite number of advantages but also disadvantages, and the most popular among all is fake news. Fake news did not originate from social media, but it was a problem that was previously discovered before the existence of social media was used as a critical weapon to enrich fake news to reach out to larger audiences. This study used a literature review to determine the top 6 algorithms highly used for fake news detection. Subsequently, the top 6 algorithms discovered were NB, DT, RF, SVM, KNN and Logistic Regression, which went through performance testing to determine the best algorithm. The experimental results showed that the best-performing algorithm was Decision Tree for fake news detection with an accuracy of 99.38%. Therefore, the Decision Tree algorithm may be an efficient machine learning tool to stop fake news on social media platforms.

10 Future Work

This research aims to extend this study by adapting larger fake news datasets with modern trends of machine learning algorithms such as deep learning and ensemble learning.

References

1. Berners-Lee, T., Cailliau, R., Luotonen, A., Nielsen, H.F., Secret, A.: The world-wide web. Commun. ACM **37**(8), 76–82 (1994)
2. Leiner, B.M., et al.: A brief history of the Internet. ACM SIGCOMM Computer Communication Review **39**(5), 22–31 (2009)
3. McQuail, D.: The influence and effects of mass media. Mass Communication and Society, pp. 70–94 (1977)
4. Sami, M., Sharma, N.A.: Learning computer modules using multimedia and social media platform in a developing country. In: 2021 IEEE Asia-Pacific Conference on Computer Science and Data Engineering (CSDE), IEEE, pp. 1–9 (2021)
5. Burkhardt, J.M.: History of fake news. Libr. Technol. Rep. **53**(8), 5–9 (2017)
6. Grinberg, N., Joseph, K., Friedland, L., Swire-Thompson, B., Lazer, D.: Fake news on Twitter during the 2016 US presidential election. Science **363**(6425), 374–378 (2019)
7. Carrion-Alvarez, D., Tijerina-Salina, P.X.: Fake news in COVID-19: A perspective. Health promotion perspectives **10**(4), 290 (2020)
8. Lee, R.S.: Credibility of newspaper and TV news. Journal. Q. **55**(2), 282–287 (1978)
9. Tanikawa, M.: What is news? What is the newspaper? The physical, functional, and stylistic transformation of print newspapers, 1988–2013. Int. J. Commun. **11**, 22 (2017)
10. Schlagheck, C.: Newspaper reading choices by college students. Newsp. Res. J. **19**(2), 74–87 (1998)
11. Oliver, P.E., Maney, G.M.: Political processes and local newspaper coverage of protest events: from selection bias to triadic interactions. Am. J. Sociol. **106**(2), 463–505 (2000)
12. Fowler, E.F., Ridout, T.N.: Local television and newspaper coverage of political advertising. Polit. Commun. **26**(2), 119–136 (2009)
13. Meyer, P.: The influence model and newspaper business. Newsp. Res. J. **25**(1), 66–83 (2004)
14. DeRoche, E.F.: Newspapers in education: What we know. Newsp. Res. J. **2**(3), 59–63 (1981)
15. Rundblad, G., Chen, H.: Advice-giving in newspaper weather commentaries. J. Pragmat. **89**, 14–30 (2015)
16. Abel, J.D., Wirth, M.O.: Newspaper vs. TV credibility for local news. Journal. Q. **54**(2), 371–375 (1977)
17. Layefa, G., Johnson, W.A., Taiwo, A.: Newspaper readership pattern in Ekiti state, Nigeria. IOSR Journal of Humanities and Social Science (IOSR-JHSS) **21**(5), 121–13 and 5 (2016)
18. Ullah, R.: Role of fm radios in news and information: a study of fm radios in peshawar, khyber Pakhtunkhwa. Int. J. Commu. Res. **8**(2) (2018)
19. Joshi, H., Ayyangar, G.V.: ICT: A boon for fishermen community. Journal of Global Communication **3**(1), 8–13 (2010)
20. Bijsterveld, K., Dieker, M.: A captive audience: Traffic radio as guard and escape. Journal of Radio & Audio Media **22**(1), 20–25 (2015)

21. Irivwieri, J.W.: Information needs of illiterate female farmers in Ethiope East local government area of Delta State. Library hi tech news (2007)
22. Chamberlain, D.: Television interfaces. Journal of popular film & television **38**(2), 84–88 (2010)
23. Machill, M., Köhler, S., Waldhauser, M.: The use of narrative structures in television news: An experiment in innovative forms of journalistic presentation. Eur. J. Commun. **22**(2), 185–205 (2007)
24. Porter, D.: Internet culture. Routledge (2013)
25. Vivianl, M., Pasi, G.: Credibility in social media: opinions, news, and health information—a survey. Wiley interdisciplinary reviews: Data mining and knowledge discovery **7**(5), e1209 (2017)
26. Bandari, R., Asur, S., Huberman, B.: The pulse of news in social media: Forecasting popularity. Proceedings of the International AAAI Conference on Web and Social Media **6**(1), 26–33 (2012)
27. Heuer, H., Breiter, A.: Trust in news on social media. In: Proceedings of the 10th Nordic conference on human-computer interaction, pp. 137–147 (2018)
28. Li, R., Suh, A.: Factors influencing information credibility on social media platforms: Evidence from Facebook pages. Procedia computer science **72**, 314–328 (2015)
29. Sameera, A.: A study of modern communication methods and replacing the traditional teaching learning methods in schools in Sri Lanka. In: 4th International Conference on Social Sciences 2018, Research Centre for Social Sciences, Faculty of Social Sciences, p. 105. University of Kelaniya, Sri Lanka (2018)
30. Granik, M., Mesyura, V.: Fake news detection using naive Bayes classifier. In: 2017 IEEE first Ukraine conference on electrical and computer engineering (UKRCON), pp. 900–903. IEEE (2017)
31. Jain, A., Kasbe, A.: Fake news detection. In: 2018 IEEE International Students' Conference on Electrical, Electronics and Computer Science (SCEECS), pp. 1–5. IEEE (2018)
32. Adiba, F.I., Islam, T., Kaiser, M.S., Mahmud, M., Rahman, M.A.: Effect of corpora on classification of fake news using naive Bayes classifier. Int. J. Autom. Artif. Intell. Machi. Learn. **1**(1), 80–92 (2020)
33. Agarwal, A., Dixit, A.: Fake news detection: an ensemble learning approach. In: 2020 4th International Conference on Intelligent Computing and Control Systems (ICICCS), pp. 1178–1183. IEEE (2020)
34. Ingole, P., Bhoir, S., Vidhate, A.V.: Hybrid Model For Text Classification. In: 2018 Second International Conference on Electronics, Communication and Aerospace Technology (ICECA), 29–31 March 2018, pp. 7–15 (2018). https://doi.org/10.1109/ICECA.2018.847 4738
35. Mugdha, S.B.S., Ferdous, S.M., Fahmin, A.: Evaluating machine learning algorithms for bengali fake news detection. In: 2020 23rd International Conference on Computer and Information Technology (ICCIT), pp. 1–6. IEEE (2020)
36. Lyu, S., Lo, D.C.-T.: Fake news detection by decision tree. In: 2020 SoutheastCon, pp. 1–2. IEEE (2020)
37. Irena, B., Setiawan, E.B.: Fake news (hoax) identification on social media twitter using decision tree c4. 5 method. Jurnal RESTI (Rekayasa Sistem Dan Teknologi Informasi) **4**(4), 711–716 (2020)
38. Hakak, S., Alazab, M., Khan, S., Gadekallu, T.R., Maddikunta, P.K.R., Khan, W.Z.: An ensemble machine learning approach through effective feature extraction to classify fake news. Futur. Gener. Comput. Syst. **117**, 47–58 (2021)
39. Dinesh, T., Rajendran, T.: Higher classification of fake political news using decision tree algorithm over naive Bayes algorithm. Revista Geintec-Gestao Inovacao e Tecnologias **11**(2), 1084–1096 (2021)

40. Islam, F., et al.: Bengali fake news detection. In: 2020 IEEE 10th International Conference on Intelligent Systems (IS), pp. 281–287. IEEE (2020)
41. Faustini, P.H.A., Covões, T.F.: Fake news detection in multiple platforms and languages. Expert Syst. Appl. **158**, 113503 (2020)
42. Cușmaliuc, C.-G., Coca, L.-G., Iftene, A.: Identifying fake news on twitter using naive bayes, SVM and random forest distributed algorithms. In: Proceedings of The 13th Edition of the International Conference on Linguistic Resources and Tools for Processing Romanian Language (ConsILR-2018). ISSN, pp. 177–188 (2018)
43. Azer, M., Taha, M., Zayed, H.H., Gadallah, M.: Credibility detection on twitter news using machine learning approach. Int. J. Intell. Sys. Appli. **13**(3), 1–10 (2021)
44. Bharadwaj, P., Shao, Z.: Fake news detection with semantic features and text mining. Int. J. Natu. Lang. Comp. (IJNLC) **8** (2019)
45. Al-Ash, H.S., Putri, M.F., Mursanto, P., Bustamam, A.: Ensemble learning approach on indonesian fake news classification. In: 2019 3rd International Conference on Informatics and Computational Sciences (ICICoS), pp. 1–6. IEEE (2019)
46. Amer, A.Y.A., Siddiqui, T.: Detection of covid-19 fake news text data using random forest and decision tree classifiers. Int. J. Comp. Sci. Info. Sec. (IJCSIS) **18**(12) (2020)
47. Aphiwongsophon, S., Chongstitvatana, P.: Detecting fake news with machine learning method. In: 2018 15th international conference on electrical engineering/electronics, computer, telecommunications and information technology (ECTI-CON), pp. 528–531. IEEE (2018)
48. Yazdi, K.M., Yazdi, A.M., Khodayi, S., Hou, J., Zhou, W., Saedy, S.: Improving fake news detection using k-means and support vector machine approaches. Int. J. Elec. Comm. Eng. **14**(2), 38–42 (2020)
49. Poddar, K., Umadevi, K.: Comparison of various machine learning models for accurate detection of fake news. In: 2019 Innovations in Power and Advanced Computing Technologies (i-PACT), vol. 1, pp. 1–5. IEEE (2019)
50. Shaikh, J., Patil, R.: Fake news detection using machine learning. In: 2020 IEEE International Symposium on Sustainable Energy, Signal Processing and Cyber Security (iSSSC), pp. 1–5, IEEE (2020)
51. Jain, A., Shakya, A., Khatter, H., Gupta, A.K.: A smart system for fake news detection using machine learning. In: 2019 International Conference on Issues and Challenges in Intelligent Computing Techniques (ICICT), vol. 1, pp. 1–4. IEEE (2019)
52. Mahir, M., Akhter, S., Huq, M.R.: Detecting fake news using machine learning and deep learning algorithms. In: 2019 7th International Conference on Smart Computing & Communications (ICSCC), pp. 1–5. IEEE (2019)
53. Kesarwani, A., Chauhan, S.S., Nair, A.R.: Fake news detection on social media using k-nearest neighbor classifier. In: 2020 International Conference on Advances in Computing and Communication Engineering (ICACCE), pp. 1–4. IEEE (2020)
54. Zuliarso, E., Anwar, M.T., Hadiono, K., Chasanah, I.: Detecting Hoaxes in Indonesian News Using TF/TDM and K Nearest Neighbor. In: IOP Conference Series: Materials Science and Engineering, vol. 835, no. 1, p. 012036. IOP Publishing (2020)
55. Benamira, A., Devillers, B., Lesot, E., Ray, A. K., Saadi, M., Malliaros, F.D.: Semi-supervised learning and graph neural networks for fake news detection. In: 2019 IEEE/ACM International Conference on Advances in Social Networks Analysis and Mining (ASONAM), pp. 568–569. IEEE (2019)
56. Kareem, I., Awan, S.M.: Pakistani media fake news classification using machine learning classifiers. In: 2019 International Conference on Innovative Computing (ICIC), pp. 1–6. IEEE (2019)

57. Tiwari, V., Lennon, R.G., Dowling, T.: Not everything you read is true! Fake news detection using machine learning algorithms. In: 2020 31st Irish Signals and Systems Conference (ISSC), pp. 1–4. IEEE (2020)
58. Awan, M.J., et al.: Fake news data exploration and analytics. Electronics **10**(19), 2326 (2021)
59. Tacchini, E., Ballarin, G., Della Vedova, M.L., Moret, S., De Alfaro, L.: Some like it hoax: Automated fake news detection in social networks. arXiv preprint arXiv:1704.07506 (2017)
60. Pinnaparaju, N., Indurthi, V., Varma, V.: Identifying Fake News Spreaders in Social Media. In: CLEF (Working Notes) (2020)
61. Islam, N., et al.: Ternion: an autonomous model for fake news detection. Appl. Sci. **11**(19), 9292 (2021)

Big Data Privacy and Security

Robust Graph Embedding Recommendation Against Data Poisoning Attack

Junyan Zhong[1], Chang Liu[2], Huibin Wang[3], Lele Tian[4], Han Zhu[5]([⊠]),
and Chan-Tong Lam[5]

[1] HSBC Software Development Guangdong Ltd., Guangzhou, China
[2] Faculty of Humanities and Social Science, Macao Polytechnic University, Macao SAR, China
[3] ABB Global Open Innovation Center, Shenzhen, China
[4] Gree Electric Appliances Inc. of Zhuhai, Zhuhai, China
[5] Faculty of Applied Sciences, Macao Polytechnic Uniuversity, Macao SAR, China
HanZhu@ieee.org

Abstract. With the development of recommendation system technology, more and more Internet services are applied to recommendation systems.

In recommendation systems, matrix factoring is the most widely used technique. However, matrix factoring algorithms are very susceptible to shilling attacks (trust or espionage). The former defends methods against data poisoning attacks focused on detecting individual attack behaviors. But there are few detection methods for group data poisoning attacks. Therefore, we propose a detection method based on Graph Neural Network (GNN) and adversarial learning. We train user-item nodes and edges through a semi-supervised learning approach, improving the robustness of the GNN recommendation system. Our work can be divided into the following parts:

Firstly, we review the former recommendation systems and the graph representation learning recommendation systems. Secondly, we analyze the main vulnerabilities of the graph representation learning recommendation systems. Furthermore, the detection methods of data poisoning attacks are analyzed, and the difference between individual data poisoning attacks and group data poisoning attacks are discussed. Finally, we propose a per-process Robust-GNN semi-supervised detection model to conduct group detection on different types of attacks. In addition, we also analyze the sensitivity of the proposed methods. From the experiments results, it can be concluded that we should apply the attention mechanism to the proposed methods which makes it more generalized.

Keywords: Recommendation system · Adversarial learning · Data poisoning attack · Graph neural network

1 Introduction

With the development of the Internet, web app has generated a huge amount of data. Big companies collect those data and use it for profiling and paralytics. Those big companies are gradually benefiting from data. We have entered an information-rich era and face the problem which means information overload. Many approaches have been devised to utilize those large amounts of data. To tackle the problem of telling people what to buy, people proposed the recommendation system [1].

The recommendation system learns the user's interests by analyzing the user-item interaction data—those data are based on users' history behavior. The system can automatically recommend the user's potential interest items. With the rapid development in the number of users and items, recommending the right item to the right person has become a hard problem to be tackled. Therefore, recommendation algorithms have been developed in various systems to help people make decisions about buying items.

With the rapid development of recommendation systems, however, the security issues of recommendation systems continue to threaten their stability of recommendation systems. Many recommendation systems are vulnerable to the malicious injection of product ratings [2]. The act of malicious users injecting some targeted products rating into the recommendation system is called a data poisoning attack or data injection attack. Attackers inject biased ratings to items that affect the stability and accuracy of recommendation systems. The most common behavior of the rating data injection is that attackers intentionally increase or decrease the rating of certain types of products, thereby increasing or decreasing the probability of pushing such products to more people [3].

To prevent data poisoning attacks, various attack detection methods have been proposed. Some shopping websites are detected by robots, effectively reducing the frequency of data poisoning attacks. And also, some companies use Generative Adversarial Networks (GAN) to generate fake users for recommendation systems [4]. Those fake users would give some of the target items a fake rating. That rating data would be used for adversarial learning, which effectively strengthens the defense against data poisoning attacks.

The main idea of this paper would focus on detecting abnormal users and their behavior in recommendation systems. Abnormal users and their behaviors here mean that users use specific and identical tactics to promote or demote specific items. For example, a specific attacker can generate hundreds of fake user behavior, which will affect shopping interest distribution in the overall user profile. To avoid that data injection attack, we proposed a method based on GNN to detect abnormal users.

Obliviously, matrix factorization (MF) [5] is one of the most widely recommendation methods. The algorithm relies on the user's historical behavior data to describe the user's portrait. It can provide users with recommendations based on their previous behavior. The former recommendation systems usually build matrices between users and products and implement recommendations through matrix factorization methods. These matrices are usually sparse because customers don't rate all items. Therefore, before solving these sparse matrices for the recommendation, it is usually necessary to approximate these matrices to improve the solving efficiency.

For the graph neural network recommendation system, there is no such problem because the graph data only stores the user commodity nodes with interactive behaviors.

Graph representation recommendation systems need to represent user behavior matrix in behavior inter-action graphs before learning graph data-set. To express the interaction between the user and the product in a bipartite graph, we need to transform the user-item matrix into the user-item interaction bipartite graph. We often use the adjacency matrix of the user-item interaction bipartite graph to build our data sets. Also, we need to transform the MF recommendation system to a graph-represent learning recommendation system.

To make personalized recommendations for users based on the bipartite graph, the task of recommending items to users can be transformed into measuring the correlation between the user vertex vu and the item nodes directly connected to i_u on the graph. The value of each edge means the rating of use given to the items. Also, the edge between each user node shows the social relation between each user. We can make a recommendation based on the edge of each user's nodes. Those similarities show the correlation of each user node.

The main challenge of this idea is how to identify the problem about the interaction between users and items to users, and how to transmit user information to items. The main principles for building a model to solve these problems are as follows:

- Sample: The main problem of the composition of the Robust-GNN is how to sample neighbor nodes efficiently, which means the methods should classify the neighbor nodes with low time complexity.
- Neighbor aggregation and similarity evaluation: The main problem of the composition of the Robust-GNN is how to aggregate information about neighbors.
- Data transmission: The main problem of the data transmission of our method is how to integrate the representation of each node and the neighbor nodes' aggregation.
- Graph learning: It's hard for GNN methods to learn with deep layers. The main point of that problem is how that method learns effective information using a shallow layer network (Fig. 1).

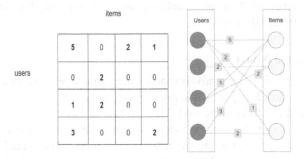

Fig. 1. Graph data collaborative filtering recommendation

Recommendation systems are vulnerable to malicious data poisoning attacks, which may attract a group of shilling attackers to intentionally insert abnormal feedback, thereby biasing the recommendation system toward their own preferences. Those attack methods may violate the modeling assumption that data is always available and that these data do reflect user interests and preferences. White-box attacks detection are based on the detection of attack signatures generated by some known attack strategies. However, fraud detection is an error-prone process due to the pursuit of high classification recall. Real users may be flagged as fraudsters, so being removed would have the opposite effect.

2 Related Work

We first need to identify common attack methods for graph-representation learning recommendation systems to better define defense methods for recommendation systems. Commonly used graph neural network attack methods are mainly divided into the following types.

2.1 Graph Graph-Data Attack Methods

2.1.1 Random Attack

The Random attack means some malicious users might randomly select some users' nodes and change the edges between users' nodes and items' nodes, thus changing the relationship in the original graph. Also, some may randomly change the edge between each user's edge. This attack is equivalent to adding random perturbations or cutting edges to the graph data. Those methods conform to a standard Gaussian distribution.

2.1.2 Targeted Attack

Targeted attacks focus on specific target nodes. We initially set several target items for the user nodes and several target user nodes for the train data-set. We refer to an attack as a form of attack in which the original graph data is injected.

Nettack is an adversarial attack model for graph node classification. This method aims to mix the normal nodes and target nodes. Nettack can change the edge distribution and node features while preserving data features to avoid the attack behaviors that are not easily detected. Therefore, targeted attack aims to imply incremental computation and utilizes the sparsity of the graph to achieve fast execution, and that method has good adaptability to different data-sets.

2.1.3 Non-targeted Attack

Non-targeted attacks aim to use adversarial learning attacks with random target nodes. The meta-learning attack is part of the non-targeted attack. We use this method as our non-targeted attack experiment method.

The general idea of meta-learning is to train a meta-learner with many tasks similar to the target task and apply it to the target task to get good initial model values. Small. Amount of data in the model. Meta attackers use this attack method to learn prior information. Based on these previews, the attack model can adapt quickly to new attack tasks, and only a small number of queries can generate adversarial examples. Specifically, the meta-attacker first trains the graph of her data using the data gradients computed by each classifier. After training, the meta-aggressor is used in the target classifier, and the fine-tuned meta-aggressor is fed as gradient information to the target classifier to generate adversarial examples.

2.2 Graph-Data Defend Methods

To prevent data poisoning attacks, many detection methods have been proposed to avoid them. Cao [6] proposed a semi-supervised method to detect data poisoning attacks. The algorithm is divided into two stages. First stage is that the method aims to train the Naive Bayes classifier with a small subset of labeled data. The second stage combines the unlabeled data with the EM algorithm to improve the former classifier, which is used to detect whether the user is the attacker or not.

The method performs well on average attack flow attacks but does not improve significantly on other attack modes. The problem is that real-world data poisoning attacks are not single-mode attacks, and detection methods should be more general [7]. Thus, it is difficult to label the attack behaviors that affect the classification of attackers [8]. Zhang [9] proposed a detection method based on k-means clustering dichotomy. The method is based on an unsupervised learning method, which overcomes the problem of poor performance when the attacker has some related items. Essentially, detectors based on unsupervised learning assume that the attackers are very similar, and the detector's accuracy also depends on whether this rule is met. Since existing detection methods aim to detect individual data poisoning attacks, the detection of group data poisoning attacks is rarely considered.

Several methods are proposed to detect group data poisoning attacks. Zhang [10] proposed a detection method based on GCN representation learning. Anelli [11] proposed a detection method based on a knowledge graph. These methods are less accurate in large cluster data sets. Some researchers focus on review detection for website reviews.

These methods differ from group data poisoning attacks in recommendation systems. The shilling group attack rates targeted items and tries to upgrade or downgrade non-targeted items to reduce the risk of being detected [12, 13]. Thus, the researchers made adjustments to the applied fraud detection method [14]. This idea inspired me to use GNN to detect data poisoning attacks.

3 Preliminaries

For detection models, we first use some existing models as baseline models. Here we use GAT and GCN and RGCN and also the GCN-SVD models as the baseline detection models. We will compare our methods' performance with those baseline methods in the following experiments.

GCN: GCN [15] is a widely used graph neural network that defines graph convolution using spectral analysis.

$$H^{(l+1)} = \sigma\left(\tilde{D}^{-\frac{1}{2}}\tilde{A}\tilde{D}^{-\frac{1}{2}}H^{(l)}W^{(l)}\right) \tag{1}$$

$$\mathbf{h}_i^{(l+1)}\rho\left(\sum_{j\in ne(i)}\frac{1}{\sqrt{\tilde{D}_{i,i}\tilde{D}_{j,j}}}\mathbf{h}_j^{(l)}\mathbf{W}^{(l)}\right) \tag{2}$$

GAT: GAT [16] is a graph network with self-attention ability to assign different neighborhood weights. The main usage of GAT is to classify graph nodes. The principle of this method is based on the attention mechanism. The main idea of GAT can be listed as follows:

(1) When operating in parallel, GAT can perform parallel processing on adjacent nodes.
(2) By adjusting the attention coefficient, the weights of adjacent nodes with different
    edge degrees connected to the node can be changed.

$$\vec{h}_i' = \sigma\left(\sum_{j \in \mathcal{N}_i} \alpha_{ij} \mathbf{W} \vec{h}_j\right) \tag{3}$$

$$\alpha_{ij} = \frac{\exp\left(\text{LeakyReLU}\left(\vec{\mathbf{a}}^T\left[\mathbf{W}\vec{h}_i \| \mathbf{W}\vec{h}_j\right]\right)\right)}{\sum_{k \in \mathcal{N}_i} \exp\left(\text{LeakyReLU}\left(\vec{\mathbf{a}}^T\left[\mathbf{W}\vec{h}_i \| \mathbf{W}\vec{h}_k\right]\right)\right)} \tag{4}$$

RGCN: RGCN [17] is specially developed for the highly multi-relational data features
of realistic knowledge bases and aims to defend against adversarial edges attack.

$$h_{N(i)}^{(l)} = \sum_{j \in N(i)} \frac{1}{\sqrt{\tilde{D}_{ii}\tilde{D}_{jj}}}\left(h_j^{(l)} \odot \alpha_j^l\right) \tag{5}$$

$$h_i^{(l)} \sim N\left(\mu_i^{(l)}, \text{diag}\left(\sigma_i^{(l)}\right)\right) \tag{6}$$

GCN-SVD: To prevent the graph's high-rank spectrum from deviating due to graph
attacks, GCN-SVD first uses SVD to perform low-rank approximation on the adjacency
matrix to purify the graph, and then uses GCN without decryption to identify false nodes.

The change in the graph attack method is that the connection matrix can effectively
utilize the deployment of high-order graphs and can only maintain low-order network
confrontation.

4 Our Methods

4.1 Pre-process GNN Supervised Detection Structure

Aiming at the problem of data poisoning detection, we propose a Robust GNN-
supervised detection model. This method is mainly divided into two parts. The first
part is to reduce the dimension of the graph data subjected to poisoning attacks through
the Truncate-SVD method, thereby reducing the probability of high-rank attacks. This
step is called graph purification. The second part is to input the purified graph data into
our semi-supervised graph clustering framework and monitor the possible attacking user
nodes by clustering and scoring outliers, so as to exclude the impact of user attacking
nodes on the scoring data.

Its structure is shown in Fig. 2. We first build a multi-relational graph based on domain
knowledge. Then, the GNN is trained using the partially labeled nodes supervised by
a supervised classification loss function. Instead of directly aggregating all relational
neighbors, we divide the aggregation part into relational and inter-relational aggregation
processes. The embedding under each relation is aggregated simultaneously during the
interrelation aggregation process. Then, the embedding for each relation is combined
during the interrelation aggregation process. Finally, predictions are made using the node
embedding method of the last layer.

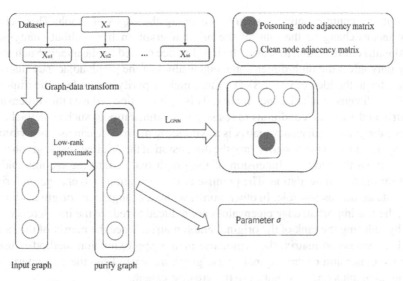

Fig. 2. Pre-process GNN supervised detection structure method

4.2 Pre-process GNN Supervised Detection Method

We use the normalized attention coefficient scores to generate linear combination features of their corresponding nodes. The aggregation process uses a linear combination process, which can be used to update node features.

More specifically, the structure of a graph neural network layer is as follows:

$$h_j^{l+1} = \sigma \left(\sum_{j \in N_j} a_{ij}^l W^l h_j^l \right) \tag{7}$$

The σ refers to the activation function of the network. The activation function we use, the RELU function or other activation function, etc., is the activation matrix of the lth layer, and $h_j^l + 1$ represents the updated activation layer. The W^l represents the weight parameter of the L layer. a_{ij}^l represents the attention parameters of the neural network and the attention parameters of node i in the j node set in the neighborhood area.

$$a_{ij}^{l-1} = \text{softmax}\left(\text{LeakyRELU}((e_{ij})^{l-1}\right) = \frac{\exp\left(\text{LeakyRELU}(e_{ij}^{l-1})\right)}{\sum_{j \in Nj} \exp\left(\text{LeakyRELU}(e_{ij}^{l-1})\right)} \tag{8}$$

The e_{ij} shows the layer update of the network, and softmax function is used to normalize the LeakyRelu activation function to avoid over-fitting.

4.3 Optimization of the Model

To optimize the model, we use dimension reduction to remove outlier eigenvalues in the sparse graph matrix. Since Nettack's attack mode tends to change the reasoning of the entire recommendation system by changing the edges of graph. This behavior usually means changing the rank of the original graph matrix without changing the original matrix information to reduce the interference caused by the attack. Such attacks usually only affect the high-dimensional eigenvalues of the graph adjacency matrix, so we can refer to the idea of GCN-SVD, which mainly purify and reduce the dimension of the high-dimensional adjacency matrix. This optimization reduces the dimension of the matrix under certain conditions to resist similar attack modes such as nettack.

Since the graph's adjacency matrix is a symmetric matrix, we can use the symmetric matrix approximation method to reduce the dimension of the original sparse graph matrix and then input the reduced dimension of the graph matrix into the recommendation system for the recommendation. The premise of this operation is to change the original matrix data as little as possible. In other words, without changing the original adjacency matrix, the less important edge eigenvalues are reduced to reduce the interference of the attack by reducing the rank of the original graph matrix. Since the matrix of the indirect graph is a symmetric matrix, the symmetric matrix approximation method is used to reduce the dimension of the original sparse graph matrix to keep the characteristics of the original graph adjacency matrix to the greatest extent.

Truncate-SVD would be suitable in this problem, which aims to reduce the dimension of the matrix to approximate the original matrix.

$$A_k = \sum_{i=1}^{k} \sigma_i u_i v_i^* \tag{9}$$

$$\|A - A_k\|_2 = \sigma_{k+1} \tag{10}$$

$$\sigma_{k+1} \leq \alpha \tag{11}$$

We also use regularization to tune the loss function so the model can avoid overfitting.

$$L_{gnn} = \frac{1}{m} \sum_{i=1}^{m} L\left(\hat{y}^{(i)}, y^{(i)}\right) + \frac{\lambda}{2m} \|w\|_2^2 \tag{12}$$

Our algorithm is shown below. First, the purified graph adjacency matrix w is initialized to the input graph adjacency matrix, and the gnn parameter σ is randomly initialized. Then, we train the graph clustering method with the loss function (12).

During training, we set the training time to τ and updated the parameter σ to minimize the loss function. We use Stochastic Gradient Descent (SGD) methods to solve this optimization problem. Finally, we can get the output parameter σ and the clean graph h. A clean graph refers to a clean adjacency matrix in which shilling attack edge values are removed from the graph. The average of item interactions will replace these maliciously tampered values.

We can use a clean graph h for recommendations without worrying about malicious attacks tampering with product ratings.

Algorithm 1: Robust-GNN recommendation detection

   Input: Purify graph adjacency w
   Output: Learned clean graph adjacency matrix and GNN parameters σ
1   initialize $w \rightarrow h_j^l$
2   Randomly initialize σ
3   **while** *stopping condition is not meet* **do**
4      $h_j^{l+1} \leftarrow \sigma\left(\sum_{j \in N_i} a_{ij}^1 W^1 h_j^1\right)$
5   for i = 1 to τ do
6        $g \leftarrow \frac{\partial L_{GNN}}{\partial \sigma}$
      Return σ, clean graph h

4.4 Model Evaluation Metric

To measure the detection metric by injecting attack edges, we use the following evaluation metric:

$$S_p = \sum_{l=1}^{L} \sum_{e_{ij} \in P} a_{ij}^l \beta \tag{13}$$

L is the total number of layers in the network, and P is the perturbed edge. Generally speaking, the smaller the S_p, the smaller the attention coefficient obtained by the adversarial editing.

Attention methods improve the robustness of targeted attacks. β is a coefficient used to adjust the attack weight.

$$\text{cosineSim}\left(\vec{a}, \vec{b}\right) = \frac{\vec{a} \cdot \vec{b}}{|\vec{a}| \times |\vec{b}|} \tag{14}$$

We utilize cosine similarity to evaluate the distance of attacker clusters. The method calculates the cosine similarity between different users, showing the similarity between attacker characteristics. If the characteristics between two nodes are very different, it can be considered that the edge is likely to be a new edge caused by malicious attacks.

5 Experiments

In this section, we evaluate the effectiveness of our methods against different adversarial attack. We aim to answer the question that how our methods perform compared to the state-of art defense methods under different adversarial attacks.

5.1 Data-Sets

We validate our proposed approach on benchmark data-sets, including Cora, Pubmed, Citeseer and Reddit (Table 1).

Table 1. Data-set description

Data-set	Nodes	Font size and style	Classes
Cora	2,485	1,433	7
Pubmed	19,717	500	3
Citeseer	1,222	3,703	6
Reddit	232,965	114,615,892	7

Cora: The data-sets have a total of 2708 samples. Each sample represents a 1433-dimensional dictionary with 1433 features per sample point.

Pubmed: Pubmed [18] contains medical-related publications, including paper features and citation-correlation relationship features.

Citeseer: The Citeseer [19] data-set contains 3312 scientific publications, which can be grouped into 6 categories. The reference network consists of 4732 links.

Reddit: Reddit [20] is a community network data-set. The node tag is the community or "Reddit" to which the post belongs.

5.2 Baseline Model

GCN: GCN [21] is a widely used graph neural network that defines graph convolution through spectral analysis. It's one of most represent methods to detect graph attack.

GAT: GAT [22] consists of an attention layer that learns weights for different neighborhood nodes.

RGCN: RGCN model node representation as a Gaussian distribution to absorb the effects of adversarial attacks. We use Chen's method [23] as our baseline methods.

GCN-SVD: GCN-SVD [24] proposes to seed GCN with a low-rank approximation of perturbation graphs.

We compare the performance of the baseline model with our proposed model.

5.3 Experiment Analysis

In order to evaluate the effectiveness of this detection model, we used targeted and non-targeted attack patterns and random attack patterns to imply a shilling attack in this experiment.

We use node classification accuracy to evaluate the effectiveness of the model. We vary the attacker's injection size and the data-set's ability to evaluate the detection model's robustness and generality. We will analyze the performance of this detection method on data-sets of different sizes.

5.3.1 Random Attack Detection Result

In experiments, we can find that our method performs better on larger-scale random attacks. It shows that the purification step of adding the graph significantly reduces the impact of random attacks (Fig. 3).

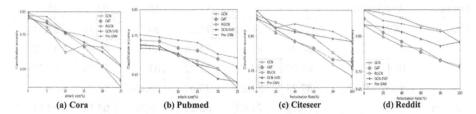

(a) Cora   (b) Pubmed   (c) Citeseer   (d) Reddit

Fig. 3. Random attack detection performance

5.3.2 Non-targeted Attack Detection Result

In the experiments in the Non-targeted attack state, we find that our method is more effective in the first three data sets.

However, the effect is not obvious in the Reddit data-set. Since the feature similarity and neighborhood relationship of the Reddit data-set are often very close, our method is very sensitive to the edge feature similarity of different types of points. Still, the learning of this feature of the relationship between the same type of points is not very good to improve the classification results, this defect should be further improved in the next work (Fig. 4).

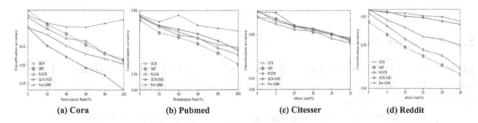

(a) Cora   (b) Pubmed   (c) Citesser   (d) Reddit

Fig. 4. Detection for non-targeted attack detection performance

5.3.3 Targeted Attack Detection Result

The experimental results of the target attack are shown in Table 2. We can see the performance of our proposed method on multiple data-sets, while comparing it with other methods and confirming the feasibility of the model. Our proposed method also achieves better performance under different attack scales, proving that our method is insensitive to the attack scale of a specific target attack and is more robust than other methods. And the performance of this method is much better than other methods on a large attack scale, indicating that it can sensitively detect targeted attacks of groups.

Table 2. Detect ion for non-targeted attack performance

Data-set	Attack size(%)	0	5	10	15	20	25
Cora	GCN	83.22	76.03	71.29	68.29	61.31	53.41
	GAT	84.95	81.44	74.61	69.31	61.96	54.72
	RGCN	81.20	77.81	72.22	67.31	59.66	51.20
	Robust-GNN	87.98	82.27	79.62	75.45	71.58	68.21
Citeseer	GCN	73.11	71.40	68.23	65.66	63.12	59.11
	GAT	75.19	73.02	71.11	70.31	62.29	59.13
	RGCN	71.23	70.93	68.44	67.63	63.71	62.97
	Robust-GNN	72.58	72.93	71.81	70.92	68.02	65.95
Pubmed	GCN	77.10	76.45	74.77	71.11	68.90	67.50
	GAT	76.30	72.32	69.54	67.21	66.30	64.20
	RGCN	71.60	75.16	73.53	71.61	70.62	66.90
	Robust-GNN	82.90	82.80	80.12	78.12	76.25	74.32
Reddit	GCN	94.10	90.11	89.13	86.24	85.28	80.83
	GAT	93.33	92.12	89.13	87.31	84.81	81.21
	RGCN	91.73	87.21	85.12	83.75	81.21	77.81
	Robust-GNN	95.20	91.41	91.20	88.25	87.23	82.28

5.4 Parameter Analysis

In this section, we will explore hyper-parameter sensitivity. In experiments, we varied the hyper-parameters of the model loss function to understand how they affect the performance of our model.

The premise we set is the Cora data-set with an attack rate of 10. The performance change of the model is shown in the following figure (Fig. 5).

We can find that increasing the values α and γ will improve the classification accuracy in the test set. This is because the parameters change the criterion of the approximated matrix. With the higher α, we can approximate the original graph adjacent matrix much better. On the other hand, γ affects the regularization of the loss function, which can avoid the over-fit of the optimization. Thus, γ within a certain range will get the optimal value. And the parameter β affects the similarity between graph edges, and a too large β will mislead the detection method.

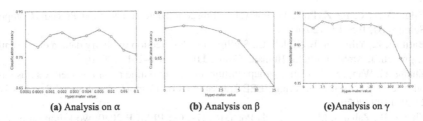

(a) Analysis on α   (b) Analysis on β   (c)Analysis on γ

Fig. 5. Parameter analysis

6 Conclusion

Graph representation recommender systems are very vulnerable to adversarial attacks. In order to deal with various attacks on graph-represented recommender systems, we propose a preprocessing based GNN detection model. This method has two parts. The first part focuses on purifying graphs by reducing the dimension of adjacent matrices. Then, the method uses a semi-supervised clustering method combined with adversarial learning to detect abnormal nodes in the purification graph and eliminate them, which finally makes the recommendation system more robust.

Our proposed method is completely different from previous attack detection methods that only focus on anomalous reputation and timestamp information. This approach allows us to detect adversarial attacks more efficiently and avoids the limitations as traditional methods assuming the attacker's feature distribution. At the same time, we also analyzed the sensitivity of the detection method.

We also propose improvements to existing models and identify future challenges. In the future, our goal is to explore more defense methods to further improve the robustness of graph-represented recommender systems.

References

1. Dhelim, S., Aung, N., Bouras, M.A., Ning, H., Cambria, E.: A survey on personality-aware recommendation systems. Artificial Intelligence Review **55**(3), 2409–2454 (2022)
2. Gu, Z., Cai, Y., Wang, S., Li, M., Qiu, J., Shen, S., Xiaojiang, D., Tian, Z.: Adversarial attacks on content-based filtering journal recommender systems. Computers, Materials & Continua **64**(3), 1755–1770 (2020)
3. Wang, H., Zhong, J., Tak, K.U.: Matryoshka attack: research on an attack method of recommender system based on adversarial learning and optimization solution. In: 2020 International Conference on Wavelet Analysis and Pattern Recognition (ICWAPR), pp. 102–109 (2020). https://doi.org/10.1109/ICWAPR51924.2020.9494616
4. Wang, Z., Gao, M., Li, J., Zhang, J., Zhong, J.: Gray-box shilling attack: an adversarial learning approach. ACM Transactions on Intelligent Systems and Technology (TIST) (2022)
5. Koren, Y., Bell, R., Volinsky, C.: Matrix factorization techniques for recommender systems. Computer **42**(8), 30–37 (2009)
6. Cao, J., Zhiang, W., Mao, B., Zhang, Y.: Shilling attack detection utilizing semi-supervised learning method for collaborative recommender system. World Wide Web **16**(5), 729–748 (2013)

7. Bilge, A., Ozdemir, Z., Polat, H.: A novel shilling attack detection method. Procedia Computer Science **31**, 165–174 (2014)
8. Batmaz, Z., Yilmazel, B., Kaleli, C.: Shilling attack detection in binary data: a classification approach. J. Ambient Intelli. Humani. Comp. **11**(6), 2601–2611 (2020)
9. Zhang, F., Wang, S.: Detecting group shilling attacks in online recommender systems based on bisecting k-means clustering. IEEE Transactions on Computational Social Systems **7**(5), 1189–1199 (2020)
10. Zhang, B., Zaharia, M., Ji, S., Ada Popa, R., Gu, G.: PPMLP 2020: workshop on privacy-preserving machine learning in practice. In: Proceedings of the 2020 ACM SIGSAC Conference on Computer and Communications Security, pp. 2139–2140 (2020)
11. Anelli, V.W., Deldjoo, Y., Di Noia, T., Di Sciascio, E., Merra, F.A.: Sasha: Semantic-aware shilling attacks on recommender systems exploiting knowledge graphs. In: European Semantic Web Conference, pp. 307–323. Springer, Cham (2020)
12. Ke, Z., Li, Z., Zhou, C., Sheng, J., Silamu, W., Guo, Q.: Rumor detection on social media via fused semantic information and a propagation heterogeneous graph. Symmetry **12**(11), 1806 (2020)
13. Sun, X., Yang, J., Wang, Z., Liu, H.: HGDom: heterogeneous graph convolutional networks for malicious domain detection. In: NOMS 2020–2020 IEEE/IFIP Network Operations and Management Symposium, pp. 1–9. IEEE (2020)
14. Chen, J., Lin, X., Shi, Z., Liu, Y.: Link prediction adversarial attack via iterative gradient attack. IEEE Trans. Computat. Soc. Sys. **7**(4), 1081–1094 (2020)
15. Feng, Y., Gai, M., Wang, F., Wang, R., Xiaowei, X.: Classification and early warning model of terrorist attacks based on optimal gcn. Chinese Journal of Electronics **29**(6), 1193–1200 (2020)
16. Tang, X., Li, Y., Sun, Y., Yao, H., Mitra, P., Wang, S.: Transferring robustness for graph neural network against poisoning attacks. In: Proceedings of the 13th international conference on web search and data mining, pp. 600–608 (2020)
17. Chen, J., Hou, H., Gao, J., Ji, Y., Bai, T.: RGCN: recurrent graph convolutional networks for target-dependent sentiment analysis. In: International Conference on Knowledge Science, Engineering and Management, pp. 667–675. Springer, Cham (2019)
18. Canese, K., Weis, S.: PubMed: the bibliographic database. The NCBI handbook **2**(1) (2013)
19. Giles, C.L., Bollacker, K.D., Lawrence, S.: CiteSeer: an automatic citation indexing system. In: Proceedings of the third ACM conference on Digital libraries, pp. 89–98 (1998)
20. Baumgartner, J., Zannettou, S., Keegan, B., Squire, M., Blackburn, J.: The pushshift reddit dataset. In Proceedings of the international AAAI conference on web and social media **14**, 830–839 (2020)
21. Jiang, B., Zhang, Z., Lin, D., Tang, J., Luo, B.: Semi-Supervised Learning With Graph Learning-Convolutional Networks. IEEE/CVF Conference on Computer Vision and Pattern Recognition (CVPR) **2019**, 11305–11312 (2019). https://doi.org/10.1109/CVPR.2019.01157
22. Veličković, P., Cucurull, G., Casanova, A., Romero, A., Lio, P., Bengio, Y: Graph attention networks. ICLR (2018)
23. Chen, M., et al.: A trend-aware investment target recommendation system with heterogeneous graph. Int. Joint Conference on Neural Networks (IJCNN) **2021**, 1–8 (2021). https://doi.org/10.1109/IJCNN52387.2021.9533535
24. Entezari, N., Al-Sayouri, S.A., Darvishzadeh, A., Papalexakis, E.E.: All you need is low (rank) defending against adversarial attacks on graphs. In: Proceedings of the 13th International Conference on Web Search and Data Mining, pp. 169–177 (2020)

A Secure Sharing Framework Based on Cloud-Chain Fusion for SWIM

Qing Wang⬤, Xin Lu⬤, and Zhijun Wu$^{(\boxtimes)}$ ⬤

College of Safety Science and Engineering, Civil Aviation University of China, Tianjin, China
2020095004@cauc.edu.com, {2018071030,zjwu}@cauc.edu.cn

Abstract. The air traffic management (ATM) data sharing has attracted extensive attention as the key content of the collaborative operation in the next generation of aviation sector, and the corresponding secure issues and controls have become research hotspots. The SWIM concept aimed at enabling the secure sharing of data among ATM stakeholders was proposed. According to the SWIM regulation on efficient, reliable and secure data sharing, this paper intends to design a data sharing framework with security protections. By sorting out the characteristics and sharing requirements of ATM big data, it is found that the sharing framework based on distributed architecture has become the optimal choice for large-scale ATM systems. On the basis of cloud storage and blockchain, the concept of ATM data security sharing based on cloud-chain fusion is proposed, the feasibility of combining the two technologies is demonstrated, and the ATM data sharing cloud-chain fusion framework named CB-ATM is constructed. CB-ATM is built on the data publishing and discovery mechanism, operation record and traceability mechanism, and data security protection mechanism. Then, the security of this framework is demonstrated in accordance with ATM data secure sharing requirements. Finally, three future research directions for ATM data sharing are proposed. This paper provides a new idea for establishing an efficient, secure and reliable ATM data sharing architecture.

Keywords: SWIM · Data sharing · Access control · Cloud-chain fusion · Secure

1 Introduction

Air Traffic Management (ATM) is the nerve center of air transport activities. In recent years, the concept of Trajectory Based Operation (TBO), which is realized through situational awareness and collaborative decision-making based on multi-party data source, has pushed the ATM business into a new stage. Situational awareness and collaborative decision-making depend on the data exchange and sharing. The SWIM concept [1, 2] was proposed as the basis for secure, efficient and reliable data sharing among multiple stakeholders. [3] presents security requirements and means to design a security architecture for SWIM. Considering the actual operation of ATM systems, there are several issues still need to be solved to meet the standard of SWIM:

(1) The storage performance of the existing ATM business system is limited, resulting in the ineffective use of a large amount of historical data.

(2) The ATM business systems are constructed separately, all kinds of information are processed separately, and the data from different sources cannot be effectively shared.
(3) Existing ATM systems are mainly services-oriented, and data security has not been given sufficient attention.

Based on the problems above, researchers have carried out related research on ATM data sharing. In order to solve the third-party trust issues in the SWIM, [4] designs a new verifiable attribute encryption access control scheme oriented to cloud storage administration centers to verify the trustworthiness of third parties. [5] proposed a reliable and distributed storage platform based on blockchain for the flight data to improve confidential data sharing under the SWIM standard. An ATM data grading method is proposed in [6], which adopts multidimensional encryption algorithm to protect the confidentiality of shared data. From the above introduction, it can be found that these studies focus on a certain aspect of ATM data sharing, such as distributed storage, data encryption, trusted issues of third parties, rather than providing a comprehensive framework to satisfy function and security needs of ATM data sharing.

Aiming at the objects of ATM data sharing, section II extracts the characteristics of ATM data, and summarizes the requirements for ATM data sharing. Section III introduces cloud storage and blockchain technology, expounds the feasibility of applying the cloud-chain fusion architecture to ATM data sharing. Section IV puts forward the three-layer architecture of the ATM data sharing on the basis of the traditional ATM architecture, and explains three security mechanisms. Section V makes a theoretical analysis of the security of the architecture. Section VI lists future research directions for ATM data sharing.

2 Data Sharing Analysis

2.1 ATM Data and Its Classification

As an integral part of the transportation system, the aviation service is characterized by multi-level organizational and highly dynamic management and cross-area operation with complex procedures, which generates massive, diverse and heterogeneous ATM data. At present, the industry and research have not yet formed a unified standard for the classification of ATM big data. This paper divides ATM big data into 9 categories according to services functions: operational data, flight data, traffic flow data, intelligence data, meteorological data, communication data, surveillance data, navigation data, and other data.

- Operation data: operation data consist of flight plan data, flight dynamic data and flight history data, among which flight plan data includes schedule plan, historical plan, next day plan, and temporary plan. The operation data may include private information, such as the execution date, flight mission, flight number, aircraft type, aircraft number, affiliated airline, departure station, stopover station, destination station, alternate station, take-off and landing time of each station, terminal building number, flight status, execution time and other information.

- Flight data: flight data is a series of flight parameters related to the flight performance and flight status of the aircraft recorded by the flight data recording equipment during the entire operation of the aircraft, including flight identification information, flight rescue information, flight operation information, and flight preference information, flight path information, other private information. Flight data plays a key role in flight accident investigation, aircraft design, maintenance, flight quality evaluation and inspection and supervision.
- Traffic flow data: The main function of air traffic flow management (ATFM) is to monitor a certain range of air traffic conditions, predict and sequence traffic flow, and reasonably control aircraft operations to maximize the use of airspace capacity of routes, areas or sectors. The traffic flow data is extracted from the flight plan, flight status and surveillance data provided by ATM systems.
- Meteorological data: the randomness of aviation operating environment makes aviation safety deeply affected by meteorological conditions. Meteorological information includes aerodrome weather reports, aerodrome forecasts, landing forecasts, takeoff forecasts, en-route forecasts, area forecasts, significant weather information, low-level weather information, aerodrome warnings, and windshear warnings. Users of meteorological data include aviation departments, flight crews, air traffic services departments, airport operations management departments, search and rescue departments, aeronautical information services departments, and other departments related to civil aviation activities.

The above four kinds of data are mostly stored in the database of ATM systems in a structured form.

- Aeronautical information data: aeronautical information data is used to support the safe, economical and efficient operation of ATM systems. Aeronautical information data can be divided into static data such as aeronautical information compilation, aeronautical charts, etc., and dynamic data such as aeronautical information circular, NOTAM, etc. Its content is: geographic data, airport data, airspace data, air traffic route data, instrument flight procedure data, radio aids/navigation system data, obstacle and terrain data, etc. Currently, the aeronautical information data has the features of large volume and heterogeneity, and is mostly presented in unstructured forms such as PDF text and HTML web pages.
- Communication data: communication services include aviation fixed service, aviation mobile service and aviation broadcasting service. Communication data is generated in the process of voice communication or data communication between ground controllers, between ground controllers and pilots, and between pilots. The communication content includes flight plan, flight dynamics, control information, weather information, air traffic control instructions, etc.
- Surveillance data: surveillance data refers to the data generated in the process of detecting, identifying and tracking aircraft (including air and airport ground targets) using ATM surveillance equipment, and is the basis for ATM and ATFM. ATM surveillance equipment mainly includes surveillance radar, automatic dependent surveillance system, multi-point positioning surveillance system, etc.

- Navigation data: navigation data refers to the data generated by the navigation equipment during the process of providing navigation services for the aircraft in ocean/desert areas, route/terminal areas, approach areas and landing areas. ATM navigation equipment mainly includes ground-based navigation systems, autonomous navigation systems, landing systems, microwave landing systems, satellite-based navigation systems.

Currently, communication, surveillance and navigation data are mostly provided in semi-structured form. For example, surveillance data using the communication protocol Asterix, which is a protocol for data exchange of structured surveillance information. Specially, communication data may also include unstructured voice data.

- Other data: other data related to ATM, such as data generated by personnel scheduling and safety management.

2.2 Features of ATM Data Sharing

This section analyzes the ATM environment from the perspective of data sharing, and extracts relating features.

(i)   ATM data is gathered from multiple sources, including communication, navigation and surveillance equipment of airports and air routes, weather radar equipment of meteorological departments, airline flight planning systems, ticket booking systems, office automation systems, etc. The data volume often reaches TB and PB levels;

(ii)   There are three types of ATM data: structured data, semi-structured data, and unstructured data. The first type, such as the flight plan in the flight planning system, is stored in the database tables; semi-structured data as mentioned above is stored in CAT062 format; and the unstructured data, such as voice data of communication data, and aeronautical charts of aeronautical information data; In addition, semi-structured data often presents the characteristics of sequence, large amount, rapidity and continuous.

(iii) ATM applications tend to have more complex types of data users, such as ATM departments, airline operation centers, airport operation centers, airspace providers, airspace users, military coordination departments, meteorological agencies, national governments departments, regulators and other users. They are both data producers and data consumers. When a user attempts to access shared data, its access scope is constrained by its business.

(iv)   Users such as aircraft and unmanned aerial vehicles (UAVs), whose storage and computing capacity are more limited than that of ground systems, have data sharing requirements as well. So, it is necessary to consider offloading most of the storage and computing costs to the cloud.

To sum up, ATM data has these basic features of large amount, multi-source, heterogeneity, which determine the features of ATM data sharing.

2.3 ATM Data Sharing Trends

In the foreseeable future, with the rapidly development of the aviation industry, ATM data sharing will show the following trends:

(i)   The change in the frequency of ATM data flow: from " limited data flow between fixed parties " to "up to million times of massive data sharing and exchange in a certain period of time ". This change makes the existing data exchange mode invalid, and a data sharing architecture that meets new sharing requirements is urgently needed.

(ii) The change in the scope of data sharing: from "ATM data will only be used in a fixed and limited security domain" to "ATM data will be used across different security domains", making it a challenge to expand the scope of ATM data distribution and retrieval;

(iii) The change in storage location of the ATM data: from "each data owner stores and manages private data separately" to "ATM data is gathered in one or more cloud storage centers for centralized storage", which puts forward new challenges for data security and data management;

(iv) The change in the access subjects of ATM data: from "the accessor of ATM data is the executor of aviation operations" to "the accessor of ATM data also includes third-party analysts and researchers". The change further expands the scope of sharing which increases the difficulty in access control.

Through the above trends, the following conclusions can be further drawn. According to services, the existing ATM data sharing can be divided into two dimensions: vertical and horizontal. Horizontal data sharing refers to the data sharing between various operational and functional departments within the same level of ATM units (such as air traffic control bureaus in different region), and data sharing is mainly executed through the data centers departments at the same level. The vertical data sharing is mainly the data sharing between the ATM bureau, the regional ATM bureau and the ATM sub-bureaus (stations), and data collection and exchange are executed through data centers at all levels and basic data nodes. The existing horizontal and vertical sharing modes can reduce the complexity of cross-domain data sharing between different levels. However, with the changes of ATM data flow frequency and data storage location, considering the expansion of data sharing scope and subject, cross data sharing will also become one of the directions in the future. Therefore, it is urgent to analyze the requirements of ATM data sharing.

2.4 Security Requirements of ATM Data Sharing

Through the analysis of ATM data sharing features and trends, it can be seen that the bottleneck of ATM data sharing is mainly presented in the following three aspects:

(i)   Cloud storage can replace the traditional local storage mode, which can solve the limited storage performance However, the separation of data ownership and control brings new security risks such as data leakage, unauthorized access, data tampering.

Therefore, an approach that enables data users to securely access outsourced data is urgently needed.

(ii) To achieve effective data sharing, a set of general shared data management methods, which includes data release, discovery, retrieval, access, etc., should be provided. However, most traditional data management solutions for sharing use a centralized architecture with a high-performance central server store and process all the ATM data, and other stakeholders need to communicate with the central server. This architecture is applied in large-scale ATM systems, and may lead to the traffic congestion and communication delay. In addition, the central server in the centralized management method is generally faced with the trust issue which may cause the data leakage.

(iii) The identity of the user should be authenticated. Malicious users and unauthorized users may masquerade as authorized users to disrupt the operation of the ATM systems. For example, Malicious user share fake data with others to interfere with ATM services.

Therefore, it is necessary to seek a solution to realize the secure data sharing in the existing ATM environment. Considering the performance requirements and security risks, a secure and feasible sharing mechanism is proposed in terms of the following needs: (i) Cloud storage can replace the traditional local storage with limited storage capacity; (ii) Methods oriented data encryption, access control, and integrity verification to ensure data security are provided; (iii) A set of general shared data management methods including data publishing, discovery and access is designed; (iv) The distributed shared data management mode replaces the centralized mode to solve the trust issue of centralized server; (v) Security constraints controls is provided to ensure that the behavior of users is credible.

3 Preliminary Knowledge

3.1 Cloud Storage

As a key branch of cloud computing technology, cloud storage can take charge of coordinating remote storage devices and providing users with data storage service [7]. Besides, cloud storages usually provide security protection means such as data encryption and data disaster recovery backup.

Due to the large volume of ATM data, the ATM participants cannot save all the data in the local database. The cloud storage has become the optimal choice due to its advantages over data storage volume, security, reliability and cost. Users outsource their data to the cloud service provider (CSP) and access data remotely over the Internet. CSP provides users with a more efficient and flexible way of data management, and gives solutions to ATM participants with limited storage and computing capacity. Therefore, multiple ATM agencies can share one or more cloud storage services according to their geographical division and service divisions. However, outsourcing the ATM data to the cloud means that users lose control on the data, which brings new security risks such as data leakage, unauthorized access, and data tampering. In addition, the multi-cloud storage mode makes it difficult to publish and retrieve data due to the isolation between multiple clouds.

3.2 Blockchain

The concept of blockchain first appeared in the Bitcoin white paper [8]. In recent years, blockchain has been extensively studied. Blockchain is a database organized in the form of blocks, and can be used in any environment that requires global and historical data recording. Blockchain has the potential to enhance data security in cloud storage systems. The cloud-chain fusion architecture can effectively complement the functions of cloud storage and blockchain. For example, by storing metadata on the blockchain, users can utilize the traceability of blockchain to verify the integrity of the original data stored in cloud storage. Blockchain can provide credible data management methods to solve the trust issue of data sharing, and the distributed nature of blockchain makes it more suitable for the distributed ATM environment. Blockchain cannot be directly applied to the ATM environment. Therefore, an efficient, flexible and reliable framework needs to be designed to take advantage of blockchain.

3.3 Feasibility of Cloud-Chain Chain Fusion Architecture

Cloud storage can meet the storage demands of ATM systems, and the distributed architecture of blockchain can avoid the performance and security problems caused by centralized architecture. Therefore, the cloud-chain fusion architecture naturally meets the needs of ATM data sharing, making it one of the best solutions. However, the research on the cloud-chain fusion architecture is still in its infancy, and the research on applying the cloud-chain fusion architecture to ATM is even rarer. Therefore, there are still many gaps in the design of the cloud-chain fusion architecture. On the basis of fully considering practical operations of ATM, this paper designs a framework for the fusion of cloud and blockchain to avoid their shortcomings and effectively utilize their technical advantages.

3.4 Ciphertext Policy Attribute Based Encryption (CPABE)

As a public key encryption algorithm, CPABE [9] introduces the concept of user attribute to implement access control. User attributes can be used to describe a user, and a set of attributes can be used to describe a group of users. The data owner encrypts the plaintext with the access control policy and data accessor decrypts the ciphertext with its private key which implicitly contains its attributes. The CPABE algorithm stipulates that users whose attributes meet the policy can correctly decrypt the ciphertext. Since a set of attributes can represent a group of users rather than a single user, it takes only on encryption operation to achieve access control to many users. Compared with traditional public key encryption algorithms, the CPABE algorithm significantly reduces the number of encryption operations but achieves the same access control effect. In addition, the algorithm supports AND, OR and threshold operations on attributes to flexibly express various access control policies. Therefore, the CPABE algorithm has broad application prospects in large-scale scenarios due to its advantage of fine-grained access control.

The basic CPABE algorithm includes four phases:

Setup: the algorithm generates the master key and public parameters through a secure parameter.

Encryption: take the public key, access control policy and the plaintext as input, and the encrypted data is the output;

KeyGen: take master key and accessor's attributes as input, and output the private key of data accessor for decryption;

Decryption: the data accessor decrypts the ciphertext with its private key.

4   The ATM Information Security Framework Based on Cloud-Chain Fusion

This paper is mainly oriented to the large-scale, distributed and dynamic ATM environment. The traditional cloud storage and blockchain have the potential to meet the demands of ATM data sharing, but existing cloud storage security mechanisms and blockchain operating mechanisms cannot be directly applied to ATM data sharing. This chapter proposes an ATM data sharing framework with three mechanisms based on cloud-chain fusion.

4.1   ATM Data Sharing Framework

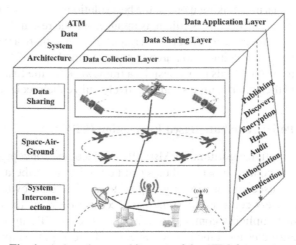

Fig. 1. A three-layer architecture of the ATM data system

As is shown in Fig. 1, a three-layer model of the ATM data system is provided according to the data flow direction across ATM systems, which includes a data collection layer, a data sharing layer, and a data application layer.

Data collection layer: data in this layer includes two types: the first type is the data collected and preprocessed by the ATM cyber-physical systems such as the ADS-B system, and the second type is the data generated by the service systems, such as the ATC automation system.

Data sharing layer is to realize data sharing, providing data storage, data publishing, data retrieval, and related security assurance methods such as authentication, authorization, encryption, hash operation and audit. The data sharing layer is the focus of this paper.

Data application layer provides decision support, operation coordination, operation command, and information services for each ATM business department.

The data sharing layer plays is a crucial component of ATM data model, and a framework named CB-ATM is constructed to implement the function of the sharing layer. Based on the above analysis, it can be seen that CB-ATM needs to provide three functions: (i) Data publishing and discovery mechanism (DPAD) based on cloud-chain fusion. The data owner publishes the data identification to the blockchain through this mechanism, and the data user can locate and access the corresponding data in the cloud storage through the data identification; (ii) The operation record and traceability mechanism (ORAT) based on cloud-chain fusion. The data publishing records of the data owner and the access records of the data users are stored in the blockchain, and the traceability of the operation records is also provided; (iii) Data security assurance mechanism (DSPS) based on cloud-chain fusion. DSPS provides access control, integrity verification, data encryption and other methods to prevent potential data security issues during data sharing.

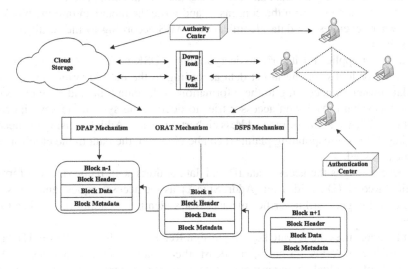

Fig. 2. Framework of CB-ATM

The framework of CB-ATM is shown in the Fig. 2. Participants of CB-ATM include ATM departments, airline operations centers, airport operations centers, airspace providers, airspace users, military coordination departments, meteorological agencies, national government departments, regulatory authorities and cloud storage. From the perspective of data sharing, participants include data providers and consumers; from the perspective of data ownership, they can be considered as data owners and accessors. These participants are commonly referred to as data users. In this framework, the semi-trusted cloud is the actual storage location of the ATM data, and data users can upload and download the ATM data from the cloud. Data users serves as the blockchain network nodes and the content of blockchain ledger is the metadata of ATM data and historical operation records. The consensus mechanism of the blockchain ensures that the ledger cannot be tampered with, and the smart contract ensures that the user's operation is credible. The specific process of data sharing is as follows:

- In order to share data, data users must first apply to the authentication center for a pair of keys {PK_u, SK_u} for identity authentication, where PK_u can be considered as the user's identity.
- The owner encrypts its data file symmetrically, and performs hash operation on the data ciphertext to obtain the data ciphertext and hash value.
- The owner uploads the data ciphertext to the cloud storage, and gets the data address DAddr returned by the cloud storage.
- The owner customizes the access policy, and conducts CPABE on the symmetric key Data_KEK and storage address based on the access policy to ensure that only accessors who satisfy the access policy can obtain the ATM ciphertext.
- The owner packages the data identity Data_Id, the data hash value, the symmetric key ciphertext {DKEK}$_{CT}$, address ciphertext {Data_Addr}$_{CT}$, data type, data subtype, data attribute, etc. as metadata and broadcasts them to the blockchain.
- The blockchain nodes form the consensus, and write the metadata into the block.
- The owner generates the data identification AMIS according to the result from the blockchain.
- The accessor applies for its private decryption key DSK to the authority center.
- The accessor looks for the target data according to the data identifier provided by the data owner, or according to the information of the data type and attributes saved in the blockchain. And then accessor tries to decrypt the symmetric key ciphertext {Data_KEK}$_{CT}$ and the storage address ciphertext {Data_Addr}$_{CT}$ using the decryption key. If the corresponding plaintext can be obtained, the data in the cloud storage can be accessed.
- The accessor signs the access data ID and data address with its private key forming the field Req = {Data_Id, Data_Addr, SignA} as the access request and gives it to the cloud storage. Until it verifies the accessor's identity, it cannot return data to the accessor.
- Cloud Storage uses the private key SK_c to sign Req to form the field Res = {Data_Id, Data_Addr, SignA, PK_u, SignC}, broadcasts the signature of the data accessor. After each node of the blockchain verifies that the signature is correct, this item is written into the block.
- The accessor downloads the data and uses the hash value to verify its integrity.
- The accessor decrypts the ciphertext of the target data with the symmetric key DKEK and obtains the plaintext.

4.2 Data Publishing and Discovery Mechanism (DPAD)

Data owners publish the ATM metadata to the blockchain through the data publishing mechanism, and synchronize the ledger and metadata through a consensus mechanism.

DPAP mechanism provides data management function by the ATM data identification. ATM data identification is a hierarchical ATM metadata index structure (AMIS), which provides an independent, open and credible structural standard for self-naming identification and data sharing indexing in the ATM environment, which lay the groundwork for sharing between data owners and data consumers. The standard structure of AMIS is based on the metadata structure, which is defined as: data ID, hash value, ciphertext of symmetric key, ciphertext of storage address, data type, data subtype, data attribute, etc. The standard structure of AMIS is as follows:

#[Data_Id].[Block_Num].[Block_offset].[HASH].[Data_KEK].[Data_Addr]. [Data_type].[Data_subtype].[Data_attribu te1]...[Data_attributen].

[Block_Num] is the serial number of the block where the metadata is located, and [Block_offset] is the offset of the metadata in the block whose serial number is [Block_Num].

Data users can retrieve the ATM data in the following two ways: (i) data users locate the corresponding metadata through the prefix of the data identifier, and access the original file in the cloud storage according to the address and key information in the metadata; (ii) data users retrieve data types and attributes in the blockchain ledger to find metadata that may meet their needs, and then access the original files in cloud storage through the address and key information in the metadata.

4.3 Operation Record and Traceability Mechanism

The function of the ORAT mechanism is to generate reliable operational logs for the supervisor to audit. Both data providers, data accessors and cloud storage centers have the motivation to record operation logs dishonestly. Therefore, the ORAT mechanism uses the tamper-proof feature of the blockchain to fix the data operation records, which meets the requirements for searchability, traceability and non-repudiation. The operation logs of the CB-ATM framework include two types: data publishing logs and data access logs. The former records the publishing operation of the data provider and the record in AMIS format can be directly used as the data publishing record. Data access logs record the access operations of data accessors. For the sake of interests, data accessors may not take the initiative in reporting their own access operations. However, the access log is the proof-of-work of the cloud storage center, so cloud storage is more inclined to accurately record or even exaggerate the number of accesses in exchange for higher service fees. Therefore, the cloud storage center serves as blockchain nodes, and takes charge of broadcasting the signed access requests to all nodes as access logs. Since the access request are designed to be signed by the accessor's private key, the cloud storage center cannot forge access logs. All access requests verified by each node of the blockchain are permanently stored on the blockchain as access logs.

4.4 Data Security Protection Mechanism

Data Encryption and Access Control. The ATM data is outsourced to cloud storage centers and beyond the data owners' control. Therefore, in order to protect the availability and confidentiality of the ATM data, an CPABE method is used for access control. The owner encrypts the data locally through symmetric encryption, encrypts the symmetric key according to the access control policy through CPABE algorithm, publishes the ciphertext of the symmetric key in the blockchain, and outsources the ciphertext of ATM data to the cloud storage center simultaneously. Through the above operations, administrators of the cloud storage centers and data accessors cannot view the plaintext of ATM data, which ensures the confidentiality and availability of data.

Using CPABE to realize access control has following advantages: (i) It can be combined with symmetric encryption to ensure data confidentiality. (ii) It can achieve one-to-many access control by dividing users into multiple groups without considering the users' number. By formulating a customizable and flexible access control policy with AND, OR, NOT and threshold operation of attributes, data owners can realize long-term access control with one encryption operation, reducing their access control overhead. (iii) The user's private key is related with a random number, and different users cannot combine their keys to conduct collusion attacks; (iv) According to specific needs of various data owners, the CPABE method can be combined with various extended functions such as policy hiding [10], user revocation [11], multi-authority [12], computing outsourcing [13], making the scheme more suitable for the ATM environment. For example, considering the distributed nature of the ATM system, an CPABE scheme that supports multiple authority centers can be selected; Considering the limited computing capacity of mobile users such as drones and manned aircraft, an CPABE scheme that supports outsourced computation can be selected; In addition, by choosing an CPABE scheme with hidden policy, the privacy of the data owner is protected.

Integrity Verification. When the owner encrypts the data locally, the data ciphertext is hashed and stored on the blockchain as an item of metadata. The tamper-proof of blockchain is used to ensure the integrity of the hash value. After downloading the data ciphertext, the data accessor verifies the integrity of the ciphertext. If the data has not been tampered with, the accessor preform the decryption operation to obtain the data plaintext.

5   Function and Security Analysis

The security of ATM data sharing is briefly analyzed.

Requirements (i): provide data encryption, access control, and integrity verification methods oriented to cloud storage to ensure data security.

The data security protection mechanism in the CB-ATM framework provides an access control method based on CPABE and an integrity verification method based on hash operation. In terms of security, the CB-ATM provides ciphertext storage for confidentiality, data hash value verification for integrity, and fine-grained access control for availability.

Requirements (ii): ensure that the identity of users who participate in the ATM operation is credible;

This architecture is based on the alliance chain, and the user's identity is guaranteed to be credible through identity authentication. All users who join the alliance chain, including cloud storage centers, need to be authenticated.

Requirement (iii): the distributed shared data management replaces the centralized management to solve the problem of centralized trust;

The CB-ATM realizes distributed and decentralized data management based on blockchain with ATM participants as nodes, avoiding the trust issue caused by traditional centralized data management methods.

Requirement (iv): provide security constraints to ensure that the behavior of users participating in data sharing is credible;

The CB-ATM records data publishing operations and data access operations in the blockchain based on the operation record and traceability mechanism, which ensures that the operation records cannot be tampered with. In particular, since an access operation is the interaction between a cloud storage center and a data accessor, in order to prevent the data accessor from not submitting its own access operation to the blockchain, the CB-ATM stipulates that the cloud storage center takes the accessor's access request as the access record and broadcast it to the blockchain. Since the access request is signed by the accessor, the cloud storage center cannot forge the signature, which ensures the authenticity of all access records. Since all records are stored in the blockchain, any node can trace the above records, thus preventing users from conducting dishonest behavior.

Requirement (v): on the basis of satisfying the above requirements, protect user privacy as much as possible.

The ATM data is mostly business data, so data owners are more concerned with data confidentiality than privacy. In the CB-ATM, since the data access control policy contains description of the data accessor's attributes, malicious users may infer the data users' identities according to attributes in the access policy. Therefore, the CB-ATM framework can adopt CPABE with hidden policy as a solution.

To sum up, the design of CB-ATM framework meets all the secure requirements of ATM data sharing.

6 Future Research Directions

6.1 Entities' Attributes Mining and Attribute-Authority Relation Mining Based on Deep Learning

The CB-ATM framework performs access control utilizing CPABE algorithm and taking the users' attributes and access control policies as input. Firstly, the extraction and definition of attributes of ATM stakeholders are the key to the algorithm. The accuracy of attribute extraction affects access control performance especially in the ATM environment with a large number of entities. Secondly, to ensure that a policy can express the data owner's true purpose, a reference that describe the relationships between attributes and authority should be defined in advance for data owners to use. Although mining the universal set of user attributes and the relationships between attributes and authority are foundational work, there is little research on it. Since few scientists or experts have a complete understanding of the large-scale ATM environment, this issue cannot be settled through traditional expert evaluation method. How to automatically mine the attributes and relationships between attributes and authority has become a top priority. With the development of deep learning and convolutional neural networks, this problem can be addressed. By applying deep learning methods to access control logs, identity databases and test cases of ATM business systems, the attributes and relationships between attributes and authority can be efficiently and comprehensively mined.

6.2 The Decentralized CPABE Method for Access Control Based on Homomorphic Encryption and Blockchain

CPABE has been considered as the optimal choice for access control in the ATM environment, and the algorithm requires a fully trusted center to generate public parameters and user private keys. However, two issues have been raised: (1) the so-called trusted center may not be trustworthy in reality and may leak secret information; (2) the trusted center may be inaccessible because of single point of failure. As a decentralized system, blockchain provides a solution to the problem of single points of failure. Since the private parameters of CPABE should be kept secret, the CPABE algorithm cannot be deployed on smart contracts that are open and transparent to all blockchain nodes. Homomorphic encryption technology can directly perform some operations on ciphertext instead of plaintext. Therefore, homomorphic encryption can generate key ciphertext for users under the premise of ensuring the confidentiality of secret parameters. How to combine homomorphic encryption and blockchain to implement decentralized access control will be a research direction.

6.3 The Data Privacy Protection Based on Computation Offloading and Secure Multi-party Computation

Existing data sharing is performed by data accessors downloading the data to their local, which compromises the owner's control over the data. Computation offloading technology can be used to offload computation from the accessor to the owner. Multiple data owners can collaborate to perform calculations based on their own local data through secure multi-party computation technology. These two technologies can make it possible to share the results of calculations rather than the original data. With the development of computation offloading and secure multi-party computation technology, a novel sharing solution will become a research direction.

7 Conclusion

This paper firstly summarizes the existing problems of data sharing in the ATM environment, analyzes the data types and characteristics, and refines the development trend and security requirements of ATM data sharing. By introducing the principle and security mechanism of blockchain and storage, the feasibility of cloud-chain fusion is analyzed. The secure sharing framework based on cloud-chain fusion is proposed with the data publishing and discovery mechanism, the operation record and traceability mechanism, and the data security assurance mechanism. Finally, the security of CB-ATM framework is analyzed. This paper provides a new idea for the secure and reliable data sharing in ATM, and puts forward several related research directions.

Acknowledgment. This research was funded by Fundamental Research Funds for the Central Universities of China (No. 3122022081).

References

1. ICAO: Manual on System Wide Information Management (SWIM) concept. In: International Civil Aviation Organization, Tech. Rep. Doc 10039 (2014)
2. Meserole, J., Moore, J.: What is System Wide Information Management (SWIM). IEEE Aerosp. Electron. Syst. Mag. **22**(5), 13–19 (2007). https://doi.org/10.1109/maes.2007.365329
3. Stephens, B.: Security architecture for system wide information management. In: 24th Digital Avionics Systems Conference, p. 10, vol. 2 (2005). https://doi.org/10.1109/DASC.2005.1563474
4. Wu, Z., Nie, J., Yin, Y., Wang, H.: Verified CSAC-based CP-ABE access control of cloud storage in SWIM. In: 2021 IEEE 19th International Conference on Embedded and Ubiquitous Computing (EUC), pp. 72–78 (2021). https://doi.org/10.1109/EUC53437.2021.00019
5. Dehez Clementi, M., Larrieu, N., Lochin, E., Kaafar, M.A., Asghar, H.: When air traffic management meets blockchain technology: a blockchain-based concept for securing the sharing of flight data. In: 2019 IEEE/AIAA 38th Digital Avionics Systems Conference (DASC), 1–10 (2019). https://doi.org/10.1109/DASC43569.2019.9081622
6. Wu, Z., Liu, L., Yan, C., Xu, J., Lei, J.: The approach of SWIM data sharing based on multi-dimensional data encryption. In: 2017 25th International Conference on Software, Telecommunications and Computer Networks (SoftCOM), pp. 1–6 (2017). https://doi.org/10.23919/SOFTCOM.2017.8115587
7. Wu, J., Ping, L., Ge, X., Wang, Y., Fu, J.: Cloud storage as the infrastructure of cloud computing. Int. Conf. Intell. Comp. Cognitive Informatics **2010**, 380–383 (2010). https://doi.org/10.1109/ICICCI.2010.119
8. Nakamoto, S.: Bitcoin: A Peer-to-Peer Electronic Cash System. https://bitcoin.org/bitcoin.pdf. Accessed 1 Oct. 2022
9. Bethencourt, J., Sahai, A., Waters, B.: Ciphertext-policy attribute-based encryption. In: 2007 IEEE Symposium on Security and Privacy (SP'07), pp. 321–334 (2007). https://doi.org/10.1109/SP.2007.11
10. Hui, C., et al.: An efficient and expressive ciphertext-policy attribute-based encryption scheme with partially hidden access structures. Comput. Netw. **133**, 157–165 (2018). https://doi.org/10.1016/j.comnet.2018.01.034
11. Li, J., et al.: User collusion avoidance CP-ABE with efficient attribute revocation for cloud storage. IEEE Systems Journal **12**(2), 1767–1777 (2017). https://doi.org/10.1109/JSYST.2017.2667679
12. Banerjee, S., et al.: Private blockchain-envisioned multi-authority CP-ABE-based user access control scheme in IIoT. Computer Communications **169**, 99–113 (2021). https://doi.org/10.1016/j.comcom.2021.01.023
13. Ning, J., et al.: Auditable sigma-time outsourced attribute-based encryption for access control in cloud computing. IEEE Transactions on Information Forensics and Security **13**(1), 94–105 (2017). https://doi.org/10.1109/TIFS.2017.2738601

Privacy-Protective Distributed Machine Learning Between Rich Devices and Edge Servers Using Confidence Level

Saki Takano[1]($\boxtimes$), Akihiro Nakao[2], Saneyasu Yamaguchi[3], and Masato Oguchi[1]

[1] Ochanomizu University, 2-1-1 Otsuka, Tokyo, Japan
saki-t@ogl.ocha.ac.jp, oguchi@is.ocha.ac.jp
[2] The University of Tokyo, 7-3-1-1 Hongo, Bunkyo-ku, Tokyo, Japan
nakao@nakao-lab.org
[3] Kogakuin University, 1-24-2 Nishi-shinjuku, Suhinjuku-ku, Tokyo, Japan
sane@cc.kogakuin.ac.jp

Abstract. Many recent studies have focused on using the personal information collected by edge devices for machine learning on servers while protecting privacy. In most cases, a high-performance server aggregates and manages all data. However, users may refuse to pass on their personal information to an external server owing to the risk of information leakage. To address this concern, we propose a distributed machine learning model that does not extract any sensitive data from the edge device. In the proposed model, edge devices also run machine learning and integrates learning results obtained at edge servers with those obtained at edge devices by comparing their confidence levels. To validate the proposed model, we performed experiments on facial image recognition using Jetson Nano. Experimental results confirm that the proposed model enables the use of personal data for machine learning without transferring any sensitive information to the edge server. With this learning model, each user could use personal information securely and could receive the best match results.

Keywords: Edge Computing · Distributed Machine Learning · Federated Learning · Internet of Things

1 Introduction

Owing to the spread and performance improvement of smartphones and IoT devices, significant amounts of data are being accumulated on edge devices. In addition, machine learning has come to be used in various situations, such as displaying recommendations and image recognition. Therefore, machine learning on large amounts of data containing personal information collected by edge devices while protecting privacy is becoming increasingly necessary and challenging.

In cloud computing, which is currently the mainstream computing model, and edge computing [1], which has attracted attention as a new computing model,

C.-H. Hsu et al. (Eds.): DataCom 2022, LNCS 13864, pp. 142–154, 2023.
https://doi.org/10.1007/978-981-99-2233-8_10

training is performed on a high-performance servers. Low-spec edge devices are used only for collecting data and transferring them to the server. However, the data collected by edge devices may contain sensitive information such as personal data. There is a risk that sensitive information may be leaked or falsified through attack methods such as membership inference attacks [2] or data poisoning [3]. Privacy concerns arise when extracting data collected by an edge device. In addition, there is increasing concern around privacy, as witnessed, for example, by the establishment of the EU General Data Protection Regulation (GDPR) [4]. There could be a growing resistance to the transfer of personal data to servers. Therefore, edge servers can only use the training results on general data, which makes it impossible to use optimal training results for each edge device.

The objective of this study is to enable machine learning with data collected by edge devices while ensuring the protection of sensitive data. The advent of rich clients with relatively high-performance CPUs and GPUs has made it possible to run machine learning on edge devices. However, since the specifications of edge devices are significantly lower than those of edge servers. Therefore, we use a machine learning model that complements the specifications of edge devices by sending the results of learning on edge servers to edge devices. We propose a method that integrates the training results of general data on an edge server with the training results of personal data on an edge device by comparing confidence levels. Through experiments using facial images as training data and Jetson Nano as an edge device, we confirmed the possibility of training on sensitive data securely. Furthermore, the proposed model does not require general data on the edge server for machine learning on the edge device. Therefore, we believe that our model has advantages in terms of communication cost.

2   Related Work

In this section, we introduce edge computing, the original idea of the proposed model, and federated learning, which assumes machine learning on edge devices as well.

Edge Computing. Edge computing is a computing model in which edge servers are placed at the network edge for data processing [5,6]. The advantages of edge computing include its low latency, distribution of the load on a cloud server, and a reduction in the amount of data sent from the edge devices to the server [7]. Because of these advantages, edge computing has been applied to IoT applications, such as smart cities [8,9] and intelligent transport systems [10]. Edge computing enables the development of real-time responsive systems, which cannot be implemented using cloud computing.

One of the challenges of edge computing is how to handle the raw data collected by edge devices. Sending raw data from the edge device, the source of the data collection, to the edge server for machine learning raises privacy problem and increases communication costs because data is transferred from the edge device to the edge server. To address these problems, the introduction of user authentication protocols [11] or data compression and feature extraction [12] on edge devices have been considered. However, these approaches extract data from the edge device, which is not desirable for users, who do not want to share any information stored on their devices.

Federated Learning. Federated learning, a distributed machine learning model that also conducts machine learning on devices, has been proposed [13–15]. In federated learning, the learning model is first trained on the cloud and the resulting training model is distributed to each device. Each device uses the unique collected data for further training and sends the information about the changes to the cloud. The cloud then averages the changes collected from each device and improves the original learning model to improve it. In this manner, the raw data collected by each device is not shared with anyone. This method enables the utilization of the data on a device for machine learning while ensuring privacy. Federated learning differs from edge computing in that it is a privacy-aware computing model in which information from edge devices is aggregated onto the cloud and managed centrally.

A study on the implementation of federated learning to the Google Keyboard suggested that it is possible to realize machine learning across devices and the cloud without sharing the unique data on a device [16]. Federated learning is expected to have applications also in various other fields, such as sensitive information sharing in the medical field [17], healthcare applications [18], communication during driving [19], and the use of data acquired from sensors in smart cities [20].

Although federated learning is said to be secure, the parameters obtained from the training are sent to the cloud. These parameters contain some information about the training data. It means that even though the raw data remains on the device, there is still a risk of information leakage. Owing to this insufficient privacy protection in federated learning, it is possible to decrypt the private data collected by the device from the parameters sent to the cloud [21]. Studies have shown that original images trained on a device could be recovered clearly from the parameters sent to the cloud [22,23]. Therefore, it is undesirable to use federated learning on highly confidential data.

3 Research Issues and the Proposed Method

3.1 Research Issues

Privacy protection is the most critical problem in machine learning on data stored on user devices. Conventional learning methods aggregate all or part of the information on a server and manage it centrally. Therefore, there is some risk of information leakage. From the privacy protection perspective, it is secure to use a method that does not transfer any information collected by an edge device, including encrypted parameters, to a server.

Furthermore, the data collected by each edge device may be biased toward the personal information of the device owner. However, the results obtained through training should be able to handle a wide range of both general and personal data. For example, in a monitoring service that uses video images collected by sensors installed at home to identify behavior, only information specific to the household is collected from the sensors, such as the actions of owners and placement of objects, which is personal information. Therefore, significant knowledge about personal data can be obtained, and the owner's actions can be accurately determined. On the other hand, if the system lacks knowledge about general data, it may become difficult to identify actions when a stranger visits to the house or when a person moves unusually. With biased data on edge devices, challenges remain in obtaining training results covering a wide range of data types.

3.2   Proposed Method

With the advent of rich clients, complex processing such as machine learning can be enabled on edge devices. Therefore, we propose a distributed machine learning model suitable for rich clients to address the aforementioned problems. In particular, The proposed method is based on offloading some of the machine learning tasks performed on edge servers in the edge computing model to edge devices.

Comparison with Previous Research. In our previous study [24], we proposed a model in which the edge device receives the results trained on the edge server and some general data on the edge server, and then the edge device inherits the training using the data containing personal data. This model works with edge servers but does not transmit any sensitive information out of the edge device. The implementation results suggest that the proposed model provides accurate training results quickly by receiving approximately 30% of the general data on the edge server and inheriting the training on the edge device. However, this model requires transferring some of the data on the edge server to the edge device to obtain results corresponding to both general and personal data. This is not desirable in terms of communication costs when training with huge amounts of data.

Therefore, we consider methods like ensemble learning, in which multiple models are used to improve the accuracy. Ensemble learning is a method to generate a high-accuracy training model by integrating several models, each of which has low accuracy [25]. Bagging is a technique that aggregates training results of several models trained in parallel using a mean value for regression problems and majority vote for classification problems [26,27].

Proposed Model. We integrate the training results on the edge server with those on the edge device using the confidence level of the model. The confidence level indicates degree of certainty of the prediction. Figure 1 shows the proposed model.

We train the learning model using general data on the edge server, and create a checkpoint file to store the training weights. The edge device trains using the collected personal data. When the edge device such as a smartphone moves and

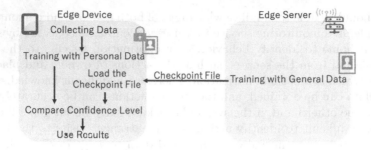

Fig. 1. Proposed Model

connects to the edge server, it receives the checkpoint file created on the edge server. Then, it compares the confidence level obtained from the training results on the edge device with that obtained by loading the checkpoint file received from the edge server. In particular, the edge device loads the model trained on the edge server using general data and the model trained on the edge device using personal data. Next, the data required to judge is input to both models. Confidence levels are calculated for the results of both models, and the result with the higher confidence level is accepted as the correct result. In this manner, we expect to improve the training accuracy using the training results on the edge device for predictions about personal data and the training results on the edge server for predictions about general data.

Contribution. The proposed model builds a unique model for each edge device and is different from the conventional learning models in which the cloud manages all the training results on the edge devices and creates a single model on the cloud. It has the advantage that personal information collected at the edge devices is processed only within the edge device, preventing the transfer of any information to the edge servers. Therefore, there is no risk of information leakage from servers or during communication between edge devices and servers. This model enables the use of personal information while addressing the privacy issues that arise when conventional methods send a part of the information to the server.

4   Implementation and Evaluation of Proposed Model

4.1   Dataset

We used facial images similar to those that would be expected in real-world applications to evaluate the performance of the proposed approach. We used Labeled Faces in the Wild (lfw) [28], which contains jpg images collected from the Internet and sorted into folders for each person. After extracting faces from each photo and removing images that failed to extract properly, we used 20% of each folder as test data. The remaining images were used as the training data and blurred to increase the number of images nine-fold.

Table 1. Specifications of the edge server

OS	Ubuntu 18.04 LTS
CPU	Intel Core i7-8700
GPU	GeForce RTX 2080Ti
Memory	32 Gbyte

Table 2. Specifications of Jetson Nano

OS	Ubuntu 18.04 LTS
CPU	Quad-core ARM A57 @ 1.43 GHz
GPU	128-core Maxwell
Memory	4 GB 64-bit LPDDR4 25.6 GB/s

4.2 Experimental Environment

Table 1 lists the specifications of the edge server, and Table 2 lists the specifications of the Jetson Nano used as the edge device. Jetson Nano is a small AI computer board with a GPU. Smartphones and various IoT devices are expected to adopt similar systems in the near future.

We used TensorFlow for machine learning and connected Jetson Nano and the edge server via Ethernet.

4.3 Preliminary Experiments

To clarify the specifications of the edge server and edge device, we compared the times required for the machine learning process. For the preliminary experiment, we selected 33 individuals from lfw, each with 30 images. To create the dataset, we extracted faces from these images and divided them into training and test data. Figure 2 compares the execution times required to obtain 65% accuracy on the edge server with that on the edge device.

The execution times were 7 min for the edge server and 143 min for the edge device, which is approximately 20 times longer. Notwithstanding its slow speed, machine learning was performed exclusively within the edge device, thereby allowing training with confidential data. However, there is a limit to training on the edge device only, and cooperation with the edge server is necessary.

4.4 Experiment 1 (Used only Personal Data for Training on Edge Device)

Outline of Experiment (Experiment 1). We ran the proposed model with the edge device holding only sensitive personal images collected by it. In this experiment, we selected 30 individuals from lfw as general data for training on the edge server and assumed that Tony Blair's images in lfw as personal

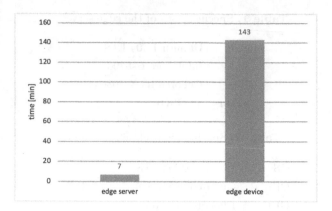

Fig. 2. Execution times of the machine learning process on the edge server and edge device

information for training on the edge device. For each of the 30 individuals used in the edge server, we prepared about 23 training and about 6 test datasets. Because edge devices are expected to collect many images of their owners, we prepared 86 training and 21 test datasets of Tony Blair.

At the edge server, training is sufficiently conducted in 100 epochs using general data that does not contain personal information. Because the specifications of the edge server are high enough to train a lot in a short time, we set the number of epochs that could obtain the upper limit of the accuracy. After training, the edge server sends the checkpoint file containing the training weights to the edge device. Simultaneously, training is conducted at the edge device in 20 epochs using personal data. When the edge device receives the checkpoint file, it loads the model to compare the confidence level of the model trained with the general data on the edge server with the model trained with the personal data on the edge device.

Results (Experiment 1). Figure 3 shows the accuracy at each step. The accuracy is measured using the test data without personal data on the edge server and using the test data including both general and personal data on the edge device. We prepared about 6 images for each of the 30 individuals as test data on the edge server. On the edge device, we added 21 personal test images to this test dataset.

On the edge server, it was possible to achieve 70% of the training on general data. After transferring the checkpoint file to the edge device and testing with the test data containing personal information on the edge device, the accuracy decreased to 62% because of the inability to deal with personal data. In contrast, the training result on the edge device was 11%, which could handle personal data but not general data. A comparison of the confidence levels resulted in an accuracy of 34%. Because the confidence level of the training results on the edge device was higher than that of the edge server, the system could identify

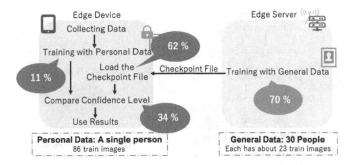

Fig. 3. Accuracy when using only personal data for training on the edge device (Experiment 1)

personal data. However, for general data, the training results obtained from the edge device often identified the wrong person with a high confidence level, resulting in low overall accuracy.

Discussion (Experiment 1). If we use the data of only one individual for training on the edge device, all test images would be identified as that of the individual with a high confidence level. Consequently, confidence level comparisons often result in incorrect identification of general test data.

Therefore, we considered including data of multiple individuals when training on the edge device. However, transferring general data from the edge server to the edge device every time is not desirable from the viewpoints of the capacity of the edge device and communication cost. Therefore, we considered including individuals who differed from those trained on the edge server. This approach is based on the assumption that the training data on the edge server will be replaced by the latest data one after another; however, the edge device uses images acquired previously when downloading the application for the first time.

4.5 Experiment 2 (Adding Four Individuals Different from the Edge Server)

Outline of Experiment (Experiment 2). We prepared the same dataset as in Experiment 1 for the edge server. For the edge device, in addition to the training data used in Experiment 1, we prepared four more individuals in lfw different from the general data used on the edge server. Each individual has 15 images. The test data were the same as in Experiment 1. On the edge server, training was conducted as in Experiment 1. On the edge device, training was conducted in 20 epochs.

Results (Experiment 2). Figure 4 shows the accuracy at each step. Training on the edge device yielded an accuracy of 11%. In particular, while the system could identify personal data with 95% accuracy, it was not able to

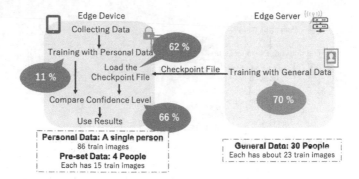

Fig. 4. Accuracy when using four people in addition to personal data for training on the edge device (Experiment 2)

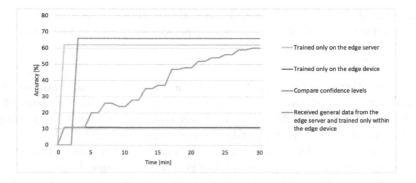

Fig. 5. Details of the training accuracy (Experiment 2)

handle general data. A comparison of the confidence levels showed an accuracy of 66%. In detail, it was able to identify personal data with an accuracy of 76%. Because the confidence level of the result trained on the edge device was higher than that on the edge server, these experimental results indicate that the proposed approach was able to identify personal data with a high probability. As for general data, a correct result trained on the edge server was often more confident than an incorrect result trained on the edge device. Consequently, the overall accuracy of the proposed approach was good.

Accuracy Analysis (Experiment 2). Figure 5 shows the accuracy with the horizontal axis representing the time from just after the checkpoint file is received at the edge device. The yellow graph depicts the accuracy when training on the edge server is just loaded without comparing confidence levels. The blue graph depicts the results trained on the edge device alone without comparing confidence levels. The red graph depicts the accuracy when using the comparison of confidence levels. Training on the edge server alone yields an accuracy of 62% and fails to deal with personal data, whereas training on the edge device alone yields an accuracy of only 11% and fails to deal with general data. In contrast, by comparing confidence levels, we could achieve well-balanced training results for both personal and general data in a short time.

In addition, the green graph depicts the results of training solely at the edge device by preparing all the data of the edge server on the edge device. Because the performance of the edge device was lower than that of the edge server, it took significantly longer to improve the accuracy, indicating that the help provided by the edge server is effective. Moreover, it is possible to conduct training on the edge device before connecting to the edge server because we do not use the data on the edge server for training on the edge device. For example, in Experiment 2, we could save 9 min. Therefore, it is possible to obtain accurate results immediately, contributing to the realization of real-time applications.

Discussion (Experiment 2). By including some non-personal data on the edge device, we could obtain results compatible with both general and personal data. The non-personal data can be different from the person to be identified. Therefore, we only have to transfer the checkpoint file (16 MB) to the edge device. Our proposed model has advantages in terms of the capacity of the edge device and communication costs. Furthermore, we can immediately obtain good results by training on the edge device when the device is not in use.

4.6   Consideration About the Amount of Training and Data

In Experiment 2, as an example, four individuals were used as preset data on the edge device, and trained with 100 epochs on the edge server and 20 epochs on the edge device. To clarify the relationship between accuracy and the number of datasets or the amount of training, we varied the following three factors: the number of epochs of training on the edge device, the number of epochs of training on the edge server, and the number of preset individuals on the edge device. Other factors were the same as in Experiment 2. The results are listed in Tables 3, 4, 5 and 6.

In all cases, as we trained with more epochs on the edge devices, learning became more responsive to personal data but the model faced difficulty in identifying general data. As we increased the amount of training at the edge server or the number of individuals on the edge device, the result was influenced more by general data trained at the edge server but less by personal data trained on the edge device. Therefore, there is a trade-off between improving the accuracy of general data trained on the edge server and improving the accuracy of personal data trained on the edge device. Setting the appropriate number of datasets and amount of training can achieve good accuracy for both general and personal data.

Table 3. Results of varying the amount of training at the edge device (Epochs at the edge server: 40, Preset data: 4 individuals)

Epoch	20	40	100
Accuracy after comparing confidence levels	60 %	56%	48%
(of which, the accuracy of identifying personal data)	81%	86%	90%

Table 4. Results of varying the amount of training at the edge device (Epochs at the edge server: 40, Preset data: 8 individuals)

Epoch	20	40	100
Accuracy after comparing confidence levels	66%	62%	60%
(of which, the accuracy of identifying personal data)	67%	71%	76%

Table 5. Results of varying the amount of training at the edge device (Epochs at the edge server: 100, Preset data: 4 individuals)

Epoch	20	40	100
Accuracy after comparing confidence levels	66%	62%	49%
(of which, the accuracy of identifying personal data)	76%	81%	86%

Table 6. Results of varying the amount of training at the edge device (Epochs at the edge server: 100, Preset data: 8 individuals)

Epoch	20	40	100
Accuracy after comparing confidence levels	66%	64%	61%
(of which, the accuracy of identifying personal data)	62%	76%	90%

5   Summary and Future Work

We investigated a distributed machine learning model suitable for rich clients to enable training while ensuring privacy of personal data on edge devices. We proposed a model that runs machine learning on the edge device and compares its confidence level with machine learning on the edge server. Based on experimental demonstrations using Jetson Nano as the edge device and facial images as training data, we found two advantages of this approach. First, privacy protection is achieved by processing personal information within the edge device itself without sharing it with the edge server. Second, the execution time and communication cost are reduced because training on the edge device does not need to use general data on the edge server to obtain good accuracy for both general and personal information. The results indicate that there is a trade-off between improving the accuracy of general and personal information. We achieved good accuracy by appropriately determining the number of preset datasets and the amount of training.

In future research, we will consider feeding information back from edge devices to edge servers while protecting privacy.

References

1. Taleb, T., Samdanis, K., Mada, B., Flinck, H., Dutta, S., Sabella, D.: On multiaccess edge computing: a survey of the emerging 5G network edge cloud architecture and orchestration. IEEE Commun. Surv. Tutorials **19**(3), 1657–1681 (2017)
2. Shokri, R., Stronati, M., Shmatikov, V.: Membership inference attacks against machine learning models. CoRR, Vol. abs/1610.05820 (2016)
3. Hong, S., Chandrasekaran, V., Kaya, Y., Dumitraş, T., Papernot, N.: On the effectiveness of mitigating data poisoning attacks with gradient shaping. CoRR, Vol. abs/2002.11497 (2020)
4. European Parliament and The Council of the European Union. The general data protection regulation (GDPR). https://eur-lex.europa.eu/eli/reg/2016/679/oj. Accessed 10 Apr 2021
5. Murshed, M.S., Murphy, C., Hou, D., Khan, N., Ananthanarayanan, G., Hussain, F.: Machine learning at the network edge: a survey. ACM Comput. Surv. (CSUR) **54**(8), 1–37 (2021)
6. Shi, W., Cao, J., Zhang, Q., Li, Y., Lanyu, X.: Edge computing: vision and challenges. IEEE Internet Things J. **3**(5), 637–646 (2016)
7. Satyanarayanan, M.: The emergence of edge computing. Computer **50**(1), 30–39 (2017)
8. Chen, N., Chen, Y., Song, S., Huang, C.T., Ye, X.: Poster abstract: smart urban surveillance using fog computing. In: 2016 IEEE/ACM Symposium on Edge Computing (SEC), pp. 95–96 (2016)
9. Tang, B., et al.: Incorporating intelligence in fog computing for big data analysis in smart cities. IEEE Trans. Ind. Inf. **13**(5), 2140–2150 (2017)
10. Lin, J., Yu, W., Yang, X., Yang, Q., Fu, X., Zhao, W.: A real-time En-route route guidance decision scheme for transportation-based cyberphysical systems. IEEE Trans. Veh. Technol. **66**(3), 2551–2566 (2017)
11. Lee, J., Kim, D., Park, J., Park, H.: A multi-server authentication protocol achieving privacy protection and traceability for 5G mobile edge computing. In: Proceedings of the 39th IEEE International Conference on Consumer Electronics (ICCE 2021) (2021)
12. Wang, S., et al.: A cloud-guided feature extraction approach for image retrieval in mobile edge computing. IEEE Trans. Mob. Comput. **20**(2), 292–305 (2021)
13. Yang, Q., Liu, Y., Chen, T., Tong, Y.: Federated machine learning: concept and applications. ACM Trans. Intell. Syst. Technol. (TIST) **10**(2), 1–19 (2019)
14. Li, L., Fan, Y., Tse, M., Lin, K.-Y.: A review of applications in federated learning. Comput. Ind. Eng. **149**, 106854 (2020)
15. Chen Zhang, Yu., Xie, H.B., Bin, Yu., Li, W., Gao, Y.: A survey on federated learning. Knowl. Based Syst. **216**, 106775 (2021)
16. Yang, T., et al.: Applied federated learning: improving google keyboard query suggestions. ArXiv, Vol. abs/1812.02903 (2018)
17. Xu, J., Glicksberg, B.S., Su, C., Walker, P., Bian, J., Wang, F.: Federated learning for healthcare informatics. J. Healthc. Inform. Res. **5**(1), 1–19 (2021)

18. Rieke, N., et al.: The future of digital health with federated learning. NPJ Digit. Med. **3**(1), 1–7 (2020)
19. Ye, D., Rong, Yu., Pan, M., Han, Z.: Federated learning in vehicular edge computing: a selective model aggregation approach. IEEE Access **8**, 23920–23935 (2020)
20. Jiang, J.C., Kantarci, B., Oktug, S., Soyata, T.: Federated learning in smart city sensing: challenges and opportunities. Sensors **20**(21), 6230 (2020)
21. Nasr, M., Shokri, R., Houmansadr, A.: Comprehensive privacy analysis of deep learning: passive and active white-box inference attacks against centralized and federated learning. In: 2019 IEEE Symposium on Security and Privacy (SP), pp. 739–753. IEEE (2019)
22. Song, M., et al.: Analyzing user-level privacy attack against federated learning. IEEE J. Sel. Areas Commun. **38**(10), 2430–2444 (2020)
23. Geiping, J., Bauermeister, H., Dröge, H., Moeller, M.: Inverting gradients-how easy is it to break privacy in federated learning? In: Advances in Neural Information Processing Systems, vol. 33, pp. 16937–16947 (2020)
24. Takano, S., Nakao, A., Yamaguchi, S., Oguchi, M.: Privacyprotective distributed machine learning using rich clients. In: 2021 International Conference on Emerging Technologies for Communications (ICETC 2021), IEICE Proceedings Series, vol. 68, no. C1–4 (2021)
25. Opitz, D., Maclin, R.: Popular ensemble methods: an empirical study. J. Artif. Intell. Res. **11**, 169–198 (1999)
26. Breiman, L.: Bagging predictors. Mach. Learn. **24**(2), 123–140 (1996)
27. Tuysuzoglu, G., Birant, D.: Enhanced bagging (eBagging): a novel approach for ensemble learning. Int. Arab. J. Inf. Technol. **17**(4), 515–528 (2020)
28. Huang, G.B., Mattar, M., Berg, T., Learned-Miller, E.: Labeled faces in the wild: a database forstudying face recognition in unconstrained environments. In: Workshop on faces in 'Real-Life' Images: detection, alignment, and recognition (2008)

A Novel Approach of Securing Medical Cyber Physical Systems (MCPS) from DDoS Attacks

Brij. B. Gupta[1,2]([⊠]), Kwok Tai Chui[3], Varsha Arya[4]([⊠]), and Akshat Gaurav[1,5]

[1] International Center for AI and Cyber Security Research and Innovation and Department of Computer Science and Information Engineering, Asia University, Taichung 413, Taiwan
gupta.brij@gmail.com

[2] Lebanese American University, Beirut 1102, Lebanon

[3] Hong Kong Metropolitan University (HKMU), Kowloon, Hong Kong
jktchui@hkmu.edu.hk

[4] Department of Business Administration, Asia University, Taichung, Taiwan
varshaarya21@gmail.com

[5] Ronin Institute, Montclair, NJ 07043, USA

Abstract. The term "Cyber-Physical Systems" (CPS) often refers to systems that are both designed and physical, as well as biological. In regard to a CPS, the evolution of physical quantities and distinct software and hardware states are usually distinguishing it over time. Continuous state variables for the physical components interspersed with discrete events may be used to represent them in general. CPS is employed in a variety of industries, including healthcare, because of its efficiency. An MCPS is a medically critical integration of a medical cyber-physical system. Continuous, high-quality treatment is made possible via the employment of these systems. Challenges include interoperability, security/privacy, and high system software assurance in the MCPS architecture. It's still early days for MCPS, thus, adequate standards and procedures must be established for their security. Also, due to their low processing capability, they are susceptible to a wide variety of cyberattacks. As a result, MCPS devices need defined protocols and paradigms to maintain their security. In this context, this paper aims to propose DDoS attack detection for the MCPS system. We used statistical approaches to identify and mitigate DDoS attack traffic in the MCPS system.

Keywords: Medica cyber physical systems · IoT · DDoS · Fog computing · Entropy

1 Introduction

Recently, there has been a tremendous uptick in study and application of Cyber-Physical Systems (CPS). There are many applications of CPS in different domains such as the medical sector [14, 14, 17, 43], energy sector, etc. The MCPSs

© The Author(s), under exclusive license to Springer Nature Singapore Pte Ltd. 2023
C.-H. Hsu et al. (Eds.): DataCom 2022, LNCS 13864, pp. 155–165, 2023.
https://doi.org/10.1007/978-981-99-2233-8_11

are the variants of the CPS that are related to the health care domain. Heterogeneity is a major problem in MCPS security. According to an estimate, by 2021, 78% of total internet traffic is due to MCPS devices [5], and by 2025 there will be 82 billion internet-connected devices in the market [19]. Latency is the main limitation of MCPS devices because some services need a quick response from the cloud server.Thus, the notion of fog computing is established to lessen processing time and latency [31,34]. Fog computing is based on decentralized computing, and any low-specification device having processing power and storage can act as a fog node [12,27]. Figure 1 represents an MCPS scenario with fog node, region 1 and region 2 contain different MCPS devices that are generating traffic, and this traffic is prepossessed by the fog node.

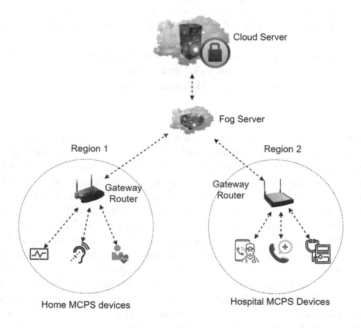

Fig. 1. Medical Cyber Physical System (MCPS) Architecture

The low computational intelligence and internet connectivity of MCPS devices makes them an easy target of different cyber attacks [1]. In this paper, we focus on the detection of DDoS attack [41] which is the deadliest and most popular cyber-attack. The DDoS attack is more than a decade-old attack, but it is still effective and can make victim's server unavailable by consuming its resources. The attacker mostly hacks the MCPS devices and then used them to generate the DDoS attack traffic, Maria [44] malware attack is a recent example of this type of attack in which the attacker generates 1.2 TBps of attack traffic from the IoT bots, in Argentina another version of Maria malware effect the IoT devices in 2017 [24]. Therefore, in recent years, researchers have been proposing many works to protect smart devices from DDoS attacks [30].

In order to improve the security of MCPS devices, we proposed a DDoS attack detection approach. The main contributions of this paper are as follows:

- We proposed a novel DDoS attack detection approach that uses the concept of fog computing to mitigate DDoS attacks.
- The proposed approach is based on statistical techniques for filtering the DDoS attack traffic.

The remaining of the paper is organized as follows. Section 2 represents the literature survey. Section 4 explains our proposed approach in detail, Sect. 5 given the analysis of our proposed approach. Finally, Sect. 6 concludes the paper.

2 Related Work

The first DDoS attack was detected in 1999, and by then it had been considered as the biggest cybersecurity threat to all major communication platforms like IoT, cloud, etc [2,13,38]. Researchers had been proposing different solutions for its detection. At first, some researchers proposed a sliding window-based detection module, in which two sliding windows were used to detect the attack traffic [33]. Later, this method is improved by adding a clustering method [11]. As hackers develop different variants of DDoS attacks these classic techniques were not able to detect the attack traffic. However, recently, the author [23] improved the sliding window technique for the detection of source IP address entropy. The proposed method quickly calculates the entropy value of incoming traffic, hence it is an efficient method for the detection of volumetric DDoS attacks.

With the development of new techniques like machine learning, deep learning [3] , and fuzzy logic, new models for DDoS detection were developed. The author [45] proposed a fuzzy logic-based DDoS detection module, which uses the combination of entropy and fuzzy logic for the identification and filtering of the attack. Some researchers used information shearing by thread intelligence and command line intelligence for the detection of attack packets [25,35]. Some researchers suggest that machine learning techniques are the most efficient way for the detection of anomalies in network traffic [2,4,7]. In this context, author [37] proposed an SVM-based technique for the detection of HTTP flooding, SYN flooding, and amplification attacks.

Sometimes the use of honeypots is effective for the detection of the DDoS attack, the author [40] proposed a honeypot-based defense model. In the proposed approach, the honeypot technique is used to store the unauthorized attempt of malicious software installation, and then a machine learning approach is used to predict the attack types. However, this technique is unable to detect zero-day attacks. The author [9] proposed DDoS attack detection based on the Online Discrepancy Test (ODIT) [42] method. In the proposed approach, the author uses the asymptotic optimality to handle a large number of training datasets. The proposed approach uses the concept of a dynamic scenario in which the number of devices keeps on changing. In [10] performance of different machine learning techniques like SVM, ANN, KNN are compared.

However, all these detection techniques need a large amount of training data and work only in a specific test scenario. The author [32] also uses the SVM technique for DDoS detection, firstly the author extracted useful features from the incoming traffic and then applied the SVM algorithm. The author [22] proposed an anomaly-based detection method using the dimensionality reduction technique, this approach can detect malicious traffic in a higher dimensionality setting. In [28] auto-encoders are used for the detection of the DDoS attack traffic. However, the proposed approach is not acceptable for large networks because auto-encoders are trained for every device present in the network.

Other than DL and ML techniques, statistical methods are also used for the detection of DDoS attack traffic. In these methods, the statistical properties of incoming traffic like probability or entropy are analyzed. These techniques are useful for the detection of volumetric DDoS attack detection because the statistical properties of network traffic change at the time of attack [15]. Mostly, the variation of the source's IP address entropy is the factor that is used by the authors for differentiating normal traffic from the DDoS attack traffic [6]. In [18] author calculates the score of the packet from the IP addresses and attributes of the incoming packets, and then combines the score with the destination IP address entropy for the identification of DDoS attack traffic. In all statistical-based DDoS attack detection methods, there is a need to selection of a threshold value beforehand. This is the main limitation most of these statistical-based techniques. To overcome this limitation, researchers proposed a technique of dynamically selection of threshold value [21,36]. Other than entropy, other statistical parameters like traffic flow variation are also used by different authors for the preparation of models for DDoS attack detection [8,29]. In [26] author proposed a load balancing technique for the mitigation of DNS flooding. The author also proposed a model through which the victim's site is reachable even if the DNS server is down. However, these techniques are not efficient for large size of networks.

As no single approach can efficiently detect the DDoS attack traffic, some authors proposed a hybrid approach. In this context, the author [20] proposed a DDoS detection approach that is based on the combination of entropy and deep learning. In the proposed approach, the deep lea ring algorithm is used to find the threshold value for entropy-based filtering of incoming packets. In another approach, the author [16] proposed an approach that is the combination of flow control and CNN algorithm. Flow maintenance is managed by statistical method and filtering is done by CNN algorithm.

3   System Model

The system model of our proposed approach is represented in Fig. 2. Each of the MCPS devices are divided into N regions, as represented in the Fig. 2. Devices in each region collect the data and transmit it to the fog node through the gateway devices. The Fog nodes are the devices that have extra computation power compared to MCPS devices. All fog nodes are connected to each other and share

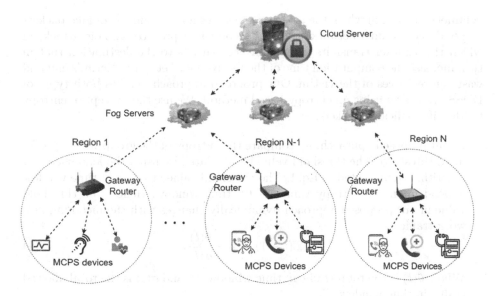

Fig. 2. System Model

the incoming traffic according to their processing power. After processing the data, the fog nodes perform the required operation and forward the important information to the cloud storage for further processing.

Definition 1. *Network* $N = \{R_N, D_N, F_N, G_i, Ln_i\}$ *represents the network where DDoS attack takes place.* $R = \{R_1, R_2, ..., R_N\}$ *are the different regions in which smart devices are present.* $D = \{D_{11}, ..., D_{1n}, D_{21}..., D_{NN}$ *are the MCPS devices present in different regions.* $G = \{G_1, G_2, ..., G_N\}$ *are the gateway devices.* $F_N = \{F_1, F_2, ..., F_N\}$ *are the fog nodes, which prepossess the incoming traffic.*

At the time of the attack, a random number of MCPS devices are infected by malicious malware and act as bots. The bots generate DDoS attack traffic. During the attack time, the following assumptions should be full filled.

Example 1. There must be a link present between the gateway devices (G_n) and fog nodes (F_N), and there is no direct communication between fog nodes (F_N) and the cloud server.

Example 2. The communication channel between fog nodes (F_N) and the cloud server is secure.

4   Proposed Methodology

Our proposed approach is divided into two parts in order to identify different types of DDoS attacks efficiently. There are two types of DDoS attacks, one is a volumetric attack in which the attacker generates a large number of fake packets to flood the victim's network, and the second is a protocol exploit attack, in which the attacker transmits the malformed packets to the destination that in turn increase the computation time of the received packet at the victim's end and wast the resources of the victim. Our proposed approach handles both types of DDoS attacks by using an entropy-based method. We use the concept of entropy to identify malicious packets.

- In our proposed approach, we compare the entropy of the group with a predefined threshold. The threshold value is calculated by using the load shedding algorithm, represented in Eq. 1. The threshold value at $(t+1)^{th}$ time window depend upon the entropy values of tth time window. Hence, the threshold value in our proposed approach dynamically changes with the incoming network traffic.

$$T(t+1) = 1 - \frac{\theta(t)}{\sigma(t)} \qquad (1)$$

Where $\theta(t)$ is the total traffic in time window 't', and $\sigma(t)$ is the total allowed traffic in time window 't'.

In light of the above-defined terms and concepts, we now explain the working of the DDoS attack module, which is the first line of defense against the DDoS attack.

- For every time window δt fog device extracts the IP address of network traffic that is generated from the MCPS devcies and places the IP addresses in different groups. This process is represented in the 5th to 12th lines of Algorithm 1
- If there is no group is available for the IP address then a new group G_{n+1} is created for the respective IP address.
- After placing the IP addresses in the appropriate groups, calculate the group probability and entropy.
- Now by using Eq. 1, we calculate the threshold value for time window δt.
- If the group entropy is greater than a threshold number, then the incoming traffic's nature has changed from the prior time frame, according to our suggested technique.
- If the group entropy is less than the threshold, then the traffic is passed unaffected.

5   Results and Discussion

In this section, we represent the implementation results of our proposed approach. For simulating volumetric DDoS attacks, we use OMNET++ [39], which is a discrete event simulator. The basic simulation environment is represented in Table 1. We use three types of nodes in the simulation; MCPS nodes, malicious

---

Algorithm 1: Incoming Packet Analysis Algorithm

---

1 **Input** : Incoming Traffic
2 **Output** : Packet Filtering
3 **Start**
4 **for** $\forall$ (T_t) **do**
5 | $T_t \rightarrow A_{IP}$, extract address
6 | **if** $A_{IP} \in B$ **then**
7 | | Dropt packet
8 | **end**
9 | **else**
10 | | **if** $A_{IP} \in G$ **then**
11 | | | classification according to IP address;
12 | | **end**
13 | | **else**
14 | | | $A_{IP} \rightarrow G_{n+1}$;
15 | | | Find Entropy;
16 | | **end**
17 | | Find Threshold T
18 | | **if** $E > T$ **then**
19 | | |
20 | | | $P_{Z_i} = max.of \{P_{Z_1}, P_{Z_2}, ..., P_{Z_n}\}$
21 | | | $Z_i \rightarrow B$;
22 | | **end**
23 | | **else**
24 | | | Pass the traffic unaffected
25 | | **end**
26 | **end**
27 **end**
28 **END**

---

devices, and fog nodes. MCPS devices generate traffic at a low rate compared to malicious devices, which want to flood the bandwidth with fake packets. We use ten different test cases to test our proposed approach on malicious users.

Table 1. Simulation Environment

Attributes	Value
Area	500×500 m^2
Time	100 sec
Malicious user data rate	$e^{0.172}$ packets/second
Legitimate user data rate	$e^{0.152}$ packets/second

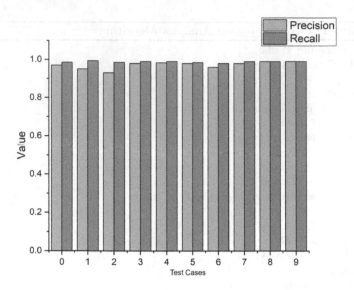

Fig. 3. Analyze of proposed approach

To check its efficiency, we calculate the following parameters:

– **Precision** - This value indicates how many packets are properly filtered as a result of using our suggested strategy. It is calculated by Eq. 2.

$$P = \frac{\phi_{tp}}{\phi_{tp} + \phi_{fp}} \tag{2}$$

– **Recall** - It measures the percentage of legitimated packets from the total undetected packets by our algorithm. It is calculated by Eq. 3

$$R = \frac{\phi_{tp}}{\phi_{tp} + \phi_{fp}} \tag{3}$$

The variation of the above-defined parameters with ten different test cases is represented in Fig. 3. From Fig. 3 it is clear that the average precision of our prospered approach is more than 98%. Hence, we can say that our proposed approach detects malicious traffic in MCPS efficiently.

6   Conclusion

We provide a detection module to prevent Distributed Denial of Service (DDoS) attacks against Medical Cyber-Physical Systems (MCPS) in this paper. The proposed approach used statistical techniques for the identification of attack traffic. The proposed approach used the concept of clustering and entropy for the mitigation of DDoS attacks. The performance of our proposed approach is measured by standard validation parameters like precision and recall, and the results emphasize the validity of our proposed approach. This study provides the backbone for DDoS attack detection in MCPS devices, and our future studies will be focused on the integration of blockchain and other latest techniques with our proposed approach.

References

1. Adat, V., Gupta, B.: Security in internet of things: issues, challenges, taxonomy, and architecture. Telecommun. Syst. **67**(3), 423–441 (2018)
2. Agrawal, N., Tapaswi, S.: Defense mechanisms against DDOs attacks in a cloud computing environment: state-of-the-art and research challenges. IEEE Commun. Surv. Tutorials **21**(4), 3769–3795 (2019)
3. Ahmed, K.D., Askar, S., et al.: Deep learning models for cyber security in IoT networks: a review. Int. J. Sci. Bus. **5**(3), 61–70 (2021)
4. Aljuhani, A.: Machine learning approaches for combating distributed denial of service attacks in modern networking environments. IEEE Access **9**, 42236–42264 (2021)
5. Bernabé-Sánchez, I., Díaz-Sánchez, D., Muñoz-Organero, M.: Specification and unattended deployment of home networks at the edge of the network. IEEE Trans. Consum. Electron. **66**(4), 279–288 (2020). https://doi.org/10.1109/TCE.2020.3018543
6. Bojović, P., Bašičević, I., Ocovaj, S., Popović, M.: A practical approach to detection of distributed denial-of-service attacks using a hybrid detection method. Comput. Electr. Eng. **73**, 84–96 (2019)
7. Chaudhary, D., Bhushan, K., Gupta, B.B.: Survey on DDOs attacks and defense mechanisms in cloud and fog computing. Int. J. E-Serv. Mob. Appl. (IJESMA) **10**(3), 61–83 (2018)
8. Cui, J., Long, J., Min, E., Liu, Q., Li, Q.: Comparative study of CNN and RNN for deep learning based intrusion detection system. In: Sun, X., Pan, Z., Bertino, E. (eds.) ICCCS 2018. LNCS, vol. 11067, pp. 159–170. Springer, Cham (2018). https://doi.org/10.1007/978-3-030-00018-9_15
9. Doshi, K., Yilmaz, Y., Uludag, S.: Timely detection and mitigation of stealthy DDOs attacks via IoT networks. IEEE Trans. Dependable Secure Comput. **18**, 2164–2176 (2021)
10. Doshi, R., Apthorpe, N., Feamster, N.: Machine learning DDOs detection for consumer internet of things devices. In: 2018 IEEE Security and Privacy Workshops (SPW), pp. 29–35. IEEE (2018)
11. Fang, F., Cai, Z., Zhao, Q., Lin, J., Zhu, M.: Adaptive technique for real-time DDOs detection and defense using spark streaming. J. Frontiers Comput. Sci. Technol. **10**(5), 601–611 (2016)
12. Gao, L., Luan, T.H., Yu, S., Zhou, W., Liu, B.: FogRoute: DTN-based data dissemination model in fog computing. IEEE Internet Things J. **4**(1), 225–235 (2016)
13. Gupta, B.B., Li, K.C., Leung, V.C., Psannis, K.E., Yamaguchi, S., et al.: Blockchain-assisted secure fine-grained searchable encryption for a cloud-based healthcare cyber-physical system. IEEE/CAA J. Automatica Sinica **8**(12), 1877–1890 (2021)
14. Haraty, R., Kaddoura, S., Zekri, A.: Recovery of business intelligence systems: towards guaranteed continuity of patient centric healthcare systems through a matrix-based recovery approach. Telematics Inform. **35**(4), 801–814 (2018). https://doi.org/10.1016/j.tele.2017.12.010

15. Herrera, H.A., Rivas, W.R., Kumar, S.: Evaluation of internet connectivity under distributed denial of service attacks from botnets of varying magnitudes. In: 2018 1st International Conference on Data Intelligence and Security (ICDIS), pp. 123–126. IEEE (2018)

16. Jia, Y., Zhong, F., Alrawais, A., Gong, B., Cheng, X.: Flowguard: an intelligent edge defense mechanism against IoT DDOs attacks. IEEE Internet Things J. **7**(10), 9552–9562 (2020)

17. Kaddoura, S., Haraty, R., Al Kontar, K., Alfandi, O.: A parallelized database damage assessment approach after cyberattack for healthcare systems. Future Internet **13**(4), 90 (2021). https://doi.org/10.3390/fi13040090

18. Kalkan, K., Altay, L., Gür, G., Alagöz, F.: JESS: joint entropy-based DDOs defense scheme in SDN. IEEE J. Sel. Areas Commun. **36**(10), 2358–2372 (2018)

19. Khan, W.Z., Aalsalem, M.Y., Khan, M.K.: Communal acts of IoT consumers: a potential threat to security and privacy. IEEE Trans. Consum. Electron. **65**(1), 64–72 (2019). https://doi.org/10.1109/TCE.2018.2880338

20. Koay, A., Chen, A., Welch, I., Seah, W.K.: A new multi classifier system using entropy-based features in DDOs attack detection. In: 2018 International Conference on Information Networking (ICOIN), pp. 162–167. IEEE (2018)

21. Kumar, P., Tripathi, M., Nehra, A., Conti, M., Lal, C.: SAFETY: early detection and mitigation of TCP SYN flood utilizing entropy in SDN. IEEE Trans. Netw. Serv. Manage. **15**(4), 1545–1559 (2018)

22. Kurt, M.N., Yilmaz, Y., Wang, X.: Real-time nonparametric anomaly detection in high-dimensional settings. IEEE Trans. Pattern Anal. Mach. Intell. **43**, 2463–2479 (2020)

23. Li, J., Liu, M., Xue, Z., Fan, X., He, X.: RTVD: A real-time volumetric detection scheme for DDOs in the internet of things. IEEE Access **8**, 36191–36201 (2020)

24. Li, J., Xue, Z.: Distributed threat intelligence sharing system: a new sight of p2p botnet detection. In: 2019 2nd International Conference on Computer Applications & Information Security (ICCAIS), pp. 1–6. IEEE (2019)

25. Liu, M., Xue, Z., He, X., Chen, J.: Cyberthreat-intelligence information sharing: enhancing collaborative security. IEEE Consum. Electron. Mag. **8**(3), 17–22 (2019)

26. Mahjabin, T., Xiao, Y., Li, T., Chen, C.P.: Load distributed and benign-bot mitigation methods for IoT DNS flood attacks. IEEE Internet Things J. **7**(2), 986–1000 (2019)

27. Mahmud, R., Kotagiri, R., Buyya, R.: Fog computing: a taxonomy, survey and future directions. In: Di Martino, B., Li, K.-C., Yang, L.T., Esposito, A. (eds.) Internet of Everything. IT, pp. 103–130. Springer, Singapore (2018). https://doi.org/10.1007/978-981-10-5861-5_5

28. Meidan, Y., et al.: N-BAIOT-network-based detection of IoT botnet attacks using deep autoencoders. IEEE Pervasive Comput. **17**(3), 12–22 (2018)

29. Min, E., Long, J., Liu, Q., Cui, J., Chen, W.: TR-IDS: anomaly-based intrusion detection through text-convolutional neural network and random forest. Secur. Commun. Netw. **2018** (2018)

30. Mustapha, H., Alghamdi, A.M.: DDOs attacks on the internet of things and their prevention methods. In: Proceedings of the 2nd International Conference on Future Networks and Distributed Systems, pp. 1–5 (2018)

31. Naha, R.K., et al.: Fog computing: survey of trends, architectures, requirements, and research directions. IEEE Access **6**, 47980–48009 (2018). https://doi.org/10.1109/ACCESS.2018.2866491

32. Nõmm, S., Bahşi, H.: Unsupervised anomaly based botnet detection in IoT networks. In: 2018 17th IEEE international conference on machine learning and applications (ICMLA), pp. 1048–1053. IEEE (2018)
33. Qing-Tao, W., Zhi-qing, S.: Detecting DDOs attacks against web server using time series analysis. Wuhan Univ. J. Nat. Sci. **11**(1), 175–180 (2006)
34. Ray, P.P., Thapa, N., Dash, D.: Implementation and performance analysis of interoperable and heterogeneous IoT-edge gateway for pervasive wellness care. IEEE Trans. Consum. Electron. **65**(4), 464–473 (2019). https://doi.org/10.1109/TCE.2019.2939494
35. Roy, K.C., Chen, Q.: DeepRan: attention-based BiLSTM and CRF for ransomware early detection and classification. Inf. Syst. Frontiers **23**, 1–17 (2020)
36. Shah, S.B.I., Anbar, M., Al-Ani, A., Al-Ani, A.K.: Hybridizing entropy based mechanism with adaptive threshold algorithm to detect RA flooding attack in IPv6 networks. In: Computational Science and Technology. LNEE, vol. 481, pp. 315–323. Springer, Singapore (2019). https://doi.org/10.1007/978-981-13-2622-6_31
37. She, C., Wen, W., Lin, Z., Zheng, K.: Application-layer DDOs detection based on a one-class support vector machine. Int. J. Netw. Secur. Appl. (IJNSA) **9**(1), 13–24 (2017)
38. Tewari, A., Gupta, B.B.: Secure timestamp-based mutual authentication protocol for IoT devices using RFID tags. Int. J. Semant. Web Inf. Syst. (IJSWIS) **16**(3), 20–34 (2020)
39. Varga, A., Hornig, R.: An Overview of the OMNeT++ Simulation Environment (2008). https://doi.org/10.1145/1416222.1416290
40. Vishwakarma, R., Jain, A.K.: A honeypot with machine learning based detection framework for defending IoT based botnet DDOs attacks. In: 2019 3rd International Conference on Trends in Electronics and Informatics (ICOEI), pp. 1019–1024. IEEE (2019)
41. Wahab, O., Bentahar, J., Otrok, H., Mourad, A.: Optimal load distribution for the detection of VM-based DDOs attacks in the cloud. IEEE Trans. Serv. Comput. **13**(1), 114–129 (2020). https://doi.org/10.1109/TSC.2017.2694426
42. Yilmaz, Y.: Online nonparametric anomaly detection based on geometric entropy minimization. In: 2017 IEEE International Symposium on Information Theory (ISIT), pp. 3010–3014. IEEE (2017)
43. Yunis, M., Markarian, C., El-Kassar, A.N.: A conceptual model for sustainable adoption of ehealth: role of digital transformation culture and healthcare provider's readiness, vol. 2, pp. 179–184 (2020)
44. Zhang, X., Upton, O., Beebe, N.L., Choo, K.K.R.: Iot botnet forensics: a comprehensive digital forensic case study on mirai botnet servers. Forensic Sci. Int. Digit. Investig. **32**, 300926 (2020)
45. Zhao, Y., Zhang, W., Feng, Y., Yu, B.: A classification detection algorithm based on joint entropy vector against application-layer DDOs attack. Secur. Commun. Netw. **2018** (2018)

LTCS: Lightweight Tree-Chain Scheme for ADS-B Data Authentication

Haoran Cui[1] , Shibo Zhu[2] , and Meng Yue[2](✉)

[1] College of Electronic Information and Automation, Civil Aviation University of China, Tianjin 300300, China
[2] College of Safety Science and Engineering, Civil Aviation University of China, Tianjin 300300, China
myue_23@163.com

Abstract. As a widely used air traffic monitoring and information transmission technology, the Automatic Dependent Surveillance - Broadcast (ADS-B) is gradually deployed to aircraft around the world. However, due to the openness of its communication protocol, it is vulnerable to malicious attacks. Aiming at the security threats of ADS-B system, this paper proposes an ADS-B data security scheme on the basis of tree-chain structure to realize the lightweight guarantee of ADS-B message reliability. Firstly, we used the idea of symmetric key delay disclosure in classical data authentication scheme to construct a tree-chain authentication model, which reduces the computation amount in authentication process and the length of key chain. Next, we used SM2 digital signature, which is more secure and computationally efficient, to authenticate the initial information in the signature phase. Compared with the original authentication scheme, our scheme improves the computation speed by about 4 times and reduces the number of keys in the authentication process, and is more applicable for ADS-B use cases with high real-time demand and tight computing resources.

Keywords: ADS-B · Cyberattack defense · Data authentication · Tree-chain scheme

1 Introduction

By 2033, according to the Federal Aviation Administration, the number of travelers in U.S. business jet is going to reach an all-time high of 1.15 billion [1].

The global economy is expected to revive soon, which will inevitably lead to an increase in the number of planes in the airspace as it becomes more crowded.

This work was supported in part by the National Natural Science Foundation of China (Nos. 62172418, U1933108, and U2133203), the Natural Science Foundation of Tianjin China (21JCZDJC00830) the Scientific Research Project of Tianjin Municipal Education Commission (No. 2019KJ117), and the Fundamental Research Funds for the Central Universities of CAUC (No. 3122021026, 3122022081).

In this regard, the infrastructure for airborne communication, navigation, and surveillance faces a significant challenge due to the increasing expansion of civil aviation worldwide. The Automatic Dependent Surveillance - Broadcast (ADS-B) system is an important air transport surveillance technology that primarily completes the extraction and processing of airplane position information and other additional information to form understandable and comprehensible background maps and trajectories. ADS-B, a crucial component of NextGen, can significantly increase air traffic control's operational effectiveness and lower the infrastructure's maintenance costs [2, 3]. ADS-B offers more precise and real-time airplane positioning data than conventional radar surveillance systems while also requiring less maintenance and having a longer lifespan [4]. Additionally, many nations have imposed rigorous guidelines for the installation of ADS-B technology. All American planes must have ADS-B equipment as of January 1, 2020 [5]. Meanwhile, since 2012, air navigation service providers in Europe have massively deployed ADS-B system [6]. ADS-B systems, which are intended to broadcast in clear text at first, have an open communication mode, making them susceptible to many forms of assaults like jamming and spoofing [7]. Researchers Slimane et al. [8] conducted interference and deception experiments on ADS-B, and the results showed that illegal message injection and other interference not only increased the work burden of control units, but also seriously affected the safety of aircraft during flight, which was very dangerous to the safe operation of civil aviation. Researchers Slimane et al. [8] conducted interference and deception experiments on ADS-B, and the results showed that illegal message injection and other interference not only increased the work burden of control units, but also seriously affected the safety of aircraft during flight, which was very dangerous to the safe operation of civil aviation. Nowadays, the majority of aircraft have transponders with ADS-B capability, making it simple to track significant flight plans. For instance, consider a scenario where an anonymous attacker could use a software radio peripheral with ADS-B reception to track the flight plan of a target aircraft as well as its exact location and altitude.

The authentication cost of the current ADS-B security scheme is too high. Our paper combines the classical data authentication protocol and improves it to reduce the computational overhead, making it more suitable for aviation links.

Our contribution is as follows:

- We combine the Timed Efficient Stream Loss-tolerant Authentication (TESLA) authentication algorithm to build a tree-chain authentication architecture to reduce the authentication cost.
- We used the SM2 algorithm with higher security and better performance to sign the initial information of the TESLA chain.
- We design a scheme for multiple aircraft in the same airspace to use different key chains for authentication, which further enhances flight security.

2   Related Works

Because there is no data authentication means in the initial stage of ADS-B design. A growing number of research personnel of civil aviation have joined in the research of ADS-B data protection mechanism, and put forward many methods to solve security problems. Unlike secure location authentication, broadcast security certification aims at presenting a security framework for ADS-B while ensuring ADS-B openness. Using cryptographic measures to secure ADS-B networks is a tried-and-true communication method [9]. Wei-Jun Pan et al. [10] proposed a solution for ADS-B data authentication based on elliptic curve ryptography and X.509 certificates, as well as symmetric key algorithms, to effectively avoid key distribution and prevent ADS-B data spoofing. The results of Richard et al. [11] show that format-preserving encryption (FPE) is suitable for ADS-B message encryption. The FPE algorithm can fuzz duplicate plaintext data and output ciphertext while maintaining high entropy security. It is also concluded that the FF3 algorithm is the most efficient in hardware and that its use can be used to improve ADS-B device encryption. Using FPE and TESLA, Haomiao Yang et al. [12] proposed a lightweight secure encryption solution that ensurse the reliability of ADS-B messages in a real airport environment. Costin et al. [13] proposed a lightweight PKI solution in which an aircraft sends multiple ADS-B messages with signed ADS-B messages, after which other participants receive multiple ADS-B messages with aircraft signatures, and the receiver retains these messages until the complete signatures are transmitted, at which point the receiver authenticates the buffered ADS-B messages. Jingxian Zhou et al. [14] propose a lightweight batch authentication algorithm for messages that ensures batch message authentication security and resists replay attacks. The identity-based batch authentication system has considerable advantages in terms of data overhead and computational cost because the point operation in the operation process is reduced.

The majority of the ADS-B security protocols in use today are built on an asymmetric encryption method with a high authentication cost. To make the ADS-B message format with limited bit resources more relevant, this paper aims to design a lightweight ADS-B data authentication structure. Additionally, Matthias et. al [7] reports that the average error rate of ADS-B messages reaches 33% due to the increasing multiplexing of different services over 1090ES data links and a message will not be sent repeatedly in ADS-B systemA, which implies that our security scheme should also be resilient to link packet loss.

3   Our Proposed Scheme

More and more researchers have applied TESLA [15] and its improved scheme to broadcast data authentication. It adopts the idea of key delay disclosure to perform data authentication, which has the advantages of small computation, low communication overhead and good anti-packet loss performance. Many researchers have improved it to make it more scalable and more suitable for wireless channel transmission. Due to the limited number of available bits and the common link packet loss in ADS-B system, TESLA and its improved scheme can be deployed in ADS-B system to ensure the data security of packets. TESLA and its improved scheme can be laid out to ensure data security.

The aircraft, as the sender, first generates a key chain of length l, then randomly selects a key K_l, and uses the pseudo-random function F to pre-calculate the whole key chain at the sender. Each key K_i can be obtained by the following method.

$$K_i = F^{l-i}(K_l) \tag{1}$$

During the construction of key chain, the whole chain can be constructed and stored at one time, or only K_l can be stored, and other keys can be generated when necessary. Considering the limited computing and cache resources of the aircraft, we adopt the solution of only storing K_l. After the key chain is generated, another pseudo-random function F' is used to generate the key K_i' used to calculate the Mac value. The calculation method of K_i' is as follows.

$$K_i' = F'(K_i) \tag{2}$$

In the TESLA chain, the delayed disclosure time of the key is critical. Before transmission, the aircraft divides the transmission time into several time intervals according to the network condition, and the duration of each interval is T_{int}. The ith time interval is represented by I_i, and the delayed release time interval of the key is d ($d = nT_{int}$). That is, the key K_i of the Mac value in the packet P_i at the ith time is disclosed after the nT_{int} time. Since all the keys are generated by the same key K_l, even if the packet of the public K_i is lost, the receiver can also deduce the K_i through the subsequent key, which ensures the robustness of the authentication scheme against link packet loss. Before data authentication, the aircraft must be guided by digital signatures to provide the receiver with the initial information required for source authentication, including a specific time interval T_i, I_i, key disclosure delay d and a key in the key chain K_j ($j<i-d$). The role of T_i, I_i, and d is mainly to achieve time synchronization, and K_j enables the receiver to verify the subsequent public key. As for the signature algorithm, we selected the SM2 signature algorithm promulgate by the Network Security Department of China in 2010. Compared with RSA algorithm, it has better performance, and has become an ISO/IEC international standard in 2018 [16].

The generation process of key chain K_i and K_i' is shown in Fig. 1.

The overall authentication architecture we built is shown in Fig. 2. In the process of flight, the plane packs its speed, longitude, latitude, heading and other information into 112bits of ADS-B packets. Firstly, SM2 digital signature is used for initial authentication of authentication information. For the detailed digital signature process of SM2, please refer to related research in [16]. Then, continuous packets in the same period are transmitted through the tree structure to generate the root hash, and HMAC-SHA256 operation is performed on each

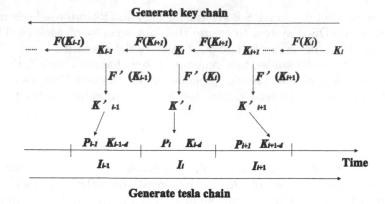

Fig. 1. TESLA Key Chain.

root hash. In this way, the integrity and authenticity of the entire ADS-B packet data are ensured. In this way, the secutity of the entire ADS-B packet data are ensured.

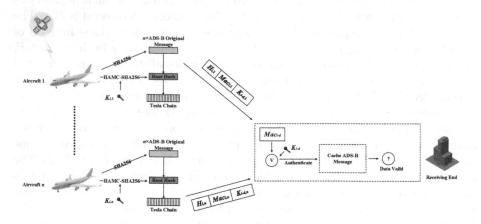

Fig. 2. Overall authentication architecture.

In order to build a lightweight tree-chain TESLA scheme, we first through the hash tree structure building certification group, at the sender, the real-time message data flow block, each with a total of n ADS-B messages, according to the root node of the tree structure to generate data block after the hash value of D_i, the choice of n will influence the computation and communication overhead, for example, with the increase of n, The computation overhead of the overall packet flow is reduced, but the communication overhead is increased. Here, $n = 4$ is selected to introduce the method of generating root hash using hash tree structure in detail. The root hash generation method is shown in Fig. 3.

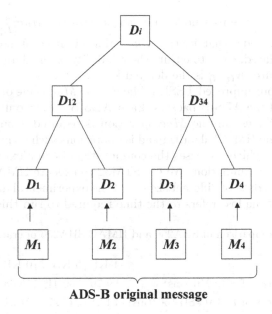

Fig. 3. Generation method of root hash.

In the tree structure calculation, the summary value of each ADS-B packet M is used as the leaf node of the authentication tree, D_i is generated by D_{12} and D_{34}, and D_{12} and D_{34} are generated by D_1 to D_4, respectively. The calculation process is as follows.

$$D_{12} = h\left(D_1\|D_2\right), \tag{3}$$
$$D_{34} = h\left(D_3\|D_4\right), \tag{4}$$
$$D_i = h\left(D_{12}\|D_{34}\right). \tag{5}$$

On the sending end, each ADS-B packet can be sent after the tree structure is generated. In our scheme, each ADS-B packet does not need to perform an operation of Mac value, and each packet only needs to carry other sibling nodes in the tree structure when it is sent. For example, packet M_1 carries D_2 and D_{34} during transmission. After initialization, the packet P_i is sent at the ith time interval I_i. With the purpose of cutting down the communication overhead during authentication and avoid the influence of high communication overhead on the packet update frequency, we truncate the hash value and Mac value, which are denoted as D^{trunc} and Mac^{trunc}. The composition of data packets in the TESLA chain is as follows.

$$P_i = \left\{D_i^{trunc}, i, Mac_{(K_i, Di)}^{trunc}, K_{i-d}\right\} \tag{6}$$

D_i is the hash of the root node to be authenticated. $Mac^{trunc}_{(K'_i,D_i)}$ is the Mac value of the root node, that is, the Mac value of the root node in each tree structure is calculated, so as to ensure the reliability of the data of all leaf nodes in the tree structure. $K_{(i-d)}$ is the delayed key.

Therefore, in our improved TESLA scheme, the Mac value of a root node can authenticate multiple ADS-B packets. Each ADS-B packet only needs to carry extra log^n_2 hash values, and no Mac operation is required. Compared with the hash algorithm, the HMAC algorithm adds operations such as padding and message combination, which increases the computational complexity. This has also been proved by test simulation. We use STM32 to execute HMAC-SHA256 and SHA256 to process data of different sizes, and the experimental data are recorded in Table 1. Here, time loss refers to the time required to run this algorithm.

Table 1. Comparison of SHA256 and HMAC-SHA256 operation speed.

Data size	1 KB	5 KB	10 KB	15 KB
The time loss of SHA256/(ms)	59.79	280.41	575.68	856.45
The time loss of HMAC-SHA56/(ms)	74.21	347.27	721.31	1030.47

Therefore, our scheme reduces the computational overhead in the authentication process. At the same time, it also reduces the number of key generation and the frequency of disclosure. Contrast with standard TESLA, the number of the keys generated by our scheme is $\frac{1}{n}$, thus reducing the cache space for the key chain opened by the communication parties.

At the receiver end, the receiver first caches the received root node Di and its corresponding leaf nodes M_1-M_4. When the key K_i corresponding to P_i is revealed, the receiver first uses D_i and K_i to verify Mac value. If the verification succeeds, it indicates that the root node is credible. After the root node is verified, the leaf node can generate D'_i according to its sibling nodes. If $D_i = D'_i$, the leaf node is proved to be trusted, so as to secure ADS-B data.

Considering that there are usually multiple aircraft in an ATC controlled airspace to transmit ADS-B data in real time, there is a key chain selection problem when using our proposed tree-chain TESLA scheme for data authentication. Of course, different airplanes can use the same key chain to generate Mac values, that is, different airplanes transmit the same key at each authentication moment. The advantage of this method is that the authentication cost is low, and all airplanes only need to initialize the authentication once, because all airplanes share a key chain. The receiver only needs to receive a correct key to realize ADS-B data authentication for all aircraft, but using the same key chain may lead to replay attacks by attackers. In addition, the aircraft acts as a high-speed transmitter, arrival time of ADS-B messages at the receiving end will change with the specific environment, the signal transmission delay may lead to the deviation of key disclosure time of different aircraft at a certain authentication time, which requires high time synchronization, these are all air link environment must be considered.

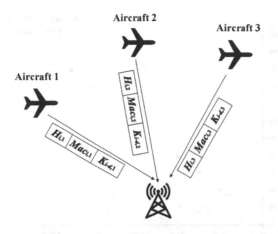

Fig. 4. Multi-key chain authentication strategy.

Aiming at the disadvantage of using the same key chain for different aircraft in the same airspace. In our scheme, using different aircraft generate different key chain to authenticate the Mac value, thus further improves the reliability of the system. Figure 4 reveals the combined authentication with different key chains is shown in Fig. 4, where $Mac_{i,n}$ represents the Mac value transmitted by the nth TESLA chain in the ith time slot.

In a word, our scheme reduces the number of Mac operations in the standard TESLA scheme by constructing a tree-chain TESLA authentication chain, and also reduces the length of the key chain, thereby reducing the computation overhead in the standard TESLA scheme. By constructing a multi-key chain data authentication mechanism, we can avoid the replay attack of attackers and accurate time synchronization. And then ensure the safety of aviation data.

4   Performance Analysis

With the purpose of appraising the performance of our proposed tree-chain authentication scheme, simulation simulations were performed on a laboratory computer (AMD Ryzen 5 3500U 2.10 GHz processor, 16.0G bytes memory, Windows 10 operating system). Firstly, we calculated the calculation time of tree-chain TESLA and compared it with the standard TESLA scheme. It shows the experimental data in Fig. 5. The experiment reveals that compared with the standard TESLA algorithm, the computational overhead of tree-chain scheme is reduced by about 4 times when the same number of ADS-B packets are processed. This is because this scheme adopts a tree-chain scheme, which uses hash operation to replace redundant HMAC operation. As shown in the above analysis, the complexity of HMAC operation is higher than that of hash operation. Therefore, our proposed tree-chain scheme is more suitable for ADS-B application scenarios with limited computing resources and high real-time data requirements.

At the same time, in order to testify the effectiveness of tree-chain scheme in data authentication of ADS-B packets, we selected an aircraft from Tianjin to

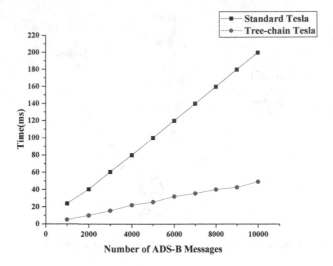

Fig. 5. Comparison of calculation time between tree-chain Tesla and standard Tesla scheme.

Nanjing and injected false information into a section of the flight path, as shown in Fig. 6. We wrote a program in python to compare MAC values of ADS-B data using the tree-chain scheme in this paper, so as to determine the authenticity of messages, and the authentication effect is shown in Fig. 7. Obviously, our method successfully removes the injected false signals and can effectively guarantee the security of aviation data.

In Table 2, we compare the performance of the standard TESLA scheme, and the tree-chain TESLA scheme proposed in this paper. Where, C_S represents the computational cost of a signature, C_V represents the computational cost of a signature verification, C_H represents the computational cost of a hash operation, C_M represents the computational cost of an HMAC operation, m is the overall number of ADS-B packets to be authenticated, n is the number of ADS-B messages in a tree structure, in an authentication architecture, there are m/n authentication trees. As shown in Table 2, by building a tree-chain structure, we reduce the computation overhead of the sender and the receiver. Meanwhile, one Mac value can authenticate several ADS-B packets, reducing the length of the key chain in the TESLA authentication architecture. In order to further reduce the latency of the receiver, the receiver can cache the authenticated hash values in the leaf nodes of the hash tree. For example, if the second leaf node of a hash tree in the chain is the first data packet to arrive, the authenticator can determine the hash value of the following nodes in the hash tree after authentication: intra-group root hashes D_i, D_2, D_1, D_2 and D_{34}. Then, when the first leaf arrives, we only need to determine whether the equation: $D_i = D_i'$ is true. If it is true, the first packet M_1 in the tree structure is credible. By caching the authenticated nodes, the computation of the receiver can be further reduced to some extent.

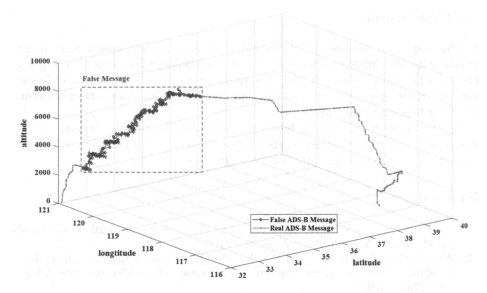

Fig. 6. ADS-B 3D track with false information injected.

Table 2. Performance comparison between tree-chain TESLA and standard TESLA scheme.

Authentication Scheme	Standard TESLA	Tree-chain TESLA
Overall Encryption Cost	$m\left(C_H + C_M\right) + C_S$	$\left(\frac{m}{n}\right)\left[(2n-1)C_H + C_H + C_M\right] + C_S$
Communication Cost/per packet	$Mac^{trunc} + K$	$\frac{Mac^{trunc}}{n} + \frac{S}{m} + Hlog_2^n + \frac{K}{n}$
Overall Verification Cost	$m\left(C_H + C_M\right) + C_V$	$\left(\frac{m}{n}\right)\left[(n + nlog_2^n + 1)C_H + C_M\right] + C_V$
Length of Key Chain	m	$\frac{m}{n}$

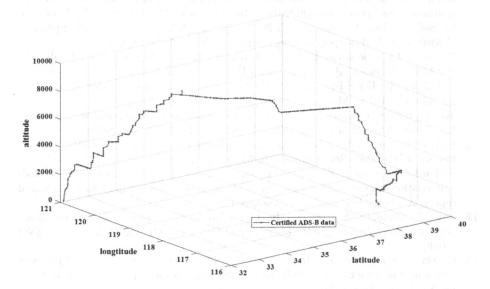

Fig. 7. ADS-B 3D track certified by our scheme.

5 Conclusion

In this paper, we design a tree-chain ADS-B data authentication scheme by combining SM2 digital signature and TESLA authentication method to respond the security vulnerabilities. At the same time, we adopt the scheme that different aircraft in the same airspace use different key chains for data authentication, which further improves the security.

In the future work, we will design certificateless state secret signature algorithm based on identity-based cryptosystem to reduce the complex certificate management process in the authentication process.

References

1. D.O.T., F.A.A.: FAA Aerospace Forecast: Fiscal Years 2013–2033. Technical report, Federal Aviation Administration (2013)
2. Wu, Z., Guo, A., Yue, M., Liu, L.: An ADS-B message authentication method based on certificateless short signature. IEEE Trans. Aerosp. Electron. Syst. **56**(3), 1742–1753 (2020)
3. Atienza, E., Falah, R., Garcia, S., Gutíerrez, L.: ADS-B: an air navigation revolution. Technical report, Universidad Rey Juan Carlos (2013)
4. Ali, B.S.: System specifications for developing an automatic dependent surveillance-broadcast (ADS-B) monitoring system. Int. J. Crit. Infr. Prot. **15**, 40–46 (2016)
5. Post, J.: The next generation air transportation system of the united states: vision, accomplishments, and future directions. Engineering **7**, 427–430 (2021)
6. Rekkas, C.: ADS-B and WAM deployment in Europe. In: Tyrrhenian International Workshop on Digital Communications - Enhanced Surveillance of Aircraft and Vehicles, Capri, pp. 35–40. IEEE (2011)
7. Schäfer, M., Lenders, V., Martinovic, I.: Experimental analysis of attacks on next generation air traffic communication. In: Jacobson, M., Locasto, M., Mohassel, P., Safavi-Naini, R. (eds.) ACNS 2013. LNCS, vol. 7954, pp. 253–271. Springer, Heidelberg (2013). https://doi.org/10.1007/978-3-642-38980-1_16
8. Slimane, H.O., Benouadah, S., Al Shamaileh, K., Devabhaktuni, V., Kaabouch, N.: ADS-B message injection attack on UAVs: assessment of SVM-based detection techniques. In: IEEE International Conference on Electro Information Technology, pp. 405–410. IEEE, Mankato (2022)
9. Wu, Z., Shang, T., Guo, A.: Security issues in automatic dependent surveillance - Broadcast (ADS-B): a survey. IEEE Access **8**, 122147–122167 (2020)
10. Pan, W.J., Feng, Z.L.: ADS-B data authentication based on ECC and X.509 certificate. J. Electron. Sci. Technol. **10**, 51–55 (2012)
11. Richard, C.: Secure ADS-B: towards airborne communications security in the federal aviation administration's next generation air transportation system. Technical report, Air Force Institute of Technology (2014)
12. Yang, H., Zhou, Q., Yao, M., Lu, R., Li, H., Zhang, X.: A practical and compatible cryptographic solution to ADS-B security. IEEE Internet Things J. **6**(2), 3322–3334 (2019)
13. Costin, A., Francillon, A.: Ghost in the air (traffic): on insecurity of ADS-B protocol and practical attacks on ADS-B devices. In: Proceedings of the Black Hat USA, pp. 1–12. Las Vegas (2012)

14. Zhou, J., Yan, J.: Secure and efficient identity-based batch verification signature scheme for ADS-B system. KSII Trans. Internet Inf. Syst. **13**(12), 6243–6259 (2019)
15. Perrig, A., Canetti, R., Tygar, J.D., Song, D.: Efficient authentication and signing of multicast streams over lossy channels. In: Proceedings of the S&P 2000, pp. 56–73. IEEE, Berkeley (2000)
16. ISO/IEC 14888–3:2018: IT Security techniques—Digital signatures with appendix—Part 3: Discrete logarithm based mechanisms (2018). https://www.iso.org/obp/ui/#iso:std:iso-iec:14888:-3:ed-4:v1:en. Accessed 12 Nov 2018

Electronic and Remote Voting Systems: Solutions to Existing Problems – An Experimental Approach to Secure Voting Platforms on Endpoints

Sagar Swamy Rajan and Neeraj Anand Sharma[✉]

Department of Computer Science and Mathematics, The University of Fiji, Lautoka, Fiji
20170003@student.unifiji.ac.fj, neerajs@unifiji.ac.fj

Abstract. The need for secure delivery solutions on endpoints has become essential as true and neutral outcomes can be provided by the systems themselves. This has arisen due to several discrepancies found in the manual voting systems and various vulnerability assessments done on the existing electronic and remote voting systems. Though these systems provide the convenience of voting using any endpoint desired, there are still loopholes that are not looked into that can harm the endpoint as well as the end user as well. The paper will be looking into the reasons why a secure endpoint delivery platform for electronic and remote voting systems is needed we experiment using a random online voting system and then test in to two phases which are the effectiveness of the antivirus software to invoke a protected browser and the second phase of the test the same online voting system on the same localhost environment by the use of the alternative of the On Vue Software such as the safe exam browser.

Keywords: Endpoint · Online Voting · Remote Voting · Security

1 Introduction

Electronic and Remote Voting systems have been around for quite some time which allows the convenience of voting to be done anywhere at any endpoint at any point in time. The availability of these systems at the polling venues has not been fully rolled out due to security concerns mainly regarding physical, network, and information security. To conclude the above-mentioned concern, a few questions and concerns must be explored.

Firstly, there are concerns about endpoint security. These concerns mainly include the physical security of the device, authentication, and whether the antivirus software installed in the endpoint has updated virus definitions. Endpoints have the typical form factors of desktops, laptops, and mobile devices such as tablets or smartphones. Secondly, the security protocols such as the Transport layer security, secure socket layer certificates, and hypertext transfer protocol secure being viable enough also come into question as threat actors now have leveled up into feigning the trust of the end user through the use of rogue protocols using techniques such as phishing attacks [1]. Thirdly, private browsing

C.-H. Hsu et al. (Eds.): DataCom 2022, LNCS 13864, pp. 178–193, 2023.
https://doi.org/10.1007/978-981-99-2233-8_13

mode is an option if any end user chooses to vote on an endpoint unfamiliar to the user as there might be fear of anonymous data collection by the web browser on the local machine on the cache data folder or a threat actor who may intercept the transmission between the host and the client on the end user thus eavesdrop or modify the contents of the transmission to carry out the desired attack. This also leads to the question whereby of a threat actor whose sole purpose is credential harvesting or eavesdropping for either malicious purposes or fun strike gold [1, 2]. The value of the information or data extracted would depend on various factors such as in the case of credential harvesting common passwords to various platforms. Other factors of value also included are the contents or information gathered through the eavesdropping activity carried out by the threat actor.

Moreover, if there is some form of endpoint security mechanisms the end-user has such as the use of antivirus software and uses the web browsers provided by the antivirus software vendor, the question of whether the end user is protected enough from the threat the users will face comes into play as well [3]. In addition, would multifactor authentication systems which are deemed very effective for protection during authentication on various platforms be able to protect the user against various attacks such as phishing or man-in-middle attacks for the threat actor to harvest credentials or obtain vital information from those credentials especially passwords from various other platforms the end user uses [4, 5, 45].

Finally, experiments in two phases will be done to test out some theories for a secure delivery platform for voting. The first test consisted of invoking a protected browser window using the antivirus software installed on a Windows-based localhost machine. In this test case, a randomly selected online voting system will be configured on the various antivirus software applications to invoke the antivirus to open the protected browser window if the address of the online voting system is centered on the address bar of the web browser. The second test case is the use of the Safe Exam Browser [1]. This Browser will be configured to allow the site to pass through and then allow the users to vote thus in theory getting to an alternative manner of using the On Vue and Respondus Lockdown Browser which would otherwise require a lot of bypasses for the site to be passed through that browser.

2   Literature Review

Similar research in this area mainly focused on how to secure the backend and authentication mechanisms. These included the remote and electronic voting applications to be developed through secure programming techniques such as DevSecOps which ensures security integrations in every stage of the software development life-cycle [6]. Other techniques included the use of blockchain technology to secure web transactions between the host and the endpoint [7]. Dual blockchain architecture has also been considered whereby the web transactions and the storing of the voting data both use different consensus algorithms [8]. Consensus algorithms such as proof of work, proof of stake, proof of burn, and proof of byzantine fault. However, when examined the proof of work and proof of stake fits the purpose of the voting systems use case [9, 10]. Proof of burn could be considered in extreme circumstances when polling outcomes have to be delivered in real-time and requirements do not need any data stores thus not requiring any audit.

Many authentication mechanisms such as the use of biometrics mainly consist of facial and fingerprint recognition and multifactor authentication systems such as the use of Captcha and One-time Passwords had also been discussed along with the level of protection they offer if implemented correctly [11, 12]. Some endpoint security methods for electronic voting terminals were also discussed such as the use of live operating systems such as Linux-based distributions or the use of windows to go which does not store any session data in the cache memory and restores itself to a clean slate state once booted [13]. However, applications such as Reboot Restore Rx which is a windows-based application that allows the endpoint to restore to the point of the first installation do provide the same functionality as a live Linux-based distribution. Other methods of authentication included the use of the Aadhar card used in India as the source of truth but in terms of the use case, it is a smart card-based authentication system that allows the user to securely login to the application along with the user credentials and start the voting process [13].

In addition, network hardening security measures such as the use of network security appliances such as firewalls which can be both stateful and stateless [14], and demilitarized zones [15] provide an extra layer of security by separating the hosts and other network appliances in an isolated network configuration from the demarcation point. But when looking at the endpoint security for electronic and remote voting platforms, both the end user and the endpoint must be secured. The end-user has to be aware of the various means to protect themselves such as phishing, spear phishing, vishing, and many more social engineering attacks which would leave the end user compromised.

Moreover, many forms of security improvement measures include such as password changes and complexity [16], multifactor authentication practices [12], and also security evaluation through the use of the antivirus software installed on the endpoint

3 Research Methodology

3.1 Why Do We Need to Secure Content Delivery Systems for Voting?

Electronic and or remote voting systems are as vulnerable as the other types of systems that are out there currently in the world. Due to the nature of the system and the information and or the data, it stores or carries is as sensitive to the level of any individual's health and financial data but to a larger scale whereby it determines a country's future. The level of security required for these systems thus needs to be higher than other systems but similar in nature to the security levels of financial data and or health data. When it comes to the question as to why there is a need for a secure content delivery platform for electronic or remote voting, there are several factors that come into play some of which may sound trivial but do play a key role in determining the necessity for it. According to Teague, electronic or remote voting systems cannot be made after research was done on how prone to cyberattacks the Australian voting system was [17]. Considered, that security measures from both the end users and the host end have to be ensured to make the systems secure. The factors which do have an effect will be explained in more detail in the latter parts of this paper. The first factor involves the end user itself and their practices in terms of authentication in general. If put into perspective in everyday life, several end users save passwords in the web browsers making it susceptible to credential harvesting either through access to the physical system itself or by the threat actor through a man-in-the-middle attack [5]. Keeping the above-mentioned in mind, the other act involves the end user willingly or voluntarily giving login credentials to any individual in terms of helping the end user out with the login and or the other processes involved in navigating or using the system itself on behalf of the user. A recent incident whereby this kind of behavior has been observed is on the mobile money platform M-Paisa whereby the users were subject to a vishing attack. This attack consisted of the threat actor impersonating Vodafone Fiji officials and asking for a onetime password from the end user, which is the only multifactor authentication mechanism to access the account to gain a financial advantage [4]. More end-user practices include the use of desk pads or notepads to write down various login credentials to various platforms. If left unattended, threat actors may inconspicuously be able to use those credentials to gain access to those systems for malicious purposes. The third factor involves the systems end or the host end which includes the use of security protocols such as Secure Socket Layer Certificates and or Transport Layer Security Certificates, and Hyper-Text Transfer Protocol Secure which are used to ensure secure content is displayed on the web browser.

In addition, the use of various security appliances such as endpoint antivirus and anti-malware software on the host machine along with other network configuration practices such as subnetting, Virtual Local Area Networking, appropriate firewall configuration whether stateful or stateless which use of intrusion detection and or prevention systems and or setting up of demilitarized zones for critical components such as the database server with the appropriate level of encryptions[43], file server, web and DNS servers [18]. Furthermore, the myth of private browsing considered to offer secure browsing experiences has also been busted [1]. The revelation came through the experiments through the use of forensic tools which were mostly for extraction of browsing activity and or possibilities of credential harvesting [19]. Private browsing by nature works in the same way the normal browsing mode works but does not store any cookies or any trackers but still leaves the user vulnerable to the attacks as in the normal browsing mode. In conjunction, web browsers provided by antivirus were also considered for the voting use case. After various studies, the only common factor which comes into play is the web browsers provided by the antivirus vendors are only effective against the threats provided that the virus definitions are updated [3].

Therefore, the need for a secure content delivery platform for electronic and or remote voting comes into the picture. This not only allows the prerequisites of the systems to be checked but also allows a secure connection between the endpoint and the host to be created once the browser window is launched. It also creates application locks to disallow any background applications which are running the application would deem that those applications are collecting data that could be sent to the threat actor [20].

3.2 Is Multifactor Authentication not a Viable Option to Secure Platform Delivery?

Multifactor authentication systems by definition are systems that allow a user to log into any system using the user credentials provided also using an alternate form of authentication typically a one-time password or secondary device authenticating smartphones or linking any account to allow secure logins to the system [12]. Many forms of multi-factor authentication include a smart card, biometric, and or token-based authentication typical with access and control systems such as doors to facilities and or corporate organizations in conjunction with active directory services [11]. These authentication mechanisms make use of role-based access control features of the active directory services. Selected web applications make use of biometric authentication such as fingerprint and facial recognition to allow access to the application to carry out role-based activities assigned to the user.

However, the question which arises after looking at the basic and or the complex nature of the multifactor authentication systems is whether is it still deemed safe or is it still prone to human error whether intentional or unintentional [21]. Human error refers to the various phishing attacks a threat actor could carry out on the end user which include social engineering attacks such as phishing, vishing, spear-phishing, and many more [45]. A recent example of a phishing attack comes from the Mobile money platform M-Paisa whereby the end users were subject to a vishing attack. This attack is carried out by impersonating the officials from Vodafone Fiji asking users to give in their identification number and their one-time password to access the account to gain financial advantage from the end user [4, 22]. Another example of a phishing attack is an online loan scam whereby the targets are individuals which are financially unstable and do not have any sort of collateral or security in order to meet the requirements of the standard loan process. In these scams the users are susceptible to get loans from shell organizations run by the threat actors and the use payment methods such as telegraphic money orders or platforms such as PayPal in order to avoid detection and continue fraudulent activities under the radar [44].

Such other examples of a phishing attack include the use of the phishing emails such as claims from individual banks about a security breach and typically asking for a password reset provided by a link given by the threat actor which redirects to the rogue host used by the threat actor for credential harvesting. Fingerprint harvesting also is a type of attack whereby the fingerprints of the individual could also be harvested based on the objects the target individual has touched and used to login into the systems along with the already harvested credentials.

Fingerprint smudge spoofing is another type of attack used to guess the commonly pressed letters, numbers, or symbols, is to determine the patterns of the credentials used mostly applicable on smart devices or the commonly used letters or numbers on the keyboard [23].

Physical credential harvesting methods include the installation of keyloggers into systems or the search and discovery of credentials written on desk pads, notepads, and or pieces of paper. All of these above mentioned are some of the techniques and ways which could be used to defeat multifactor authentication systems along with man-in-middle-attacks. According to Grimes, in an initial presentation whereby 12 ways showed how multifactor authentication systems could be defeated through the use of tools such as Brute force, freezing of hardware components such as memory sticks, and many more [24].

3.3 Do Antivirus Web Browsers Provide Protection for Voting?

The antivirus software is only deemed to be effective in its disinfection powers if only the virus definitions are updated [3]. Similarly, the web browsers provided by the vendors themselves rely on the virus definitions of the software to be effective in securing against the cyber threats current and emerging [3]. The functionality of these web browsers remains the same throughout with the added functionality of the antivirus software integration running in the background. Most of these browsers come with the browsers compressed within the online installer software itself. If the browsers are not present in the installer package, then the installer package would suggest a web browser to be installed on the computer which would download via the download manager integrated into the installer package.

Typical examples of the web browsers recommended to be installed by the software are mostly Google Chrome or Opera. These direct download installers from the antivirus software installer package also allow the antivirus security extensions to be automatically installed in the background initialize when the web browser is launched. However, standalone offline installers of the software do not offer these services as offline installers are typically used for faster installation of the software and or used for installation on end points with no internet connectivity during the time of the installation. In the case of the post-installation of the antivirus software and the launch of the application such as the web browser a prompt for the activation of the security extensions for the protection services to begin or would require manual installation of the security extensions to be installed in the web browsers and then manually start the service. Some vendors offer a protected browsing window without additional web browser software.

It uses the same web browser but opens an additional browser window establishing a secure connection between the host and the endpoint acting as intrusion prevention, and intrusion detection, the firewall also performs the duties of the antivirus role protecting the user from cyberattacks such as phishing, invalid or expired certificates, malware and many more [14]. Other functionalities provided are secure keyboards and password managers which use encrypted passwords to allow secure logins into the web application. This kind of security is typically present for sites such as social media, and communication if enabled but come pre-activated for site types such as eCommerce sites and online banking [25].

However, it has also been noted that sites that deal with telemedicine or online patient information systems and also in this case electronic and remote voting are yet to receive the kind of protection offered for the protested browsers by the antivirus vendors as these applications do have very sensitive data and in the hands of the threat actors could wreak havoc for the individual whose data has been extracted or the organization if batches of information have been extracted from the system [3].

3.4 Are TLS, SSL, and HTTPS Are not Viable Options for Voting Platforms?

Security protocols and or authentication certificates such as Secure Socket Layer, Transport Layer Security, and Hyper-Text Transfer Protocol Secure are some of the protocols which are used in web applications websites to make them secure for the end user to access them securely at the desired endpoints [26]. These protocols by nature operate with the transport layer of the open systems interconnect model to achieve security and packet transmission efficiency. The SSL/TLS protocols work by obtaining digital certificates from a certificate authority that authenticates using a set of private and public keys. These keys authenticate and verify the validity of the certificates [26].

However, some studies have shown that rogue protocols could also be used by threat actors to make the connections secure to the rogue host through the use of phishing techniques [27]. These make use of the same authentication mechanisms used by the genuine certificates but changes in the address or encryption methods which redirect the end user to the rogue host [1]. Even though SSL certificates could be freely obtained via the certificate authorities it still needs to be verified and validated to know whether the certificate obtained is genuine or not. These could be done through the use of SSL certificate checker tools which would also allow for detecting anomalies with the certificate installation as well as checking for common vulnerabilities [28]. Moreover, antivirus software also plays a vital role in checking the validity of the certificate as shown in an example in Fig. 2, and other common vulnerabilities, therefore protecting the end user and the endpoint from any looming threats that the site might be carrying [18]. Therefore, the emphasis on updating the virus definitions is given as antivirus protection is only as effective if the virus signatures are present in the virus definitions database [3].

4 Experiment

4.1 Test Case Theories

The test case theories are first to initialize the protected browsers offered by the antivirus software vendors. The criteria for this test phase are as follows.

A. Phase 1

i.   Antivirus software to be installed either as trial or as paid editions (trial editions would be used for this test case)

- Common antivirus solution vendors to be used. This would be products vendors commonly used by the individuals in the fiji market base.

ii. After installation virus definitions to be updated to the latest virus definitions

- This is to ensure that the updated virus definitions would enable to detect the threats which would otherwise have been missed by the previous antivirus solutions installed on the localhost environment. *Additionally, a full scan of the localhost machine has been done as well to allow these threats to be detected.*

iii. The antivirus software settings to be configured to allow the protected browser to be initialized once the address of the systems is entered.

- This is to allow the site to be detected and then apply the appropriate protection levels as configured in the application settings. These settings refer to the hardened security levels provided by each antivirus solution software. *All of the antivirus solutions used for the test had been configured to maximum security levels in order to get detections done at an aggressive scale for the threats.*

iv. A table to be used in order to store results with columns labelled, antivirus software, edition used, virus definitions updated, protected browser available and whether the site was able to invoke the protected browser mode after the address of the system was entered into the web browser.

- The table reduces the need for the screenshots to be provided as the results are encapsulated in the table with the above-mentioned criteria as the headers. **Screenshots have been taken in order to keep as reference.**

B. Phase 2

i. The safe exam browser to be acquired from the official website
ii. Browser to be installed and configured in order to allow the site to parse and then allow the site to be displayed and surfed.
iii. Demonstration of how the site works with safe exam browser.

4.2   Test Case 1 – Configuration and Use of Antivirus Solutions for Protected Browser Mode

In this test, the system was configured on a windows-based localhost environment on a physical machine with a windows 11 operating system. For the site to be accessed, the XAMPP stack [2] had to be installed for the system to work. A set of files provided by the system developer which also included the database which had to be with the system to be configured with MySQL and then the system to initialized by invoking the web root address of the system stored in the htdocs folder in the Apache install directory on the local disk.

The antivirus solutions used are trial editions of the premium range of the antivirus software range as the free editions do not provide the functionality which is required in order to carry out the test. This experiment will also answer the factors of how effective the various antivirus solutions when it comes to endpoint security. Exceptions to the test made that the common antivirus software vendor solutions being used in the fiji market base have been used and the same localhost machine being used for each test. No virtual machines were used in order to carry out this test.

Criteria above-mentioned has been used in order to make sure that test results can be deemed valid in integrity of the test not being compromised.

In addition to the criteria, a full scan of the local host machine was also done in order to find out threats present on the machine in order to prove the point of effectiveness of the antivirus software after which a full scan was done with malware bytes antimalware in order to see if any threats were left out by the antivirus software scans (Table 1).

Table 1. The test results as shown in the table below

Antivirus Software Name	Edition Used	Trial/Free/Licensed	Virus Definitions Updated	Protected Browser Available	Protected Browser Initiated	Full Scan Run After Installation
Kaspersky	Total Security	Licensed	Yes	Yes (Kaspersky Safe Money)	Yes	Yes
Eset	Endpoint Security	Trial	Yes	Yes	Yes	Yes
Avira	Prime	Trial	Yes	Yes (as add on)	No	Yes
BitDefender	Total Security	Trial	Yes	Yes (Bit Defender Safe Pay)	Yes	Yes
Avast	Premium Security	Trial	Yes	Yes (as add on)	No (Blocked All Apache Ports)	Yes
McAfee	Total Protection	Trial	Yes	Yes (as add on)	No(Extension did not detect site)	Yes
Trend Micro	Internet Security	Trial	Yes	Yes (as add on)	Yes	Yes
Norton	360 plus	Trial	Yes	No	No(Trial expired after few minutes of installation)	Yes
Sophos	Home Premium	Trial	Yes	Yes (as add on)	Yes	Yes
AVG	Internet Security	Trial	Yes	Yes(As add on)	Yes	Yes
Total AV	Pro	Trial	Yes	No	No (Protected Browser Function Not Available)	Yes
Comodo	Internet Security	Trial	yes	No	No (Protected Browser Function Not Available)	Yes

(*continued*)

Table 1. (*continued*)

Antivirus Software Name	Edition Used	Trial/Free/Licensed	Virus Definitions Updated	Protected Browser Available	Protected Browser Initiated	Full Scan Run After Installation
Smadav	Pro	Trial	Yes	No	No (Protected Browser Function Not Available)	Yes
Panda	Pro	Trial	Yes	Yes(As add on)	Yes	Yes
360	Total Security	Trial	Yes	Yes(As add on)	No(Extension did not detect site)	Yes

As shown in the table above, the eleven out of fifteen antivirus solutions have protected browser functionalities as separate browsers or as extensions which could be installed on the web browsers and eight out fifteen antivirus solutions were not able to invoke the protected browsers due to the reasons being either not having the feature, mis-advertised trial times or the ports have been blocked even after the exception being added to firewall to allow the ports or the resource.

These in turn tends to make a very good validation across the range of the antivirus software as to features which could be deemed necessary to be inclusive into the free versions of the antivirus software as well as many end users would not want to get subscriptions to these solutions.

During the testing period, discoveries of many features of various antivirus software have also been explored to find out the other functionalities which the vendors have to offer apart from the basic antivirus software functions.

However, it has been found that subscription-based models for antivirus solutions tend to provide more customization options in terms of the level of protection needed by the end user.

4.3 Test Case 2 – Using the Safe Exam Browser

For this test to be carried out, windows 11-based localhost environment which was a physical machine. The safe exam browser will be installed and configured for the site to be parsed through the browser and used the site on the browser with the levels of security provided by the browser. The browser has also been reconfigured to allow multiple displays for capturing the screenshots required for this particular test. Safe exam browser is known to be a secure examination delivery platform similar to the one used by Pearson Vue or Respondus Lockdown Browser [1]. This browser is an open-source and free alternative to the above mentioned and provides the same functionality whether paired with a learning management system or used as a standalone browser. The test for this phase is to parse the site through the browser and demonstrate the use of the site in a secure content delivery browser such as Safe Exam Browser. The images below show the configuration of the browser and the site after being parsed through the browser (Fig. 1, Fig. 2, Fig. 3).

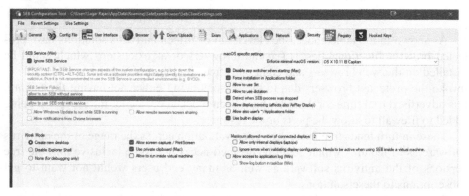

Fig. 1. Safe Exam Browser Configuration

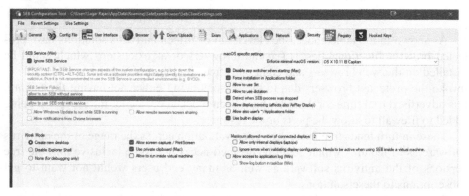

Fig. 2. Additional Safe Exam Browser configuration required for the test

Fig. 3. Online Voting System showed on the Safe Exam Browser

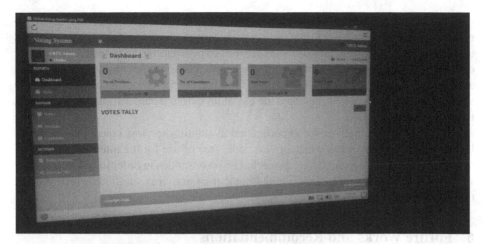

Fig. 4. Inside the site after login on the Safe Exam Browser

As shown above, the site can parse through the Safe Exam Browser successfully. With the required configuration being done. This is done for the demonstration purposes of what kind of secure delivery platforms are needed for electronic or remote voting purposes on the various endpoint.

5 Challenges Faced

The challenges which were faced in the duration of this research and experimental approach the firstly narrowing down the already broad area of the endpoint to just the desktop-based endpoint so that the scope of the research was not broad and could be done within the time frame given. Literary works were especially difficult to find as to get the appropriate papers the topics were broken down into very minute aspects. These included the searches from various web searches which included the use of google scholar, IEEE explore, Springer, ProQuest Access provided by the University of Fiji, various vendors, and trusted websites and blogs which have provided sources from various research papers or journals and books which would then be reviewed and then information being sorted out and disseminated in the paper accordingly.

Online voting systems which are free and or could be used for demonstration purposes on both GitHub and normal web searches and the configuration of the servers and the software required which include the use of XAMPP, WAMP, Moodle, and Respondus Lockdown Browser. This includes the bypassing of various mechanisms so that the site could be parsed through the lockdown browser without the use of Moodle. The configuration of the antivirus software in this case Kaspersky Total Security Safe Money Application [27] to demonstrate the use of the protected browser when the web address of the site has been entered into the address bar of the web browser. Acquisition of the Athena-based exam delivery browser from Pearson Vue had proved to be unsuccessful due to proprietary software issues and the denial of the request due to the purpose being deemed as non-neutral in nature.

Bypassing the Respondus Lockdown browser to work without a Learning Management System took a lot of time and did not yield any of the desired outcomes which led to the alternative of using the safe exam browser to be used for the purpose intended for demonstration. Taking Screenshots while the browser sessions are running. Even though as shown in Fig. 4 the allow screenshots option has been checked it still did not allow any screenshots to be taken therefore the use of an external camera was required to get the screenshots required.

Looking for alternatives for experimental evaluation for test phase 2 as there are limited number of browsers which are available free of use for the intended purposes.

Antivirus solutions which have protected browser modes in order to increase sample size of test phase 1 as there are a limited number of antivirus solutions which provide that functionality.

6 Future Works and Recommendations

The future works for this experiment in the case of future researchers are for the further study onto development of more secure platforms of voting. This however would be possible as there would be many more tools or resources available which would enable much better outcomes than what is being derived or done today. In addition, the other factor which also must be considered is that when in the development of any system or platform both the back and front ends are equally important and should be secured adequately. This could be achieved by an emphasis on secure programming techniques to be implemented or reviews to be done whilst the software in question is being developed using DevSecOps.

Moreover, emphasis on cybersecurity awareness and human training in terms of how humans can be defended against the various phishing attacks carried out by the threat actors. Trainings like these would also enable users to tackle the real-life situations which would also allow them to differentiate between a scam or phishing attack such as vishing in order to not fall prey to the threat actors trap again putting the emphasis on very attacked people [45].

This is important not for only the online voting platform but for various systems which the end-user has access on day-to-day way of life as the digital world is now the normal which has been embraced during the covid and post-covid times.

The emphasis on endpoint security is also important in this part as well as these are assets that contain data gold. The data gold in this aspect relates access to databases which contain critical information about any user or individual which could be used by the threat actor in order to gain financial advantage directly from the end user in the form of ransom or sell them to other threat actors or organizations again for financial benefits.

Endpoints in this case also refer to the devices the end users use on the day-to-day way of life as well as the hosts which allow access to client endpoints.

7 Conclusion

If there were any means to secure any systems then the first thing to secure is the human aspect as the human is the weakest link in any system which is out there. This is the concept of very attacked people as anybody could be considered as a risk regardless of their status [45]. As threat actors gain more insight into various authentication and social engineering techniques, awareness, prevention and adoption of protective cybersecurity measures are key. In the case of the electronic and remote voting systems, the human link would be the most important in making decisions to bring into power the people they trust. The above-mentioned are various factors that have explained why is there a need for a secure delivery platform for voting. Phase one of the tests has concluded that the platform can be invoked by the antivirus software to be switched to a protected browser regardless of the web browser used by the antivirus software solutions as it works with all web browsers While phase two used an alternative approach to using the On Vue software which is the Safe Exam Browser. This test also succeeded as the site was able to parse through the browser and allow the site to be displayed and used as intended thus demonstrating the means of a secure content delivery platform. Even though there were many challenges faced as above-mentioned, it was a great experiment to work on to show the importance of endpoint security and the use case of the secure content delivery platform for systems such as electronic or remote voting. However, this could also serve as an idea for other critical systems such as the Patient Information Systems.

References

1. KeyFactor: HTTPS Phishing Attacks: How Hackers Use SSL Certificates to Feign Trust – Keyfactor. 11 Oct 2021. [Online]. Available: https://www.keyfactor.com/blog/https-phishing-attacks-how-hackers-use-ssl-certificates-to-feign-trust/. Accessed 28 Aug 2022
2. A study on private browsing in windows environment. Zulfaqar J. Def. Sci. Eng. Technol. **3**(1), 15–22 (2020)
3. Shoeb, M.: Is private browsing in modern web browsers private? Jan (2018)
4. Wu, Y., Gupta, P., Wei, M., Acar, Y., Fahl, S., Ur, B.:Your secrets are safe: how browsers' explanations impact misconceptions about private browsing mode. In: WWW 2018, Lyon, France (2018)
5. Delaney, J.: The effectiveness of antivirus software, Aug (2020)
6. F. News: Do not share M-PAiSA PIN and OTP – FBC News. Fiji Broadcasting Corporation, 20 Sep 2022. [Online]. Available: https://www.fbcnews.com.fj/business/do-not-share-m-paisa-pin-and-otp/. Accessed 25 Sep 2022
7. Mallik, A.: Man-in-the-middle-attack: understanding in simple words. J. Pendidikan Teknologi Informasi **2**(2), 109–134 (2018)
8. VMware: What is DevSecOps? I DevSecOps vs. DevOps I VMware. [Online]. Available: https://www.vmware.com/topics/glossary/content/devsecops.html. Accessed 25 Aug 2022
9. National Institute of Standards and Technology: Blockchain I NIST. National Institute of Standards and Technology [Online]. Available: https://www.nist.gov/blockchain. Accessed 14 May 2022
10. Enhancing electronic voting with a dual-blockchain architecture. Ledger 6 (2021)
11. Douglas, J.: Proof-of-stake (PoS)Iethereum.org. Ethereum.org, 14 June 2022 [Online]. Available: https://ethereum.org/en/developers/docs/consensus-mechanisms/pos/. Accessed 16 June 2022
12. Hooda, P.: Proof of work (PoW) consensus – GeeksforGeeks. GeeksForGeeks, 11 May 2022 [Online]. Available: https://www.geeksforgeeks.org/proof-of-work-pow-consensus/?ref=lbp. Accessed 22 May 2022

13. Ahmad, M.: Security, usability, and biometric authentication scheme for electronic voting multiple keys. Int. J. Distrib. **16**(7), 16 (2020)
14. Microsoft Corporation: What is: Multifactor Authentication. Microsoft Corporation [Online]. Available: https://support.microsoft.com/en-us/topic/what-is-multifactor-authentication-e5e 39437-121c-be60-d123-eda06bddf661. Accessed 3 June 2022
15. Adewale Olumide S., Boyinbode Olutayo, K., Adekunle, S.E.: A review of electronic voting systems: strategy for a novel. Inf. Eng. Electron. Bus. 12 (2020)
16. Cisco: What is a firewall? – Cisco [Online]. Available: https://www.cisco.com/c/en/us/pro ducts/security/firewalls/what-is-a-firewall.html. Accessed 28 Sep 2022
17. Barracuda Networks: What is a DMZ (networking) |Barracuda Networks [Online]. Available: https://www.barracuda.com/glossary/dmz-network. Accessed 28 Sep 2022
18. National Institute of Standards and Technology: NIST Special Publication 800-63B. NIST, June 2017 [Online]. Available: https://pages.nist.gov/800-63-3/sp800-63b.html. Accessed 25 June 2022
19. Porup, J.: Online voting is impossible to secure. So why are some-CSO. CSO, 2 May 2018? [Online]. Available: https://www.csoonline.com/article/3269297/online-voting-is-imp ossible-to-secure-so-why-are-some-governments-using-it.html. Accessed 27 Aug 2022
20. National Institute of Standards and Technology: Securing web transactions TLS server certificate management. NIST Special Publication 1800-16, June (2020)
21. Lim, J.: SOK: on the analysis of web browser security. arXiv, 31 Dec 2021
22. R. MALWADE: VIRTUAL BROWSER May 2020
23. Das, S., Wang, B., Tingle, Z., Camp, L.J.: Evaluating user perception of multi-factor authentication: a systematic review. In: Proceedings of the Thirteenth International Symposium on Human Aspects of Information Security and Assurance, 19 Aug 2019
24. Dawabsheh, A., Eleyan, D., Jazzar, M., Eleyan, A.: Social engineering attacks: a phishing case simulation. Int. J .Sci. Technol. Res. **10**(3) (2021)
25. Saguy, M., Almog, J., Cohn, D., Champod, C.: Proactive forensic science in biometrics: Novel materials for finger- print spoofing. Wiley Online Library, 7 Oct 2021
26. Grimes, R.: KB. KnowBe4 [Online]. Available: https://www.knowbe4.com/hubfs/KB4-11W aystoDefeat2FA-RogerGrimes.pdf. Accessed 28 Aug 2022
27. Kaspersky Labs Gmbh: Safe Money [Online]. Available: https://support.kaspersky.com/KIS 4Mac/16.0/en.lproj/pgs/85291.htm. Accessed 25 Aug 2022
28. Internet Society: What is TLS & how does it work?|ISOC Internet Society. Internet Society [Online]. Available: https://www.internetsociety.org/deploy360/tls/basics/. Accessed 1 June 2022
29. National Institute of Standards and Technology: PHISHING|NIST, 24 Feb 2022. [Online]. Available: https://www.nist.gov/itl/smallbusinesscyber/guidance-topic/phishing. Accessed 21 Aug 2022
30. McKay, K.A.: NIST.SP.800-52r2.pdf, Aug 2019 [Online]. Available: https://www.goo gle.com/url?sa=t&rct=j&q=&esrc=s&source=web&cd=&ved=2ahUKEwiFtNz447b6AhUc yzgGHep5DqAQFnoECAMQAQ&url=https%3A%2F%2Fnvlpubs.nist.gov%2Fnistpubs% 2FSpecialPublications%2FNIST.SP.800-52r2.pdf&usg=AOvVaw3m4Wk8V1Z0pHz8X850 XTp5. Accessed 5 Sep 2022
31. U.S. Department of Justice: Identity theft. U.S. Department of Justice [Online]. Available: https://www.justice.gov/criminal-fraud/identity-theft/identity-theft-and-identity-fraud. Accessed 5 June 2022
32. Shahzad, B., Crowcroft, J.: Trustworthy electronic voting using adjusted blockchain technology. IEEE Access **7**(24488), 12 (2019)
33. Qureshi, A., Megías, D., Rifà-Pous, H.: SeVEP:secure and verifiable. IEEE Explore **7**, 19266–19290 (2019)

34. Newell, S.: Online Voting Threatens. AAAS EPI Center (2021)
35. Peifer, D.: SSL_Spoofing-OWASP [Online]. Available: https://owasp.org/www-pdf-archive/ SSL_Spoofing.pdf. Accessed 7 Sep 2022
36. Irshad, S.: Identity theft and social media. Int. J. Comput. Sci. Netw. Security **18**(1), 43–55 (2018)
37. Hamad, M.: Mitigation of the effect of standard networks attacks in SSL encrypted traffic by encrypted traffic analysis. VFAST Trans. Math. **6**(1), 15–22 (2018)
38. Carnegie Mellon University: The official CAPTCHA site. Carnegie Mellon University (2010) [Online]. Available: http://www.captcha.net/. Accessed 1 June 2022
39. Kaspersky Gmbh: Safe money, 7 Feb 2022. [Online]. Available: https://support.kaspersky. com/KIS4Mac/16.0/en.lproj/pgs/85291.htm. Accessed 22 Aug 2022
40. Noronha, C.: Online voting system (2021)
41. ETH Zurich, Educational Development and Technology (LET): Safe exam browser – about (2021–2022). [Online]. Available: https://safeexambrowser.org/about_overview_en. html. Accessed 15 Oct 2022
42. Apache Friends: About the XAMPP Project (2022) [Online]. Available: https://www.apache friends.org/about.html. Accessed 11 Oct 2022
43. Praneeta Prakash, P.P.M.: Cybercrime threats loom, Fiji Broadcasting Corporation (2022). Available at: https://www.fbcnews.com.fj/news/new-cyber-threats-to-emerge-with-developing-technologies/. Accessed 11 Oct 2022
44. Kreetika Kumar, K.K.M.: Fijians lose thousands due to cyber-loan scam, Fiji Broadcasting Corporation. Available at: https://www.fbcnews.com.fj/news/fijians-lose-thousands-due-to-cyber-loan-scam/. Accessed 11 Oct 2022
45. Choi, T.: Gaining the advantage over attackers: How very attacked people figure into your security equation, Proofpoint (2022). Available at: https://www.proofpoint.com/us/corpor ate-blog/post/gaining-advantage-over-attackers-how-very-attacked-people-figure-your-sec urity. Accessed 3 Nov 2022

Research on the Mechanism of Cooperative Defense Against DDoS Attacks Based on Game Theory

Tong Wang[1], Zihan Lai[2], Weiqing Yu[2], and Zhijun Wu[2(✉)]

[1] College of Electronic Information and Automation, Civil Aviation University of China, Tianjin, China
2021021023@cauc.edu.cn
[2] College of Safety Science and Engineering, Civil Aviation University of China, Tianjin, China
zjwu@cauc.edu.cn

Abstract. Distributed Denial of Service (DDoS) attacks are one of the biggest threats in the era of cloud computing and big data. This paper mainly studies the defense methods of DDoS attacks for cloud computing platforms and big data centers, proposes a cooperative defense DDoS attack mechanism based on game theory, and studies the DDoS attack defense methods based on Software Defined Network (SDN) to ensure the security of cloud computing platforms and big data centers.

Keywords: DDoS attacks · Game theory · SDN · Collaborative

1 Introduction

1.1 A Subsection Sample

DDoS attack is a distributed and coordinated large-scale attack. It mainly attacks influential websites, such as websites of commercial companies, search engines, and government departments, and is highly destructive. Well-constructed attacks can even reach 600 Gbps of attack traffic, enough to flood the access bandwidth of any network platform. In the face of such a large-scale DDoS attacks, a single defense system is almost powerless, causing huge economic losses and negative social impacts.

The traffic of DDoS attacks is normal and behaves naturally, using the open structure of the network to allow attack packets to reach any selected target. Therefore, the solution to defend against DDoS attacks has always been a difficult problem in the field of network security research. The main reason for DDoS attacks is the lack of effective control and authentication mechanisms in the current network. This research uses SDN technology and uses a dedicated SDN controller to manage and control all functions of virtual and physical networks. Since SDN security policy realizes the security isolation and control of network traffic, it supports deeper packet analysis, network monitoring and traffic control, which is very beneficial for defending against network attacks.

C.-H. Hsu et al. (Eds.): DataCom 2022, LNCS 13864, pp. 194–203, 2023.
https://doi.org/10.1007/978-981-99-2233-8_14

This paper proposes a cooperative mechanism for DDoS attacks defense based on game theory [3] and a method for DDoS attacks defense based on SDN. By applying SDN to the control and cleaning scheme of DDoS attack traffic, SDN's visualization and flexible control over the network can quickly discover the source of attack traffic, and effectively control the traffic of DDoS attack at the source, network and victim ends, so as to achieve rapid blocking. At the same time, by using the "agile" feature of SDN, intelligent drainage and cleaning can also be achieved to realize the goal of effectively defending against DDoS attacks [4]5.

This paper is divided into four parts, and the organization of the remaining parts is as follows: Sect. 2 classifies and summarizes the problems in the currently existing DDoS attack defense methods, and then analyzes the development trend of DDoS attack defense research; Sect. 3 proposes a defense model of DDoS attack based on game theory, which is a cooperative defense system of multiple defense subjects and is fully competent for DDoS attack detection and defense; Sect. 4 summarizes the work done in this paper.

2 Analysis of Research Status and Development Trends

From the large-scale outbreak in 1998 to the rampant in 2016, the scale of DDoS attacks continued to rise, approaching 1 Tbps, constantly challenging the Internet's defense measures and systems. Attackers are constantly seeking new methods and vectors that can cause network-crippling attacks. At present, in addition to the five major carriers of HTTP/s, DNS (DNSSEC), TCP, UDP and GRE, there are also many new attack vectors such as Black-Nurse and ICMP attacks [1, 2], and the Internet of Things (IoT) has also become an important means for attackers to organize botnets. The cruel reality of network attacks (similar to the DDoS attack incident on the US Internet in the early morning of October 22, 2016) shows that the existing defense mechanisms against DDoS attacks have certain defects, and new defense mechanisms and methods need to be further studied.

2.1 Problems (Defect Analysis)

No matter how DDoS attacks evolve, their organization remains the same. It always adopts a hierarchical structure model, including: Attackers, Handlers, Bots, and Victims. From the perspective of network layering, they can be divided into three components: the attack source end, the attack network end (accomplice network and puppet network) and the attack victim end [5]. Therefore, from the perspective of defending against DDoS attacks, the defense methods can be classified into three types according to the location of defense deployment: source-oriented defense, network-oriented defense, and victim-oriented defense [2].

At present, according to the form of defense against DDoS attacks and the location of defense deployment, existing defenses can be classified into centralized, distributed, single, and hybrid. Most of the current research results are to propose a new type of hybrid defense mechanism, because it has been proved that deploying a centralized defense system at a single defense location is difficult to achieve the desired defense effect. The hybrid (distributed) defense mechanism is currently the best way to defend against DDoS attacks. It is a measure against DDoS attacks that cooperates with multiple defense nodes deployed in different locations, and can complete the detection, response and defense of DDoS attacks in real time. The ultimate goal of hybrid defense is to detect DDoS attacks as early as possible before they reach the victim, accurately identify the source of the attack, and prevent DDoS attacks at the source. According to the analysis of the above research status, it is concluded that there are certain problems in the current defense mechanism.

Defense Method Based on Source Side. The goal of source-based defense methods is to detect and filter attack traffic at the attack source, preventing network users from being involved in DDoS attacks.

There are three main reasons why the defense method based on the origin of the attack source is not effective. First, the attack sources are widely distributed in different domains, so it is difficult to accurately detect and filter the attack traffic for each attack source; Second, at the origin of the attack, the attack traffic flows from various distribution locations like a turbulent stream into the normal traffic, and has not yet converged into a large damaged traffic, so it is difficult to distinguish the normal traffic from the illegal traffic; Third, deploying defense systems at the source is highly controversial and expensive.

Defense Method Based on Network Side. The defense method based on attacking the network side is mainly deployed inside the network, and is mainly installed in the routers of each autonomous domain. Its purpose is to detect and prevent DDoS attacks in the intermediate network to achieve the best defense against DDoS attacks.

Problems existing in the defense method based on attacking the network side: First, it usually occupies a large storage space and brings high processing overhead to the router. Moreover, when the router performs redundant detection and response along the attack path, the memory space and processor overhead will become larger, bringing a huge additional burden to the router.

Defense Method Based on Destination Side. The defense method based on the destination side is mainly deployed at the end of the network, at the front end of the attacked victim, and directly faces the large-scale attack traffic.

Existing defense methods based on attack targets all have problems: First, the defects of low detection rate and delayed response; Second, setting defenses along the attack path, resulting in a waste of network resources on the attack path; Third, unable to deal with huge attack traffic causes a large proportion of attack traffic to reach the victim.

The above three defense methods only complete defense at a single end and belong to centralized defense methods. Due to the lack of effective cooperative communication means between the end and the end, the three ends cannot be united together, so their defensive effects are limited.

Defense Method Based on Hybrid Operation. The hybrid defense method combines the attack source side, network side and victim side defenses to complete the defense at the three ends [7]. The existing hybrid defense methods have certain shortcomings: first, due to the need to maintain coordinated communication between defense points distributed on the entire network, it occupies a large amount of resources and has certain complexity; second, due to the different suppliers of network equipment, the specifications and interfaces among various network equipment are not unified, and it is difficult to form a coordinated defense system; third, in order to ensure the coordination between various defense points, it is necessary to ensure trusted communication between each device.

2.2 Analysis of Development Trend

Most of the attack detection algorithms for DDoS in the current research results are applied to the victim end of the attack, which can only achieve the detection effect and cannot resist the attack [6]. This paper proposes to use the characteristics of centralized control of SDN architecture to realize real-time monitoring of traffic at the source of the attack. At the same time, it realizes abnormal detection of access layer and abnormal detection of link traffic, thus forming a multi-defense system. It can detect attacks as early as possible, gradually filter DDoS attack traffic, and realize the detection and defense of DDoS attacks at the network layer at the source side.

According to the current research results, the defense against DDoS attack traffic mostly adopts the technology of "traffic pulling + cleaning". Traditional traffic diversion is based only on the shortest route, regardless of whether the traffic diversion path has enough available bandwidth to accommodate attack traffic, which will cause congestion on the links involved in the diversion path. It is equivalent to further amplifying the attack effect of DDoS. Based on SDN defense against DDoS attacks, the calculation of the diversion path should not only consider the shortest path, but also comprehensively consider the maximum available bandwidth of the diversion path and the maximum available bandwidth of the cleaning center. And use multi-path diversion to disperse the traffic at the source of the attack, making "traffic cleaning" more efficient, and ensuring the smoothness of the network.

Looking at the current research results, the development trend of DDoS attack defense research is shown in the following aspects:

- Since DDoS attacks are widely distributed, effective distributed solutions must be adopted for their defense. Therefore, the coordinated defense scheme of the source, the network, and the destination is adopted.
- The proposed DDoS attack defense mechanism must have the function of defending against external and internal attacks at the same time, has good scalability, and can be widely used.
- Propose a systematic defense against DDoS attacks, which can solve the problems caused by DDoS attacks from the perspective of the system, and the defense system cannot cause damage to normal user traffic.

The cooperative defense system meets the above requirements. It combines the game theory of attack and defense with the SDN structure, and can provide high-end network confrontation and monitoring functions for the complex giant network environment. Based on game theory, the attributes of various data packets can be distinguished through

SDN controllers and switches. At the same time, it combines source address authentication (preventing IP spoofing) and filtering technology to complete detection at the victim end, response at the source end and defense at the network end to achieve the best comprehensive defense effect and achieve defense against DDoS attacks [9].

3 Defense Against DDoS Attacks Based on Game Theory

The types of DDoS attacks (rates and carrier protocols, etc.) are constantly changing, but their organizational form has not changed. Usually, attackers launch large-scale and destructive attacks on victims through handlers controlling batches of puppet machines [8].

3.1 Overall Design Idea

The research of DDoS attacks model includes two contents:

- Organizational Model of DDoS Attack. From the perspective of organizational structure, it mainly studies the specific form of DDoS attack, and analyzes the relationship between attackers, handlers, puppets and victims in the DDoS attack hierarchy. They are divided into three components: the source side, the attack network side (the handlers network and the puppet network), and the destination side. The characteristics of normal traffic and attack traffic of the network in the three terminals are respectively studied.
- The Generation Model of DDoS Attack. From the perspective of big data analysis of network traffic, study the inherent non-linear relationship between organizations of various layers of DDoS attack, reveal the process of DDoS attack traffic inflow and aggregation, and analyze the characteristics of attack traffic changes throughout the attack process. Aiming at the distributed characteristics and hierarchical organization structure of DDoS attacks, the mechanism of collaborative defense against DDoS attacks proposed in this paper is shown in Fig. 1.

Figure 1, a model-driven game between DDoS attack and defense is designed to achieve end-to-end confrontation under the coordinated defense mechanism.

Aiming at the three-end network of DDoS attacks, analyze the game process between attack and defense in the three-end network, design an end-to-end cooperative defense system for DDoS attacks, and study the possibility of the defense system between the attack source side, the network side and the victim side. Based on information communication and cooperative operation, a cooperative DDoS attacks defense model under the framework of SDN is proposed. The model research of cooperative defense against DDoS attacks includes four contents:

- Defense mechanism: research the cooperation mode between the defense systems between the terminals.
- Collaborative communication: research the trusted communication between the defense systems between the terminals [10].

- Attack-defense game: study the game relationship between attack and defense in the three-end network.
- Defense architecture: study the architecture of defense against DDoS attacks that includes attack traffic control, analysis, and filtering technologies under the SDN framework.

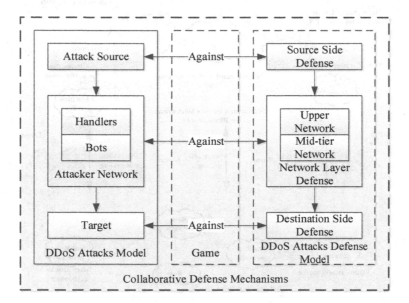

Fig. 1. DDoS attack collaborative defense mechanism.

3.2 Collaborative Defense Scheme

According to the main research content formulated, this paper designs a game theory-based defense against DDoS attacks. The DDoS attacks defense model based on SDN architecture proposed in this paper is based on game theory, which is called the multi-layer network game model MNADG (Multi-Network Attack Defense Game), as shown in Fig. 2.

The model shown in Fig. 2 is a defense system in which multiple defense entities (source defense, network defense, and destination defense) cooperate. It comprehensively considers the means and strategies available to both the offensive and defensive sides, as well as their corresponding benefits and costs. That is to calculate the Nash equilibrium of the mixed strategies adopted by both attackers and defenders, and obtain an ideal coordinated defense strategy with good defense effect and reasonable defense cost.

In the game model of Fig. 2, the attacking and defending sides are set as a $ADG = (N, S, U)$. Among them, the $N = (P_1, P_2, \cdots\cdots, P_n)$ subset is the set of game subjects, that is, the decision-making subjects involved in the game by both offense and defense, and the makers of the strategies on both sides of the offense and defense; $S = (S_1, S_2, \cdots\cdots, S_n)$ the subset is the set of strategies of the game subjects; it is the set $U = (U_1, U_2, \cdots\cdots, U_n)$ of utility functions, which includes Different benefits and costs for different strategies.

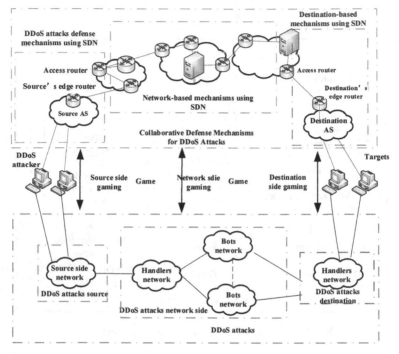

Fig. 2. Model of collaborative defense against DDoS attacks based on SDN framework.

The model evaluation includes two aspects:

- "attack benefit", "attack cost", "attack damage degree", "detection risk" and "defense probability" corresponding to various means adopted by attackers quantify.
- Quantify the "defense benefits", "deployment costs", "operation costs", "negative effects of defense systems" and "residual effects" corresponding to different defense methods adopted by defenders. Then carry out quantitative analysis to calculate the Nash equilibrium of the attacking and defending sides of the model.

3.3 SDN-Based Victim Side Defense Against DDoS Attacks

Based on the first two layers (source end and network end) of defense provided by the SDN controller, the system for defending against DDoS attacks at the victim end captures the traffic of the victim end through the edge router, and performs comprehensive attack detection based on the network traffic information provided by the SDN controller. If the presence of DDoS attack traffic is detected, the detector feeds back to the edge router and warns the defense system. Defense systems that receive an alert will react quickly, filtering traffic and limiting the rate at which edge routers pass.

Figure 3 shows the method of SDN-based victim side defense against DDoS attacks.

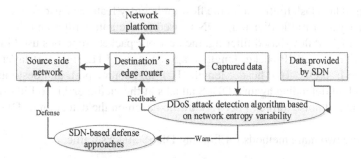

Fig. 3. SDN-Based victim-side defense against DDoS attacks.

Under the SDN framework, the network entropy rate is used to detect DDoS attacks at the victim end. The main steps are:

- On the basis of the nonlinear traffic model of DDoS attacks established based on deep learning neural networks, the overall control and traffic analysis capabilities of SDN are used to analyze normal network traffic data and DDoS attack traffic data.
- Extract the instantaneous and average queue traffic information of router queues, collect network traffic data for processing, and extract the traffic characteristics required for network entropy rate processing.
- According to the extracted features, send them as input into the established DDoS attack neural network model, and set appropriate thresholds for attack detection.
- According to the detection result information, IP tracking and packet marking are carried out through the victim edge router. And use the global information provided by SDN and the marking of some suspicious traffic in the previous layer to accurately distinguish attack traffic from normal traffic. According to the detection results of each TCP flow, it is divided into three kinds of traffic: normal traffic, attack traffic and suspicious traffic. The purpose of traffic division is to mark the attacking TCP traffic according to the detection result of the attacking traffic, and then filter (discard) the attacking TCP data packets.

In order to count the traffic characteristics of the victim network, SDN is used to monitor its bidirectional traffic. The recorded data of the three types of traffic are stored in three Hash tables respectively for comparison with the network traffic. Among them, normal traffic refers to traffic generated by links with good behavior in previous observations; Attack traffic refers to traffic that violates normal behavior initiated by deliberate attackers using forged addresses and other means, also known as abnormal traffic; Suspicious traffic refers to the ambiguous traffic that does not exist in previous observation records or cannot be determined as attack traffic and needs further judgment.

The traffic hash table is based on the result of attack traffic detection, and three traffic tables are established to store the statistical record data of normal traffic, attack traffic and suspicious traffic respectively. That is, the methods of whitelisting, grey listing and blacklisting are used to mark different traffic. According to the content of the mark, choose whether to filter or let the processed TCP flow to achieve the purpose of filtering DDoS attack traffic. In the method of filtering DDoS attack traffic based on TCP traffic, in addition to the Hash traffic table, the flow table entry feature is also used.

On the basis of traffic division, SDN is used to accurately filter and limit traffic at key nodes. In TCP flow-based filtering, the network packet properties used include: IP header length, overall IP packet length, fragmentation, TTL, transport layer protocol type, source IP prefix, TCP header length, TCP tag, source port, and destination port. The research of defending against DDoS attacks at the victim end is to filter out DDoS attack traffic and noise traffic in network traffic based on the detection of DDoS attack traffic.

There are two main methods for filtering DDoS attacks traffic:

- On the basis of SDN-based traffic analysis, mark the TCP traffic of DDoS attacks in network traffic, and then realize filtering based on TCP flow.
- According to the periodicity of normal TCP flow, Using the network traffic model established based on neural network, comb filter technology is used in the frequency domain to obtain normal TCP traffic and filter out DDoS attacks traffic.

4 Conclusion

Cloud computing and big data are two important industrial growth points in the field of information technology after the Internet. At present, the development of cloud computing and big data faces many key issues, the most critical issue is information security. Among the security challenges faced by cloud computing, cloud computing platforms and big data centers are attacked very prominently [11]. Currently, DDoS attacks are one of the biggest threats to cloud computing and big data security. A well-organized DDoS attack can reach 1 Tbps of attack traffic, which is enough to flood the access bandwidth of any server in cloud computing platforms and large data centers. With the rapid development of cloud computing and big data, more and more organizations are beginning to use virtualized data centers and cloud services, and new vulnerabilities have emerged in enterprise infrastructure [4].

Based on game theory, this paper adopts SDN structure and big data analysis technology, which can process the huge network traffic data and also deal with specific data packet attributes. The implemented security functions include: basic packet analysis and filtering, and sophisticated, advanced intrusion detection and emergency response. Therefore, it is fully competent in the detection and defense of DDoS attacks. The specific manifestations are in the following aspects:

The position of defense: realize the coordinated implementation of defense measures at the source side, network side and victim side, and the three sides operate strictly together.

Coordinated operation: the defense system can mobilize various components in the network at any time, participate in the defense against DDoS attacks.

Traffic protection: The defense system has a good protection effect on normal network traffic, ensuring minimal impact on normal traffic.

Defense performance: The defense system has a high detection rate and a low false alarm rate and missed alarm rate, to maximize the suppression of DDoS attacks.

References

1. Hoque, N., Bhattacharyya, D.K., Kalita, J.K.: Botnet in DDoS attacks: trends and challenges. IEEE Commun. Surv. Tutor. **17**(4), 2242–2270 (2015)
2. Zargar, S.T., Joshi, J., Tipper, D.: A survey of defense mechanisms against distributed denial of service (DDoS) flooding attacks. IEEE Commun. Surv. Tutor. **15**(4), 2046–2069 (2013)
3. Li, Y., Quevedo, D.E., Dey, S., Shi, L.: SINR-based DoS attack on remote state estimation: a game-theoretic approach. IEEE Trans. Control Netw. Syst. **4**(3), 632–642 (2017)
4. Yan, Q., Yu, F.R., Gong, Q., Li, J.: Software-defined networking (SDN) and distributed denial of service (DDoS) attacks in cloud computing environments: a survey, some research issues, and challenges. IEEE Commun. Surv. Tutor. **18**(1), 602–622 (2016)
5. Wang, X.L., Chen, M., Xing, C.Y., Sun, Z., Wu, Q.F.: A software-defined security network mechanism to defend against DDoS attacks. J. Softw. **27**(12), 3104–3119 (2016)
6. Rezvani, M., Sekulic, V., Ignjatovic, A., Bertino, E., Jha, S.: Interdependent security risk analysis of hosts and flows. IEEE Trans. Inf. Forensics Secur. **10**(11), 2325–2339 (2015)
7. Kallitsis, M., Stoev, S.A., Bhattacharya, S., Michailidis, G.: AMON: an open source architecture for online monitoring, statistical analysis, and forensics of multi-gigabit streams. IEEE J. Sel. Areas Commun. **34**(6), 1834–1848 (2016)
8. Li, Y., Shi, L., Cheng, P., Chen, J., Quevedo, D.E.: Jamming attacks on remote state estimation in cyber-physical systems: a game-theoretic approach. IEEE Trans. Autom. Control **60**(10), 2831–2836 (2015)
9. Yuan, Y., Yuan, H., Guo, L., Yang, H., Sun, S.: Resilient control of networked control system under DoS attacks: a unified game approach. IEEE Trans. Industr. Inf. **12**(5), 1786–1794 (2016)
10. Wan, M., Zhang, H.K., Shang, W.L., Shen, S., Liu, Y.: Research on the defense method of integrated identity network map cache DoS attack. Chin. J. Electron. **43**(10), 1941–1947 (2015)
11. Xue, R., et al.: Preface to the special issue on cloud computing security research. J. Softw. **27**(6), 1325–1327 (2016)

Detection of Malicious Node in VANETs Using Digital Twin

Varsha Arya[1][✉], Akshat Gaurav[2], Brij B. Gupta[3,4][✉], Ching-Hsien Hsu[5,6,7], and Hojjat Baghban[5]

[1] Insights2Techinfo, Jaipur, India
varshaarya21@gmail.com
[2] Ronin Institute, Montclair, NJ 07043, USA
[3] International Center for AI and Cyber Security Research and Innovation
and Department of Computer Science and Information Engineering, Asia University,
Taichung 413, Taiwan
gupta.brij@gmail.com
[4] Lebanese American University, Beirut 1102, Lebanon
[5] Department of Computer Science and Information Engineering, Asia University,
Taichung, Taiwan
[6] Department of Computer Science and Information Engineering, National Chung
Cheng University, Chiayi, Taiwan
[7] Department of Medical Research, China Medical University Hospital, China
Medical University, Taichung, Taiwan

Abstract. Vehicular ad-hoc network (VANET) plays an essential role in helping the development of smart cars and intelligent transportation systems. By easing congestion and speeding up data transfer, VANET makes it possible for connected cars to function more smoothly. However, VANETs are affected by different types of cyber attacks, such as distributed denial of services (DDoS) attacks. A digital twin (DT) is a replica of a physical system that operates in tandem with the actual thing, allowing for continuous monitoring and management. The DT prepares the way for the monitoring of a physical entity on a regular basis and for its automated management. The improved efficiency in keeping tabs on the physical world is largely attributable to DT. For this reason, academics are advocating for its use in a variety of settings. In this research, we use DT to solve the problem of identifying and stopping malignant nodes on a VANET infrastructure. In this paper, we proposed a framework that uses the concepts of DT for the identification of malignant nodes. Our suggested approach employs machine learning to distinguish between regular traffic and attack traffic.

Keywords: Digital Twin · DDoS · VANET

1 Introduction

VANET includes communication between smart vehicles; because of this, it has become an important part of intelligent transport systems. After the introduction

C.-H. Hsu et al. (Eds.): DataCom 2022, LNCS 13864, pp. 204–212, 2023.
https://doi.org/10.1007/978-981-99-2233-8_15

of smart vehicles and small IoT devices, the work in the field of VANET is gaining momentum. VANET is made up of both fixed units located along the side of the road (RSU) and moving vehicles with their own on-board systems (OBU). Using the on-board unit (OBU), the car may have conversations with nearby nodes (V2V) or the roadside unit (RSU) (V2I), as represented in Fig. 1. VANET allows for either "one-hop" communication between adjacent cars or "multihop" communication in which vehicles relay the message they have received from other vehicles. You can link your vehicle's data to a cloud server using an RSU, or you may utilize the RSU to extend your communication range.

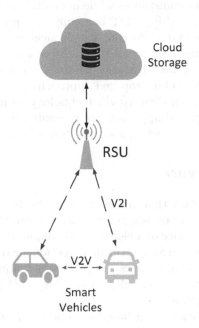

Cloud Storage

RSU

V2I

V2V

Smart Vehicles

Fig. 1. VANET Architecture

However, the working of VANETs is affected by a variety of cyber attacks such as distributed denial of services attacks (DDoS) [1,19]. During a DDoS attack, the attacker uses many nodes, or smart devices to conduct a synchronized denial of service (DoS) attack against a target or targets. Due to the DDoS attack victim's resources are exhausted and it will not able to give its services to legitimated nodes [20].

A primary protection against DDoS attacks is to develop an efficient attack detection technique [21]. However, automated DDoS attack detection is challenging since DDoS traffic sometimes looks identical to legitimate traffic. In recent times some researchers have tried using Machine Learning techniques to detect DDoS attacks. However, machine learning techniques have the following drawbacks:

- Machine learning methods are not effective against low-rate attacks
- The performance of machine learning techniques is dependent on the selection of attack features.
- They are not able to detect many types of DDoS attack variants.
- They require a large quantity of data for training the model.

Hence, researchers proposing different solution for the detection of DDoS attacks [9,16] in VANETs. Recently, the concept of DT has gained the attention of researchers. The concept of a DT was initially used in NASA's integrated technology roadmap, which called for the construction of two identical spacecrafts to reflect the spacecraft's circumstances while in orbit. The name for the spacecraft on the ground is "Twin." [14]. A DT is a copy of a product or manufacturing system that is kept up-to-date so that its physical and functional characteristics are accurately represented at all times. After analyzing the importance of DT applications, we proposed a framework for detection of malicious nodes in the VANET environment. Our proposed approach uses the concept of fog computing in conjunction with digital twin technology to identify attacker nodes. The details of our proposed approach are presented in Sect. 3. The result and discussion are presented in Sect. 4, and Sect. 5 finally concludes the paper.

2   Literature Review

There are many researchers that are working on the development of smart vehicles [2,3,10] and DT concepts using many cutting-edge technologies. In [15], the authors examine the viability of a cloud-based commercial DT that incorporates an embedded control system and intrusion detection for the fourth industrial revolution. In another research, authors [18] propose a unique metaverse-supported digital twin strategy using mobile edge computing (MEC) and ultra-reliable and low-latency communications.

Authors in [8] advocate a fog-based method to identify DDoS attacks. The proposed approach is used for the real-time identification of DoS attack nodes. Authors in [5] proposed DDoS detection in IoT through boosting. Also, the authors in [13] review different DDoS attack detection methods. In another work, authors [11] proposed DDoS attack detection through entropy and SDN.

To detect DDoS attacks in the IoT, a novel machine-learning technique is proposed by the authors [7]. The authors also compare different machine learning and neural network algorithms for attack detection.

The authors [4] created a whole new IDS for SDN, which is deployed through the controller. There are two parts to the planned IDS. The first component, an advanced Signature-based IDS, examines requests and determines whether or not a specific group of hosts is behaving normally; if the latter is the case, the hosts in question are sent to a second module, which inspects their outgoing packets. The second part of the program analyzes the behavior of open connections and gives a definitive answer as to whether or not they are acting normally.

In order to identify flooding assaults rapidly in a client-server setup, the authors [17] suggest an online approach. The proposed system is made up of five different phases. The module that monitors for suspicious behavior determines the Shannon entropy by treating the Internet Protocol address as a random variable. When the calculated entropy falls below a certain threshold, suspicious behavior is flagged. Chebyshev's theorem is used for the threshold calculation. As such, we offer a dynamic threshold system to monitor legal traffic and adapt accordingly. We used simulations and a publicly accessible data set to assess the effectiveness of the suggested approach. The detection rate, false alarm rate, accuracy, and overall accuracy of the proposed system are all higher than those of previous research in the same general area. In another work, authors [6] suggested employing fuzzy sets to enable autonomous cars to provide personal mobility in the metaverse.

The authors [7] show that a wide range of machine learning methods, including neural networks, can identify DDoS attacks in IoT network traffic when trained with features based on IoT-specific network characteristics. These findings suggest that inexpensive machine learning methods applied to flow-based, protocol-agnostic traffic data may be used by home gateway routers or other network middleboxes to identify local IoT device sources of DDoS automatic assaults.

The authors [11] devised a low-overhead defense against DDoS assaults by using the differences in entropy between attack traffic and regular traffic. An approach to lessening the impact of the assault was also presented by the authors. The suggested technique has a high detection rate and a low false positive rate. In order to simulate attacks of varying severities, authors use a mininet emulator and open flow switches.

The author [12] suggests a way to prevent these assaults from occurring in the first place and examines some existing approaches to stopping them. Selective cloud egress filter (SCEF) is a paradigm proposed by the authors that uses predefined modules to respond to identified threats. If an attack is discovered, the SCEF notifies the VMM of which VMs are involved in the attack so that they may take targeted countermeasures.

The authors [19] offer a two-pronged approach: first, the use of objective and subjective trust sources and the use of Bayesian inference to aggregate them, allowing the hypervisor to form believable trust relationships with guest Virtual Machines (VMs). The authors build a trust-based maximin game on top of the trust model, with DDoS attackers seeking to detect as little of the cloud system as possible and the hypervisor trying to optimize this detection within a constrained budget. The game's answer instructs the hypervisor on how to allocate detection work among virtual machines (VMs) in real time so as to optimize protection against DDoS assaults. The experimental findings show that compared to the current detection load distribution methodologies, our system improves detection rates, reduces false positives and negatives, and uses less resources (CPU, memory, and bandwidth) during DDoS assaults.

The authors [13] examine a robust and economical strategy for protecting against DDoS attacks. This discussion presents a threat analysis of distributed denial of service attacks (DDoS) and some innovative, recently suggested response techniques from experts working in a variety of fields. The most common measures used to assess the effectiveness of these safeguards are also discussed.

3   Proposed Methodology

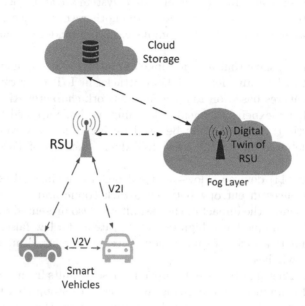

Fig. 2. Proposed Architecture

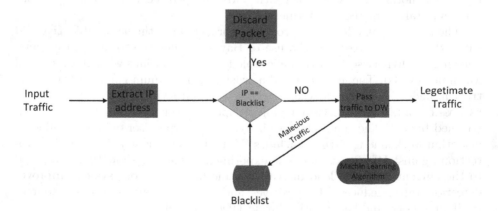

Fig. 3. Blockdiagram of Proposed Approach

In this subsection, we present a brief analysis of our proposed framework. In our proposed framework, the digital twin of RSU is stored in the fog layer.

Due to the storage of DT in the fog layer, it is easy to implement a detection algorithm. The proposed framework is presented in Fig. 2. As specified in Fig. 2, the DT of physical RSU controls its physical counterpart. Then in the DT of the RSU detects the malicious node with the help of a machine learning technique. Finally, the details of the malignant nodes are passed to the physical RSU, and that malicious node is blocked.

3.1   Phase 1

As represented in the Fig. 3 and Algorithm 1, at this phase, physical RSU analysis of the incoming packets. For every time window, ΔT, IP addresses are parsed from incoming traffic and checked against the blacklist. If the IP address of the packet belongs to the blacklist, it means that the packet is from the malicious node and that traffic is discarded.

3.2   Phase 2

The first phase is used to discard the malicious traffic according to the blacklist. However, the second phase updates the blacklist; due to this, our proposed phase dynamically detects the DDoS attack traffic. In the second phase, the features of the packets are extracted, and SVM-based machine-learning techniques are used to analyze that feature. The machine learning-based technique updated technique updates the blacklist after every time window ΔT, as represented in Algorithm 2.

Algorithm 1: Phase 1 Algorithm

Input : Incoming traffic
Output : Identify Malicious traffic
Begin
for (ΔT) **do**
    IP address is extracted
    $\mathbb{IP} \in \{ip_1, ip_2, \cdot, ip_k\} \leftarrow \mathbb{T}$
    if $ip_k == \mathbb{IP}_b \in \{ip_{b1}, ip_{b2}, ..., ipbk\}$ **then**
      | Discard packet
    end
    else
      | Pass the packets to DW
    end
end
End

---

4   Results and Discussion

OMNET++ was used to create a model and run a simulation of the VANET network. A traffic generator based on recurring events. Tensorflow was run on

---

Algorithm 2: Phase 2 Algorithm

Input : Incoming traffic
Output : Identify Malicious traffic
Begin
$\mathbb{M} \leftarrow \varnothing$
for (ΔT) **do**
  Extract features
  $\mathbb{F} \in \{f_1, f_2, f_3....f_m\} \leftarrow \mathbb{IP} \in \{ip_1, ip_2, \cdot, ip_k\}$
  Pass the feature to machine learning algorithm
  $\mathbb{M} \leftarrow \mathbb{F}$
  for $i \leq k$ **do**
    if $ip_i ==$ *malacious* **then**
      | Discard packet and update $\mathbb{B}$
    end
    else
      | Forward p_i
    end
    i++
  end
end
End

---

a 64-bit Intel i5 CPU with 16 GB of RAM in a Windows 11 environment to analyze the OMNET++ data set. We used accuracy, precision, recall, and the F1 score to find the performance of our proposed approximation. The results of the analysis is presented in Fig. 4.

- **Precision**- Forwarded packets' percentage of legitimate packets is determined by this metric.

$$Precision(\delta P) = \frac{\Delta T}{\Delta T + \Delta F} \tag{1}$$

where True positive is ΔT, false positive is ΔF

- **Recall**- Indicating how many valid packets are allowed to go via the proposed method.

$$Recall(\delta R) = \frac{\Delta T}{\Delta T + \Delta \hat{F}} \tag{2}$$

Where $\Delta \hat{F}$ is false negative.

- **Accuracy**- It assesses how well our method could work.

$$Accuracy = \frac{\Delta T + \Delta \hat{T}}{Total Packets} \tag{3}$$

- **F-1** - It evaluates how well the strategy works.

$$F - 1 \; score = Geometric \; mean \; of \; \delta P \; and \, \delta R \tag{4}$$

Where true negative is $\Delta \hat{T}$

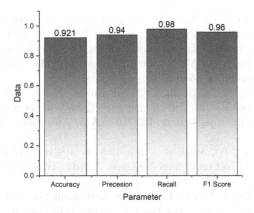

Fig. 4. Simulation results

5   Conclusion

A digital twin (DT) is a computer simulation that perfectly replicates the entity in the digital world. Due to this property, DT gains importance in the research hand industry world. Considering the rise of metaverses, digital twins have taken on more significance. In this context, we proposed a malicious node detection technique in the VANET environment with the help of DT. Our proposed approach uses the concept of machine learning to differentiate malicious traffic from normal traffic. In the future, we aim to implement our proposed approach in a real environment.

References

1. Abbas, N., Nasser, Y., Shehab, M., Sharafeddine, S.: Attack-specific feature selection for anomaly detection in software-defined networks, pp. 142–146 (2021). https://doi.org/10.1109/MENACOMM50742.2021.9678279
2. Akl, N., El Khoury, J., Mansour, C.: Trip-based prediction of hybrid electric vehicles velocity using artificial neural networks, pp. 60–65 (2021). https://doi.org/10.1109/IMCET53404.2021.9665641
3. Al-Hilo, A., Ebrahimi, D., Sharafeddine, S., Assi, C.: Vehicle-assisted RSU caching using deep reinforcement learning. IEEE Trans. Emerg. Top. Comput. (2021). https://doi.org/10.1109/TETC.2021.3068014
4. Barki, L., Shidling, A., Meti, N., Narayan, D.G., Mulla, M.M.: Detection of distributed denial of service attacks in software defined networks. In: 2016 International Conference on Advances in Computing, Communications and Informatics (ICACCI), pp. 2576–2581. IEEE, Jaipur (2016). https://doi.org/10.1109/ICACCI.2016.7732445
5. Cvitić, I., Perakovic, D., Gupta, B.B., Choo, K.K.R.: Boosting-based DDoS detection in internet of things systems. IEEE Internet Things J. **9**(3), 2109–2123 (2021)
6. Deveci, M., Pamucar, D., Gokasar, I., Köppen, M., Gupta, B.B.: Personal mobility in metaverse with autonomous vehicles using Q-rung orthopair fuzzy sets based OPA-RAFSI model. IEEE Trans. Intell. Transp. Syst. (2022)

7. Doshi, R., Apthorpe, N., Feamster, N.: Machine learning DDoS detection for consumer internet of things devices. In: 2018 IEEE Security and Privacy Workshops (SPW), pp. 29–35 (2018). https://doi.org/10.1109/SPW.2018.00013
8. Erskine, S.K., Elleithy, K.M.: Secure intelligent vehicular network using fog computing. Electronics 8(4), 455 (2019)
9. Gupta, B.B., Li, K.C., Leung, V.C., Psannis, K.E., Yamaguchi, S., et al.: Blockchain-assisted secure fine-grained searchable encryption for a cloud-based healthcare cyber-physical system. IEEE/CAA J. Automatica Sinica 8(12), 1877–1890 (2021)
10. Khoury, J., Amine, K., Saad, R.: An initial investigation of the effects of a fully automated vehicle fleet on geometric design. J. Adv. Transp. 2019 (2019). https://doi.org/10.1155/2019/6126408
11. Mishra, A., Gupta, N., Gupta, B.: Defense mechanisms against DDoS attack based on entropy in SDN-cloud using pox controller. Telecommun. Syst. 77(1), 47–62 (2021)
12. Shidaganti, G.I., Inamdar, A.S., Rai, S.V., Rajeev, A.M.: SCEF: a model for prevention of DDoS attacks from the cloud. Int. J. Cloud Appl. Comput. (IJCAC) 10(3), 67–80 (2020)
13. Singh, A., Gupta, B.B.: Distributed denial-of-service (DDoS) attacks and defense mechanisms in various web-enabled computing platforms: issues, challenges, and future research directions. Int. J. Semant. Web Inf. Syst. (IJSWIS) 18(1), 1–43 (2022)
14. Talkhestani, B.A., Jung, T., Lindemann, B., Sahlab, N., Jazdi, N., Schloegl, W., Weyrich, M.: An architecture of an intelligent digital twin in a cyber-physical production system. at-Automatisierungstechnik 67(9), 762–782 (2019)
15. Tarneberg, W., Skarin, P., Gehrmann, C., Kihl, M.: Prototyping intrusion detection in an industrial cloud-native digital twin. In: 2021 22nd IEEE International Conference on Industrial Technology (ICIT), Valencia, Spain, pp. 749–755. IEEE (2021). https://doi.org/10.1109/ICIT46573.2021.9453553
16. Tewari, A., Gupta, B.B.: Secure timestamp-based mutual authentication protocol for IoT devices using RFID tags. Int. J. Semant. Web Inf. Syst. (IJSWIS) 16(3), 20–34 (2020)
17. Tsobdjou, L.D., Pierre, S., Quintero, A.: An online entropy-based DDoS flooding attack detection system with dynamic threshold. IEEE Trans. Netw. Serv. Manage. 19(2), 1679–1689 (2022). https://doi.org/10.1109/TNSM.2022.3142254
18. Van Huynh, D., Khosravirad, S.R., Masaracchia, A., Dobre, O.A., Duong, T.Q.: Edge intelligence-based ultra-reliable and low-latency communications for digital twin-enabled metaverse. IEEE Wireless Commun. Lett. 11, 1733–1737 (2022). https://doi.org/10.1109/LWC.2022.3179207
19. Wahab, O.A., Bentahar, J., Otrok, H., Mourad, A.: Optimal load distribution for the detection of VM-based DDoS attacks in the cloud. IEEE Trans. Serv. Comput. 13(1), 114–129 (2017)
20. Yuan, X., Li, C., Li, X.: DeepDefense: identifying DDoS attack via deep learning. In: 2017 IEEE International Conference on Smart Computing (SMARTCOMP), pp. 1–8. IEEE (2017)
21. Zhou, Z., Gaurav, A., Gupta, B.B., Lytras, M.D., Razzak, I.: A fine-grained access control and security approach for intelligent vehicular transport in 6G communication system. IEEE Trans. Intell. Transp. Syst. 23, 9726–9735 (2021)

Big Data Analytics and Applications

The Storage and Sharing of Big Data in Air Traffic Management System

Yuan Zhang[1] , Qing Wang[1] , Jiahao Li[2] , and Zhijun Wu[1]([⊠])

[1] College of Safety Science and Engineering, Civil Aviation University of China, Tianjin, China
{2020071044,2020095004,zjwu}@cauc.edu.cn
[2] College of Electronic Information and Automation, Civil Aviation University of China, Tianjin, China

Abstract. With the continuous development of aviation business and informatization, the storage and sharing mechanism based on big data will play a more important role in the next generation Air Traffic Management (ATM) system. On the basis of analyzing the traditional aviation network, this paper proposes a new network structure for the storage and sharing of aviation big data to solve the transmission bottleneck, information security and other problems existing in the current network, and effectively ensure the safe and efficient operation of air traffic transportation. The structure is information-centric, with publish and subscribe as the main transmission paradigm, and includes multiple levels such as security, policy, data content and application. The main research contents of this paper are as follows. (i) Analyze the development trend of the new generation of ATM and the problems existing in the current aviation network, and in this context, propose the network structure for aviation big data. (ii) Design the policy layer of the new network structure, including content naming mode, routing mode and caching mode. (iii) Design the security layer of the new network structure, including data security, privacy protection and guarantee service, analyze the application of the new aviation network in specific aviation services.

Keywords: Air Traffic Management · Big Data · Storage · Sharing · Collaborative Decision Making

1 Introduction

With the annual increase in the global aviation business volume and the continuous deepening of the degree of informatization, the sharing requirements and its solutions of aviation data are also changing gradually. For example, the Federal Aviation Administration (FAA) proposed the concept of Collaborative Decision Making (CDM) [1–3], which aims to enable airlines to better participate in Air Traffic Management (ATM) and strengthen information exchange to reduce flight delays, traffic congestion and other issues; the International Civil Aviation Organization (ICAO) proposed the concept of System Wide Information Management (SWIM) to solve the problem of distributed sharing of aviation data in a decentralized way [4]. The development and application of

C.-H. Hsu et al. (Eds.): DataCom 2022, LNCS 13864, pp. 215–229, 2023.
https://doi.org/10.1007/978-981-99-2233-8_16

these projects show that aviation data is no longer limited to point-to-point information interaction, but to the development of system-wide interoperability. This development trend makes aviation data exhibit the characteristics of big data, namely, Volume, Velocity, Variety and Value [5]. Taking the ATM business of Civil Aviation of China as an example, the amount of information generated by more than 50 ATM sub-bureaus (stations) under the ATM department is at PB level every year [6]. Therefore, the aviation industry will be the natural owner of big data. The storage and sharing of aviation big data will become a fundamental issue for the next generation of ATM, and its solutions will have a guiding influence on all aviation related stakeholders [7].

In terms of the current aviation data sharing demand, the demander does not care about the routing or storage mode of the data, but is more concerned about whether the data can be acquired timely, accurately and efficiently. Especially with the rapid increase of aviation data, the traditional network architecture has natural defects such as transmission bottleneck and information security, and the aviation network established on the basis of it will always have drawbacks. Therefore, a new network structure for big data sharing and storage should be designed to enable global aviation users to share data efficiently and further explore the value of aviation data, so as to ensure the safe operation of aircraft.

Firstly, this paper introduces the existing aviation network situation, and analyzes the way of data storage and sharing as well as the existing problems, and then puts forward an aviation big data network architecture based on the concept of next generation ATM, and analyzes and designs its strategy, security and other levels. Finally, this paper lists the specific application scenarios of aviation big data sharing and storage architecture.

2 The Architecture of Storage and Sharing for Aviation Big Data

In order to solve the transmission bottleneck and security problems of the traditional network, this paper takes the data content as the center and adopts a new network architecture on the basis of the traditional network layer.

2.1 New Aviation Network Architecture

The traditional network architecture, such as OSI and TCP/IP, which is widely used at present, the information sharing mode is host-centered [8], which is related to the development history of information technology, but also brings the bottleneck problem to information sharing under the background of big data. In the foreground of increasing aviation business volume and rapid expansion of mobile demand, aviation network will also face the problem that its architecture does not meet the development needs. Therefore, it is very necessary to design a new data sharing and storage mechanism suitable for the background of aviation big data.

The new aviation network system should solve the problems of routing scalability, security and data dynamics faced by the traditional network. Therefore, the new network adds the policy layer to the traditional network layer, and fully supports the data content layer, so as to no longer make the network layer protocol become the bottleneck of sharing. In addition, the new network architecture will add a security layer separately, making the network security performance become a natural attribute of the system. The new network architecture is shown in Fig. 1.

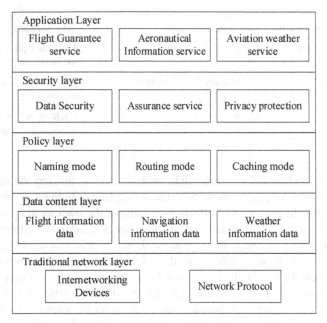

Fig. 1. New aviation network architecture.

The aviation network architecture in Fig. 1 is divided into five layers [9]. Firstly, the traditional network layer provides internetworking devices and network protocols. This layer completely adopts the network devices and protocols of the network layer and below it of the original OSI network structure. The middle three layers in the architecture belong to the scope of the new aviation network. Among them, the data content layer includes all information data in the aviation business, which is divided into flight information data, navigation information data and weather information data. The policy layer needs to provide the naming mode, routing mode and caching mode of aviation data. The security layer provides modules to ensure network security based on data content, including data security, privacy protection and other supportable services. The top aviation application layer provides basic application services and can be applied to various aviation data stakeholders, including flight guarantee services, aeronautical information services, and aviation weather services.

Compared with the traditional network, the architecture of the new aviation network has obvious differences in transmission paradigm, information naming, routing mode and data cache, as shown in Table 1.

Table 1 compares the main differences between the two networks. The new network is different from the traditional network, and the transmission paradigm uses the paradigm of publish and subscribe, that is, the transmission of information is driven by "events", the information subscribers and information publishers can communicate

Table 1. Differences between traditional network architecture and new network architecture.

	Traditional Network Architecture	New Shared Network Architecture
Transmission paradigm	Req/resp paradigm	Sub/pub paradigm
Information naming	Rely on Address/Port	Multiple optional naming methods (hierarchical/flat)
Routing mode	Unstructured routing mode	Structured/unstructured routing mode
Data cache	Caching on the server	Caching in a possible intermediate node

asynchronously, and the information will be pushed to subscribers by the network transmission mechanism, which is conducive to the decoupling of both parties and the saving of network traffic. In the aspect of information naming, the traditional network depends on address and port, and information must have specific address and port number to be correctly transmitted, while the new network has a variety of alternative ways and is independent of address, which makes the information demander can no longer pay attention to where the information is obtained from but only pay attention to the content. In addition, the routing mode of the traditional network is unstructured, which leads to the maintenance of a large number of routing tables on the router, which is not conducive to the access of mobile information. The new network can choose structured or unstructured routing mode according to the requirements. Finally, in the aspect of data caching, the traditional network only stores data on the server, and the demands for data must go to the endpoint to obtain data for every request, while the new network will use the new caching mechanism to cache the data on the intermediate nodes, so that the data demander can get the relevant data in the shortest path. Therefore, the new aviation network can solve the weak links of the traditional network in the big data environment.

2.2 Design of Policy Layer in New Aviation Network

Combined with the current situation and development trend of ATM, this subsection will design and introduce the three parts of naming, routing and caching in the policy layer.

Naming Method. ATM is mainly divided into airspace management, air traffic service and flow management, involving intelligence, control, alarm, traffic, airspace and other types of aviation data [10]. In order to avoid the problem of "information island" caused by data heterogeneity and enhance the ability of data sharing and situational awareness among civil aviation systems, the next generation ATM systems proposed by Europe and the United States have formulated standardized data models for different data types, such as navigation, flight, weather, etc., so that ATM data is no longer heterogeneous. On the basis of the above model, the data between different information domains can be arbitrarily combined, and the service information only needs to focus on the purpose of the data, not the source. This information composition is the basis of information naming in the new network [11]. The composition of the service information is shown in Fig. 2.

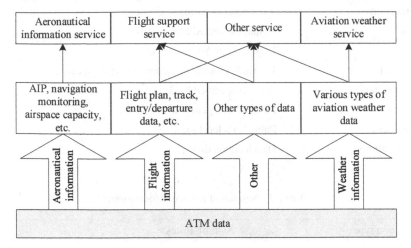

Fig. 2. Information composition mode.

Since the new network uses information naming to replace the function of IP address and takes information as the center of the network, the naming of service information is the basis of information interaction. Aviation networks connect various aviation systems around the world, which contain a large amount of aviation information, and with the further development of the aviation industry, the amount of information is still growing rapidly. In order to avoid the expansion of the routing table caused by massive information, affecting the normal operation of the system, the new network combines the characteristics of ATM data and selects the hierarchical naming method with high aggregation, Uniform Resource Locator (URL), as the naming method of service information.

ATM data mainly comes from aviation agencies such as ATM bureaus, airlines and airports, and contains a variety of fixed types of attribute information, such as: the source, urgency and valid period of ATM data, the aircraft's Globally Unique Flight Identifier (GUFI) and the current control sector, the four-character code of the airport, etc. In this paper, common attributes in ATM data are extracted as the basic elements of service information naming. The commonly used attributes and their values are shown in Table 2, in which the attributes are subordinate and cannot be arbitrarily combined.

The naming rules for service information are shown in Table 3.

As shown in Table 3, naming elements refer to the attribute information of ATM data, which enhances the semantics of naming and facilitates users to find and subscribe the required information. Since the network nodes use the longest prefix matching method to match the service information by selecting the items that match the most high-order elements in the given name, the information should be named according to the distinction degree of the attributes. According to the above rules, the information is named with its specific type as the head to indicate its purpose. After that, according to the purpose, content and so on, different types of information have different naming methods. For

Table 2. Attribute definition in ATM.

Attribute name	Value
Organization	ATM bureaus, airlines, airports, …
Region	China, the United States, Russia, …
City	Beijing, New York, Moscow,…
Department	Dispatch, control, flight service report room,…
Flight number	Aircraft-specific GUFI
Urgency	Flat report, urgency, distress
Release time	Publisher's location time
Term of validity	Data location time

Table 3. Naming of service information.

Information type	Naming Rules
Flight plan	/Information type/institution/departure city/flight number/date/remarks
Track information	/Information type /GUFI/ regulated sector/date/remarks
Navigation information compilation	/Information type/target (route/airport)/validity period/remarks
Weather information	/Information Type/Country/City/Urgency/Date/Remarks

example, aircraft sorties are represented by flight numbers in flight information, sources of information are identified through organizations in aeronautical information, and areas of representation are determined based on information in weather information. There are many types of services in the aviation system, and only a few typical service naming methods are given in the table, which will be illustrated below.

Flight plans can be divided into pre-flight plans and next-day flight plans. Airlines need to report pre-flight plans to the ATM department on a regular basis, and the next-day flight plans need to be provided to the flight service report room between 8:00 and 22:00 on the previous day for review against the pre-flight plans. The information provided by this service can be named /Flight Plan/Air China/Beijing/CA3202/171209 according to the defined naming method, which represents the flight plan information of Flight CA3202 from Beijing issued by Air China on December 9, 2017.

Aeronautical information compilation is a publication authorized by the state, which mainly contains persistent navigation data related to routes and airports, providing necessary basic information for domestic and foreign pilots and operators. The information provided by this service can be named /AIP/ZBAA/180101/Runway, which represents the runway information marked in the AIP by Beijing Capital International Airport, with a valid period until January 1, 2018.

As can be seen from the above naming rules, through hierarchical naming, different levels of information aggregation can be realized, and visitors can directly match multiple information through prefixes. For example, senior managers of airlines can access flight plan information at the institutional level, while ATM intelligence personnel can only access such information at the regional level.

Caching Method. While performing name resolution and information routing, service nodes in the new network also need to cache copies of various types of information passing through the node into the local CS to achieve separation of content and location and improve network transmission efficiency. The caching method mainly involves two aspects, one is the cache placement strategy to determine the cache location of information in the transmission path, and the other is the cache replacement strategy in a single node. This subsection will introduce the caching method in the new network from the above two aspects.

Cache Placement Strategy. The ATM system has a large amount of data. If the information is cached on all nodes passing along the road, it will lead to a large amount of information redundancy, resulting in a huge storage overhead of information copies, and the cache hit rate is low. Different from the common Internet, the ATM system can be divided into a number of relatively independent information domains according to regions, functions and other factors, and it has the natural community characteristics [12], that is, the internal nodes of a community are relatively tightly connected, and the connections between communities are relatively sparse. According to the community of information, it is divided into groups with similar attributes, which can extract useful information from the network intuitively and conveniently. In view of the above characteristics, the information in the new network will be cached at the important nodes in the information domains that it passes through, thus effectively alleviating the storage pressure and improving the cache hit rate.

The betweenness of nodes [13] is a key indicator to describe the importance of nodes in the network. In this paper, the betweenness is used to determine the important nodes in the community. The mathematical definition of betweenness is as follows:

Assuming $G = (V, E)$ is an undirected graph with n vertices, the betweenness of node t is

$$C_{(t)} = \sum_{s \neq p \neq t \in V} \frac{\sigma_{sp(t)}}{\sigma_{sp}} \tag{1}$$

where σ_{sp} is the shortest path number from vertex s to vertex p, and $\sigma_{sp(t)}$ is the shortest path number of two points passing through node t. The larger the node betweenness (the greater the proportion of the shortest path through the node), the more important the node is in the network and the more network resources it controls. Figure 3 is a basic example of system cache placement, which shows the process of weather information provided by the meteorological department of East China ATM Bureau to the dispatching department in Beijing through Air China Shanghai Branch. The above example will be extended to describe most of the situations in the system.

The information routing in Fig. 3 involves three information domains, and the network topology in the information domain is undirected graph. By calculating the betweenness of each node in the undirected graph, it is possible to determine the important nodes in each information domain, such as B3 nodes and C5 nodes, have the highest importance in their respective domains. The information is cached by selecting the node with a large betweenness in each information domain in the transmission path. It is worth noting that the betweenness of each node in domain A is the same. In this case, the new network selects the cache node with the dynamic probability P = 1/N, where N is the total number of nodes with the same betweenness in the path.

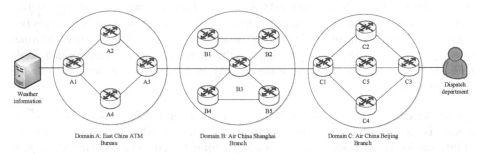

Fig. 3. Example of cache placement.

Cache Replacement Strategy. Compared with the total amount of ATM service information, the cache capacity of nodes in the network is very small, especially in the aviation hub area. During peak periods, massive data will flow through the service nodes in the aviation hub area, and massive access requests from aviation users will arrive there. In this case, the contents of nodes will be frequently replaced, and the Interest packet cannot hit *the* cache content after it arrives, which affects the overall performance of the system. Therefore, the new network needs to design a cache replacement strategy according to the information characteristics and business processes in the ATM network.

Compared with the ordinary Internet, the service information in the ATM system is divided according to the type of service, and the purpose is clearer. All kinds of information will flow in the system in strict accordance with the flow direction stipulated by the aviation business process, which has strong directivity. Most importantly, the timeliness of different types of information is very different. Based on the above characteristics, the new network is classified according to the timeliness of service information, and implements the Last-Recently-Used (LRU) [14] strategy on the same level of information.

The ATM system contains a lot of real-time information, such as route information, etc. This kind of information has a strong timeliness and will be updated in a short time, most of which cannot be reused. In addition, the system also contains some persistent information such as airports, air routes, etc., which will not be easily changed and can be reused within a specified time period. ATM information can be roughly divided into long-term information, short-term information and real-time information according to its timeliness. The information timeliness division is shown in Table 4.

Table 4. Division of information timeliness.

Aging Level	Information Types
Long term (L)	Basic airport information, route information, pre-flight plans,…
Short term (S)	The next day's flight plan, basic information of the aircraft, information on arrival/departure,…
Real time (RT)	Track information, airspace capacity, emergency weather information,…

The service node divides the local CS into multiple independent storage spaces according to the timeliness classification. As shown in Table 4, the CS is divided into three parts: L, S, and RT. When the nodes cache, the information can only be cached in the corresponding storage space and cannot occupy other space. Since the flow direction of ATM information is relatively fixed, the size of the divided storage space depends on the proportion of the information in each level to the total information. In addition, the LRU policy is implemented for independent storage spaces. When the cache entry hits, the entry is moved to the space header; when the space is full, the tail information is discarded. The above-mentioned cache replacement strategy can not only ensure that the cache information in the node is timely updated, but also ensure that the persistent information will not be replaced by real-time information, thereby effectively improving the cache utilization in the new network.

2.3 Design of Policy Layer in New Aviation Network

The new aviation network security architecture is a systematic summary of all aspects of network security. The security layer architecture will comprehensively consider the security issues and security requirements of the new aviation network and put forward corresponding solutions.

The specific network security architecture is shown in Fig. 4. The security layer design of the new aviation network is a high-level architecture design for network security based on the data content layer and the policy layer. The architecture is divided into three aspects, namely data security, privacy protection and guarantee service. Among them, the first two include malicious attack defense and security policy mechanism. The guarantee service regards emergency response and disaster backup as reusable services in the concept of security-as-a-service, providing security guarantees in special/crisis situations, making the network highly reliable. The design of the security mechanism will be described separately below.

Data Security. Data security is the content that the cyber security layer considers and designs from the security threat of data on the new aviation network. The new aviation network adopts new shared content and policies, and will face new security threats. Among them, DOS, content virus and cache pollution are malicious attacks that the new aviation network will face, and corresponding defense methods need to be spe-cially designed. At the same time, set security policies for security naming and forward-ing and application security to ensure data security.

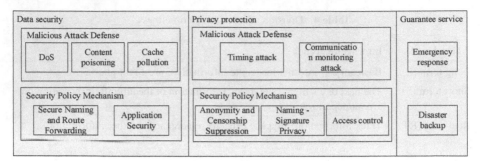

Fig. 4. New aviation network security architecture.

Dos. DoS will try to overwhelm network services with a large number of requests. In the new civil aviation network, DoS attacks will target content providers or edge routers. To defend against such attacks, we need to design the security layer in two ways, namely, rate-limiting way and static model way. The rate limiting method detects whether there is a DoS attack by detecting the timeout rate of interesting packets in the PIT of the router or the size of the PIT. When a suspicious attack is detected, the arrival rate of interested packets will be limited. According to this, two speed-limiting methods are designed, that is, each side monitoring method and PIT size limiting method. In the monitoring method, the monitoring method detects attacks by the number of overtime interest packets and the ratio of interest packets arriving at the router to the data packets sent by it, and prevents attacks by restricting the reception of malicious interest packets. In the method of controlling PIT size, the router will continuously detect PIT, and once the PIT size exceeds the threshold, the router will enter the defensive mode. The static model method relies on the static information and port status of the router's PIT to identify abnormal traffic patterns. If any item is abnormal, the router will trigger the defense mechanism, which will identify. The port where the target prefix and the most matched prefix interest packets arrive, and limit the request rate of this port.

Content Virus Attack. The content virus attack uses invalid content to fill the router cache, resulting in real content being nowhere to be stored in the node cache. Therefore, an attacker needs to inject content into the network by controlling one or more intermediate routers. The injected content has a valid name but no payload. To deal with such attacks, the cyber security layer will design several defense mechanisms, including joint signature authentication mechanism and user independence mechanism. Joint signature authentication requires the router to authenticate the content signature by cooperating with each other and it will authenticate all data packets that need to be forwarded. User independence mechanism will rely on additional request fields, data packets or user feedback to defend against content virus attacks. Therefore, the customer can choose to feedback the legality of the received content, or include the public key enabled by the provider in the request package for authentication.

Cache Pollution Attack and Security Naming and Routing Forwarding. Cache mechanism plays an important role in improving network transmission efficiency in new civil aviation network. In the cache of routers, some contents are frequently requested, while others are relatively rarely requested. The caching mechanism caches the popular content, thus reducing the request delay and network load, so that users can call the content at a small cost. However, cache pollution attacks can take advantage of this to destroy the natural request frequency and frequently request content that is not frequently requested. Cache contamination attacks are mainly divided into two ways: locality disruption and false locality. In the local disruption method, the attacker constantly requests new or rarely accessed content to destroy the locality of the cache. The attacker's goal is to change the distribution of local cache popularity. Repeat requests to a set of infrequently used content to increase the popularity of a content collection. In a defense against the former, the router would be designed to store content with a certain popularity or to store content that can be predicted periodically. The cache pollution of false locality method can be caused by the cooperation between malicious content providers and content consumers. Malicious content providers will store their content in the routing cache, and malicious content consumers will change the content popularity of the local cache. Therefore, in the defense design of the security layer, monitoring equipment can be set up to capture malicious requests from routers for potential threats, and then these requests can be summarized into a blacklist by routers.

Among the security policy mechanisms on the security layer, new networks need to be customized for naming methods, routing and forwarding. Secure naming methods will protect against the above content virus attacks, and secure routing and forwarding are aspects that must be considered at the security layer of any network. The design of secure naming adopts both RSA and IBC encryption methods.

The encryption method of RSA ensures the source of content by using the public key or signature of the content provider. The IBC method will bind the content name to the public key of the corresponding provider. Since the new aviation network adopts a publish-subscribe information sharing method, in order to prevent malicious publishers from generating false routing, it is necessary to design secure routing and anti-DOS self-routing mechanism and key management method. Two methods of secure forwarding are designed, including creating secure namespace mapping and ensuring the security of forwarding plane, which can make the interest packets forwarded by name prefix not in the FIB table of router.

Privacy Protection. The new aviation network not only provides efficient information sharing, but also faces serious risks of privacy leakage, so privacy protection is another important content of security layer design. There are many kinds of privacy problems in Internet, but the impacts of these problems are different. For example, because the information flow in aviation network is relatively fixed, and publish/subscribe is the main information interaction mode in the system, in the interaction process, except for the transmission of the initial data packet, the transmission time of the subsequent data packet cannot reflect the cache delay. In this interactive mode, the impact of sequential attack on the system is not obvious by using accurate time measurement to distinguish cache hits and determine the cache location of content. Communication monitoring attacks like this are secondary privacy issues in the network. This subsection focuses on the two main issues of naming and signature privacy protection and access control in Fig. 4.

Naming And Signature Privacy Protection. The new aviation network uses a hierarchical method to name information to enhance the aggregation and readability of the name, but this naming method has a strong semantic correlation with the content or publisher identity, which will generate a large amount of private information. If the user uses the real name to initiate a request for information, it is very likely to cause privacy leakage. By mapping real names to Hash names, the new network can prevent the above problems and realize the self-verification of system information.

The user first visits the authority, finds the corresponding Hash name in the directory according to the real name, and returns the name and signature information to the user. The user can use the public key to authenticate the signature. After authentication is successful, the user can save the name for next use, and use the name to build an Interest package to initiate a request for service information. After several routes between service nodes, the requested information is eventually returned to the user as a packet. In this step, the user can hash the returned data and compare the results with the saved name. If the content of the two is the same, it means that the information is true, and the user can use this information; if it is different, it means that the information may be maliciously tampered with during transmission, and the user needs to re-request the information.

If the service information is divided into multiple data packets, Merkle Tree can be considered to store the name of such information, which is convenient for users to access and verify [15]. In addition, the change of the data in the data packet will lead to the change of the corresponding Hash name. If a large amount of data is changed frequently, the update of the name and directory will have a large computational overhead. However, since most of the data in the ATM system is read-only data, the above defects will not have a significant impact on the system.

Access Control. The ATM system contains a large amount of confidential data involving the airspace information of member states and the commercial privacy of aviation operators. Any kind of privacy data leakage will have a greater impact on the aviation security and interests of member states. Access control is the key technology to solve the above problems.

Similar to other large-scale distributed networks, the new aviation network contains massive data, and has the characteristics of user node movement and real-time update of accessible resources. Different from the traditional network, the new aviation network adopts the function of information naming instead of IP address, and it has evolved from end-to-end communication mode to host-to-network mode. Therefore, aviation users can only obtain information through naming rules, and cannot know the location of the service publisher. In view of above characteristics, the new network adopts an Attribute-Based Access Control (ABAC) [16] scheme, which not only ensures the security of private data, but also ensures that authorized users in the system can obtain the corresponding service information at the correct time no matter where they are.

Because the naming of service information in the new network has good aggregation and is convenient for hierarchical division, the network formulates corresponding access policies by naming different information types divided to reduce redundant policy information. In the process of policy formulation, the subject, object, environment and other information should be described strictly according to the actual ATM business process, with the attributes in the system as the core. XACML [17] is a typical descriptive language under ABAC, which has good generality, cross-platform and extensibility, and is suitable for new aviation networks with multiple information domains and a large number of cross-domain access.

In the process of permission determination, the access control server first converts the original access request containing user attribute information into an attribute-based access request, and then determines the access result by associating the request with the attributes in the policy. Among them, attribute association is an important part of realizing permission determination. The tree access structure in the XACML strategy can be transformed into a matrix form by using the Linear Secret Sharing Scheme (LSSS) [18], thereby realizing flexible attribute association functions.

3 Application Analysis of New Network Structure

With the airport as the center, the Airport-Collaborative Decision-Making (A-CDM) system integrates the relevant data of airport, air traffic control and airlines, improves the efficiency of flight operation and realizes the sensible resource allocation through the perception of the general trend [19]. Through A-CDM, flight operation can be more standardized and transparent, so as to maximize resource utilization and achieve more efficient operation. Collaborative decision-making is the core of A-CDM. However, with the increasing number of flights and the continuous introduction of new aircrafts, the amount of data is increasing. Therefore, the big data processing capability of data collaboration platform has become a major bottleneck of A-CDM system. In order to make the system more optimized and better achieve the purpose of big data storage and sharing, the new network architecture is applied.

The purpose-based new network information naming method can not only achieve more efficient information integration, but also achieve faster information query. The airport, air traffic control and other information are named according to the category, so that the information is no longer heterogeneous, which can improve the efficiency of data integration and reduce the calculation consumption. In addition, due to the characteristics of A-CDM collaboration, it is necessary to design a network transmission of a large amount of information. Therefore, the loose cache placement strategy designed according to the community characteristics of the aviation system can reduce the network pressure and improve the cache information hit rate, and the cache replacement strategy of the new network architecture can also improve the cache utilization. Secondly, with the development of the information age, data security has become more and more important. Especially for large systems, security has become a key consideration while ensuring their own efficiency. The security layer set in the new network architecture can provide certain security for the A-CDM system and resist common attacks. Therefore, the new network architecture can not only achieve more efficient collaboration for A-CDM system, but also make it more secure.

4 Conclusion

Based on the analysis of the network bottlenecks and security problems faced by the existing civil aviation network, this paper proposes a new network structure for the storage and sharing of aviation big data in the new generation of ATM. The structure adopts content-oriented naming, routing and caching at the policy layer to solve the transmission bottleneck problem of traditional aviation networks. At the same time, in the security layer design of the new aviation network, the corresponding defense mode and protective policy mechanism are designed to deal with the various attacks and security requirements in the aspects of data security, privacy protection and guarantee service. The new aviation network structure can provide the necessary infrastructure and development space for aviation big data, and play a major role in the next generation of ATM.

Acknowledgment. This research was funded by the joint funds of National Natural Science Foundation of China and Civil Aviation Administration of China (U1933108) and the National Natural Science Foundation of China (62172418), the Natural Science Foundation of Tianjin China (21JCZDJZ00830), the Fundamental Research Funds for the Central Universities of China (3122021026, ZXH2012P004), and the and the Open Fund of Key Laboratory of Civil Aircraft Airworthiness Technology (SH2021111907).

References

1. Yan, R.: Concept and analysis of civil aviation collaborative decision-making (CDM). Chinese Sci. Technol. Terminol. **14**(6), 50–53 (2012)
2. ICAO: Manual on System Wide Information Management (SWIM) Concept, Doc. 10039. https://www.icao.int/airnavigation/IMP/Documents/SWIM%20Concept%20V2%20Draft%20with%20DISCLAIMER.pdf (2014)
3. Hilbert, M.: Big data for development: a review of promises and challenges. Dev. Policy Rev. **34**(1), 135–174 (2016)
4. Zhang, Z.B.: The concept, characteristics and application of air traffic management big data. J. China Civil Aviation Flight Academy **26**(6), 18–21 (2015)
5. Fisher, D., DeLine, R., Czerwinski, M., Drucker, S.: Interactions with big data analytics. Interactions **19**(3), 50–59 (2012)
6. Signore, T.L., Girard, M.: The aeronautical telecommunication network (ATN). In: Military Communications Conference, MILCOM 98. Proceedings, pp. 40–44. IEEE (1998)
7. Huang, H.Q., Xue, P.: Research on the construction of national aviation telecommunication network. Comput. Eng. Design **29**(6), 1355–1357 (2008)
8. ICAO: Global Air Traffic Management Operational Concept, Doc.9854 (2005)
9. George, X., Christopher, N.V., Vasilios, A.S., et al.: A survey of information-centric networking research. IEEE Commun. Surv. Tutorials **16**(2), 1024–1049 (2014)
10. Huang, T., Liu, J., Huo, R., Wei, L., Liu, Y.J.: A review of future network architecture research. Chinese J. Commun. **35**(8), 184–197 (2014)
11. Chai, W.K., He, D.L., Psaras, I., Pavlou, G.: Cache less for more in information-centric networks(extended version). Comput. Commun. **36**(7), 758–770 (2013)
12. Jelenkovic, P.R., Radovanovic, A., Squillante, M.S.: Critical sizing of lru caches with dependent requests. J. Appl. Probab. **43**(4), 1013–1027 (2006)
13. Baugher, M., Davie, B., Narayanan, A., Oran, D.: Self-verifying names for read-only named data. In: Proceedings of IEEE Conference on Computer Communications Workshops (INFOCOM WKSHPS), vol. 12, pp. 274–279(2012)
14. Hu, V.C., Richard Kuhn, D., Ferraiolo, D.F.: Attribute-based access control. Computer **48**(2), 85–88 (2015). https://doi.org/10.1109/MC.2015.33

15. Moses, T.: eXtensible Access Control Markup Language (XACML) Version 2.0. OASIS Standard (2005)
16. Liu, Z., Cao, Z.F.: On effciently transferring the linear secret-sharing scheme matrix in ciphertext-policy attribute-based encryption. IACR Cryptology ePrint Archive, vol. 374 (2010)
17. EUROCONTROL, Airport Collaborative Decision Making (A-CDM)[EB/OL]. http://www.eurocontrol.int/articles/airport-collaborative-decision-making-cdm (2017)
18. Düsseldorf, A.: Airport Collaborative Decision Making (A-CDM) Brief Description Process Description. https://www.munich-airport.de/de/micro/airport_cdm/media/download/dus_brief_descrip_en.pdf (2014)
19. Huang, J.: The exploration in establishment of A-CDM system and my thoughts. Civil Aviat. Manag. **08**, 17–19 (2017)

Automated Recognition and Classification of Cat Pain Through Deep Learning

Yang Yang and Richard O. Sinnott$^{(\boxtimes)}$ (iD)

School of Computing and Information Systems, The University of Melbourne, Melbourne,
VIC 3010, Australia
rsinnott@unimelb.edu.au

Abstract. Unlike humans, pets are unable to vocalize the details of specific pain
they may be experiencing. Rather, this can only be determined through physical
clues, behaviours and/or potential noises that the animals might make. For some
animals, this may be obvious but for others this is often far less easy to identify.
One example of the latter is cats. A cat in pain may appear to be simply sub-
dued. This paper explores different methods used to detect cat pain automatically
based on an international scale for pain assessment and classification for cats. A
targeted (labelled) data set collected from veterinary practices across Melbourne
is utilized in combination with diverse deep learning techniques including You-
Only-Look-Once (YOLO) [1], Single Shot Detection (SSD) [2] and inceptionV3
[3] to automatically classify the potential pain of cats. We achieve an overall accuracy of 93% for pain classification using an enhanced multi-model approach and
combining different machine learning models.

Keywords: Cat pain · Automated pain detection · Transfer learning · YOLO ·
SSD · InceptionV3

1 Introduction

Cats are one of the most popular household pets. They are often considered as aloof
and do not visibly show many types of emotions. A happy purring cat often appears
as a sleepy and/or restful cat. An angry cat is somewhat more visible with baring of
teeth, hissing and raised hackles (piloerection). However, it can be extremely difficult
to identify cats that might be experiencing pain. Only expert veterinary clinicians can
reliably distinguish the minor differences between a cat that might be suffering from a
cat that might just be resting. The physical (visual) manifestation of pain in cats includes
a slight change in the ear positions and the form of the muzzle. To help tackle this,
international pain scales such as the Glasgow Composite Measure Pain Scale (CMPS-
Feline) for cats [4] have been established to classify cats that might be in pain. These
scales cover a range of criteria including movement patterns (or lack thereof), the sounds
the cat might be making, as well as visual clues (position of the ears and the muzzle
shape) as shown in Fig. 1.

C.-H. Hsu et al. (Eds.): DataCom 2022, LNCS 13864, pp. 230–240, 2023.
https://doi.org/10.1007/978-981-99-2233-8_17

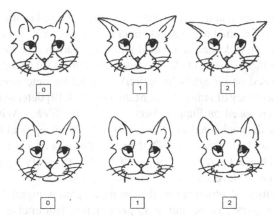

Fig. 1. CMPS-Feline pain scale illustrating cats with increasing pain left to right with ear positioning (top) and muzzle shape (bottom)

The ability to automate the process of identifying pain in cats would be highly beneficial, both to ease the continuous monitoring demands of staff working in animal hospitals and more importantly, to ease the potential suffering of cats. Such a system might be used to increase the drugs used for their associated pain management for example.

In this paper we explore how deep learning methods can be used to whether a cat might be in pain or not. The rest of this paper is structured as follows. In Sect. 2, we present related work. In Sect. 3 we present the preparation of the datasets used for pain classification. In Sect. 4, we introduce the initial and enhanced (combined) deep learning models that were explored and we present their associated results. Finally in Sect. 5 we draw conclusions on the work as a whole and identify potential areas of future work.

2 Related Work

Although cats are one of the most popular household pets, identifying and classifying their pain has hitherto not received much attention. Compared to other animals such as dogs, cats do not visibly show diverse and explicit emotions [5]. It is generally difficult to assess the level of pain a cat may be experiencing. Development of automatic pain assessment scoring tools would be highly beneficial [6]. To support this, different behaviour-based cat pain scoring instruments have been put forward. The UNESP-Botucatu multidimensional composite pain scale [7] and the Glasgow composite measure pain scale-feline (CMPS-Feline) [4] are two such examples that have both been proven to be effective in clinical use. The two approaches have various overlap in their approach and data required for capturing the different signals that might be used to identify pain. The CMPS-Feline has been adopted here. This approach uses a range of criteria to assess a cat including the behaviour, movement, noises and visual clues. It is the latter aspect here that forms the basis for this paper: can we identify a cat in pain based on the images shown in Fig. 1 through the application of diverse deep learning methods.

There are two common approaches that have been explored to identify animal pain: automatic detection of animal actions and direct use of diverse raw data. For the former approach, the detection tasks can be divided into deep learning methods and traditional computer vision methods. Tuttle et al. [8] trained and optimised a Convolutional Neural Network (CNN) based on Google's InceptionV3 model for detection of pain in mice. They achieved an accuracy of almost 99%. Mahmoud et al. [9] detected nine pain related action units of sheep based on Support Vector Machines (SVM). With a dataset comprising 480 images, they achieved an accuracy of 67% for sheep pain classification. For horses, Sardinha et al. [10] trained a CNN detecting the area of a horse's ears, eyes and mouth separately. They achieved an accuracy of 75.8% in classifying animal pain based on these three individual levels and 88.3% for binary tasks.

For the second method utilising raw data as input, pain recognition work is usually based on binary tasks, i.e., is the animal in pain or not. Hummel et al. [11] explored a landmark-based approach for horses. They annotated images with 44–54 landmarks, which were used to crop four regions of interest of horses for classification. In the action unit detection stage, a deep learning strategy based on You-Only-Look-Once (YOLO) model and traditional approaches such as scale invariant feature transform (SIFT) was adopted. They achieved an F1-score of up to 81%. Andersen et al. [12] focused on automatic detection of horse pain based on raw videos and performed an end-to-end binary pain recognition based on a dual-stream Recurrent Neural Network.

However, research on automatic cat pain recognition through deep learning methods are less well explored than other species. Finka et al. [13] detected action units of cats based on a dataset comprising 48 geometric landmarks that were annotated manually. Feighelstein et al. [14] made a comparison of this method based on the Resnet50 model. Both approaches reached a comparable accuracy of 72%.

Sinnott et al. [15] developed solutions for identifying the species of pets and their associated emotion (mood). This work did not focus on pain however, but other more obvious pet-based emotions, e.g., happy, sad, angry.

The work on automated approaches for pain classification of cats based on deep learning has not yet been rigorously explored – predominantly due to the lack of data that can be used to train (data hungry) deep learning models.

3 Data Collection

3.1 Data Collection

Collection of videos and images of cats that may be in pain is challenging since it would be clearly unethical and inhuman to inflict pain on cats and record their reactions. To tackle this, the work focused on collaboration with different veterinary practices around Melbourne including the University of Melbourne Veterinary School and the Lort Smith Animal Hospital. To identify cats in pain, there is a need for clearly labelled and accurate data of cats that may be in pain. For the lay person this would be challenging to recognise, but for trained veterinarians this is possible. To accommodate this, experienced veterinarians captured videos of cats who had recently undergone diverse surgeries and were recovering in the associated animal hospital. These data sets were labelled based on the CMPS-Feline scale. The vets were advised that the videos should ideally be of reasonably high quality and well lit. Videos of at least 15 s duration were requested. The videos themselves were labelled as follows: *11-12-2021-A-19-14112244* (for cat A video taken on 11 December 2021 where it was assessed with a pain score of 19/20 on the CMPS-Feline scale where the breakdown of this scale was Q1 = 1, Q2 = 4, Q3 = 1, Q4a = 1, Q4b = 2, Q5 = 2, Q6 = 4, Q7 = 4. Here Q1 is related to the sounds the cat is making; Q2 related to how relaxed the cat appears to be; Q3 related to whether it might be licking a wound/sensitive area, Q4 a manual classification of the visual information shown in Fig. 1, Q5 related to how and whether it responds to stroking, e.g., if it is relaxed or aggressive, Q6 relates to observational behaviour, e.g., if it bites or lashes out, and Q7 for the overall impression of the cat. In this work we focus explicitly on automatic classification of Q4 based on the example shown in Fig. 1.

Eight cats with different health conditions had videos captured using the above classification scheme. These were labelled and checked by different veterinarians. Other training data of cats (without pain) obtained from the Internet were used to augment this data set, e.g., to identify the muzzle and ears of cats more generally. The number of frames in each video was one of the key aspects of the data preparation. A healthy cat will typically be more active compared to those that might be in pain. For a cat in pain, the cat is typically quiet and non-moving, hence a given set of images extracted from a video of the cat may comprise repetitive data. To address this and after various experiments, 120 frames for each healthy cat video and 80 frames for those cats in pain was used as the basis for the data collection.

Frames comprising images of the cat's facial area from the front were chosen wherever possible – since a key observation for pain classification was the muzzle, which can only be observed from the front. This cannot always be guaranteed in the real world however, so to improve the robustness of the model, images from side angles were also included to train the models.

The lack of authoritative labelled data was a key issue, since deep learning depends on access to and use of large quantities of data for training. The gold standard data here was the labelled data from the veterinarians. To enlarge the dataset, other images were obtained and labelled directly based on self-judgement and the appearance of the cat's face and the degree it met the representative examples shown in Fig. 1. The total number of images used in this work included 840 frames from the gold standard veterinarian-labeled videos. These were randomly apportioned into a training, validation and testing dataset in the ratio 4:1:2 respectively.

According to the scoring criteria of the CMPS-Feline, the action units (i.e., ears/muzzle) contain three discrete scores that could be assigned a value of: 0, 1 and 2. A larger number represents a larger possibility of pain. Both individual and general object detection was adopted. For individual object detection, the labels consisted of the body part and the pain score. For example, an ear with pain score 1 was annotated as "e1". For general detection, the labels included "ears" and "muzzle", i.e., without the related pain scores. Therefore, six classes were used based on the dataset used for individual detection while two classes were used for general object detection. Two separate datasets with only the area of the cat's ears and muzzles were also prepared to train an InceptionV3-based model used for transfer learning respectively.

4 Model Training

4.1 Basic Model Training

Figure 2 below shows the process of individual detection of the six classes by YOLO (version 5) and Single Shot Detection (SSD version 300) respectively. Considering that the number of action units and pain scores was not large, in the first approach, these models were trained to detect and classify the action units of cats and the related pain score directly.

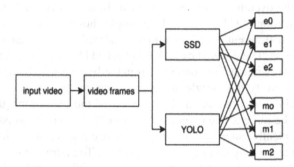

Fig. 2. Pipeline of Individual Ear and Muzzle Detection

The training dataset with 480 images and 960 labels was prepared for the training stage. After training, the two trained models were validated using a data set comprising 120- labelled images. One of the challenges with this approach was the processing of input video with the SSD300 model, since YOLOv5 supports video input directly. The input video was converted into frames based on the frame per second (in the ratio of 120/80 as described previously for pain/no pain respectively), and these were sent to the SSD model for prediction. Finally, these frames were recombined into video.

The mean average precision (mAP) results for YOLOv5 and SSD300 are shown in Table 1 below. As seen, the average mAP@.5..95 of YOLOv5 was 94.6%, while the average mAP@.5:.95 was 69.9%. The mAP of the SSD300 model was 90.2%.

Table 1. Performance of YOLO and SSD models

YOLOv5	all	e2	m2	e1	m1	e0	m0
mAP@.5	94.6%	93.3%	80.8%	98.5%	98.3%	98.5%	98.5%
mAP@.5:.95	69.9%	66.1%	57.8%	91.1%	71%	77.7%	56%

SSD300	e2	m2	e1	m1	e0	m0
AP	90.3%	59.7%	96%	97.5%	95%	93%
mAP	90.2%					

The training results for YOLOv5 are shown in Fig. 3 below. The training and validation loss decreases rapidly for the first 50 epochs, and they start to drop slowly and become stable at epoch 200. Similarly, for precision and recall, the values go up rapidly for the first 50 epochs before gradually stabilising.

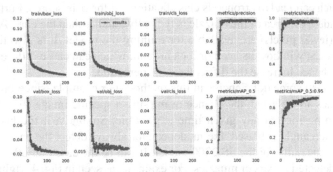

Fig. 3. Training and validation loss, precision and recall for YOLOv5

Discussion

For the first approach (based solely on YOLOv5 and SSD300), the ears and muzzles of cats are detected with the pain scores calculated directly by the YOLOv5 and SSD300 models. The model performances were acceptable (over 90%). Examples of the outputs of this approach and the challenges are shown in Fig. 4.

Fig. 4. Output of individual detection (left) and wrong detection of ears (right)

One key finding was that the performance of YOLOv5 was slightly better than SSD300 for object detection. The primary reason for this was that the training and fine-tuning of the model are dependent on the amount of data. Some parameters such as values of minimum and maximum size and the aspect ratio cannot be learnt automatically with limited data sets. They need to be manually adjusted during the model training.

It can also be observed that the detection results for muzzles are generally worse than ears. An object detection model must classify six classes, but half of these are similar. For cat ears, the pain scores totally depend on the angle of the ears. Flattened ears represent a higher pain score while pricked/vertical ears are likely to indicate a cat that is not in pain. This kind of feature with a clear boundary is easier for object detection models to learn by adding more training epochs. Compared to ears, it is harder to classify the different status of muzzles. In the CMPS-Feline scale, the criteria for this action unit are somewhat ambiguous since different cats may well have different shaped muzzles for example, which can lead to erroneous classifications of the pain scores. Furthermore, in a given cat video, the area of the muzzle is typically smaller than the ears. As such, less information (fewer pixels) are available for training the model. It is also the case that sometimes the cat will bow its head or look around, which can cause different angles of a muzzle and hence increase the difficulty in its detection.

There are also some deficiencies in this method. For example, since only a sample of video frames are selected, the chance of missing a specific image (frame) based on the cat's head position at any given time is possible. Similarly, if the background is dim or the video angle is biased, the model cannot always detect the ears and muzzles successfully, especially for the SSD300 model. It can be the case that other objects are erroneously detected as ears or muzzles. For example, as seen in Fig. 4 (right), the towel beneath the cat is detected as the ears and these are classified with a pain score of 2. This problem arises both due to the number of classes and the limited amount of data. Therefore, it was decided that the object detection model should only focus on detection of the action units (ears and muzzles) and not attempt to classify the pain score.

4.2   Enhanced Model Training

Figure 5 below shows the pipeline used for general detection of ears and muzzles using YOLOv5 and SSD300 respectively, and the subsequent classification for three pain scores undertaken with InceptionV3.

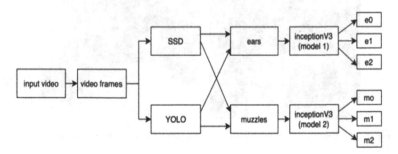

Fig. 5. The final pipeline for ear/muzzle detection and pain classification

In this approach, two object detection models are trained. The processes are similar to that shown in Fig. 2. After training YOLOv5, the model is used to crop the image areas including ears and muzzles. To enhance the two datasets required for inceptionV3 transfer learning, these cropped images are verified manually, e.g., removing the towel example shown in Fig. 4. The training of inceptionV3 is based on these datasets.

A further difficulty encountered in this method is the stitching of the object detection model and the classification model. In the detection (or prediction) process of the object detection model, the output is only the action unit. The information of this area such as the location will be sent to the inceptionV3 model for further classification of the pain score. Since the input and output can be different for these models, appropriate adaptations need to be made between the cropped data.

The mAP results for YOLOv5, SSD300 and inceptionV3 based on this enhanced approach are shown in Table 2 below. In this case, the average mAP@.5 of YOLOv5 was 95.4%, while the average mAP@.5:.95 was 71.3%. As previously, the prediction performance of the ears was better than muzzles. The mAP of the SSD300 model was 90.8% and both ear and muzzle had the same results, which was lower than YOLOv5. Applying the pre-trained inceptionV3 model for classification task achieved an accuracy in training and validation of 100%. This also performed well with the test dataset which had an accuracy of 93%.

Table 2. mAP for YOLOv5 ear/muzzle detection (top), SSD300 for ear/muzzle detection (middle), and classification of pain accuracy using inceptionV3 (bottom)

YOLOv5	all	e	m
mAP@.5	95.4%	98.5%	92.4%
mAP@.5:.95	71.3%	78.6%	63.9%

SSD300	e	m
AP	90.8%	90.8%
mAP	90.8%	

InceptionV3 training/validation accuracy	100%
Final accuracy	93%

Discussion

As mentioned, the enhanced approach uses YOLOv5 and SSD300 for detecting the ears and muzzles of cats. These are then fed into the pain classification model based on inceptionV3. Compared to the basic method, more frames are detected with the correct action units from the input videos due to the object detection models focusing on the recognition of specific object detection classes. A simple comparison between these two methods can be seen in Fig. 6 below. The advanced method can detect and classify more action units given the same pictures or videos compared to the previous methods using only object detection models.

There are several reasons for the improved model performance with this approach. For example, the focus on general detection with YOLOv5 and SSD300 improves the recognition rate of action units (ears and muzzles). One of the adjustments made with this method is the output of object detection models. Instead of providing the body parts and pain scores at the same time, the task of object recognition models in this method focus on detecting the area of action units and sending them to the corresponding inceptionV3 model. The performance of general detection with YOLOv5 and SSD300 is better than the individual detection. This is because the retrained general classes eliminate the influence of similar individual classes - to some extent. The possibility

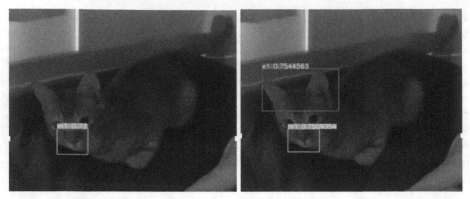

Fig. 6. Output of YOLOv5 individual detection (left) and YOLOv5 detection + inceptionV3 classification (right)

of mixing up the general classes and other irrelevant objects at the object detection stage is therefore reduced. This initial detection stage provides the foundation for the subsequent classification of the model performance. Another benefit of this approach is the separation of action unit recognition and classification using transfer learning. Instead of constructing and training a CNN model from scratch, the inceptionV3 model provides a powerful and proven CNN that provides the basis for transfer learning and hence for pain classification. As noted in Table 2, it achieves an accuracy of 93%.

However, the improvement of the accuracy for object recognition is not without some drawbacks. For example, it leads to more waiting and processing time for each video. This is mainly due to the data conversion and transportation between the object detection models and the classification model. The input to the inceptionV3 model should be processed as images prepared by the earlier stages. The models themselves have been trained on Google Colab. Whilst a high-performance GPU can save time for training, the temporary data generated in the object detection stage can only be stored in Google Drive with an associated reduced read and write speed. For each frame of video, the object recognition model will read and write once and then the inceptionV3 model will also read and write once. The I/O processing time is therefore much longer than the detection and classification time.

There are also some obvious shortcomings for the approaches. Clearly, for the training of deep learning models, it is necessary to leverage a large dataset comprising diverse, heterogeneous and authoritative data. However, to the best of our knowledge, such a data set for cat pain does not exist To enlarge the dataset, some data have been manually annotated without the supervision of professional veterinarians, which may lead to the generation of erroneous annotations. Uncertainty and personal bias for pain classification exists. This can result in the wrong pain score category of an action unit which will directly impact on the model performance for pain classification.

5   Conclusions and Future Work

In this paper, different deep learning methods were explored with regard to their ability to recognize and classify the pain level of cats in an automated fashion. The datasets were prepared and annotated by veterinarians experienced in animal and especially treatment of cats that are in pain from post-operative surgery. These were used for model training. The first approach focused on detecting cat body parts and associated pain scores directly. This achieved a reasonable overall result with the mAP of SSD300 reaching 90.2% and YOLOv5 achieving 94.6%. There were some limitations with this approach however including potential for skipped frames and attempting to have object detection models support classification. A second enhanced approach using inceptionV3 and transfer learning was explored. This was based on a general detection of cat ears and muzzles using YOLOv5 and SSD300 and classification using inceptionV3. The overall performance of this approach improved to achieve an accuracy of 93%.

There are several improvements that can be implemented for the future. As mentioned, it is clearly necessary to enlarge the amount of professionally labelled data to improve the accuracy and robustness of the deep learning models. A shared public cat pain dataset provided by vets or pet hospitals would greatly boost the research efforts and opportunities in this under-explored field. Other pain assessment scales such as the FGS (Feline Grimace Scale) [16] could be used to assess pain scores based on the position of different body parts such as ears, whiskers and the head, as well as considering orbital tightening and muzzle tension. The landmarks of the cat's facial expression would be another way to assess different pain levels as well as any vocalizations the make [17].

Exploration of other deep learning models could also be undertaken including use of multi-phase approaches such as Faster-RCNN [18]. There is a rapid evolution in deep learning and many lightweight and more accurate models are continually emerging. Exploring and exploiting these solutions would be a direct and obvious extension to the work here.

Development and delivery of this solution as a mobile application that could be used in veterinary practices and animal hospitals, e.g., attached to the cage where the animal is recovering, would be a further extension and ultimately the ideal endpoint for this work. This could include acoustic classification capabilities and body movement and behavioural responses.

Acknowledgments. The authors would like to thank the collaborators at Lort Smith and the Veterinary School at the University of Melbourne for provision of the data.

References

1. Jocher, G.: Ultralytics/YOLOv5: v3.1. Zenodo (2020). https://doi.org/10.5281/zenodo.415 4370
2. Liu, W., et al.: SSD: single shot multibox detector. In: Leibe, B., Matas, J., Sebe, N., Welling, M. (eds.) ECCV 2016. LNCS, vol. 9905, pp. 21–37. Springer, Cham (2016). https://doi.org/ 10.1007/978-3-319-46448-0_2

3. Szegedy, C., Vanhoucke, V., Ioffe, S., Shlens, J., Wojna, Z.: Rethinking the inception architecture for computer vision. In: Proceedings of the IEEE Conference on Computer Vision and Pattern Recognition, pp. 2818–2826 (2016)

4. Reid, J., Scott, E.M., Calvo, G., Nolan, A.M.: Definitive Glasgow acute pain scale for cats: validation and intervention level. Vet. Rec. **180**(18), 449 (2017). https://doi.org/10.1136/vr.104208

5. Hernandez-Avalos, I., et al.: Review of different methods used for clinical recognition and assessment of pain in dogs and cats. Int. J. Vet. Sci. Med. **7**(1), 43–54 (2019)

6. New app developed in Montreal to measure pain in cats. Montreal (2022). https://montreal.ctvnews.ca/new-app-developed-in-montreal-to-measure-pain-in-cats-1.5750733

7. Brondani, J.T., et al.: Validation of the English version of the UNESP-Botucatu multidimensional composite pain scale for assessing postoperative pain in cats. BMC Vet. Res. **9**(1), 1–15 (2013)

8. Tuttle, A.H., et al.: A deep neural network to assess spontaneous pain from mouse facial expressions. Mol. Pain **14**, 1–9 (2018). https://doi.org/10.1177/1744806918763658

9. Mahmoud, M., Lu, Y., Hou, X., McLennan, K., Robinson, P.: Estimation of pain in sheep using computer vision. In: Moore, R.J. (ed.) Handbook of Pain and Palliative Care, pp. 145–157. Springer, Cham (2018). https://doi.org/10.1007/978-3-319-95369-4_9

10. Sardinha, D.S., et al.: Pain assessment in horses using automatic facial expression recognition through deep learning-based modelling, pp. 1–12 (2021). https://doi.org/10.1371/journal.pone.0258672

11. Hummel, H.I., Pessanha, F., Salah, A.A., van Loon, T.J., Veltkamp, R.C.: Automatic pain detection on horse and donkey faces. In: Proceedings - 2020 15th IEEE International Conference on Automatic Face and Gesture Recognition, FG 2020, pp. 793–800 (2020). https://doi.org/10.1109/FG47880.2020.00114

12. Andersen, P.H., et al.: Towards machine recognition of facial expressions of pain in horses. Animals **11**(6), 1643 (2021). https://doi.org/10.3390/ani11061643

13. Finka, L.R., et al.: Geometric morphometrics for the study of facial expressions in non-human animals, using the domestic cat as an exemplar. Sci. Rep. **9**(1), 1–12 (2019). https://doi.org/10.1038/s41598-019-46330-5

14. Feighelstein, M., et al.: Automated recognition of pain in cats automated recognition of pain in cats. Sci. Rep. **12**(1), 1–10 (2022)

15. Sinnott, R.O., Aickelin, U., Jia, Y., Sinnott, E.R.J., Sun, P.Y., Susanto, R.: Run or pat: using deep learning to classify the species type and emotion of pets. In: IEEE Conference on Computer Science and Data Engineering, Gold Coast, Australia (2021)

16. Evangelista, M.C., et al.: Facial expressions of pain in cats: the development and validation of a Feline Grimace Scale. Sci. Rep. **9**(1) (2019). https://doi.org/10.1038/S41598-019-55693-8

17. Ntalampiras, S., Kosmin, D., Sanchez, J.: Acoustic classification of individual cat vocalizations in evolving environments. In: 2021 44th International Conference on Telecommunications and Signal Processing (TSP), pp. 254–258. IEEE (2021)

18. Ren, S., He, K., Girshick, K., Sun, J.: Faster R-CNN: towards real-time object detection with region proposal networks. In: Advances in Neural Information Processing Systems, vol. 28 (2015)

Perceiving Airline Passenger Booking Lifecycle with the Utilization of Data Warehouse

Prashneel Gounder and Kunal Kumar[✉]

Department of Computer Science and Mathematics, The University of Fiji, Lautoka, Fiji
KunalK@unifiji.ac.fj

Abstract. Today, expansive ventures depend on database frameworks to oversee their information and data. These databases are valuable for conducting day-by-day trade exchanges but do not provide information that could be used for analysis to make a strategic decision. A data warehouse also known as an informational database act as a central repository that accumulates historical data from various sources and multiple systems across the company, the analysis of which fosters strategic decisions. Data mining techniques and algorithms in conjunction with business intelligence tools were utilized to analyze, predict, forecast and make logical sense of the integrated data. The applicability of data warehouse was across various functional areas and different types of business. For instance, some domains of use cases with the likes of Health, Retail, Finance, Service, Manufacturing and so forth. This paper examined various implementations of data warehouses in the aviation industry and proposes a data warehouse design. The plan was clarified with a meticulous case study on comprehending airline passenger booking at various stages of its lifecycle through a data warehouse design utilizing the four-step dimensional modelling methodology enabling smart revenue management for airlines. The primary beneficiaries of this article are academics, data warehouse and database administrators, data scientists (data mining and Business intelligence specialist), airline operators, management team, and functional silos across the business who would need passenger-booking intakes to make strategic decisions.

Keywords: Snowflake Schema · Data warehouse for airlines · Analyzing Passenger Booking Record · Aviation · Data Mining · Business Intelligence · Sales Booking Record (SBR) · Dimensions and Fact · Fourth Dimensional Modelling

1 Introduction

In this fast challenging and dynamic era, technological innovation plays a pivotal role in the success of any company. Therefore, businesses continuously invest and explore opportunities to optimize processes and create greater value with the data collected over the years. With data in an electronic medium competitive advantage can be attained through analysis via businesses intelligence and decision support utilities that extensively contribute to the business's bottom line. Fiji's air transport industry, which includes airlines and their supply chain, is predicted to contribute $465 billion in GDP. Based on IATA's report published in 2018, in the next 20 years, the "current trends" scenario predicts a 75 percent increase in this revenue. An additional 1.1 billion dollars would be generated because of this. By 2038, there will be a million passenger departures. If this condition were satisfied, an increase in demand would support around 116,400 employment and $3.9 billion in GDP [1]. To cater for this boom in demand for air travel, airlines would need smart systems and technologies to facilitate the decision-making process quickly and accurately with a competitive advantage. OLTP database systems lack analytical capabilities and are unable to handle heterogeneous data from multiple source systems. Thus, organizations invest in data warehouses that form the backbone for the company's data needs.

As defined by the father of the data warehouse (Bill Inmon) - "A data warehouse has integrated subject-oriented, time-variant and has non-volatile data collection to support for management's decision-making process" [2]. Further breaking down this definition subject-oriented, data in the warehouse can be classed into a specific subject area. In a service-based industry, data is analyzed against time/status/Sales etc. Moreover, integrated data is centrally stored and is ingested from multiple sources. For instance, passengers' information such as name. Address and other details can be from the booking system, flight/uplift detail from the depart control system (DCS), and refund details from the refunds system which is consolidated and stored centrally. Furthermore, time-variant, data ingested in the data warehouse have a timestamp, which can be used as parameters for queries and analysis. This enables users to benchmark performance as of that date and other enhanced capabilities such as comparison year-to-date (YTD) or trend analysis of the last X months or years. Finally, nonvolatile data, whereby data in the warehouse is historical and is in its final form, is never to be manipulated. The process of data warehouse development is an iterative cycle of scoping, developing and deploying.

A deeper analysis of airline booking data from sources such as CRM and Loyalty, booking engines, departure control systems and web and social media channels provide a better understanding of booking patterns such as peaks and off peaks. Consequently, realigning strategies to meet high and low demands. Arline fares are usually classed into three categories namely, Business (J class), Economy (Y class) and First (F class) each of which is associated with booking classes. Factors such as aircraft capacity, sector type and flight date and time are attribute to the number of classes accompanying each flight. The holy grail of any airline business is to increase yields with fares and seat occupancy with a greater degree of control over the types of fares sold [4]. With frequent changes in fares, fare-repricing variables such as passenger booking data, anticipated data, inventory, and currency conversion rates at various points of sale are disseminated across multiple source OLTP databases. These OLTP sources do not provide insights to identify prices that match the customer's viewpoint and their overall impact on the company's financials. This paper exhibits a comprehensive design layout of the data for an airline industry that aids in the analysis of passenger booking throughout its lifecycle enabling smart revenue management. The ETL process (Extract, Transform and Load) has been documented to ingest data from multiple sources into a staging area, transform data based on conversion rules and logic, and push it to a central repository known as the Data warehouse. The data warehouse would provide a repository to capture sales booking records (SBR) (also known as passenger booking records) as a snapshot, the analysis of which helps airlines to evaluate the impact on their bottom line. The following are the objectives of this study:

1. Explore implementation and successful use cases of adoption of the data warehouse by the aviation industry.
2. Identify opportunities and challenges with the implementation and adoption of the data warehouse platform.
3. Design and propose a data warehouse architecture for airlines. The proposed data warehouse will aid airlines to analyze passenger bookings and undertake tactical and strategic decisions to capitalize on opportunities and overcome challenges in the arena of revenue management
4. Propose recommendations and ideas to successfully integrate and expand the data warehouse to other functional silos within the organization.

Following the introduction to the research problem, the paper is structured in the following manner: Sect. 2 entails the research methodology outlining the chronology and stages of research in constructing a data warehouse for this paper. Section 3 covers related work in the data warehouse discipline for airlines with successful use cases. Sections 4 and 5 highlight the challenges and benefits associated with the adoption and implementation of data warehouses. Next, Sect. 6 analysis and presents a data warehouse design with a snowflake schema to be used by airlines. Kimball's fourth dimensional modelling step has been incorporated to structure the design process. The design provides a comprehensive framework that lays the foundation for business intelligence revealing commercial insights for strategic airline decision-making. Section 7 provides future scope for this data warehouse and recommends suggestions to further expand the warehouse as a living ecosystem for the data needs of the organization. Finally, the paper concludes in Sect. 8.

The denouement of this research will benefit airline operators in implementing a data warehouse to trace passenger booking throughout its lifecycle. Additionally, it provides a platform to perform advanced analysis, prediction and forecasting to benchmark a company's performance against key performance indicators (KPIs). Consequently, take action to mitigate risk, and provide better services and promotions thus increasing the company's profitability. Functional silos and analysts would benefit from the ease of access to historical data and integrated data whereby capabilities such as slice and dice or drill up and down, YTD analysis would be a click away to make an informed decision.

2 Research Methodology

A thorough evaluation of written works was undertaken in reputable repositories such as but not limited to Google Scholar, IEEE Xplore, Springer, ResearchGate, and Science Direct was conducted. The usage of catchphrases ("Using Data Warehouse in the Airline Industry") AND ("Analyzing Passenger Booking using Data Warehouse", "Designing Data Warehouse for Airline") was the gold standard for these enquiries. Titles, keywords, and abstracts were used to map searches. Furthermore, data and article references from Airline sites, GDS Reports, IATA website are used to back up findings with statistics.The difficulties faced and options presented in implementing the usage of the data warehouse by the airline were explored. In addition, interviews with subject matter experts involved in data analysis were conducted. The feedback from these interviews revealed current issues, and data needs of the company and offered suggestions for implementing a data warehouse.Following the elicitation of requirements, a data warehouse design was proposed. The design incorporated four steps dimensional modelling methodology. With the implementation of a data warehouse, decision support systems and other BI tools could leverage data analysis that empowers the management team to make informed strategic decisions.

3 Related Work

3.1 Data Warehouse Implementations

Literature has reiterated the importance of data warehouses in a competitive and dynamic environment such as the airline industry enabling competitive advantages with the ability to make quick and informed decisions [4–6]. In addition, the literature also identifies the lack of quality data to facilitate the decision-making process as a challenge in the aviation industry [4–6]. [6]. Girsang et al. proposed a data warehouse using the nine-step methodologies by Kimbal to monitor the sales order lifecycle. The proposed design was attained taking into consideration the analysis and reporting requirements to monitor sales, refunds, orders, and inventory. The author's recommended an OLAP analysis using Pentaho data warehouse integration to analyze and reveal insights to make customers more loyal resulting in increased profits. [6]. The authors further elaborate on how to build the data warehouse using the nine-step methodologies by Kimbal. Abdallah et al. [7] highlight the use of data mining with classification techniques to predict the future demand for parts that will be required by an airline to perform aircraft maintenance. The source for this analysis was an airline data warehouse.

Chung et al. explained how business intelligence assists in making effective strategies and helps industries plan their business, reduce stock, and increase profitability by using demographic data and trend analysis of customers' demand for purchasing. Another research on Continental Airlines [9, 10] shows how the dynamics of the business can transform with real-time data warehousing in conjunction with business intelligence. Continental has gained over a $500 million increase in revenues and cost savings in areas like marketing, fraud detection, demand forecasting and tracking, and enhanced data centre management after investing $30 million in hardware and software over six years.

Moreover, another research paper proposed new systems based on big data technology (Data Lake) to facilitate decision-making at SATA Airlines. The Data lake technology supports the storage of large volumes of data in its native format ingesting customer-centric data from internal and external sources [11].

Similarly, Sachidanand et. al. [12] discuss how businesses can make optimal use of business analytics. Retrieving these insights involves realigning business processes and strategies to embed an analytical mindset and capabilities. The research was supported by three use cases where business analytics is utilized in medical, financial and supply chain management. Frank Acito et al. [13] presents a unique analytics system capable of processing queries over large volumes of aviation data. The system was built by Boeing Research and Technology (BR&T) Advanced Air Traffic Management (AATM) that stores Aircraft Situation Display feed to IBM DB2 data warehouse for further descriptive, predictive and conceivably prescriptive analysis. Tulinda et al. [14] propose an integrated aviation data warehouse on big data technology to combat airline operational problems. The author further elaborates on the use of analytical utilities to enhance aircraft performance, crew resourcing, enhance safety procedures. The authors [15, 16] explicitly demonstrate that predictive models with sparse, fine-grained data yield low predictive performance. The article is supported by empirical results with data extracted from nine different predictive applications.

Additionally, [17] proposed a novel destination management information system (DMIS) using business intelligence and data warehousing technologies. Alfredo et al. proposed a data warehouse for flight booking systems for online travel agencies helping to gain significant insights into customer behaviour using the procedures developed by Kimball. [18]. Donnelly [19] built a data warehouse to prove that flights can be impacted by certain weather conditions. The writer also queried data using BI tools to gain insights into the data warehouse. Hopfgartner et al. presented critical factors for the success of deploying a data warehouse and its adoption in the arena of sales forecasting and planning [20]. Jayashree and Priya proposed factors to consider in data warehouse design for the supply chain with a supporting case study to trace the order lifecycle [21]. Likewise, Ragulan and Subash et al. [22] also proposed a data warehouse design for sales and distribution. The paper also detailed the data migration, ETL, data indexing and loading processes. Girsang et al. discussed the implementation of the OLAP database and data warehouse using the nine-step method elaborated by Kimball and Ross. Dashboards were built using the information from the data warehouse [23].

Jian-bo and Chong-jun evaluated requirements, functions and architectures for data warehouse and business intelligence for Shanghai Airport Group and compared it with other types of data warehouse architectures. The authors proposed data bus architecture for airport development which evolves with the business need as opposed to a one-time development [24]. Bahadir and Karahoca took an experimental approach to perform data mining using a dataset from the data warehouse to compare the accuracy of different algorithms. The authors mentioned limitations with the volume of the dataset to run the mining algorithms [25]. Himmi et al. [26] shed light by presenting a case study as to how big data warehouse technology can be used in the airline industry to bolster profits and improve efficiency. Hueglin and Vannotti used information from a data warehouse to conduct data mining and determine the probability of passenger "no-shows" revealing passenger behaviour [27]. Jiang et al. developed a Customer-Centric E-Business (CCEB) System Meta Model that interfaced with a passenger data warehouse [28]. This paper lacked the technical specification of the model and the interface. Choosing the right data warehouse is critical during the design phase it can have performance implications based on the data integrated into the warehouse. Sidi et al. proved the benefits of star schema with faster query execution and response time, simpler, and easy to understand query when using bitmap index [29].

The environment in which airlines operate is very dynamic as business, profitability and survival are driven by many external factors. COVID-19 pandemic has demonstrated the volatility of an airline where revenue equated to almost zero with groundings and travel sanctions. Therefore, airlines must be empowered with BI and decision support tools to strategically make an informed decisions. Concisely, it can be concluded that while most papers focus on the implementation of data warehouses in business as a living ecosystem, there was not much emphasis on its adoption or implementation by the airline industry in recent years. In addition to this, none of the papers focused on resolving the challenge of tracing the passenger-booking lifecycle that would unlock smart revenue management. This paves a justification for further research in this arena.

3.2 Airline Usecases

Airline data is collected from heterogeneous platforms with the likes of departure control systems, refund systems, customer relationship management systems (CRM), and booking platforms. To get a holistic view of these data, information has to be integrated and analyzed which is accomplished through the use of a data warehouse. The below section discusses some arenas in which data warehouses have been adopted by airlines.

One of the use cases of a data warehouse in aviation was by American Airlines (AA) in the area of aviation safety data analysis. AA in conjunction with MITRE Corporation utilized its Aviation Safety Data Mining Workbench analysis to evaluate its Airline Safety Action Program (ASAP). This analysis involved evaluating its pilot incident report, and risky takeoff landing approaches to revamp its takeoff and land checklist. As a result of such analysis, AA was able to attain a higher safety rating and significantly improved its maintenance reliability, evaluate pilot workload and boost efficiency across the company [30]. on the other hand, AA also did not let the COVID-19 pandemic go to waste. During the pandemic, AA refocused its usage of the data warehouse from a historical perspective to a real-time one. This is accomplished with the usage of Microsoft Azure cloud, Teradata Vantage cloud analytics and data warehousing solutions. Not only, does this approach increase profitability but improves customer service and satisfaction [31].

Moreover, tech giants such as Oracles have also realized the importance and demand for data warehouses in the airline industry. Oracle's Airline Data Model (OADM) offering provides an off-the-shelf data warehouse that can integrate historical and transactional data from several source systems for advanced BI capabilities. OADM is specifically designed for airline's environment, thereby data formats and industry-specific metrics match the context of airlines. Thus significantly reducing time and efforts for the data cleansing process enabling faster deployment and compatibility with other airlines systems [32]. In a similar context, Amazon Redshift offers a fully managed petabyte, a column-oriented cloud data warehouse built for storing and analyzing massive data sets at scale. Redshift hooks into SQL-based clients and BI tools to provide information for analysis in real time. Redshift offers advantages such as faster query response time on large datasets, a pay-as-you-use model as opposed to upfront infrastructure and software setup cost, flexibility with scalability and ETL services Pentaho Data integration [33].

Furthermore, with a successful implementation of the data warehouse, Continental Airlines revamped its business with increased revenue and savings to a record US

$500 million. The real-time data warehouse technology was a key metric in attaining this success enabling a faster decision-making process. The data warehouse ingested data from 25 operational and 2 external systems either in real-time or in batches [34]. Next, with a data warehouse, Swiss International Airlines can make faster pricing decisions. This boosted the company's profit margins and passenger uplifts [35]. Similarly, Air France-KLM with its big data technology and mining algorithm can increase revenue for origin/destination bookings, forecast "no shows" and cancellations and manage overbooking caps by analyzing passenger profiles in its data warehouse [36].

4   Challenges Whilst Implementing

This section entails challenges whilst implementing a data warehouse for the company.

1. Data quality - Data cleaning becomes a challenge due to the heterogeneous data integration with information across multiple systems with different schemas and relational database environments that have run through the ETL process and are translated into a common language. More so, integration with both on-premise systems and cloud systems brings in an additional layer of complexity [37]. This requires an extensive understanding of data dictionaries from multiple systems. The integration between data sources can only be achieved if requirements are scoped and the dimensions of the facts are documented at early stages. Physical Design- the limitation of the physical design of the data warehouse introduces some common problems such as index selection, data partitioning and creation of data views. These aspects of the data warehouse are key determinants of performance specifically with execution time for highly expensive queries via decision support systems. In addition to this, poor design leads to other problems such as inconsistency in the data, longer ETL processes, and restrictions on the expansion of the data warehouse to ingest data from other silos/sources [38].
2. Data warehouse management- identifying expensive, deadlock queries, and managing scheduling resources are constraints related to data ware management. Other aspects include performance, scalability, and recoverability [39]. For instance, setting up a failover environment, how quickly can a data warehouse recover from an error state or failure and checkpoint issues with the ETL process with the rollback affecting many underlying data views and indices.
3. Interoperability issues – the ability to ingest data using common standards or processes can be a hurdle and possesses serious data integrity issues when integrating a legacy system that does not support a mechanism for interfacing [40].
4. Security Issues- the decision on which security measure to be implemented to safeguard the data must be carefully made as one solution may not be ideal for the entire organization. Besides this, blanket or global encryption introduces performance degradation and requires the management of a complex encryption key that resists ease of access to the needed information. Moreover, securing exposure of data warehouse via BI tools (via the internet (web data mining) [41]. Company sensitive data can be exploited with web breaches.

5. Investment and expertise- the incorporation of a data warehouse as a living ecosystem in the business is time-consuming and resource-intensive. This requires collaboration across various silos, and in-depth analysis of source data to effectively and efficiently convert tacit knowledge into explicit. In many instances company,'s may not have the needed expertise to set up and maintain data and thus opt to engage a third-party implementation specialist which comes at an added cost to the business. Furthermore, as the data warehouse consumes historical data from multiple sources the underlying huge infrastructure investment is required for optimized performance [42]. In addition to this, with organizational backup, failover and replication strategies this cost exponentially increases. All of these requirements come at an expense of significant investment in infrastructure, people which small and medium-sized companies may not be able to sustain. On the other hand, retaining technical data warehouse analysts and specialist is another challenge that many organizations encounter.

6. Requirements change-information needs of the organization change over time as the airline industry is dynamic which further introduces complexity in the design of the data warehouse. For example, if the requirement changes to ingesting more elements or use of a different source, the data warehouse design should be flexible to accommodate this change [43]. Additionally, there should be infrastructure capacity planning in place to sustain this growth in data. On the other hand, network expansion plans airline mergers and acquisitions, subsidiaries setup and airline code shares are common in aviation which induces more complexity in the data integration.

5 Benefits of Data Warehouses

There is a clear indication as to why operational databases are segregated from data warehouses. The DW typically support Online Analytical Processing (OLAP) over summarized, historic and consolidated data whereas operational databases support Online Transaction Processing (OLTP) with day-to-day activities which are structured and repetitive. There are significant returns with investments in implementing a data warehouse which is summarized below.

1. Enables complex analysis and visualization via a multidimensional model. For instance, in a passenger booking warehouse, the time of booking, country of sale/point of sale, agent, booking, and sector are dimensions of utmost importance. The dimensions are hierarchical such as the time dimension can be split into a day-month-quarterly-year hierarchy, booking as the RBD-Cabin hierarchy [44]. With the hierarchical composition OLAP operation such as rollup and drill down or slice and dice operations and pivoting can be performed which is restricted by the relational format in operational databases.

2. OLAP operations are independent of the OLTP databases. Executing expensive and complex queries against the OLTP would result in and deteriorate performance and in the worst cases, service outages which would affect the day-to-day activities [45].

3. The data warehouse integrates data from multiple systems and includes historical whereas operational databases are restricted to current data. An example of one such application is that - understanding trends and forecasts, requires historical data that would be absent from operational databases [46].

4. Inconsistencies with data integration from multiple systems can be corrected with a data warehouse via the ETL layers. Therefore, the data is standardized and is consistent in representation, codes and formats.

6 Analysis and Result

The proposed data warehouse for airlines that captures passenger booking records is covered in this section below. Kimball's four steps dimensional modelling methodology has been used to structure the design of the warehouse. This would be the model used to push the data into the dimensional warehouse optimized for reporting and analytics.

6.1 Business Requirement Analysis

The transactional database for the booking system is optimized for data integrity to support and store daily transactional data but is a nightmare to create reporting queries as multiple complicated joins are involved. Besides this, expensive reporting queries will have a performance impact on the transactional system thus affecting business day-to-day business. The structure of the transactional database limits integration with multiple sources and is restrictive with drill-through analysis to the lowest level, the analysis of which reveals more insights for strategic decision-making. This paves a strong justification for the airline data warehouse.

The proposed data warehouse architecture is ideal for the airline industry for smart revenue management. Data from source systems such as departure control systems, airline revenue management systems, booking engines, refund systems and any other data sources that house passenger bookings data will be consolidated into a central repository. ETL layer performs the necessary conversion, data cleansing, and error handling to standardize the data into a staging area before loading it into the warehouse. Various data query tools, report writers, BI and visualization tools query the warehouse to provide the needed information to analysts and management users for strategic decision-making. The snowflake schema was employed in this research. This technique explains dimension-to-dimension, which has the benefit of storing the available memory capacity. The fact table will be aided by the dimension table in displaying the data needs that the analyst desires to increase e-travel business optimization.

6.2 Business Process Selection

The proposed data warehouse would facilitate decision-making in the arena of passenger booking management. Key tasks involved in this process are:

- Passenger makes a booking by purchasing a ticket with the airline via either of the channels (agent, web, sales office).
- Passenger provides personal details such as name, passport, travel dates, sector(s) travelling, requests ancillary and special handling services (optional) and makes payment.
- Passengers may opt to change the itinerary with a change in dates, sector(s) travelling

- If the passenger decides not to travel, he/she claims a refund (penalties may be applicable depending on the class fare)
- Passenger utilizes the booking by travelling and the status of the coupon is updated as flown
- If the status of the coupon is unutilized past planned travelled dates, coupon(s) is/are marked as expired based on the airline's expiration policy.

These changes in the status of booking records will need to be tracked and analyzed enabling smart revenue management. Data analysis provides yields with flight to passenger ratio, unutilized or unsold seats to identify more revenue opportunities via targeted campaigns and promotions; total cash outflow with refunds, daily revenue inflow with daily sales analysis, and calculate forward sales liability.

6.3 Grain Declaration

The data loaded in the table is at the atomic level. The granularity is at the event level. With a new booking, an event number and version is generated in the source and subsequent changes or updates generate new events. These events would be ingested into the source. Preference for most airlines would be to capture, monitor and analyze revenue for all the routes operated by the airline. Thereby the grain of the warehouse is sales booking information by day by the route.

In addition to this, the granularity is supported by the proposed data warehouse as booking records are stored at the coupon/sector level. This is the lowest level, which can be drilled down to any booking record.

6.4 Dimension Identification

Each dimension has a surrogate key for each record to uniquely identify the record within the dimensional model and is independent of the source key. The idea of associating a surrogate key with each record is that, as data is ingested from heterogeneous platforms the definition and meaning of the business/primary key would vary across different sources, which would create inconsistencies with duplication. Therefore, a surrogate key is used to uniquely identify the record.

The dimensions are Type 2 slow-changing dimensions (SCD) where row versioning has been incorporated to track history. Each record in the fact table is included with an Expiry Date (ExpDate), timestamp and flag status (Current flag) to reflect the recency of the record. The data in the source system are event-based. As passenger booking (PNR) goes through various changes (changes in status, cancellations, and changes in the sector) there are new records generated to reflect the changes. Therefore, to trace and report on tickets since their inceptions maintaining historical data is critical. In addition to this, an ETL load data time stamp is included to reflect when data is ingested into the data warehouse.

The dimensions for the proposed warehouse is summarized in Table 1 below whereby primary/surrogate keys are denoted by PK and foreign keys are denoted by FK and cardinalities (1:1) denoting one-to-one relationship and (1:M) denoting one-to-many associations between the tables. Dimensions documents and coupons have sub-dimension to

Table 1. Dimension Definition

Name	Keys	Description	Relationship
Dim_Event	Event_ID PK	Updates to booking records trigger a new event each time. These events will be used to capture the historical updates to the booking record	Fact_Booking -Dim_Event (1:1)
Dim_Document	Document_ID PK	A passenger booking record is regarded as a document. The Document dimension captures itinerary information, passenger bio details, aggregation of fare, taxes, commission, discounts that are part of the document	Fact_Booking-Dim_Document (1:1) Dim_Document- Dim_Coupon (1:M)
Dim_DateTime	DateID PK	The date dimension is used to slice data to the lowest level	Fact_Booking -Dim_DateTime (1:1)
Dim_Coupon	Coupon_ID PK Document_ID FK RouteID FK	The Coupon dimension is a component of the ticket that captures the "good for passage"- the sector information that the passenger is entitled to travel as per the booking	Dim_Document- Dim_Coupon (1:M) Dim_Route-Dim_Flight (1:1)
Dim_Flight	FlightID	Captures Flight Details at Coupon Level	Dim_Route-Dim_Flight (1:1)

(*continued*)

Table 1. (*continued*)

Name	Keys	Description	Relationship
Dim_Crew	CrewID PK FlightID (PK, FK)	Captures Operating Crew Information	Dim_Flight –Dim_Crew (1:M)
Dim_Route	RouteID	Each Coupon in the document is associated with a Sector. This is captured in the route information	Dim_Route- Dim_Coupon (1:1)
Sub Dimensions (Fare, Commission, Taxes, FOP, Fees)	ID fields for respective Dimension PK DocumentID FK CouponID FK	Stores Fare, Commission, Taxes, FOP, Fees) at document and coupon level	A document and coupon have a (1:M) relation with these sub dimensions. For instance, with any dollar value transactions are captured in natural, published and base currencies

capture fare, fees, commission and taxes. These financial components of any booking are recorded in payment and base/natural currency, therefore normalizing the relation to ensuring referential integrity.

6.5 Fact Identification

The Fact Table of the proposed warehouse is "booking" with the fact being Total and Net Sales for the day by Sector. Measures associates with the Fact table are Total Fare in Base/Accounting and Natural/Payment Currency, Total Taxes in Base and Natural Currency, Total Commission in Base and Natural Currency, Total Discount in Natural and Base Currency and Net Fare/Revenue in Base and Natural Currency. The Net Fare measures are formulated whereby Net Fare = Total Fare - Commission - Discount - Taxes.

6.6 Analysis

With the implementation of the proposed warehouse, airlines should be able to conduct the following analysis for strategic decision-making.

- Origin and Destination – to monitor and trace source markets
- Total Sales by Location on given Day – Monitor daily revenue and induce promotions and campaigns in low performing sectors.
- Net Sales by Location on a given Day- Monitor net income with trend analysis. Compare with daily KPI and take initiatives to capitalize on opportunities.
- Sales by Channel –monitor and implement targeted campaigns via different channels

- Daily Uplift Analysis – Compare Total Uplifts per sector with Total Capacity.
- Agent Analysis – monitor performance of agents by location and implement incentives to further boost sales via agents (Fig. 1).

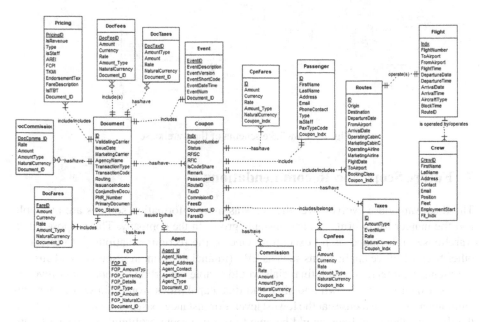

Fig. 1. ERD Data model for the OLTP System

6.7 Hosting Platform and Schedule

The data warehouse will be hosted on the Windows platform with Microsoft SQL Server 2019 platform as the underlying database. There are two databases involved in this architecture. Data from multiple sources (historical) are ingested into a staging database at scheduled intervals. SQL Server Integration Services (SSIS) provides the ETL layer for the proposed warehouse. Posting conversion and transformation data is pushed into a central repository as a warehouse. The architecture can be further expanded over multiple farms for failover, redundancy and high availability. The data warehouse is backed up weekly with a full backup and incremental backup schedules running daily as a night job.

6.8 Snowflake Schema

(See Fig. 2).

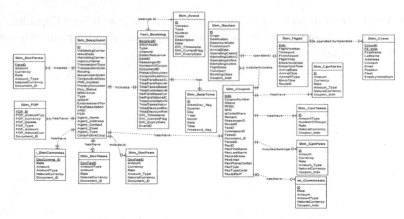

Fig. 2. Snowflake schema of the warehouse

7 Future Scope and Recommendations

The data warehouse evolves over the years as more information sources are available and the hunger for information and insights grows in the company. The proposed data warehouse in this paper is no exception. One of the recommendations is to integrate other back-of-office applications such as ERP (financials), human resources and aircraft maintenance. Integration with financials would enable the airline to benchmark revenue against expenses. Drill down and slice and dice capabilities would allow the management team to view expenses at the lowest level. For instance, based on data analysis from the data warehouse airlines would be able to retrieve route profitability, predict future demand, introduces discounts and competitive pricing through targeted marketing, and provide enhanced customer experience. Besides this, airlines may get insight into price sensitivity and what a client is ready to spend on a plane ticket by creating and analyzing individual profiles of passengers including information such as lifestyle purchase decisions, travel behaviors, and even passenger financial condition. In addition to this, as the aircraft is the most expensive asset for any airline, insights and strategic information such as return on investments, and fleet expansion needs would be a click away.

To quickly adapt to evolving demands and factors impacting business decisions, another recommendation as part of the future scope is to integrate data in near real-time. For example, implementing dynamic pricing and selling holiday packages as part of ticketing offerings via e-commerce channels. Furthermore, to make optimal use of insights from data analytics tools, data analysts and scientists need to be abreast with the latest developments in the market. Therefore, continuous training and upskilling are essential with a documented system operating procedure and data dictionary of the warehouse. This ensures that critical information is retained and passed onto successors with employee exits.

Next, the research area may be expanded to incorporate a reporting platform with integration to business intelligence, data mining and decision support tools. This integration would provide insights into the data in form of dashboards, and canned or Adhoc reports. Finally, proposing a data bus architecture for a data warehouse that evolves with the business need as opposed to a one-time development. This would cater for future expansion in the data needs of the airline.

8 Conclusion

With the nonstop advancement, innovation and business process optimizations and carriers will proceed to extend in the volume of commerce. The extensive volume and growth of information available from various sources pose a challenge to quicker analysis and the turnaround time for strategically making decisions. Embedding business intelligence capabilities with a data warehouse plays a pivotal role in decision-makers forming a more opportune and viable, more scientific and sensible business decision.

In addition to this, research has proposed a data warehouse architecture for airlines that will assist in smart revenue management using four steps dimensional methodology. As part of the research future scope and enhancements have been proposed that could become building blocks of the enterprise data warehouse. It is without a doubt that the successful implementation and adoption of a data warehouse in the aviation industry paves a foundation for a more lucrative and opportunistic business model. Information to support decision-making and capitalize on opportunities is a few clicks away without the dependency on technical staff and expertise.

References

1. Iata.org (2022). https://www.iata.org/en/iata-repository/publications/economic-reports/fiji-value-of-aviation/. Accessed 04 July 2022
2. The Data Warehouse: From the Past to the Present – DATAVERSITY. DATAVERSITY (2022). https://www.dataversity.net/data-warehouse-past-present/. Accessed 04 July 2022
3. Dou,X.: Big data and smart aviation information management system. Cogent Bus. Manage. 7(1), 1766736 (2020). https://doi.org/10.1080/23311975.2020.1766736. Accessed 3 July 2022
4. Nenadović, A.: Data warehouse for global air transport development. In: Symorg 2016, pp. 180–187 (2016). http://symorg.fon.bg.ac.rs/proceedings/2016/papers/DATA%20SCIE NCE%20AND%20BUSINESS%20INTELEGENCE.pdf#page=3. Accessed 16 Apr 2022
5. Yilma, G., Kumar, D., Kemal, M., Debele, G.: Leveraging big data analytics for airlines: personalization and smart pricing (2018). https://www.researchgate.net/publication/335444 692_Leveraging_Big_Data_Analytics_for_Airlines_Personalization_and_Smart_Pricing. Accessed 16 Apr 2022
6. Girsang, A., Isa, S., Puspita, A., Putri, F., Hutagaol, N.: Business intelligence for evaluation e-voucher airline report. Int. J. Mech. Eng. Technol. (IJMET) 10(2), 213–220 (2019). https://iaeme.com/MasterAdmin/Journal_uploads/IJMET/VOLUME_10_ISSUE_2/ IJMET_10_02_024.pdf. Accessed 16 Apr 2022
7. Karam, Z.: A Study on applying data mining in airline industry for demand forecasting by predicting item criticality (2018). https://bspace.buid.ac.ae/bitstream/handle/1234/1248/201 5128179.pdf?sequence=1. Accessed 16 Apr 2022
8. Chung, P., Chung, S.: On data integration and data mining for developing business intelligence. In: 2013 IEEE Long Island Systems, Applications and Technology Conference (LISAT) (2013). https://doi.org/10.1109/lisat.2013.6578235. Accessed 16 Apr 2022

9. Watson, H., Wixom, B., Hoffer, J.: Continental airlines flies sky high with business intelligence (2004). https://www.academia.edu/26484864/Continental_Airlines_Flies_Sky_High_with_Business_Intelligence. Accessed 16 Apr 2022

10. Watson, H., Wixom, B., Hoffer, J., Anderson-Lehman, R., Reynolds, A.: Real-time business intelligence: best practices at continental airlines. EDPACS **40**(6), 1–16 (2009). https://doi.org/10.1080/07366980903484935. Accessed 16 Apr 2022

11. Oliveira, Â., Mendes, A., Gomes, L.: Big data in SATA airline finding new solutions for old problems. Int. J. Comput. Sci. Inf. Secur. (IJCSIS) **14**(6) (2016). https://repositorioaberto.uab.pt/bitstream/10400.2/7650/1/Big_Data_in_SATA_Airline_finding_new_sol.pdf. Accessed 16 Apr 2022

12. Singh, S., Singh, N.: Big data analytics. In: 2012 International Conference on Communication, Information & Computing Technology (ICCICT) (2012). https://doi.org/10.1109/iccict.2012.6398180. Accessed 4 July 2022

13. Acito, F., Khatri, V.: Business analytics: why now and what next? Bus. Horiz. **57**(5), 565–570 (2014). https://doi.org/10.1016/j.bushor.2014.06.001. Accessed 4 July 2022

14. Larsen, T.: Cross-platform aviation analytics using big-data methods. In: 2013 Integrated Communications, Navigation and Surveillance Conference (ICNS), pp. 1–9 (2013). https://doi.org/10.1109/ICNSurv.2013.6548579

15. Ayhan, S., Pesce, J., Comitz, P., Sweet, D., Bliesner, S., Gerberick, G.: Predictive analytics with aviation big data. In: 2013 Integrated Communications, Navigation and Surveillance Conference (ICNS), pp. 1–13 (2013). https://doi.org/10.1109/ICNSurv.2013.6548556

16. Junqué de Fortuny, E., Martens, D., Provost, F.: Predictive modeling with big data: is bigger really better? Big Data **1**(4), 215–226 (2013). https://doi.org/10.1089/big.2013.0037. Accessed 4 July 2022

17. Höpken, W., Fuchs, M., Höll, G., Keil, D., Lexhagen, M.: Multi-dimensional data modelling for a tourism destination data warehouse. In: Cantoni, L., Xiang, Z. (eds.) Information and Communication Technologies in Tourism 2013, pp. 157–169. Springer, Heidelberg (2013). https://doi.org/10.1007/978-3-642-36309-2_14. Accessed 16 Apr 2022

18. Alfredo, Y., Girsang, A., Isa, S., Fajar, A.: Data warehouse development for flight reservation system. In: 2018 Indonesian Association for Pattern Recognition International Conference (INAPR) (2018). https://doi.org/10.1109/inapr.2018.8627015. Accessed 16 Apr 2022

19. Donnelly, I.: Correlation of airline flight delays with weather conditions (2018). http://norma.ncirl.ie/3450/1/iandonnelly.pdf. Accessed 16 Apr 2022

20. Hopfgartner, E., Schuetz, C., Schrefl, M.: A case study of success factors for data warehouse implementation and adoption in sales planning. In: AMCIS 2017 (2017). https://www.semanticscholar.org/paper/A-Case-Study-of-Success-Factors-for-Data-Warehouse-Hopfgartner-Sch%C3%BCtz/426e1293a2c471902d3f235b137f82684d9b608a. Accessed 16 Apr 2022

21. Jayashree, G., Priya, D.: Design of visibility for order lifecycle using datawarehouse. Int. J. Eng. Adv. Technol. **8**(6), 4700–4707 (2019). https://doi.org/10.35940/ijeat.f9171.088619. Accessed 16 Apr 2022

22. Balasingham, R., Subash, R.: Designing a data warehouse system for sales and distribution company (2021). https://www.researchgate.net/publication/349098830_Designing_a_Data_Warehouse_System_for_Sales_and_Distribution_Company. Accessed 16 Apr 2022

23. Girsang, A., Arisandi, G., Elysisa, C., Saragih, M.: Decision support system using data warehouse for retail system. J. Phys. Conf. Ser. **1367**(1), 012007 (2019). https://doi.org/10.1088/1742-6596/1367/1/012007. Accessed 16 Apr 2022

24. Jian-bo, W., Chong-jun, F.: Research on airport data warehouse architecture. Int. J. Bus. Humanit. Technol. **2**(4) (2012). https://www.ijbhtnet.com/journals/Vol_2_No_4_June_2012/12.pdf. Accessed 16 Apr 2022

25. Bahadir, C., Karahoca, A.: Airline revenue management via data mining. Glob. J. Inf. Technol. Emerg. Technol. **7**(3), 128–148 (2017). https://doi.org/10.18844/gjit.v7i3.2834 Accessed 16 Apr 2022

26. Arcondara, J., Himmi, K., Guan, P., Zhou, W.: Value oriented big data strategy: analysis & case study. Hdl.handle.net (2022). http://hdl.handle.net/10125/41277. Accessed 16 Apr 2022

27. Hueglin, C., Vannotti, F.: Data mining techniques to improve forecast accuracy in airline business. In: Proceedings of the Seventh ACM SIGKDD International Conference on Knowledge Discovery and Data Mining - KDD 2001 (2001). https://doi.org/10.1145/502512.502578. Accessed 16 Apr 2022

28. Jiang, D., Yu, D., Li, D., Qian, D.: Airline customer-centric E-business (CCEB) system meta model and data warehouse. In: Proceedings of 7th International We-B (Working For E-Business) Conference 2006 e-Business: how far have we come? (2006). https://researchbank.swinburne.edu.au/file/573ca290-d506-42d0-aca7-b83 33851210f/1/PDF%20%28Published%20version%29.pdf. Accessed 16 Apr 2022

29. Sidi, E., El, M., Amin, E.: Star schema advantages on data warehouse: using bitmap index and partitioned fact tables. Int. J. Comput. Appl. **134**(13), 11–13 (2016). https://doi.org/10.5120/ijca2016908108

30. Nazeri, Z.: Application of aviation safety data mining workbench at american airlines. The MITRE Corporation (2022). https://www.mitre.org/publications/technical-papers/application-of-aviation-safety-data-mining-workbench-at-american-airlines. Accessed 04 July 2022

31. American Airlines flies its data warehouse to the cloud. SearchDataManagement (2022). https://www.techtarget.com/searchdatamanagement/news/252509924/American-Airlines-flies-its-data-warehouse-to-the-cloud. Accessed 04 July 2022

32. Oracle.com (2022). https://www.oracle.com/technetwork/database/options/airlines-data-model/airlines-data-model-bus-overview-1451727.pdf. Accessed 04 July 2022

33. Cloud Data Warehouse – Amazon Redshift – Amazon Web Services. Amazon Web Services, Inc. (2022). https://aws.amazon.com/redshift/. Accessed 04 July 2022

34. Anderson-Lehman, R., Watson, H., Wixom, B., Hoffer, J.: Continental airlines flies high with real-time business intelligence. MIS Q. Execut. **3**, 163–176 (2004)

35. Mendes, A., Guerra, H., Gomes, L., Oliveira, Â., Cavique, L.: Big data in SATA airline: finding new solutions for old problems. Hdl.handle.net (2022). http://hdl.handle.net/10400.3/4080. Accessed 03 July 2022

36. Asharaff, M.: Study of data warehouse architecture. Glob. Sci. J. **10**(2) (2022). https://www.globalscientificjournal.com/researchpaper/Study_of_Data_Warehouse_Architecture.pdf. Accessed 4 July 2022

37. Four-Step Dimensional Design Process. Kimball Group (2022). https://www.kimballgroup.com/data-warehouse-business-intelligence-resources/kimball-techniques/dimensional-modeling-techniques/four-4-step-design-process/. Accessed 04 July 2022

38. Iqbal, M., Mustafa, G., Sarwar, N., Wajid, S., Nasir, J., Siddque, S.: A review of star schema and snowflakes schema. In: Bajwa, I., Sibalija, T., Jawawi, D. (eds.) INTAP 2019. Communications in Computer and Information Science, vol. 1198, pp. 129–140. Springer, Singapore (2020). https://doi.org/10.1007/978-981-15-5232-8_12

39. McKelvey, N., Curran, K., Toland, L.: The challenges of data cleansing with data warehouses. In: Effective Big Data Management and Opportunities for Implementation, pp. 77–82 (2016). https://doi.org/10.4018/978-1-5225-0182-4.ch005. Accessed 3 July 2022

40. Bellatreche, L., Chakravarthy, S.: A special issue in extending data warehouses to big data analytics. Distrib. Parallel Databases **37**(3), 323–327 (2019). https://doi.org/10.1007/s10619-019-07262-1

41. Wu, L., Yuan, L., You, J.: Survey of large-scale data management systems for big data applications. J. Comput. Sci. Technol. **30**(1), 163–183 (2015). https://doi.org/10.1007/s11390-015-1511-8. Accessed 4 July 2022

42. https://joinup.ec.europa.eu/sites/default/files/document/2018-05/SC508DI07171%20D05.02%20Big%20Data%20Interoperability%20Analysis_v1.00.pdf

43. Risks and challenges of data access and sharing. Oecd-ilibrary.org (2022). https://www.oecd-ilibrary.org/sites/15c62f9c-en/index.html?itemId=/content/component/15c62f9c-en. Accessed 04 July 2022

44. Venkatraman, S., Venkatraman, R.: Communities of practice approach for knowledge management systems. Systems **6**(4), 36 (2018). https://doi.org/10.3390/systems6040036. Accessed 4 July 2022

45. Chen, E.T.: Implementation issues of enterprise data warehousing and business intelligence in the healthcare industry. Commun. IIMA **12**(2), Article 3 (2012). https://scholarworks.lib.csusb.edu/ciima/vol12/iss2/3

46. Andiyappillai, N.: Factors influencing the successful implementation of the warehouse management system (WMS). Int. J. Comput. Appl. **177**(32), 21–25 (2020). https://doi.org/10.5120/ijca2020919787. Accessed 4 July 2022

Utilizing an Airline Data Warehouse for Website Data Analytics: A Conceptual Design

Ravnesh Kumar and Kunal Kumar[✉]

Department of Computer Science and Mathematics, The University of Fiji, Lautoka, Fiji
KunalK@unifiji.ac.fj

Abstract. As a result of the Covid-19 outbreak, airlines are focusing more on online booking engines, which require airlines to segment clients, target personalized offers, and monitor channel performance, advertising spend, goal conversion, and campaign effectiveness using web analytics data. To accommodate all of these aspects, as well as quick responses to current and future demands, enhanced planning, and alignment with corporate decision-making, a data warehouse is required. This study will illustrate how to integrate website data into a data warehouse as well as its data model using the snowflake schema. A thorough case study on understanding airline digital booking engine data at different stages of its lifecycle through a data warehouse architecture using the four-step dimensional modelling approach, allowing smart revenue management for airlines, provided more clarification of the strategy. This post will mostly benefit the airline's digital team, data warehouse and database administrators, digital analysts, revenue management team, and functional segments throughout the organization that use digital passenger-booking inputs to make strategic choices.

Keywords: Google Analytics · Data warehouse in airlines · ETL Process · schema · reporting schema · digital marketing analytics · E-Commerce · fourth step dimensional modelling · Data Analytics · Web Matrices

1 Introduction

One of the main drivers for airlines has been online marketing, and there has been a lot of interest in employing web analytics to assist and determine user behavior, the impact of website design and marketing creativity on online conversions and adoration. Most businesses aren't investing enough in evaluating data from digital platforms these days. Even when businesses have sufficient funds to invest in measuring technology, they frequently fail to devote sufficient resources and effort to make the tools work for them [1]. Customer loyalty on the other hand might be difficult to come by in today's world, with so many flying options available. However, the more information you have about your consumer and their purchasing motivations, the more you will be able to influence their purchasing decisions. To do so, marketing management must gather and analyze a large amount of data about their customers, which is often housed in airline line-of-business apps.

C.-H. Hsu et al. (Eds.): DataCom 2022, LNCS 13864, pp. 259–274, 2023.
https://doi.org/10.1007/978-981-99-2233-8_19

Because of the epidemic, airlines have shifted their focus to selling online rather than through traditional channels such as reservations and travel agencies. This creates a challenge to get meaningful data that allows the airline to change direction in an instant when the business climate and client demand change more unexpectedly. Web Analytics combines statistics, data mining algorithms, and methodological procedures. E-Commerce analysts draw several pallets of data sources to find the flawless combination that will return actionable insights. From the airline's perspective, data is analyzed from the past 5 years against the next 5 years to find trends and design pricing, routing and budget strategies for the next 3 to 6 years onwards. However, there are certain drawbacks with online analytical applications and self-service analytics tools like spreadsheets and dashboards where data is obtained from a single source [2].

With so much rivalry in the airline-to-airline digital market, a data warehouse is required to allow marketing and analytics teams to compile data on the number of site users and their user behaviors. Data warehouses are a new and primarily focused technology that is currently being employed in practically every industry to improve business performance. This would help in driving more extensive analysis and market assessment hence maximizing the value of the website.

Campaigns driven from different social media platforms such as Facebook, Google, Instagram, data get easily consolidated into web analytics platforms like Google Analytics. Yet, these platforms' reporting and dashboard pages are confined to a specific time period and provide minimal insight into user and campaign performance. This paper is focused on the conceptual architectural design of the airline's web analytics data warehouse, data integration, challenges, and benefits, and drives digital analysts more into extensive analysis and market assessment.

Data is transforming airlines from pre-flight through post-flight operations in the aviation industry, including booking, seats, luggage, boarding, ground transportation, and customer experience. With real-time data access, the findings of this study will help digital marketers analyze user experience, and campaign behavior, and develop user journeys. As a result, timely reactions to present and future demands, improved planning and alignment with business decision making, and a clear understanding and monitoring of the major performance drivers relevant to the aviation sector are all enhanced. The results will also aid in propelling the aviation sector to new heights by assisting them in meeting consumer demands, real-time performance dashboards, and proactive maintenance in any way feasible.

The following is a breakdown of the paper's structure. The second section delves into the research methods used in the Kimbal Technique. In Sect. 3, the literature studies are described based on a series of questions linked to this study, as well as the reasons why airlines require data warehouses (DWH) and the obstacles encountered with planning and designing. The results and analysis are presented in Sect. 4, which contains the DWH conceptual design, the kind of schema employed, the suggested architecture, and the DWH data model. Section 5 identifies the research's limitations on the research topic. Section 6 examines the research's future scope and suggestions, as well as mode design and DWH improvement. Section 7 closes the paper with concluding remarks.organizations can choose the best method for implementation in their individual organisations respectively.

2 Research Methodology

Research is entirely based on Google Analytics data which is used as a repository to capture online user behavior. The study has adopted Kimbal Technique which goes through several steps to achieve the expected results. For this study, the data warehouse was conceptualized through Kimball's fourth step of dimensional modelling. Identifying a business process, selecting a grain, determining dimensions, and determining a fact table are the fourth steps in the dimensional modelling method (Fig. 1).

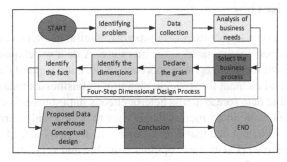

Fig. 1. Research methodology

During the design of a dimensional model, there are four crucial considerations to make:

- Select the business process. This step outlines the business processes required to leverage the data warehouse to establish the dimensions and facts at the end of the modelling.
- Declare the grain. Declared grain can be used to identify the contents of the fact table. Grain will map the information requirements based on the data warehouse design.
- Identify the dimensions. The needs of the fact table are met by dimension tables. The development of the dimension table makes the fact table's aims easier to understand and interpret.
- Identify the facts. The fact table is the physical representation of the data warehouse and the primary focus of business requirements. The results of business operations that should meet all needs will be displayed in the fact table. The fact table is a table that typically contains numbers and historical data, with the key being particularly unique because it serves as the primary and foreign keys relationship for the current dimensional relations.

The hybrid design methodology was practised to re-engineer Google Analytics data schema, business goals and integrated data-driven approach. This methodology assists in setting up a strategy to overcome unstructured data, retuning ETL processes to get structured into the data warehouse.

As a foundation for developing a data warehouse, business optimization challenges become identification findings. Data is gathered through the airline's web analytics as well as the examination of literature for support. The study also proposes the conceptual design of an analytics data warehouse for an airline, particularly on the e-commerce side of the airline.

Through a diverse understanding of business needs in e-travel, business optimization produces an analysis of how to better it and business need becomes the foundation for the design of a data warehouse using the above four-step dimensional modelling. The data warehouse design outcomes are expected to be the airline's response to the requirement to improve e-commerce optimization.

3   Literature Review

The importance of a data warehouse in a competitive digital market environment like the aviation sector has been emphasized in the literature. A data warehouse has evolved as a significant platform for the integrated approach of decision support data in businesses and become a crucial element for strategic planning in businesses today [3]. It has also been highlighted that data spread across heterogeneous data sources is difficult to clean, filter, transform, and store in a structure that is easy to access and interpret [4, 5].

Researchers also mentioned that with Google's restrictions placed on Google Analytics, it is difficult to work with basic options available and very little data available to work on dashboards [6, 7].

The authors also propose a better way to deal with the concerns through robust, in-house data storage with qualitative and quantitative storage capability for predicting future demands on electronic commerce in the aviation industry [8, 9].

Data analytics is emphasized as a critical topic in data warehousing. Given the complexity and volume of data in warehouses, the requirement for specialist software to perform sorting and searching functions is examined [10–12]. Researchers [13] also studied an online travel company that data warehouse development has the purpose to develop a big picture of customer behavior and provide quick and accurate information for management for the best decision.

In further research into the tourism industry, the authors presented ideas on a methodological framework for digital marketing intelligence and automation through data warehousing in obtaining economic benefits [14, 15]. Pandey also explains that due to the pandemic, businesses have moved the focus toward e-commerce and marketers needs to develop marketing communication plan through digital data warehousing. This would boost target-market customers for insights and future direction [16]. Papers [17–19] discuss the airline's efficiency through a campaign which is critical to allow digital analysts to obtain information about online competitors and satisfy their customers' demands and preferences.

Raj through her analytical study based a theoretical view on data retention and non-volatile storage while contrasting transactional systems with data warehouses for keeping historical records [20]. A study on Continental Airlines states that Data should not change once it is stored in the data warehouse since it is non-volatile. In a nutshell, data in a data warehouse is stable [21]. Further research was done on Continental Airlines which has transformed its industry position from "worst to first" and subsequently from "first to favourite" with real-time data warehousing and business intelligence (BI) that supports an ambitious Go Forward business plan [22].

Moreover, a segmentation study was done for the airline's domestic bookings which use the data bus architectural model to maintain data dimension consistency and the gradual completion of data warehouse construction following business development needs [21]. Studies done by Fangyi explain the combination of data mining technology with customer segmentation theory to highlight the process of air cargo customer segmentation to improve the application level of customer relationship management in the air cargo industry. Some domestic literature has provided a prototype of an air cargo data warehouse, and using this prototype, conducted an OLAP analysis, and achieved some practical results on air freight customer behavior [23].

The authors examined airlines' traditional data warehouse solutions which tend to be a problem when there's large customer behavioral data. The analytics necessitates the collection of data from various sources however, with growing data volume this gets worse in terms of agility and flexibility [24, 25]. Nair also explained that business analytics will assist managers in gaining deeper insights for successful business operations by allowing them to make fact-based decisions, resulting in increased competitiveness, however, it also has been stressed the major challenge is in the storage, integration, and reconciliation of data from various divergent sources across several business activities, as well as continual updates to the data warehouse [26, 27].

Furthermore, a study on Data Management shows the challenges faced with data integration. Query optimization, insufficient resources, and skilled professionals are some of the challenges because data integration necessitates high-level professionals who understand the data model and which tools to use [28, 29]. The authors from [30, 31] advocate the need for designing and building machine learning-based models for ETL-based data integration which can help organizations have potential systems in place for decision-making. It is strongly recommended for organizations to improve their ETL solutions' procedures, and that more robust analytic solutions are needed to enable effective and efficient decision-making.

To conclude, the goal of a Data Warehouse is to give decision-makers consistent, reliable, and timely data in a manner that enables easy retrieval, exploration, and analysis for analytical, planning, and assessment purposes. Due to the pandemic and market competition, airlines have shifted their focus more on selling online compared to offline channels like reservations and travel agents. Precision in terms of client targeting would be crucial. This would necessitate a combination of data and technology to identify growing sectors in the target market.

3.1 The Need for Data Warehouse in Digital Space?

The cold, hard reality is that most advertising groups depend on simple spreadsheets and dashboard tools for information "capacity", examination, perception, and announcing. And keeping in mind that that is just fine with small data volumes, self-service analytics tools like spreadsheets and dashboards won't be able to handle an ever-growing magnitude of marketing data [32]. The number of marketing tools used by the average company is continually increasing. There are a few ad platforms, CRM, CMS, many social media platforms, an email system, and perhaps a few more tools and platforms, in addition to one or two analytics systems. All of these technologies are designed to make our jobs as marketers, business owners, or data analysts easier and more efficient

[33]. In practice, however, one would wind up with systems that don't interact properly with one another and nearly never agree on key criteria. This may cause confusion and disagreement among teams, resulting in a situation where no one knows which tool or numbers to believe at the end of the day [34].

Decision Support; Data warehouse's have evolved as a significant platform for the integrated approach of decision support data in businesses and become the crucial point for strategic planning in businesses today [3]. Data warehouses provide an infrastructure that creates a process of accessing unrelated data sources, cleaning, filtering, and transforming the data and storing the data in a structure that is easy to access and interprets [5]. Afterwards, the information is used for querying, reporting, as well as data analysis. Data warehousing has also evolved as an effective tool for transforming data into meaningful information, providing management and analysts with better accessibility to integrated and archived data from heterogeneous data sources to aid planning and decision-making. While working with web analytical applications like Google Analytics, provides a basic option to work on such as standard reports, and very little or no access to raw data to work on the dashboards [6, 7]. Therefore, marketing data warehousing can store a huge amount of historical intelligence which could be analyzed at different periods, aid in forecasting and trends can be a game-changer for digital marketers [8].

Data Quality Relate to Better Communication Success; Data quality assurance ensures that your marketing plan is founded on correct data regarding your marketing activities. A data warehouse helps you check the quality and integrity of your client data for marketing reasons by converting data from numerous sources into a single format. This helps you to detect and reduplicate data, as well as keep track of records that aren't kept up to date. Programs for quality assurance can be costly and time-consuming. Using such a data warehouse can eliminate many of these headaches, and the cost reductions alone can be enough to justify the investment. Poor data is not only a problem for your business, but it also reduces the overall profitability of your operations [14, 15].

In this regard, it provides a greater opportunity for marketers to develop a marketing communication plan and adapt to the reality of their target-market customers' expectations. For an airline, efficiency in the campaign is critical as it allows digital analysts to obtain information about online reputation and competitors, allowing them to improve the campaigns they're running in the market to satisfy the demands and preferences of their customers [17, 18].

Data Retention and Non-Volatile; Every piece of data in a data warehouse is associated with a specific time. A data warehouse is used to store historical data. In a data warehouse, for example, records from 3 months, 6 months, 12 months, or perhaps even older can be retrieved. This is in contrast to a transactional system, which typically just keeps the most recent data. A transaction system, for example, may save a client's most recent address, whereas a data warehouse may store all addresses linked with a customer [20]. Data should not change once it is stored in the data warehouse since it is non-volatile. If there has been an insert, update, or delete in the database, a different version of the data is stored in the data warehouse. As a result, the actual data is never changed. In a nutshell, data in a data warehouse is stable.

Emphasis on Growth Segments; In the post-pandemic commercial context, accuracy in terms of client targeting would be crucial. Finding growing sectors in the customer base will necessitate the use of data and technology. It is necessary to examine the older target section to narrow the most promising target segment even further [35]. This new targeted target segment (also known as growth segments) would result in a higher conversion rate with less resource investment, as well as the lowest cost per conversion. In addition to retargeting and customized services, behavioral targeting utilizing client digital footprints would seem to be a game-changer for businesses. The behavioral targeting method should be used to define the growth segments inside the existing target segment. To be successful in digital marketing, the majority of the spending must be allocated to these growth sectors [16, 36].

3.2 Challenges Faced

One of the most challenging and considerable investments into data warehousing is ETL(extract, transform, load) system. A distinctive ETL system may be useful for managing structured data that is up-to-date and relevant for business insights and decision-making. However, dealing with faster streams, time-sensitive data, on the other hand, demands a different approach and a lot of tuning to the ETL system, since high availability, low latency, and horizontal scalability are three essential elements that must be addressed in a near real-time context [37].

Change in business needs or processes also impacts data warehouse designs [38]. The change in development is considered complex and challenging when doing an overhaul during:

- Pre-deployed stage of a data warehouse: is concerned with the examination of the organization and its operations. It is conceivable to detect a need for data that does not exist in the company today and must be derived to meet the data warehouse's requirements at this point.
- Post-deployed stage of a data warehouse: a stage concerned with the actual use of the data warehouse that has previously been implemented The data warehouse may identify new possible strategies for the organization, which may necessitate a restructuring of the organization's procedures.

Furthermore, security is another factor that contributes to the challenges of data warehouses. Data security issues are linked to security issues. Because all communications are reliant on an internet connection, security issues are also related to Internet security in general. As stated by the authors 'K. Buntak, M. Kovacic and M. Mutavdzija' [39], "The existing encryption methods are no longer sufficient to ensure a satisfactory level of security. Likewise, there is a lack of adequate software solutions for managing, analyzing, and printing such a large amount of data."

4 Results Discussion

To conclude, the goal of a Data Warehouse is to give decision-makers consistent, reliable, and timely data in a manner that enables easy retrieval, exploration, and analysis for analytical, planning, and assessment purposes. Due to the pandemic and market competition, airlines have shifted their focus more on selling online compared to offline channels like reservations and travel agents. Precision in terms of client targeting would be crucial. This would necessitate a combination of data and technology to identify growing sectors in the target market.

4.1 Data Warehouse Conceptual Design

Multidimensional databases used in analytical processing are known as data warehouses. The traditional architecture is typically based on a multi-level strategy, with (a) the data source layer containing mixed databases that can be internal or external to the information system, (b) the data warehouse layer storing cloned and aggregated data, and (c) the analytic layer running the applications used to perform analysis and deploy reports and dashboards for business managers. An ETL (Extraction, Transformation, and Loading) stage is required in this architecture to extract data from sources, execute transformation and cleaning activities, and ultimately feed the data warehouse [40]. The requirement approach becomes more supportive when designing reports and dashboards for the digital marketing team to study further user behavior.

4.2 Snowflake Schema

One technique of structuring a data warehouse with a normalization procedure for existing dimension tables is the snowflake schema which was applied in this research. In this design, data dimensions are the source of information that will be used to make decisions.

This scheme explains dimension-to-dimension, which has the capability of storing the allocated memory capacity, normalized tables reducing data redundancy and speeds up the processing of data analysis needed [33]. The dimension table will assist the fact table in displaying the data needs that the analyst desires in order to boost the airline's ecommerce company optimization. To improve user behavior and online transactions, a data warehouse with a snowflake structure was designed in this study.

4.3 Proposed Infrastructure Architecture

For the web analytical data warehouse, the study has adopted two-level architecture that can be observed as:

• data source layer, a connection to google analytics database which hosts raw data.
• data warehouse layer holds data that has been synthesized and aggregated.

The analytics layer can be added as an unobserved layer to the data warehouse which uses OLAP (On-Line Analytical Processing) operators to execute the applications required to build and publish dashboards containing reports and charts (Fig. 2).

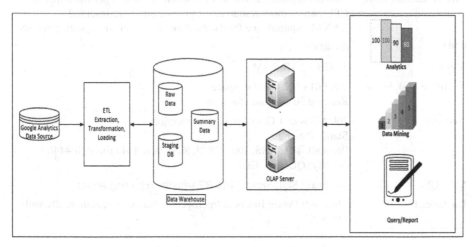

Fig. 2. Proposed DWH Architecture

1. Infrastructure Requirements

Airlines integrating the transactional database with other data sources are all collated and stored in a data warehouse through ETL processes. The data model is built in such a way that it can aggregate data from all of these sources and make business choices based on it. Based on calculated factors such as risks and cost-benefit analysis, Airlines have options to use a cloud-based data warehouse or build and maintain an on-premise system. In an on-premise data warehouse, the airline implements one of the various data warehouse systems – either open-source or paid solutions – on their infrastructure and the estimated requirements would be (Table 1):

Table 1. Infrastructure requirements

Component	Required
Operating system	Based on airlines infrastructure, airlines may choose: Microsoft Server Red Hat Enterprise Linux Or other operating systems that are compatible with Microsoft SQL Database

(continued)

Table 1. (*continued*)

Component	Required
Virtual machine (VM)	This component can run in a virtual environment, provided that the CPU and memory resources for your instance are reserved 2 * VM required, one for database and the other for reporting service
CPU	8 - 40 CPU cores
Memory	32 GB - 2 TB RAM
Available Disk Space	200 GB - 512 GB disk space Keeping 50 GB aside for logs
Network	100 Mbps or 1 Gbps Ethernet connection Static IP address Ports 80, 443, 1098, 1099, 3873, 8083, and 4444 through 4446 For MySQL, port 3306
MS SQL	Microsoft SQL Server 2016 R2 with the reporting server
Dashboard	Microsoft Power Business Intelligence that can integrate easily with MS SQL

The Airline does not have to worry about establishing or managing a data warehouse while using a cloud-based data warehouse service. The supplier creates and maintains the data warehouse, and all of the features necessary to run it are offered via online APIs. AWS Redshift, Microsoft Azure SQL Data Warehouse, Google BigQuery, Snowflake, and others are examples of such services.

2. ETL (Extract, Transform, Load)

Bringing source data into your data warehouse without any modifications is a solid ETL strategy however, data needs to place in staging tables and transformed as per business requirements, which can be moved further into summary or reporting tables. Google Analytics offers an API integration opportunity to automate complex reporting and configuration tasks from which other systems can integrate and pull data [41].

To achieve this, airlines can directly use MS SQL Server Integration Services (SSIS). MS SSIS is a framework for implementing enterprise-level data integration and data transformations. SSIS enables to copy or download files, load data warehouses, cleanse and extract data, and manage SQL Server objects and data using Integration Services [42]. The ETL service may then be built on the same DWH database server, with the scheduler and failover notification enabled.

Furthermore, airlines also have the option to migrate ETL service on a cloud platform such as MuleSoft, which is an open-source platform that makes data integration simple. Businesses can spend less time thinking about database and application connectivity and more time concentrating on key business operations by leveraging MuleSoft's Anypoint Platform. DataWeave, a component of the Anypoint Platform, is a strong data integration tool that provides simple yet powerful integration capabilities for ETL workflows and high-performance data mapping activities [43].

3. Data Refresh

Every user interaction, including pageviews, screen views, events, and ecommerce transactions, can be transmitted to Analytics as a separate hit. As a result, a single session might provide a large number of hits and every hit on Google Analytics servers gets monitored. In other words, data present in Google Analytics are real-time data. ETLs can be scheduled based on business requirements to retrieve data from the Google Data source which could be hourly or every 30 min depending on the latency and duration of extraction.

The Google Analytics Reporting API v4 allows programmatic access to Google Analytics report data in a single request with two date ranges. However, to prevent the system from getting more data than it can manage and to maintain a fair allocation of system resources, Google places limitations and quotas on API calls. A refresh rate can then be calculated based on API pricing schemes and quota allotment.

4.4 Design with Snowflake Schema

The snowflake approach is used in the construction of the e-commerce customer-behaviour data warehouse for business optimization, as illustrated in Fig. 3 below.

The snowflake data model allows defining hierarchies using smaller, normalized relational tables as sub-dimensions which helps to eliminate data redundancy and speed up data analysis processes. In terms of scalability and resource independence, the Snowflake schema is more elastic, requiring less time to recover and having fewer risks of failure. The query to extract data from several dimensions and sub-dimensions, however, has certain complexity [44].

1. Fourth Step Dimensional Model

The business processes chosen in the data warehouse are User location, systems information, personal and acquisition details and pages & session data. These processes determine the high-level user behaviour on the website. The determination of the grains is defined in the four dimensions defined below for the data model. The fact table identified for the website analytics DWH design is the session table shown in Fig. 3 which captures every session detail of the user who visits the webpage.

Location dimensions; These are the most important dimensions that determine where the user visited closely relating to the geolocation. Country and City tables are used to store 'real' location data, language table is used to collect data on different site editions the website accessed from. This helps in targeting certain campaigns as a user could be in a different country but accessing a different site edition. Service Provider table stores the unique service provider name in the dictionary.

The location aspects give a clear image of where a website performs best and may be further broken down by city, website language, and service name. This greatly aids

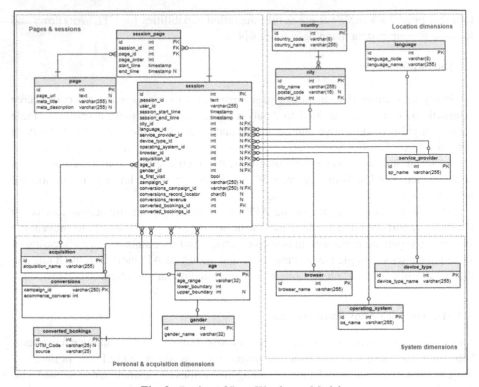

Fig. 3. Design of Data Warehouse Model

marketing in determining their target market and providing appropriate information and advertisements.

System dimensions; The system dimensions topic area has the same format as the "location dimensions" subject area, which has three dictionaries that each describe a single session. A list of device types used by a site visitor, such as desktop, tablet, or mobile, will be stored in the device type dictionary. The operating system dictionary will only hold all of the device's operating systems, not versions. The browser dictionary keeps track of all the different browsers that a user could use to view a website. NULL is used where data does not exist in the data tables. The system aspects provide clear information to the marketing team on how to present their website, as well as how to make future campaigning or targeting decisions based on the system usage.

Personal & acquisition dimensions; Personal & acquisition dimensions hold information that is more specialized to a given usage, such as an age group with upper and lower boundaries. The path that a visitor took to get to the page is stored in the acquisition table. The converted bookings table includes information about online transactions, including the campaign code that initiated the click and the source from which it originated. This dimension aids marketing in establishing the tone of the campaign and identifying the right people to target.

Pages & sessions – FACT TABLE; The section that holds data on pages and sessions is known as the pages and sessions dimension. Each page's metadata and unique page links are stored in the page table. All pages and sub-pages that were accessed during each session are stored in the session page database. The session to which the record relates, as well as the page that was opened by a specific click.

The session table, also known as the fact table, captures every session detail of the user who visits the webpage. For an airline, the record_locator is the most important grain that determines how a customer is related to the airline, its flight, at the airport and to what countries. Every information is recorded with a timestamp, although NULL is used when data is missing from the data tables. Because of the large number of entries stored in them, the session and session page tables are by far the most important. The session page table will have the most entries.

5 Limitations

Most recent publications studied, some have highlighted the adoption as a living ecosystem, a few articles have indicated the need for a data warehouse in the organization and others have presented the importance of data warehouse and web analytics in businesses. There's a lack of research on the airline's side of the business itself, digital marketing to be specific. Therefore, this paper would be focused more on the airline's web analytical data integration into the data warehouse as well as present an overall web analytics data warehouse architecture through a theoretical approach.

6 Future Scope and Recommendations

The model we've discussed in the proposal might be thought of as a simplified version of the Google Analytics model. Needless to say, there are several ways to improve on our proposal. Adding a couple of additional DWH-like tables to a model might be one solution. To reuse these records when querying historical details, we may aggregate data weekly or monthly. We could drastically minimize the number of reads necessary when querying the session table this way.

Secondly, in terms of future scope, incorporating an airline booking data source (as shown in Fig. 4) that maintains all booking and passenger-level detail is a must. This connects the dots between transactional data from Google Analytics and booking level and passenger data. This provides the digital marketing team with a more customized picture of how to target their campaigns and to appropriate audiences.

Additionally, further study in the field of web analytics, online user behavior, and how this might be incorporated into data warehouses (DWH) is required in the airline industry. There has to be more research on how OLAP may improve marketing analytics and decision-making. How DWH can improve user insights, advertise more effectively, and reach a larger audience.

The integrated flight data dimension is shown above, which is connected to the transformed record locator, provides a more detailed and granular view of tailored data. This helps marketing to analyze and build path journeys to trigger promotions, vouchers, abandon cart emails and so on.

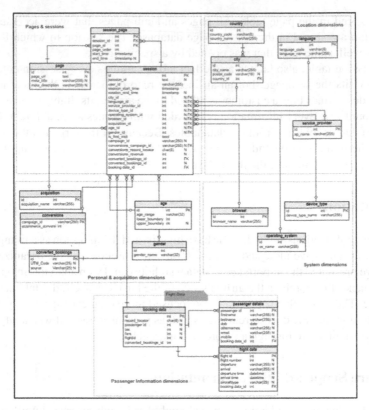

Fig. 4. Constellation Schema, future enhancement

7 Conclusion

With the competition in the airline-to-airline digital market, there is a need for a data warehouse to allow marketing and analytics teams to consolidate data from hetero-geneous data sources including advertising channels like Facebook and Google, web analytics platforms like Google Analytics and drive more into extensive analysis and market assessment. Even though the majority of articles focused on data warehouse implementation in the company as a living ecosystem, the airline sector has not been a major adopter or implementer in recent years. Furthermore, none of the publications attempted to address the problem of airlines' digital marketing and analytics data. This establishes a case for more research in this field. Building a data warehouse from all of the airline's important data sources is an efficient approach to obtaining the data neces-sary to make business-critical decisions. Building a data warehouse, on the other hand, involves a larger initial investment than a normal on-shelve product or preconfigured dashboard, and it will also allow marketing management to address any query about consumers by combining data from all tools.

References

1. Mishra, S.: Web Analytics (2016). https://docuri.com/download/web-analytics_59a8d410f 581719e12acc9bd_pdf
2. 4 Benefits of Using Web Analytics for Small Business Owners. Brand24 (2017). https://brand24.com/blog/4-benefits-of-using-web-analytics-for-small-business-owners
3. Alsqour, M., Owoc, M.L.: The role of data warehouse as a source of knowledge acquisition in decision-making. An empirical study. In: Mercier-Laurent, E., Owoc, M.L., Boulanger, D. (eds.) AI4KM 2014. IAICT, vol. 469, pp. 21–42. Springer, Cham (2015). https://doi.org/10.1007/978-3-319-28868-0_2
4. Nemati, H.R., Steiger, D.M., Iyer, L.S., Herschel, R.T.: Knowledge warehouse: an architectural integration of knowledge management, decision support, artificial intelligence and data warehousing, pp. 143–161 (2002)
5. Watson, F.H., Ariyachandra, J.C.: Data warehouse governance: best practices at blue cross and blue shield of North Carolina. Decis. Support Syst. 435–450 (2004)
6. Gaur, L., Singh, G., Kumar, S.: Google analytics: a tool to make websites more robust (2016)
7. Dibrova, A.: Website analysis with Google Analytics (2013). http://www.diva-portal.org/smash/get/diva2:1482124/FULLTEXT01.pdf
8. Jain, S., Sharma, S.: Application of data warehouse in decision support and business intelligence system (2019)
9. Girsang, A.S., Isa, S.M., Puspita, A.D., Putri, F.A., Hutagaol, N.: Business intelligence for evaluation e-voucher airline report. **10**(02) (2019)
10. Abimbola, B.: Trends in data warehousing technology. **1**(3) (2021)
11. Bahri, S., Zoghlami, N., Abed, M., Tavares, J.M.R.S.: Dimensions of automated ETL management: a contemporary (2019)
12. Zykov, S.V.: Agile patterns and practices. Managing Software Crisis: A Smart Way to Enterprise Agility, pp. 107–134 (2018)
13. Alfredo, Y.F., Girsang, A.S., Isa, S.M., Fajar, A.N.: Data warehouse development for flight reservation system (2018)
14. Ramos, C.M.Q., Matos, N., Sousa, C.M.R., Correia, M.B., Cascada, P.: Marketing intelligence and automation – an approach associated with tourism in order to obtain economic benefits for a region (2017)
15. Naydenova, I., Kovacheva, Z., Kaloyanova, K.: Important data quality accents for data analytics and decision making (2021)
16. Pandey, N.: Digital marketing strategies for firms in post COVID-19 era: insights and future directions (2021)
17. Geria, A.A.G.A., Maheswari, A.I.A., Pemayun, A.A.G.P.: Social media as promotion trend for increasing tourist visit towards digital era. Int. J. Soc. Sci. Hum. (2018)
18. Fan, S., Lau, R.Y., Zhao, L.: Demystifying big data analytics for business intelligence through the lens of marketing mix. Big Data Res. **2**(1) (2015)
19. Aversa, J., Hernandez, T., Doherty, S.: Incorporating big data within retail organizations: a case study approach. **60** (2021)
20. Sinha, R.: Analytical study of data warehouse. **8**(1) (2019)
21. Bouaziz, S., Nabli, A., Gargouri, F.: From traditional data warehouse to real time data warehouse (2017)
22. Anderson-Lehman, R., Watson, H., Wixom, B.: Flying high with real-time business intelligence
23. Yin, F.: Study on customer segmentation intelligent (2019)
24. Yilma, G., Kumar, D., Kemal, M., Debele, G.: Leveraging big data analytics for airlines: personalization

25. Larsen, D.T.: Cross-platform aviation analytics using big-data methods (2013)
26. Nair, B.C.: Business analytics – leveraging the power of data (2019)
27. Soundararajan, R., Singh, K.: Winning on HR analytics: leveraging data for competitive advantage (2017)
28. Offia, C.E., Crowe, M.: A theoretical exploration of data management and integration in organisation sectors (2019)
29. Chandra, P., Gupta, M.K.: Comprehensive survey on data warehousing research (2018)
30. Kumar, G.S., Kumar, M.R.: Dimensions of automated ETL management: a contemporary literature review (2021)
31. Gustavo, M.V., Cunha, I., Pereira, A.C.M., Oliveira, L.B.: DOD-ETL: distributed on-demand ETL for near real-time business intelligence (2019)
32. Hassan, A.: Review of industries need to depend on data warehouse for decision making and taking benefit from it (2021)
33. Ariawan, P.A., Ardiada, D., Sudarmojo, Y.P.: Design of library data warehouse using OLTP result of services analysis. **3**(1) (2018)
34. Prabawa, N.A., Arimbawa, D.A.K., Janardana, I.G.N.: Analysis and design data warehouse for e-travel business optimization. **4**(1) (2019)
35. Habes, M., Alghizzawi, M., Ali, S.: The relation among marketing ads, via digital media and mitigate (COVID- 19) pandemic in Jordan (2020)
36. Hwang, E.H., Nageswaran, L., Cho, S.-H.: Impact of COVID-19 on omnichannel retail: drivers of online sales during pandemic (2020)
37. Sabtu, A., et al.: The challenges of extract, transform and load (ETL) for data integration in near real-time environment. **95**(22) (2017)
38. Holgersson, J.: Data warehouse development - an opportunity for business process improvement (2002)
39. Buntak, K., Kovacic, M., Mutavdzija, M.: Internet of things and smart warehouses as the future of logistics. **13**(3) (2019)
40. Ross, K.R.: The Data Warehouse Toolkit: The Definitive Guide to Dimensional Modeling, 3rd edn. (2013)
41. Analytics Integration I Google Developers. https://developers.google.com/analytics/devgui des/integrate
42. SQL Server Integration Services (2022). https://docs.microsoft.com/en-us/sql/integration-ser vices/sql-server-integration-services?view=sql-server-ver16
43. MuleSoft I Integration Platform for Connecting SaaS and Enterprise Applications. Mulesoft. https://www.mulesoft.com/
44. Akid, H., Frey, G., Ayed, M.B., Lachiche, N.: Performance of NoSQL graph implementations of star vs. snowflake schemas. **10** (2022)
45. Jian-bo, W., Chong-jun, F.: Research on airport data warehouse architecture. **2**

Multi-platform Performance Analysis for CRUD Operations in Relational Databases from Java Programs Using Hibernate

Alexandru-Marius Bonteanu[1] and Cătălin Tudose[2(✉)]

[1] "Politehnica" University of Bucharest, Bucharest, Romania
[2] Luxoft, Bucharest, Romania
catalin.tudose@gmail.com

Abstract. A data set is a collection of information about something. Almost every application nowadays needs data persistence to maintain track of its status in the event of a problem. Databases are the primary component of an application for storing data and can be of two types: SQL or NoSQL. SQL (Structured Query Language) is a query language used in most relational databases to create, read, update, and delete entries (CRUD operations). In the relational database model, data is organized in a collection of tables, with rows as entries and columns as a specific property of the entry. New relational database management systems have emerged over time. From this perspective, a comparison of some of the most popular relational database management systems linked to a Java application using Hibernate is worthwhile. The time for each CRUD action is evaluated since they are the most often utilized operations for thousands and hundreds of thousands of entries. Depending on the bulk of operations, changing the database management system may be beneficial.

Keywords: framework · relational database · object-relational mapping · Hibernate · MySQL · Oracle · SQLServer · PostgreSQL · performance

1 Introduction

The experiment is around accessing relational databases using Java programs. Any application may require data persistence, which may be accomplished via an Object Relational Mapping (ORM) that maps a Java class to a database table [1].

When developing a new application, there are several relational database management systems to choose from. Each has its own set of advantages and downsides, resulting in a trade-off, as practically everything in the realm of computer science does.

The goal of this research is to profile combinations of the Hibernate framework with the most prominent relational database management systems (RDBMS). Previous research concentrated on MongoDB, the most popular non-relational database management system [2, 3] The major topic will be the speed and complexity of the code for performing batches of CRUD actions.

C.-H. Hsu et al. (Eds.): DataCom 2022, LNCS 13864, pp. 275–288, 2023.
https://doi.org/10.1007/978-981-99-2233-8_20

There are various articles discussing which RDBMS to use, with pros and downsides for each, but no practical review. Any developer could be interested in combining RDBMSs and frameworks [4].

The recommended method is to run a medium-complexity application with several RDBMSs, using the Hibernate framework, and timing how long it takes to execute varied quantities (thousands to hundreds of thousands) of each CRUD action. This provides us with a clear picture of how different technologies function better for efficient access to a relational database in a Java program. The key goal is to establish how quickly an application can access data and how easily this may be accomplished.

2 Background

The data in relational databases is structured in tables. Each table entry should have a unique identifier known as the Primary Key (PK). Columns are data properties that are defined when a table is built. Foreign Keys link related tables together (FK). The structure is thoroughly discussed in the book "Relational database theory" [5]. For example, we have a Student table with a unique number as the PK and the properties Name, Address, Date of birth, and Class. However, the Class is also a table with a unique number as a PK and properties such as Name, Difficulty, and Number of hours. The Class column in the Student table will retain the PK of the relevant entry in the Class table to keep data organized. This implies that the class identification in the Student table will be an FK.

Commands are classified into four types:

- data definition language (DDL) – to define and modify the database and tables structure
- data query language (DQL) – to interrogate the database tables for specific information (the SELECT command)
- data manipulation language (DML) – to insert, delete and update the tables
- data control language (DCL) – to control user's access to the database

The implementation focuses on the DQL and DML operations, the core activities of an application. The SELECT command is used for reading, and the INSERT, UPDATE, and DELETE commands are used to create, update, and delete data from the database.

Object Relational Mapping provides various benefits over JDBC that make the developer's job easier: it conceals SQL interaction, allows development using objects rather than database tables, has the same model implementation for all RDBMSs, requires less code to complete the same task, and works on top of JBDC.

A JDBC driver is used to connect to a database in Java applications. The database management system specifies this driver, which must be present in the application's setup. When setting the database connection, developers must additionally provide a dialect so that queries are written in the correct language.

There are several Relational Database Management Systems (RDBMSs) in the SQL industry, but four are particularly popular:

- MySQL
- PostgreSQL

- Oracle SQL
- Microsoft SQL Server

The syntax is slightly different, but we can do our database actions with any of them. Each has its own tool for monitoring and modifying data via a graphical user interface. Finally, a comparison with the evaluation of a medium-complexity Java program will be performed. Joins will be an important part of our program. A join is an action performed between two tables that share an attribute. In the preceding example of the Student and the Class, if the developer wants to access not only the specifications of one student but also the number of hours of his class, he just considers the number of hours from the Class table entry whose ID corresponds to the Class ID from the Student table.

Optimization approaches may emerge as a result of the testing. If an application is running slowly, the database management system might be tweaked to improve speed.

In his thesis "Performance assessment of Java Object-Relational Mapping tools" [6], Haseeb Yousaf examines different ORM frameworks such as OpenJPA, EclipseLink, and Hibernate on an Ubuntu operating system. He ran five queries on a table: one by ID (PK), three by distinct type characteristics, and one by two attributes combined. According to the data, Hibernate is the quickest of the three frameworks from 10000 to 160000 records, while OpenJPA is the slowest. As the number of records grows, EclipseLink becomes closer to Hibernate.

Another paper by Ismail Hossain [7] examines the top five relational database management systems: MySQL, Oracle, PostgreSQL, SQLite, and Microsoft SQL Server. The first test he does is to time each of them during installation. Oracle and SQL Server appear to be the most sluggish, whereas SQLite and MySQL install in less than five minutes. The second test he does is to time each CRUD action on a different amount of entries. Based on his studies, Oracle appears to be the most sluggish when it comes to reading information from the database, but rather adept at updating and deleting. MySQL's update and delete performance is substantially inferior to Oracle's, with very long execution times. According to Ismail Hossain's research, PostgreSQL appears to be the greatest choice for a developer. SQLite and Microsoft SQL Server are the other two options for establishing a new application.

Both of the works described above compare at the same technological level. One is used to compare different ORM frameworks, while the other is used to determine which relational database management system is the fastest.

This research will attempt to combine all of the technologies outlined in the preceding studies to produce a more complex assessment based on the RDBMS and the Hibernate framework, which will work together to optimize access to a relational database from a Java application.

Similar work was done at the University of Oradea [8], but in a different programming language (.NET), comparing the execution times and memory usage of an application based on three distinct ORM frameworks accessing SQLServer.

The following technologies are used to evaluate how a developer might optimize access to a relational database:

- Java programming language
- Oracle RDBMS

- PostgreSQL RDBMS
- Microsoft SQL Server RDBMS
- MySQL RDBMS
- Hibernate
- JUnit – Java testing library
- Maven – Java package manager

Java [9] is a well-known programming language that allows you to create an end-to-end application, including both the server side and the graphical user interface used by the application's clients. As a popular language, there are a large number of libraries and frameworks built for it, as well as a large number of developers.

Oracle is a well-known RDBMS created by Oracle Corporation. Many key applications with large amounts of data, such as Netflix, LinkedIn, and eBay, use this technology. Oracle's Procedural Language for SQL (PL/SQL) is a wrapper for traditional SQL.

PostgreSQL is a SQL language extension. It supports a variety of data formats, including Numeric, String, JSON, XML, and designing your own. As previously said, developers may incorporate non-relational data, which is an important feature. Because of the psycopg database adapter, this relational database management system is typically favored by Python developers, but it may also be utilized in Java programming.

Microsoft SQL Server is the company's solution for relational database administration. Transact-SQL (T-SQL) is its own dialect that provides for transactional leverage and adequate error handling. The wrapper also includes procedural programming.

MySQL is the Oracle open-source software for relational databases. Many developers consider it the most popular since it is simple to use, free, and has a vast community. The installation procedure is quick, and it can be used on practically any computer running an operating system, without a lot of resources to function.

Hibernate is an open-source ORM framework. It is the most widely used framework for implementing the JPA standard. The application and the database communicate via a session in which CRUD activities are performed. It offers transactions, which are produced from sessions, that must be begun and committed when all activities are completed to persist changes in the database.

JUnit was selected as the testing framework. It is the most widely used testing extension. It defines a test and the procedures that must be executed before and after each test in a class, or before and after executing all the tests in one class.

Maven is an integration tool for combining the core JDK with various frameworks. An XML file is used to define the dependencies. Maven accesses remote repositories containing these dependencies. Maven downloads these dependencies to a local repository, making them usable from the application under development.

3 Architecture

The purpose of this analysis is to assist developers and architects in making the best decision for relational database management systems in Java applications. As a result, the proposed solution was achieved by generating a Hibernate framework configuration file and altering the database connection settings. For each combination and CRUD action, test cases were built.

Following a series of tests and adequate assessment, the pros and disadvantages of the many ways that the implementation intends to create will be assessed. This procedure will be presented in the assessment section, where all measurements will be graphically and numerically reported.

The database connection and dialect are very simple to switch across relational database management systems. The configuration file contains the database settings. For adequate database comparison, the suggested solution proposes switching only three characteristics: the dialect, the database driver, and the URL. This analysis is intended for Java professionals who wish to increase their understanding of how things function when connecting with a database and how they might be improved for a better speed.

The study considers four main RDBMSs: MySQL, Oracle, SQLServer, and PostgreSQL. The ORM framework is in charge of mapping Java objects to database models. It directs the flow of data until it reaches the database. Once data is stored in a database, the relational database management system takes care of it. Each RDBMS has its optimization strategies for data retrieval and writing. Despite having a considerable influence on efficiency, it is the most easily replaced owing to common configuration files.

RDBMSs provide drivers that enable developers to connect to the database. This driver facilitates communication, but it also requires a language that the RDBMS understands. Specifying the dialect is the solution to this problem - it refers to the SQL instructions that the ORM framework should convert before sending them to the RDBMS.

A configuration file describes these two configurations, as well as the route to the database (URL). Every framework has its means of describing these attributes.

By merging all of these components, end-to-end component communication is achieved. It begins with the Java application, which obtains the framework JARs through Maven and connects with the database via a set of properties.

The evaluation will be carried out by developing a medium-complexity betting application with the following primary entities: tickets, bets, and matches. The implementation part will go through these entities.

The most crucial part of any CRUD process is time. The testing will quantify the time for each stated combination, allowing for a duration comparison.

After gathering all of the results, they will be organized in tables to ease analysis. Based on that, the solution will deliver relevant information to the audience by building some more appealing graphs using the collected figures.

4 Solution Implementation

The implementation's major goal was to construct a medium-complexity application. It was decided to have a plot in the backdrop to make things more intriguing.

The app focuses on a soccer betting service concept. This implies that testing is carried out by constructing a large number of tickets, each with its own set of bets and related matches, and mimicking their behavior for the database and the ORM framework.

The project's three primary entities are where the CRUD operations are tested (Fig. 1):

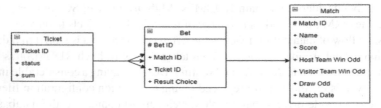

Fig. 1. Data Model.

A single ticket can include several bets (a one-to-many connection), and each bet is based on a single match (one-to-one relationship).

For the Hibernate implementation, it was necessary to configure a `SessionFactory`. From this factory object, Hibernate gets `Session` objects to create transactions. It has its configuration file called "hibernate.cfg.xml" where the connection details and setup properties are declared. The `SessionFactory` is created through this file. The flow continues by creating transactions from the session, where the operations are executed.

For each CRUD operation, a transaction is initiated, marking the time when it was started. Then the operation is executed and afterward the finishing time is set. The difference between these two moments represents the execution time for each operation, measured in milliseconds.

What is special about this implementation is that for the read operation, it is needed to create a query to get the desired entities. This is achieved by using the `Criteri-aBuilder`, `CriteriaQuery`, and `TypedQuery` classes. On the last one, there is a method `getResultList()` which retrieves all the entities matching the query.

The data mocking procedure for the test cases is another common aspect of the project. It implies a match builder method used in a bet builder method, which is then utilized in a ticket builder method. On top of that, a mechanism for issuing a variable number of tickets was developed to facilitate the testing of different data sets.

To assess their efficiency, various technologies that can express a complete flow between a relational database and a Java application were chosen. They are significant in many production applications since the comparison with actual and popular components should be of interest.

The JPA standard serves as the foundation for all ORM systems. This facilitates the mapping of a Java class to a database table by providing certain annotations that perform this operation in the background.

```java
@Data
@Entity
@Builder
@Table(name = "tickets")
@AllArgsConstructor
@NoArgsConstructor
public class Ticket {
    @Id
    @GeneratedValue(strategy = GenerationType.IDENTITY)
    private Long id;
    private TicketStatus ticketStatus;
    private Double sum;
    @OneToMany(cascade=CascadeType.ALL)
    private List<Bet> bets = new LinkedList<>();
}
```

The Java Persistence API [10] is present in the code above, representing a betting ticket, via the annotations below:

- `@Entity` -> used to mark the class as data that can be persisted in the database
- `@Table` -> used to mark the name of the corresponding database table
- `@Id` -> used to mark the primary key for the tickets table
- `@GeneratedValue` -> used to describe how the primary key is populated
- `@OneToMany` -> used to describe a one-to-many relationship between the ticket and the bet entities

The code above contains four additional annotations that are part of the Lombok library. Their goal is to eliminate boilerplate code by creating constructors, getters, setters, and a builder for this class. This data entity is comparable to the other two for bets and matches.

The Hibernate solution has a file named "hibernate.cfg.xml", where the configuration is described:

```
<hibernate-configuration>
    <session-factory>
        <property name="hibernate.connection.driver_class">
            oracle.jdbc.driver.OracleDriver
        </property>
        <property name="hibernate.connection.url">
            jdbc:oracle:thin:@localhost:1521/DB12c
        </property>
        <property name="hibernate.dialect">
            org.hibernate.dialect.Oracle12cDialect
    </property>
        <property name="hibernate.connection.username">oracle</property>

        <property  name="hibernate.connection.password">admin</property>

        <property  name="hibernate.connection.pool_size">50</property>

        <property  name="show_sql">false</property>

        <property  name="hibernate.hbm2ddl.auto">create</property>
    </session-factory>
</hibernate configuration>
```

This file provides the database URL, user information for connecting, and the RDBMS driver. The dialect is also given here so that the application and the database may communicate in the same language. The above example is for a connection to an Oracle database.

5 Solution Evaluation

The laptop setup on which the time of the CRUD operations was measured is:

- CPU: Intel i7 – 6700HQ @ 2.6 GHz
- RAM: 8 GB
- Operating System: Windows 10 Pro 64-bit

The requirements were to install all of the technologies specified in Sect. 3 and to devise a method for accurately measuring execution time. To determine the precise time before and after each CRUD action, the suggested solution uses the `System.nanoTime()` function. The time in milliseconds is given by dividing the difference by 10^6. Other procedures that occurred during the testing were not taken into account when the measurements were computed.

Hibernate's logs were deleted to minimize execution time because displaying them in the console takes a long time. All CRUD activities were carried out sequentially, in a single unit test, in the following order: create the entries, update them, read them, and lastly remove them.

The tests on the development of a betting service were designed to measure the length of each CRUD action for a different number of tickets, each carrying one bet on one match. These were the ticket numbers: 1000, 2000, 5000, 10000, 20000, 50000, 100000, 200000, and 500000.

To maintain the activities running on all three database tables, the update operation modified the ticket's status, the bet's outcome selection, and the name of the match. This increased the application's complexity.

These tests were done on each combination of Hibernate and relational database system, resulting in four distinct situations (1 ORM framework and 4 RDBMSs). The analysis of the data may provide developers with a better understanding of how to optimize their application to obtain better timings, whether it is a little application (10-20k entries) or a larger one (up to 500k entries).

Tudose Cătălin and Odubășteanu Carmen did some comparable work on a single database table [11], comparing the same framework plus Hibernate and Spring Data JPA on a MySQL RDBMS. The intention was to expand on this research study with a more complicated application, additional relational database management systems, and hundreds of thousands of entries.

For a better overall picture, the findings for each combination examined were translated into the tables below, from which related graphs by CRUD operation were constructed. Each pair will be interpreted further to determine its pros and downsides (Tables 1, 2, 3, 4 and Figs. 2, 3, 4, 5).

Table 1. MySQL – Hibernate Execution Times.

Number of operations	Execution times (ms)			
	Create	Read	Update	Delete
1000	2470	125	1325	1253
2000	4554	138	1873	1922
5000	7456	168	3629	4159
10000	11004	177	6577	7793
20000	18374	191	12409	15337
50000	40688	278	31887	40001
100000	74397	325	63205	78410
200000	141294	466	126576	158083
500000	352569	876	324282	394135

Table 2. Oracle – Hibernate Execution Times.

Number of operations	Execution times (ms)			
	Create	Read	Update	Delete
1000	3176	195	1424	1868
2000	5436	223	1871	2706
5000	10231	264	3347	6438
10000	16900	302	6025	14139
20000	28865	444	11561	30267
50000	65406	878	28601	112778
100000	125629	1306	56481	368699
200000	251595	2259	111793	1278305
500000	617148	5191	278557	7422952

Table 3. SQLServer – Hibernate Execution Times.

Number of operations	Execution times (ms)			
	Create	Read	Update	Delete
1000	2200	139	932	2126
2000	3340	154	1437	5803
5000	6391	162	2905	27133
10000	10724	173	5510	102812
20000	18227	186	10045	273914
50000	39076	218	25955	359862
100000	72904	307	51129	979468
200000	142407	425	98792	3121897
500000	370316	548	251087	17313278

Table 4. PostgreSQL – Hibernate Execution Times.

Number of operations	Execution times (ms)			
	Create	Read	Update	Delete
1000	1293	131	606	947
2000	2130	142	1002	1799

(continued)

Table 4. (*continued*)

Number of operations	Execution times (ms)			
	Create	Read	Update	Delete
5000	4241	169	2094	6264
10000	7204	176	3776	18384
20000	12739	193	7217	59161
50000	29389	202	17682	314171
100000	59067	310	39052	1188371
200000	109056	420	69723	4668658
500000	265081	977	174504	28132449

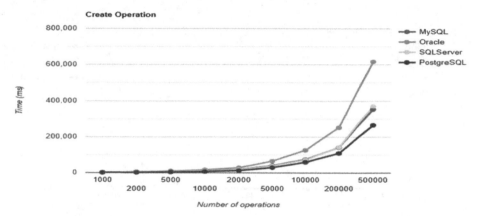

Fig. 2. Create execution times.

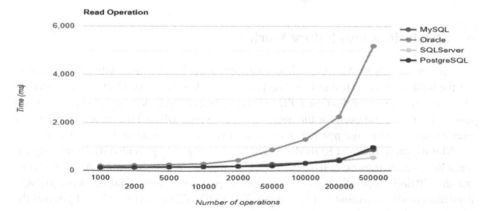

Fig. 3. Read execution times.

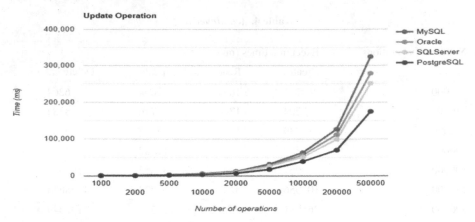

Fig. 4. Update execution times

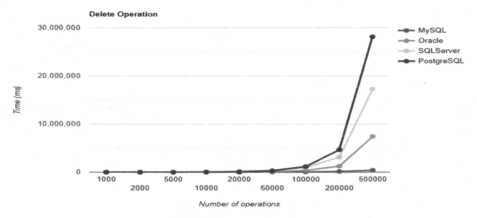

Fig. 5. Delete execution times

6   Conclusions and Future Work

The first combination (MySQL - Hibernate) appears to be effective, with an overall time for the 500k operations test of less than 1200 s (less than 20 min). The CREATE process takes somewhat longer than the UPDATE procedure. READ is extremely quick, taking less than one second even for the most demanding test. DELETE appears to double its execution time when the number of operations is doubled, making it fairly linear.

Moving on to the next RDBMS utilized for testing, one provided by Oracle, significant differences may be noted. The DELETE process takes almost 2 h on 500k items, but the CREATE operation, which is likewise time-consuming relative to the MySQL implementation, is around 12 times faster. The UPDATE operation, which bypasses the MySQL implementation, is a benefit for this design.

READ and UPDATE continue to outperform the other two RDBMS implementations for the SQLServer combo.

PostgreSQL appears to be the best choice for a small number of entries (less than 5k), however, when the number of entries grows, developers may consider switching the RDBMS. The deletion is significantly worse at 500k entries than it was in the prior combination. The benefits of a larger number of entries can be seen in the three additional CRUD procedures, setting a new record. The deletion overhead is so significant that it may be a compelling argument not to use this RDBMS in the specified scenario. PostgreSQL results are more intriguing in a Java application because of its relationship with the Python programming language.

MySQL provides excellent overall performance. Although it has a slower speed than PostgreSQL for creating, reading, and updating entries, it saves a significant amount of time on the delete process (over 70 times faster).

SQLServer and PostgreSQL have the fastest update execution speeds. In every case, reading entries from a database is quick. SQLServer has the best reading, while Oracle has the worst, however, this cannot be used to decide which technology to use to develop an application. Because the difference between these two is less than 5 s for 500k entries. Oracle is the slowest of the four RDBMSs in terms of insertion.

All of these tests were designed to analyze the performance of various RDBMSs in conjunction with the Hibernate framework to assist developers who are starting a new application as well as those who are dissatisfied with the performance of their present application.

SQLServer is the finest RDBMS for reading data, however, it performs poorly when it comes to deletion. Oracle appears to be worth a try when working with even more entries than the testing in this article have attempted because it performs better as the number of entries increases.

The research would not be complete without expanding these findings or investigating how the combinations respond in various situations. It is intended to perform the tests in the future using additional common frameworks such as JPA or Spring Data JPA.

Another intriguing aspect is the time of framework method execution. The most time-consuming calls will be identified and examined in this manner. JMeter, an Apache performance testing tool, might be useful for this type of job.

Finally, there are several drivers for the same RDBMS. It'll be fascinating to watch how things alter when you switch between these drivers. Adding indexes and composite primary keys to the data model, as well as investigating execution discrepancies, might further the research.

References

1. Keith, M., Schnicarol, M.: Pro JPA 2, Object-relational mapping, pp. 69–106. Apress (2009)
2. Truică, C.O., Boicea, A., Trifan, I.: CRUD operations in MongoDB. In: International Conference on Advanced Computer Science and Electronics Information. Atlantis Press, Beijing (2013)
3. Truică, C.O., Rădulescu, F., Boicea, A., Bucur, I.: Performance evaluation for CRUD operations in asynchronously replicated document oriented database. In: Conference on Control Systems and Computer Science. Bucharest (2015)
4. Sumathi, S., Esakkirajan, S.: Fundamentals of Relational Database Management Systems. Springer, Heidelberg (2007)

5. Atzeni, P., De Antonellis, V.: Relational Database Theory. Benjamin-Cummings Publishing Co., Inc. (1993)
6. Yousaf, H.: Performance evaluation of Java object-relational mapping tools (2012)
7. Ismail Hossain, M.M.: Oracle, MySQL, PostgreSQL, SQLite, SQL Server: performance based competitive analysis (2019)
8. Zmaranda, D., Pop-Fele, L., Gyorödi, C., Gyorödi, R.: Performance comparison of CRUD methods using NET object relational mappers: a case study. Int. J. Adv. Comput. Sci. Appl. 55–65 (2020)
9. Arnold, K.: The Java Programming Language. Addison Wesley Professional (2005)
10. Tudose, C.: Java Persistence with Spring Data and Hibernate. Manning (2022)
11. Tudose, C., Odubășteanu, C.: Object-relational mapping using JPA, Hibernate and Spring Data JPA. In: Conference on Control Systems and Computer Science, Bucharest (2021)

Enhancing Data Warehouse Efficiency by Optimizing ETL Processing in Near Real Time Data Integration Environment

Kunal Maharaj[1][✉] and Kunal Kumar[2]

[1] Department of Information Technology, National Training and Productivity Centre, Fiji National University, Lautoka, Fiji
kunal.maharaj@fnu.ac.fj
[2] Department of Computer Science and Mathematics, University of Fiji, Lautoka, Fiji
KunalK@unifiji.ac.fj

Abstract. The importance of data towards business process enhancement is perhaps the most important element. Successful utilization of data collected enables business organizations to visualize relationships between business processes, identifying not only solutions to problems but also opportunities based on current trends, to make effective decisions and gain competitive advantage. The digital era has resulted in the continuous generation of volumetric data from various sources such as IoT devices, social media API's and so on. These sources, combined with other core data sources for any respective business such as Online Transaction Processing (OLTP) are needed in real-time for effective decision making. This study identifies techniques which will optimize the real-time data warehouse ETL processes for the overall efficiency of the data warehouses implemented by business organizations. Due to the complex nature of data (structured, semi-structured and unstructured), this study proposes a unified model for efficient ELT processes which can be implemented for robust near-real data warehousing. Based on a significant review of the literature, this paper identifies and recommends instances where ELT and pushdown processes work optimally in real-time.

Keywords: Near-real time data integration · ETL process · Pushdown technology · Data warehousing

1 Introduction

The key to survival for any business is the ability to make informed decisions regarding its business processes. Aligning strategies to meet and deliver customer requirements escalates the growth of any business and also enables a strong competitive advantage in the industry. The main component in identifying requirements, trends and approaches are to acquire data and discover knowledge, as opposed to simply gaining information, from the data. Acquisition of data in the digital age has become relatively easy due to the practical implementations of technological platforms and systems. Handling data from numerous sources, in high volumes and great velocity in itself is challenging for

C.-H. Hsu et al. (Eds.): DataCom 2022, LNCS 13864, pp. 289–304, 2023.
https://doi.org/10.1007/978-981-99-2233-8_21

business organizations. The constant injunction of real-time data from sources such as IoT devices, API's and OLTP systems, along with a mix of raw, structured and unstructured data increases the complexities in extracting fresh data for quick and informed decision making. Aside from the infrastructure, the involved extraction, transformation and loading processes for quick insights and reports need to be optimized. This will not only reduce the cost of data management but also enable lightweight, quick, efficient and reliable data warehouses.

While several studies have been proposed to achieve efficient data warehousing, various approaches have been implemented to optimize ETL processes for near-real data integration. The key to efficient data warehousing is to achieve low latency, high availability and horizontal scalability [1]. Several techniques have been proposed to achieve these characteristics, such as query optimization and data quality improvements [2]. Many simple and dedicated frameworks have also been developed [3, 4] to achieve near-real data warehouse efficiency.

The availability of various techniques to approaching an optimal solution has paved diverse methods to implement a working solution in the near-real time data integration. Performance degradation at each step is the primary focus, to reduce the impact on continuously streamed data and process data as they are generated. The conceptual overview of data warehousing has enabled several solutions, presenting researchers with many routes to devise optimal solutions, however, limited work has focused on optimizing each of the ETL processes singularly. Various studies have computed cost models to benchmark real-time streaming to improve data latency issues and better resource utilization [5].

This paper aims to contribute to the knowledge base by identifying techniques presented in several works of literature, which will optimize the real-time data warehouse ETL processes for the overall efficiency of the data warehouses implemented by business organizations. Due to the complex nature of data (structured, semi-structured and unstructured), in our study, we propose a unified model for efficient ELT processes which can be implemented for robust near-real data warehousing. Based on a significant review of literature, we identify and recommend instances where ELT and pushdown ELT processes work optimally in real-time, based on which, different business organizations can choose the best method for implementation in their individual organisations respectively.

2 Research Methodology

The key to survival for any business or organization in this digital age is the ability to store, analyse and produce meaningful information which can form the basis of knowledge discovery out of the continuous data being acquired from transaction processing and analytical systems. A Data warehouse acts as a repository which stores strategic data from several sources and enables leaders to make data-driven decisions [6], having integrated and converted data by applying various tasks and technical processes to it.

The volume of data increases exponentially every day, hence, data in warehouses need to be maintained systematically in the form of extraction, transformation and loading. One of the key factors in designing ETL tools is to factor in the reality of heterogeneous data sources with structured and unstructured data sources such as emails, pdf files,XML's, flat files and so on [7]. Transformation requires filtering and aggregating data from the source. One of the key optimisation concerns during this process is filtering 'dirty' data with anomalies such as duplicate records, missing values, and misspellings along with different formats and definitions of data types and variables [8].

The data warehouse concept is evolving rapidly, since the advent of real-time big data and cloud computing [9], hence, it is a challenging task to maintain the quality of data given the constant injunction of real-time data to the ever-present historical data in the warehouse. The near real-time data warehouse environment has the added challenge of enabling access to source data quickly for advanced data analytics. Low latency, high availability with minimum disruptions as well as scalability are integral characteristics of a near real-time environment [10, 11].

RealTime data warehouses face many challenges such as the impact on the system performance. However, the biggest challenge lies in enabling ETL to extract data in real-time mode. Most of the ETL tools are designed to operate in batch mode and aggregation operations on the data set realistically cannot be synchronised [12]. To add to this challenge, data sources have evolved significantly, adding to the challenges of efficient ELT processes. Third-party data sources, such as social media data, Google API and live streaming add to the complexity of real-time data integration in data warehouses. These data sources cannot be overlooked by companies in their quest to retrieve accurate information from data warehouses. Traditional ETL tools have a limitation to such data. Secific ETL tools need to be invested in by respective organisations. These tools should readily connect to the continually evolving open data sources with minimum interaction from users in its data extraction and processing functionalities [13]. Where traditional ETL tools are effective in batch processing of structured data, the real-time continuous flow data demands tweaking these tools massively with focus on low latency and high availability and horizontal scalability [14, 15].

Some of the challenges in optimizing ETL tools when working with third-party sources, such as SaaS providers, include integration with respective APIs which is not only different for every application but is also undergoing constant changes. The same is the case for social media platforms. For instance, 'Meta' needs to frequently update its reporting API's due to their 'move fast and break things' approach'.

ETL tools used to achieve these tasks can be developed in-house by respective organizations or purchased, with a range of high-end software available in the market to some open-source ELTs that can be considered [16]. Some of the factors that need to be considered when selecting and developing an ETL tool include the ability to support various data from multiple sources by inflicting minimal burden on the sources [17, 18], compatibility with other tools, usability and functionality as well as performance and scalability [19] where the system can adjust to sudden changes to the volume of data without impacting the performance of the overall environment. Horizontal scaling is an approach that targets performance efficiency by reducing data interruptions on separate independent servers whilst requiring significantly low coordination between systems.

2.1 Data Warehouse Implementations Factors for Consideration in Optimizing ETL Tools for Near Real-Time Data Integration

- Extraction

Real-time ETL tools have to deal with voluminous data. As such, extraction from real-time systems is done in stages, thus changing the environment into the near real-time, onto a staging area and not directly into the data warehouse so that validation can be done [1, 2, 5]. Data extraction is the most delicate and important phase of the ETL process for data integration from heterogeneous sources [8]. There are several ways data can be extracted in real-time, of which, partial extraction without update notifications is deemed to put minimal stress on the sources and the staging area. Partial extraction is an extension of the Change Data Capture (CDC) log-based technique applied in near real-time integration. This method of extraction has minimal impact on the source database, which usually would get overloaded otherwise due to the continuous influx of real-time data and reading data for extraction [4, 8]. A pre-processing framework for real-time data warehouses was designed [6] to this conflict between real time-data loading and real-time query, separating historical and real-time ETL and a dynamic storage area with a bi-link for mirroring. The process of allocating and creating mirror allocation is illustrated below in Fig. 1, where a node is created for the data image and initialized. Real-time ETL tool then checks if the data does not already exist in the storage area due to a request from OLTP (Online Transaction Processing System), a new mirror link is created and allocated storage space is based on the size of the data, otherwise, a corresponding mirror link is created and the image node is inserted and updated in the real-time storage area.

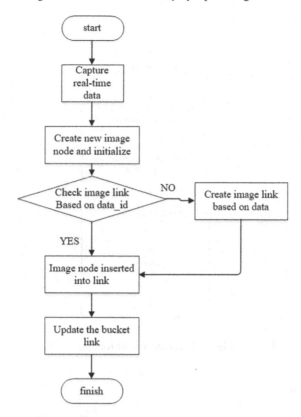

Fig. 1. Dynamic Mirror Creation and Allocation

Figure 2 illustrates the release process of data from the pre-processing framework to be uploaded to the data warehouse. If the data does not meet the validation check, the process is terminated, otherwise, the image is updated and the node is recycled.

A similar conceptual design is explored by [9], with the only difference being the intermediary staging area which stores results obtained from lightweight transformations.

Parallel flow of data from the source is one of the optimisation techniques suggested by [6, 7, 9] while having considered the design, [10] have proposed the distributed on-demand ETL, a tool which they customize after buying off the shelf ETL tool and tweaking it to include a unified programming model built upon a unified technology independent distributed and parallel architecture. While [11] suggests creating a message broker and in-memory cache, [9] develops a parallel architecture for partitioning the flow of data over several nodes, and in doing so, can increase the throughput and response time of the actual data integration. One of the key drawbacks in both the systems implemented, however, is the lack of testing on data from third-party sources. Optimisation of ELT tools for extraction purposes also needs to consider resources such as memory requirements, response time, and synchronisation. [9] has also iterated that new ETL tools should also focus on the execution of queries in sequential order.

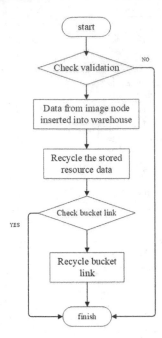

Fig. 2. Dynamic Mirror Release

- Transformation

    Data transformation deals with validation and usually requires processes such as cleaning, filtering, standardization, row and column transposing, joining, splitting, and sorting, before loading the data into the warehouse [13]. Optimizing queries can greatly enhance the efficiency of ETL tools and processes. Writing an accurate query is crucial in a real-time environment. These queries can become very complex and have an overall impact on the system performance which can affect throughput and quick access to information. This point is stressed using an instance of the NULL and BLANK data in storage tables and how in the real-time transformation [12, 13], a conflict can arise due to several definitions in data types over data sources. 70% of the performance issues can be eliminated directly using query optimization. Using insert statements with multiple values is one of the techniques as it significantly reduces the overhead involved in processing [14]. It also ensures high speed in loading data from files. Furthermore, implementing the Cartesian join optimization and performing predictive filtering before using join significantly reduces the size of the join. Predictive pushdown enables filtering before data is pushed through the network or filtered in memory and greatly enhances throughput. There are very few ETL tools in the market that can perform real-time join on unstructured data [15, 16]. Finally, [17] encourages the use of the group-by optimization technique where grouping is performed before conditional statements. This ensures a greater measure of cost reduction as the logic behind this technique is based on the fact the grouping reduces the cardinality of the relation.

- Loading

As the final step in the ETL process, newly transformed data should be loaded to the warehouse. Although most of the optimization process focuses on extraction and transformation, [6] states clean data needs to be stored in a format that is light in weight such as those formats being commonly used applications, for instance, text files, excel files, JSON, XML or databases. Incremental loading is the most efficient way of loading data in a near real-time environment, [14–16] as opposed to initial load where a lot of verification processes have to be performed on redundancy and full refresh type of loading which utilizes a lot of computational resources to periodically refresh the process of loading for verification.

The objective of researching the ETL domain in this paper has been to identify the challenges being faced in real-time ETL processes and ways of optimizing the ETL tools which make data warehousing more efficient. While a tremendous amount of work is continually being done by organizations and service providers to optimize the ETL process, there has been no formalization of any ETL tool with a generalized concept that can be universally accepted. Most of the tools bought off the shelves and those provided by cloud service providers are not only costly but. Most organisations are now beginning to consider the ELT process over ETL, where, after importing unprocessed data gets loaded and cleaning is delayed until needed. New transformation rules and the ability to test and enhance queries after loading raw data are some ways ELT proves to be more efficient [21–23]. A summary of optimization techniques has been tabulated in Table 1 below, where techniques proposed in the literature for ETL process optimization towards data warehouse efficiency have been taken into consideration.

Table 1. ETL Optimization Techniques based on the literature reviewed.

Summary of Findings on Performance Optimization

Process	Optimization Techniques	References
Extract	Design a pre-processing framework for real-time data warehouses	[1, 2, 4, 11, 12]
	Create bi-link storage for mirroring	[1–5, 7, 8, 19]
	Create a distributed on-demand ETL tool to enable parallel flow of data	[9, 10, 14, 15, 19]
Transform	Caching the validation process on near-real time data by identifying real-time sources	[4, 5, 10, 11, 16, 17]
	Merging attributes with schemas from other sources during conditional pre-processing	[3–5, 9, 11, 16]
	Re-writing queries with real-integration in consideration	[5, 9, 19]
Load	Continuous Realtime Loading with Data Integration	[4–6, 15–17]

(continued)

Table 1. (*continued*)

Summary of Findings on Performance Optimization

Process	Optimization Techniques	References
	Initial Entry in a temporary table with sequential identifier attribute	[3, 5, 17–19]
	Use of Temporary replicated tables for recent queries	[4, 6, 11–13, 17, 18, 20]
	File format of most commonly used applications	[7, 20–23]

The ETL process of a real-time environment is full of challenges due to the ever-growing data sources with complex unstructured data. The objective of this paper is to devise the best working strategy for data warehousing needs of real-time environment with optimization of real-time ETL tools.

3   Optimization of Near-Real Time Data Warehousing Processes

The ETL process of a real-time environment is full of challenges due to the ever-growing data sources with complex unstructured data. The objective of this paper is to devise the best working strategy for data warehousing needs of real-time environment with optimization of real-time ETL tools.

Data warehouses are built and implemented by businesses and organisations to act as a central repository. The general motivation behind such investments is driven by the importance of data being generated by several data sources, such as Online Transaction Processing Systems (OLTP), data captured from IoT devices as well as data acquired from the use of third-party applications such as social media API's. The technological revolution has ensured the significance of the effective use of data for businesses to gain competitive advantage by analysing trends and retrieving knowledge, as opposed to, just information from data analytics. For this reason, the demand for access to fresh and most recent data is of utmost importance and the challenges to access and truncate data from heterogeneous sources efficiently are an ongoing concern.

Near-real time data components can prove to be complicated, from the operational and maintenance perspective, when integrated into the overall data warehouse environment, as it is significantly different compared to the traditional design and environment. The data warehouse's ability to achieve near-real time processing is solely based on designs with the ability to incorporate low latency, high availability, minimum disruptions and relatively high scalability.

The following section aims to optimize each of the processes related to obtaining efficient data warehousing processes suggesting optimization techniques tailored and custom designed for every business organization, based on the type and size of the organization, various types of data involved, number of sources as well as the volume of data being utilized from these respective sources.

3.1 Near-Real Time Data Integration

Regardless of the type and size of business organization, due to the ambidextrous era, the acquisition of data and its sources has evolved. More and more sources are being integrated into the traditional sources for efficient decision making which involves the identification of market trends and discovering issues and opportunities. One of the key challenges in near-real time data integration occurs in streamlining data structure from sources into a single field of vision. Understanding the structure of raw and unstructured data being streamed, the logic and the desired output will help reduce the complexities by significantly eliminating redundancies and increasing the quality of data being dealt with.

Managing the continuous flow of data in a real time environment utilizes a significant amount of resources. Bottlenecks can develop simply due to overloading as a result of the high volume of data being integrated, hence, a parallel flow of data can be invoked in the initial phase. The figure below illustrates the means and the need for invoking a parallel flow of data, where data can be temporarily stored in the staging tables. The number of staging tables depends on the number of sources data is being integrated from. Ideally, the relationship between the number of tables and sources should be linear and one-to-one, however, for cost effective measures, multiple sources can be integrated to share staging tables. This technique may impact the rate of flow of data, hence, a trade-off is advisable between the cost of implementation and the rate of flow of data.

3.2 Optimizing the Extraction Process of Near-Real Time Data

Real time data flow causes congestion at some stage regardless of the high-end systems and their capabilities, over a given time, depending on the volumetric data. One of the proven ways to address this issue is to optimally employ streamlined processing. Streaming processes increase the efficiency of the transformation performance at staging tables. A continuous stream of data is generated by the sources and processed at the implemented stages without having to store the data and create a cache buffer. This ensures efficiency, since there is minimal load on the systems from the computational aspects, enabling a significantly lighter and much faster process.

The data extraction process faces several other challenges which significantly affect the performance of near-real time data warehousing. The need to constantly refresh the data warehouse to ensure new and changed transactions are processed, so as not to create repetition and redundancy, the change data capture approach takes precedence over parallel flow and metadata management methods for the sole reason that the volume of data can be reduced. Based on the preferences of the respective organization, we recommend the use of either timestamp-based or log-based technique for change data capture. Where data is being extracted from many sources, timestamp based approach proves to be more efficient as the timestamp of the last extract is stored and the refresh buffer compares it to identify any changed records. The log based approach is ideal where less number of sources are being used with infrequent data generation. A log for every extraction is maintained the system checks the previous logs for duplication when refreshing the records to ensure only new and changed records are entered.

Furthermore, resource contention occurs during extraction when the data sources are frequently being accessed for extraction. To avoid the source systems' interruption due to frequent access, dataflow controllers should be considered. Such performance deterioration should be avoided for a quicker flow of data. While initially extracted data is being processed, due to the voluminous data, temporary storage may well be used for buffering purposes. The data buffer serves as additional storage for the continuing extraction in real time mode. Alternatively, the storage buffer can be used conditionally, allowing extraction to take place from here. Regardless of the options available for buffering, such streams of data flow enable enhanced optimization of the extraction process in near-real time processing.

3.3   Enhancing the Transformation Process of Near-Real Time Data

As opposed to traditional warehouse environment, near-real time requires frequent transformations. This process can be quite cumbersome due to the quality of data from certain real-time such as third-party API's and IoT devices. Queries needed to extract meaningful information needs to be kept simple and relatively light. Dealing with NULLS and BLANKS is a continuous challenge, as the same query operation is run over multiple sets of 'flowing' data in rapid succession. In the events where irregularities occur due to unstructured and missing structs, the refresh frequency of the entire operation will heavily be impacted, thereby, delaying the overall ETL process.

Query optimization plays a crucial role during transformation, as transformation may require cleaning, filtering, standardization, validation, transposing, joining, splitting and sorting repetitively (Sreemathy, J TALEND). Indexing is a good way to enhance query optimization. There are several open-source indexing algorithms available, which can be integrated for performance tuning. Therefore, we will rather be focusing, using Table 1, on the commonly used queries and optimization techniques for each of these queries rather than the indexing algorithms. Optimizing queries improves the operational speed of processes.

1. INSERT Statement

     Ideally, the most efficient way is to copy multiple, evenly sized data to improve ETL runtimes. We recommend the use of an Insert statement with multiple values. Consequently, the Insert statement can also be used with Select, as a set-based operation. This technique increases the execution speed of procedural operations.
2. JOIN Operator

     To reduce the number of rows, predicate pushdown for filtering can be imposed to reduce the size of the join. We recommend invoking the cache data along with the join operator. Moreover, Cache should be attributed to metadata tables, as these tables ideally provide business key-related information descriptively.
3. LOOKUP Statement

     We discourage the use of the Lookup statement entirely, as it processes each row is processed one at a time. Iterations, depending on the number of rows in the source, thus, significantly increase the duration of execution. The lookup function can be achieved using the Join statement, by grouping the number of rows.

4. GROUP-BY Statement

The group-by clause comes in handy when applying conditional statements. Grouping reduces the cardinality of a relation. If grouping is applied before the condition, it significantly reduces the cost of subsequent joins.

5. HASH JOIN Statement

Index scans are the fastest ways to retrieve required rows. For this, a common practice is the use of nested loops, however, we recommend the use of hash joins over nested loops, as loops work best when the dataset is relatively small. For a larger dataset, using nested loops, especially 'WHERE' clause in a statement often confuses unnecessary indexes. For this reason, functions should be avoided when using the 'WHERE" clause in an expression.

6. WITH Clause

The WITH clause can be effectively used to split complex queries, especially with the SELECT statement. Debugging statements and testing performance can also be achieved using the respective clause. The resulting smaller statements are much faster to run.

7. Direct-Path INSERT

The direct-path Insert statement is efficient over a simple Insert statement and can be utilized during the loading process. For this reason, we did not include a direct-path insert statement earlier to avoid ambiguities. Since data is always appended at the end of the table during loading, the direct-path insert statement achieves the results more efficiently as it avoids the use of free space and does not require access to log information. The particular statement can also be used to merge rows and tables, however, only when foreign key constraints are not enabled in target tables.

In addition to query optimisation, the transformation process can be optimized further at different stages. As elaborated earlier, the effective use of staging tables during extraction can be extended further to accommodate the storage of transformed data temporarily by allocating memory to the staging tables. The dynamic staging area is an extension of the effective use of staging tables. In contrast, for organizations using pushdown technology, this process can be eliminated, as data is directly loaded without staging and transformation.

Finally, the Master Data Repository, which provides context, and validates source records can also be optimized for efficient data warehousing. Since the source data in real time environment is always recent data, the undesired overhead created due to reading all master data can be eliminated by simply introducing cache master data. The cache master data can be incorporated within the in-memory sources or be read from the master data table.

3.4 Enhancing the Loading Process of Near-Real Time Data

Reducing the run time rate of the ETL process is one of the crucial measures of efficiency in data warehousing. The near-real time data becomes historic once initial staging and loading occur. Larger organisations with frequent demand for information can opt for dedicated and separate ETL processes, with different sets of staging tables. This technique may cause resource contention, however, a simple strategy such as replication of data warehousing tables eliminates the duel issue between historic and real time data.

Incremental loading is by far the adopted means. We recommend the use of incremental loading using timestamps, ensuring recent and changed records is extracted only. This eliminates the need to run Lookup clauses for the validation process, which significantly reduces the time and maintains a lightweight process established. While most of the resource contention occurs during the extraction and transformation processes, ensuring only required data is loaded helps maximise efficiency in near-real time environment. A good understanding and identification of the type of data required help in establishing the significance of the desired data. Effective use of master data can ensure that business critical and sensitive data required for information can be validated with the provision of support for business purposes.

Finally, since near-real time environment produces very high volumes of data, data aggregation techniques need to be carefully implemented, so as not to overload the computational capabilities of the systems. Along with significance-based loading, loading a fixed number of records ensures a lighter load on the system performance. Since the number of records may be quite high, employing aggregation techniques can significantly reduce the number of records by merging one or more dimensions of data. The aggregation concept can also be implemented at several stages of the ETL process, including the pre-processing stages to reduce the data complexities using set-based operations.

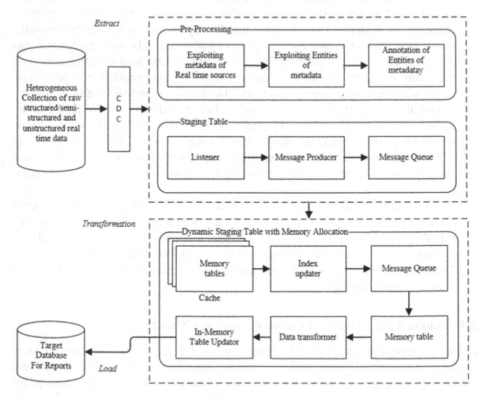

Fig. 3. Conceptual Model with Optimized ETL Processes

Figure 3 disseminates a conceptual model of the ETL process based on the optimization techniques presented for each of the respective processes.

3.5 Efficient Design Targeting Specific Needs of Independent Data Warehousing

Real-time data integration poses constant challenges to the efficiency of data warehouses. The constant influx of data fed into warehouses and the challenges of automating the transformation process to generate meaningful analytics is the presiding factor. The single optimal goal is to achieve lightweight reports using the most recent data. Depending on the number, and the nature of data sources, as well as the size of data warehouses, the ETL process can be smartly stitched. Rather than transforming the data before loading, efficiency, in the form of throughput, can be achieved simply by switching the transformation and loading process. Thereby, depending on the nature of data sources and the size of warehouses, the ELT process can also be utilized.

In the previous section, the primary focus was the optimization of respective ETL processes. Using the techniques for each of the respective processes, data warehouse efficiency can be significantly improved by determining which one of the two methods to employ in the respective warehouse. This section focuses on instances where ELT can be used instead, to achieve greater efficiency. As organizations with huge quantities of structured, semi-structured and unstructured data look to invest in the cloud, loading the data straight after extraction is optimal since throughput is obtained in rapid succession. Since the majority of the processes using ETL is carried out while data is still in the pipeline, ELT ensures that transformation is carried out for analysis once all the data reaches the warehouse. In this way, lightweight queries can be used to generate required reports, since the processing environment, data cube dimensions with aggregations and schemas are already deduced.

Based on the computational requirements and system capabilities, the voluminous nature of real-time integration causes bottlenecks in processing takes precedence over overloading. ELT prioritizes the transfer speed. Regardless of the quality of data, using ELT would mean loading all the data in the warehouse. Complexities surrounding the data warehouse's storage capability can arise an issue depending on the platform employed. To resolve this issue, a separate staging area needs to be allocated which can temporarily store a predefined size of real-time data. Upon transformation, the stage can be cleared by moving the data into the historical section of the warehouse. Table 2 summarizes scenarios where optimal methods can be effectively employed to achieve maximum efficiency.

Table 2. Factors to consider between ETL and ELT for data warehousing.

Specificity and Demands - DW	ETL	ELT
Conceptualized View	Transformation demands preprocessing, therefore, data is presented in a structured manner	Does not require transformation before loading, as real-time data can be moved directly into the warehouse
	The bulk of the processing is staged before loading, and analysis with clean schemas ensures the accurate and timely delivery	Both, Structured and Unstructured, data is kept indefinitely, which enables multiple transformations
	Data is processed on separate servers. Although resources are constraining, raw data does not pass staging to be stored in the warehouse	Data is handled with less stringency, cleansing, enriching and transformations can occur whenever needed
	Compliance violations with data is never possible. Ensures continuity, with a well-defined flow for the ongoing process	Real-time integration is handled more efficiently with less stress on system requirements
Real-Time Integration	Mirroring technique enables secondary processing servers which can achieve a faster loading due to staging	Real-time integration is achieved quicker as data is loaded directly, and transformations can be handled with simpler queries
Throughput	Data loaded into the system is transformed, ensuring only structured data is available in the warehouse	Developing diverse light-weight reports from analysis due to the availability of both, structured and unstructured data
Scalability	Truncation during transformation and specificity with methods as demanded by particular deployment ensure reducing bottleneck issues	Raw datasets can be infinitely queried due to data retention ability
Workflow staging	Pre-processing eliminates several data handling issues such as dealing with NULLS and BLANKS	Simultaneous loading and transformation with real-time data

4 Limitations

Various optimization techniques have been carefully analysed and presented for each of the processes involved in a data warehouse environment, however, for the model to be widely accepted, it needs to be implemented in a real time data warehouse.

5 Conclusion

Near-real integration in data warehouses poses significant challenges where multiple sources, with complex data, need to be handled efficiently for fresh and quick analysis. This paper looked at the optimization processes at each significant process level by extensively reviewing related literature, based on which a unified model was proposed, which will significantly increase the near-real time data warehousing. The next phase will be to take our research further by implementing the proposed model in a real time data warehouse.

References

1. Iata.org (2022). https://www.iata.org/en/iata-repository/publications/economic-reports/fiji-value-of-aviation/. Accessed 04 July 2022
2. Swapnil, G.: ETL in Near-real-time Environment: A Review of Challenges and Possible Solutions, ResearchGate.com (2020)
3. Gupta, A., Arun, S.: Proposed techniques to optimize the DW and ETL query for enhancing data warehouse efficiency. In: 5th International Conference on Computing, Communication and Security (ICCCS), Patna (2020)
4. Anderson, O., Thomsen, C., Kristian, T.: ETL processing by simple specifications. In: Proceedings of the 20th International Workshop on Design, Optimization, Languages and Analytical Processing of Big Data co-located with 10th EDBT/ICDT Joint Conference (2018)
5. Mehmood, E., Tayyaba, A.: Challenges and solutions for processing real-time big data stream: a systematic literature review. IEEE Access **8** (2020)
6. Sabtu, A., et al.: The challenges of extract, transform and load (ETL) for data integration in near real-time environment. J. Theor. Appl. Inf. Technol. **95**(22), 6314–6322 (2017)
7. Yingchi, M., Xiafang, L.: Real-time data ETL framework for big real-time data analysis. In: IEEE International Conference on Information and Automation, Lijiang (2015)
8. Sreemathy, J., Deebika, R., Suganthi, K., Aisshwarya, T.: Data integration and ETL: a theoretical perspective. In: 7th International Conference on Advanced Computing and Communication Systems, Coimbatore (2021)
9. Biswas, N., Sarkar, A., Mondal, K.C.: Efficient incremental loading in ETL processing for real-time data integration. Innov. Syst. Softw. Eng. **16**, 53–61 (2020)
10. Gang, C., An, B., Liu, Y.: A novel agent-based parallel ETL system for massive data. In: Chinese Control and Decision Conference (CCDC), Yinchuan (2016)
11. Mudassir, M., Raghubeer, K., Dayanand, R.: Towards comparative analysis of resumption techniques in ETL. Indonesian J. Inf. Syst. **3**(2), 82–93 (2021)
12. Machado, G.V., Cunha, Í., Pereira, A.C., Oliveira, L.B.: DOD-ETL: distributed on-demand ETL. J. Internet Serv. **6**, 10–21 (2019)
13. Pooja, W., Vaishali, D.: Challenges and solutions for processing real-time big data stream: a systematic literature review. IEEE Access **8** (2020)

14. Sreemathy, J., Joseph, I., Nisha, S., Chaaru, P., Gokula Priya, R.M.: Data integration in ETL using TALEND. In: 2020 6th International Conference on Advanced Computing and Communication Systems (ICACCS), Coimbatore (2020)
15. Jintao, G., Liu, W., Du, H., Zhang, X.: Batch insertion strategy in a distribution database. In: 8th IEEE International Conference on Software Engineering and Service Science (ICSESS), Beijing (2017)
16. Abhishek, G., Arun, S.: A comprehensive survey to design efficient data warehouse for betterment of decision support systems for management and business corporates. Int. J. Manag. (IJM) **11**(7), 463–471 (2020)
17. Berkani, N., Bellatreche, L., Carlos, O.: ETL-aware materialized view selection in semantic data stream warehouses. In: 12th International Conference on Research Challenges in Information Science (RCIS), Nantes (2018)
18. Suleykin, A., Panfilov, P.: Metadata-driven industrial-grade ETL system. In: IEEE International Conference on Big Data (Big Data), Atlanta (2020)
19. Diouf, P.S., Boly, A., Ndiaye, S.: Variety of data in the ETL processes in the cloud: state of the art. In: IEEE International Conference on Innovative Research and Development (ICIRD), Bangkok (2018)
20. Kar, P., Mukherjee, R.: A comparative review of data warehousing ETL tools with new trends and industry insight. In: IEEE 7th International Advance Computing Conference (IACC), Hyderabad (2017)
21. Qu, W., Stephan, D.: Incremental ETL pipeline scheduling for near real-time. Datenbanksysteme für Business, Technologie und Web (2017)
22. Ali, S.M.F., Wrembel, R.: From conceptual design to performance optimization of ETL workflows: current state of research and open problems. VLDB J. **26**(6), 777–801 (2017). https://doi.org/10.1007/s00778-017-0477-2
23. Thangam, A.R., Peter, S.J.: An extensive survey on various query optimization technique. Int. J. Comput. Sci. Mob. Comput. **5**(8), 148–154 (2016)
24. Santos, R.J., Bernardino, J.: Optimizing data warehouse loading procedures for enabling useful-time data warehousing. In: Proceedings of the 2009 International Database Engineering & Applications Symposium, pp. 292–299 (2009)

Big Data Visualization Tools, Challenges and Web Search Popularity - An Update till Today

Anal Kumar[1]([⊠]) [iD] and A. B. M. Shawkat Ali[2] [iD]

[1] Fiji National University, Nadi, Fiji
`anal.kumar@fnu.ac.fj`
[2] The University of Fiji, Lautoka, Fiji
`shawkat.ali@ieee.org`

Abstract. In today's culture, when everything is recorded digitally, from online surfing habits to medical records, individuals produce and consume petabytes of data every day. Every element of life will undergo a change thanks to big data. However, just processing and interpreting the data is insufficient; the human brain is more likely to find patterns when the data is shown visually. Data analytics and visualization are crucial decision-making tools in many different businesses. Additionally, it creates new opportunities for visualization, reflecting imaginative problem-solving with the aid of large amounts of data. It might be challenging to see such a large amount of data in real time or in a static manner. In this paper, the authors discuss the importance of big data visualization, the issues, and the use of several large data visualization techniques. The enormous data mine cannot become a gold mine until sophisticated and intelligent analytics algorithms are applied to it, and the findings of the analytical process are presented in an effective, efficient, and stunning way. Unsurprisingly, a plethora of Big Data visualization tools and approaches have emerged in the last few years, both as independent apps or plugins for data management systems and as a component of data management systems. The dataset obtained from Google Trends is prepared and experimented upon to visualize the Web search trends for Microsoft Power BI, Tableau, Qliikview, Infogram and Google Charts. Through this data visualization experiment various insights have been obtained that illustrates how sharply Power BI is gaining popularity as compared to rather modest trend of Tableau and other Data Visualization tools. Furthermore, the authors provide more insight on top listed countries searching for various Data Visualization tools and categorizing various Data Visualization tools of interest based of geographical locations. On account of these issues, this article provides an overview of the most popular and frequently used visualization tools and approaches for large data sets, concluding with a summary of the key functional and non-functional characteristics of the tools under consideration with a detailed comparative analysis of various Data Visualization tools web search trends.

Keywords: Data Visualization · Tableau · Power BI and Qlikview

1 Introduction

In recent years, Big Data has caught the interest of a wide range of businesses, including academia, IT firms, and governments [1]. Due to various variables such as the Internet of Things (IoTs), sensors in our environment, and the digitization of all offline documents such as our medical history, the rate of data growth has accelerated tremendously in recent years. Big Data has shown its value to the world in such a short period of time that practically all IT and non-IT firms now save all of the data they generate. Businesses are already struggling to store vast amounts of data, but processing, interpreting, and presenting it in useful ways is a task for the future [2].

The phrase Big Data has multiple dimensions since it refers not only to the quantity of data but also to the variety of it sources and the speed with which data is analyzed. The 3Vs [3, 4], illustrated in Fig. 1, is a widely used model to characterize Big Data. It depicts the three main characteristics of Big Data: volume, velocity, and variety. Each of the aforementioned characteristics complicates typical data management activities. For example, when the volume grows, data extraction and storage, as well as data processing, become more difficult (cleansing, analysis, etc.). In order to cope with the increased volume of data in a typical scenario, both storage systems and analytics algorithms must be scalable. In addition, the variety dimension complicates data storage and analysis because of the integration of data with different structures.

According to the Economic Times, huge firms who use Big Data analytics outperform their counterparts who do not [5]. Many of the visualization tools described in the literature are essentially analytics tools with an increasingly important visualization component. The Big Data imperative's [6] challenges to data management have a significant impact on data visualization. The "bigness" of enormous data sets, as well as their variety, contribute to the complexity of data representation [7], making drawing methods particularly difficult: Consider the popular social network Facebook, where nodes represent people and links represent interpersonal connections; we should note that nodes can be accompanied by information such as age, gender, and identity, and links can be of various types, such as colleague relationships, classmate relationships, and family relationships.

This work is based on a similar paper by Caldarola and Rinaldi [7], which offered a paradigm based on qualitative analysis of Big Data solutions. In a certain case, software solutions for storing Big Data were investigated, while data and information visualization tools were examined in a similar manner here. The remainder of this paper is structured as follows. The second section presents the typical model characterizing the dimensions of Big Data and the technological solution with a focus on the visualization issue. The third section introduces the evaluation framework adopted for the comparison of the Big Data visualization solutions, whereas the fourth section illustrates the results of the comparison carried out on the most widespread existing tools, based on the predefined criteria. Finally, the last section draws the conclusions, summarizing the major findings, and opens new directions for further researches in future works.

2 Literature Review

Checkland and Holwell [8] quoted the definition of data as "a representation of facts, concepts or instructions in a formalized manner suitable for communication, interpretation, or processing by humans or by automatic means". Data is considered as the building blocks upon which any organizations growth upturns [9].According to Yaqoob, Hashem, Gani, Mokhtar, Ahmed, Anuar and Vasa [10] the volume of data generated and stored in today's digital world had gradually evolved within a shorter time frame. Massive advances in computer science area emerged and accumulated vast amount of data in unstructured format forming big data [11]. "Big Data" in general sense is used for describing collection, processing, analyzing and visualizing with large data sets [12]. According to the English Oxford Dictionary [13] definition "Big Data" is "extremely large data sets that may be analyzed computationally to reveal patterns, trends, and associations, especially relating to human behavior and interactions". There are numerous formal and informal definition of Big Data [14].

According to Han, Yonggang, Tat-Seng and Xuelong [14] "Big Data" does not only mean large volume of data however there are three types of definition which plays an important role in determining how big data is regarded. Attributive Definition: IDC [15] is expertise in the area of Big data which describes "Big data technologies as a newer generation of technologies and architectures that are specifically designed for extraction of values from very large volumes of data, by permitting high-velocity capture, discovery, and/or analysis". This definition used 4 features of Big Data including volume, value, velocity and variety resulting in the wide use of "4Vs" definition [16–18]. Comparative Definition: According to a report [19] produced by Mckinsey in 2011, the definition of big data was expressed as "datasets whose mass is beyond the capacity of typical database software tools to capture, store, manage, and analyze." This definition incorporates the evolutionary aspect of which dataset can be considered as big data. Architectural Definition: According to Makrufa [20] "Big Data" is where the volume of the data, velocity or data representation have limited ability to perform analysis effectively for efficient processing. According to Hu [14] big data can also be further categorized into big data science and big data framework. Big data science [21] is "the study of techniques that covers the acquisition, conditioning, evaluation and exploration of big data" whereas big data frameworks [22] are "software libraries with their related algorithms that enables distributed processing and analysis of different components which plays an important role to process, handle and store large data.".

Graphics is one of the most significant approaches for exploring data and presenting results which are often very effective at information communication [23]. Data visualization originated from ancient needs which was needed for human survival in the form of hunting where humans kept track of the statistics on what kind of animals are to be hunted with its objectives. The human mind is very visual, historically there were visuals alphabets like Phaistos, Sumerian, Assyrian cuneiform which were based on visuals rather than on sounds [24]. Data visualization uses images to represent information and in considered one of the powerful means of studying data. According to Few and Edge [25] data visualization are undermined in today's world due to lack of understanding. Data visualization deals with data presentation in graphical format making the information ease of understanding to help explain facts in order to determine the course of action [26]. Sadika [26] suggested that real-time data visualization can enable users to proactively respond to the arising issues related to large datasets. According to Tukey [27], effective visualization provides better understanding of user's own data in order to communicate their insights to others. Data visualization has been used in vast fields historically from probability [28], statistics [29] and astronomy [30]. According to Ali, Gupta, Nayak and Lenka [31] the most important feature for visualization should be interactive where the users shall be able to freely interact with the visualization. In today's era the environment where industries operations are drastically changing with complexity due to the huge volume of data generated significantly. These high volumes of data hold important insights that can significantly help industries and organizations in shaping up business, understanding pattern trends and predictive analysis [32]. Due to the evolution of complexity of big data there is a need for data visualization [33].

According to Azzam [34] data visualization is defined as "a process based on qualitative or quantitative data that results in an images that is a representative of raw data that is readable by viewers and supports exploration, examination, and communication of the data". Engebretsen [35] described data visualization as a technology or set of technologies like a clock, compass or map that can transform the way human views and relates to reality. Graphical representation of numeric information is not a new concept however its importance evolved from the widespread use of data and statistics in the 19th century [36]. The greatest strength of data visualization is reduced data errors and increase amount of data access speed [33]. Data visualization is a newer approach to data integration that expertise's in decision making that can change the way people experience information [24]. According to Alexander [37] the three major principles of data visualization which supports the scalability and operational efficiency for big data environments are partitioning, isolation and encapsulation.

Over the years wide variety of Data Visualization tools has been developed to analyze dataset in many fields including medical [38], environment science [39, 40], decision making [24, 41], agriculture [33] and fraud investigation [42].

Tableau: is one of the most widely used interactive data visualization tool today in the market that focuses on business intelligence and highly used by data analytics industry [43]. According to Ali [31] Tableau uses a user friendly interface and range of visualization features and functionalities to customize visuals supporting most data formats and connection to servers. Hoelscher [44] suggested that Tableau is useful in driving decision making process. There are no programming skills required for basic calculation and statistics with the intuitive user interface provided. Tableau significantly stands apart from other sophisticated data visualization tools with the integration of queries, exploration and visualization of data into a single process [41]. Tableau is used by many corporations, journalists, and nonprofits to help people see and understand data. Tableau has been always the best data visualization tool due to its "drag-and-drop" interface which draws out its simplicity for usage among users with no programming background or knowledge [43].

Power BI integrates an ecosystem that provides unique features empowering benefits that can be directly accessed by the application itself [45]. According to Widjaja [46] Power BI offers "data warehouse capabilities such as data preparation, data discovery and interactive dashboards". Krishnan [47] states that Power BI has the capability to combine various databases, files and web services in order to make changes and fix issues automatically. According to Ali [31] Power BI stands apart from other visualization tools, as users can use natural language to query the data where there is an additional option to run R script. Diamond, Michael and Angela [48] mentioned that there were two obstacles when creating Power BI dashboard.

Qlikview: is one of the most ease of use Business Intelligence tools for converting data into knowledge. Qilkview is combination of quick and click which means that the application is super-fast and ease of use at the same time [49]. Qlikview was used in a study to address the common challengers using commercially available software in the classroom [50].

2.1 Problem Statement, Objectives and Methodology

This section reviews the most popular solutions and provides an explanation of the assessment criteria listed below, each of which aims to provide a response to a specific query. It begins by explaining the fundamental categories that define the existing huge data visualization tools. This section reviews the most popular solutions and provides an explanation of the assessment criteria listed below, each of which aims to provide a response to a specific query. It begins by explaining the fundamental categories that define the existing huge data visualization tools followed by Scope which offers details about the application or range of the tool, attempting to address the following query: Is this a developer tool or a presentation tool? Among the solutions surveyed, the authors divide them into two broad categories: presentation tools, which are primarily used for presentation through desktop (stand-alone) or web-based applications, and development tools, which are primarily software libraries (APIs) or programming language modules (such as Python or Java modules), and which are primarily used for extending an application by using methods and routines provided ad hoc by the library. The software group displays the type of the analytical solution. It makes a distinction between desktop applications (standalone programs that cannot be extended), web-based programs or services, software libraries (such as web-based Javascript libraries), and software frameworks (complex software applications with a plugin or add-ons-based mechanism to extend them in order to connect the framework to existing data storage or analytics solutions). The visualization's framework answers the question of what kind of graphical object the tool is intended for. As a result, it offers details about the main widget or visual for the tool. Although the tool is often detached from one or more widgets, many solutions are not limited to a single graphical component. Furthermore, the paper discusses the operating system of the tool (such as Linux, Windows, or Mac OS X), as well as if it is web-based. The license for the product is stated as follows: commercial and open source under a variety of licenses (such as the GNU GPL and the Apache License); Flexibility. This criterion relates to horizontal scaling techniques used by the tools to accommodate very large data collections. Some of the solutions deal with issues like the program's capacity to connect to a Hadoop instance that is processing a sizable dataset or the usage of a pay-as-you-go cloud. Scalability and latest release date criteria refer to the extensibility of tools with add-ons or plugins and the ability to connect to existing storage solutions. For example, Plottly can connect to Matlab and R through specific client connections and can be dynamically extended in various ways using the Javascript API.

The goal of this research is to give a comprehensive overview of the literature and industry practices in relation to Big Data Visualization, as well as to establish a conceptual framework for constraint management. The study has the following sub-objectives in particular:

To provide a comprehensive review of sources and characteristics of constraints commonly found in Big Data Visualisation Tools and Software's.
To provide a comprehensive review of current industry practices and researches in relation to Data Visualisation and to develop a conceptual framework for selecting Data Visualization tools.
To identify the top searched and most popular Data Visualization tool that is of interest to users based on web search trends. The findings of this study will be useful to industry practitioners and software suppliers in establishing better data visualization practices and technologies.

The literature review and conceptual modeling are the key research methods used in this study. The first step toward a "zero-constraint" environment is to identify and classify constraints using a structured approach. This research will look at several forms of restrictions in Data Visualization Tools. This research paper explains the characteristics of constraints commonly found in Big Data Visualisation Tools and Software's. It is assumed that a real time operating system with a priority based scheduling is used which is common in modern embedded systems. The method is fully software based and no additional hardware or customization to existing kernel is required. The main objective of the proposed method is to detect and classify various characteristics of constraints commonly found in Big Data Visualisation Tools and Software's. Furthermore, In the proposed method the authors proceed with identifying the top searched and most popular Data Visualization tool that is of interest to users based on web search trends. The dataset obtained from Google Trends is prepared and experimented upon to visualize the Web search trends for Microsoft Power BI, Tableau, Qliikview, Infogram and Google Charts. Through this data visualization experiment various insights have been obtained that illustrates how sharply Power BI is gaining popularity as compared to rather modest trend of Tableau and other Data Visualization tools. Furthermore, the authors provide more insight on top listed countries searching for various Data Visualization tools and categorizing various Data Visualization tools of interest based of geographical locations.

2.2   Data Comparison and Analysis

Since almost everyone utilizes Google in some way, some more or less than others, it has ingrained itself into peoples' daily lives. With more than 1.5 billion users globally, it is the best and most widely used search engine. In actuality, Google handles about 40,000 searches every second on average. This demonstrates how Google has truly embedded itself into people's daily online lives, becoming the go-to resource whenever someone has a question or query about a certain subject. Visualizing and identifying patterns in search behavior across Google Search, Google News, Google Images, Google Shopping, and YouTube is vital when evaluating the popularity of Data Visualisation tools. A trend graph of the searched subject over the chosen period of time is produced using data indicating the frequency of certain searches during the specified time period, enabling user's authors to analyze the findings. Authors have done an analysis and comparative studies by using the Search Volume Index graph to view the queries of 5 distinct Data Visualization tools simultaneously. To compare relative popularity, each piece of data is divided by the total number of searches for the region and time period it covers. Otherwise, the top-ranked locations would always be those with the largest search volume. The generated values are then scaled on a scale from 0 to 100 according to the proportion of searches for each topic to searches for all topics. Different regions with the same search interest for a phrase do not necessarily have the same overall search volumes, according to the study (Fig. 2 and Table 1).

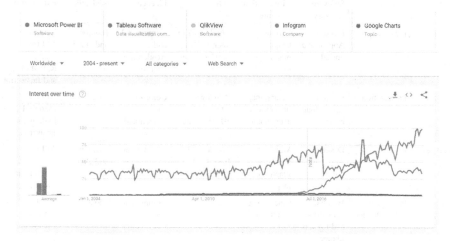

Fig. 1. Scatter Chart shows how sharply Power BI is gaining popularity as compared to rather modest trend of Tableau.

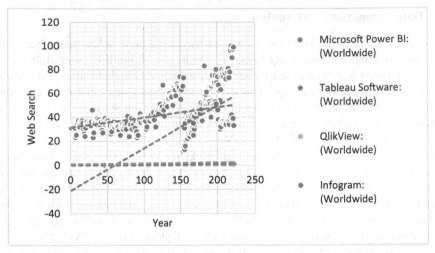

Fig. 2. X Y Scatter Chart shows how sharply Power BI is gaining popularity as compared to rather modest trend of Tableau.

Table 1. Evaluation framework of selected Natural fixed features for the surveyed visualization tools.

Name	Usage	Software category	Visualization structure	O.S	Licence	Scalability	Extensibility
Tableau	Presentation	Desktop App., cloud hosted	Various Charts, graphs and maps	Windows 7 or later, OSX 10.10 or later	Commercial and Academic license	Hadoop and cloud	DBs Drivers, API for Matlab, R, Python and Javascript
Infogram	Presentation	Desktop App., cloud hosted	Charts, map, images and even videos	Windows 7 or later, OSX 10.10 or later	Commercial and educational license	Cloud	API for Matlab, R, Python and Javascript
QlikView	Presentation	Desktop App., cloud hosted	Various Charts, graphs and maps	Windows 7 or later, OSX 10.10 or later	Commercial	Hadoop and cloud	API for Matlab, R, Python and Javascript
Plottly	Presentation + Developers	Web tool, JavaScript and Python library	Charts, plot and maps	Web Based	Commercial and Community	Cloud	API for Matlab, R, Python and Javascript
Power BI	Developers	Desktop App., cloud hosted	Various Charts, graphs and maps	Windows 7 or later, OSX 10.10 or later	Free, Pro, and Premium Per User	Cloud and Hadoop	DBs Drivers, API for Matlab, R, Python and Javascript

2.3 Discussion and Conclusion

The creation of graphics, diagrams, or animations to convey a message from the insight observed depends heavily on the visualization of data. This study has given a preliminary assessment of the most popular Big Data visualization tools currently available. As was seen in the preceding sections, a great number of solutions are open-source projects demonstrating the great interest that the community of developers has in such topics. The comparison test between the three data visualization tools reveals that Power BI scores for connectivity, data management, embedded analytics, augmented analytics, mobile business intelligence capabilities, OS and technical support, as well as security, according to the research conducted by the authors. Tableau also excels in data management, data visualization, reporting, queries, operating system support, embedded analytics, and geographic analytics. The categories of data management, queries, IOT and mobile analytics, and security are all areas where Qlik View excels. The first limitation is the study is limited to big data visualization based on Web Search data from Google trends and maybe some papers are skipped. The second limitation of the proposed research is that the search process was performed in using top 5 most commonly data Visualisation tools and it does not consider many other tools that are present currently. The reason was to focus on only top most used visualization tools. This work identified a number of outstanding questions and concerns that might inform future research in the field of data visualization, recognizing the uniqueness of data visualization tools. Heterogeneous data visualization, which contributes to data integration and big data process issues, will be a part of future studies. Since they demand a lot of data processing and storage space, both of them are crucial and challenging to display and analyze in large databases.

References

1. Jin, X., Wah, B.W., Cheng, X., Wang, Y.: Significance and challenges of big data research. Big data research 2(2), 59–64 (2015)
2. Center, I.I.: Big data visualization: turning big data into big insights. White Paper., 1–14 (2013)
3. SAS, Visualization, data:making big data approachable and valuable. Whitepaper, Source: IDG Research Services, pp. 1–4 (2012)
4. Mohanty, S., Jagadeesh, M., Srivatsa, H.: Big Data Imperatives: Enterprise 'Big Data'warehouse',Bi'implementations and Analytics. Apress, New York (2013)
5. Bhanu, S.: Companies adopting big data analytics to deal with challenges. The Economic Times (2013)
6. Caldarola, E.G., Picariello, A., Castelluccia, D.: Modern enterprises in the bubble: why big data matters. ACM SIGSOFT Softw. Eng. Notes 40(1), 1–4 (2015)
7. Caldarola, E.G., Picariello, A., Rinaldi, A.M.: Experiences in wordnet visualization with labeled graph databases. In: Fred, A., Dietz, J.L.G., Aveiro, D., Liu, K., Filipe, J. (eds.) IC3K 2015. CCIS, vol. 631, pp. 80–99. Springer, Cham (2016). https://doi.org/10.1007/978-3-319-52758-1_6
8. Checkland, P., Holwell, S.: Data, capta, information and knowledge. In: Introducing Information Management: The Business Approach, pp. 47–55. Elsevier London (2006)
9. Elgendy, N., Elragal, A.: Big data analytics: a literature review paper. In: Perner, P. (ed.) ICDM 2014. LNCS (LNAI), vol. 8557, pp. 214–227. Springer, Cham (2014). https://doi.org/10.1007/978-3-319-08976-8_16

10. Yaqoob, I., et al.: Big data: from beginning to future. Int. J. Inf. Manage. **36**(6), 1231–1247 (2016)
11. Tang, L., Li, J., Du, H., Li, L., Wu, J., Wang, S.: Big data in forecasting research: a literature review. Big Data Research **27**, 100289 (2022)
12. Emmanuel, I., Stanier, C.: Defining big data. In: Proceedings of the International Conference on Big Data and Advanced Wireless Technologies, pp. 1–6 (2016)
13. "Engish Dictionary" Oxford Lexico.https://www.lexico.com/definition/big_data. Accessed 14 July 2022
14. Hu, H., Wen, Y., Chua, T.S., Li, X.: toward scalable systems for big data analytics: a technology tutorial. IEEE Access **2**, 652–687 (2014). https://doi.org/10.1109/ACCESS.2014.2332453
15. Gantz, J., Reinsel, D.: Extracting value from chaos. IDC iview **1142**(2011), 1–12 (2011)
16. Lustberg, T., et al.: Big data in radiation therapy: challenges and opportunities. Br. J. Radiol. **90**(1069), 20160689 (2017)
17. Matturdi, B., Zhou, X., Li, S., Lin, F.: Big Data security and privacy: a review. China Commun **11**(14), 135–145 (2014)
18. Biswas, R.: "Atrain distributed system" (ADS): an infinitely scalable architecture for processing big data of Any 4Vs. In: Acharjya, D.P., Dehuri, S., Sanyal, S. (eds.) Computational Intelligence for Big Data Analysis. ALO, vol. 19, pp. 3–54. Springer, Cham (2015). https://doi.org/10.1007/978-3-319-16598-1_1
19. Manyika, J., et al.: Big Data: The Next Frontier For Innovation, Competition, and Productivity. McKinsey Global Institute, Washington (2011)
20. Hajirahimova, M.S., Aliyeva, A.S.: About big data measurement methodologies and indicators. Int. J. Mod. Educ. Comput. Sci. **9**(10), 1 (2017)
21. Dahdouh, K., Dakkak, A., Oughdir, L., Ibriz, A.: Improving online education using big data technologies. Role Technol. Educ. (2020)
22. Mohanty, H., Bhuyan, P., Chenthati, D.: Big Data: A Primer. Springer, Berlin (2015). https://doi.org/10.1007/978-81-322-2494-5
23. Chen, C.-H., Härdle, W.K., Unwin, A.: Handbook of Data Visualization. Springer, Berlin (2007). https://doi.org/10.1007/978-3-540-33037-0
24. Aparicio, M., Costa, C.J.: Data visualization. Commun Design Quart. Rev. **3**(1), 7–11 (2015)
25. Few, S., Edge, P.: Data visualization: past, present, and future. IBM Cognos Innovation Center (2007)
26. Sadiku, M., Shadare, A.E., Musa, S.M., Akujuobi, C.M., Perry, R.: Data visualization. Int. J. Eng. Res. Adv. Technol. (IJERAT) **2**(12), 11–16 (2016)
27. Tukey, J.W.: Exploratory Data Analysis. Reading, MA (1977)
28. Hald, A.: A History of Probability and Statistics and their Applications before 1750. John Wiley & Sons, Hoboken (2005)
29. Porter, T.M.: The Rise of Statistical Thinking, 1820–1900. Princeton University Press, Princeton (2020)
30. Riddell, R.C.: Parameter disposition in pre-Newtonian planetary theories. Arch. Hist. Exact Sci., 87–157 (1980)
31. Ali, S.M., Gupta, N., Nayak, G.K., Lenka, R.K.: Big data visualization: tools and challenges. In: 2016 2nd International Conference on Contemporary Computing and Informatics (IC3I), pp. 656–660. IEEE (2016)
32. Muniswamaiah, M., Agerwala, T., Tappert, C.: Data virtualization for decision making in big data. Int. J. Softw. Eng. Appl. **10**(5), 45–53 (2019)
33. Mathivanan, S., Jayagopal, P.: A big data virtualization role in agriculture: a comprehensive review. Walailak J. Sci. Technol. (WJST) **16**(2), 55–70 (2019)
34. Azzam, T., Evergreen, S., Germuth, A.A., Kistler, S.J.: Data visualization and evaluation. N. Dir. Eval. **2013**(139), 7–32 (2013)

35. Engebretsen, M., Kennedy, H.: Data visualization in society (2020)
36. Friendly, M.: A brief history of data visualization. In: Handbook of Data Visualization, pp. 15–56. Springer, Berlin (2008). https://doi.org/10.1007/978-3-540-33037-0_2
37. Bogdanov, A., Degtyarev, A., Shchegoleva, N., Korkhov, V., Khvatov, V.: Big data virtualization: why and how? In: CEUR Workshop Proceedings (2679), pp. 11–21 (2020)
38. Kilimba, T., Nimako, G., Herbst, K.: Data everywhere: an integrated longitudinal data visualization platform for health and demographic surveillance sites. In: Proceedings of the 6th ACM Conference on Bioinformatics, Computational Biology and Health Informatics, pp. 551–552 (2015)
39. Grainger, S., Mao, F., Buytaert, W.: Environmental data visualisation for non-scientific contexts: Literature review and design framework. Environ. Model. Softw. **85**, 299–318 (2016)
40. Kumar, O., Goyal, A.: Visualization: a novel approach for big data analytics. In: 2016 Second International Conference on Computational Intelligence & Communication Technology (CICT), pp. 121–124. IEEE (2016)
41. Murphy, S.A.: Data visualization and rapid analytics: applying tableau desktop to support library decision-making. J. Web Librariansh. **7**(4), 465–476 (2013)
42. Dilla, W.N., Raschke, R.L.: Data visualization for fraud detection: practice implications and a call for future research. Int. J. Account. Inf. Syst. **16**, 1–22 (2015)
43. Wesley, R., Eldridge, M., Terlecki, P.T.: An analytic data engine for visualization in tableau. In: Proceedings of the 2011 ACM SIGMOD International Conference on Management of data, pp. 1185–1194 (2011)
44. Hoelscher, J., Mortimer, A.: Using Tableau to visualize data and drive decision-making. J. Account. Educ. **44**, 49–59 (2018)
45. Knight, D., Knight, B., Pearson, M., Quintana, M., Powell, B.: Microsoft Power BI Complete Reference: Bring your Data to Life with the Powerful Features of Microsoft Power BI. Packt Publishing Ltd, Birmingham (2018)
46. Widjaja, S., Mauritsius, T.: The development of performance dashboard visualization with power BI as platform. Int. J. Mech. Eng. Technol., 235–249 (2019)
47. Krishnan, V.: Research data analysis with power BI (2017)
48. Diamond, M., Mattia, A.: Data visualization: an exploratory study into the software tools used by businesses. J. Instr. Pedagogies **18** (2017)
49. Shukla, A., Dhir, S.: Tools for data visualization in business intelligence: case study using the tool Qlikview. In: Satapathy, Suresh Chandra, Mandal, Jyotsna Kumar, Udgata, Siba K., Bhateja, Vikrant (eds.) Information Systems Design and Intelligent Applications. AISC, vol. 434, pp. 319–326. Springer, New Delhi (2016). https://doi.org/10.1007/978-81-322-2752-6_31
50. Podeschi, R.: Experiential learning using QlikView business intelligence software. Baltimore, Maryland, USA (2014)

The Australian Digital Observatory: Social Media Collection, Discovery and Analytics at Scale

Richard O. Sinnott[✉] [iD], Qi Li, Abdul Mohammad, and Luca Morandini

School of Computing and Information Systems, The University of Melbourne, Melbourne, VIC 3010, Australia
rsinnott@unimelb.edu.au

Abstract. The Australian Digital Observatory was funded by the Australian Research Data Commons in 2021. The goal of the project was to establish the national social media data repository for Australia. This includes collection of social media data at scale, in the first instance from numerous platforms including Twitter, Reddit, FlickR, FourSquare and YouTube. This paper describes the technical architecture of the ADO platform and provides examples of the capabilities that are offered for data discovery, analysis and subsequent download of targeted social media data to support diverse research purposes, noting that the platform needs to respect the terms and conditions of the various social media platforms on data licensing and use, i.e., direct user access to the original raw data is not possible as this would violate the licensing arrangements of the various platforms. We present a case study in the utilization of the platform.

Keywords: Social media · Twitter · Reddit · FlickR · FourSquare · YouTube · topic modelling · sentiment analysis · Cloud · couchDB

1 Introduction

Across the world, individuals use social media on a daily basis. This is also the case for the population of Australia. Many researchers and organisations require access to such data for a wide range of purposes. This can be from a diverse array of domain-specific research concerns, e.g., predicting the outcome of elections or the fluctuations in the stock market based on evolving population sentiment, understanding movement patterns of the population using the location information often captured in social media, through to computational challenges and demands in training computer scientists in how best to deal with big data processing and developing scalable solutions on the Cloud. Unfortunately, it is the case that many researchers only collect small amounts of social media data since they can be overwhelmed with the amount of data that can be collected and its associated storage and analysis demands. The Australian Digital Observatory (ADO – www.ado.eresearch.unimelb.edu.au) was funded by the Australian Research Data Commons (ARDC – www.ardc.edu.au) to tackle this issue. The ADO aim was to establish *the* national social media data repository for Australia. By harvesting data at scale from multiple social media platforms, the aim was to support diverse research communities in their social media discovery, access and usage needs. This paper provides an overview of the ADO project and the technical implementation of the platform that has been realized. Example case studies in the utilization of the platform are also presented.

The rest of this paper is structured as follows. Section 2 provides an overview of related work in social media data collection and curation platforms. Section 3 introduces the ADO platform and the key requirements that have shaped its technical realization. Section 4 illustrates the benefits of the platform through a representative case study. Finally, Sect. 5 draws conclusions on the work as a whole and identifies areas of future work.

2 Related Work

Social media is a rich source of data that researchers and organizations from many diverse disciplines increasingly incorporate into their daily research and business needs. However, researchers, particularly with limited funds or lack of computational skills/resources, face many hurdles when attempting to use such data, especially when dealing with data at scale. Social media data sets are typically voluminous, heterogeneous, available across multiple diverse and independent platforms, have veracity and bias challenges and are often produced and consumed at high velocity. In this context, whilst many researchers and research communities have attempted to establish their own data collection and storage systems, for many this works initially but rapidly overwhelms their associated computational resources, e.g., the laptop or PC that they may have use for collecting and analyzing data.

To tackle this issue various researchers have explored data collection and associated data curation approaches targeted specifically to the needs and demands of social media. Behesti et al. [1] established the DataSynapse solution based on a data (knowledge) lake. This solution provided the foundation for big data analytics by automatically curating raw social data and preparing it for future insights. These include algorithms to transform social items, e.g., tweets into contextualized and curated items. This work focused specifically on Twitter, Facebook, GooglePlus and LinkedIn, however many of these platforms do not share data directly (through APIs) and hence the data can only be obtained through scraping websites directly, which violates the terms and conditions of the social media platforms. A further challenge with such an approach is that social media data is live and continually growing and whilst capturing and storing historic data in a well curated manner is beneficial and important, it is the case that many researchers wish to access data related to things that are happening at the present time, e.g., to understand the pulse of cities [2].

Early approaches such as [3] investigated social media curating activities based on the Pinterest platform and the way in which they related to digital libraries. They explored issues such as the nature of popular pins and categories on Pinterest and their associated provenance. This work focused largely on Pinterest however and did not seek to develop a broader multi-social media platform solution.

The QURATOR project [4] focused on development of a platform that could be used to provide services to address the challenges in curating digital content more generally.

This work was not targeted to social media specifically, however there were overlaps with data aggregation and downstream use that are aligned with the overarching goals of ADO.

The CrowdCorrect project [5] established a social media data curation pipeline by automating the process for cleaning and curating social media data and preparing it for downstream data analytics. This included automatic feature extraction, correction and enrichment. They applied this to urban social issues based on Twitter data with specific focus on government budgets. This work largely focused on Twitter data however and not the broader social media data landscape.

[6] utilized diverse sources of social media data. However, the focus here was to potentially identify the same users across different platforms and not to provide a resource for others to access and use in the social media usage demands. The work considered Twitter and Instagram and use of a range of matching criteria, e.g., similarity of user account names, images, topics etc.

Works such as [7–10] focus on establishing collections (corpus) of social media and connections across such platforms data, however these do not tackle the larger scale integration of diverse social media data and how such data can be discovered, accessed and used for downstream data processing to support the research needs of diverse communities. Rather they focus on demands on establishing a specific corpus of social media [7]; supporting diverse aspects such as labelling the credibility of social media data for researchers exploring topics such as fake news [8], or they focus on a single annotated collection of social media data such as sentiment of YouTube comments [9] or collections of annotated tweets from Twitter [10]. In the case of [10], whilst 97 million annotated tweets may be useful to researchers who are unfamiliar with the Twitter APIs and not able to access and collect such data themselves, such solutions do not meet the challenges facing the research community in understanding what this data might comprise, and more importantly what topics it might include and how these differ from current opinions on those topics as reported in social media. This is a key focus of the ADO project – namely, to be a living all-encompassing reflection of the social media activity across Australia.

3 Australian Digital Observatory Design and Implementation

The first question in development of the ADO platform was what social media data it should include. There are many diverse social media platforms existing today. Rather than attempting to scrape websites and hence violate terms and conditions of these platforms, the project decided to focus on those platforms that offered a publicly accessible APIs and to only collect social media data across Australia. The social media platforms selected included: Twitter, Reddit, FlickR, FourSquare and YouTube comments. Previous work also utilized Instagram however, the Instagram APIs have since been removed as a result of the Cambridge Analytica scandal [11].

In the case of Twitter, the full Twitter archive has been made accessible for academic use since 2021. This requires formal approval and an academic license to access and use. The platform makes available approximately 10m tweets across Australia per month. Platforms such as FlickR and FourSquare are less utilized in Australia, however they typically include location information, e.g., hotels and locations that individuals are checking in to (FourSquare) or tagging of the location of images/photographs (FlickR). The information in Reddit is not as rich as others, e.g., Twitter which is used extensively and includes rich metadata including information such as the tweet text, the time the tweet was sent, the language tweeted, the user profile and follower/followee information. Indeed, a single 280-character tweet can include over 9kb of metadata, which has numerous privacy issues [12, 13]. Reddit instead has various subgroups and discussion topics/threads and does not explicitly offer features to filter for those that post in Australia only. The subgroup names and content are used to select posts that are made across Australia, e.g., subgroups related to sports specific to Australia or named locations such as Melbourne.

The system architecture as shown in Fig. 1 is cloud-native in all of its components. The underlying Cloud infrastructure provided by ARDC comprises eight virtual machines providing a total of 120GB RAM and at present 8TB of storage. The various components are managed by a Kubernetes container orchestration platform (https://kub ernetes.io). A ReSTful API, secured by a JSON Web Token-based authorization system (https://jwt.io), acts as the only gateway to the back-end software, which is designed as a Function-as-a-Service (serverless) application. The system is based on the Knative FaaS framework (https://knative.dev) and the Camel-K cloud-integration platform (https://camel.apache.org). All of the ADO microservices are integrated by an Istio-based service mesh that manages authentication, load-balancing, ingress points, and service-level security. To deal with the volume of data, a distributed data solution has been adopted based on a clustered CouchDB offering. The 4-instance CouchDB database holding the social media posts and topic models is sharded (12 shards) and replicated (2 replicas).

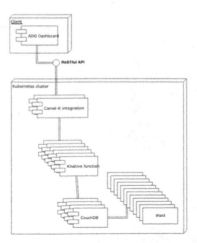

Fig. 1. ADO Architecture

The ADO platform itself comprises key capabilities: social media aggregation including counting of social media posts and sentiment analysis at diverse spatial aggregation levels; topic modelling based on Bidirectional Encoder Representations from Transformers (BERT) [14], term search and analysis and support for subsequent data download and raw data access. We consider these in turn.

3.1 ADO Social Media Aggregation

The ADO platform provides users with the ability to aggregate over social media collections in different ways: by location; by time, by seasonality and by the language of the social media posts (if available). This is shown in Fig. 2. These aggregations are controlled by a start/end date used to specify the period over which the aggregation is required. The location aggregation results are visualised through maps and bar charts (Fig. 2 top left). At present, there are three geographic levels that are available for location-based data aggregation: State, Greater Capital City Statistical Area (GCCSA) and suburb area level. These spatial levels are defined by the Australian Bureau of Statistics. Each social media document in the database also contains a sentiment property. This is given as a score of the sentiment of the text in the document in the range -1(very negative) to + 1 (very positive). The sentiment can also be aggregated across all the different spatial levels. In this case, the sentiment is given as the total sentiment of all social media posts divided by the number of documents over which the overall sentiment is calculated. The seasonality aggregation supports two types of aggregation level: day of week and hour of day. This is based on the number of posts / mean sentiment for each day/hour respectively (Fig. 2 top/middle right). As seen several hundred thousand posts are made daily across Australia.

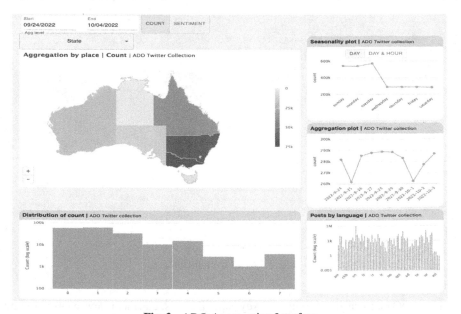

Fig. 2. ADO Aggregation Interface

The language used for social media posts is also aggregated when it is available, e.g., Twitter, (Fig. 2 bottom right), noting that this is a logarithmic scale since most posts are in English, i.e., over 1 million posts are made in English, but less than 20k posts made in other (non-English) languages. Nevertheless, as can be seen from the x-axis, Australia is a multi-cultural society and there are many languages that are used daily.

3.2 ADO Topic Modelling

The ADO platform also supports topic modelling. The topic modelling pipeline is run every day, on a day's worth of social media data. The topic modelling uses BERTopic, to generate a list of topic clusters. These clusters simulate the trending topics of a given day, and each cluster is associated with up to 30 representative terms – from which the topic of the cluster can be extrapolated as shown in Fig. 3 (top). In order to track the evolution of topics over time, a network graph was deemed most suitable to link clusters over consecutive days. In a topic network graph, a node is a topic cluster on a given day, and edges are formed by linking similar topic clusters based on the threshold. This threshold is the minimum number of common terms for an edge to exists between two nodes (or clusters) – note this may not necessarily be the exact same terms, but at least a given number of terms must match over consecutive days. Given a low threshold, nodes can have multiple edges (Fig. 3 (bottom)). Each node is also assigned to a group, which is determined by examining all the paths where the node is present and selecting the longest path as the grouping that the node is assigned to.

Topic clusters that belong to the same group fall on the same x-axis, whilst the y-axis reflects the date of the topic cluster. The radius of a given node is proportional to the number of documents present in that cluster. As seen on the right of the topic graph of Fig. 3, a panel is supported where tweets of certain topic groupings can be inspected. The groups can be explored based on the top terms of the selected group. A selection of tweets that are also present in the group are used for visual inspection.

The complete list of tweet identifiers (*tweetIds*) for subsequent raw data access (hydration) can be downloaded by clicking the download button underneath the embedded tweets panel (Fig. 3 bottom right). Specifically, given a list of *tweetIds*, the raw tweets themselves can be harvested by specifying them as an input parameter using standard Twitter data access libraries such as Tweep/Twitter4J. This model of using ADO for discovery of social media posts related to specific topics and subsequently allowing to download their *tweetIds* addresses the Twitter policy of sharing of social media data, i.e., ADO is used for discovery of tweets and does not provide direct access/sharing of the tweets themselves.

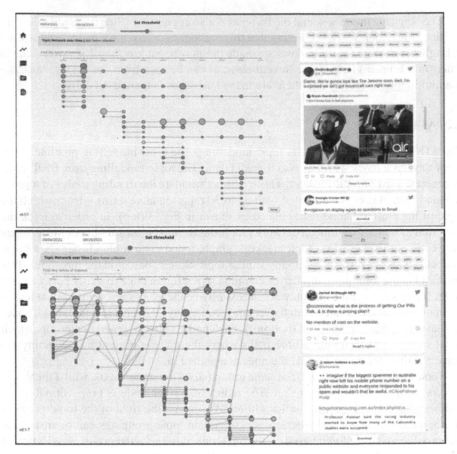

Fig. 3. ADO Topic Modelling (top/bottom shows 15 vs 5 terms in common respectively)

3.3 ADO Search Term Analysis

Outputs of the ADO topic modelling pipeline includes the frequency of terms, as well as word embeddings for each day. This allows to analyse the frequency of terms and interact with the associated word embedding models. Word embeddings are representations of words in a numeric manner, typically as n-dimensional vectors. These can be used to capture the semantic and syntactic properties of words and to compare the semantic similarity of words, e.g., a *queen* is a *woman* as well as richer and more complex semantic scenarios and relationships. In the ADO pipeline, the *word2vec* library [15] was used to build word embeddings for all terms in the vocabulary derived from the social media corpus, as well as support word embeddings. The ADO platform provides an interface to interact with these models through targeted query terms and selected periods of interest. Figure 4 shows the term analysis front end.

The panel on the left shows the result of a summation of cosine similarity of similar terms to the term "covid", in the date period specified. This can be useful as a mechanism to gauge public perception about certain themes, at certain periods of time based on examining the closest, or most similar words of interest. The terms are then further sorted based on this measure. A word cloud is also produced along with a heatmap for the frequency of appearance of the term on specific days. In this case terms such as "vaccin", "infect", "viru" and "jab" are strongly associated with the term "covid". It is noted that the terms themselves are stemmed, i.e., the terms vaccine, vaccination etc. as might occur in social media posts are reduced to "vaccin".

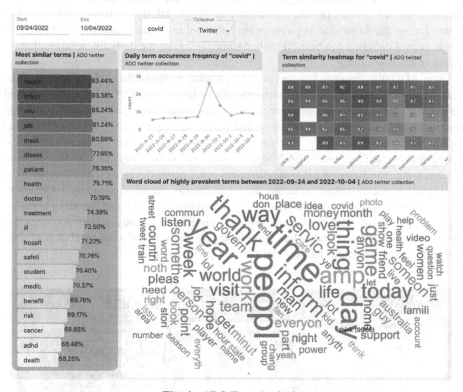

Fig. 4. ADO Term Analysis

Researchers can also search for terms directly, e.g., all posts that mention the term "covid". In this case, a range of posts are returned (if the term is found). These are constrained by the associated use selected data range. The option to directly download the identifiers of the posts is also supported. This is realized as a comma-separated-variable (csv) file. This data can then be used to acquire the actual raw social media data by the researchers – so called *data hydration*.

4 Exemplar Case Study in the Use of the Australian Digital Observatory

To understand the utility of the ADO platform, we present a representative case study in the targeted access to and usage of social media data. Across Australia over the last few years, the property market has seen a period of exponential growth driven primarily by the low cost of borrowing money. However recently there has been a gradual increase in the cash rate set by the Reserve Bank of Australia (RBA) to meet the challenges of rising inflation. In this context, understanding the impact of this on the average citizen, e.g., their ability to make mortgage payments is important. Whilst Government agencies such as the ABS capture precise information on the population at large, the day-to-day issues facing the Australian population are less easy to acquire. Social media provides one source of data that can be used to shed some light onto the daily financial challenges facing many households.

The ADO platform can be used to access a wide range of data related to this topic. Searching for content based on search terms "rba", "hous", "cost", "inflat" over a targeted period, e.g., before/after the most recent increase in the cash rate results in large amounts of related data sets being identified as relevant. Specifically, over 42,000 social media posts are identified as relevant over the period 1st – 15th September 2022 – noting that the rate increased by 0.5% on 7th September. Such data sets are from official agencies, e.g., the RBA (@RBAInfo, financial news networks as well as a diverse array of official/unofficial sources including the population as exemplified in Fig. 5. Clearly to understand individual household financial issues requires official and reporting agencies to be flagged as such in the downstream data analytics, i.e., these are from accounts that are not representative of individual households that may be affected by changes in the cash rate. Such filtering is an essential part of the data analysis.

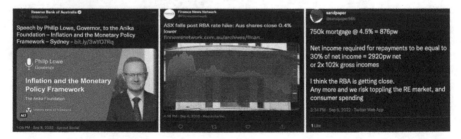

Fig. 5. Examples of Discovered Content

Such content can also be contextualized within a broader social context. For example, considering the median weekly income and median monthly mortgage repayments as shown in Fig. 6 from the Australian Bureau of Statistics. One can identify those areas where individuals are more likely to struggle in paying their monthly mortgages, i.e., where the income is relatively low and the mortgage repayment is relatively high. Targeting social media collection and analysis to those specific areas can provide an on-the-ground assessment of the individual households in the specific areas.

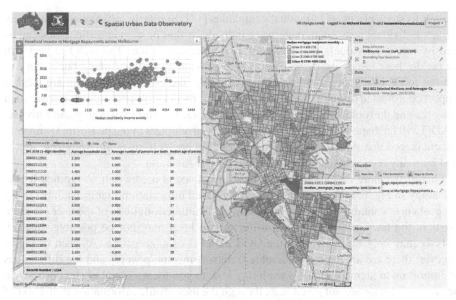

Fig. 6. Mortgage Stress around Melbourne

5 Conclusions and Future Work

The ADO platform provides a single access point for researchers requiring access to large-scale social media data across Australia. The platform currently comprises 136m posts and over 130Gb of data from a range of social media platforms. These have been collected since mid-2021. This is growing daily. By far the main social media resource thus far is Twitter – this is much more widely used than other platforms across Australia (or at least those social media platforms that offer an external API that allows data harvesting).

There are a range of associated challenges with the work. Firstly, the volume of data collected and stored is continually growing and pushing the technical boundaries of the underpinning Cloud infrastructure. The NeCTAR Research Cloud is a general-purpose cloud resource that is used by many diverse research communities for Infrastructure-as-a-Service cloud activities. As such, it has not been designed for rapid input/output where network and disk latency must be minimized due to the volume and velocity of the data. This I/O performance can impact on the clustered database solution due to the read/write performance needed when handling load balancing and data synchronization issues across multiple servers. To minimize the impact of this, the ADO platform currently restricts the date range that can be selected. At present this is set to an upper limit of 21 days. This is not an elegant solution and alternatives are being considered. One possibility would be to migrate the platform to Amazon Web Services (AWS), however thee associated costs would be prohibitive and not coverable by the ARDC grant.

There are also many open issues that are being explored with regards to social media: fake news and privacy are two such hot topics. The ability to share information has never been easier. This can cause many issues such as influencing elections [16] through to stock prices of individual companies [17]. Similarly, privacy and the ability to track individual movement patterns or individuals that post on specific topics can be used by many individuals, businesses and Governments alike. The ADO project will not tackle these issues itself, however it will provide a rich data playground that can be used to explore many such topics. For example, the user networks that are used to support coordinated opinion shaping through social media requires ways to discover such networks and the topics they are promoting/attacking. The future planning and activities of ADO will be shaped by the end user community of adopters of the platform. Ultimately it is envisaged that ADO will become an enduring and self-sustaining platform that is used by many researchers and communities across Australia.

One of the more recent challenges in utility of social media data as typified by the case study in Fig. 6, is the amount of location-based information that is available. Very few posts now contain location information, e.g., latitude/longitude of the user location. As such, the finer grained analysis at the suburb level may not be possible. Instead, analysis may only be possible at the GCCSA level of aggregation. As seen in Fig. 6 however, there are areas of considerable (relative) income/poverty and the differences are important to identify. Work is exploring how to geo-locate social media posts when the precise lat/long are not given, e.g., through the user profile information or the text of the post more generally.

Currently ongoing extensions to the work include support for full-text search capabilities. This will allow users to search for social media documents through rich combinations of post authors, dates, hashtags, and text using logical connectors based upon the Apache Lucene syntax. The platform is also exploring new models for visualization and how best to understand voluminous amounts of evolving data. As one example, [18] shows how dynamically evolving topic graphs can be visualized based on a topological perspective, where peaks and troughs of topic virality can be explored, reflecting the highly dynamic changes in the social media landscape.

Acknowledgments. The authors would like to thank the collaborators involved in the ADO project at Queensland University of Technology and the University of New South Wales. Acknowledgments are also given to the ARDC for the ADO funding.

References

1. Beheshti, A., Benatallah, B., Tabebordbar, A., Motahari-Nezhad, H.R., Barukh, M.C., Nouri, R.: Datasynapse: a social data curation foundry. Distrib. Parallel Databases **37**(3), 351–384 (2019)
2. Zarro, M., Hall, C.: Exploring social curation. D-Lib Mag. **18**(11/12), 1 (2012)
3. Cunliffe, G., Liang, C., Sinnott, R.O.: Using social media to understand city-wide movement patterns and behaviours. In: IEEE International Conference on Social Network Analysis, Management and Security (SNAMS 2020), Paris, France, December 2020
4. Rehm, G., et al.: QURATOR: innovative technologies for content and data curation (2020). arXiv preprint: arXiv:2004.12195
5. Beheshti, A., Vaghani, K., Benatallah, B., Tabebordbar, A.: Crowdcorrect: a curation pipeline for social data cleansing and curation. In: Mendling, J., Mouratidis, H. (eds.) CAiSE 2018. LNBIP, vol. 317, pp. 24–38. Springer, Cham (2018). https://doi.org/10.1007/978-3-319-929 01-9_3

6. Wang, Z., Sinnott, R. O.: Linking user accounts across social media platforms. In: IEEE/ACM International Conference on Big Data Computing, Applications and Technologies, Leicester, UK, December 2021

7. Rüdiger, S., Dayter, D. (eds.) Corpus Approaches to Social Media, vol. 98. John Benjamins Publishing Company, Amsterdam (2020)

8. Mitra, T., Gilbert, E.: Credbank: a large-scale social media corpus with associated credibility annotations. In: Proceedings of the international AAAI conference on web and social media, vol. 9, no. 1, pp. 258–267 (2015)

9. Uryupina, O., Plank, B., Severyn, A., Rotondi, A., Moschitti, A.: SenTube: a corpus for sentiment analysis on YouTube social media. In: Proceedings of the Ninth International Conference on Language Resources and Evaluation (LREC2014), pp. 4244–4249, May 2014

10. Petrović, S., Osborne, M., Lavrenko, V.: The Edinburgh twitter corpus. In: Proceedings of the NAACL HLT 2010 Workshop on Computational Linguistics in a World of Social Media, pp. 25–26, June 2010

11. Isaak, J., Hanna, M.J.: User data privacy: Facebook, Cambridge Analytica, and privacy protection. Computer 51(8), 56–59 (2018)

12. Wang, S., Sinnott, R.O.: Protecting personal trajectories of social media users through differential privacy. Comput. Secur. 67, 142–163 (2017)

13. Humphreys, L., Gill, P., Krishnamurthy, B.: How much is too much? Privacy issues on Twitter. In: Conference of International Communication Association, Singapore, June 2010

14. Tenney, I., Das, D., Pavlick, E.: BERT rediscovers the classical NLP pipeline (2019). arXiv preprint: arXiv:1905.05950

15. Church, K.W.: Word2Vec. Nat. Lang. Eng. 23(1), 155–162 (2017)

16. Walton, C.: Spies, election meddling, and disinformation: past and present. Brown J. World Aff. 26, 107 (2019)

17. Hamurcu, C.: Can Elon Mask's Twitter Posts about cryptocurrencies influence cryptocurrency markets by creating a herding behavior Bias? Fiscaoeconomia 6(1), 215–228 (2022)

18. Morandini, L., Sinnott, R.O.: Mapping the chatter: spatial metaphors for dynamic topic modelling of social media. In: FOSS4G Conference, Florence, Italy, August 2022

A Web Application-Based Infant Health Monitoring System for Parents & Medical Professionals

Zain Buksh[(⊠)] and Neeraj Anand Sharma[(⊠)]

Department of Computer Science and Mathematics, School of Science and Technology,
The University of Fiji, Lautoka, Fiji
20180393@student.unifiji.ac.com.fj, neerajs@unifiji.ac.fj

Abstract. In order to co-monitor child and infant health while they are under their parents' care, a user-focused design methodology has been developed in this paper and utilized to create a prototype web application. Having created the website application prototype based on the preliminary findings of a user study while incorporating other research publications as well. It enables parents and medical staff to jointly monitor and manage a child's health. Families and medical experts also may communicate consistently thanks to the proposed web application. Additionally, it enables the monitoring of kids' physical development and well-being. The easily accessible data provided by the suggested designed system also enables medical personnel to perform duties more effectively. Additionally, the chosen medical specialists will be better equipped with accurate data to diagnose health-related problems.

Keywords: Website · Biofeedback · Sensors · Database · Healthcare

1 Introduction

Many innovative methods have been created recently to make daily life for people and business operations easier as technology continues to advance. Such technologies vary in terms of their intended utilization, the target client base they cater to, and the technological infrastructure they make use of, which would include websites, software, Hardware, and android applications. Despite the existence of all the preceding technologies, there is still a shortage of technologies that allow simple and safe interactions between parents and medical experts regarding the health and habits of children when they are at or away from home. Whenever a child develops a medical illness such as infections, obesity, breathing problems, or behaviour issues that might have an adverse effect on how well they do in school and in later life, parents frequently place a high priority on their health. As a result, many parents are nervous about how to keep an eye on young kids while they are at home [1].

Home healthcare and monitoring systems of clinical information have recently become more important due to technological advancement. It is a common implementation to monitor patients' at-home healthcare, especially for infants and babies. The mechanism used to examine the observations is the health monitoring system. When dynamic characteristics like natural frequencies are used as the observations, exploratory modal analysis is one of the most appropriate care monitoring techniques. According to the World Health Organization (WHO) Every infant, worldwide, has an entitlement to high-quality comprehensive neonatal healthcare. Babies have the right to be fed, to be kept warm, to be safeguarded from harm and illness, and breathe properly. All infants should have access to the crucial care that every baby needs in the first few days after delivery, known as essential newborn care. Both at home and a medical facility, it is necessary [2].

This project aims to create a prototype for a web application that will be used by caregivers and medical specialists to monitor and record the health complications of the child both at home and away. The program enables medical personnel to receive updates on the medical issues of individual patients at any time, based on data entered on the platform. Temperature, or baby fever, is among the most crucial physiological variables to measure in such monitoring systems. Infants' alterations in body temperature play a significant part in the identification and management of illnesses. Rapid febrility in general can harm a baby's crucial organs. Therefore, it is important to constantly check your body temperature. Babies that were born prematurely or with weak bodies may experience excessive sweating or cooling as a result of being unable to regulate their environment's temperature. For these infants, the ideal body temperature ought to be 36 to 38°. Cardiovascular pulses are another important characteristic to monitor. Infants can die suddenly from cardiac arrhythmia; hence it may be necessary to regularly monitor the infant's heartbeat rhythm. Parents can be informed via a vibrating notification on a smartwatch. Bluetooth technology is used to connect this item to the android-based smartphone. Additionally, it may send SMS to receive messages and set reminders for each tool. The greatest alternative for informing the parent is through a smartphone device with notifications enabled. The website can be used in combination with these features.

2 Literature Review

Technologies have had a big impact on how medical services have been produced and provided to the public. Well over the past few years, many technologies for monitoring children's behavior and health in schools have been created. Their utilization of various technologies varies among them all. All of them, nonetheless, serve the same goal of protecting child safety, whether they are at home, playing outside, getting looked after by a caregiver or maid, or traveling to and from school. For instance, a technology for monitoring children throughout public bus transfers and drop-offs was devised recently to protect their welfare and to alert families and officials if a child were missing from the collection or drop-off [3]. Research by [4, 15] identifies the use of mobile apps as a means to monitor children's online activities. Related to this, research [5] that tracks a child's health does not allow for parent and health professional co-monitoring and doesn't take into consideration while kids are away from home, although having a similar goal. The technology was particularly concerned with monitoring and keeping track of a child's blood sugar levels if they had diabetes. When it's time for the child to monitor their readings, it transmits a notification, and it also informs and notifies the parent in real-time. Families can use the software in their daily lives, according to the results of the original study review. Although they could see what their child's blood level was and if they had completed their testing or not, several respondents noted that it made monitoring simple and pleasant for them [5].

Software for diabetes-specific health monitoring has already been available for a while. Several diabetic care apps available on the App Store were examined in the research. The findings indicate that these programs were mostly utilized by individuals, and the information they gather cannot be used to create patient health records. Moreover, technology has undoubtedly changed and enhanced how individuals manage their diabetics, particularly with regard to taking their medications on schedule and often testing their blood sugar levels [6]. The usage of smartphone apps to track the health of children has been described in a number of researches. Sendra et al. [7]. Investigation of the efficacy of smart architecture designed to keep an eye on a student's wellbeing while being in school. In this research, kids were given wireless wearable gadgets that could measure their temperatures, heartbeat, and blood pressure. Such gadgets were connected with instructors' and parents' cell devices to maximize their usefulness. Irrespective of where the children were, their use made it simple to keep an eye on their health.

Chen et al. [8] looked into the use of wearable sensors to track the health of those who are wearing it. The studies suggest that earlier approaches were not practical. The usage of clothing that is connected to online cloud databases and cellular services, according to their argument, might offer great tracking for those with chronic diseases in an emergency. This apparel is versatile; therefore, it may also be used to keep an eye on kids. Asthma represents one of the most prevalent chronic conditions in small children and is extraordinarily challenging to manage [9]. In one research, the usefulness and viability of utilizing cell devices to monitor and control breathing problems were evaluated. Individuals were instructed to take a measurement of their peak flow and submit it to a web application system; if they did not do so before sunrise, they received short messaging reminders [10].

There are additional mobile embedding technologies that can be used to remotely monitor people's health, according to another research as well. The methods for designing and creating smartphone apps, including gyroscopes and accelerometers, that are used to monitor individuals remotely were examined by Paraa et al. [11] The efficiency of apps that could be used to measure environmental factors like moisture, temperatures, sound, and brightness that might have an impact on health, on the contrary side, was studied by Garcia et al. [12]. By examining related preliminary studies, this work makes a contribution to closing the important gaps in child health monitoring system that permits co-monitoring among parents and medical professionals concerning both the child's health and early disease diagnosis. Furthermore, we included the final user in the consumer design process for these prototypes.

3   Methodology

The study's main objective was to determine if an application is necessary to keep track of children who have medical issues. To assist parents, keep track of their children's health, it will also be an added advantage to investigate the functionality that medical professionals and parents would want to see in an application. The design, implementation, and validation of a WEB-based Infant Health tracing system serve as the key research method for this research project. To better design and build the suggested solution, the literature research will be utilized to comprehend existing health tracing procedures, healthcare monitoring apps used in Fiji, and other comparable applications. The main sources of information for this project will be credible sources such as published journal articles and online web databases. The SDLC (System Development Life Cycle) strategy will guide the progression. The time frame for this research is August through November 2022. Based on the literature review and research, an initial prototype design and procedures will be developed.

4 Primary Objective

The suggested system might function as a web service for healthcare monitoring; in other terms, it may represent a fresh approach to tracking children's health online, particularly in Fiji where these technologies are not readily available. The four important elements of the proposed solution are the database system, the graphical user experience (GUI), the decision analysis features, and the feedback data. Figure 1 depicts these elements.

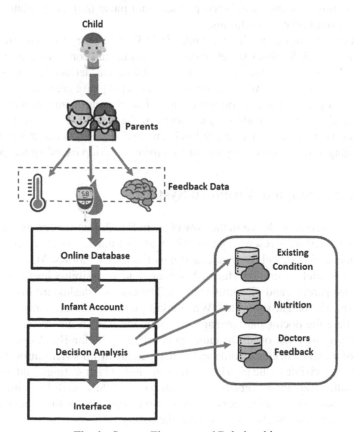

Fig. 1. System Elements and Relationships

Using sophisticated instruments that ensure the child's convenience, this system analyses biofeedback statistics from a child's body and digitally connects it to an internet database that may be utilized in the same location as the baby's residence or school. or at a different location, such as a general doctor's office. To make the most appropriate decision possible at the correct time, the Decision analysis Technique, which serves as the system's core element, is supplied input from the child's medical profile and the semantic database server. A child's health status under the proposed model has three primary components: existing conditions, nutritional information, and doctor feedback information.

4.1 Feedback Data

Typically, the biofeedback technique is used by the deployment of several sensor types that reflect the data source and ensure the genuine aspect of the feedback approach. Since biofeedback data can provide crucial information about the biological, physical and development of a child, some diseases and medical conditions have been treated with biofeedback technology. There are several medical related data that can be recorded by health monitoring website to help the medical professional to better understand the medical condition. For instance, blood pressure and pulse frequency related data can help diagnose heart related conditions.

Heart Rate was introduced by academics in [13], it had step by step directions for users in relation to biofeedback to help individuals to take full control of their responsive behaviors, which are associated with various Using ECG data, determine emotional states like stress or rage use. [13]. Additionally, scientists in [14] have created a transportable biofeedback gadget for posture correction and rehabilitation of infants with scoliosis. It is a non-medical gadget made for kids between the ages of 3 and 10 to alert them to adjust their posture. Similar research has been conducted except uses a biofeedback system utilizing a real-time solitary sensor to improve desktop users' spinal position.

5 Prototype Design of Proposed System

The software concept, as shown in the flow chart in Fig. 2, was created using the information we gathered from research papers and was customized for every child's health status. An application model was made, and it works with Windows, Mac, and Android phones. In the model, several interfaces, dashboard and accessibility levels are available for physicians, parents, and IT administrators. The doctor's dashboard displays all the data that a specific parent submitted. When a kid profile is chosen, a range of choices opens up where the doctor may manage statistics, interact on the accounts they have chosen, and acquire a list of all the children enrolled in the family. A doctor can also keep track of a child's health records and notify parents of important information. The filed children are visible to the physicians in the household list settings, and infants with recorded health issues are denoted by a red alert bar. A child's portfolio, which includes a photograph, basic information, contact details, and a summary of their medical history, is displayed after a doctor chooses one from the listing.

A practitioner can utilize the "manage health" submenu or webpage to solely examine kids who have documented medical issues. Based on it, a listing of infants within the same household who have certain medical issues displays. The physician can choose any kid to examine the child's overall health status, which may include the child's name, medical issues, prescribed medications, and choices for a medication record. Once the prescribed medication has been given to the kid, the doctor can enter it in the medication log option. Under the child's medical profile, a doctor may also provide a message for the parents. An alternative for notifications reminders is provided at the base of the design. This feature notifies the physicians in a tailored manner when to provide the prescription to any children who need it throughout the day. Depending on the details the parents gave on the timing of their children's medicine, this choice will show. Additionally, parents get access to all of their enrolled kids. They may write a letter to the physicians immediately and can monitor their temperature, pulse rate, notifications, and updates.

Every child has a special biography that details individual health issues, pharmaceutical requirements, potential treatments, and sugar levels. They may also examine their child's medication logs on a monthly or weekly basis and submit any sick note paperwork. The once-a-week option displays a chart that provides an overview of the child's well-being and prescription use during the week. Parents who choose the bimonthly option can download or export records that show when prescriptions were taken or skipped in addition to any remarks from the doctors.

The information and technology professionals of the hospital or any member of the clinic management can control the admins' profiles. The administrator account can sign up new children, inspect and administer the children, and notify families. Additionally, it can handle data management, handle child information, control hospital staff members, and broadcast emails to parents or physicians. The administrator is also in charge of keeping track of the child's medical history and any relevant medical conditions and prescriptions (Table 1).

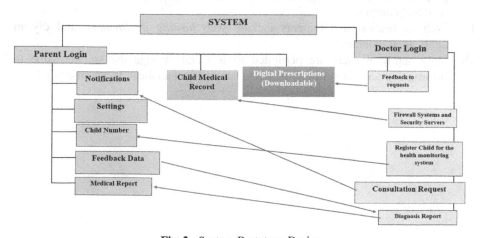

Fig. 2. System Prototype Design

Table 1. The Stakeholders and access levels

Stakeholder	Purpose	Access Type
Doctor	To provide feedback to parents	Full Access
Admins	Manage the system records and provide overall administrative support	Full Access
Parents	To Input data such as Heartrate, glucose level, etc.	Partial Access

In every instance, the software prototype enables customization by allowing admins, families, or physicians to adjust the program's color schemes and letter sizes. Additionally, they may control or modify their personal information, such as their user accounts, contact information, photographs, and logins, as seen on various screens from the suggested monitoring program model and design.

5.1 Requirements

Core Requirements
The Core requirements features of the web application system are as follows:

I. ***Purpose of the Project:*** Healthcare System is mainly used to track the child's average body temperature over a period of time and cardiac pulses using the appropriate sensors. Such content is recorded and saved so that it is always available for authorized individuals to access and evaluate remotely.
II. ***Data management requirement:*** The system supports data analysis and supports graphical reporting through database records and tabular interface that is easy to read and interpret.
III. Web application requirements include web ***hosting deployment*** and distant application monitoring.
IV. Only approved users are permitted to use and manage the software due to information security restrictions and to keep patient medical data confidential.

Functional Requirements

- Caretaker and the Parents should be able to login and interact with the system using Android, IOS and windows-based systems.
- Parent Login should be able to input data such as (Heart Rate, Blood Pressure, Sugar Level, Temperature, sleep hours, Breathing Problems and etc.)
- Parents should be able to request a consultation with the doctors and medical professionals.
- The Parents and guardians should be able access the system once the web application is hosted online.
- The website should show to the parents that the data upload was successful and waiting for the doctor's response.
- The Website Should be able to synchronize with databases.

Non- Functional Requirements

- The User Interface should be easily Understandable and users should be able to use without any additional training.
- The Website should have an SSL Certificate (HTTPS).
- All the features should be developed before implementing.
- The Website should be fast, responsive and Accessible.

Use Case Specifications
The entities participating in the software's use instances are described in the use case model. Refer to Fig. 3 Below.

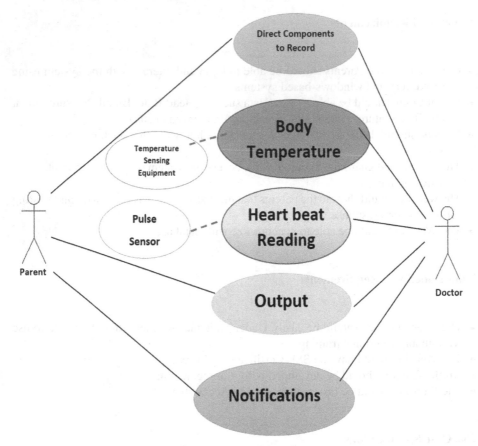

Fig. 3. System Use Case Diagram

Process Specifications

The procedures are depicted in the flow chart. The website collect data from the parents and record it in a database; whenever the readings exceed a specific threshold, notifications are sent. Refer to Fig. 4.

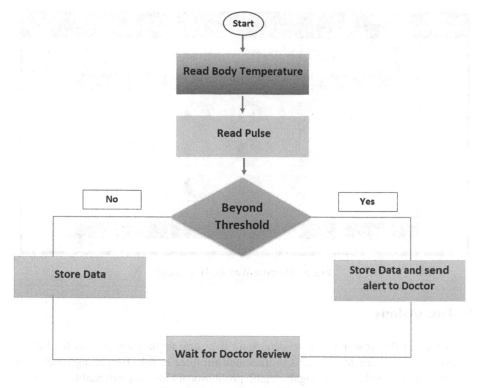

Fig. 4. System Process Diagram

Application

The experimental application was developed using the Microsoft and Apple-compatible Visual Studio 2019 (ASP.NET, C#). In the design, admins, parents, and doctors each have their own login and password with a unique interface and levels of access. A Master page was created to keep the User Interface design uniform (Figs. 5, 6, 7, 8, 9 and 10).

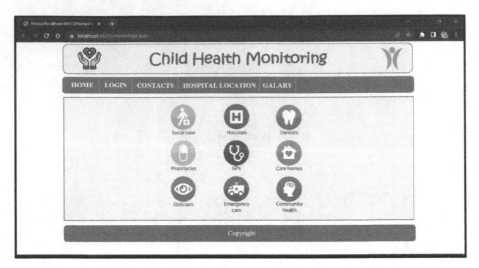

Fig. 5. Hospital Website Homepage

6 Discussions

The focus of this research was to determine if a web application system for kids is necessary to help parents and kids to track and monitor health. By getting input from physicians and families regarding the health problems of kids, this will enable consistent communication between parents, physicians, and health authorities. The outcomes of our research indicated that several school-aged and non-school aged infants develop health concerns, and as a consequence, there is a critical need for an efficient method of enabling doctors to co-manage child health with the guardians while they are at home. This may be done by giving administrators access to an app that keeps track of their children' medical conditions, prescriptions, and care requirements. Based on the findings, a web application prototype is designed to track kids' medical status and improve parent-doctor interaction. Due to the fact that almost all doctors and parents routinely use smartphones and laptops and are familiar with a variety of smartphone browser apps, the app will be useful to both groups of people.

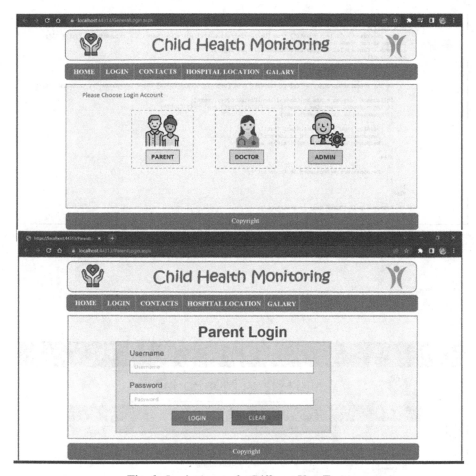

Fig. 6. Login Access for Different User Types

Furthermore, our research showed that such a program is required to make other medically related tasks and activities—including delivering medical notifications and completing clinical information convenient. The program will also take care of a few other relevant requirements, such as logbook for medical professionals and administrators as well as providing families with an insight of their child's medical situation. Integrating healthcare and communication analytics is crucial since consumers would only have to utilize one system instead of switching between multiple applications or distinct platforms. The most important shortcoming in this research was the little amount of research literature that was accessible through various other platforms, especially concerning Fiji. In the future, it is intended to put the app into use and assess its usability, effectiveness, and capacity to support efficient co-monitoring and administration of infant medical issues between parents and doctors.

```
SqlConnection conn = new SqlConnection(ConfigurationManager.ConnectionStrings["RegistrationConnectionString"].ConnectionString);
            conn.Open();
            string checkuser = "select count(*) from [UserRegistrationData] where UserName='" + txtUserName1.Text + "'";
            SqlCommand com = new SqlCommand(checkuser, conn);
            int temp = Convert.ToInt32(com.ExecuteScalar().ToString());
            conn.Close();
            if (temp == 1)
            {
                conn.Open();
                string checkPasswordQuey = "select password from [UserRegistrationData] where UserName='" + txtUserName1.Text
+ "'";

                SqlCommand passCom = new SqlCommand(checkPasswordQuey, conn);
                string password = passCom.ExecuteScalar().ToString().Replace(" ", "");
                if (password == txtPassword1.Text)
                {
                    Session["New"] = txtUserName1.Text;
                    Response.Write("Password is correct");
                    Response.Redirect("UserOfficalPage.aspx");
                }
                else
                {
                    Response.Write("Password is incorrect");
                }
            }
            else
            {
                Response.Write("User Name is incorrect");
            }
```

Fig. 7. Code for Login Pages

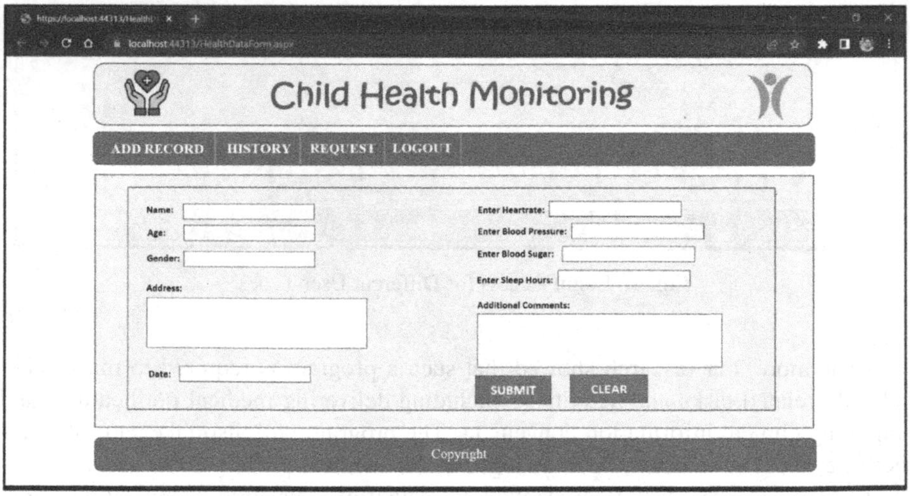

Fig. 8. Data Entry Page

```
public partial class HealthDataEntryPage03 : System.Web.UI.Page
    {
        protected void Page_Load(object sender, EventArgs e)
        {
            if (IsPostBack)
            {
                SqlConnection conn = new SqlConnec-
tion(ConfigurationManager.ConnectionStrings["RegistrationConnectionString"].ConnectionString);
                conn.Open();
                string checkuser = "select count(*) from [HealthData] where Data #='" + txtAccNum.Text + "'";
                SqlCommand com = new SqlCommand(checkuser, conn);

                conn.Close();

            }
        }

        protected void btnSubmit_Click(object sender, EventArgs e)
        {
            try
            {
                SqlConnection conn = new SqlConnec-
tion(ConfigurationManager.ConnectionStrings["RegistrationConnectionString"].ConnectionString);
                conn.Open();
                string insertQuery = "insert into [HealthData] (PatientName, PatientAge, PatientGender, PatientAddress, Entry-
Date,
                            PatientHeartRate, PatientBloodPressure, PatientBloodSugar, SleepHours, Comments)
                            values (@PatientName, @PatientAge, @PatientGender, @PatientAddress, @EntryDate
                            @PatientHeartRate, @PatientBloodPressure, @PatientBloodSugar, @SleepHours, @Comments)";

                SqlCommand com = new SqlCommand(insertQuery, conn);
                com.Parameters.AddWithValue("@PatientName ", txtPatientName.Text);
                com.Parameters.AddWithValue("@PatientAge ", txtAge.Text);
                com.Parameters.AddWithValue("@PatientGender ", txtGender.Text);
                com.Parameters.AddWithValue("@PatientAddress ", txtAddress.Text);
                com.Parameters.AddWithValue("@EntryDate ", ddlEntryDate.Text);
                com.Parameters.AddWithValue("@PatientHeartRate ", ddlHeartRate.Text);
                com.Parameters.AddWithValue("@PatientBloodPressure ", ddlBloodPressure.Text);
                com.Parameters.AddWithValue("@PatientBloodSugar ", ddlSugar.Text);
                com.Parameters.AddWithValue("@SleepHours ", ddlSleepHours.Text);
                com.Parameters.AddWithValue("@Comments ", ddlComments.Text);

                com.ExecuteNonQuery();
                Response.Write("Data Saved in Database");
                lblSaved.Text = "Data Saved in Database";
                conn.Close();
            }
            catch (Exception ex)
            {
                Response.Write("Error:" + ex.ToString());
```

Fig. 9. Code for Data Entry and SQL Database Entry

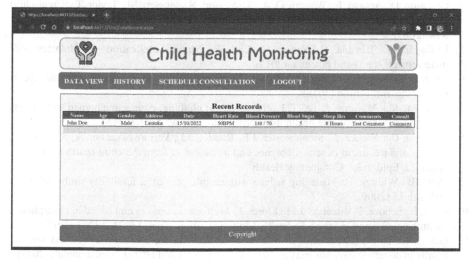

Fig. 10. Doctors Side Record Viewer Interface

7 Conclusion

This research paper has suggested a customized health advisory platform for child care has been suggested in this article. We have built the knowledge base, the graphical interface, and the architecture design. The system can monitor children's well-being in real-time and offer parents a helpful tool for modifying their children's lifestyles for improved health and well-being, according to the results of the system's early evaluation with caregivers.

With the upcoming work, it is intended to incorporate biofeedback devices into the system and examine real-time performance. In addition, to offer more precise suggestions by the medical professionals, we will also look at the idea of including information about the children's surroundings. Finally, a thorough feasibility study including the software's three key stakeholders (parents, medical professionals, and admins) is required to confirm the system's viability.

References

1. Riley, A.W.: Evidence that school-age children can selfreport on their health. Ambul. Pediatr. **4**, 37–380 (2004). https://doi.org/10.1367/a03-178r.1
2. W. H. O. (WHO), Improving early childhood development, World Health Orgnization, 5 March 2020. https://www.who.int/publications/i/item/97892400020986. Accessed August 2022
3. Al-Lawati, A., Al-Jahdhami, S., Al-Belushi, A., Al-Adawi, D., Awadalla, M., Al-Abri, D.: RFID-based system for school children transportation safety enhancement. In: IEEE 8th GCC Conference & Exhibition (2015)
4. Gammon, D., Årsand, E., Walseth, O. A., Andersson, N., Jenssen, M., Taylor, T.: Parent-child interaction using a mobile and wireless system for blood glucose monitoring. J. Med. Internet Res. (2005)
5. El-Gayar, O., Timsina, P., Nawar, N., Eid, W.: Mobile applications for diabetes self-management: status and potential (2015)
6. Sendra, S., Parra, L., Lloret, J., Tomás, J.: Smart System for childrens chronic illness monitoring. Inf. Fusion (2018)
7. Chen, M., Ma, Y., Song, J., Lai, C.F., Hu, B.: Smart clothing: connecting human with clouds and big data for sustainable health monitoring. Mob. Netw. Appl. (2016)
8. Spee-Van Der Wekke, J., Meulmeester, J.F., Radder, J.J., Verloove-Vanhorick, S.P.: School absence and treatment in school absence and treatment in from the child health monitoring system. J. Epidemiol. Community Health
9. Holtz, B., Whitten, P.: Managing asthma with mobile phones: a feasibility study. Telemed. e-Health **15** (2009)
10. Parra, L., Sendra, S., Jiménez, J.M., Lloret, J.: Multimedia sensors embedded in smartphones for ambient assisted living and e-health. Multimed. Tools Appl. 13271–13297 (2015)
11. García, L., Parra, L., Romero, O., Lloret, J.: System for monitoring the wellness state of people in domestic environments employing emoticon-based HCI. J. Supercomput. (2017)
12. Ahuja, N., Raghavan, V., Lath, V., Pillai, S.: Heart rate variability and its clinical application for biofeedback. In: 17th IEEE Symposium on Computer-Based Medical Systems (2004)
13. Archibald, D., Vemula, K., Anburajan, M., Vpr, S.K.: Portable biofeedback device for rehabilitating children with scoliosis between ages of 3–10 years. In: 3rd International Conference on Electronics Computer Technology (2011)

14. Breen, P.P., Nisar, A., ÓLaighin, G.: Evaluation of a single accelerometer based biofeedback system for real-time correction of neck posture in computer users. In: Annual International Conference of the IEEE Engineering in Medicine and Biology Society (2009)
15. Sharma, N.A., Kumar, K., Ali, A.S.: A digital monitoring system for parents. In: 2019 IEEE Asia-Pacific Conference on Computer Science and Data Engineering (CSDE), Melbourne, VIC, Australia (2019)

Impact of Business Analytics and Decision Support Systems on E-commerce in SMEs

Ziad Almtiri[1,3](✉), Shah J. Miah[2](✉), and Nasimul Noman[3](✉)

[1] Department of Management Information Systems, Taif University, Taif,
Kingdom of Saudi Arabia
ziad_almtiri@outlook.com
[2] Newcastle Business School, University of Newcastle, Newcastle, NSW, Australia
shah.miah@newcastle.edu.au
[3] School of Information and Physical Sciences, University of Newcastle, Newcastle, NSW,
Australia
nasimul.noman@newcastle.edu.au

Abstract. With the advancement in the marketing channel, the use of e-commerce has increased tremendously therefore the basic objective of this study is to analyze the impact of business analytics and decision support systems on e-commerce in small and medium enterprises. Small and medium enterprises are becoming a priority for economies as by implementing some policies and regulations these businesses could encourage gain development on an international level. The objective of this study is to analyze the impact of business analytics and decision support systems on e-commerce in small and medium enterprises that investigate the relationship between business analytics and decision support systems in e-commerce businesses. To evaluate the impact of both on e-commerce the, descriptive analysis approach is adopted that reviews the research of different scholars who adopted different plans and strategies to predict the relationship between e-commerce and business analytics. The study contributes to the literature by examining the impact of business analytics in SMEs and provides a comprehensive understanding of its relationship with the decision support system. After analyzing the impact of business analytics and decision support system in SMEs, the research also highlights some limitations and provide future recommendations that are helpful to overcome these limitations.

Keywords: Business Analytics · Decision support system (DSS) ·
E-commerce · ICT · SMEs · Enterprise resource planning (ERP)

1 Introduction

Electronic commerce offers electronic mechanism to improve the efficiency and effectiveness of different aspects of a product or service. It includes various digital aspects such as for design, production, marketing, and sales by utilizing current and emerging information technologies. In the contemporary era, small and medium enterprises (SMEs) must understand the adoption of information and communication technology

(ICT) which is significant to improve their ways of development. Different E-Commerce channels are providing services to e-retailers who could select the products and add them to carts then check out based on their needs [1]. Furthermore, E-Commerce provides advanced methods that could help businesses to start economic growth and achieve the goals that are set out by the management. With the adoption of advanced communication technology, businesses could enable faster and cheaper communication and increase business operations that play a significant role in the development of e-businesses.

Business analytics is an extensive form of using data, statistical and quantitative analysis, and explanatory and predictive models that are used to make decisions and take actions in the business. Several businesses are striving to release their business policies and strategies for adopting better business analytics techniques that could make effective marketing campaigns, revenue forecasting, and automation system that will improve the performance of the business [2].

The other aspect is Decision Support System DSS which is an umbrella term used to explain the computer application that is used to improve the user's ability to decide for business [3]. The term is used to explain the system that is based on computer design and help the management to make a decision based on data knowledge and communication that could identify the problem and make the decision to solve these problems. DSS could be divided into different categories such as driven DSS, data-driven DSS, document driver DSS, knowledge driving DSS, model drive DSS, web-based DSS, and spreadsheet-based DSS. Decision support systems are widely used in several organizations as small and medium enterprises have a common tendency to implement the experience and techniques that could gain from large organizations [4]. The early development of DSS was introduced in the 1970s and primarily generated management information from the operating system. The decision support system is commonly based on four components the model-based, the database, the user interface, and the user central [5].

The advancement in technology is used in the computation part of the data of an organization that provides easy access to data and flexible control that provides a variety of analytical tools. The basic objective of DSS is to improve the ability to decide by increasing the efficiency of management with reliable data [6]. The practices based on DSS could be hardly separated from the computer-based system as it is mostly integrated with the system based on operational databases, spreadsheets, report generators, and an executive support system. It includes the data and model-oriented system reporting system and other group decision support systems that are continuously growing the businesses of small and medium enterprises. These tools are used to solve the problem of SMEs just like large corporations as the use of information systems is helpful to overcome the problems and provide support to small and medium businesses according to the perspective of social and economic development. A few types of research have been conducted to analyze the decision support system requirement in the context of using information technology in SMEs. The management of SMEs is mostly disappointed with the use of software as there is the inability of adapting the software according to the needs of the customers therefore it may differentiate the problems of small businesses from large enterprises. SMEs usually have limited resources and a lack of skillful managerial staff therefore the failure risk is increased as compared to large corporations.

The implication of a decision support system in SMEs provides a productive domain and introduces an improved level of computer-based decision support. The management of SMEs is usually involved in day-to-day operations therefore it is required to include an analytical approach that will provide a strong decision based on business analytics and provide information to adopt the software that is suitable and could be effectively used by management to resolve the concerned problems.

E-commerce businesses required basic support for e-business transactions therefore E-commerce systems are required to become standard between suppliers and manufacturers. The E-Commerce system is based on computers and the internet, therefore, statistics represent that increasing interest in international shopping is also promoting the concept of e-commerce, therefore, manufacturers and retailers are required to improve their efforts to develop their operations in the international market [7]. The effects of manufacturers and retailers could improve the performance of SMEs as an E-commerce system permits them to perform the functions quickly at a low financial cost. The basic element in improving the efficiency of e-commerce is improved internal and external procedures as all the management activities and decisions are made according to the requirements of targeted customers therefore businesses could obtain optimal solutions for the problems and implement the procedural structure based on modeling and simulation. For organizations that are operating according to the E-commerce business model, it is considered appropriate to follow the business modeling as a central part of the projects.

The significance of e-commerce could be analyzed with the help of using a new business model that explains the benefits of the e-commerce system according to the perspective of SMEs [8]. The expanded scope and use of the new model highlight the needs of the customers and also provide information about the increase in demand that required deciding by the management. Information communication technology (ICT) is becoming a basic decision-making support system in SMEs as these technologies are based on an E-Commerce system and improved the ERP and CRM system of the business which is helpful to obtain the objectives of management. Currently, most organizations are based on the decision-making support modules and tools that are based on DSS and provide information that how these systems could be used in the development that is appropriate in specific conditions and could be classified as an intelligent decision support system.

1.1 Problem Statement

With the advancement in the internet, E-Commerce is considered a new way of doing business therefore it has the potential to change the economic activity and social environment of business. It has a huge impact on the performance of large corporations including their communication, finance, and retail trading, and holds a promise in specific areas to improve and put positive impacts. Similarly, small and medium organizations are also required to develop customized products and services that are based on the requirements of the customers, and the management of these companies is required to use proper market research and make a decision about the manufacturing or trading of the products and services that are according to the needs of the businesses. The paper emphasizes analyzing the problem related to finding the relationship between E-Commerce and decision support systems and finding the impact of business analytics and decision support systems on e-commerce networks adopted by small and medium enterprises.

1.2 Objectives of Study

By considering these facts the basic objective of the study is presented as analyzing the impact of business analytics and decision support systems on e-commerce at SME businesses. E-Commerce is the basic support of online shopping as it increases transactional efficiency and effectiveness and in the advanced era, it provides an understanding of the adoption of ICT and digital channels that are used by businesses. An E-commerce system is developed to support the management of SMEs. The result is required to review the literature to find out the following objectives:

- To learn about eCommerce channels adopted by small and medium enterprises.
- To find out the relationship between e-commerce business analytics and decision support systems and find out the impact of business analytics and decision support systems on e-commerce in SMEs.

The success and continuous development of small and medium organizations are significant for the growth of the economy but the problems could not be ignored therefore it is significant for the management of the organization to collect data and analyze the area where the problem may occur [8]. The use of information system could increase the attention of customers toward SMEs and also provides support to small businesses to prepare policies according to the analyzed data. The management of businesses is considered to use software packages that are helpful to improve the ability to meet the requirements of customers and reduce the failure risk that is appropriate for the development of SMEs. The improving use of e-commerce and marketing channels provides a great influence on the decisions of management. The influence of DSS could not be ignored on E-Commerce as it is a business activity that is developed to support business activities therefore the customers are required to meet their needs and requirements and it could not be possible without the implication of business. Data analytics provide information about the market data and figures that are analyzed with the help of a decision support system and interpret the results that help the management to make decisions [4].

While implementing The E-Commerce system, it is significant to link the system of the organization with the decision support system and other information systems that are used by the organization as all the changes in the e-commerce system could be made and it could make sure that the data is consistently following the instruction of management. Enterprise resource planning (ERP) is an appropriate strategy for international operations as it is based on different facilities and integrates the business procedures in different departments [2]. The major benefits of ERP are based on improving the coordination in the functional department and increasing efficiencies of doing business. The objective of this software is to collect the information that is processed by the management through a decision support system and make a decision that is beneficial for the organization. Briefly discuss the impact of decision support systems and business analytics, it would be explained that it provides a positive impact as it is used to improve the alignment of strategies and operations that improve productivity and reduce cost. The development of e-commerce in small and medium organizations could provide better relations with existing customers and also increase sales through reliable channels. These impacts are also helpful to develop the E-Commerce business on an international level and meeting the management standards of a large corporation that are based on achieving the goals of creating a relationship with customers, effective supply chain management, and operation management that could be refined with the help of information system management [1].

2 Literature Review

The impact of Business Analysis and Decision Support systems in e-commerce in SMEs is more critical with respect to company growth and development. A computerized information system that assists a business or business with its management, operations, and planning by organizing, collecting, and analyzing data is known as a decision support system (DSS) [1]. The majority of the time, DSSs are tasked with gathering data pertaining to sales, anticipated earnings, and stock levels. This information is utilized to create databases with pre-set links so sales data from different periods can be compared and analyzed [2].

A successful DSS makes it simple to incorporate data from a wide variety of sources, including, but not limited to, written records, raw data, management reports, business models, and the individual experiences of workers, and makes small enterprises more effective toward growth and development [3].

The DSS applications for Business Analysis and Decision Support systems at e-commerce in SMEs can be used in various contexts, including evaluating bids for engineering, agricultural, or rail construction projects, making medical diagnoses, checking credit loan applications, and the business of businesses [4].

Managers of Business Analysis and Decision Support systems at e-commerce in SMEs have various options for putting DSS programs to use. Most of the time, business strategists tailor a DSS to their requirements and then utilize it to analyze various processes and procedures. Sales and stock are examples of these processes, and both can benefit from the assistance that DSS programs can provide in improving the supply chain flow. Managers also benefit from DSS software since it assists them in planning and thinking about the potential implications of changes.

DSS may be beneficial because it can analyze a SMEs stock and assist the company in making the most of its asset listing [5].

In Business Analysis and Decision Support Systems at e-commerce in SMEs, Tracking trends and doing in-depth analyses of sales data to develop forecasts is another possible application of a decision support system. Because the system is simple to operate, planners have access to a diverse set of tools that can assist them in making judgments on customer data [6].

DSS software can also be used to make predictions about an SME's future or to obtain a comprehensive grasp of the factors that contribute to the expansion of a business. These two shows demonstrate the adaptability of the powerful program being used. This could be useful in challenging circumstances, the resolution of which needs a high level of financial prediction, such as when determining predicted and actual expenses and revenue [3].

Business Analysis and Decision Support Systems at e-commerce in SMEs or their Managers are continually working toward helping their companies expand. They achieve this goal by locating novel possibilities and resolving existing issues. Managers must make strategic decisions since managing a business in its various guises requires a variety of specific activities. When there is a lot of competition in a business sector, it can be difficult for managers to decide what actions to take. Regarding business-to-consumer (B2C) electronic commerce (e-commerce), managers may have difficulty deciding what actions to take when millions of people buy things directly from company websites. Therefore, DSS is the best approach to incorporate into their SMEs [7].

Studies showed that customers would look at several e-commerce websites before purchasing online to gain more knowledge and make educated decisions. When retailers and end users do business with each other directly over the internet, this type of transaction is known as "business-to-consumer" or "B2C" e-commerce. This is a pretty popular method utilized when conducting business activities online [8].

Therefore, if you want to meet the demands of any shift in the external business environment, you must create a robust business strategy. Taking care of these things in business is a popular choice for many businesses because it helps them maintain their current success level [9]. However, much small business (SME) owners and managers are poor planners whose short-term goals are unspecific and based on human intuition [10]. Such challenges can only be overcome with technological support and solutions, often out of reach for small businesses (SMEs). Researchers have also found that when organizations of all sizes fail to account for the influence that information technology will have on their operations, business performance suffers (IT) [11]. Many businesses nowadays are creating or deploying their information technology systems (DSS), such as a decision support system, to maintain a competitive advantage in their respective industries (DSS) with respect to improving their Business Analysis and to better utilize Decision Support Systems at e-commerce in SMEs [12].

Few SMEs use information technology artifacts as strategic decision support (DSS) tools to better their business decisions. This has only recently become more widespread [13]. The absence of plans is most noticeable in how their websites have been implemented with modern technology's useful features [14]. The resources available to small enterprises (SMEs) are often somewhat restricted, and their managerial staff members have a lower level of expertise. Because of this, the likelihood of the collapse of a small business is increased because such companies do not always have access to the information they require [15], In specific knowledge about the operating environment of a business. Consequently, research on the design of IT artifacts for managerial decision support systems (DSS) is essential for improving business strategies [1].

In most cases, socioeconomic variables, rather than business changes, have been the focus of research on small enterprises (SMEs). There hasn't been a lot of research done on the requirements for decision-making (DSS) processes that micro and small firms have when developing IT products. Researchers tend to draw the same conclusions regarding experience and methodologies used in large organizations and apply them to small businesses, even though DSSs are extensively utilized. They do this without taking into consideration the fact that the DSS requirements for small enterprises are unique. This is still the case even though there are a great many distinct types of groupings [16]. Although strategic judgments are more crucial, most small businesses use decision support systems (DSS) to make tactical ones. Due to the unpredictability of their environments, small businesses have a hard time making long-business strategic decisions. Considering this when comprehending the intuition and judgment decision-makers employ in DSS design [13].

Many business processes can benefit from implementing E-Commerce because of the potential for increased efficiency and productivity. The challenges of modern E-commerce extend beyond technological ones into the realm of business. A decision support system (DSS) is "an interactive information system that gives information, models, and data manipulation tools to aid in making decisions in semi-structured and unstructured contexts." Online trade can take numerous shapes, each with its own set of advantages and disadvantages, costs, and levels of difficulty, depending on the needs of the business [15].

Multiple studies have shown that the e-commerce sector is highly competitive and constantly evolving. To thrive in today's market, firms must maintain a competitive edge through the introduction of new products and services, as well as the efficient management of operational processing using a decision support system. In addition, for businesses to maintain their success in the modern digital age, they need to adapt to the constantly advancing state of technology quickly [2].

Business Analysis and Decision Support Systems for e-commerce in SMEs are one of the most successful strategies, despite their inverted U-curve shape, fluctuating nature, and variety of approaches based on several factors. Business Analysis and Decision Support Systems in e-commerce in SMEs strategy could help businesses capture new ideas from external resources to keep up with the growing demand for their products [7].

If SME's access to the Decision Support System, E-commerce platforms can effectively manage their human resources, particularly those who work in IT support. The success of enterprises that operate as E-commerce platforms is mainly dependent on the IT support teams because the primary purpose of these teams is the collecting and process information [7].

Failures may be exceedingly costly in the information technology business, which places a significant amount of responsibility on the shoulders of the project manager to ensure that they do not occur. The authors of the study also stated that an agile project management system, provided with the appropriate level of oversight, can assist in ensuring that managers deal with problems as they emerge and refrain from providing incorrect updates on the status of their projects. The agile methodology places a strong emphasis on adaptability and rapid iteration when it comes to the process of developing a new and beneficial product or service. An IT project can be finished more quickly and with fewer complications, if its status is tracked correctly, according to [7], who found that this was also the case. This makes it easier for managers to avoid costly escalations and lowers the risk of failure. Therefore, scientific and methodical evaluations of product developments and IT project management in a dynamic environment are essential to improve the economics of doing business online.

If there will be a discussion about business analytics then simply it is stated as "the process of discovering meaningful and actionable insight in data." Business analytics is considered a relatively new term that is going to be famous among the nation to introduce various new and innovative ideas to enhance the knowledge of the individual for the accurate decision support system. If its history will be searched in the business world then there is nothing that can be searched and observed for this. Before starting a more specific discussion about business analytics and exploring its raking and stages for the process of decision support system, the analytics perspectives must be discussed that are much closer to the specific stage of decision making. Generally, business analytics is defined as the science and art of discovering, analyzing, and identifying novel insight from a wide range of data by considering sophisticated statistical models, machine learning, and mathematics for supporting more timely and accurate decision support systems at E-commerce [9].

Also, Things can benefit the e-commerce of SMEs by enhancing customer experience as well as providing reliable product and service delivery. Combining data can create new methods that can benefit SMEs. It is important to understand small and medium businesses contribute a large portion of a nation's gross domestic product. This indicates that these businesses have to maintain their growth. One way they can maintain this growth is through business analytics. The wide accessibility of business analytics has made it possible for small and medium businesses to adopt recent technologies to improve their performance and revenues. SMEs are making great steps by using the business analytics of decision support systems. With the use of smart technology, these businesses can efficiently utilize their resources, improve market share, as well as boost revenue. As such, many SMEs are using decision support systems in E-commerce as one of their business strategies.

Therefore, in the terms of business analytics, this discussion is all about decision support systems at E-commerce in SMEs as well as problem-solving. Due to the rapid growth of technology, business analytics can be stated in very simple a word that is "the particular process for discovering actionable and meaningful full insight in the data. The key objective of business analytics is to generate learning, knowledge, and understanding. Collectively, it is used to referee the particular insight for supporting the evidence that is based upon the decision-making for the process of performance management. By considering the aspects of evolution, it has been started several years ago and it also refers to the process of the competencies, practices, applications, and technologies that are being involved in order to attain such kinds of particular objectives. Therefore, several people are getting confused by merging the terms and concepts that are relatively similar to their meanings as well. Intentionally, sometimes it has been driven by vested interest and involved technology [10].

Today, in business decision-making is moving towards the particular point at which the accepted practices are all about the first understanding of the specific numbers as well as what they are revealing for it. It also includes the particular aspects that are utilized for this insight to deriving the decision of intelligent business. The approaches are also can be replaced where the action has been taken by people which is considered to feel better and right after that it is also used to identify the numbers that are used to analyze and see its work. Hence, the process of business analytics must be driven toward an accurate decision support system of E-commerce in SMEs. It also plays an essential role in the organizational landscape. This document explores the various aspects of business analytics as well as a decision support system in E-commerce. It also explores the positive effects of business analytics and decision support systems along with the negative aspects of business analytics and decision support systems. Both of these points and aspects are being discussed by considering the decision support system process [11].

2.1 Theoretical Content

There are many disadvantages of Business Analytics. There are many issues that can be described that can be mentioned for the main issue of why business analytics go wrong and such as when we make decision support system it can be wrong. There are many issues and problems that can be the main issue for that. We will discuss them one by one. One of the main issues is human judgment. Another main issue may be mentioned as a lack of governance of decision-making. If we do not mention another main issue like organizational culture then it will be a big problem for us. Now we will be in this position to describe what are the main and prominent issues and problems that can be the main resin of becoming business analytics become proof wrong. One of the main reasons is people.

2.2 People

People may be facing a different types of Bias on the basis of different levels of issues like age, gender, and ethnicity. Many people face, Bias. For example, a huge amount of people apply for the post of pacific jobs. But approximately a huge number of candidates have the same qualification, skills, and experience but they received a response from the organization to much more than the candidates of those people that applied with the name of African Americans names. So, we can now in this position to explain if the data set can be biased data set that it will consider it will be could be wrong. Because it is basically available on the basis of data set. That belongs to the biased data set [12].

2.3 Governance

Governance is also the main issue that can make Business Analytics become wrong. In governance, the main resign is Insufficient legislation. When a un insufficient legislation is available then it needs to be proper legislation for proper governance. Without law, it is very difficult to manage a single person, poor judgment, or an organization. Without proper legislation, it is impossible to manage of management of people. A proper way for the success of business analytics is to require governance and make in mind it is impossible to maintain governance. Social media need legislation. Now it is a big issue for humans. Without proper legislation, it is very difficult to manage individuals and manage accounts, and management and decision-making are impossible [13].

So, if proper governance and rules and regulation is available then it is possible that Business Analytics give a positive response otherwise it will give a negative result and all issue that tackle on the basis of Business Analytics become wrong. All over the world people spread propaganda against different religions on the basis of freedom. [14].

2.4 Culture

Culture is also the main issue for Business Analytics and decision support systems in E-commerce. If the culture of the organization will not support then different actions taken on Business Analytics will be negative. So, we need a proper and positive culture to maintain and implementation of proper Business Analytics. If the culture of the system. Now it describes the history that most organization required and tries to get maximization of profit. The organization tries to maximize profit. As a result of getting more profit quality of products or services is compromised. Day by day Quality is going to decrease and need. It is all about due to culture. So, we have to mature culture so that our different, Business Analytics will become positive [15].

2.5 Technology

Technology is also making a big impact on Business Analytics and decision support systems in E-commerce it is very important to take very careful to get data from systems or databases. Data on different social media can be created or hacked. After that, it can be used for a negative type of people so it is very important to secure data on any system. People have a very low level of human visibility. it is also a very low-level decision support system. it also depends on a different ethical basis.

There is an important link between the use of the human decision support system and business analytics. This link has been neglected oftentimes despite such importance. The research on the connection between business analytics and decision support systems.

Positive arguments for business analytics and decision support Systems.

In order to explain and explore the benefits and positivity of business analytics and decision support systems in E-commerce three important points are discussed. These three aspects are people, governance, and culture. The aspects of business analytics and decision support systems also require introducing positivity to the requirements. It has been analyzed that business analytics must be coordinated across the groups of several stakeholders to empower the trust gap which is existed currently among the parties. In order to do this as well as perform this in a good way, humanity and society will be prepared for responding to the business analytics that is related to the ethical demands and that will have required to grow variety and complexity in the future.

2.6 People

If the aspects and points of the decision-support system and business analytics in E-commerce must have been discussed to highlight the individuals who are involved in this particular process of business analytics. First of all, the discussion is entirely about the professionals of business analytics who are accountable for this morally as well. It has been indicated in various studies that the technology of big data is neutral ethically. Even sometimes, it is not considered a built-in perspective to explain what is right or wrong and what is bad or good in its utilization. There are several codes of ethics that existed relevant to the computer sciences and data analytics. By adopting all of these data analytics businesses can get access in good ways. Even if the individual will be utilized in their organization the business performance can be easier as compared to various other aspects. For the profession of analytics, the absence of the framework can be the cause of leaving voiding by which individuals are not clear on the particular consistent standards for their productivity within the organization and working with their colleagues as compared to other disciplines or industries [16].

2.7 Governance

This section is entirely a discussion about the rules, laws, and regulations that can be enforced for business analytics in decision-making. It has been argued by the houses of cultures, common digital, support committees, and media that for the technology companies the era of self-regulation must end. The SMEs were trusted to self-regulate for too long a process in the field of growing data and analytics SMEs. In the field, the public interest has been undermined as well as highlighting the several benefits of analytics. It also offers an exclusive overlook to society; it includes exceptional user experience as well as fraud prevention. One of the most important positive steps is the implementation of the GDPR general data protection regulation for protecting the individual's privacy rights in the EU. A powerful message has been sent out by regulation for the process of the data related to the level of care that is expected at the time of the handling of data of individuals.

2.8 Overall Culture

The culture is discussing the documented ethical principles that are required for enhancing the productivity of the organization. Additionally, ethically minded business analytics can be employed through various methodologies. The culture of careful ESR can be reinforced in the SMEs.by considering the publication and development of ethical principles that have been utilized as the points of the references that are against the framing of the analytics activities.

Summing up all the discussion it is concluded that business Analytics plays a very important role in the progress of the systems. But it will become negative if it is implemented without the proper way. It became wrong and gives negative results if it is not managed properly. We discuss in detail if people have to face a different level of baseness like gender, discrimination on skin colour, or if the business is based on belonging to a different culture and gender then will going go wrong for diction making and business analytics become a not good decision support system way [17]. The governess is also taken an important role in positive decision-making way. In governess, it also needs proper legislation and proper way of Rules and regulations. It is not possible without proper rules and laws required for social media for the respect of other religions.

3 Limitations and Future

The present work aimed to investigate the impact of business analytics and decision support systems on e-commerce in SMEs. Business analytics are highly adopted in business organizations to improve decision-making systems. Business analytics are useful for e-commerce businesses as they can provide information about online shopping trends and comprehend shifts in customer behavior. Data-driven decisions are usually beneficial for business organizations to help them improve their user experiences and expand business operations in profitable directions. Although, the appropriate selection of these analytics and support systems is possible through detailed research projects. Therefore, a research project studying business analytics and decision support system is highly important for business organizations dealing with online shopping or e-commerce business operations. In this research, the main emphasis is given to secondary information collection using authentic and relevant research articles and other sources from academic literature. Even the several measures were taken into consideration to determine the high authenticity, originality, fairness, and accuracy of the research outcomes still this research project is lacking in some areas. Lacking is representing critical issues that can influence the research outcomes or at least comply with the ethical standards set for a high-quality research paper in the respective field. In this section, these issues are discussed as limitations of this research project. Followed by these limitations, this section will also discuss future work.

Starting with the research project limitations, there are three main limitations of this research project which are discussed here. Firstly, the entire focus of this research project is on two variables only. Sometimes, there can be other mediating factors and variables which may have influenced the outcomes and results for these selected variables of research interest (business analytics and decision support systems). Regarding business analytics, its suitability and adaptability for an e-commerce business are essential for meaningful research findings. Otherwise, inappropriately selected business analytical approaches and methodologies can inappropriately influence their impact on e-commerce business operations executed by small and medium-sized business organizations. In this research project, we did not give sufficient attention to various business analytics and relevant suitability for e-commerce businesses. The obtained information is presenting a general scenario only. In the selection process, we only checked whether the research project contains knowledge of business analytics in e-commerce (SME) businesses or not. We did not define this criterion in more detail to study other factors and variables such as adaptability and suitability which represents a major limitation of this project [18].

The second major limitation associated with this research project is linked to the data collection methodology and research designs. In this project, we have obtained secondary information from the literature to extract research findings on this topic. Relying on secondary research data is not sufficient to originate actual research findings. Regarding such important research topics, a mixed-method approach could be utilized to enhance the relevancy, validity, and reliability of the research findings. In the research project, secondary research data should be combined with primary research to critically assess the actual impact of business analytics and decision support systems in e-commerce businesses in the SME sector. Primary research data could be extracted by using the interview or survey approaches. Regarding this relevant e-commerce companies could be invited to share their experiences with business analytics and decision support systems (if they have implemented both or at least one of these variables at their workplace). A combination of secondary and primary research data can cover this research limitation [18].

The third and most important limitation of this research project is linked with the generalization of extracted research findings. In this research project, we have not classified e-commerce companies into different geographical segments or countries. Variation in geographical locations relates to the economic situation and variation in social factors (e.g., familiarity with advanced technology, the tendency towards technological adoption, and awareness levels). Diversity in geographical locations emphasizes the inclusion of geographical details in the research project. Obtaining information from various research articles may not satisfy the requirements for research findings generalization. The inclusion of research articles from diverse geographical segments may have the tendency to a specific geographical segment or county if articles included from that segment or country are greater in number. In this situation, the generalization of research findings will not meet the high reliability and validity status. Thus, it represents the major limitation of the research project [19].

Moving to future work, a new research trend is evident in existing literature under which researchers are obtaining primary research findings from original respondents regarding their challenges and adopted mitigation strategies. In these research studies, researchers are emphasizing the identification of various challenges experienced by the management of e-commerce businesses in the SME sector. These challenges will be related to the adoption, selection, and assessment of business analytics and decision support systems at the workplace. In the future, we can also direct this research project in this direction. Somehow, we can also include new variables of research interests in future work to promote its usability in academic and commercial sectors. Research findings of the future research project will aware the management of e-commerce businesses take effective decisions regarding the selection of business analytical approaches and systems while understanding the expected challenges behind this huge change. Moreover, it will open a new path for future researchers to study challenges and issues with strategic solutions in the SME sector while studying the cases of e-commerce businesses dealing with business analytics and decision support systems. In the future, we will also work on a separate research project indicating the situation of the same research variables with a specific geographical context. We aim to study e-commerce SME businesses adopting business analytics and decision support systems in the Middle East region. Currently, the middle east is an emerging market with high potential for e-commerce business. Several new e-commerce businesses from small and medium-sized sectors have recently expanded their businesses as large corporations with B2B business models. This situation is an indicator of high potential in this market segment. Consequently, considering the growing market of e-commerce business in Middle East emerging markets we will focus our future research project on this segment. Conclusively, a research project on the Middle East will add worth to the existing literature and bring forth applicable findings for the commercial sector (e.g., management of e-commerce businesses from the SME sector) to grow their businesses and sustain their growth trends.

4   Recommendation

Considering the above discussion, literature review findings, limitations, and future work a few recommendations are stated below. These recommendations are subdivided into two parts. In the first part, recommendations are presented for the audience or readers of this research project. On the other hand, recommendations shared in the second part of this research project are for researchers to improve their research work for the future.

4.1 Recommendations for the Audience

Firstly, eCommerce management should try to record their sales transaction and frequency of sales data in internal databases. This data can be supportive of the data analeptics. In the business analytics of e-commerce businesses, managers are supposed to use historical data for the identification of patterns and trends to discover new findings related to their executed business operations and customer buying patterns. Storing data in secure internal databases with historical series can be beneficial for the management of e-commerce businesses to use in business analytics. Without having sufficient data, business managers may not be able to extract meaningful and highly reliable information for their business. For example, if the offered product is linked with seasonality then data from one year is not sufficient. Managers should make sure to keep records of sales data and other informative content for more than one year to identify each trend in seasonality. Thus, using business analytics managers of e-commerce businesses will be able to estimate future demands and requirements for inventory or stocking. This kind of information is also useful in determining the reorder point and improving the supply chain decisions to smoothly complete all business operations.

Secondly, data regarding electronic commerce should be also converted into categorical variables for better visualizations of results in the decision support system. For example, if an e-commerce business is offering two flavors for a single product, then both should be presented in the same graph or chart to determine customer preferences. Such visualizations (e.g., pivot tables, pivot charts, and time series charts) are useful in the decision-making process for the future direction and modifications of the e-commerce business.

Thirdly, academic researchers working on a similar research project should consider earlier discussed research limitations. The information available in this research article is generalized using secondary research data which may have differences from the actual research findings of the selected geographical context of the next researchers. Therefore, researchers are advised to consider the above limitation of this research project to enhance the chances of producing a highly reliable and valid research project for the academic literature. Furthermore, some findings may also get change with the passage of time. Currently, the technological situation is dynamic therefore, we are uncertain about the future impact of this research project. Future researchers using this project for their research project should also consider this issue. Research findings would be useful for general information only therefore, these findings should not be based on a research project in a different context while ignoring the social and technological variabilities.

Fourthly, research findings suggest that e-commerce business managers should also cover diversity-based methods if business operations are linked with infrequent purchases. Seasonality and infrequent purchases from these e-commerce websites sometimes cause challenging situations for business managers to extract meaningful findings from the qualitative data to further use in the decision-making process. In this situation, business managers should also consider relevant algorithms and business analytics approaches that comply with infrequent and seasonal sales.

4.1.1 Recommendations for Researchers

This section is entailing information about key recommendations for the researchers to improve their research projects in the future. These recommendations are mainly drawn by considering the limitation section as these limitations are required to be eliminated and properly managed for a future research project. The most important and relevant recommendations for the researchers are stated below:

Firstly, researchers should further research this topic by continuously studying variations in business analytics and decision support systems in the same context. Researchers should cover this information by using the empirical research approach. A number of e-commerce websites should be selected by using clearly defined research criteria to collect original responses from the research population. In the defined criteria researchers should cover e-commerce business size, business model, and suitability for the advanced decision-making processes. The selected businesses should have experience with at least one of these: business analytics or decision support systems. In the selection process companies having long-term experience should be preferred to companies having short-term experience with business analytics and decision support systems. An appropriate selection of e-commerce businesses for the SME sector will be beneficial for this research project in the future.

Secondly, researchers should also include information about the selected research articles in a systematic literature review format. Under this format, researchers should share information about the research groups, county, research journal, and year of publication. Such information is highly important in a secondary research project.

Thirdly, future research projects should also include information about other research variables which can work as mediators for this research project. Regarding decision support systems, researchers should also cover details on security measures and management systems at workplaces for the obtained data from e-commerce websites. Moreover, a detailed research project in the future should also cover fuzzy decision support systems for the risk assessment and management of e-commerce businesses in the SME sector. Real-coded genetic algorithms used in e-commerce businesses are also supportive of the implementation and functionality of fuzzy neural networks which need to be further studied while determining the impact of decision support systems and business analytics on e-commerce businesses [20]. Thus, by working on these recommendations this project can be made a better and improved version for future researchers and research audiences interested in this topic.

5 Conclusion

The widespread adoption of E-Commerce has the potential to boost the productivity of a great many business activities. The technological and commercial challenges of e-commerce are significant in businesses globally. Solving one of these issues is not easy.

The term "decision support system" refers to "an interactive information system that delivers the information, models, and data manipulation capabilities to assist in making decisions in semi-structured and unstructured settings." This is so since "an interactive information system that delivers the information, models, and data manipulation capabilities to aid in making decisions in semi-structured and unstructured settings" Decision support systems are defined as "information systems that give information, models, and data manipulation tools to aid in the process of making decisions". There are a variety of approaches to e-commerce that can be used depending on the requirements of the business; each may involve a varying degree of complexity and cost. Depending on the method selected, the business may incur the quantity of either.

To make informed decisions regarding the day-to-day operations of their firms and the long-term business plan for those organizations, decision-makers in small businesses need to have access to effective decision support systems. These decisions could mean the difference between business and failure for the companies. The decision-making technologies that are currently available give a wide variety of system provisions for managerial decisions. They continue to have a limited capacity to cope with the cognitive business requirements of decision-makers, which is particularly problematic for small businesses competing in the online consumer market. Today's small enterprises must still contend with various obstacles to survive and thrive in their respective industries. Some of these difficulties are attributable to the ever-changing nature of the business climate, the continually rising capabilities of technology, and the ever-evolving tastes of clients. Small business needs to have an interactive website that gives them access to a platform comparable to what larger organizations have for them to tackle these problems. Often, the owners and managers of small businesses may not have access to the information required to maintain their current websites. This can make it difficult for them to keep their websites up to date. Because of this, it may be challenging for them to maintain the information on their websites current. More than half of the retail establishments take part in promotional activities on the websites of local small companies. This percentage is higher than it is in the United States. Even though it is essential for managers to have a digital strategy that uses effective websites, social media, and mobile applications, most owners and managers do not have confidence in their ability to make strategic judgments regarding fundamental problems such as this one. This is even though managers need to have a digital strategy.

Many managers still do not have a digital strategy, even though this is exceptionally vital for them to have. The impact of Business Analysis and Decision Support Systems in e-commerce in SMEs is one of the best strategies for growth and development. In relation to designing an exclusive managerial support system in the operation of e-commerce for SMEs, a vital task would be to conduct a design study in future for capturing insights of the decision-making problems [for example, 21, 22], through adopting modern research methodology, such as design science principles [23–28].

References

1. Wang, D., Luo, X.R., Hua, Y., Benitez, J.: Big arena, small potatoes: a mixed-methods investigation of atmospheric cues in live-streaming e-commerce. Decis. Support Syst. **158**, 113801 (2022)

2. Khan, S.A., Hassan, S.M., Kusi-Sarpong, S., Mubarik, M.S., Fatima, S.: Designing an integrated decision support system to link supply chain processes performance with time to market. Int. J. Manag. Sci. Eng. Manag. **17**(1), 66–78 (2022)
3. Wang, H., Wang, S.: Teaching tip: improving student performance by introducing a no-code approach: a course unit of decision support systems. J. Inf. Syst. Educ. **33**(2), 127–134 (2022)
4. Lin, J., Li, L., Luo, X.R., Benitez, J.: How do agribusinesses thrive through complexity? The pivotal role of e-commerce capability and business agility. Decis. Support Syst. **135**, 113342 (2020)
5. Kustiyahningsih, Y., Anamisa, D.R., Mufarroha, F.A.: Decision support system for mapping SMEs batik Bangkalan facing industry 4.0 using the SMART method. In: Journal of Physics: Conference Series, vol. 1869, no. 1, p. 012103. IOP Publishing (2021)
6. Okfalisa, O., Anggraini, W., Nawanir, G., Saktioto, S., Wong, K.: Measuring the effects of different factors influencing the readiness of SMEs towards digitalization: a multiple perspectives design of decision support system. Decis. Sci. Lett. **10**(3), 425–442 (2021)
7. Wang, D., Li, G.: The best decision for E-Commerce funds transfer based on cloud computing technique. Mathematical Problems in Engineering (2022)
8. Yadav, H., Soni, U., Gupta, S., Kumar, G.: Evaluation of barriers in the adoption of e-commerce technology in SMEs: a fuzzy DEMATEL approach. J. Electron. Commer. Organ. (JECO) **20**(1), 1–18 (2022)
9. Azvine, B., Nauck, D., Ho, C.: Intelligent business analytics—a tool to build decision-support systems for businesses. BT Technol. J. **21**(4), 65–71 (2021)
10. Lytras, M.D., Raghavan, V., Damiani, E.: Big data and data analytics research: from metaphors to value space for collective wisdom in human decision making and smart machines. Int. J. Semant. Web Inf. Syst. (IJSWIS, 2017) (2017)
11. Mikalef, P., Pappas, I., Krogstie, J., Pavlou, P.: Big data and business analytics: a research agenda for realizing business value. Elsevier (2020)
12. Bichler, M., Heinzl, A., van der Aalst, W.M.: Business analytics and data science: once again? (2017)
13. Liu, Y., Han, H., DeBello, J.: The challenges of business analytics: successes and failures (2018)
14. Laursen, G.H., Thorlund, J.: Business Analytics for Managers: Taking Business Intelligence Beyond Reporting. John Wiley & Sons, Hoboken (2016)
15. Cho, I., Wesslen, R., Karduni, A., Santhanam, S., Shaikh, S., Dou, W.: The anchoring effect in decision-making with visual analytics. In: 2017 IEEE Conference on Visual Analytics Science and Technology (VASTIEEE), pp. 116–126 (2017)
16. Seddon, P.B., Constantinidis, D., Tamm, T, Dod, H.: How does business analytics contribute to business value. Inf. Syst. J. 237–269 (2020)
17. Kustiyahningsih, Y.: Decision support system for mapping SMEs batik Bangkalan facing industry 4.0 using the SMART method. In: Journal of Physics: Conference Series, Volume 1869, 2nd Annual Conference of Science and Technology (ANCOSET 2020) (2021)
18. Abbott, M.L., McKinney, J.: Understanding and Applying Research Design, p. 446. John and Wiley & Sons, Hoboken (2013)
19. Kuo, R., Chen, J.: A decision support system for order selection in electronic commerce based on the fuzzy neural network supported by real-coded genetic algorithm. Expert Syst. Appl. **26**(2), 141–154 (2004)
20. Vahidov, R., Ji, F.: A diversity-based method for infrequent purchase decision support in e-commerce. Electron. Commer. Res. Appl. **4**(1), 1–16 (2005)
21. Miah, S.J., McKay, J.: A new conceptualisation of design science research for DSS development. In: Proceedings of the 20th Pacific Asia Conference on Information Systems (PACIS 2016), 2016, Taiwan (2016)

22. de Vass, T., Shee, H., Miah, S.J.: IoT in supply chain management: opportunities and chal-lenges for businesses in early industry 4.0 context. Oper. Supply Chain Manag. Int. J. **14**(2), 148–161 (2021)
23. Miah, S.J., Gammack, J.: Ensemble artifact design for context sensitive decision support. Australas. J. Inf. Syst. **18**(2), 5–20, 29 (2014)
24. Miah, S.J., Ahamed, R.: A cloud-based DSS model for driver safety and monitoring on Australian roads. Int. J. Emerg. Sci. **1**(4), 634–648 (2011)
25. Miah, S.J., Gammack, J.: A Mashup architecture for web end-user application designs. In: Pro-ceedings of the 2nd IEEE International Conference on Digital Ecosystems and Technologies, Thailand, 26–29 February 2008
26. Miah, S.J.: An ontology based design environment for rural decision support Unpublished PhD Thesis, Griffith Business School, Griffith University, Brisbane, Australia (2008)
27. Miah, S.J.: A new semantic knowledge sharing approach for e-government systems. In: Pro-ceedings of the 4th IEEE International Conference on Digital Ecosystems and Technologies, pp. 457–462, Dubai, United Arab Emirates, 13–16 April 2010
28. Aghdam, A.R., Watson, J., Cliff, C., Miah, S.J.: Improving theoretical understanding towards patient-driven healthcare innovation: online value co-creation perspective: a systematic review. J. Med. Internet Res. (2020). https://doi.org/10.2196/16324

Big Data Managements and Services

Task Offloading and Resource Allocation in Satellite Terrestrial Networks: A Deep Deterministic Policy Gradient Approach

Yuhan Wang[(✉)] and Qibo Sun[(✉)]

State Key Laboratory of Net working and Switching Technology,
Beijing University of Posts and Telecommunications, Beijing, China
{yhanwang,qbsun}@bupt.edu.cn

Abstract. Low Earth Orbit (LEO) satellite network, as a crucial part of
6G key technology, can provide high network coverage for mobile communications. Due to the rotation and limited resource of satellites, it
still challenging to improve QoE with satellite network. To address the
above issue, this paper takes advantage of the computation resources provided by terrestrial users, satellites and cloud to achieve better Quality
of Experience (QoE). Firstly, we propose a novel edge computing architecture based on satellite-terrestrial integration. Secondly, we formulate
the task offloading and resource allocation problem under this architecture as an optimization problem of maximizing the QoE-aware utility.
Since the problem is a mixed integer nonlinear programming (MINLP)
problem, we proposes a Deep Deterministic Policy Gradient (DDPG)-
based Optimization Algorithm for Task Offloading and Resource Allocation (DATR). The DATR algorithm decomposes resource allocation
from offloading decision to reduced complexity. The Lagrangian multiplier method is used to achieve the optimal allocation of edge node
resources; The offloading decision problem is solved by the DDPG algorithm. Simulation results show that our algorithm outperforms baselines
in terms of QoE indicators.

Keywords: Satellite Edge Computing · Task Offloading · Deep
Reinforcement Learning · Quality of Experience

1 Introduction

Although densely deployed small cells in 5G networks can improve coverage
and capacity, constructing communications infrastructure to serve underserved
areas like remote mountain areas is costly. In addition, terrestrial communication infrastructure is vulnerable to natural disasters like earthquakes. Therefore,
as a low-cost, low-latency and high-coverage communication solution, satellite
network becomes a powerful complement to terrestrial networks.

Supported by the Fundamental Research Funds for the Central Universities.

With the rapid development of satellite network, its propagation delay has reached the millisecond level [15]. Furthermore, satellites are equipped with computation resources nowadays. Exploiting the communication and computation resource to serve underserved areas becomes a promising solution. Despite the enormous potential benefits brought by satellites, there are still many challenges should be addressed. First, due to the limited resource of a satellite, a reasonable resource allocation algorithm is required. Second, the rotation of satellites makes the link between satellites and ground unstable, resulting in low quality of user experience (QoE) [5].

To address the above issues, we first propose a novel edge computing architecture based on satellite-terrestrial integration. The architecture is illustrated in Fig. 1. Then, we formulate the resource allocation and task offloading problem under the newly proposed architecture as a QoE-aware utility maximization problem. On this basis, we proposes Deep Deterministic Policy Gradient (DDPG)-based Optimization Algorithm for Task Offloading and Resource Allocation (DATR) to achieve better QoE. The contributions of our study are as follows:

1. We propose an edge computing architecture based on terrestrial-satellite-cloud fusion. For the proposed architecture, we study the problem of task offloading and resource allocation for users to maximize QoE under the high dynamics and resource constraints of satellites. We formulate the problem as a QoE-aware utility maximization problem.
2. Since the problem is a mixed integer nonlinear programming (MINLP) problem, we proposes a DATR algorithm to split the problem into two sub-problems: First, the optimal allocation of computing resources is achieved by the Lagrangian multiplier method; Second, the offloading decision problem is solved by DDPG algorithm.
3. We simulate the proposed algorithm and compare it with other benchmark algorithms. Simulation results demonstrate that our method has excellent performance in terms of QoE indicators.

2   Related Work

In recent years, satellite networks gradually applied in the field of edge computing. [13] uses a game theory algorithm to solve the offloading problem in Low Earth Orbit (LEO) satellite network to minimize the processing delay and energy consumption of the task. [12] proposes a dual-edge satellite-terrestrial network architecture, and uses the Hungarian algorithm to optimize the processing energy consumption and delay of the task. [15] integrates computing resources through dynamic network virtualization technology to improve QoS for mobile users. The above traditional optimization algorithms such as game theory and Hungary need to obtain optimal results through a large number of iterations, and the computational time complexity is high. Different from the above studies, we use deep reinforcement learning algorithms to solve task offloading decisions.

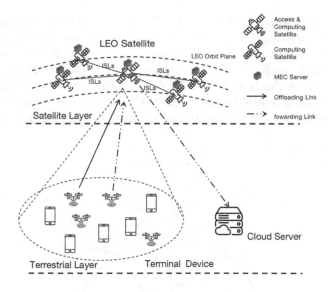

Fig. 1. Satellite-terrestrial fusion network edge computing system model.

It not only reduces the time complexity of the algorithm, but also has better performance in dealing with the time-varying satellite Multi-Access Edge Computing (MEC) environment.

Current research in the field of satellite MEC focuses on reducing task processing delay and energy consumption, while ignoring the user experience quality. [1] optimizes QoE by reducing latency, but ignores that system power consumption will reduce battery life, thereby affecting the QoE. [9] achieves the trade-off between latency and energy consumption through Lyapunov optimization, but ignores the time-varying of user preferences. We model the quality of user experience as a QoE-aware utility to dynamically adapt to the user's preference difference, and the maximization of a QoE-aware utility is taken as the optimization goal to improve the QoE.

3   System Model and Problem Formulation

3.1   System Model

Network Model: Our proposed satellite-terrestrial fusion edge computing model is shown in Fig. 1, which includes N ground users (UEs), K LEO satellites and ground cloud servers. UE are distributed in remote areas covered by satellites and without supported by ground communication facilities. Both UE and cloud server are connected to satellites through wireless links, and each LEO satellite is equipped with a lightweight MEC server. Adjacent satellites form satellite constellations by establishing inter-satellite links, communicate with each other through ISLs. The intermediate node satellites act as access satellites to undertake forwarding and computing services, while the orbiting satellites only provide computing services. The tasks can be executed locally, offloaded to LEO satellites, or forwarded to cloud server via relay satellite for execution.

In the system, each UE will generate a task $W_i \triangleq (U_i, D_i, C_i, T_i^{max})$, U_i denotes the size of the task model, D_i denotes the size of the task input, C_i denotes the required central processing unit (CPU) cycles to accomplish the task, T_i^{max} denotes the maximum tolerated delay, and all tasks are indivisible [14].

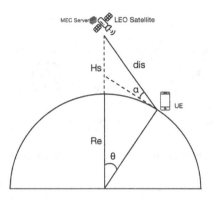

Fig. 2. Geometric relationship between ground users and LEO satellites.

LEO Satellite Coverage Model: Due to the high-speed movement of the satellite, it must maintain a geometric visual relationship with the ground user for normal communication, as shown in Fig. 2. R_e denotes the radius of the earth, H_s denotes the orbital altitude of satellite s, and dis denotes the geometric distance between UE and LEO satellite. The communication window between the LEO satellite and UE can be represented by the elevation angle α [7]:

$$\alpha = \arctan \left(\frac{\cos \Delta\omega \cos \epsilon_t \cos \epsilon_s + \sin \epsilon_t \sin \epsilon_s - \frac{R_e}{R_e + H_s}}{\sqrt{1 - (\sin \epsilon_t \sin \epsilon_s + \cos \Delta\omega \cos \epsilon_t \cos \epsilon_s)^2}} \right) \tag{1}$$

where $\Delta\omega = \omega_t - \omega_s$, ω_t and ϵ_t are the longitude and latitude of the UE, ω_s and ϵ_s are the longitude and latitude of the LEO satellite. The geocentric angle θ between the LEO satellite and UE can be expressed as:

$$\theta = arccos \left(\frac{R_e}{R_e + H_s} \cdot \cos \alpha \right) - \alpha \tag{2}$$

Similarly, as shown in Fig. 2, the distance expression between the satellite and UE can be calculated as:

$$dis = \sqrt{R_e^2 + (R_e + H_s)^2 - 2 \cdot R_e \cdot (R_e + H_s) \cdot \cos \theta} \tag{3}$$

Satellite-Terrestrial Communication Model: Since there is only one access satellite in the system, when multiple users choose to offload tasks to the satellite, they need to share spectrum resources. According to Shannon's formula, the uplink transmission rate from user i to satellite k can be defined as:

$$R_{i,k}^{up} = B_{i,k} \log_2 \left(1 + \frac{P_i h_{i,k}}{\sigma^2}\right) \tag{4}$$

where $B_{i,k}$ denotes the channel bandwidth from user i to satellite k, P_i denotes the uplink transmit power allocated for user i, σ^2 is the additive white Gaussian noise power, $h_{i,k}$ is the channel gain from user i to satellite k and $h_{i,k} = dis^{-\varpi}$, ϖ is the path loss factor [8]. The data scale of tasks is generally much larger than the scale of the result [10]. Therefore, we ignores the transmission delay of returning the result.

Task Computing Model: In the system model, tasks generated by the UE can be executed locally, at the edge of the LEO satellite, or at the cloud server.

   1) Local Computing. For local computing, f_i^{loc} represents the CPU clock cycle of user i's local device. The time delay for user i to perform the task locally can be expressed as:

$$T_i^{loc} = \frac{C_i}{f_i^{loc}} \tag{5}$$

The energy consumption for user i to perform the task locally can be expressed as [3]:

$$E_i^{loc} = \kappa C_i (f_i^{loc})^2 \tag{6}$$

κ represents the energy coefficient, it depends on the chip architecture [6].

   2) Satellite Edge Computing. For satellite edge computing, the task processing delay should include transmission delay, propagation delay and task processing delay. $f_{i,k}^{mec}$ is the computing power allocated to user i by satellite k, and the task processing delay of user i on satellite k can be expressed as:

$$T_{i,k}^{mec} = \frac{U_i + D_i}{R_{i,u}^{up}} + 2 \cdot \frac{dis}{c} + \frac{C_i}{f_{i,k}^{mec}} + T_{u,k}^{ISL} \tag{7}$$

where c represents the speed of light, $2 \cdot \frac{dis}{c}$ represents the uplink and downlink propagation delay, $T_{u,k}^{ISL}$ represents the average round trip time from accessing satellite u to offloading satellite k transmission tasks, the round trip time can be estimated using the average of historical information [4]. In addition, the energy consumption of user i to satellite k is:

$$E_{i,k}^{mec} = \frac{U_i + D_i}{R_{i,u}^{up}} \cdot P_i + \left(2 \cdot \frac{dis}{c} + \frac{C_i}{f_{i,k}^{mec}} + T_{u,k}^{ISL}\right) P_i^f \tag{8}$$

where P_i^f is idle power of user i, and P_i is uplink transmit power of user i.

   3) Terrestrial Cloud Server Computing. Since the users are located in a remote area without the coverage of communication facilities, so the user needs to forward the task to the ground cloud server through the relay satellite for execution. The cloud server has abundant computing resources, so the computing delay of tasks is not considered. Therefore, the delay of the cloud server processing tasks can be expressed as:

$$T_i^{cloud} = \frac{D_i}{R_{i,u}^{up}} + \frac{D_i}{R_i^{cloud}} + 4 \cdot \frac{dis}{c} \tag{9}$$

where R_i^{cloud} indicates the transmission rate of the satellite forwarding task i, $4 \cdot \frac{dis}{c}$ denotes the sum of uplink and downlink propagation delays for tasks and computation results. In addition, the computing energy consumption of task i on the cloud server is:

$$E_i^{cloud} = P_i \cdot \frac{D_i}{R_{i,u}^{up}} + \left(\frac{D_i}{R_i^{cloud}} + 4 \cdot \frac{dis}{c} \right) P_i^f \tag{10}$$

To sum up, the task processing delay for user i can be expressed as:

$$T_i^{mc} = x_i T_i^{loc} + \sum_{k=1}^{K} y_{i,k} T_{i,k}^{mec} + z_i T_i^{cloud} \tag{11}$$

where x_i indicates whether task i is executed locally, $y_{i,k}$ indicates whether task i is executed in satellite k, z_i indicates whether task i is executed in cloud server, and $x_i, y_{i,k}, z_i \in \{0,1\}$. Similarly, the processing energy consumption for task i can be expressed as:

$$E_i^{mc} = x_i E_i^{loc} + \sum_{k=1}^{K} y_{i,k} E_{i,k}^{mec} + z_i E_i^{cloud} \tag{12}$$

3.2   Problem Formulation

Considering the user's QoE, we analyze the problem of building task offloading from both subjective and objective aspects. First, the subjective aspect is mainly influenced by user preferences. Due to differences in user characteristics, users have different preferences for services. Therefore, we introduce a delay-sensitive coefficient $\nu \in [0,1]$ to represent user preferences. For users who prefer low latency $\nu > 0.5$, and users who prefer low energy consumption $\nu < 0.5$.

Secondly, the objective aspect is mainly influenced by the computing resource status of LEO satellites f^{load}: users will preferentially offload to nodes with more remaining resources.

For the problem of computing resources, we introduce a load balancing factor to improve the resource utilization of satellites. Based on user preferences, we build a QoE-aware utility function. It denotes the latency and energy consumption benefit of task offloading compared to local execution. The QoE-aware utility function can be expressed as:

$$\phi_i(x_i, y_i, z_i, f_{i,k}^{mec}) = (1 - \delta) \frac{E_i^{loc} - E_i^{mc}}{E_i^{loc}} + \nu \delta \frac{T_i^{loc} - T_i^{mc}}{T_i^{loc}} \tag{13}$$

where $\frac{E_i^{loc}-E_i^{mc}}{E_i^{loc}}$ represents energy consumption benefit, $\frac{T_i^{loc}-T_i^{mc}}{T_i^{loc}}$ represents the delay benefit. δ is used as a weight parameter to achieve a trade-off between delay and energy consumption, and $\delta \in [0,1]$. Specifically, δ represents the task type, and ν represents the user preferences.

We abstract the QoE maximization problem as the QoE-aware utility maximization problem, which is defined as follows:

$$\max_{x_i,y_i,z_i,f_{i,k}^{mec}} \sum_{i=1}^{N} \phi_i(x_i, y_i, z_i, f_{i,k}^{mec}) \tag{14}$$

$$s.t. \quad T_i^{mc} \leqslant T_i^{max} \tag{14a}$$

$$x_i, y_{i,k}, z_i \in 0,1 \tag{14b}$$

$$x_i + \sum_{k=1}^{K} y_{i,k} + z_i = 1 \tag{14c}$$

$$\sum_{i=1}^{V_k} f_{i,k}^{mec} \leq F_k^{max}, \quad \forall k \in K \tag{14d}$$

Here, (14a) represents delay constraint. (14b), (14c) represent binary offloading decisions. (14d) represents the computing resource constraint of satellite k, and V_k represents the number of users offloaded to satellite k. Since computing resources are continuous variables, also offload decisions are integer vectors, the goal function is a MINLP problem.

4 DDPG-Based Optimization Algorithm for Task Offloading and Resource Allocation

To solve the optimization problem, we decouple it into two sub-problems: computing offloading and resource allocation.

4.1 DDPG-Based Optimization Algorithm for Task Offloading

For the offloading problem, we propose a model framework, which includes a load balancing module and a deep reinforcement learning module.

Load Balancing Module. In order to improve the utilization of LEO satellite resources, we introduce load balancing coefficients to assist offloading decisions. In the decision-making process, the load balancing coefficient is used as the penalty item of the model reward function to achieve a balanced distribution of task requests. The load factor of LEO satellite k can be expressed as:

$$L_k(t) = \frac{\sum_{i \in k} C_i}{f_k^{mec}} \tag{15}$$

The total load balancing factor for all LEO satellites in the same time slot can be expressed as:

$$L = \frac{\sum_{m \in M}(L_k - |E|)^2}{K} \tag{16}$$

where $|E|$ is the mean value of the load factor of all edge servers.

Reinforcement Learning Module. We transform the offloading problem of maximizing the QoE-aware utility into a Markov decision process model, which mainly includes state, action, and reward.

1) State: We consider N terrestrial users, M LEO satellites and a cloud server in time slot T. At any time slot t, each user will generate a computing task. Therefore, the system state at any time slot t is defined as:

$$S_t \triangleq \{seq_t, f_t^{load}\} \tag{17}$$

where seq_t represents the task request vector at time t, f_t^{load} represents the computing resources of the LEO satellite at time t.

Algorithm 1: DDPG-based optimization algorithm for task offloading

---

Input: Critic and Actor learning rate α_{Critic}, α_{Actor}; Experience replay buffer B_m, mini-batch size N; Gaussian distributed behavior noise $\mu_e = n_0$

Output: *Actor* Network $\mu(s|\theta^\mu)$

1　Initialize the weights θ_μ and θ_Q, target network Q' and μ', and weights $\theta^Q \leftarrow \theta^{Q'}$ and $\theta^\mu \leftarrow \theta^{\mu'}$;

2　**for** *episode* $i = 1,...,E$ **do**

3　　Reset simulation parameters and obtain initial state S_1;

4　　**for** $t = 1,...,T$ **do**

5　　　Choose an action by $a_t = \mu(S_t|\theta^\mu) + n_t$ with noise n_1;

6　　　According to action, allocate resources by (20), (30);

7　　　Perform action a_t get reward r_t and next state S_{t+1};

8　　　**if** B_m *is not full* **then**

9　　　　Store(S_t, a_t, r_t, S_{t+1}) to B_m;

10　　　**end**

11　　　Randomly replace a transition (S_t, a_t, r_t, S_{t+1}) in B_m ;

12　　　Randomly simple a mini-batch L (S_t, a_t, r_t, S_{t+1}) from B_m;

13　　　Let $y_i = r_i + \gamma Q'(s_{i+1}, \mu'(s_{i+1}|\theta^{\mu'}), \theta^{Q'})$;

14　　　Update *Critic* network's θ^Q by $L(\theta^Q) = \frac{1}{N}\sum_i(y_i - Q(si, ai|\theta^Q))^2$;

15　　　According to (21) update *Actor* network's θ^μ;

16　　　Update the *Critic* and *Actor* target network by $\theta^{Q'} \leftarrow \tau\theta^Q + (1-\tau)\theta^{Q'}, \theta^{\mu'} \leftarrow \tau\theta^\mu + (1-\tau)\theta^{\mu'}$:

17　　**end**

18　**end**

---

2) Action: Since the DDPG algorithm deals with the decision problem on the continuous action space, the action that the agent chooses is a high-dimensional discrete action. Therefore, the discrete action is processed continuously here:

$$a_t = \{a_{0,t}, a_{1,t}, a_{2,t}, ..., a_{n,t}\} \quad a_{i,t} \in \{0, M+2\} \tag{18}$$

where $a_{i,t}$ denotes the offloading decision of user i. When $a_{i,t} \in \{0, 1\}$, the task is executed locally; when $a_{i,t} \in \{1, M+1\}$, the task is executed on LEO satellite; when $a_{i,t} \in \{M+1, M+2\}$, the task is executed on cloud server.

3) Reward: we consider the objective function as the reward for the action. In addition, the load balancing coefficient and the number of task timeouts are used as penalty items to train the network model. The reward function can be expressed as:

$$r_t = \sum_{i=1}^{N} \phi_i - \gamma_1 \frac{\eta}{N} - \gamma_2 L \tag{19}$$

where γ_1 and γ_2 represent the penalty factor of task timeout and load balancing state, and η represents the number of non-local offload task timeouts.

$$P_{i,k} = \left(\frac{D_i + U_i}{\sum_{l \in V_k} D_l + \sum_{j \in V_k} U_j}\right) P_k \quad \forall i \in V_k \tag{20}$$

$$\nabla_{\theta^\mu} J \approx \frac{1}{N} \sum_i \nabla_a Q(s, a|\theta^Q)|_{s=s_i, a=\mu(s_i)} \nabla_{\theta^\mu} \mu(s|\theta^\mu)|_{s=s_i} \tag{21}$$

DDPG-based optimization algorithm for task offloading is shown in the Algorithm 1. Since the general reinforcement learning algorithm can't solve the high dimensional discrete action space, we adopts the DDPG algorithm to make the offloading decision. The power is allocated by (20), where V_k represents users who forwarded or offloaded by the access satellite k.

4.2   Resource Allocation Optimization Algorithm

According to our system model, the QoE-aware utility (13) can be organized as:

$$\phi_i = 1 - \left(\frac{1-\delta}{E_i^{loc}} E_i^{ec} + \frac{\nu\delta}{T_i^{loc}} T_i^{ec}\right) \tag{22}$$

Let:

$$\psi_i = \frac{1-\delta}{E_i^{loc}} E_i^{ec} + \frac{\nu\delta}{T_i^{loc}} T_i^{ec} \tag{23}$$

Combined with the objective function (14), it can be seen that the objective function optimization problem can be transformed into:

$$\min_{x_i, y_i, z_i, f_{i,k}^{mec}} \sum_{i=1}^{N} \psi_i(x_i, y_i, z_i, f_{i,k}^{mec}) \tag{24}$$

Since the LEO satellite resource allocation and offloading decisions are decoupled, it is assumed that offloading decisions are known when solving the resource allocation problem. In addition, because the resource problems of different satellites are independent of each other, we simplify the problem to a resource allocation for a single satellite. The formula (5), (6), (11) and (12) can be substituted into (24) to get:

$$\min_{f_i^{mec}} \sum_{i=1}^{V} \frac{\frac{1-\delta}{E_i^{loc}} C_i P_i^f + \frac{\nu\delta}{T_i^{loc}} C_i}{f_i^{mec}} + \zeta \tag{25}$$

$$s.t. \quad \sum_{i=1}^{V} f_i^{mec} \leq F^{max} \tag{25a}$$

$$T_i^{mc} \leqslant T_i^{max} \tag{25b}$$

where ζ denotes a constant term, V denotes ths users who offloaded to satellite node. Let $g(f_i^{mec}) = \frac{\frac{1-\delta}{E_i^{loc}} C_i P_i^f + \frac{\nu\delta}{T_i^{loc}} C_i}{f_i^{mec}}$, the second derivative of it can be obtained:

$$\frac{\partial g}{\partial (f_i^{mec})^2} = \frac{2(\frac{1-\delta}{E_i^{loc}} C_i P_i^f + \frac{\nu\delta}{T_i^{loc}} C_i)}{(f_i^{mec})^3} > 0 \tag{26}$$

$$\frac{\partial^2 g}{\partial f_{i,k}^{mec} \partial f_{j,k}^{mec}} = 0 \quad i \neq j \tag{27}$$

From (26) and (27), the Hessian matrix of $g(f_i^{mec})$ is positive definite, so (25) is a convex problem. Next, we will use KKT condition to solve it.

The Lagrangian function of (25) can be expressed as:

$$L(f_i^{mec}, \lambda) = \sum_{i=1}^{V} g(f_i^{mec}) + \lambda(F^{max} - \sum_{i=1}^{V} f_i^{mec}) + \mu(T^{max} - T_i^{mc}) \tag{28}$$

where λ and μ represent the Lagrangian multiplier, and the derivative of the Lagrangian function is:

$$\frac{\partial L(f_i^{mec}, \lambda)}{\partial f_i^{mec}} = -\frac{\frac{1-\delta}{E_i^{loc}} C_i P_i^f + \frac{\nu\delta}{T_i^{loc}} C_i}{(f_i^{mec})^2} - \lambda + \frac{\mu C_i}{(f_i^{mec})^2} \forall i \in V \tag{29}$$

By setting (29) Lagrangian gradient equal to 0, the optimal computing resource allocation is solved as follows:

$$(f_i^{mec})^* = \sqrt{\frac{\mu^* C_i - \frac{1-\delta}{E_i^{loc}} C_i P_i^f - \frac{\nu\delta}{T_i^{loc}} C_i}{\lambda^*}} \tag{30}$$

For (30), the subgradient method can be used to solve [2]. Through continuous iteration, the subgradients of (31) and (32) can be made convergence to optimal λ and μ, as shown in Algorithm 2. Finally, the optimal computing resource allocation can be obtained by substituting the λ and μ into (30).

Algorithm 2: QoE maximization iterative resource allocation

Input: The Lagrangian multiplier λ, μ; Step size $t1$, $t2$;

Output: Optimal computing resource allocation $(f_i^{mec})^{opt}$

1 Initialize $\lambda_0 > 0$, $\mu_0 > 0$, $\varepsilon > 0$, t_1 and t_2;

2 $m = 0$, $\lambda^{(0)} = \lambda_0$, $\mu^{(0)} = \mu_0$

3 Repeat $\leftarrow$ *Layer*1

4 $\quad m = m + 1$

5 $\quad$ According to $\lambda^{(n-1)}$, $\mu^{(n-1)}$ and (30) to compute $(f_i^{mec})^*$

6 $\quad$ According to (31), (32) update $\lambda^{(n)}$ and $\mu^{(n)}$

7 $\quad \Delta\lambda = \lambda^{(n)} - \lambda^{(n-1)}$, $\Delta\mu = \mu^{(n)} - \mu^{(n-1)}$

8 Until $|\Delta\lambda| \leq \varepsilon$, $|\Delta\mu| \leq \varepsilon$

$$\lambda^{(n+1)} = [\lambda^{(n)} - t_1^{(n)}(F^{max} - \sum_{i=1}^{V} f_i^{mec})]^+ \tag{31}$$

$$\mu^{(n+1)} = [\mu^{(n)} - t_2^{(n)}(T^{max} - T_i^{mc})]^+ \tag{32}$$

5 Simulation Experiment and Result Analysis

5.1 Simulation Experiment Environment

In this section, we introduce the simulation-related experimental parameters, and conduct simulation validation and performance evaluation of our task offloading algorithm. In the simulation, the software environment is Python 3.9 and Tensorflow, and the hardware environment is MacBook Pro, M1 Pro processor. There are 5 LEO satellites and 10 ground users in the satellite edge computing environment. The rest of the simulation parameters in the experimental environment are set according to the reference [11], as shown in Table 1.

5.2 Task Offloading and Resource Allocation Policy Validation

In this section, a comparative experiment with DATR will be conducted. We set three benchmark algorithms: 1) Offloading strategy based on no load balancing factor (NLBF): remove the load balancing module from our algorithm framework; 2) Greedy-based resource allocation methods assist in offloading strategies (GBRA): use greedy algorithm for resource allocation; 3) Greedy algorithm based computational offloading strategy (GACO): all users offload tasks to LEO satellites for execution.

Figure 3(a) shows the relationship between different satellite computing resources and the QoE-aware utility. For the GACO, its QoE-aware utility performance mainly depends on the computing resources of the satellite, so its benefit performance is poor. Due to the lack of load balancing factor, the utilization of computing resources by the NLBF is not as good as that of the DATR, so

Table 1. Simulation experimental parameters

Parameters	Values
Channel bandwidth B	20 MHz
Task model size U	$[50, 500]$ KB
Task input data size D	$[10, 50]$ KB
Required CPU cycles C	$[500, 1500]$ Mcycles/s
user preferences ν	$[0, 1]$
Task delay constraint T^{max}	$[0.5, 1]$ s
LEO satellite altitude H_s	784 Km
Transmit power P	0.8 W
User equipment idle power P^f	0.05 W
User device cpu cycles f^{loc}	800 MHz
LEO satellite cpu cycle f^{mec}	10 GHz
Noise power σ^2	-174 dBm/Hz
LightSpeed c	299792458 m/s

the QoE-aware utility is low. Also, the greedy algorithm does not consider the impact of QoE, so the GBRA is slightly worse. Our proposed DATR still has good performance with the least computing resources.

Figure 3(b) shows the change curve of QoE-aware utility under different numbers of terrestrial users. In experiment, $f^{mec} = 30$ GHz, $P = 2.4$ W. As the number of users increases, the resources allocated to each user decrease, so the QoE-aware utility shows a downward trend. In the stage of large number of users, NLBF performs worse than GBRA. Therefore, for the offloading problem with a large number of users, load balancing can bring greater performance optimization than resource allocation. Due to the lack of load balancing and resource allocation, GBCO performance declines as the number of users increases. As shown in figure, our proposed DATR can achieve excellent performance even with the largest number of users.

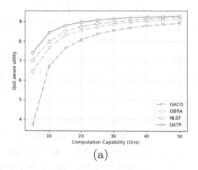
(a)

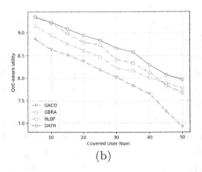
(b)

Fig. 3. (a)The QoE-aware utility with different computing resources. (b)The QoE-aware utility with different number of users.

6 Conclusion

In this paper, we first propose a novel edge computing architecture based on satellite-terrestrial integration. For the proposed architecture, we study the problem of task offloading and resource allocation for users to maximize QoE under the high dynamics and resource constraints of LEO satellites. We formulate the problem as a QoE-aware utility maximization problem. Since it is a MINLP problem, we propose a DATR algorithm to find the near-optimal solution. The DATR algorithm decouple the problem into two sub-problems: first, use the Lagrangian multiplier method to achieve the optimal allocation of computing resources for LEO satellites; second, use the DDPG algorithm to solve the offloading decision problem. Simulation results show that our algorithm outperforms baselines in terms of QoE indicators.

References

1. Buddhika, T., Stern, R., Lindburg, K., Ericson, K., Pallickara, S.: Online scheduling and interference alleviation for low-latency, high-throughput processing of data streams. IEEE Trans. Parallel Distrib. Syst. **28**(12), 3553–3569 (2017)
2. He, C., Li, G.Y., Zheng, F.C., You, X.: Energy-efficient resource allocation in OFDM systems with distributed antennas. IEEE Trans. Veh. Technol. **63**(3), 1223–1231 (2013)
3. Li, H.: Multi-task offloading and resource allocation for energy-efficiency in mobile edge computing. Int. J. Comput. Tech. **5**(1), 5–13 (2018)
4. Mao, Y., Zhang, J., Letaief, K.B.: Dynamic computation offloading for mobile-edge computing with energy harvesting devices. IEEE J. Sel. Areas Commun. **34**(12), 3590–3605 (2016)
5. Meng, Q., Wang, K., Liu, B., Miyazaki, T., He, X.: QoE-based big data analysis with deep learning in pervasive edge environment. In: 2018 IEEE International Conference on Communications (ICC), pp. 1–6. IEEE (2018)
6. Miettinen, A.P., Nurminen, J.K.: Energy efficiency of mobile clients in cloud computing. In: 2nd USENIX Workshop on Hot Topics in Cloud Computing (HotCloud 10) (2010)
7. Pelton, J.N.: The future of communications satellites. In: Satellite Communications. SpringerBriefs in Space Development, pp. 95–104. Springer, New York (2012). https://doi.org/10.1007/978-1-4614-1994-5_8
8. Rappaport, T.S., et al.: Wireless Communications: Principles and Practice, vol. 2. prentice hall PTR, Hoboken, New Jersey (1996)
9. Ruan, L., Liu, Z., Qiu, X., Wang, Z., Guo, S., Qi, F.: Resource allocation and distributed uplink offloading mechanism in fog environment. J. Commun. Netw. **20**(3), 247–256 (2018)
10. Shi, Q., Zhao, L., Zhang, Y., Zheng, G., Yu, F.R., Chen, H.H.: Energy-efficiency versus delay tradeoff in wireless networks virtualization. IEEE Trans. Veh. Technol. **67**(1), 837–841 (2017)
11. Tang, Q., Fei, Z., Li, B.: Distributed deep learning for cooperative computation offloading in low earth orbit satellite networks. China Commun. **19**(4), 230–243 (2022)

12. Wang, Y., Zhang, J., Zhang, X., Wang, P., Liu, L.: A computation offloading strategy in satellite terrestrial networks with double edge computing. In: 2018 IEEE International Conference on Communication Systems (ICCS), pp. 450–455. IEEE (2018)
13. Wang, Y., Yang, J., Guo, X., Qu, Z.: A game-theoretic approach to computation offloading in satellite edge computing. IEEE Access **8**, 12510–12520 (2019)
14. Yang, L., Cao, J., Yuan, Y., Li, T., Han, A., Chan, A.: A framework for partitioning and execution of data stream applications in mobile cloud computing. ACM SIGMETRICS Perform. Eval. Rev. **40**(4), 23–32 (2013)
15. Zhang, Z., Zhang, W., Tseng, F.H.: Satellite mobile edge computing: improving QoS of high-speed satellite-terrestrial networks using edge computing techniques. IEEE Netw. **33**(1), 70–76 (2019)

Attendance Monitoring and Management Using Facial Recognition

Shanil Chetty[✉] and Neeraj Anand Sharma[✉]

Department of Computer Science and Mathematics, The University of Fiji, Lautoka, Fiji
{shanilc,neerajs}@unifiji.ac.fj

Abstract. When it comes to recognizing a specific person, nothing beats seeing their face. Face recognition technology is useful because it can use a person's unique facial characteristics as biometrics. Tracking who was present when is often the most challenging part of the job. Teachers traditionally have taken attendance by calling out students and recording their physical presence or absence. These conventional approaches, however, are laborious and time-consuming. In this research, a fully fetched system is being designed, that will take into account student/course creation as well as enrollment. Together with this, attendance will be taken using facial recognition, recorded and sent to the teacher via email. The system uses FisherFace Algorithm with EmguCV Library and WinForms C# for development. In addition, the projection method is based on Fisher's Linear Discriminant. This method provides well-separated classes in a low-dimensional subspace, despite the fact that the lighting and facial expressions can change substantially. The computing requirements for the Eigenface technique, which is another method, are quite similar to those for the previous methodology. This method involves projecting the picture space in a linear fashion onto a subspace that has fewer dimensions. However, a vast number of studies have demonstrated that the "FisherFace" approach, which was proposed, has error rates that are lower than those of the Eigenface methodology, which was utilized for tests. This was found to be the case when comparing error rates between the two methods.

Keywords: EmguCV · FisherFace · WinForms · facial · attendance · monitoring

1 Introduction

The timing of when employees and students clock in and out of an organization, as well as the precise regions of the business in which they are responsible for their responsibilities, are both tracked by attendance systems, which are utilized in businesses of every kind. There are a lot of positive outcomes that can result from putting in place an attendance system for your company. There was once a time when instructors and employers tracked attendance at school and work using physical registers to keep track of who showed up each day. Those who have attended classes that made use of attendance registers, on the other hand, are aware of how straightforward it is to game this method of keeping track of attendance by recording each other's attendance as "present." The industry

C.-H. Hsu et al. (Eds.): DataCom 2022, LNCS 13864, pp. 379–397, 2023.
https://doi.org/10.1007/978-981-99-2233-8_27

as a whole saw a sea change in how it recorded the presence of personnel after the advent of the attendance tracking system. The system's capacity to simplify and speed up the process of registering attendance is a gift to proprietors of both educational institutions and commercial enterprises. The Eigenface method is another popular option for recognizing people's faces, and it works by linearly projecting the image space onto a feature space with a limited number of dimensions [6–8]. When it comes to face recognition, however, the Eigenface method—which uses principal components analysis (PCA) for dimensionality reduction—produces projection directions that optimize the total scatter across all classes, i.e., across all images of all faces. In other words, it produces projection directions that produce the best results for face recognition. Since PCA chooses the projection that results in the greatest total scatter, it is able to maintain fluctuations that are not desirable and are caused by factors such as lighting and facial expression. As can be seen in Figs. 1, 2, 3 and 4, according to Moses et al. [9], the changes between the images of the same face due to illumination and viewing direction are nearly always larger than image variations due to changes in face identity.

2 Literature Review

When compared to a database of stored photos, a person's face can serve as a reliable biometric identifier. Attempts to automate a solution to this problem have met with difficulty because to the impact of factors including age, lighting, and facial expression. Even though it isn't the most reliable biometric method, facial recognition has many useful applications. Autonomous, user-friendly, and functional, facial recognition is a game changer. The proposed solution [2] uses facial recognition technology to automatically and unobtrusively keep track of when students and staff members are present. Webcams are used to record employees and students. Photographic characteristics of people's faces [2].

a. **Attendance automation using face recognition biometric authentication**

Soniya et al. (2017) [4] In this paper, the authors suggest an Adriano-UNO and camera-based IoT-based system. To speed up the process of registering new users, they are setting up the system to function as a student database, which includes allowing users to contribute new entries. PCA is employed for both feature detection and facial recognition. If pupils leave class and don't return within 15 min, they are deemed absent. Face tracking and face positioning are utilized for facial recognition. Face tracking is used to determine the optimal placement based on the face's dimensions (height, width, and pixel width). They made a graph showing the frequency with which FMRs (which occur when a real match is obtained) and FNMRs (which occur when a genuine user is blocked) occur.

The device in question employs a camera with a 300k pixel resolution and light sensors to activate 4 LEDs in the dark. You can adjust the camera's sharpness, image quality, brightness, and saturation. The biggest negative is that it is incredibly time-consuming to take attendance for a large number of people because they take attendance one student at a time [3].

b. Vision-Face Recognition Attendance Monitoring System for Surveillance using Deep Learning Technology and Computer Vision

Harikrishnan et al. (2019) [4] proposed a Surveillance Attendance Monitoring System that Uses Deep Learning and Computer Vision to Identify People by Their Faces. The camera can be placed in a discreet location, and it will take pictures for recognition purposes, which it will then check against a face database and an attendance mark in an Excel sheet. Finally, the system achieves an overall recognition accuracy of up to 74%. Here, local binary pattern histograms are employed as the recognizer (abbreviated as LBPH). Furthermore, Local Binary Pattern Histogram (LBPH) is used for picture recognition; this method involves sliding a 3×3 matrix window across an image and deriving the pixel value from the matrix's center. Unfortunately, the system's precision is only just adequate.

c. Study of Implementing Automated Attendance System Using Face Recognition Technique

Three primary procedures have been used to put into action the suggested system. Face detection and extraction is the initial procedure. By posing in front of the camera, the user's presence can be detected and used as data. The image is then transformed to greyscale after the face has been identified. The next phase entails acquiring knowledge and refining skills with regards to facial imagery. The process begins with providing the system with a training set of facial photos. It is processed with the PCA method. All the training images are transformed into points in a subspace identified by principal component analysis. The final stage is the spotting and labeling. The test face, or recognized face, is taken from the front of the image in this process. Next, we recalculate the Eigen value of the test face and compare it to the closest neighbor's data we have on file. A distance function between the projected test face and each projected training set is used to determine the closest neighbor. Here "Squared Euclidean Distance" is used as the metric of distance. When a face is matched, data is pulled from the system that corresponds to it. To record that person's presence, the system time is entered into the log table [5].

d. Face Recognition-based Lecture Attendance System

Two cameras, one mounted on the ceiling and used to detect where students are seated, and another placed around the room, record each student's face as they enter and exit the classroom (Fixed in front of the seats). The camera is focused on a certain seat in order to acquire a clear shot of the person sitting there. Face images are recoded into the database after being improved and identified. Each student's relationship to their assigned seat is represented as a vector of values. In order to assess attendance, facial recognition data collected through constant observation is analyzed. The student's attendance and grade are both recorded in the system [6].

e. Implementation of classroom attendance system based on face recognition in class

A camera in the system records scenes in the classroom and sends them to a separate module where they can be enhanced. The accuracy of the face detection algorithm was evaluated across a range of test photos featuring a variety of facial poses and lighting conditions. In order to detect many faces in a classroom photo, an algorithm is first trained on face photos. After that, PCA is utilized for facial recognition. Using an Eigen face approach, we extract the faces from the image and check them against our database. The enrolment procedure gathered and stored photographs of each student's face to create a database of facial template data. Attendance is taken by checking off each student's face against a database. The system has a timetable add-on that can pull in information such course name, period, day of the week, and time of day. When teachers enter the classroom, they need only launch the executable file to begin taking attendance [7].

3   Research Methodology

There are two distinct phases in facial recognition: processing, which takes place before recognition and includes techniques like face identification and detection, and recognition, which includes feature extraction and matching. In this section, we investigate four pattern classification strategies for the purpose of resolving the face recognition issue. We do so by contrasting two approaches that have garnered a great deal of attention in the field of face recognition research—namely, the FisherFace and Eigenface methods—with newer strategies that were developed by the authors themselves. Using the framework of the pattern classification paradigm, we tackle this problem by thinking of each of the pixel values in a sample image as a coordinate in a space with a high dimension.

Face recognition uses a variety of algorithms. Below are a few of them:

1. Eigenfaces
2. Fisher Face
3. Local binary patterns histograms

a. **Eigenfaces**

Because correlation algorithms are famously resource-intensive, both in terms of computing power and space for data storage, it makes perfect sense to explore for solutions that reduce the dimensionality of the data. In the field of computer vision, a methodology known as principal components analysis (PCA) [6, 7, 8, 14] [17] is utilized frequently as a method for simplifying difficult issues, particularly in the area of facial recognition. PCA methods, which are also known as Karhunen-Loeve methods, select a linear projection that maximizes the information gain for all samples that are projected in order to achieve this goal.

In a more formal sense, let's imagine we have N sample photos to work with $\{x_1, x_2, \ldots, x_N\}$ utilizing n-dimensional image values and supposing that each image corresponds to a set of c classes $\{X_1, X_2, \ldots, X_c\}$. The n-dimensional image space can be linearly transformed into an m-dimensional feature space, where m > n. Using recently developed feature vectors $Y_k \in R^m$ are characterized by the linear mapping.

$$y_k = W^T x_k \quad k = 1, 2 \ldots, N$$

where $W \in R^{n \times m}$ is a matrix with orthonormal columns.

If the total scatter matrix ST is defined as

$$S_T = \sum_{k=1}^{N} (x_k - \mu)(x_k - \mu)^T$$

where n is the number of sample images, and $\mu \in R^n$ is the mean image of all samples, then after applying the linear transformation W^T, the scatter of the transformed feature vectors $\{y_1, y_2, \ldots, y_N\}$ is $W^T S_T W$

In PCA, the projection W_{Opt} is chosen to maximize the determinant of the total scatter matrix of the projected samples, i.e.,

$$W_{opt} = \arg \max \left| W^T S_T W \right|$$

$$= [w_1 \, w_2 \ldots w_m]$$

where $\{w_i | \, i = 1, 2, \ldots, m\}$ is the set of n-dimensional eigenvectors of S_T corresponding to the m largest eigenvalues.

The eigenvectors are called Eigenpictures in [6] and Eigenfaces in [7, 8] because their dimensions match those of the source images. Eigenface is identical to correlation if N is the number of images in the training set and m is selected to represent the reduced feature space.

The problem with this approach is that it maximizes the within-class dispersion, which is undesirable for classification, as well as the between-class scatter, which is good. Keep in mind the advice of Moses et al. [9] that emphasizes how much of a difference in image quality can be brought about by changes in ambient light. Accordingly, if you provide PCA with a collection of face photographs taken under varying lighting circumstances, it will produce principal components (i.e., Eigenfaces) in the projection matrix W_{Opt} that account for this variation. The projected space may not have distinct clusters of classes, and instead the various demographics may blur together.

It has been claimed that reducing the amount of variation in the illumination by concentrating just on the three primary components that are of the most significance can help. The removal of the first main components, which indicate the fluctuation owing to illumination, is supposed to be an effective method for enhancing projected sample grouping, as stated by the theory. On the other hand, it is highly improbable that the first few basic components correspond solely to variations in lighting; as a consequence, discriminatory information may be lost.

b. Fisher Faces

The aforementioned method is able to capitalize on the fact that the intra-class variation occurs in a linear region of the picture space under certain hypothetical situations that have been idealized. You can tell that each category is convex by drawing a line down the center of it and observing the result. We are able to reduce the number of dimensions without giving up our capacity to linearly separate them when we use linear projection. Because of this, linear approaches to dimensionality reduction are more likely to be used, which is critical for the face identification challenge because of the sensitivity of the problem to changes in lighting. By utilizing the labeled training set, you will be able to optimize the dimensionality reduction strategy that you use for the features. On the other hand, we contend that class-specific linear techniques for dimensionality reduction and straightforward classifiers in the condensed feature space have the potential to outperform the Linear Subspace methodology and the Eigenface method. A good example of a class-specific technique is the Fisher's Linear Discriminant (FLD) [5, which seeks to "shape" the scatter so that it is more reliable for classification purposes. Using this method, you will select a value for W that lies within the interval [1], and it will be chosen so that it will optimize the ratio of between-class dispersion to within-class scatter.

$$S_B = \sum_{i=1}^{c} (\mu_i - \mu)(\mu_i - \mu)^T$$

and the within-class scatter matrix be defined as

$$S_W = \sum_{i=1}^{c} \sum_{x_k \in X_i} (x_k - \mu_i)(x_k - \mu_i)^T$$

where μ_i is the mean image of class X_i, and N_i is the number of samples in class X_i. If S_W is non-singular, the optimal projection W_{opt} is chosen as the matrix with orthonormal columns which maximizes the ratio of the determinant of the between-class scatter matrix of the projected samples to the determinant of the within-class scatter matrix of the projected samples, i.e.,

$$W_{opt} = \frac{arg\ max\left|W^T S_B W\right|}{w\left|W^T S_W W\right|}$$

$$= [w_1 w_2 \ldots w_m]$$

where $\{w_i|\ i = 1, 2, \ldots, m\}$ set of generalized eigenvectors of S_B and S_W the m largest generalized
eigenvalues $\{\lambda_i|- = 1, 2, \ldots, m\}$ i.e.,

$$S_B w_i = \lambda_i S_W w_i, \quad i = 1, 2, \ldots,$$

Note that there are at most $c - 1$ nonzero generalized eigen-values, and so an upper bound on m is $c - 1$, where c is the number of classes.

We demonstrate the usefulness of class-specific linear projection by employing a low-dimensional model of the classification problem. In this model, the data pertaining to each class are arranged in a linear subspace, and the model is then projected onto a two-dimensional plane. Figure 2 presents a comparison of the performance of principal component analysis (PCA) and fuzzy linear modeling (FLD) when used to a problem with two classes and random disturbances applied to samples from each class in a direction that is perpendicular to a linear subspace. There is a total of 20 of them, making N equal to 2, yet there is only 1 of them, making m equal to 1. As a consequence of this, individuals belonging to each category have a propensity to congregate in the direction of a central line in the 2D feature space. In order to translate points from a two-dimensional space to a one-dimensional one, principal component analysis and tensor linear regression have both been utilized. When the two projections are compared side by side, it is easy to see that PCA muddles up the classes to the point where they are unidentifiable. PCA is superior to FLD when it comes to simplifying the classification process in terms of total scatter, but FLD shines when it comes to simplifying the classification process by reducing the amount of scatter between classes. PCA is superior to FLD when it comes to simplifying the classification process in terms of total scatter.

One of the issues that must be addressed while developing a solution to the facial recognition problem is the fact that the within-class scatter matrix $S\_W \in R^{(n \times n)}$ always and only one. This is due to the fact that the rank of SW is at most $N - c$, and the number of photographs in the training set N is often significantly less than the number of pixels in each image n. This indicates that there is a value of W that may be selected such that the projected samples have no within-class scatter. To get over the problem of using just one SW, we propose an alternative criterion (4).

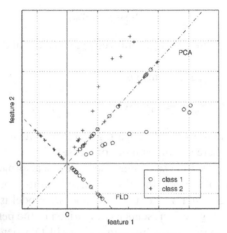

Fig. 1. An examination of the similarities and differences between principal component analysis (PCA) and Fisher's linear discriminant (FLD) for a two-class situation where the data for each class is located close to a linear subspace.

To circumvent this issue, we employ a technique we call FisherFace, which involves projecting the picture set to a lower dimensional space in order to generate a nonsingular within-class scatter matrix SW. To do this, we first use the usual FLD specified by (4), which reduces the dimension of the feature space to c, and then use PCA to lower the dimension to $c - 1$.

c. Local Binary Patterns Histograms (LBPH)

For the purpose of this method's training, grayscale images are essential. This method, in contrast to other algorithms, does not use a thorough approach [1].

d. Parameters

LBPH uses the following parameters:

i. Radius:
    The radius around the central pixel is usually depicted by a circular local binary pattern whose radius is either 1 or 1.

ii. Neighbors:

The average number of sample points surrounding the central pixel (8 in this case). The number of sample points will increase in tandem with the computing cost.

iii. Grid X:

The horizontal number of cells is denoted by the X grid. As the number of cells rises, which boosts the dimension of the feature vector, the grid becomes more acceptable.

iv. Grid Y:

Grid Y indicates the number of cells present in the vertical direction. As the number of cells rises, the grid becomes more precise, which increases the dimension of the feature vector [10].

e. Algorithm Training

For the disclosed method to use the provided information for perceiving an input image and producing an output, a training dataset having facial images of the to-be-recognized humans and their unique identities is required. Identification documents must share the same photograph [11].

f. Computation of the Algorithm

The first step involves producing a similar-looking intermediate image with enhanced face features. Sliding window theory is used with the aforementioned variables to reach this goal [12].

A facial photo is converted to grayscale. The brightness of each pixel is contained in a 3×3 matrix, also called a 3×3 window (0–255). Then we look at the threshold, which is the matrices' midpoint [9]. Each of the eight neighboring values will be reset based on this value. There is a unique binary value assigned to each neighbor of the core value. Whenever the value is greater than the cutoff, the outcome is 1. The alternative is zero [13].

g. Extraction of Histogram

The image captured in the preceding phase is separated into numerous grids using the Grid X and Grid Y parameters. The image can be used to derive the histogram in the way depicted below:

Each histogram will only have room for 256 values (0–255), which represent the intensity of each pixel, because the image is in grayscale [7, 10]. Next, a new, expanded histogram is made for each original histogram. The final histogram for an 8x8 grid will consist of 16,384 points. The histogram, in the end, is a representation of the actual image's attributes [14].

The research questions identified from the study and that will be answered in this research is:

1. Can a system be created to facilitate the entire process from student registration to enrolment and attendance using facial recognition?
2. How will the face be detected?
3. How will the face be uniquely identified?
4. How will the face be recognized upon being saved in the system?

4 Experimental Results and Discussions

a. **Algorithm Framework**

We demonstrate and explain each of these facial recognition methods here, utilizing two separate databases. Many of the common databases did not suffice for testing the predictions we had regarding the relative performance of the algorithms under consideration. Therefore, we have relied on a Harvard Robotics Laboratory database where the illumination conditions have been carefully altered. Second, we've built a database at Yale that accounts for differences in lighting and facial expression.

Variation in Lighting
As for the initial trial run, we hypothesized that face recognition algorithms would fare better if they took use of the fact that, regardless of how drastically the lighting conditions vary, images of a Lambertian surface lie in a linear subspace. Hallinan's image database from the Harvard Robotics Laboratory [7, 14] is used to evaluate the four methods described in Sect. 2 in terms of their recognition error rates. For each of the thousands of images in this collection, the subject is seen staring directly into the camera's eye. We then took a random sample of 150 steps across the space of light source directions, which is limited by spherical angles. For an illustration of this, see Fig. We pulled 330 pictures from here, and 5 of them are humans (66 of each). We divided the information into five groups to examine the results of various lighting conditions.

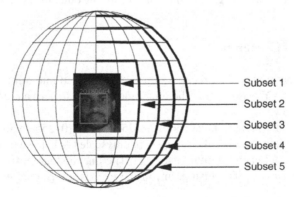

Fig. 2. The directions of the light sources for Subsets 1 through 5 are shown by the lines of longitude and latitude that have been highlighted. On the right-hand side of the graphic, at each point where a longitudinal line and a latitudinal line connect, there is a corresponding image stored in the database.

Thirty photos make up the first subset, and all of them have light sources whose directional angles are less than or equal to 150°, with the axis of illumination also aligning with the optical axis of the camera. Subset 2 consists of 45 photos with light sources located 300 on either the long or short axis relative to the camera. Subset 3 consists of 65 photos with light sources located at a distance of 450°, measured in either the long or short axis, relative to the camera.

In the fourth set of photographs, the light source is located 600, or more, degrees away from the camera's axis. Subset 5 consists of 105 photos with the light source located at a distance of 750°, measured in either the long or short axis, from the camera. A closest neighbor classifier was used for all classification in all tests. Each person's training photos were mapped onto a feature space. Face areas were used as cropping targets, with the head's outline removed. 2 The photos were normalized so that the mean and variance were both zero before being put through the Eigenface and correlation tests. An example of the Eigenface method's output with ten principal components is provided. As it has been speculated that the first three principal components are primarily attributable to illumination variance, and that recognition rates can be improved by eliminating them, error rates utilizing principal components four through thirteen are also displayed.

Using the Harvard Dataset, we performed both extrapolation and interpolation analyses. Each tactic was preconditioned on Subset 1 data and then put to the test on Subsets 2 and 3. Since there are 30 photos in the training set, the correlation algorithm is quite close to Eigenface's 29-principal-components method. In Fig. 5 we can see the results of this experiment. Subsets 1 and 5 were used for training in the interpolation experiment, whereas Subsets 2, 3, and 4 were used for testing. The final outcome of this experiment is depicted in Fig. 2 (Table 1).

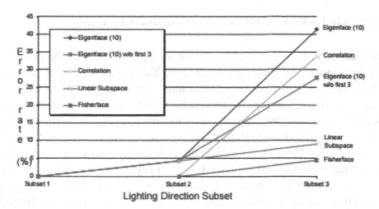

Fig. 3. Extrapolation: The graph and table below display how well each approach performs under extreme light source conditions when trained on images with near frontal illumination (Subset 1).

These two experiments reveal a number of interesting points:

1. When lighting is approximately frontal, all algorithms function perfectly. Off-axis lighting, however, causes a noticeable performance gap between the two class-specific approaches and Eigenface.

Table 1. Extrapolating from Subset 1

Method	Reduced Space	Error Rate (%)		
		Subset 1	Subset 2	Subset 3
Eigenface	5	0.0	31.15	47.71
	11	0.0	4.41	41.52
Eigenface w/o 1st 3	5	0.0	13.31	41.53
	11	0.0	4.44	27.71
Correlation	130	0.0	0.02	33.94
Linear Subspace	16	0.0	4.44	9.25
FisherFace	5	0.0	0.05	4.61

2. Because performance improves with the size of the eigenspace, it has been pointed out that the Eigenface approach is no better than correlation when the number of Eigen-faces is equal to the size of the training set. This is also supported by actual evidence.
3. Eliminating the first three major components in the Eigenface technique improves its functionality under varying illumination conditions.
4. The Linear Subspace approach is just as accurate as the FisherFace one, but it takes three times as long and requires three times as much storage space.
5. The FisherFace approach needed less computing time and had lower error rates than the Eigenface method.

b. Variation in Facial Expression, Eye Wear, and Lighting

We devised experiments to see how the techniques fared in a different set of circumstances using a second database developed at the Yale Center for Computational Vision and Control. In a single session, ten photographs were taken of each of the sixteen subjects against a plain background. There were both men and women involved, and several of the men had facial hair. One subject is depicted ten times in Fig. 3. The first picture was captured with natural light, and the subject was in a neutral expression while wearing spectacles. The second picture is the original without the spectacles. It was the person's own glasses that were utilized if they were worn regularly, or someone else's glasses were borrowed if none were used regularly. Photos 3–5 were taken after the subject's neutrally expression face was illuminated from three angles using a Luxolamp. The final five photos were taken in natural light and feature a range of expressions (happy, sad, winking, sleepy, and surprised). The images were adjusted to have a mean of zero and a variance of one for the Eigenface and correlation tests. Images were manually cropped and centered at two distinct sizes: The complete face and some of the backgrounds were visible in the wider photographs, whereas the brow, eyes, nose, mouth, and chin were visible in the more tightly cropped images but the occluding contour was cut off.

Error rates were determined using the "leaving-one-out" technique [4]. Taking a human image out of the dataset and creating a dimensionality reduction matrix W was found to increase classification accuracy. Images were projected into the constrained area for categorization after the test image was removed from the database. To accomplish this identification, a closest neighbor classifier was employed. The training set subjects are each projected from ten photos, whereas the test subject is projected from nine.

Eigenface's effectiveness has a tendency to shift as more fundamental features are added to the algorithm. We began by comparing and contrasting the FisherFace approach, the Linear Subspace method, and the Eigenface method. After that, we carried out an experiment to determine the optimal number of principal components. We compare the error rate before and after eliminating the first three PCs in Fig. 8, along with the number of PCs required to analyze the significantly smaller data set.

Figure 4 provides a graphical representation of the relative effectiveness of each of the algorithms. The error rates that were accomplished via the utilization of FisherFace were noticeably lower than those that were accomplished through the utilization of previous methods. It would appear that the FisherFace technique chooses a set of projections that performs well in a wide range of settings, such as with or without glasses, in addition to differences in lighting and facial expression. This would be an advantage for the FisherFace approach.

This latest illumination test, in contrast to the ones detailed in earlier sections of this paper, demonstrates that the Linear Subspace technique performs less admirably. Images are displaced from a linear subspace whenever there is variation in face expressions. Due to the fact that the FisherFace approach disregards non-essential parts of the image, the projections W that are produced hide the areas of the face that are subject to significant change. As an illustration, the region surrounding the lips is disregarded since it shifts so significantly in response to various facial expressions. Because of their greater consistency through time, the nose, cheekbones, and brow are more important features for recognition. This is in contrast to the eyes and mouth, which exhibit some degree of individual variation. Because projection directions have a tendency to reduce within-class dispersion for all classes, we presume that the FisherFace methods' projection directions will have a comparable level of effectiveness when it comes to recognizing faces that are not part of the training set.

Full-face photos gave the greatest results for any of the facial recognition systems. When we used the FisherFace approach, we were able to reduce the number of inaccurate predictions from 7.3% to 0.6%. Because the overall contour of the face is such a major factor in face recognition, the method is trained on the entire face, and the pixels that correspond to the occluding contour of the face are selected as good characteristics for dis- discriminating between individuals. If the background or hair styles had been different, it is likely that the identification rates for the full-face photographs would have been substantially lower. In fact, it is possible that these rates would have been even lower than those for the closely cropped images (Tables 2 and 3).

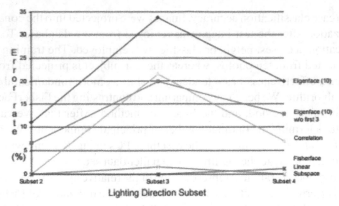

Fig. 4. Interpolation: The graph and table below illustrate how each technique performs under intermediate lighting circumstances when trained on photos from both near frontal and severe illumination (Subsets 1 and 5).

Table 2. Interpolating Between Subsets 1 and 5

Method	Reduced Space	Error Rate (%)		
		Subset 2	Subset 3	Subset 4
Eigenface	5	53.4	75.5	53.1
	11	11.12	34.0	20.1
Eigenface w/o 1st 3	5	31.12	60.1	29.41
	11	6.8	20.1	12.91
Correlation	130	0.1	21.56	7.21
Linear Subspace	16	0.0	1.51	0.01
FisherFace	5	0.01	0.01	1.21

c. **User Interface**

Student Registration - This is where a student is registered with all their important details entered into the system. Their face is saved in the process which is later used to mark the attendance. As seen in Fig. 6, Student's information is captured together with that, the face is saved.

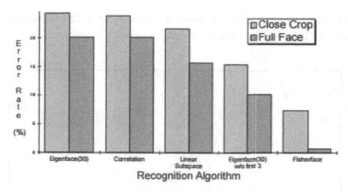

Fig. 5. When the algorithms were applied to the Yale Database, which comprises a variety of facial expressions and lighting conditions, the graph and table that corresponds to it indicate the relative performance of the algorithms.

Table 3. "Leaving-One-Out" of Yale Database

Method	Reduced Space	Error Rate (%)	
		Close Crop	Full Face
Eigenface	30	25.41	20.46
Eigenface w/o 1st 3	30	16.35	11.83
Correlation	160	24.92	21.3
Linear Subspace	48	22.67	16.62
FisherFace	15	7.32	0.62

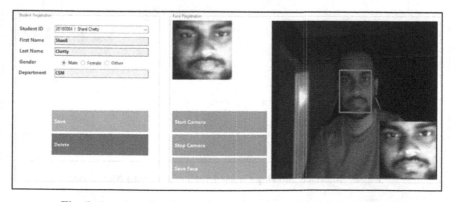

Fig. 6. Interface showing student registration and facial data capture

Student Enrolment - This is where a particular student is added to their subject/course and this ensures that all students are added before attendance is taken. As seen in Fig. 7,

Subject field can be used to select the subject, and student field to be used to select the student, after which the student can be added to a particular subject.

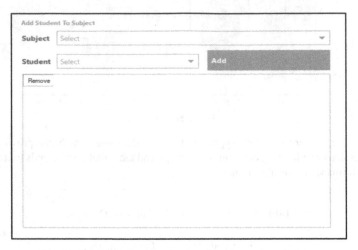

Fig. 7. Interface showing Student Enrolment into Subject

Subject - This is where individual courses are created with important details and key identifier. Figure 8 shows create course and auto attendance marking. Using which, a course can be created a fixed time can be scheduled for auto attendance.

Fig. 8. Interface Showing Course Creation and Auto Attendance

Attendance Report – Fig. 9 shows where all the attendance report are provided for different subjects/courses based on date and time.

Fig. 9. Interface Showing Attendance Report

Attendance - This is the most important part of the application as this window captures the face in real-time and tries to match it with the face data stored in the database as shown in Fig. 10.

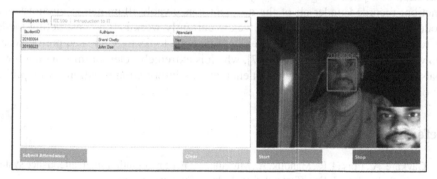

Fig. 10. Interface Showing a Successful Attendance

d. **Features**

Some key features include an automated attendance schedule, sending attendance via email, Student enrolment, and an Accuracy tracker. These features make up the attendance system and ensure that it is ready to be used in an operational University environment.

5 Conclusion

In conclusion, the system designed through this research is a fully fletched system which ensures that student and subject is created and registered with each other. After which the student's facial data is stored and later used to be identifies and marked present. In addition to this, this system also emails the results to the respective teacher/lecturer. There are multiple rooms of environment as this application could be further enhanced and be made as a mobile application which would then be easier for students to take their own attendance. In addition, other algorithms could be tested with this system to see which performs better and later multiple algorithm properties could be used to derive a new algorithm. All four research questions were answered using experimental methods and the system is fully function with the ability to create students/courses, enroll students into courses, detect faces, extract features from faces to identify them uniquely and recognize faces while taking attendance. Despite all of the testing that has been done, there are still interesting open questions; for example, I'm keen to see how well the FisherFace approach fares with enormous data sets. Other interesting open questions include: How open-minded should one be to different degrees of illumination if they can only ever see a particular individual in one? Therefore, new face detection methods are required to support the algorithms presented in this research because existing approaches are likely to fail under extreme illumination conditions such as those shown in Sub-sets 4 and 5 of Fig. 2. Last but not least, all of the recognition systems that have been supplied perform poorly when there is a preponderance of shadowing, indicating that there may be a requirement for strategies that model or hide the shadowed parts. The collection of n-pixel images of an object of any shape and with an arbitrary reflectance function, recorded under all of the different conceivable illumination circumstances, produces a convex cone in !R", and we are currently working on constructing models for representing this data. This convex lighting cone looks to be located pretty close to a low-dimensional linear subspace [7], which is extremely relevant information for the goals of this work. As if that weren't enough, this information is extremely helpful for the objectives of this work.

References

1. Gavkare, A., Prasad, R., Mandlik, A., Mutkule, A.: Face recognition smart attendance system-a survey. Int. Res. J. Eng. Technol. (2022). https://www.irjet.net/
2. Sayeed, S., Hossen, J., Kalaiarasi, S.M.A., Jayakumar, V., Yusof, I., Samraj, A.: Real-time face recognition for attendance monitoring system 1. J. Theor. Appl. Inf. Technol. **15**(1) (2017). https://www.jatit.org/
3. Soniya, V., Sri, R.S., Titty, K.S., Ramakrishnan, R., Sivakumar, S.: Attendance automation using face recognition biometric authentication. In: 2017 International Conference on Power and Embedded Drive Control (ICPEDC), 2017, pp. 122–127 (2017). https://doi.org/10.1109/ICPEDC.2017.8081072
4. Harikrishnan, J., Sudarsan, A., Sadashiv, A., Ajai, R.A.S.: Vision-face recognition attendance monitoring system for surveillance using deep learning technology and computer vision. In: 2019 International Conference on Vision Towards Emerging Trends in Communication and Networking (ViTECoN), 2019, pp. 1–5 (2019).https://doi.org/10.1109/ViTECoN.2019.8899418
5. Kar, N., Deb Barma, M., Saha, A., Pal, D.: Study of implementing automated attendance system using face recognition technique. Int. J. Comput. Commun. Eng. 100–103 (2012). https://doi.org/10.7763/IJCCE.2012.V1.28

6. Patole, S., Vispute, Y.: Automatic Attendance System Based On Face Recognition (2017). https://doi.org/10.15680/IJIRSET.2016.0608042
7. Gomes, C., Chanchal, S., Desai, T., Jadhav, D.: Class attendance management system using facial recognition. In: ITM Web of Conferences, vol. 32, p. 02001 (2020). https://doi.org/10.1051/itmconf/20203202001
8. Bhatti, K., Mughal, L., Khuhawar, F., Memon, S.: Smart attendance management system using face recognition. EAI Endorsed Trans. Creat. Technol. 5(17), 159713 (2018). https://doi.org/10.4108/eai.13-7-2018.159713
9. Munigala, S., Mirza, S., Naseem Fathima, Z.: Automatic attendance management system using face recognition. In: IJCSN-Int. J. Comput. Sci. Netw. 8(2) (2019)
10. Alghamdi, R., Alsubaie, W., Alharthi, R., Alghamdi, W., Alboaneen, D.A., Alqahtani, N.F.: A smart attendance system for Imam Abdulrahman Bin Faisal University using facial recognition. In: Journal of Physics: Conference Series, vol. 1627, no. 1 (2020). https://doi.org/10.1088/1742-6596/1627/1/012004
11. Lukas, S., Mitra, A.R., Desanti, R.I., Krisnadi, D.: Student attendance system in classroom using face recognition technique. In: 2016 International Conference on Information and Communication Technology Convergence, ICTC 2016, pp. 1032–1035, November 2016. https://doi.org/10.1109/ICTC.2016.7763360
12. Krishnan, M.G., Babu, S.: Implementation of Automated Attendance System using Face Recognition. Int. J. Sci. Eng. Res. 6(3) (2015). http://www.ijser.org
13. Singh, A., Bhatt, S., Gupta, A.: Automated attendance system with face recognition (2021). http://www.ijeast.com
14. Bhagat, S.: Face recognition attendance system. Int. J. Res. Appl. Sci. Eng. Technol. 10(1), 280–283 (2022). https://doi.org/10.22214/ijraset.2022.39702

Reinforcement Learning-Based Task Scheduling Algorithm for On-Satellite Data Analysis

Junji Qiu[✉] and Qibo Sun

State Key Laboratory of Net working and Switching Technology,
Beijing University of Posts and Telecommunications, Beijing, China
{junji23,qbsun}@bupt.edu.cn

Abstract. To leverage the explosively growing computing capacity of satellites, this paper envisions a novel computing paradigm – on-satellite data analysis. By directly dispatching data analysis logic to satellites and executing on them, this paradigm enables bandwidth-friendly and privacy-preserving ground-space computing, avoiding the need to download large amounts of (sensitive) data to ground stations. However, the intermittent connectivity between satellites and ground stations and hard-to-predict hardware status pose challenges to data analysis processes, especially the long tail phenomenon caused by struggling satellites. To facilitate this paradigm, we proposed a reinforcement learning-based scheduling algorithm that does not rely on real-time hardware status, and redundantly schedules tasks to more satellites based on real-time feedback. What's more, the algorithm dynamically adjusts the time for redundant scheduling, rather than setting a specific landmark. Simulation results show that the proposed algorithm outperforms baselines in optimizing task execution time and satellite resource consumption under various task arriving intervals.

Keywords: Satellite data analysis · Task scheduling · Reinforcement learning

1 Introduction

The rapid growth number of Low Earth Orbit (LEO) satellites has brought enormous benefits to end users. As of July 2022, SpaceX has launched over 3,000 LEO satellites, providing Internet services to over 500,000 users [2]. Analyzing data generated/captured by satellites brings a lot of benefits. For example, Barmpoutis et al. detected real-time natural disasters using satellite imagery data [6]. Aragon et al. used satellite data for real-time analysis of agriculture [5].

Most of the existing data analysis paradigms download satellite data to ground stations, upload it to the cloud, and then analyze them through high-performance servers. However, this paradigm faces the following challenges:

Supported by the Fundamental Research Funds for the Central Universities.

1. Satellite data may contain private information that can not be freely transmitted. For example, in smart urban computing, the data scientists perform data analysis based on sensitive data, such as bio-metrics, locations, and itineraries [12].
2. The volume of satellite data is explosively growing [1]. Only the satellites for Earth observation collect hundreds of Gigabytes of data per day [16]. Downloading such an amount of satellite data to ground stations dominate the downlink bandwidth, thus affecting other services on satellites. In addition, the fast motion of satellites might incur hours of latency for downloading data to ground stations, making the end-to-end data analysis latency unpredictable [19].

Fortunately, the increasing computation capacity of LEO satellites opens up a huge space for performing on-space data analysis. In this paradigm, when a data analysis request arrives, the ground station sends the data analysis code to connected satellites. The satellite then runs the analysis code based on its own data and sends the analytical results back to the ground station. Compared to raw data, the post-analysis results are typical of less footprint and contain less sensitive information while meeting the needs of data analysts. For example, the original image captured by satellites might be hundreds of MBs. But the extracted image features might only be a few KBs.

However, how to schedule the analytics task in the volatile satellite environment efficiently is still challenging due to the long tail phenomenon. The long tail phenomenon is, when massive distributed nodes process the same analytics task, the execution time of the weaker node is significantly longer than the average time usually caused by the limited computation capacity or inactive mode, thus delaying the overall data analysis process. Ananthanarayanan et al. analyzed the long tail phenomenon in Google's MapReduce clusters and found that completion times among similar tasks are greatly different. Stragglers inflate the job completion time by 34% at median [4]. The above phenomenon can be even more severe in space due to (1) the connection between the satellite and the ground station may be lost at any time due to electromagnetic interference or orbital periodic motion and (2) different satellites have diverse status that affects computation capacity.

There have been lots of studies on how to reduce the negative impact of long tail phenomenon in data analysis by optimizing scheduling algorithms. For example, blacklist strategy is one of the most common algorithms [3]. With this mechanism, nodes with long execution time will be put into a blacklist without tasks assigned to them in the future [21]. However, the blacklist strategy relies heavily on differentiating straggler nodes, therefore a wrong strategy may cause large deviations and can't reveal actual results. Another common algorithm is redundant scheduling [20], which dispatches sub-tasks to nodes exceeding the required number. By adding sub-tasks, the probability of tasks being blocked due to waiting for struggling nodes is reduced, thereby reducing task execution time. To determine a redundancy value, most of the existing research is based on high-frequency information exchange (e.g., task progress and node status).

It is unable to achieve this in the satellite environment due to the instability of satellites. Based on above analysis and observations, this paper studies how to efficiently schedule analytics tasks in the volatile satellite environment, and makes the following contributions.

1. For on-satellite data analysis, we proposed a reinforcement learning (RL)-based redundancy scheduling algorithm. The algorithm reduces the negative impact of the long tail phenomenon on the execution of distributed tasks in space and optimizes the task execution time with the low satellite computation cost.
2. We simulated the proposed algorithm with different task arriving intervals, and compared the results with baselines. The result shows that the proposed algorithm realizes joint optimization of task execution time and satellite computation cost.

The rest of this paper is structured as follows. In Sect. 2, we briefly introduce the related work. We define our system model in Sect. 3. In Sect. 4, we present our RL-based algorithm and give its implementation. We show our evaluation results in Sect. 5. At last, we conclude this paper in Sect. 6.

2   Motivation and Related Work

There has been a low of studies on how to mitigate the long tail phenomenon in existing data analysis frameworks. Ananthanarayanan et al. [3] determined whether a node is on the blacklist or not by monitoring the machine for a given time interval, and employed temporal prediction for scheduling. However, the results showed that the system performance is much lower than that of other algorithms. The LATE algorithm [22] and the Mantri [4] algorithm are two representative algorithms for speculative execution in existing data analysis frameworks. In speculative execution algorithms, a scheduler determines which node is the potential "straggler" according to real-time feedback (e.g., node's heartbeats), and redundantly dispatches the same number of straggler to more nodes to avoid the long tail phenomenon. However, these algorithms require nodes to upload their real-time status frequently, which is hard to be adopted on satellites due to the unstable connection and severe power issues. In addition, the above algorithms heavily rely on the characteristics of the Map stage and the Reduce stage to estimate the task execution progress. However, there is no such general framework for on-satellite data analysis thus it's hard to implement.

Dean et al. proposed a general mechanism based on cloning to reduce the impact of the long tail in MapReduce framework [9]. When a task is almost finished, the scheduler performs secondary scheduling for late sub-tasks. However, this algorithm cannot adaptively change the strategy in different clusters. What's more, the secondary scheduling process is performed too late (e.g., when receiving 90% of total results). A potential optimization to improve the system performance is to re-schedule sub-tasks to more devices earlier than their origin time. Xu et al. proposed a smart cloning algorithm in low-load environments to reduce overall latency when it is difficult to estimate task execution time. However, this algorithm does not take resource consumption into account.

In satellite scenarios, there are also some scheduling strategy studies. In order to solve the problem of waiting for a long time for the result to be returned, Razmi et al. proposed an asynchronous version of the FedAvg [17] algorithm [18]. In the above algorithm, the ground station performs aggregation every time it receives a result, avoiding long waits. But it is only suitable for federated learning. For on-satellite data analysis, it still cannot avoid the long tail phenomenon.

For on-satellite data analysis, it is difficult for the scheduler to implement refined strategies as current data analysis models due to the lack of real-time status. In this paper, we design a scheduling policy *without any prior knowledge of tasks and hardware status*. In the following sections, we consider how to optimize redundant scheduling strategies without prior knowledge to mitigate the long tail phenomenon.

3   System Model

3.1   Model Workflow

Figure 1 provides an overview of our model's workflow. In our data analysis model, each satellite can only perform one sub-task at the same time to avoid inference to other high-priority tasks on the satellite. We assume that data scientists submit a set of tasks $J = \{J_1, J_2, .., J_N\}$ to the ground scheduler at an interval of λ. When task J_i arrives, the ground scheduler splits it into multiple sub-tasks and then puts them in the waiting queue. All sub-tasks in the waiting queue will be sent to idle satellites. After executing the task, satellites return their results to the ground scheduler for further aggregation. At last, data scientists receive the aggregated results from the ground scheduler.

3.2   Problem Formulation

Considering the intermittent links between satellites and the ground scheduler, we borrow the idea of clone execution algorithm in MapReduce framework [9] and design a two-stage redundancy scheduling algorithm to mitigate long task execution time.

We assume that the target result number of task J_i is m_i, meaning that data scientists require to get the aggregated result from m_i satellites. For the first stage, the redundancy number is defined as k_i^1, and the secondary redundancy number is defined as k_i^2. The ground scheduler sends $m_i + k_i^1$ sub-tasks at the beginning of task J_i. When the ground scheduler receives the p_i-th results returned by satellites, it starts the secondary scheduling round and sends k_i^2 sub-tasks. The task J_i completes once the ground scheduler receives m_i results. At this point, the ground scheduler automatically sends the request to kill the remaining sub-tasks on satellites.

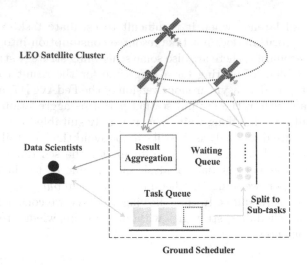

Fig. 1. The workflow of the analytical model.

When performing on-satellite data analysis, task execution time directly affects user experience. A long task execution time might even make the analytics results outdated. The satellite computation cost indicates the total cost spent by the satellites serving a task. In such a computing framework, the computation cost is positively related to the user's payment cost. It is obvious that the short execution time and low satellite computation cost can effectively improve the availability of the system. Therefore, we select the task execution time and the satellite computation cost as indicators for our algorithm evaluation.

For task J_i, the computation time S_i is defined as follows:

$$S_i = C_i - A_i \tag{1}$$

where A_i is the time when task J_i comes to the cluster. C_i is the completion time of task J_i. Task completion time C_i can be represented as the time when the m_i-th result returns to the ground scheduler.

The satellite computation cost is denoted as E_i and is computed as the total time spent by the satellites serving a task [13]. It is defined as follows:

$$E_i = \sum_{\xi_i^j \in F_i} (f_i^j - s_i^j) + \sum_{\xi_i^j \in D_i} (C_i - s_i^j) \tag{2}$$

where F_i represents a list of completed sub-tasks, and D_i represents a list of in-process sub-tasks when task J_i is completed. The ξ_i^j is the j-th sub-task of task J_i. The s_i^j and f_i^j represent the start time and completion time of ξ_i^j, respectively.

Simply increasing the scheduling redundancy can efficiently reduce the task execution time [8,23]. However, the incurred computation cost also challenges the system's efficiency. The close correlation between scheduling redundancy and computation cost makes us decide to optimize both of them at the same time.

Algorithm 1. RL-Based Redundancy Scheduling Algorithm

Input: Sequence length N
Output: Policy parameter θ
1: Initialise θ arbitrarily
2: **for** each episode **do**
3:   **for** $i = 1$ to N **do**
4:     Choose action a_i from $\pi_\theta(s_i, a_i)$
5:     Take action a_i, observe r_i, s_{i+1}
6:   **end for**

7:   **for** $i = 1$ to N **do**
8:     $R_i = \sum_{i'=i}^{N} \eta^{i'-i} \cdot r_{i'}$
9:   **end for**
10:   $b = \sum_{i=1}^{N} \frac{R_i}{N}$
11:   **for** $i = 1$ to N **do**
12:     Update θ based on Equation 9
13:   **end for**
14: **end for**

Therefore, we defined utility U_i to measure the overall cost of task J_i. U_i is defined as follows:

$$U_i = S_i + \mu \cdot E_i \tag{3}$$

where μ is the computation cost coefficient.

In order to optimize multiple tasks in the system, we defined the optimization objective is to minimize the average utility of a set of tasks. It means that for a set of tasks $J = \{J_1, J_2, .., J_N\}$, our algorithm needs to find a set of variables $(k^1 = \{k_1^1, k_2^1, ..., k_N^1\}, k^2 = \{k_1^2, k_2^2, ..., k_N^2\}, p = \{p_1, p_2, ..., p_N\})$ to minimize the average utility of all tasks. As shown in Eq. 4:

$$\min_{(k^1, k^2, p)} \sum_{i=1}^{N} (C_i - A_i) + \mu \cdot \sum_{i=1}^{N} \sum_{\xi_i^j \in F_i} (f_i^j - s_i^j) + \sum_{\xi_i^j \in D_i} (C_i - s_i^j) \tag{4}$$

4 RL-Based Task Scheduling Algorithm

We propose our RL-based task scheduling algorithm in Algorithm 1. The intermittent network connection and unpredictable network bandwidth make it difficult for the ground scheduler to collect the system states of satellites to navigate the scheduling process. Without any prior information, it is impossible to leverage the traditional deep learning-based scheduling algorithm or statistical model to make scheduling decisions. Therefore, we determine to employ an RL-based algorithm to guide the scheduling process.

RL can effectively learn from experience in the case of such stateless transition probability models [10]. RL can be divided into two categories: policy iteration and value iteration. Among them, the policy iteration algorithm has been widely used in scheduling due to its strong convergence and better effect when facing continuous action space [15]. Therefore, we select the policy gradient algorithm, a representative algorithm of policy iteration, to jointly optimize the task execution time and satellite computation cost.

The elements in RL are defined as follows:

- **State** refers to the sum of all running sub-tasks and sub-tasks in the waiting queue divided by the total number of satellites with connection. Since each satellite only runs one sub-task at the same time, the state definition above can represent the current system load.

- **Action** contains three parameters. For task J_i, the action a_i contains (1) the first stage redundancy number k_i^1; (2) the secondary redundant scheduling time p_i; and (3) the secondary redundant number k_i^2. The action is defined as follows:

$$a_i = (k_i^1, p_i, k_i^2) \tag{5}$$

- **Reward** is represented by r_i in the following equation.

$$r_i = U_i - \bar{r} \tag{6}$$

where U_i represents the utility of task J_i and the $\bar{r}$ represents the historical average utility. By using differentiated reward instead of standard reward, it can reduce the error caused by different sequence lengths of different iterations [10].

The basic idea of the policy gradient algorithm is to use the observed rewards to learn policy parameters based on gradient descent. Consider a set of consecutively arriving tasks J. For task J_i, the scheduler collects the reward r_i obtained by using the action a_i at the state s_i. After a set of tasks are all completed, the parameter θ of the strategy $\pi_\theta(s_i, a_i)$ is updated based on the reward r_i, where θ represents the probability of selecting a_i at state s_i. The updated definition of θ is as follows:

$$\theta \leftarrow \theta + \alpha \cdot \sum_{i=1}^{N} \nabla_\theta log \pi_\theta(s_i, a_i) \cdot v_i \tag{7}$$

where α is the learning rate. $\nabla_\theta log \pi_\theta(s_i, a_i)$ represents the degree of deviation from the action a_i at the state s_i, and the v_i is used to measure the quality of the current action. In traditional policy gradient algorithms, the v_i is simply defined as the reward of the task J_i. However, not only the action but also newly arrived tasks bring changes to the cluster load. It makes the state unstable and causes the gradient variance to be too large. To solve this problem, the definition of v_i is modified as follows:

$$v_i = \sum_{i'=i}^{N} \eta^{i'-i} \cdot r_{i'} - b \tag{8}$$

where b is the baseline. By introducing the baseline, the gradient variance of the policy gradient algorithm can be effectively reduced [11]. Besides, the baseline can avoid unfairness to unselected strategies due to the random selection of strategies in the early stage. In this paper, the baseline is defined as the average value of all rewards in the current iteration. The introduction of η is to give a separate weight to the action, distinguish different actions, and enhance the reward and punishment effect of the algorithm. Therefore, the update of θ can be modified as follows:

$$\theta \leftarrow \theta + \alpha \cdot \sum_{i=1}^{N} \nabla_\theta log \pi_\theta(s_i, a_i) \cdot (\sum_{i'=i}^{N} \eta^{i'-i} \cdot r_{i'} - b) \tag{9}$$

Table 1. Dataset overview

	Device number	Response number
Dataset 1	804	47,950
Dataset 2	1,150	75,632

Table 2. Simulation parameters

Parameter	Value
Policy weight η	0.95
Learning rate α	0.01
Resource consumption coefficient μ	0.1
Sequence length N	100

5 Evaluation

5.1 Overview of Datasets

We use a previous mobile phone-based federated analytics dataset [23] to evaluate our algorithm in this study. We select the dataset for two reasons. First, there is no public dataset for such a new paradigm – on-satellite data analysis. Second, we find that mobile devices share similar characteristics with LEO satellites: (1) they might have intermittent connections with cell stations caused by out-of-power problem or frequent movement; (2) a lot of mobile devices will connect to a central server and then process specific on-device tasks. Concretely, in that system, mobile devices receive data analysis code from a central server, execute the code locally, and only send post-analysis results back to the server.

We use two sub-datasets as shown in Table 1. The task execution time distribution of the two selected datasets had large deviations. As shown in Fig. 2, dataset 1 has shorter task execution time, and its 80-percentile (p80) execution time is within 30,000 ms. Dataset 2 performs poorly – the p60 execution time exceeds 100,000 ms. The above observations reveal that there is a huge potential for optimizing task execution time.

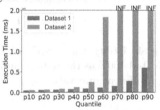

Fig. 2. Distribution of task execution time. P_n represents n-th percentile of the data.

5.2 Setup and Baselines

We use Ubuntu 18.04 system, Python 3.6, and TensorFlow 2.0 as the simulation environment. Parameters of our RL-based scheduling algorithm are shown in Table 2.

We select the following baselines as in [23].

- **OnceDispatch.** Dispatch sub-tasks with a fixed redundancy rate at the initial scheduling stage. This algorithm is adopted in traditional federated learning systems to facilitate model convergence [7,14].
- **IncrDispatch.** The IncrDispatch borrows the idea from the traditional MapReduce framework's redundant scheduling strategy [9]. At the beginning

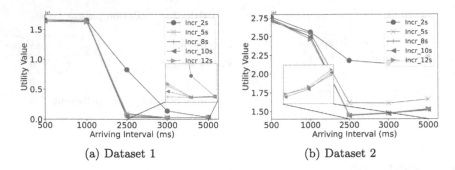

(a) Dataset 1   (b) Dataset 2

Fig. 3. Utility value with varying task arriving intervals using IncrDispatch. We selected 8-second as the wake-up interval for dataset 1 and dataset 2 because it performed well on different datasets and task arriving intervals.

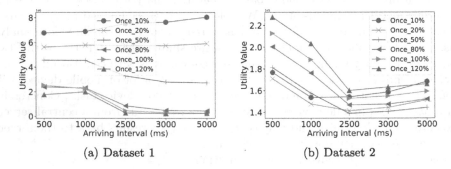

(a) Dataset 1   (b) Dataset 2

Fig. 4. Utility value with varying task arriving intervals using OnceDispatch. We selected 100% as the redundancy rate due to the well performance on different datasets and different intervals.

of a task, only a fixed number of sub-tasks are sent to the satellite. After a fixed wake-up interval, the scheduler adaptively sends sub-tasks to more satellites with the same number of in-process sub-tasks.

We first select diverse parameters for OnceDispatch and IncrDispatch and compare their utility values in Figs. 3 and 4. Task arriving interval affects system loads and computation cost on satellites. Thus, we select the p50 execution time (2,500 ms) of dataset 2 as the basic interval and expand it to more intervals. Based on the results, we select 100% as the redundancy rate for OnceDispatch and 8s as the wake-up interval for IncrDispatch, which perform well on different datasets and different intervals, for later comparison.

5.3   Scheduling Algorithm Performance

We present the performance of algorithms under varying task arriving intervals in this section. Figure 5 shows that the increase of task arriving interval leads to a reduction in average utility value. The utility value of our proposed algorithm is

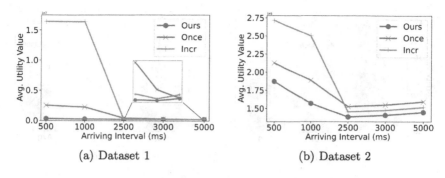

(a) Dataset 1   (b) Dataset 2

Fig. 5. Utility value comparison.

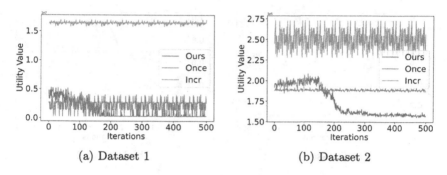

(a) Dataset 1   (b) Dataset 2

Fig. 6. Utility value comparison of each iteration.

lower than that of the baselines under different task arriving intervals. Notably, our algorithm shows better performance with a low task arriving interval.

We use task arriving interval λ of 1,500 ms for further analysis. Figure 6 shows the relationship between the average utility value and the iteration number when λ is 1,500 ms. At the initial stage, the utility value is high due to the existence of the stochastic policy. But as the number of iterations increases, the average utility value decreases and tends to keep stable after 200 iterations.

Figure 7 shows the maximum, minimum, and average task utility values. In summary, our proposed algorithm not only significantly reduces the average utility value, but also reduce the utility value in the worse case. This means that this algorithm also improves the usability of the overall system.

In addition, we also evaluate our algorithms for time-sensitive data analysis tasks. We assume that the p70 execution time is the time limit for receiving all results, that is, tasks that complete before the time limit are treated as success tasks, and vice versa. Figure 8 shows the average success rate of tasks. The main observation is that initially, the success rate is low due to the random behavior unknown to the system state. However, as the number of iterations increases, the success rate gradually increases through the adjustment based on the utility value.

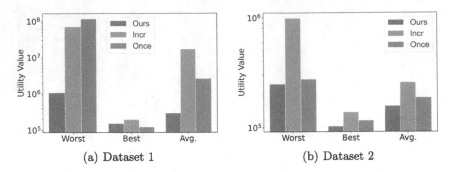

(a) Dataset 1   (b) Dataset 2

Fig. 7. Utility values when λ=1,500 for the worse, best and average cases.

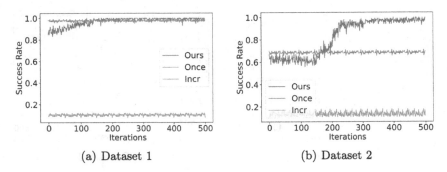

(a) Dataset 1   (b) Dataset 2

Fig. 8. Success rate comparison of each iteration. Task arriving interval $\lambda = 1,500$.

6   Conclusion

In this paper, we envisioned a new paradigm – on-satellite data analysis, and proposed an RL-based redundancy scheduling algorithm to mitigate the long tail phenomenon during the data analytic task. During the scheduling process, we used the policy gradient algorithm to adapt task completion time variation caused by intermittent network connectivity and dynamic in-space environment. The experimental results show that the proposed algorithm not only alleviates the long tail phenomenon, but also achieves joint optimization on task completion time and on-satellite computation cost.

References

1. Data in space: the exabytes from orbit. https://blog.westerndigital.com/data-in-space-exabytes-satellites-in-orbit/ (2021)
2. Starlink - wikipedia. https://en.wikipedia.org/wiki/Starlink (2022)
3. Ananthanarayanan, G., Ghodsi, A., Shenker, S., Stoica, I.: Effective straggler mitigation: attack of the clones. In: 10th USENIX Symposium on Networked Systems Design and Implementation (NSDI 13), pp. 185–198 (2013)

4. Ananthanarayanan, G., et al.: Reining in the outliers in {Map-Reduce} clusters using mantri. In: 9th USENIX Symposium on Operating Systems Design and Implementation (OSDI 10) (2010)
5. Aragon, B., Houborg, R., Tu, K., Fisher, J.B., McCabe, M.: Cubesats enable high spatiotemporal retrievals of crop-water use for precision agriculture. Remote Sens. **10**(12), 1867 (2018)
6. Barmpoutis, P., Papaioannou, P., Dimitropoulos, K., Grammalidis, N.: A review on early forest fire detection systems using optical remote sensing. Sensors **20**(22), 6442 (2020)
7. Bonawitz, K., et al.: Towards federated learning at scale: system design. Proc. Mach. Learn. Syst. **1**, 374–388 (2019)
8. Chen, Q., Liu, C., Xiao, Z.: Improving mapreduce performance using smart speculative execution strategy. IEEE Trans. Comput. **63**(4), 954–967 (2013)
9. Dean, J., Ghemawat, S.: Mapreduce: simplified data processing on large clusters. Commun. ACM **51**(1), 107–113 (2008)
10. Du, H., Zhang, S.: Hawkeye: adaptive straggler identification on heterogeneous spark cluster with reinforcement learning. IEEE Access **8**, 57822–57832 (2020)
11. Greensmith, E., Bartlett, P.L., Baxter, J.: Variance reduction techniques for gradient estimates in reinforcement learning. J. Mach. Learn. Res. **5**(9) (2004)
12. Huang, A., et al.: Starfl: hybrid federated learning architecture for smart urban computing. ACM Trans. Intell. Syst. Technol. (TIST) **12**(4), 1–23 (2021)
13. Joshi, G., Soljanin, E., Wornell, G.: Efficient replication of queued tasks for latency reduction in cloud systems. In: 2015 53rd Annual Allerton Conference on Communication, Control, and Computing (Allerton), pp. 107–114. IEEE (2015)
14. Learning, F.: Collaborative machine learning without centralized training data (2017)
15. Mao, H., Schwarzkopf, M., Venkatakrishnan, S.B., Meng, Z., Alizadeh, M.: Learning scheduling algorithms for data processing clusters. In: Proceedings of the ACM Special Interest Group on Data Communication, pp. 270–288 (2019)
16. Marta, S.: Planet Imagery Product Specifications. Planet Labs, San Francisco, p. 91 (2018)
17. McMahan, B., Moore, E., Ramage, D., Hampson, S., y Arcas, B.A.: Communication-efficient learning of deep networks from decentralized data. In: Artificial Intelligence and Statistics, pp. 1273–1282. PMLR (2017)
18. Razmi, N., Matthiesen, B., Dekorsy, A., Popovski, P.: Scheduling for ground-assisted federated learning in leo satellite constellations. arXiv preprint arXiv:2206.01952 (2022)
19. Vasisht, D., Shenoy, J., Chandra, R.: L2d2: low latency distributed downlink for LEO satellites. In: Proceedings of the 2021 ACM SIGCOMM 2021 Conference, pp. 151–164 (2021)
20. Xu, H., Lau, W.C.: Optimization for speculative execution in big data processing clusters. IEEE Trans. Parallel Distrib. Syst. **28**(2), 530–545 (2016)
21. Yadwadkar, N.J., Choi, W.: Proactive Straggler Avoidance Using Machine Learning. University of Berkeley, White paper (2012)
22. Zaharia, M., Konwinski, A., Joseph, A.D., Katz, R.H., Stoica, I.: Improving mapreduce performance in heterogeneous environments. In: Osdi, vol. 8, p. 7 (2008)
23. Zhang, L., Qiu, J., Wang, S., Xu, M.: Device-centric federated analytics at ease. arXiv preprint arXiv:2206.11491 (2022)

Optimizing Data Stream Throughput
for Real-Time Applications

Kusuma Amilineni[1], Po-Yen Hsu[2], Ching-Hsien Hsu[1,3]($\boxtimes$), Hojjat Baghban[1],
Wen-Thong Chang[1], and Nithin Melala Eshwarappa[3]

[1] Department of Computer Science and Information Engineering, Asia University, Taichung,
Taiwan
109121022@live.asia.edu.tw, hojjatbaghban.eed06g@nctu.edu.tw
[2] Department of Mechanical Engineering, National Chung Cheng University, Chiayi, Taiwan
poyhsu@alum.ccu.edu.tw
[3] Department of Computer Science and Information Engineering, National Chung Cheng
University, Chiayi, Taiwan
chh@cs.ccu.edu.tw, nithincse141@alum.ccu.edu.tw

Abstract. Many problems, like recommendation services, website log activities,
commit logs, and event sourcing services, are often very high volume and high
velocity as many activity messages are generated. Various cloud vendors offer
services for building message transport and processing pipelines. We present the
Apache Kafka optimization process for using Kafka as a messaging system in high
throughput and low latency systems. Experiments are conducted with various configurations for observing their effects on performance metrics. The performance,
Durability, and reliability trade-offs of Apache Kafka are presented for various
data rates, resource utilization, and configurations on how to utilize resources more
economically and choose the best Kafka configuration for use cases. This research
presents by tuning configuration parameters leveraged throughput by 19%.

Keywords: Apache Kafka · stream computing · throughput optimization ·
latency optimization · real-time application

1 Introduction

There are millions of information sources over the internet, and data is produced faster
and faster in both volume and velocity, so there is a need to adopt performance solutions
for message transport systems. Typically, the computations are arranged with many
components, often implementing push-pull or producer-consumer design patterns. An
example application of such Website activity tracking is a use case to rebuild a user
activity tracking pipeline as a set of real-time publish-subscribe feeds. In Web site activity
(views, searches) is published to topics. These feeds are available for subscription/pull for
various use cases, including real-time processing, monitoring, and loading into Hadoop
or offline data warehousing systems for offline processing and reporting [1]. In, Batch
processing data is collected, stored at the warehouse, and processed in large batches

C.-H. Hsu et al. (Eds.): DataCom 2022, LNCS 13864, pp. 410–417, 2023.
https://doi.org/10.1007/978-981-99-2233-8_29

at convenience [2]. Batch processing is used for historical data, where latencies are in minutes to hours. Historical data is used for complex analytics; it does not respond in real-time. Streaming data is continuous and is processed in small batches (KB) the most recent data is delivered with a delay in milliseconds to different consumers.

Apache Kafka is an event streaming platform [3]. It is an open source developed at LinkedIn to process views and search log data with delays of a few milliseconds, and its design features are high throughput, scalability, low latency, and persistence. Social networking site Line uses Apache Kafka; hundreds of billions of messages are procedure and consumed on various applications like threat detection and data analysis. Many studies on benchmarks measure Apache Kafka's performance and latency in different configuration parameters like the number of partitions, broker, and batch size. The new version of Apache Kafka supports batching and linger time. This study discusses the performance matrix by tuning linger time, ACK and batch-size parameters. It will help users to utilize resources more economically to enhance throughput and provide advice on setting configuration parameters.

2 Related Work

Jay kreps et al. [4] are the engineers who developed Kafka at LinkedIn; at that time, they used data feeds to show users who viewed their profiles and related searches. LinkedIn used Kafka as a persistent store for writing log records to topics. In [5] discussed that Kafka supports online and offline message subscriptions. Kafka's replication of log records solved the problem of losing records when servers failed and followers were up to date with the leader [6]. Dobbelaere et al. [7] compared Apache Kafka to RabbitMQ frameworks for standard features of both systems and highlighted the best use cases of Kafka and RabbitMQ. Kafka applications like retail data produced through order, sale, and shipment are considered stream data [8]; if data of the Kafka cluster needs to be processed and then written back to Kafka, using Kafka streams would be a good choice [9]. In Big data applications [10, 11], multiple partitions of Apache Kafka and Spark in stream processing provide better fault tolerance [12] when both can recover in parallel.

However, explicit social relation is not always available in recommender systems, and it, if exists, is always sparse and noisy [7]. Recent studies [10, 11] have shown the success of finding reliable implicit friends to make social recommendation. Ma et al. [10] propose to identify the top-k similar users of each user from the user-item rating matrix by calculating the Pearson Correlation Coefficient between them, when the explicit social relation is not available. Taheri et al. [11] build a novel recommendation model Hell- TrustSVD which uses Hellinger distance to extract implicit social relations in the user-item bipartite network.

In [10], Le Noac'H et al. evaluated several configurations and performance metrics of Apache Kafka for users to avoid bottlenecks and tune configurations for stream processing for big data applications. In [13], the authors evaluated the performances of Kafka on a large scale with different cluster configurations recommended by Confluent Kafka and Azure. Topic partitioning process for a given topic. Wu et al. [14] discussed the batch size impact on the performance of Kafka. They deployed Apache Kafka on docker tested relation batch size and latency, adding network failure and network delay. Using the ANN model, they predicted message loss with network delay, they proposed batch processing method in both excellent and poor network conditions, and experimental analysis showed improved throughput. H. Wu et al. [15] analyzed the structure and work-flow of Apache Kafka, the performance prediction matrix of cloud services by configuration parameters of the number of brokers, partitions in a topic, and batch size of messages.

Apache Kafka Producer API latency optimizations discussed by wiatr et al. [16], the performance test to measure Apache Kafka's impact on the system. Results show the impact of memory allocation on CPU usage, by lowering the memory can reduce CPU usage.

3 Overview

Apache Kafka is a data event streaming platform; its system architect is shown in Fig. 1. It is an open-source distributed system consisting of Kafka servers and client machines communicating over a TCP layer. Kafka System can be deployed on-premises, VMs, Containers, and cloud.

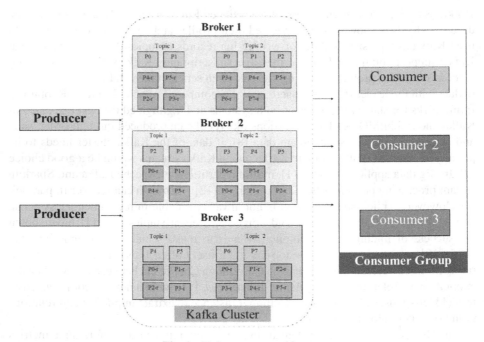

Fig. 1. Kafka system architecture

Topic 1 has six partitions for brokers 1, 2, 3 and their replicas. P0, P1, P2, P3, P4, and P5 are leader partitions, with two replicas of each partition, so if one of the brokers fails, replicas of other brokers will be elected as new leaders. Only leader partitions write/read messages with producer and consumer. Kafka partitions of the topic are load balanced over three brokers. Allows the producer to write messages in parallel.

In the above Kafka architecture, consumers belong to the same consumer group. Consumers split the work and fetch messages parallelly from different partitions from a subscribed topic. One consumer can consume from one or more partitions, but one partition is consumed by only a consumer of every consumer group. Consumer refers to offsets for current read messages.

4   Methodology for Performance Optimization

Producer Throughput
In the performance matrix, Producer throughput is the number of records delivered to the broker in each interval. In Apache Kafka, the Producer receives messages from the data source; the producer starts batching messages to send in a signal request. These batched messages go to the same partition. The topic must be created before sending messages to the cluster; the number of partitions for a topic is a crucial parameter for enhancing the throughput [15]. A producer can parallel send messages to multiple partitions; partitions are load-balanced on different brokers. We assume that enough messages are sent to the producer for batching. Before sending messages to leader partitions, the producer waits for messages to fill the batch as configured by default, batch. Size is 16 KB, where the batch size is the maximum size of bytes of each message batch sent before waiting out is reached, as shown in Fig. 2.

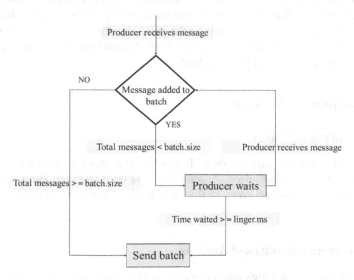

Fig. 2. Producer message batching flow

Linger. ms is the maximum time the producer waits to batch messages before sending the batch. By default, linger. ms is 0. It is essential to turn batch size and linger time parameters to increase producer batching to reach a maximum batch size; increasing linger waiting time can help producers fill the batch. Large batches can increase throughput and reduce the number of requests to the producer and CPU cycles on the broker; the trade-off is latency.

Algorithm 1: Producer message batching

Input: Message
Output: Messages are batched and sent to the broker
1.   **Begin**
2.   Producer receives message
3.   Messages were added to Batch
4.   **While** (Total messages >= Batch. Size or Time waited >= linger.ms)
                                      //waited for messages
5.   send the batch
6.   **End**
7.   **End**

The producer writes messages to the leader broker partition and waits for the broker to send an acknowledgement to know that messages are successfully written to brokers before sending the next messages/batch. Broker response time affects the producer throughput; acks is the parameter configuration that defines the number of brokers that need to respond before the producer sends the next batch. The newer version of Apache Kafka 3.0 later, by default, has acks = all, meaning the leader partition and its replicas need to acknowledge that message is written successfully. Acks = 1, only leader broker partition acknowledges and responds to the producer for every written request without waiting for followers' Responses. Acks = 0; the producer sends messages without waiting for acknowledgment from the broker.

5   Experimental Analysis

5.1   Experimental Settings

We run a performance matrix test on a MacOS M1 chip machine with 8 CPUs, 8 GB of RAM, and 256 GB of disk space. Apache Kafka is built from the latest version 3.1.0, Java runtime environment correto-11.0.15.9.1. Kafka cluster of 3 brokers using Kafka as service.

5.2   Experimental Results and Analysis

We study use cases with a high volume of data, with Kafka configuration parameters like batch size, and linger wait for varying record sizes and the number of records sent in a batch. Our topics with six partitions, a replication factor of 3, and data retention of 24 h. Apache Kafka performance matrix varies significantly depending on the message type, and the compute power of machines like CPU and memory. Apache Kafka producer configurations – default values, 16,384 is the default batch. Size, the latest version of Kafka supports acknowledgment acks = all by default, and linger.ms = 0.

5.2.1   Effect of Batch Size and Linger Wait to Throughput

The relation between batch size and linger wait to throughput. The exact number of messages are sent in different batch sizes with linger wait of default 0 and a delay of 30 ms, 60 ms, and 90 ms. In Fig. 3, we can observe that batching messages significantly increased the throughput; a little wait of a millisecond on moderate/high load helps to optimize throughput instead of sending single messages to the broker. Linger has a minimal impact with smaller batches. However, larger batch size with linger wait has high throughput while configuring linger wait 0 to 90 ms improves throughput by 19%.

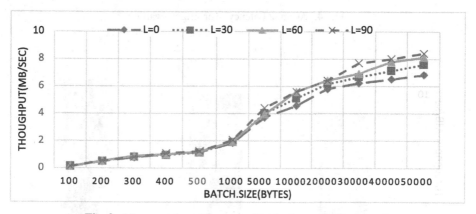

Fig. 3. Messages throughput over Batch sizes with Linger wait

5.2.2   Effect of Batch Size and Linger Wait to Latency

In Fig. 3 and Fig. 4, we observe batching and linger to optimize the throughput at the expense of latency. At linger.ms = 0 messages are sent as soon as they are received, less time wait to fill batch, then latency is less.

5.2.3   Effect of Acknowledgement on Throughput

In Fig. 5, we observe the relation between other acknowledgments and throughput. For messages of the same size, high throughput and low latency are achieved when producers do not wait for an acknowledgment. However, there is a greater chance of losing data in this case. More acknowledgments mean the producer must wait before sending messages. The fewer acks required by the producer, the higher the throughput; here trade-off is durability: acks = all with a replication factor of N and Min. in sync. Replicas M can tolerate N-M brokers going down for topic availability purposes.

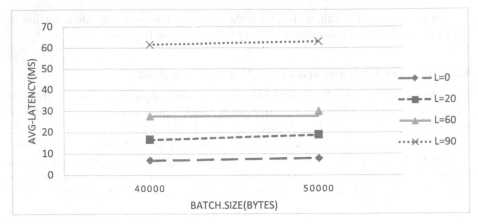

Fig. 4. Average Latency over lingers waiting

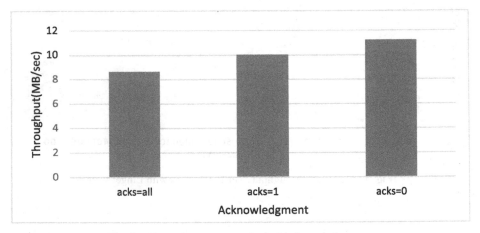

Fig. 5. Throughput compression of Acknowledgements

6 Conclusions

In this paper, we evaluated Apache Kafka performance matric for different configuration parameters on the producer side. By tuning the batch size and linger wait, overall throughput is increased by 19%. However, adding a long wait will affect the latency. Acknowledgment acks = all, wait for confirmation of broker and replicas, compromises on slight throughput but ensures availability and durability.

In future work, we will analyze more configuration parameters in Apache Kafka, study how to utilize resources more economically, and choose the best Kafka configuration for use cases.

References

1. Sagarkar, M., et al.: A Study of distributed event streaming & publish-subscribe systems
2. Das, T., et al.: Adaptive stream processing using dynamic batch sizing. In: Proceedings of the ACM Symposium on Cloud Computing (2014)
3. John, V., Liu, X.: A survey of distributed message broker queues. arXiv preprint arXiv:1704. 00411 (2017)
4. Goodhope, K., et al.: Building linkedin's real-time activity data pipeline. IEEE Data Eng. Bull. 35(2), 33–45 (2012)
5. Kreps, J., Narkhede, N., Rao, J.: Kafka: a distributed messaging system for log processing. In: Proceedings of the NetDB. vol. 11 (2011)
6. Wang, G., et al.: Building a replicated logging system with Apache Kafka. In: Proceedings of the VLDB Endowment, vol. 8, no. 12, pp. 1654–1655 (2015)
7. Dobbelaere, P., Esmaili, K.S.: Kafka versus RabbitMQ: a comparative study of two industry reference publish/subscribe implementations: industry paper. In: Proceedings of the 11th ACM International Conference on Distributed and Event-Based Systems (2017)
8. Hiraman, B.R.: A study of apache kafka in big data stream processing. In: 2018 International Conference on Information, Communication, Engineering and Technology (ICICET). IEEE (2018)
9. Langhi, S., Tommasini, R., Della Valle, E.: Extending kafka streams for complex event recognition. In: 2020 IEEE International Conference on Big Data (Big Data). IEEE (2020)
10. Le Noac'H, P., Costan, A., Bougé, L.: A performance evaluation of Apache Kafka in support of big data streaming applications. In: 2017 IEEE International Conference on Big Data (Big Data). IEEE (2017)
11. Tun, M.T., Nyaung, D.E., Phyu, M.P.: Performance evaluation of intrusion detection streaming transactions using apache kafka and spark streaming. In: 2019 International Conference on Advanced Information Technologies (ICAIT). IEEE (2019)
12. Ramalingam, G., Vaswani, K.: Fault tolerance via idempotence. In: Proceedings of the 40th Annual ACM SIGPLAN-SIGACT symposium on principles of programming languages (2013)
13. Raptis, T.P., Passarella, A.: On efficiently partitioning a topic in Apache Kafka. arXiv preprint arXiv:2205.09415 (2022)
14. Wu, H., et al.: A reactive batching strategy of apache kafka for reliable stream processing in real-time. In: 2020 IEEE 31st International Symposium on Software Reliability Engineering (ISSRE). IEEE (2020)
15. Wu, H., Shang, Z., Wolter, K.: Performance prediction for the Apache Kafka messaging system. In: 2019 IEEE 21st International Conference on High Performance Computing and Communications; IEEE 17th International Conference on Smart City; IEEE 5th International Conference on Data Science and Systems (HPCC/SmartCity/DSS). IEEE (2019)
16. Wiatr, R., Słota, R., Kitowski, J.: Optimizing Kafka for stream processing in latency sensitive systems. Procedia Comput. Sci. 136, 99–108 (2018)

Miscellaneous Topic of Big Data

MagicBatch: An Energy-Aware Scheduling Framework for DNN Inference on Heterogeneous Edge Servers in Space-Air-Ground Computation

Di Liu[1,2], Zimo Ma[1], Aolin Zhang[1], and Kuangyu Zheng[1,2(✉)]

[1] Department of Mathematics and Theories, Peng Cheng Laboratory, Shenzhen, China
[2] School of Electronic and Information Engineering, Beihang University, Beijing, China
{diliu,mazimo,aolin2000,zhengky}@buaa.edu.cn

Abstract. With the fast development of space-air-ground computing scenarios, large UAVs, airships or HAPS (high altitude platform station), and satellites, are in the trend to have more powerful computation resources (e.g., heterogeneous types of GPUs), and can act as edge servers in the air. They are increasingly used for a large number of deep neural networks (DNN) inference applications, such as disaster monitoring, remote sensing, and agriculture inspection. However, these edge servers in the air always have a very limited energy supply. Thus, how to reduce their energy consumption to extend their working hours, while meeting the delay requirements of DNN inference tasks becomes a very important demand.

In this paper, we propose MagicBatch, an energy-aware scheduling framework for DNN inference workloads on edge servers (with heterogeneous GPUs) in the air. MagicBatch is based on our key finding, that various GPUs can have different energy and latency performance under different DNN inference batch sizes. Thus, MagicBatch is designed in two phases: In the offline analysis phase, it analyzes the execution latency and energy consumption performance of different DNN inference tasks on heterogeneous GPUs; In the online scheduling phase, we propose a heuristic energy-aware scheduling algorithm (PSO-GA) to better allocate heterogeneous GPU computing resources to various inference tasks. Evaluation on our emulation testbed shows that MagicBatch can achieve more than 31.3% energy savings and 41.1% throughput improvement compared with the state-of-the-art methods.

Keywords: DNN inference · Heterogeneous GPUs · Energy-aware scheduling · Space-air-ground computation · Edge computing

1 Introduction

Witnessed the emerging Space Internet like Starlink, OneWeb, together with the increasing coverage and computing demands at remote areas, the space-air-

© The Author(s), under exclusive license to Springer Nature Singapore Pte Ltd. 2023
C.-H. Hsu et al. (Eds.): DataCom 2022, LNCS 13864, pp. 421–433, 2023.
https://doi.org/10.1007/978-981-99-2233-8_30

ground networks have received more attention. With the development of deep learning technology, a large number of DNN inference applications, such as disaster (e.g., flood, fire) monitoring, remote sensing, and agriculture inspection, etc., are deployed at the edge of the network. Most of them are computation-intensive and require sub-second-level short latency. Directly using the DNN models on mobile devices may fail to meet the latency requirements. To alleviate the latency bottleneck, a better solution is to use the emerging edge computing paradigm [3]. Large unmanned aerial vehicles (UAVs), airships, HAPS (High Altitude Platform Station), or satellites are having increasingly improved heterogeneous computation resources (e.g., different CPUs, GPUs, FPGAs, ASICs), and can be used as edge servers to provide extensive computing support for various DNN applications. However, for either UAVs, HARPs, or satellites, due to their very limited battery capacities, they are usually energy constrained.

For edge servers, the deployment of multiple heterogeneous GPUs are emerging, and is becoming a possible future trend. On one hand, new generations of GPU innovated quickly, and common edge servers always equipped with different generations and types of GPUs. On the other hand, parallel computing capabilities enable outdated types of GPUs to still speed up DNN inference tasks compared with mobile devices, and even have the advantage of cost-effectiveness. Thus, the heterogeneous characteristics of GPU clusters on edge servers are not unusual [5].

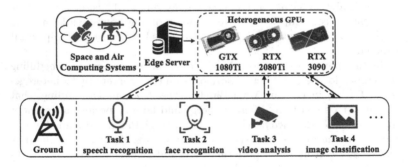

Fig. 1. Scenario: Ground devices submit various DNN tasks to the edge server in space or air with heterogeneous GPUs. (GPU types as GTX 1080Ti, RTX 2080Ti and RTX 3090, are merely heterogeneous examples we used in our emulation experiments)

Figure 1 shows a proposed working scenario of the edge servers in space-air-ground computation scenario. Ground devices send DNN inference requests to the edge server, and the edge server returns the results after completing the inference tasks on the heterogeneous GPUs. In order to make full use of parallel computing resources of GPUs, multiple DNN inference requests are usually combined into a batch for execution. Higher system throughput and GPU resource utilization can be achieved by increasing the batch size and processing more inference tasks in parallel. However, a large batch size results in a longer execution latency, which may violate the deadline of the tasks. There-fore, the scheduler needs to consider appropriate batch size selection based on the trade-off between throughput and execution latency. Batch size also affects the energy consumption of GPUs when executing DNN inference tasks. Unfor-tunately, existing works have not paid attention to the potential of scheduling various DNN inference tasks on heterogeneous GPUs to save energy.

In this paper, we propose MagicBatch, an energy-aware scheduling framework for DNN inference workloads on heterogeneous edge servers in space-air-ground computing scenarios. We first analyze the inference performance of several clas-sical DNN models on heterogeneous GPUs in detail. Then, a heuristic scheduling algorithm PSO-GA is designed to assign heterogeneous GPUs to various DNN inference tasks, thereby saving total energy consumption. Specifically, the con-tributions of this paper are as follows:

- We test and analyze the performance of various DNN inference tasks on some heterogeneous GPUs in detail, which confirm a key finding, that different GPUs could have different energy efficiencies and execution latencies, even running the same computation task. The analysis results are also used to predict the execution latency and energy consumption.
- We propose MagicBatch, a DNN inference tasks scheduling framework for heterogeneous edge servers. It leverages an energy-aware heuristic scheduling algorithm PSO-GA to reduce the energy consumption of edge servers while meeting the latency requirements of inference tasks.
- We evaluate the performance of MagicBatch through hardware experiments. The experimental results show that MagicBatch can significantly reduce the energy consumption of edge servers and improve the system throughput.

The rest of this paper is organized as follows. Section 2 surveys the related work. Section 3 identifies the latency and energy consumption performance char-acteristics of batching inference. Section 4 shows the design of MagicBatch. The performance evaluation of MagicBatch is conducted in Sect. 5. Finally, conclu-sions of this paper are provided in Sect. 6.

2   Related Work

Some existing works focus on the heterogeneity of GPU clusters [6,9,11]. HetPipe [11] can effectively train large DNN models by using virtual workers composed of multiple heterogeneous GPUs. Gavel [9] is a heterogeneous-aware GPU cluster scheduler, which supports higher average input job rates and lower average job completion time. BytePS [6] is a unified distributed DNN training acceleration system that achieves optimal communication efficiency in heterogeneous clusters. However, these works focus on DNN training tasks rather than inference tasks with higher latency requirements.

Some schedulers aim at balancing throughput and QoS [2,4] in DNN inference workloads. Ebird [2] enables the GPU side prefetching mechanism and elastic batch scheduling strategy to improve the responsiveness and throughput of deep learning services. Kalmia [4] adopts a preemption-based scheduling method to reduce the deadline violation rate of DNN inference tasks with heterogeneous QoS requirements and achieve high system throughput. However, these works do not consider the optimization of energy consumption.

The energy consumption of GPUs is considered in some studies [8,12]. BatchDVFS [8] combines batch size selection with DVFS to maximize throughput while meeting the power cap. EAIS [12] adaptively coordinates batching processing and DVFS according to fluctuating workloads to minimize energy consumption and meet the latency SLO. However, the heterogeneity of GPUs in edge servers has not been fully considered in these works.

3   Batch Performance Analysis

In this section, we introduce the motivation experiment, by measuring the throughput, execution latency, and energy consumption of three heterogeneous GPUs when they execute inference tasks of two DNN models in different batch sizes.

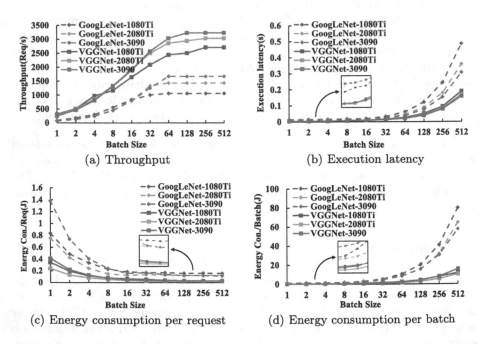

Fig. 2. Throughput, execution latency, and energy consumption curves of heterogeneous GPUs executing inference tasks of diverse DNN models.

Throughput: Figure 2(a) shows the relationship between throughput and batch size. It can be seen that the throughputs of all these GPUs with different CNN tasks fluctuate at a high level after a sharp increase when the batch size rises from 1 to 64. This is because the computing resources of GPUs have not been fully utilized when the batch size is small. At this stage, increasing the batch size enables the GPUs to execute more DNN inference tasks in parallel. When the workload of a batch exceeds the parallel processing capacity of the GPUs, the increase of the batch size cannot contribute to a higher throughput. Besides, we also find that GPUs with advanced architectures do not always perform better when executing different DNN inference tasks.

Execution Latency: Figure 2(b) indicates the variation of execution latency with batch size. Specifically, execution time is positively correlated with batch size. The reason is simple. Although the batching strategy enables the GPUs to process more inference tasks in parallel at a time, the increase in batch size leads to longer execution time for individual batches, resulting in higher latency of requests. Thus, larger batch sizes imply higher system throughput, while smaller batch sizes imply higher task responsiveness.

Energy Consumption: Figure 2(c) and 2(d) show the variation of energy consumption with batch size. It can be seen from 2(c) that the energy consumption for processing a single DNN inference task decreases with the increase of batch size, because parallel processing improves the effectiveness of GPU computing resources. Although a larger batch size may lead to higher execution power, the overall time to complete the same number of inference tasks decreases, so energy consumption can be reduced. Moreover, for both DNN tasks (VGGnet or GooglNet) as batch size increases, there are some crossing points (e.g., batch size 128 and 256) on the energy consumption between different types of GPUs (e.g., GPU 2080Ti and 3090), which means higher-end GPU (e.g. 3090) does not always have worse energy efficiency than lower-end ones (e.g. 2080Ti).

From the above analysis, it can be seen that heterogeneous GPUs have different characteristics in terms of throughput, latency, and energy consumption when executing DNN inference tasks. Besides, the performance of advanced GPUs is not always optimal. In this case, there is a lot of room for optimization in terms of energy consumption when scheduling different DNN inference tasks on heterogeneous GPUs.

4   MagicBatch Design

4.1   Overview

MagicBatch is an energy-aware scheduling framework for DNN inference tasks deployed on edge servers with heterogeneous GPU computing resources. Mobile devices continuously send inference requests to the edge server, while the server invokes MagicBatch to schedule the inference tasks to the appropriate GPU for execution, and sends the results back to each device. Figure 3 shows the overview of MagicBatch framework, which mainly consists of an offline analysis phase and an online scheduling phase.

In the offline analysis phase, MagicBatch measures and analyzes the performance of executing different inference tasks on multiple heterogeneous GPUs in

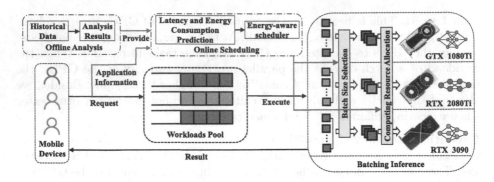

Fig. 3. Overview of MagicBatch framework.

different batch sizes, including throughput, execution latency, and energy consumption. The analysis results obtained in the offline analysis phase will be used in the online scheduling phase.

In the online scheduling phase, MagicBatch obtains application information of mobile devices (including the type of DNN models, task arrival rate, and task deadline) and assigns a task waiting queue for each device in the workloads pool. The inference requests of each device are added to their respective task queues and wait for execution. Then, MagicBatch predicts the latency and energy consumption for executing inference tasks in different batch sizes based on the results obtained from offline analysis phase (Sect. 4.2). A heuristic scheduling algorithm is designed to select batch size and allocate computing resources to minimize energy consumption while meeting delay requirements of tasks (Sect. 4.3).

4.2 Performance Prediction

We predict the latency and energy consumption of inference tasks according to the analysis results obtained in the offline analysis phase.

In the MagicBatch framework proposed in this paper, the inference requests of each device are first added to their respective task queues according to the order of arrival and then executed on the assigned GPU. Therefore, the latency of completing an inference request consists of two parts, the time spent waiting in the task queue and the time spent executing on the GPUs. Let $T_{request}$ represent the total latency, it can be expressed as:

$$T_{request} = T_{wait} + T_{execution} \tag{1}$$

where T_{wait} denotes the waiting latency. $T_{execution}$ can be obtained from the offline analysis phase.

The time to wait in the task queue consists of two parts: the time to wait for subsequent requests and the time to wait for the assigned GPU to be idle. Figure 4 shows the complete process of an inference request. Suppose that at

t_1, a new inference request is added to the task queue. In order to implement batching inference strategy, the request needs to wait for later requests. At t_2, the number of tasks reaches the pre-setting batch size, these tasks are combined into a batch. However, the new batch cannot be executed immediately, because the GPU allocated to it may be busy at this time (such as t_3). Until t_4, the GPU finishes processing the last batch. The new batch of tasks finishes waiting and starts to be executed. It should be noted that in practice, the processing speed of GPU devices is much greater than the task arrival rate of inference requests from mobile devices. Therefore, without loss of generality, the latency of waiting for the GPU to be idle is negligible.

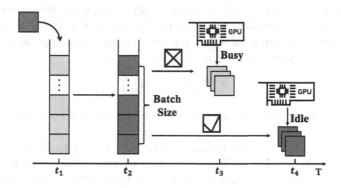

Fig. 4. The whole execution process of an inference request.

For each inference request in the same batch, the waiting time in the task queue is different, and the computation time on the GPU is the same. Therefore, as long as the first request in a batch does not exceed the upper latency limit, all tasks in the batch can be considered to meet the latency requirement. Let T_{wait}^{first} denotes the waiting time of the first arriving task, it can be expressed as:

$$T_{wait}^{first} = \frac{(B-1)}{r} \tag{2}$$

where r represents the task arrival rate.

All requests in a batch are executed in parallel on the GPU, so the energy consumption can be regarded as equal. Let $E_{request}$ represents the energy consumption for a request:

$$E_{request} = \frac{E_{batch}}{B} \tag{3}$$

where E_{batch} can be obtained from the offline analysis phase.

4.3 Scheduling Algorithm

We first describe the optimization problem to be solved, and then design a heuristic algorithm PSO-GA to find an approximate optimal solution to the problem.

(1) Problem formulation

Assume that the GPU cluster of the edge server consists of N types of heterogeneous GPUs, and the number of GPUs of each type is G_n ($1 \leqslant n \leqslant N$). The current number of mobile devices sending inference requests to the edge server is M, each device's requests are executed separately by the same GPU. The inference tasks of device m ($1 \leqslant m \leqslant M$) have the same task arrival rate r_m and deadline D_m. δ_n^m represents whether the inference tasks of m are executed on the n-type GPUs. If yes, $\delta_n^m = 1$ then otherwise $\delta_n^m = 0$. b_n^m denotes the optimal batch size for the inference tasks of m to process on the n-type GPUs. Without loss of generality, within a fixed duration τ, the system can be considered stable.

As can be seen from the previous discussion, execution latency and throughput increase monotonically with increasing batch size, while energy consumption does the opposite. Therefore, choosing the largest batch size that satisfies the latency requirement can guarantee minimum energy consumption at this time. The latency constraint can be expressed as:

$$T_{request}^{n,m} \leqslant D_m \tag{4}$$

where $T_{request}^{n,m}$ represents the latency of executing the inference task of device m on n-type GPUs.

From (4), we can get the optimal batch size b_n^m for the inference tasks of device m on n-type GPUs. Then, according to the offline analysis results, we can obtain the energy consumption of a single task when executing the tasks of device m on n-type GPUs under the batch size b_n^m, expressed in $E_{request}^{n,m}$. In a duration τ, the GPUs' total inference energy consumption E_τ is shown in (5):

$$E_\tau = \sum_{m=1}^{M} \sum_{n=1}^{N} \delta_n^m \cdot E_{request}^{n,m} \cdot r_m \cdot \tau \tag{5}$$

Now we can get an optimization problem (P) as the following form:

$$(P) : minE_\tau \tag{6}$$

$$s.t. : T_{request}^{n,m} \leqslant D_m \tag{7}$$

$$\sum_{n=1}^{N} \sum_{g=1}^{G_n} \delta_n^m = 1, \sum_{m=1}^{M} \delta_n^m \leqslant G_n \tag{8}$$

$$M \leqslant \sum_{n=1}^{N} G_n \tag{9}$$

$$1 \leqslant m \leqslant M, 1 \leqslant n \leqslant N \tag{10}$$

where constraint (6) represents minimizing the sum of the energy consumption of all GPUs on the edge server. Constraint (7) means that no matter which GPU the inference task is executed on, the deadline cannot be exceeded. Constraint (8) means that the tasks of each device can only be executed on one GPU, and the number of GPUs allocated cannot exceed the total number of GPUs of this type. Constraint (9) means that the number of mobile devices that the server can accept cannot exceed the total number of GPUs.

For this optimization problem, the complexity of solving this problem increases rapidly as the number of servers accepting tasks increases. Meanwhile, the utility function (6) is a nonlinear function, so it is essentially an NP-hard nonlinear integer optimization problem. Therefore, we design a heuristic algorithm that can provide a low-complexity near-optimal solution to this problem.

(2) PSO-GA algorithm

PSO algorithm and GA algorithm are two classical optimization algorithms. PSO algorithm is easy to fall into local optimum, while GA algorithm has poor local search ability, resulting in low search efficiency in the later stage. Therefore, we combine PSO with GA to find the optimal scheduling strategy from a global perspective. Specifically, we use a particle to represent a scheduling strategy, and then iterate through the update strategies of PSO and GA, respectively, until an approximate optimal solution is found.

In this paper, GPU scheduling is a discrete problem, so we need to design a suitable coding scheme to improve the search efficiency and the performance of the PSO-GA optimization algorithm. Inspired by [7], we adopt a device-GPU nesting strategy for coding. Each particle represents a candidate scheduling scheme. The $i-th$ particle can be represented as follows:

$$X_i = (x_{i1}, x_{i2}, ..., x_{iM})$$ (11)

where x_{im} denotes the tasks of device m are executed by an n-type GPU, which can be expressed as follows:

$$x_{im} = (n, m)_{im}$$ (12)

After getting the coding results, we design fitness functions to evaluate the performance of particles. MagicBatch aims at minimizing the energy consumption of GPUs on the edge server, so we directly use the energy consumption model as the fitness function of PSO-GA algorithm. It should be noted that the number of GPUs allocated cannot exceed the total number of such GPUs, so not every particle can represent a feasible solution in the problem space. Therefore, We first divide the particles into two categories according to whether the restrictions are met, and then design a fitness function for each category of particles. When the number of GPUs allocated does not exceed the total number of such GPUs, fitness is the energy consumption value of the scheduling method represented by the particle. Instead, the fitness value is set to infinity. The final function expression is shown in (13):

$$F(X_i) = \begin{cases} E^\tau(X_i), & if \, \forall n, G_n^{alloc} \leqslant G_n \\ \infty, & else \end{cases}$$ (13)

In each iteration, we first generate children through crossover and mutation of genetic algorithm. Then we select particles with good fitness to form a new group and update the speeds and positions of particles according to (14) and (15). With the continuous iteration of the PSO-GA algorithm, we can finally find the approximate optimal scheduling strategy of the GPUs.

$$v_i = v_i + c_1 \cdot rand() \cdot (pbest_i - x_i) + c_2 \cdot rand() \cdot (gbest_i - x_i) \qquad (14)$$

$$x_i = x_i + v_i \qquad (15)$$

5 Evaluation

5.1 Experiment Setup

In this section, we evaluate the performance of MagicBatch with real hardware testbed as emulation for the edge sever in the space or air. The arrival rate and deadline of tasks are randomly generated. We use VGGNet-16, GoogLeNet, ResNet-101, and DenseNet as models of inference tasks. The GPUs used in the experiment are Nvidia GTX 1080Ti, Nvidia RTX 2080Ti and Nvidia RTX 3090. The data set used in the experiment is CIFAR-10 and can be changed when necessary.

We evaluate the performance of MagicBatch from two aspects. First, we compare the proposed PSO-GA scheduling algorithm with the two baselines. (1) **FCFS:** The GPUs are numbered from small to large according to their advanced nature, and the idle GPUs with smaller numbers are allocated first. (2) **Greedy:** The tasks of each device are scheduled to be executed on the GPU with the lowest energy consumption among the currently idle GPUs.

Then, we compare MagicBatch with state-of-the-art baseline **TensorFlow Serving** (TF-Serving). We implement the scheduling policy in the official guide of TF-Serving [10], where batch size is a constant. We set it as 32, which is recommended in many papers [1,2,4]. When the number of tasks in the queue is equal to the target batch size, these tasks will be combined into a batch for execution. In addition, the scheduler will wait at most 30ms, otherwise, even if the number of tasks in the queue is insufficient, the existing tasks will be processed.

5.2 Effectiveness of MagicBatch

(1) Scheduling algorithm performance

Figure 5(a) shows the energy consumption performance of PSO-GA scheduling algorithm finally used for MagicBatch and other baselines. With the increase of the number of tasks, the energy consumption is increasing for all algorithms. PSO-GA algorithm maintains the lowest energy consumption. This is because

FCFS algorithm does not consider the difference in energy consumption of heterogeneous GPUs, resulting in high energy consumption. Greedy algorithm allocates the current task to the GPU that consumes the least energy during execution. However, this allocation method is not comprehensive. For a simple example, suppose there are two tasks task1 and task2. The optimal energy consumption for them to execute on GPU1 and GPU2 is 100 J, 110 J and 50 J, 200 J respectively. For the greedy algorithm, the first task 1 is placed on the GPU1 with the lowest energy consumption, and the second task 2 can only be placed on the GPU2, so the total energy consumption is 300 J. Compared with these baselines, the PSO-GA algorithm can consider the problem from a global perspective. Although task 1 is not placed on GPU1, task 2 saves more energy on GPU1. As the number of tasks increases, the situation becomes more complex, but such scheduling algorithm can minimize the overall energy consumption.

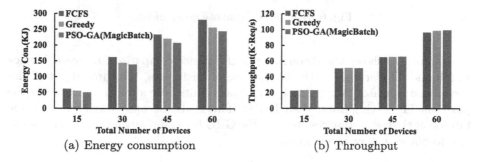

(a) Energy consumption   (b) Throughput

Fig. 5. Performance comparison of different scheduling algorithms. PSO-GA is the scheduling algorithm used by our MagicBatch framework.

Figure 5(b) shows the throughput performance of scheduling algorithms. With the increase of access customers, the throughput of the server also increases. It should be noted that the optimization target of PSO-GA algorithm is total energy consumption. Therefore, the throughput may decrease slightly. But experimental results show that our scheduling algorithm can still achieve similar results with the other two scheduling algorithms, which shows that our scheduling algorithm is effective.

(2) Overall performance

Figure 6(a) shows the performance comparison of MagicBatch and TF-Serving in terms of energy consumption. Similarly, with the increase of the number of tasks, the energy consumption of the GPU cluster is also increasing. The energy consumption is always lower when MagicBatch is adopted than TF-Serving is adopted (the optimization is more than 31.3%), which reflects the advantages of the batching strategy. MagicBatch can select the optimal batch size according to the arrival rate and deadline of tasks in the scheduling process, and TF-Serving always maintains a fixed batch size. However, the batch size set in the initial stage is usually conservative, which leads to the fact that the parallel processing capacity of GPU is not fully utilized in the actual operation process, resulting in higher energy consumption.

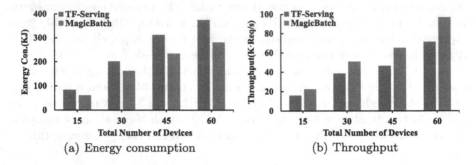

(a) Energy consumption   (b) Throughput

Fig. 6. Overall performance comparison.

Figure 6(b) shows the throughput performance comparison between Magic-Batch and TF-Serving. With the increase of customers, the throughput of the server also increases. MagicBatch can always contribute a much higher throughput than TF-Serving (more than 41.1%). This is also because MagicBatch makes full use of the computing resources of the GPU by adaptively adjusting the batch size to obtain higher throughput.

6   Conclusion

More and more DNN applications are deployed on the heterogeneous edge servers in the space-air-ground networks. It is a significant challenge to energy-efficient schedule various DNN inference tasks on the GPU clusters. In this paper, we propose an energy-aware scheduling framework MagicBatch for DNN inference on heterogeneous edge servers. We model the energy consumption optimization problem of GPU clusters as an integer linear programming problem and propose a heuristic scheduling algorithm PSO-GA to allocate appropriate GPU computing resources for inference tasks. The experimental results show that MagicBatch can achieve more than 31.3% energy savings and 41.1% throughput improvement compared with existing methods.

References

1. Crankshaw, D., Wang, X., Zhou, G., Franklin, M.J., Gonzalez, J.E., Stoica, I.: Clipper: a low-latency online prediction serving system. In: 14th USENIX NSDI, pp. 613–627 (2017)
2. Cui, W., Wei, M., Chen, Q., Tang, X., Leng, J., Li, L., Guo, M.: Ebird: elastic batch for improving responsiveness and throughput of deep learning services. In: 37th ICCD, pp. 497–505. IEEE (2019)

3. Dinh, H.T., Lee, C., Niyato, D., Wang, P.: A survey of mobile cloud computing: architecture, applications, and approaches. Wirel. Commun. Mob. Comput. **13**(18), 1587–1611 (2013)
4. Fu, Z., Ren, J., Zhang, D., Zhou, Y., Zhang, Y.: Kalmia: a heterogeneous QoS-aware scheduling framework for DNN tasks on edge servers. In: IEEE INFOCOM 2022, pp. 780–789. IEEE (2022)
5. Jiang, J., Cui, B., Zhang, C., Yu, L.: Heterogeneity-aware distributed parameter servers. In: Proceedings of the 2017 ACM International Conference on Management of Data, pp. 463–478 (2017)
6. Jiang, Y., Zhu, Y., Lan, C., Yi, B., Cui, Y., Guo, C.: A unified architecture for accelerating distributed DNN training in heterogeneous GPU/CPU clusters. In: 14th USENIX OSDI, pp. 463–479 (2020)
7. Lin, B., Huang, Y., Zhang, J., Hu, J., Chen, X., Li, J.: Cost-driven off-loading for DNN-based applications over cloud, edge, and end devices. IEEE Trans. Industr. Inf. **16**(8), 5456–5466 (2019)
8. Nabavinejad, S.M., Reda, S., Ebrahimi, M.: Coordinated batching and DVFS for DNN inference on GPU accelerators. IEEE Trans. Parallel Distrib. Syst. **33**(10), 2496–2508 (2022)
9. Narayanan, D., Santhanam, K., Kazhamiaka, F., Phanishayee, A., Zaharia, M.: Heterogeneity-aware cluster scheduling policies for deep learning workloads. In: 14th USENIX OSDI 2020, pp. 481–498 (2020)
10. Olston, C., et al.: TensorFlow-serving: flexible, high-performance ML serving. arXiv preprint arXiv:1712.06139 (2017)
11. Park, J.H., et al.: HetPipe: enabling large DNN training on (Whimpy) heterogeneous GPU Clusters through integration of pipelined model parallelism and data parallelism. In: USENIX ATC, pp. 307–321 (2020)
12. Yao, C., Liu, W., Tang, W., Hu, S.: EAIS: energy-aware adaptive scheduling for CNN inference on high-performance GPUs. Futur. Gener. Comput. Syst. **130**, 253–268 (2022)

Understanding Syntax Errors in C Sharp Using Game-Based Techniques at Tertiary Level

Ravishek Raj and Neeraj Anand Sharma[✉]

Department of Computer Science and Mathematics, School of Science and Technology,
The University of Fiji, Lautoka, Fiji
20180306@student.unifiji.ac.fj, neerajs@unifiji.ac.fj

Abstract. Programming is one of the most popular and demanding courses in universities around the world for students to build a strong foundation for their future in the field of computer science. Unlike other subjects, computer science is more of a practical field than a theoretical one, which requires practical experience to learn rather than theoretical knowledge, which can be forgotten if the teachings are not put into practice by students. When new students enroll in a programming course for the first time, about half of the students pass the course on the first try, while most of the students that pass obtain the minimum grade for passing the course. This is because students find it hard to cope with programming with limited guidance in a short period of time, whereas not all students can get lecturers to help when they get stuck on an error while learning to code. The purpose of this study is to see if there is a need for a strategy to help students new to programming learn about and identify common errors in C-sharp programming and improve their coding abilities using a game-based learning application. The study will also discuss which type of game application will be the most effective in gaining the interest of students, allowing them to actively use the application to improve their experience in coding while outlining a rough idea of what a game-based learning application should contain for others to use as a guide to help in their research.

Keywords: Code Review · Game-Based Learning · Gamification · Introductory Programming · Syntax Errors

1 Introduction

Computer science is a growing field now more than ever in these times of technological advancements where computers and computer systems are used in every field, from rocket science to agriculture [1] and garbage collection services [2], as the use of computers and applications available that were created through programming has helped make jobs in other fields more efficient, organized, safer, and easier to carry out daily activities. For the creation of an application to make jobs and people's lives easier or even more fun, an application requires the use of programming languages to code and structure the application line by line so it can function properly. Over the years, more advanced and complex computer systems and applications have been developed compared to a decade ago, and as the system gets more complex to design, so does the coding

© The Author(s), under exclusive license to Springer Nature Singapore Pte Ltd. 2023
C.-H. Hsu et al. (Eds.): DataCom 2022, LNCS 13864, pp. 434–450, 2023.
https://doi.org/10.1007/978-981-99-2233-8_31

aspect too, where the code can go from a few tens of lines to tens of thousands of lines of code, and in bigger and more advanced applications, can contain millions of lines of code to run an application system correctly. For example, Google's system uses more than 2 billion lines of code to work correctly, while only the browser application for Google Chrome uses around six to seven million lines of code to access the larger part of the system [3]. The number of lines of code increases daily as Google is constantly trying to make its applications easier to use and have a wide variety of functions.

With the advancement of computer applications and systems, the process of creating simple applications and websites has become easier than what was required a couple of years ago. Compared to before, information websites, which required days of coding and designing, can be made in a couple of hours with the help of applications such as WordPress, where all the code required to build an information or e-commerce website is available within the applications in the form of plug-ins and the users are only required to assign the information or drag and drop the function into an already built template [4]. Using plug-ins can be easy to create simple websites and applications, but it is not feasible to use them to build complex applications for advanced job settings, such as using the internet of things in monitoring systems in hospitals, which require multiple systems to work in synchronicity and need to be connected by manual-code to avoid errors. Thus, manual coding to create applications and websites is preferred as it allows more complex applications to be developed and can be fine-tuned however the user desires.

Computer science courses are one of the most versatile courses available at universities, where students taking double majors or minors are required to have some form of computer-based knowledge to further their studies. This is especially true for commerce students, and depending on the university, computer-based courses could take up to half of the courses available at a university, leading to most students enrolling in computer-related courses. Depending on the university and the structure of its programs, some majors will require students to enroll in introductory programming courses before they can graduate or further their studies. Programming courses are not the easiest courses to do as they contain complex code, commands, and logic that need to be structured properly to give a proper and correct result. Without prior proper knowledge and understanding of programming, some students tend to drop out of the course midway or fail on their first try at programming. Of those who pass these courses on the first try, the majority have their grades at the lowest possible passing grade. Some of the common reasons for low grades, dropouts, and failures are because students are not able to understand coding logic; correct placement of "symbols, brackets, and operators"; misspelling; and assignment of values to variables, which are common errors that occur when coding. To reduce the risk of dropping out, failure rate, and low grades in introductory programming courses, a strategy or application that helps students understand programming language and common errors made while coding before enrolling in programming courses, as well as help students better identify errors in the code while reducing the error rate while coding, must be implemented.

The key focus of this study is to develop and try to research and implement a Game-based Learning (GBL) application where, firstly, new or pre-university students can interact to understand the C-sharp programming language and identify if they can cope with programming, thereby reducing dropout and failure rates in introductory programming courses and deciding whether to enroll in the course or not. Secondly, those programming students enrolled in introductory programming courses can better understand programming and some of the common errors made in the coding process. And finally, students can better identify errors in codes and improve their coding ability while reducing the rate of errors when coding. The paper includes the following sections, Sect. 2 discusses some of the literature in this area, Sect. 3 discusses the methodology used in this research, Sect. 4 discusses statical data for game-based learning improvements on students learning abilities, Sect. 5 highlights on the game application design and concept, Sect. 6 discusses some ways GBL can be applicable to teaching students, Sect. 7 introduces some of the limitations identifies in this research, Sect. 8 includes discussion, and finally Sect. 9 concludes the paper.

2 Literature Review

2.1 Programming Trends and Issues

One of the major issues which are frustrating for new programming students in universities nowadays is missing and misplaced symbols in the code while programming or logical errors in the code during the programming process. Most universities today usually elect the C programming language, C-sharp or C++, to teach new students coding. C programming is more highly preferred as C programming is a more "procedure-oriented low-level programming language which can be broken down into functions and can be used in both application development and system development, which other languages such as Java cannot" [5]. Students usually think programming courses are the most difficult to cope with, as they usually have the largest dropout rates compared to other computer-based units offered by universities. This is because most students are unable to cope with a new type of information called coding languages, which has a lot of rules associated with it and can get confusing at times [6].

2.2 Introductory Programming Students' Failure and Dropout Statistics

Programming is not the easiest course in computer science courses, but it is also not the hardest. As long as students have a basic understanding of mathematics and logic, they can easily pass the unit without having high school knowledge of computer science. Having the largest enrollment rate in some universities compared to other courses also leads to a large drop-out and failure rate due to a lack of understanding of introductory programming courses, especially for students who had limited contact with computers before enrolling in a computer science course. The most recent study carried out in 2018 through 2019 called "Failure rates in introductory programming: 12 years later" by Jens Bennedsen et al., did a comparison of the failure rates of students in programming courses from 33% in 2007 to the current failure rates in 2019. It was discovered that only around 78% of students complete the introductory programming course, with a failure and dropout rate of 28% in developed countries [7], while the dropout and failure rates in developing countries are as high as 50% [8, 9].

2.3   Students and Programming Issues

Over the years, multiple computer science researchers and developers have tried to create applications, strategies, and algorithms to help in identifying problems in the code and code correction software, but looking for the error is still best when the programmer does it themselves to learn from their mistakes. Not all students enrolling into computer science and programming course have prior computer science knowledge as there are times students from other subject fields enrolls into programming courses, when a student starts university in an undergraduate level, they usually receive a maximum of four courses per semester with 20 h per week for lecture or 5 h per course during a week [10], since programming is more of a practical course than theory it requires more guidance for new students and most of the time these students are not able to keep up with the pace of the teaching as new information on the coding language is taught weekly before moving to a new concept and one lecturer for a class of usually 30 students or more is unable to point out every student mistakes individually and guide them in the five hours they have together, this usually leads to students dropping out of the course mid-way or failure, which leads to students to redo the course again when available as Introductory courses are usually compulsory. The technical issue for programming students is programming concepts [11], such as placement of code and symbols, as well as defining terms that require time to understand with guidance from someone or an application that can help the students put the concept into practice.

2.4   What Aspect Would Reduce Dropout and Failure Rate?

Multiple studies conducted by researchers in various situations [12–14] found that games and quizzes (Game-Based Learning) is the most effective way to teach students something new other than one-on-one guidance sessions by lecturers to help new programming students with little to no experience in coding better understand coding and some of the simple mistakes made during writing code. The main focus of this study is to find out what can be done to allow new programming students to properly understand programming languages before they withdraw from the course mid-way or before they try to start a programming course without any experience while improving their coding skills and error identification ability during coding.

2.5   Similar Research Done

A similar and most recent research study done to develop a quiz-type game to allow engineering students to identify errors in code via a code review process was by Baris Ardic et al. [12]. In the study, the author created a serious game to help students improve their code review abilities. The application created was too confusing for the students to use and lacked an introduction for the application inside the game for users to understand its functions. Another similar paper using the same logic as Guimaraes [15] discusses the gamification of the code review process, where users try to find errors in a code in an already defined array as a group. The application and process lacked a game element when mentioned as a gamification process, resulting in its shortcomings. Other similar studies that use error identification using code review include "Modern Code Review"

[16], an early antipattern library to detect errors in a code [17]. Currently, there is no better strategy or software available today that can help students identify errors in code than the code review process.

2.6 Game-Based Learning and Gamification

Over the years, there have been various studies carried out on game-based learning and gamification, mostly literature-based with limited experimental and application studies carried out on C-sharp game-based learning. Krenare Pireva Nuci et al. [18], in 2021, carried out a study for a game-based digital quiz to improve students' learning during the COVID-19 pandemic. The results showed an increase in the learning curve of 73% compared to 57.5% for regular teaching methods. The outcome of the study proved that GBL increases students' learning frequency.

2.7 Other GBL Strategies for Increasing Students' Performance

There have been some alternative strategies suggested by some researchers and authors to improve students' knowledge of programming and other subjects so that the number of students that drop off from the course halfway is reduced while also decreasing the failure rate in an introductory unit in universities. Rodrigo Pessoa Medeiros et al. [19] conducted a review of a hundred papers to create an understanding of "introductory programming related issues" and formulated two issues that impact students in introductory programming courses; one "programming related skills," which is the problem-solving skills of the students; and two "general education skills," which are the students' critical thinking ability to analyze and interpret a problem. Ching-Huei Chen et al. [20] tried to implement a strategy of "student-generated questioning" where students in-depth go over a concept during class before moving on with the lecture, and the results were that students showed better performance in their subjects. There are many strategies stated by researchers to improve students' performance in introductory programming [8], but not all are feasible.

2.8 Positive Effects of Video Games

Video games are usually seen as a form of entertainment [21] for individuals and are usually seen by some to have a negative impact [22] on a student's performance. Too much gaming can have a negative effect on a student's mind and mental health when it becomes addictive, but moderate usage and the correct combination of video games can have a positive effect on a student's academic performance [23]. Over the years, some researchers have seen the benefits of games on a student's ability to make better judgments in a critical moment. Some of the positive impacts' researchers observed from students were "better cognitive abilities; better multi-tasking ability; improved problem-solving skills and logic; fast and accurate decision-making abilities; better observation skills and memory of conceptual knowledge." These greatly affected the student's ability to learn positively [24–26].

3 Methodology

The focus of the study was on data pertaining to game-based learning and programming languages in the education system. Information, data, and literature that fell into the categories of these two topics were carefully researched to keep the study's scope within a limited field. The primary sources of information for this study were authentic conference papers found online in pdf format from these and other credible platforms, as well as online credible database libraries such as IEEE Xplore, Google Scholar, and the Association for Computing Machinery digital library. The information will be gathered using a qualitative approach via a literature search of related topics targeting reviews, documents, reports, conferences, and journals related to the field of computer science programming and learning with games and quiz applications. This is a topic that has had limited experimental studies conducted and is mostly covered in literature reviews. Some of the information gathered will come from former programming students' experiences and personal experiences they personally experienced when students were first introduced to the programming courses. The data will be analysed by looking at the similarities between each author's methods and the results they came to in their respective studies. The information gathered will be from 2017 to 2022, but some information that predates 2017 will be used, such as historical and factual information that did not change over time. This study will concentrate on errors in coding made by students' inexperience with misspellings, missing and misplaced symbols, and logic errors during the coding process, as well as aspects used in GBL that improve students' abilities. The study will first examine similar studies to determine what type of application would be best for teaching students about programming errors and then design a prototype application from the data gathered and understood from past literature.

4 Evaluation Data

According to a survey conducted on teachers who used game-based learning techniques on students, 81% of the teachers responded that they felt students were more actively involved in the interactive session, 65% of the teachers stated that they noticed that some students' social skills improved during GBL sessions, and 68% of the teachers felt that the students had developed and improved their problem-solving skills [29].

Using GBL on a 19-year-old student from the Massachusetts Institute of Technology in 2010 showed that the student retained around 90% of what he had learned, and GBL increased the student's theoretical knowledge by about 11% and boosted the student's self-confidence by 20% over the short period the study was conducted [29, 30]. The figure below shows four tests conducted by Krenare Pireva Nuci et al. in 2021 for regular teaching methods vs. quiz-based learning methods [18] (Figs. 1 and 2):

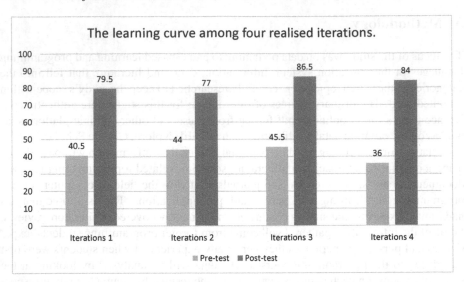

Fig. 1. Tests carried out on Traditional learning vs GBL

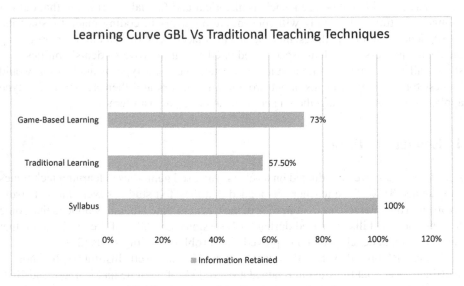

Fig. 2. Average of the four tests conducted

It was observed that 80% of students prefer game-based learning techniques over traditional teaching methods for learning in schools [27, 28]. During the COVID-19 pandemic, two groups of students were taught using traditional teaching methods and GBL. The results showed an increase in the learning curve of 73% compared to 57.5% for regular teaching methods. The outcome of the study proved that GBL increases students' learning frequency by 15.5% seen in the tests compared to traditional teaching methods [18] (Fig. 3).

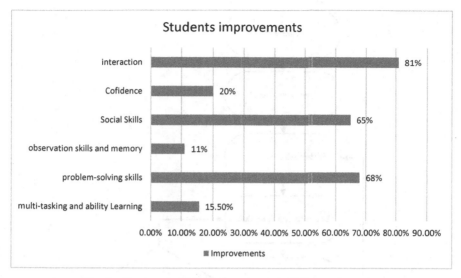

Fig. 3. How much GBL improved certain abilities of students

5 Game Application Design and Concept

The GBL application will target students aiming to join an introductory programming unit after high school. The programming language used will be C-sharp, and the first half of the game will contain a brief tutorial for the introduction of the application and programming concepts to get the user used to coding terms and functions, while the second half will be able to put what they have learned in the tutorial into actual practice (Fig. 4).

5.1 Game Content

To allow new programming students to learn coding and its concepts and be able to identify errors in coding while improving their skills at the same time, the game application needs to be divided into two main sections. First, an introduction to the C-sharp coding language; concepts, logic, and errors related to the programming language, which will be the tutorial section of the GBL application; second, the quiz section, where the student can test out the tutorial information in practical experience. Before the start of each new concept in C-sharp programming, the tutorial will give the students what they need to know and emphasize the errors commonly made while coding. When the tutorial is finished, the application will start asking the user questions related to programming and related content, where students will have to answer the current question to continue. If the students are stuck, they can press the hint button to find what's needed to be done or refer to the tutorial to get an idea of the correct solution. If students are still unsure, they can skip the question or reconsider their decision to continue coding (Fig. 5).

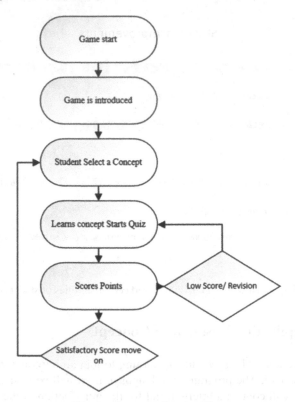

Fig. 4. Game Application Flow

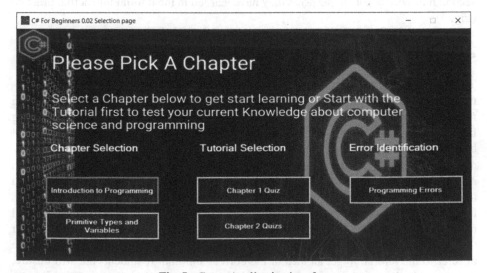

Fig. 5. Game Application interface

5.2 Gaining Student's Interest

It is very easy for students to lose interest in a game if it's not very interesting to them or not fun. The students may not want to use the application to make the game more fun and not just informative. Adding a scoring system will be most effective, as this will allow students to be more competitive with each other and challenge their friends. The way the points system will work, students will have five tries on each question on the quiz, and the number of tries remaining will be the points they score on each question. Using a hint will result in a minus one point. The sum of points in one concept learned will be the final score and a grade will be given depending on the score to encourage students or give them a recommendation.

5.3 Game Coding

The coding does not need to be complex, especially for the quiz section, as simple operators such as IF and IF ELSE can be used to determine the solution by answering the question in a text box. A multiple-choice type quiz is not efficient in helping students test their practical knowledge; it is most effective in testing conceptual knowledge. Open-answer questions with only possible solutions available would be the most effective, where students have to give solutions from the questions provided as coding follows extremely strict laws where misuse of an upper-case letter in a predefined word or value and lower-case definition would result in an error in the code example.

Int num1 = 5;
Int num2 = 6;
Txt1.text = Num1 * Num2; // the correct way to write this would be "Txt1.text = num1 * num2;"
Num1 is not the same as num1 as n is a capital letter, this error would result in the code not running properly
with errors.

For the solution to be validated in the game application, students need to write the correct solution precisely
as written in the actual code before they continue or receive a score.

```
private void btnConfirmS1_Click(object sender, EventArgs e)
        {
                string SE1 = "int score:";


                if (txtS1.Text == SE1)
                {
                    txtS1.Text = "Correct";
                }
                else
                {
                    txtS1.Text = "Incorrect";
                }
        }
```

The score from the quiz will be calculated using the IF statement while the quiz is displayed using the Switch
and Case Statement and the score will be displayed in a message box at the end of the quiz.

```
public Form3Chapter1Quiz()
        {
                InitializeComponent();
                askQuestion(questionNumber);
                    // specifying the number of questions to display
                totalQuestions = 10;
        }

        private void CheckAnswerEvent(object sender, EventArgs e)
        {
                // Program checks if the input is correct and adds plus 1 to
the score
                var senderObject = (Button)sender;
```

```
        int buttonTag = Convert.ToInt32(senderObject.Tag);

        if (buttonTag == correctAnswer)
        {
            score++;
        }

        if (questionNumber == totalQuestions)
        {
            // work out the percentage

            percentage = (int)Math.Round((double)(score * 100) /
            totalQuestions);
            // displays the percentage of questions got right in the
quiz
            MessageBox.Show(
                "Chapter 1 Quiz Ended!" + Environment.NewLine +
                "You have answered " + score + " questions correctly."
+ Environment.NewLine +
                "Your total percentage is " + percentage + "%" + Envi-
ronment.NewLine +
                "Click OK to play again or go back to the slides to
revise");
            score = 0;
            questionNumber = 0;
            askQuestion(questionNumber);
        }

    questionNumber++;
    askQuestion(questionNumber);
    }
            // displays the questions
    private void askQuestion(int qnum)

    {

        switch (qnum)
        {
            case 1:
                // Question in image form

                pictureBox3.Image = Properties.Resources.Chapter2Quiz1;
                btnA.Text = "A";
                btnB.Text = "B";
                btnC.Text = "C";
                btnD.Text = "D";
                // Specifying correct answer using tag value on number
                correctAnswer = 1;

                break;
            // next question
```

6 Practicable Use of GBL in Programming

There are many variations of GBL "student-teacher interactive sessions such as quizzes, questions and answer sessions, tests, and tutorials on applications using multiple choice, fill in the blanks, selections, sentence arrangements using drag and drop as well as precision answers input," depending on the major, some options are more preferred by students and some options are more effective for students according to their course and learning style.

Students new to programming courses usually opt for multiple-choice, fill-in-the-blanks type quizzes as they are provided with possible solutions, but these types of GBL are more effective for conceptual and theoretical knowledge than for simple explanation type information.

Students who have completed programming courses or are redoing programming courses know the selections and sentence arrangements type quizzes and questions are more important as understanding where the code goes and how it is arranged affects the outcome of the application.

Students who have completed their programming courses or are studying at a higher level know that the type of questions and quizzes that are most helpful when doing programming are the precision answers quizzes, where the user has to enter information in the correct decimal, uppercase, lowercase, and symbol order, where one mistake can cause incorrect output in the application or, in some cases, crash the application due to an error in the code.

A good informative programming quiz application requires three steps or sections to teach students about coding and the facts related to it. The first step is to teach students conceptual and theoretical knowledge, which can be taught using lectures and exercises such as multiple choice and fill-in-the-blanks. The second step is the logic that can be taught using videos and live demonstrations while also giving students selection type and sentence arrangement quiz questions to solve. In the final step, practical experience can be gained by using precision-answer questions in an application or physical test where the students need to enter the correct answer word for word, like in coding.

7 Study Limitations

The limitations faced while compiling data for this study were that, firstly, there was limited research carried out on C-sharp programming game development and implementation over the years for error identification and improving students' abilities in programming. Most of the documents available online were literature papers and strategies on how to improve students' conceptual knowledge and retain knowledgeability using quizzes, questionnaires, and in-depth discussions during classes, which were not feasible due to time constraints during lecture sessions and the schedule to follow provided by the university. The second time was limited to creating a fully working application and testing it on students, as accurate testing without bias could only be done at the start of the introductory programming course.

8 Discussion

The purpose of the research study and game application was to find out if students preferred GBL over traditional teaching methods and if GBL was more effective in teaching students. After reading through recent literature and research documents on game-based learning over the past decade, it was revealed that more than 80% [27, 28]

of students prefer game-based learning compared to traditional teaching methods for learning. A survey was carried out on an "online portal with more than three hundred teachers on game-based learning." The responses of those teachers were, in summary, as follows: 81% felt that students were more active in learning while playing; 68% responded by saying that GBL helped students develop problem-solving skills; and 65% responded that GBL improved students' social skills. In another research carried out at the Massachusetts Institute of Technology in 2010 on GBL on a 19-year-old student, the results showed that the student retained around 90% of what he had learned, increased the student's theoretical knowledge by about 11%, and boosted the student's self-confidence by 20% [29, 30]. The reason students prefer GBL over traditional methods and why it's more effective is that GBL is able to inspire its learners to be creative and think outside the box, as there is no fixed rule. GBL allows students to be more active and interactive while learning by putting the concept into action rather than just learning it theoretically, allowing them to retain information faster and longer [31]. Seeing as GBL is more effective than traditional teaching methods and preferred by most students and some teachers, using GBL on a large scale outside of experimental setups and trials can help many students improve their understanding of theoretical concepts via practice rather than just listening and jotting down points in class. It was learned that multiple choice type quizzes had more effect on conceptual knowledge while open-ended questions with specific solutions were effective for coding as misspelled and wrongly used upper and lower cases in coding could cause errors in the code.

9 Conclusion and Future Work

In this study, an optimal way to teach new programming students to learn about errors in coding and conceptual knowledge was through a game application when students did not have access to proper guidance due to various limitations. The study found that apart from their learning ability and information retaining ability, learning via gaming also improves students' decision-making skills and confidence, and has various effects on the students' social skills. After conducting research on GBL, objectives were formulated to find an effective way to create games students would find interesting and effective. Incorporating a tutorial in every section of the game seemed the most effective, as putting a concept into practice right after reading is the most effective way to allow students to retain knowledge and improve their abilities. For this study in the future, a proper fully functioning game needs to be created and tested on new students to avoid bias, and experienced programming students need to use the game application to compare results in an experimental report and find any gaps in the applications that can be filled with their responses.

Appendix

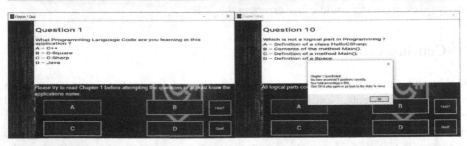

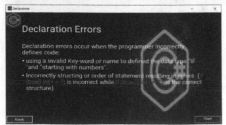
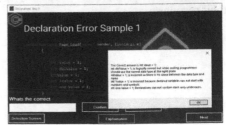

References

1. Karim, F., Karim, F.: Monitoring system using web of things in precision agriculture. In: The 14th International Conference on Future Networks and Communications (2017)
2. Yang, Z., Li, D.: WasNet: a neural network-based garbage collection management system. IEEE (2020). https://ieeexplore.ieee.org/abstract/document/9107232. Accessed 8 Sep 2022
3. How Many Millions of Lines of Code Does It Take? Visual Capitalist. https://www.vis ualcapitalist.com/millions-lines-of-code/#:~:text=Google%20Chrome%20(browser)%20r uns%20on,Collider%20uses%2050%20million%20lines. Accessed 8 Sep 2022
4. Rodas-Silva, J., Galindo, J.A., García-Gutiérrez, J., Benavides, D.: Selection of software product line implementation components using recommender systems: an application to wordpress. https://ieeexplore.ieee.org/abstract/document/8720203. Accessed 8 Sep 2022
5. geeksforgeek: Difference between Java and C language. geeksforgeek. https://www.gee ksforgeeks.org/difference-between-java-and-c-language/#:~:text=Java%20is%20more%20d ata%2Doriented,language%20using%20compiler%20or%20interpreter. Accessed 17 Sep 2022
6. Fu, X., Shimada, A., Ogata, H., Taniguchi, Y., Suehiro, D.: Real-time learning analytics for C programming language courses. In: Proceedings of the Seventh International Learning Analytics and Knowledge Conference (LAK 2017), New York, (2017.)
7. Bennedsen, J., Caspersen, M.E.: Failure rates in introductory programming: 12 years later. https://doi.org/10.1145/3324888. Accessed 7 Sep 2022
8. Margulieux, L.E., Morrison, B.B., Decker, A.: Reducing withdrawal and failure rates in introductory programming with subgoal labeled worked examples. Int. J. STEM Educ. 7(1), 1–16 (2020). https://doi.org/10.1186/s40594-020-00222-7
9. Enhancing confidence in using computational thinking skills via playing a serious game: a case study to increase motivation in learning computer programming. Faculty of Engineering, Cyprus International University, pp. 221831–221851, 22 December 2020
10. University of the Sunshine Coast Australia: How much should your child work while studying full time? UniSC. https://www.usc.edu.au/community/parent-lounge/parent-lounge-update/ 2017/june/how-much-should-your-child-work-while-studying-full-time. Accessed 17 Sep 2022
11. Qian, Y., Lehman, J.: Students' misconceptions and other difficulties in introductory programming: a literature review. ACM Trans. Comput. Educ. 18(1), 1–24 (2017)
12. Ardiç, B., Yurdakul, I., Tüzün, E.: Creation of a serious game for teaching code review: an experience report. IEEE, Munich, Germany (2020)
13. Zapata-Cáceres, M., Martín-Barroso, E.: Applying game learning analytics to a voluntary video game: intrinsic motivation, persistence, and rewards in learning to program at an early age. IEEE Access pp. 123588–123602, 14 September 2021
14. Gaining Student Engagement Through. IEEE Access pp. 1881–1892, 6 January 2022
15. Guimarães, J.P.R.: Serious game for learning code. https://core.ac.uk/display/143409158? utm_source=pdf&utm_medium=banner&utm_campaign=pdf-decoration-v1. Accessed 17 Sep 2022
16. Modern code review: a case study at Google (2018)
17. Ureel II, L.C., Wallace, C.: Automated critique of early programming antipatterns. Misconceptions, pp. 738–744, 2 March 2019
18. Nuci, K.P., Tahir, R., Wang, A.I., Imran, A.S.: Game-based digital quiz as a tool for improving students' engagement and learning in online lectures. IEEE Access 9, 91220–91234 (2021)
19. Medeiros, R.P., Ramalho, G.L., Falcão, T.P.: A systematic literature review on teaching and learning introductory programming in higher education. IEEE Trans. Educ. 62(2), 77–90 (2018)

20. Chen, C.H., Yeh, H.C.: Effects of integrating a questioning strategy with game-based learning on students' language learning performances in flipped classrooms. Technol. Pedagogy Educ. **28**(3), 347–361 (2019)
21. Reynaldo, C., Christian, R., Hosea, H., Gunawan, A.A.: Using video games to improve capabilities in decision making. In: 5th International Conference on Computer Science and Computational Intelligence, vol. 5, pp. 211–221 (2020)
22. Mustafaoğlu, R., Zirek, E., Yasacı, Z., Özdinçler, A.R.: The negative effects of digital technology usage on children's development and health. Addicta: Turkish J. Addict. **5**(2), 13–21 (2018)
23. Young adults learning executive function skills by playing focused. Cognitive Developmen, pp. 43–50 (2019)
24. Benjamin Emihovich, N.R.J.M.: Can video gameplay improve. Int. J. Game-Based Learn. **10**(2), 21–38 (2020)
25. Adair, C.: Postive effects of video games. Game Quitters (2015). https://gamequitters.com/positive-effects-of-video-games/. Accessed 19 Sep 2022
26. Bawa, P.: Game on!: investigating digital game-based versus gamified learning in higher education. Int. J. Game-Based Learn. **10**(3), 16–46 (2020)
27. Ibrahim, R., Yusoff, R.C.M., Mohamed-Omar, H., Jaafar, A.: Students perceptions of using educational games to learn introductory programming. Comput. Inf. Sci. **4**(1), 205 (2011)
28. Game-based learning is probably worth looking into (2013)
29. Designing Digitally: Game-based learning vs. traditional training. Designing Digitally. https://www.designingdigitally.com/blog/game-based-learning-vs-traditional-training#:~:text=When%20compared%20with%20traditional%20learning,learning%20retention%20up%20to%2090%25. Accessed 12 Sep 2022
30. Peter Mozelius, A.H.: Game-based learning - a long history. In: Irish Conference on Game-based Learning 2019. Cork, Ireland (2019)
31. Sami, M., Sharma, N.A.: Learning computer modules using multimedia and social media platform in a developing country. In: 2021 IEEE Asia-Pacific Conference on Computer Science and Data Engineering (CSDE), pp. 1–9. IEEE (2021)

What Makes AI Addictive? The Role of Discounting, Risk Aversion and Self-regulation

Renita Murimi[✉]

University of Dallas, Irving, TX 75062, USA
rmurimi@udallas.edu

Abstract. AI-enabled technology, with its capabilities of parsing large data sets and adaptively tuning its learning capabilities, has the potential to keep users "hooked". However, this poses a problem for child users, since their ongoing cognitive development is not adequately primed to implement self-regulation. In this paper, we evaluate the impact of technology overuse by studying its impact on limited attention resources among children. We examine the factors that make AI-enabled technology addictive for children, specifically the impact of the short-term and long-term discounting tendencies and the degree of risk-aversion prevalent among child users. Our work in this paper illustrates the unique attributes of child users of technology, and therefore calls for technology design that can enhance the user experience of children by avoiding negative outcomes associated with the over-usage and addiction of AI-enabled technology.

Keywords: Addictive AI · Future discount · Risk Aversion

1 Introduction

The scope of technology's reach into modern childhood is broad. According to recent estimates, one in three Internet users is a child [21]. The impact of technology on our society has created increasingly seamless avenues for children to interact with technology. For example, work in [2] found that the top three most popular uses of smart speakers were for search, streaming music, and IoT device control. These applications lend themselves to be used by both children and adults, and it may be inferred that the nature of technology's interactions with children are different than those with adults. As AI technology matures, the nature of interactions with such smart applications continues to evolve. AI-powered applications continuously refine their operations by sifting through millions of queries, ratings and use cases to achieve robust interactions with the humans who use them. For example, the Pew Internet Report statistics [26] indicate that the algorithms driving YouTube's recommendations encourage users to watch progressively longer and more popular content. Additionally, a fifth of the most-recommended videos were determined by researchers to be oriented toward children.

Several reasons have been posited for technology addiction, including but not limited to the efficiency of recommendation algorithms, intuitive and seamless interface

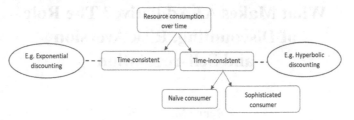

Fig. 1. Resource consumption profiles over time.

design, and low barrier to entry and participation [1]. Ongoing research into the adverse impacts of overusing Internet technologies has described the negative effects on academic work [14], as well as on social and personal performance [15]. Work in [14] described how immediate gratification afforded by social media use was a significant driver in the tendency toward developing Internet addiction. Our work in this paper seeks to quantify the impact of instant gratification and the myopic decisions that prefer short-term outcomes leading to over-usage of technology among children. In this paper, we study how self-regulation of limited attention resources, tendency to discount the future and risk-aversion impacts the decision to use technology. We propose an economic model based on discounting that studies three types of technology users: naïve users (who are unaware of their self-regulation problem), sophisticated users (who are aware of their self-regulation problem and act accordingly to maximize their utility) and time-consistent users who follow an initial disciplined plan of technology usage (see Fig. 1). We model the utility of technology usage according to an iso-elastic utility function, which has been used to study addiction and habit formation [24, 25]. Our findings indicate a clear difference between the value derived from technology usage by naïve and time-consistent users. We show that the naivete of children and their lower risk-aversion are key factors in their reduced self-regulation of limited resources. Finally, we highlight key directions for future research – explainable AI as a tool for learning with technology, regulation and accountability and the need for developing technologies that enhance the cause of ethical AI for children.

2   Related Work

Much like drugs and alcohol, Internet addiction has been studied as a clinical disorder [34]. Technology addiction has far-reaching consequences among children and adults, extending deep into their brains [9]. Neuroscientific evidence pointing to Internet addiction has shown that certain processes in the prefrontal cortex related to working memory and executive functions were reduced, similar to the outcomes in other behavioral addictions such as gambling [6]. Related research into how Internet addiction rewires structures deep in the brain and shrinks surface-level matter was described in [23]. Additional work in [8] confirmed that Internet addiction was related to impulsivity (urgency, lack of perseverance) and obsessive passion. While the vast majority of studies about Internet and technology addiction among children have been conducted from the perspective of adults, work in [31] looked at the interaction between children and technology from the perspective of children. Physical health experiences reported by children ranged from headaches, poor vision and fatigue, while mental health experiences documented included the inability to focus, adverse effects of seeing vivid imagery, aggression, and sleep problems. Although it might seem that limiting a child's access to technology might be a solution, differing guidelines on best practices can leave parents and educators at crossroads. Screen time limits, long seen as guidelines for best practices, have seen conflicting interpretations. Is an educational app excluded from screen time? Going back further, what makes an app, device or website "educational"? In [12], some children described that, in the absence of specific parental restrictions on usage, they would prefer to use the tablet "until they got tired" or "until it died".

Since modern devices are increasingly enmeshed in some kind of network, children are not able to translate the implications of their local interaction with digital technology contained in toys and other devices to a global network. Work in [5] studies exactly this conundrum, where they outline the core issues of child users – impact of digital identity on the life course of children, and data generated by child users that is analyzed by "indeterminate algorithms, for indeterminate identities". The authors also discuss how the issue of children's understanding of data persistence, tracking, and data mining is inadequate, and does not account for realistic informed consent practices.

The addiction caused from the over-usage of digital technology by children can be attributed to two broad factors. First, the design of AI-enabled technology is purposely addictive. User profiles are continuously tuned and refined to adapt to the user's activities and "reward" the user with recommendations for indulging in more of those activities, such as the endless newsfeeds, videos and notifications made available through inviting interfaces [30]. Second, children's brains work differently than adults when it comes to projecting long-term outcomes from present activity. Work in [28] studied how adolescents favor short-term outcomes in decision making. In their work, the authors described how children learn little from negative outcomes, thus advocating for the use of effective deterrents in a proactive rather than reactive learning mechanism. Since negative consequences do not serve as capable learning experiences for children, the notion of invulnerability and consequent risk-taking is higher in children. One of the key findings of their work illustrates how adolescents exhibit an optimistic bias, where they view their own risks as lesser than those of peers. Multiple factors were identified as causes of this optimistic bias, including incomplete brain maturation, as well as cognitive and developmental differences.

Our work builds upon these notions of myopic decision-making among children when it comes to interaction with AI-enabled technology, thus leading to ineffective long-term use of limited attention resources. This paper quantifies the adverse impacts of choosing the short-term outcomes of gratification from over-usage of technology by children. We use tools from economics and game theory to study how time-inconsistent behaviors by child users to study the utility of technology usage over a period of time. In the next section, we present our model for studying the behavior of child users who exhibit naïve time-inconsistent behavior, and contrast it with it that of an adult who exhibits sophisticated time-inconsistent behavior or better yet, time-consistent behavior when it comes to regulating technology usage over time.

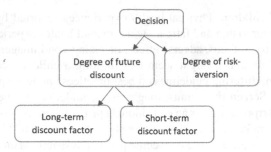

Fig. 2. Factors impacting the decision to use technology

3 Model

Consider a budget of K that reflects sparse attention resources that must be allocated to a technology activity. We consider a child to be a naïve player who is unable to project the shortcomings of spending all her time and attention resources on the technology in the current instant. Consider that our consumer receives a stream of payoffs $x_1, x_2, ..., x_T$ over the periods $t = 1, 2, ..., T$, and evaluates per-period utility function as $u(x)$. We assume three time periods, which includes the current time period t_1 and the future time periods t_2 and t_3. The allocation of the total available resources K is allocated among these three time periods is denoted as x_1, x_2 and x_3, where $x_1 + x_2 + x_3 = K$. We denote the utility of consuming x_i resources during the current time period t_i as $v_i(x_i)$.

The discounted sum of future payoffs, as evaluated in period $t = 1$ is evaluated as below, where, $\delta \in (0, 1)$ is the player's discount factor, which she uses to discount future payoffs.

$$v(x_1, x_2, ..., x_T) = u(x_1) + \delta u(x_2) + ... + \delta^{T-1} u(x_T) = \sum_{t=1}^{T} \delta^{t-1} u(x_t) \quad (1)$$

Equation (1) reflects the behavior of a time-consistent player who consistently uses the value of δ to discount payoffs from future time periods. This discounting rule, also known as exponential discounting, describes consumers who will stick to their plan for future time periods. This time-consistent behavior is in contrast to hyperbolic discounting, where a player uses an additional discount factor of $\beta \in (0, 1)$ to discount all of the future compared to present consumption.

Thus, for three time periods, the discount factor between the current time period ($t = 1$) and the next period ($t = 2$) is $\beta\delta$. The discount factor for the future time periods, i.e. between time periods $t = 2$ and $t = 3$ is δ. Since $\beta\delta < \delta$, a consumer following hyperbolic discounting discounts the payoffs from future time period in a weaker form (δ) than that in the current time period ($\beta\delta$). Hyperbolic discounting leads consumers to believe that they will follow a disciplined mode of consumption, but who will ultimately act to revise their plan of consumption. Thus, this player can be acting according to time-inconsistent behavior ($\beta < 1$), be either aware of this self-control problem, or be unaware of it. The former case where a time-inconsistent consumer is aware of her self-control problem is known as a sophisticated player $\left(\hat{\beta} = \beta\right)$, and the latter case where the time-inconsistent consumer is unaware of her self-control problem is known as a naïve player $\left(\hat{\beta} = 1\right)$. These factors used in our model (discount factors and risk aversion) that are involved in the decision to use technology are shown in Fig. 2.

Let $v(x)$ be the iso-elastic utility function given as follows, where $\rho < 1$.

$$v(x) = \frac{x^{1-\rho}}{1 - \rho} \tag{2}$$

Equation 2 represents the iso-elastic utility function. The iso-elastic utility function belongs to a class of functions known as Constant Relative Risk Aversion (CRRA), where the relative risk aversion of a utility function $u(x)$ is given by [3] as follows.

$$\text{Relative risk aversion} = -x\frac{u''(x)}{u'(x)} \tag{3}$$

A CRRA function such as the iso-elastic utility function is used to model scenarios where, as the resources increase, the consumer holds the same percentage of resources in risky assets. The use of the iso-elastic CRRA utility function has been shown to explain habit formation models [7, 29]. For our three-period scenario, the consumer's hyperbolic discounted consumption problem is given by

$$\max_{x_2,x_3} v(K - x_2 - x_3, x_2, x_3) = \frac{(K - x_2 - x_3)^{1-\rho}}{1 - \rho} + \beta\delta\frac{x_2^{1-\rho}}{1 - \rho} + \beta\delta^2\frac{x_3^{1-\rho}}{1 - \rho} \tag{4}$$

Thus, the optimization problem for allocation of limited attention resources (K) can be formulated as follows:

$$\max_{x_2} v_2(x_2, K_2 - x_2) = \frac{x_2^{1-\rho}}{1 - \rho} + \beta\delta\frac{(K_2 - x_2)^{1-\rho}}{1 - \rho} \tag{5}$$

For best response, set $\frac{dv_2}{dx_2} = 0$, and re-arranging to solve for x_2, we get

$$x_2 = \frac{K_2}{1 + (\beta\delta)^{1/\rho}} \tag{6}$$

Since allocation during the third time period is given by $x_3(K_2) = K_2 - x_2$, from Eq. (6), we get

$$x_3(K_2) = \frac{K_2(\beta\delta)^{1/\rho}}{1 + (\beta\delta)^{1/\rho}} \tag{7}$$

Backtracking to find the maximum utility during the current time period, our optimization problem is defined as

$$\max_{x_1} v_1(x_1, x_2, x_3) \tag{8}$$

Substituting Eqs. (6) and (7) into (8), we get,

$$\max_{x_1} v_1(x_1, x_2, x_3) = \frac{x_1^{1-\rho}}{1 - \rho} + \frac{\beta\delta}{1 - \rho}\left(\frac{K - x_1}{1 + (\beta\delta)^{1/\rho}}\right)^{1-\rho} + \frac{\beta\delta^2}{1 - \rho}\left(\frac{(K - x_1)(\beta\delta)^{1/\rho}}{1 + (\beta\delta)^{1/\rho}}\right)^{1-\rho} \tag{9}$$

Setting $\frac{dv_1}{dx_1} = 0$ in Eq. (9), and rearranging to solve for x_1, we get

$$x_1 = K\left\{1 + \frac{(\beta\delta)^{1/\rho}}{\left[1 + (\beta\delta)^{1/\rho}\right]^{\frac{1-\rho}{\rho}}}\left[1 + \delta(\beta\delta)^{\frac{1-\rho}{\rho}}\right]^{\frac{1}{\rho}}\right\}^{-1} \tag{10}$$

We assume three kinds of players – a child (fully naïve player), a sophisticated player that follows hyperbolic discounting, and a disciplined player (follows exponential discounting). For a disciplined player, exponential discounting with $\beta = 1$ results in

$$x_1 = K\left\{1 + \frac{(\delta)^{1/\rho}}{\left[1 + (\delta)^{1/\rho}\right]^{\frac{1-\rho}{\rho}}}\left[1 + \delta(\delta)^{\frac{1-\rho}{\rho}}\right]^{\frac{1}{\rho}}\right\}^{-1} \tag{11}$$

For a time-inconsistent player, replace β with $\hat{\beta}$ to denote the level of time-inconsistency in Eq. (10), we get

$$x_1 = K\left\{1 + \frac{\left(\hat{\beta}\delta\right)^{1/\rho}}{\left[1 + \left(\hat{\beta}\delta\right)^{1/\rho}\right]^{\frac{1-\rho}{\rho}}}\left[1 + \delta\left(\hat{\beta}\delta\right)^{\frac{1-\rho}{\rho}}\right]^{\frac{1}{\rho}}\right\}^{-1} \tag{12}$$

A sophisticated player differs from a naïve player in that $\hat{\beta}$ equals 1 for a fully naïve player, but she actually acts according to a value of $\beta < 1$. On the other hand, a sophisticated player is aware of her shortcomings when it comes to efficiently allocating sparse attention resources. Thus, $\hat{\beta} = \beta$, and $\beta < 1$ for the sophisticated time-inconsistent player. In Eq. (12), we denote the term $(\beta\delta)^{(1/\rho)}$ as the plasticity, P, of the limited attention resources available in any given time period. The next section presents our findings of the role of discount factors (β, δ), the degree of risk aversion (ρ), and the plasticity (P) on the utility derived from consuming limited attention resources.

4 Findings

From Fig. 3, we see that as the long-term discount β increases, the plasticity increases. Similarly, as the short-term discount, δ increases, the plasticity increases. This shows that the plasticity is directly proportional to the long-term and short-term discount factors. The increase in plasticity shows that the limited attention resources are not self-regulated – they can be spent on demand in as much quantity as required in the given time period. However, once spent, they cannot be recovered and subsequent time periods will suffer from a limited quantity of attention resources.

Moving onto the next time period, once again, the remainder of attention resources can be spent in an unregulated fashion, by consuming as much as required in that time period. The consequence of this direct relationship between the discount factors and the plasticity P is that fewer and fewer resources are available for consumption during

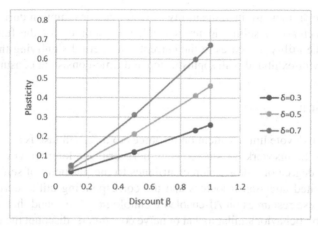

Fig. 3. Plasticity as a function of the long-term discount factor β. Higher the value of β, the higher the plasticity of limited attention resources.

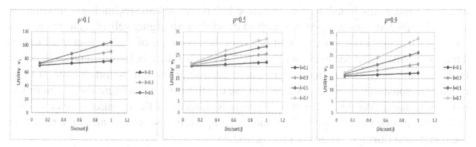

Fig. 4. The utility of consuming a resource in the current time period (v_1) as a function of the long-term discount factor β.

subsequent time periods. The resulting impact on the consumer (whether naïve, sophisticated or disciplined) is that the utility of the resource decreases in subsequent time periods, which is a prime factor in addiction. Poor self-regulation causes the consumer to consume more and more of a scarce resource without thought for the future [4, 11].

We also see that as ρ increases, the plasticity P decreases. The plasticity is related to the amount of self-regulation of attention resources over current and future time periods. Here, ρ denotes the degree of relative risk aversion in the utility function. As ρ increases, it denotes a higher risk-averse consumer whose profile becomes increasingly cautious of the consumption and therefore seeks to regulate it. Thus, the inversely proportional relationship between ρ and the plasticity P offers insights into the behavior of a naïve consumer (child) and contrasts it with increasing abilities for regulation such as those found in sophisticated consumers or time-consistent consumers.

Figure 4 shows the utility during the current time period, v_1, as a function of the long-term discount factor β. Consistent with the findings in Fig. 3 above, we see that an increase in β leads to an increase in the utility obtained by a consumer in the current time period, which ultimately leads to lower resources available for future time periods.

Similarly, with an increase in δ, the utility of resource consumption during the current time period increases resulting in fewer available resources for the future. Also, as ρ increases, the utility decreases in the current time period signifying the higher risk aversion behavior exhibited with sophisticated and time-consistent consumers.

5 Discussion

The decision to devote limited attention resources to a certain task is a consequence of several factors. In this work, we studied how short-term and long-term discount factors, as well as the degree of risk aversion contributes to the plasticity of self-regulation of expending limited attention resources and the corresponding utility derived from the spending of these resources on AI-enabled technologies. We found that, children who typically exhibit behavior similar to that of naïve consumers, discount the future heavily in favor of the present time period, which leads to increased spending of attention on the AI technology in the current time period leaving fewer attention resources for the future. Naïve users are unaware of their time-inconsistent behavior, and their lower risk-aversion tendencies translate into addictive behaviors toward technology. In contrast, sophisticated consumers – perhaps, a child or adult with higher self-regulation capabilities – still exhibits time-inconsistent behavior, but is aware of their self-control issues. Thus, a sophisticated consumer will regulate her own future behavior in order to derive higher value from their patterns of resource consumption. On the other hand, a time-consistent consumer follows a planned course of attention expenditure corresponding to a discount factor. As the discount factor increases, more of the resources are consumed in the initial time period. When the future is completely discounted, all of the resources are consumed during the current time period.

Our work classifies children as naïve users, although, adults exhibiting limited self-control could also be classified as naïve users. The reverse is also true – some children might exhibit greater awareness of their time-inconsistent behavior and therefore behave as sophisticated consumers or time-consistent consumers do with limited resources. One example of this is the Stanford marshmallow experiment [22] which suggested that children who exhibited delayed self-gratification were more capable of success in later life. This suggests that self-regulation is not entirely the domain of a certain age group, but rather is a combination of internal traits and environmental stimuli [33]. While both time-consistent and time-inconsistent users are faced with the task of self-regulation of technology consumption, the difficulty of accomplishing this over a period of time is compounded by the addictive nature of the AI-enabled technology itself.

While a sophisticated or time-consistent consumer might be able to withstand the temptation to watch another video or play the game one more time, a naïve user might find it challenging to do so [32]. The phrase "technologization of childhood" first made popular in [27] studied technology usage of children within the home, and found that parents were getting more and more comfortable with their children's increasing competence with the technology. Parents reported feeling conflicted over regulating their children's usage, and not being able to discern the right balance of technology usage. This raises important questions about the nature of regulation. Should prevalent screen time guidelines contain warnings about the impact of over-usage by children? Should the developers of technology create auto-shut off features that detect an age-appropriate user and limit activity? If this is true, it raises concerns about technology overreach leading to issues in privacy, surveillance, censorship and ultimately user freedoms. Additionally, the role of algorithmic biases cannot be overlooked. The development of technology that implements an auto-shutoff feature based on computed thresholds may be impacted by biases, errors and malfunction. Children are especially vulnerable to the adverse impacts of these effects. Proponents of early digital literacy would argue that since humans live in a networked world populated by devices, introduction to technologies should begin in childhood to ensure competence and fluency. Thus, the ethics of the relationship of children's interaction with the burgeoning AI-enabled technology in their environment is a nuanced one, whose urgency is pressing with the arrival of every new technological artifact.

5.1 Limitations

Our model for studying the behavior of naïve (child users) versus sophisticated users, or time-consistent users showed that plasticity, or the self-regulation of limited attention resources depends on the short-term and long-term discount factors as well as the degree of risk aversion. Consequently, the utility of consumers over time varied as a function of the attention resources available to them, especially for the naïve consumers. Some limitations of our work concerning the modeling of resources, the utility function, and plasticity are described below.

First, while the CRRA utility function used in our model has been widely used to model short-term choices over long-term benefits, further research into the use of other classes of functions such as increasing/decreasing absolute risk aversion (IARA/DARA) might reveal insights into the behaviors of various kinds of users. Our model could then be enhanced to study various levels of naivete, to study increasing levels of sophistication in planning and self-regulation of limited attention resources.

Second, our paper studied the allotment of limited attention resources to be allocated over a period of time. However, in practice, children live in environments with a range of spatio-temporal resources. For example, the introduction of a sport, hobby or friends might serve to reduce the time spent with a technology. Similarly, life events, seasonal patterns and broad socio-economic-political factors dictate the different environments of children around the world. Further research will help to determine the true impact of addictive technology on child behavior. For example, long-term comparisons of brain structures of children in environments not exposed to technology versus those heavily exposed to technology will shed light into how technology has altered child behavior.

Lastly, we modeled the plasticity of resource allocation as a function of the risk aversion and discount factors. However, other forms of plasticity might be defined. For example, if the resources are chosen as a combination of attention, working memory and other higher-order executive functions, plasticity of these resources would have to be incorporated into the models presented in this paper.

5.2 Future Work

Although our work has focused on the discounting and risk aversion inherent in the behavior of naïve users, our model can be extended to study how addictive technology can be improved by incorporating explainability, regulation and accountability in developing AI technologies for children. We present some directions below.

Explainable AI as a teaching tool: Our model can be extended to understanding how children learn with humans versus with technology, over a period of time. The discounting and risk aversion factors could be used to study varying levels of naivete. Additionally, since AI-driven technology is capable of learning and improving, discounting and risk-aversion can be applied to the technology as well creating a multi-dimensional model of smart agents and humans with varying levels of discounting and risk aversion. This points to the role of explainable AI not just as a tool for justifying decision-making, but also as a tool for extending the learning paradigm from being technology-assisted to being one that is technology-initiated.

Role of regulation and accountability in ethical AI development: Research over the past three decades has increasingly pointed to the asymmetry of scale inherent in technology. The power of vast networks at our fingertips has far-reaching consequences for information dissemination. Network effects disproportionately affect children, as they are faced with content in apps, social networking sites, and websites for which they might not be developmentally ready. Effective regulation and accountability measures can help to develop significant interventions for the use of technology as a positive force in children's lives.

Distributive justice in technology usage: Although AI technologies heavily influence our lives, the notion of fair resource allocation through technology has not received much attention. Distributive justice, which is defined broadly as fair allocation of resources [18], has heavily influenced work in multiple domains including copyright law [13], environmental law [17], and economic policy [16]. By developing AI algorithms that adapt to children, we can unlock the potential for AI technology to be sensitive to individual differences in variety of children's environments [10, 15]. Future work in this area will require ethical AI frameworks for collocated spaces of adults, children, bots and IoT devices in pervasive networks and will need to address key challenges that result as a consequence of unchecked AI prowess and their impact on children.

6 Conclusions

Choosing consumption of limited attention resources over time is daunting. Discounting the future is one of the reasons that consumption during the current time period seems more appealing than consumption in the future. In this paper, we studied how the consumption of limited attention resources over a period of time is a function of the amount of short-term and long-term discounting as well as the degree of risk-aversion. Characterizing children as naïve users of technology, we showed how limited attention resources would be quickly depleted in the face of low risk aversion and extreme discounting. On the other hand, more disciplined and thoughtful users could mitigate some of the effects of lack of self-regulation and myopic over-consumption in the current time period. The problem of designing technologies that do not encourage discounting the future among child users and consequent addiction is a pressing one due to their ongoing cognitive development. The consequent implications of technology design for children are of increasing importance, where children are inheriting environments embedded with AI-enabled technology of various kinds.

References

1. Alter, A: Irresistible: the rise of addictive technology and the business of keeping us hooked. Penguin (2017)
2. Ammari, T., Kaye, J., Tsai, J.Y., Bentley, F.: Music, search, and IoT: how people (really) use voice assistants. ACM Trans. Comput. Hum. Interact. **26**(3), 1–28 (2019)
3. Arrow, K.: The theory of risk-bearing: small and great risks. J. Risk Uncertain. **12**(2–3), 103–111 (1996)
4. Augeraud-Veron, E., Bambi, M., Gozzi, F.: Solving internal habit formation models through dynamic programming in infinite dimension. J. Optim. Theory Appl. **173**, 584–611 (2017)
5. Berman, G., Albright, K.: Children and the data cycle: rights and ethics in a big data world. Innocenti Working Paper WP-2017-05, UNICEF Office of Research, Florence (2017)
6. Brand, M., Young, K., Laier, C.: Prefrontal control and internet addiction: a theoretical model and review of neuropsychological and neuroimaging findings. Front. Hum. Neurosci. **8**, 375 (2014)
7. Bossi, L., Gomis-Porqueras, P.: Consequences of modeling habit persistence. Macroecon. Dyn. **13**(3), 349–365 (2009)
8. Burnay, J., Billieux, J., Blairy, S., Laroi, F.: Which psychological factors influence Internet addiction? Evidence through an integrative model. Comput. Hum. Behav. **43**, 28–34 (2015)
9. Carr, N.: The Shallows: What the Internet is Doing to Our Brains. WW Norton & Company (2011)
10. Druin, A.: The role of children in the design of new technology. Behav. Inf. Technol. **21**(1), 1–25 (2002)
11. Gomes, F., Michaelides, A.: Portfolio choice with internal habit formation: a life-cycle model with uninsurable labor income risk. Rev. Econ. Dyn. **6**(4), 729–766 (2003)
12. Hadlington, L., White, H., Curtis, S.: "I cannot live without my [tablet]": children's experiences of using tablet technology within the home. Comput. Hum. Behav. **94**, 19–24 (2019)
13. Hughes, J., Merges, R.: Copyright and distributive justice. Notre Dame L. Rev. **92**, 513 (2016)
14. Iskender, M., Akin, A.: Social self-efficacy, academic locus of control, and internet addiction. Comput. Educ. **54**(4), 1101–1106 (2010)
15. Ito, M., et al.: Living and Learning with New Media: Summary of Findings from the Digital Youth Project. John D. and Catherine T. MacArthur Foundation (2008)
16. Kaplow, L., Shavell, S.: Fairness versus welfare: notes on the Pareto principle, preferences, and distributive justice. J. Leg. Stud. **32**(1), 331–362 (2003)
17. Kaswan, A.: Distributive justice and the environment. NCL Rev. **81**, 1031 (2002)
18. Konow, J.: Fair and square: the four sides of distributive justice. J. Econ. Behav. Organ. **46**(2), 137–164 (2001)
19. Leung, L.: Predicting Internet risks: a longitudinal panel study of gratifications-sought, Internet addiction symptoms, and social media use among children and adolescents. Health Psychol. Behav. Med. **2**(1), 424–439 (2014)

20. Leung, L., Lee, P.: Impact of internet literacy, internet addiction symptoms, and internet activities on academic performance. Soc. Sci. Comput. Rev. **30**(4), 403–418 (2012)

21. Livingstone, S., Byrne, J., Carr, J.: One in Three: Internet Governance and Children's Rights, Innocenti Discussion Papers no. 2016–01, UNICEF Office of Research - Innocenti, Florence (2016)

22. Mischel, W., Ebbesen, E.: Attention in delay of gratification. J. Pers. Soc. Psychol. **16**(2), 329 (1970)

23. Mosher, D.: High wired: does addictive Internet use restructure the brain? Scientific American. https://www.scientificamerican.com/article/does-addictive-internet-use-restructure-brain/. Accessed 29 Apr 2022

24. Naryshkin, R., Davison, M.: Developing utility functions for optimal consumption in models with habit formation and catching up with the Joneses. Can. Appl. Math. Q. **17**(4), 703–719 (2009)

25. Perali, F., Piccoli, L., Wangen, K.: An extended theory of rational addiction (No. 69). Universitat de les Illes Balears, Departament d'Economía Aplicada (2015)

26. Pew Research Center – Internet and Technology Report. Many turn to youtube for children's content, news, how-to lessons. https://www.pewresearch.org/topic/internet-technology/. Accessed 29 Apr 2022

27. Plowman, L., McPake, J., Stephen, C.: The technologisation of childhood? Young children and technology in the home. Child. Soc. **24**(1), 63–74 (2010)

28. Reyna, V., Farley, F.: Risk and rationality in adolescent decision making: implications for theory, practice, and public policy. Psychol. Sci. Public Interest **7**(1), 1–44 (2006)

29. Roshan, R., Pahlavani, M., Shahiki, M.: Investigation on habit formation, risk aversion and intertemporal substitution in consumption of Iranian households by GMM approach. Int. Econ. Stud. **42**(1), 47–56 (2013)

30. Singer, N.: Can't put down your device? That's by design. The New York Times. https://www.nytimes.com/2015/12/06/technology/personaltech/cant-put-down-your-device-thats-by-design.html. Accessed 29 Apr 2022

31. Smahel, D., Wright, M.F., Cernikova, M.: The impact of digital media on health: children's perspectives. Int. J. Public Health **60**(2), 131–137 (2015). https://doi.org/10.1007/s00038-015-0649-z

32. Stern, S.E.: Addiction to technologies: a social psychological perspective of Internet addiction. Cyberpsychol. Behav. **2**(5), 419–424 (1999)

33. Yayouk, W., et al.: Genetic and environmental influences on self-control: assessing self-control with the ASEBA self-control scale. Behav. Genet. **48**(2), 135–146 (2018)

34. Young, K.: Internet addiction: the emergence of a new clinical disorder. Cyberpsychol. Behav. **1**(3), 237–244 (1998)

Two High-Performance Antenna Selection Schemes for Secure SSK Modulation in Intelligent Industrial Wireless Sensing Systems

Hui Xu[1]([✉])[ID], Benjamin K. Ng[1][ID], Huibin Wang[2][ID], Boyu Yang[3][ID], and Chan-Tong Lam[1][ID]

[1] Macao Polytechnic University, Macau SAR, Gaomeis Street, Macao 999078, China
{p2112282,bng,ctlam}@mpu.edu.mo
[2] ABB Global Open Innovation Center, Shenzhen 518000, China
astingwang@hotmail.com
[3] Beijing University of Posts and Telecommunications, Beijing 100876, China
yangboyu111@bupt.edu.cn

Abstract. Industrial wireless sensor networks (IWSNs) provide intelligent factory management with a new dimension. Reliable intelligent industrial wireless sensing systems play a vital role in ensuring the reliability and security of IWSNs. Therefore, improving the confidentiality of real-time communication of intelligent industrial wireless sensing systems and making IWSNs more intelligent has attracted widespread attention. This paper proposes two high-performance antenna selection (AS) schemes along with friendly jamming to protect the confidentiality of real-time communication of intelligent industrial wireless sensing systems based on space shift keying (SSK). Additionally, two AS schemes named the generalized Euclidean distance antenna selection (GEDAS) and the leakage-based antenna selection (LBAS) are proposed for maximizing the difference in average mutual information (AMI) between D and E. In this way, the physical layer security (PLS) of the system is further improved. Moreover, the algorithmic complexity of the two proposed AS schemes is thoroughly analyzed in this paper. The simulation results demonstrate that the performance of the proposed joint schemes is superior to the traditional random selection scheme in terms of secrecy rate (SR), secrecy capacity (SC), and bit error rate (BER). Thus, the security enhancement benefits the real-time communication of the intelligent industrial wireless sensing systems and prevents data transmission leakage.

Keywords: Intelligent industrial wireless sensing systems · Security · Space shift keying · Jamming signal · Antenna selection

Supported by organization Macao Polytechnic University.

1   Introduction

Industrial superpowers, including Germany, the United States, and Japan, have recently implemented new national policies. Industry 4.0 in Germany, industrial internet in the United States, and intelligent manufacturing system in Japan are all strategic plans for their respective manufacturing industries based on their surroundings. China, as the largest manufacturer in the world, has also put out the "Made in China 2025" national plan, which positions "smart manufacturing" as the primary path of Chinese industrial transformation and a critical starting point for implementing the national strategy [1].

Among them, industrial wireless sensor networks (IWSNs) are used to monitor and control various industrial tasks. They are committed to improving production efficiency by providing ubiquitous perception, which is the key to introducing industrial automation into industrial manufacturing intelligence [2]. Due to the deployment environment and the characteristics of IWSNs, such as resource constraints, wireless communication, security-sensitive, uncontrollable environments, and distributed deployment, there are a lot of security vulnerabilities in the networks [3]. In addition, IWSNs must also adhere to strict real-time and communication reliability requirements if they are utilized for monitoring and control. Meanwhile, this means that the system can only work effectively if the information is transmitted in real-time and in a reliable manner when the intelligent industrial sensing systems in IWSNs interfaces with the gateway. One of the challenges in the security of IWSNs stemming from the aforementioned issue is to increase the confidentiality of real-time communication of intelligent industrial sensing systems so that IWSNs can fend off attacks such as eavesdropping and session hijacking [4].

Modern communication systems have significantly benefited from developing multiple-input multiple-output (MIMO) technology. For intelligent wireless sensing systems, we can use MIMO systems to handle the massive instantaneous data transmission demands [5]. MIMO technology allows the use of receive and transmit diversity to improve the reliability of the system and can also use spatial multiplexing to enhance the transmission rate. The proposal of cooperative communication technology promotes the practical application of MIMO technology. However, MIMO technology requires multiple antennas on both the transmitter and receiver, which increases the signal processing complexity of the receiver, requires strict inter-antenna synchronization (IAS), and increases the cost. At the same time, a large number of radio frequency units lead to energy efficiency being reduced. Applying low-complexity communication methods, such as spatial modulation (SM) and space shift keying (SSK), is a promising option for intelligent wireless sensing systems. SM is proposed in [6]. The information delivered to the constellation and antenna index is mapped by the SM system. Because there is only one active antenna in each time slot, the complexity and interference issues can be resolved [7]. However, to achieve an acceptable bit error rate (BER) performance, the antenna index of SM is demodulated by the characteristics of various channels, and there are stringent restrictions on the transmission characteristics of the channel. Correspondingly, SSK is a simplified technique of

SM [8]. The antenna index of the transmitter carries the valid information of the SSK system, which reduces the complexity of the modulation and demodulation process [9]. The above modulation techniques have emerged as contenders for intelligent wireless sensing systems. The security and reliability of the information transmission process are key evaluation indicators with significant research importance and practical value to properly quantify the effectiveness of various modulation schemes in intelligent wireless sensing systems.

2 Related Work

Physical layer security (PLS) is the main topic of this paper, which exploits the randomness of the wireless channel to increase system security while significantly reducing computation costs compared to upper-layer encryption [10]. A transmitter, a legal receiver, and an eavesdropper are fully considered in the classic eavesdropping channel model of Wyner [11], which is based on secure information theory [12]. Wyner also introduced the secrecy capacity (SC) to analyze the security performance of the system, which is crucial in subsequent PLS-related research. Furthermore, it is demonstrated that when the legal channel outperforms the eavesdropping channel, the transmitted valid information can be received by the legal receiver rather than by the eavesdropper.

Examples of typical PLS improvement methods are beamforming, artificial noise (AN) approach, cooperative communication technique, precoding, and antenna selection (AS) scheme. The method achieved the maximum secure transmission performance when [13] applied beamforming technology to multiple-input single-output (MISO) systems to maximize the difference in received signal quality between legal receivers and eavesdroppers. [14] proposed a decode and forward-based cooperative relay scheme for secure transmission in a MIMO system, which considers various beamforming scenarios at the relay and derives closed-form expressions of achievable secrecy rate (SR). Furthermore, it is established that the general beamforming method surpasses null-space beamforming and ranks one in terms of SR. The authors of [15] proposed AN-aided SM systems over the Rayleigh channel. The AN is created by performing singular value decomposition (SVD) on the legal channel, which can be eliminated at the legal receiver and cause interference to the eavesdropper. Additionally, the closed-form approximation expressions and lower bounds of ergodic SR are obtained. In order to obtain system information for secure data transmission, [16,17] proposed joint jamming transmission and signal techniques for unknown eavesdropper locations in the SM system. SR and BER are two significant measures for adequately evaluating the security performance of the proposed systems. To enhance the PLS of the SM system, [18] proposed a novel precoding approach for the precoding-assisted SM (PSM) scheme. The fundamental concept behind the proposed methodology is to preprocess the data at the transmitter so that a legitimate receiver can demodulate the SM signal normally for secure communication. In [19–21], consider using a joint AS scheme and AN technique to improve the security performance of SM and SSK systems. The signal-to-leakage-to-noise

(SLNR) scheme was proposed in [19], which selected the optimal antenna according to the maximum SLNR values and increased the mutual information difference between legitimate receivers and eavesdroppers, improving the SR of the system. Furthermore, asymptotic results of the scheme show that better security performance can be achieved at the cost of increased system complexity by adding another AN. Following that, the SLNR-based scheme and AN approach are implemented in the SSK system [20]. However, the channel state information (CSI) in [20] is assumed to be perfect, which is difficult to achieve in practice. Therefore, in [21], the authors evaluated the algorithmic complexity of various AS schemes in imperfect CSI environments and the security performance of SSK systems measured by BER and SR.

To the extent that we are aware, the applications of the traditional MIMO technique and SM in PLS transmission have been widely studied. However, there is relatively little research on the PLS of the SSK system. Therefore, this paper considers improving the security of SSK-based communication and applying it to intelligent wireless sensor systems. Our main contributions are outlined below:

(1) A novel friendly jamming signal joint AS scheme based on the SSK system is proposed to ensure the communication security of intelligent industrial wireless sensor systems.
(2) A generalized Euclidean distance antenna selection (GEDAS) scheme and the leakage-based antenna selection (LBAS) scheme are proposed to boost the safety performance of the SSK system. Moreover, the complexity of the LBAS scheme and the GEDAS scheme are compared.
(3) To evaluate the security performance of the proposed schemes, the SR, SC, and BER of the proposed schemes are comprehensively compared to the traditional random selection scheme.

Notation: Bold capital letters and lowercase letters indicate matrices and vectors, respectively; $|.|$ represents the modulus operation; $(:)$ means the binomial coefficient; $\mathbb{C}^{m \times n}$ stands for the complex space of $m \times n$ dimensions. $\mathfrak{R}^{m \times n}$ denotes the realvalued space of $m \times n$ dimensional.

3   System Model

We consider intelligent wireless sensing systems where SSK is applied as the vital transmission technology. The proposed SSK system in intelligent industrial wireless sensing systems is shown in Fig. 1. A source node (S), a destination node (D), and an eavesdropping node (E) constitute the system model. S is equipped with N_a transmitting antennas for conveying confidential information to D, while E attempts to eavesdrop on the information being transmitted. D and E are each equipped with one antenna for receiving information. To satisfy the generality requirement, considering N_a is assumed not to be a power of 2, the SSK principle is not satisfied. To execute the SSK function, choosing antenna N_t from antenna N_a, where N_t is a power of 2. Thus, there is a total of $P = \begin{pmatrix} N_a \\ N_t \end{pmatrix}$

selection patterns. According to the working mechanism of SSK, one of the N_t antennas is activated in each time slot, and then mapping the transmitted valid information to the index of the active antenna. In the case of the friendly jamming signal design, the jamming signal is transmitted alongside the valid information, causing no interference to the D node because it is restricted to the null space of the legal link (from S to D link). However, due to spatial decorrelation, E is unaware of the relevant information about the legal link. As a result, the reception of E is interfered with by the friendly jamming signal.

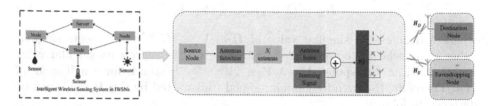

Fig. 1. System model of the proposed scheme for SSK-based communications in intelligent industrial wireless sensing systems

Each antenna in the proposed SSK system corresponds to a specific information vector, which can be written as:

$$x_j = [0...0...1...0]^T \tag{1}$$

where x_j represents a $N_t \times 1$ vector. The position of the non-zero value in the vector denotes the $j - th$ active antenna, and the transmitted power of each information vector is normalized to the unit.

When AS is applied to SSK, the received signals by D and E nodes are denoted as follows:

$$y_D = H_D T_M x_j + n_D \tag{2}$$

$$y_E = H_E T_M x_j + n_E \tag{3}$$

where $H_D \in \mathbb{C}^{1 \times N_a}$ and $H_E \in \mathbb{C}^{1 \times N_a}$ are row vectors representing the legal and illegal link (from S to E), respectively. We assume that the two links are quasi-stationary flat-fading. $T_M \in \mathbb{C}^{N_a \times N_t}$ is constituted by choosing N_t column vectors out of the identity matrix I_{N_a}, which is an optimal transmit antenna matrix to perform the SSK function for $M \in \{1, 2, ... P\} \cdot n_D$ and n_E are the additive white Gaussian noise (AWGN) at D and E nodes, with zero mean and variance δ^2.

4 Proposed Methods

This section thoroughly explains the proposed friendly jamming signal design and AS schemes. Furthermore, the SR of the proposed system is analyzed and calculated, which can be defined as the difference between the average mutual information (AMI) of the D node and that of the E node.

4.1 Friendly Jamming Signal Design

To improve the security performance of the proposed SSK system, the friendly jamming signal, which is dependent on the CSI of the lawful link, must be provided. By using SVD for the legal link [15], we can obtain the following:

$$H_D = [\lambda, 0_{1 \times (N_a - 1)}] [V_1, V_0]^H \tag{4}$$

where λ denotes the singular value of $H_D \cdot V_1 \in C^{1 \times N_a}$ represents singular value vector which is corresponded to λ. $V_0 \in C^{1 \times N_a}$ represents singular value vector which is corresponded to λ. $V_0 \in \mathfrak{R}^{N_a \times (N_a - 1)}$ stands for a null space of H_D. Therefore, the friendly jamming signal transmitted by the V_0 node can be designed to follow:

$$W = V_0 z \tag{5}$$

where $z = [z_1, z_2 \cdots z_{N_{t-1}}]^T \in \mathfrak{R}^{N_a \times (N_a - 1)}$ represents the vector of a time-varying jamming signal, whose components follow a truncated Gaussian distribution.

Because the friendly jamming signal is designed to be transmitted alongside valid information, the received signals can be expressed as follows:

$$y_D = H_D T_M x_j + H_D W + n_D = h_{Dj} + n_D \tag{6}$$

$$y_D = H_E T_M x_j + H_E W + n_E = h_{Ej} + h_{EW} + n_E \tag{7}$$

where h_{Dj} and h_{Ej} represent the valid information from S to D link and S to E link, respectively. h_{EW} denotes the jamming signal term of the E node. Considering that the jamming signal is confined in the null space of the legal link, H_D and W are orthogonal. Therefore, $H_D W = 0$. Due to spatial decorrelation, the E node is impacted by the jamming signal $H_E W$ since it lacks awareness on the CSI of the legal link.

4.2 LBAS Scheme

In this part, we introduce the proposed LBAS scheme, which can improve the security performance of the proposed SSK system even more. $\|H_D T_M e_j\|^2$ is the received signal power at the D node, while $\|H_E T_M e_j\|^2$ is the received signal power at the E node, which is the leakage of D node. For guaranteed communication performance of destination node $\|H_E T_M e_j\|^2 + \sigma^2$ should be smaller than $\|H_D T_M e_j\|^2$, where σ^2 is the AWGN power. To solve the problem described above, we define the LBAS ratio of the j-th link of the M-th combination as:

$$\varphi_j(T_M) = \frac{\|H_D T_M e_j\|^2}{\|H_E T_M e_j\|^2 + \sigma^2} \tag{8}$$

By maximizing the LBAS values, the objective is to determine the optimal T_M. Assuming all transmit antennas are irrelevant, the LBAS of each transmit antenna is different and can be expressed as follows:

$$\varphi_l = \frac{\|h_{Dl}\|^2}{\|h_{El}\|^2 + \sigma^2} \tag{9}$$

where l denotes the index of the selected antenna ($l \in \{1, 2, \ldots N_a\}$), and h_{Dl} and h_{El} denote the l-th column of links H_D and H_E, respectively. We determined the LBAS values for each antenna on the transmitter and arranged them in descending order, as shown below:

$$\varphi_{\pi_1} \geq \varphi_{\pi_2} \geq \ldots \geq \varphi_{\pi_{N_t}} \geq \ldots \varphi_{\pi_{N_a}} \tag{10}$$

where $\{\pi_1, \pi_2 \ldots \pi_{N_a}\}$ is a list of permutations of $\{1, 2, \ldots N_a\}$ in an ordered manner. Therefore, change the optimization to choose the first N_t LBAS values from (10). We can obtain the corresponding N_t antenna based on the given LBAS values. The difference between the legal and illegal link increases with increasing LBAS values. Therefore, compared to the non-AS method, this scheme can enhance the performance of the system.

4.3   GEDAS Scheme

This part introduces the proposed GEDAS scheme, which can further boost the security performance of the proposed SSK system. In accordance with the AMI of the received nodes, the GEDAS scheme is proposed. Therefore, the AMI expressions are determined first.

The signal received at the D node after executing AS on the SSK system follows the complex Gaussian distribution. Therefore, the probability density functions (PDF) can be expressed by:

$$P(y_D \mid x_j) = \frac{1}{\pi\sigma^2} \exp\left(-\frac{|y_D - h_{Dj}|^2}{\sigma^2}\right) \tag{11}$$

Because the transmitted information has an independent and identical distribution, the unconditional PDF of y_D can be obtained by:

$$P(y_D) = \frac{1}{\pi\sigma^2 N_t} \sum_{j=1}^{N_t} \exp\left(-\frac{|y_D - h_{Dj}|^2}{\sigma^2}\right) \tag{12}$$

The AMI of the S to D link is expressed as follows by combining (11) and (12).

$$I(y_D; h_{Dj}) = \int \sum_{j=1}^{N_t} P(y_D, h_{Dj}) \log_2 \frac{P(y_D, h_{Dj})}{P(y_D) P(h_{Dj})} dy_D$$

$$= \log_2 N_t - \frac{1}{N_t} \sum_{j=1}^{N_t} E_{n_D}\left[\log_2\left(\sum_{j'=1}^{N_t} \exp\left(-\frac{|\zeta_{j,j'} + n_D|^2 - |n_D|^2}{\sigma^2}\right)\right)\right] \tag{13}$$

where $\zeta_{j,j'} = h_{Dj} - h_{Dj}$.

Similarly, the AMI of the S to E link is represented as:

$$I\left(y_E; h_{Ej}\right) = \log_2 N_t - \frac{1}{N_t} \times \sum_{j=1}^{N_t} E'_{n_E}\left[\log_2\left[\sum_{j=1}^{N_t} \exp\left(-\frac{\left|Q\alpha_{j,j'} + n'_E\right|^2 - \left|n'_E\right|^2}{\sigma^2}\right)\right]\right]$$

(14)

$$n'_E = h_{EW} + n_E$$

(15)

$$Q = \delta_E\left\{\left[n'_E\left(n'_E\right)^H\right]\right\}^{-1/2}$$

(16)

where $\alpha_{j,j'} = h_{Ej} - h_{Ej'}$. Obviously, the noise term of E is comprised of AWGN and the jamming signal. The function of Q is to make the noise term of E follow the Gaussian distribution with a mean value of zero and a variance of δ^2 [24]. Therefore, the signal received by the E node follows the complex Gaussian distribution. Consequently, the AMI of the E node can be calculated in the same method as the AMI of the D node.

After acquiring the AMI expressions for D and E nodes, the SR of the proposed scheme may be determined utilizing the definition in [20], which can be represented as:

$$R_s = \max\left\{0, I\left(y_D; h_{Dj}\right) - I\left(y_E; h_{Ej}\right)\right\}$$

(17)

The lower bound of $I\left(y_D; h_{Dj}\right)$ can be computed using Jensen's inequality [22] as follows:

$$I\left(y_D; h_{Dj}\right)_{LB} = \log_2 N_t + 1 - \frac{1}{\ln 2} - \frac{1}{N_t} \times \sum_{j=1}^{N_t} \log_2\left(\sum_{j'=1}^{N_t} \exp\left(\frac{-\left|\zeta_{j,j'}\right|^2}{2\sigma^2}\right)\right)$$

(18)

In the high signal-to-noise ratio (SNR) areas, σ^2 is close to 0, thus $\frac{-\min_{j\neq j}\left|\zeta_{j,j}\right|^2}{2\sigma^2}$ becomes the dominant term in the process of calculating AMI [22]. Therefore, the minimum Euclidean distances, $d_{1\min} = \min_{j\neq j'}\left|\zeta_{j,j'}\right|^2$ and $d_{2\min} = \min_{j\neq j'}\left|\alpha_{j,j'}\right|^2$ determine the AMI of D and E nodes, respectively. The proposed GEDAS scheme proposes a novel selection pattern that maximizes the minimum Euclidean distances over the legal link or minimizes the minimum Euclidean distances over the illegal link [23]. As a consequence, the proposed GEDAS method is as follows:

$$\boldsymbol{T}_{M^*} = \underset{\boldsymbol{T}_M \in \{\boldsymbol{T}_1, \boldsymbol{T}_2, \cdots \boldsymbol{T}_P\}}{\arg\max} \min_{j\neq j'}\left|\zeta_{j,j'}\right|^2$$

(19)

$$\boldsymbol{T}_{M^*} = \underset{\boldsymbol{T}_M \in \{\boldsymbol{T}_1, \boldsymbol{T}_2, \cdots \boldsymbol{T}_P\}}{\arg\min} \min_{j\neq j'}\left|\alpha_{j,j'}\right|^2$$

(20)

where $\boldsymbol{T}_{M^*}$ denotes the optimal selection. We propose two selection patterns, as illustrated in (19) and (20), and then choose the pattern with the higher R_s. This maximizes the AMI of the D node or minimizes the AMI of the E node. As a result, the SR of the proposed SSK system is enhanced further.

4.4   Complexity Analysis

The complexity of the two proposed AS methods is calculated in this part. There are two parts to LBAS scheme complexity. The first part determines all the LBAS values, and the second is the sorting process. Therefore, the complexity of the LBAS method can be lowered to $O(N) + O(N \log_2 N))$ without sacrificing the security performance of the proposed system. The complexity of GEDAS is divided into three parts. The complexity of computing the minimum Euclidean distance is the first component, which is $3N_a$. The second part is the search complexity to find the best pattern, and the complexity is $\left(N_t^2 + 3N_t + 3\right) 2^{N_a - N_t} - \frac{N_a^2 + 5N_a + 8}{2}$. The third is to calculate the complexity of the two modes of SR, and the complexity is $2P \left[N_a^2 (1 + N_t) + 2N_a \left(N_t^2 + 1\right)\right]$. Therefore, the complexity of GEDAS scheme can be expressed as $3N_a + \left(N_t^2 + 3N_t + 3\right) 2^{N_a - N_t} \frac{N_a^2 + 5N_a + 8}{2} + 2P \left[N_a^2 (1 + N_t) + 2N_a \left(N_t^2 + 1\right)\right]$.

5   Simulation Results

In this section, the security performance of the proposed scheme is assessed from three perspectives, SR, SC, and BER. The simulation's outcomes are displayed in Fig. 2. We utilize the MATLAB tool for the Monte Carlo tests and assume that the link is quasi-stationary flat fading that obeys the Rayleigh distribution. Additionally, it is assumed that the input bits have an equiprobability distribution and that the noise is an AWGN.

To better demonstrate the performance of the proposed scheme, we compare two proposed schemes with the traditional random selection scheme [24]. Specifically, we analyze the SR of the LBAS scheme, GEDAS scheme, and random selection scheme under various transmit antennas N_a and N_t. The SC of the three AS schemes and the SC of the conventional SSK system are fully calculated. In addition, the BER values of the two proposed AS schemes under different transmit antennas are comprehensively analyzed.

As shown in Fig. 2(a), we set different (N_a, N_t) pairs, (6,4), (10,8), for three AS schemes. In the high SNR region, the SR values of the three AS schemes tend to saturate as the SNR values rise. As the number of $(N_a, N_t))$ increases, the SR values of the GDEAS scheme and LBAS scheme improve significantly, and the value SR of the randomly selected scheme is also enhanced. It can be inferred that the SR values will increase as the number of (N_a, N_t) increases. Moreover, in the case of the same (N_a, N_t) values, the SR values are in descending order: GEDAS scheme, LBAS scheme, and random selection scheme. In addition, the SR of the two proposed AS schemes in different (N_a, N_t) are better than the SR of the random selection scheme.

The SC against SNR for the three AS schemes and the traditional SSK system are shown in Fig. 2(b). We can observe that the SC values of the three AS schemes rise as the SNR values rise. LBAS scheme, GEDAS scheme, and random selection system are ranked in decreasing order of SC performance. Thus, the proposed

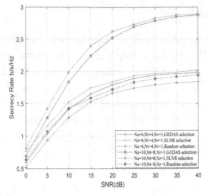

(a) The SR versus SNR with varying N_a
and N_t under three AS schemes

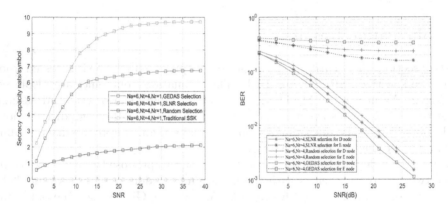

(b) The SC versus SNR under three AS   (c) The BER versus SNR under three AS
schemes and traditional SSK.   schemes for various receivers.

Fig. 2. Simulation results of the proposed method.

GEDAS and LBAS schemes have the potential to further increase the security
of the SSK system.

The BER performance of the proposed LBAS scheme, the GEDAS scheme,
and the random selection scheme with the identical (N_a, N_t) values are comprehensively compared in the simulation in Fig. 2(c). It can be shown that the
BER values of all three AS systems drop as the SNR values increases. The BER
values of the three AS methods for E nodes varied slightly. In the 27dB area,
the BER values of the three AS schemes at the E node are all close to 10^{-1},
and normal communication cannot be guaranteed. Therefore, it is verified that
the designed friendly jamming signal has no influence on the normal reception
of the D node and causes interference with the reception of the E node.

6 Conclusion

This paper proposed two high-performance AS schemes that can be used in intelligent wireless sensing systems. In the proposed scheme, a friendly jamming signal and AS techniques are applied to the secure SSK to promote the confidentiality of intelligent wireless sensing systems. In the friendly jamming design part, the jamming signal is designed by SVD decomposition and can be cancelled by utilizing the CSI of the legal link. In AS part, we proposed two high-performance AS schemes. The LBAS scheme selects antennas to improve system performance according to the maximized LBAS values. The GEDAS scheme further enhances the security of the system by maximizing the Euclidean distance for the legal link or minimizing the Euclidean distance for the illegal link. It is evident that the GEDAS scheme can achieve similar SR performance to the LBAS scheme and lower BER but at the cost of increased algorithmic complexity. In addition, simulation results reveal that the two proposed AS schemes are far superior to the traditional random AS schemes in terms of SR, SC, and BER performance. It can be concluded that the proposed schemes can be considered for secure information exchange and reliable communication in future intelligent wireless sensing systems.

References

1. Yang, D., et al.: Assignment of segmented slots enabling reliable real-time transmission in industrial wireless sensor networks. IEEE Trans. Ind. Electron. **62**(6), 3966–3977 (2015)
2. Wang, H., Yu, F., Li, M., Zhong, Y.: Clock skew estimation for timestamp-free synchronization in industrial wireless sensor networks. IEEE Trans. Industr. Inf. **17**(1), 90–99 (2021)
3. Hang, N.T.T., Trinh, N.C., Ban, N.T., Raza, M., Nguyen, H.X.: Delay and reliability analysis of p-persistent carrier sense multiple access for multi-event industrial wireless sensor networks. IEEE Sens. J. **20**(20), 12402–12414 (2020)
4. Farag, H., Sisinni, E., Gidlund, M., Österberg, P.: Priority-aware wireless fieldbus protocol for mixed-criticality industrial wireless sensor networks. IEEE Sens. J. **19**(7), 2767–2780 (2018)
5. Mietzner, J., Schober, R., Lampe, L., Gerstacker, W.H., Hoeher, P.A.: Multiple-antenna techniques for wireless communications-a comprehensive literature survey. IEEE Commun. Surv. Tutor. **11**(2), 87–105 (2009)
6. Zhang, J., Björnson, E., Matthaiou, M., Ng, D.W.K., Yang, H., Love, D.J.: Prospective multiple antenna technologies for beyond 5G. IEEE J. Sel. Areas Commun. **38**(8), 1637–1660 (2020)
7. Mesleh, R., Haas, H., Ahn, C.W., Yun, S.: Spatial modulation-a new low complexity spectral efficiency enhancing technique. In: 2006 First International Conference on Communications and Networking, pp. 1–5. IEEE, China (2006)
8. Mesleh, R.Y., Haas, H., Sinanovic, S., Ahn, C.W., Yun, S.: Spatial modulation. IEEE Trans. Veh. Technol. **57**(4), 2228–2241 (2008)
9. Jeganathan, J., Ghrayeb, A., Szczecinski, L., Ceron, A.: Space shift keying modulation for MIMO channels. IEEE Trans. Wirel. Commun. **8**(7), 3692–3703 (2009)

10. Mukherjee, A., Fakoorian, S.A.A., Huang, J., Swindlehurst, A.L.: Principles of physical layer security in multiuser wireless networks: a survey. IEEE Commun. Surv. Tutor. **16**(3), 1550–1573 (2014)

11. Shannon, C.E.: Communication theory of secrecy systems. Bell Syst. Tech. J. **28**(4), 656–715 (1949)

12. Wyner, A.D.: The wire-tap channel. Bell Syst. Tech. J. **54**(8), 1355–1387 (1975)

13. Shafiee, S., Ulukus, S.: Achievable rates in Gaussian MISO channels with secrecy constraints. In: 2007 IEEE International Symposium on Information Theory, pp. 2466–2470. IEEE, France (2007)

14. Mirzaee, M., Akhlaghi, S.: Achievable secrecy rate of wiretap channels incorporating multi-input-multi-output amplify and forward relaying. IET Commun. **10**(3), 300–308 (2016)

15. Yu, X., Hu, Y., Pan, Q., Dang, X., Li, N., Shan, M.H.: Secrecy performance analysis of artificial-noise-aided spatial modulation in the presence of imperfect CSI. IEEE Access **6**, 41060–41067 (2018)

16. Goel, S., Negi, R.: Guaranteeing secrecy using artificial noise. IEEE Trans. Wirel. Commun. **7**(6), 2180–2189 (2008)

17. Wang, L., Bashar, S., Wei, Y., Li, R.: Secrecy enhancement analysis against unknown eavesdropping in spatial modulation. IEEE Commun. Lett. **19**(8), 1351–1354 (2015)

18. Guan, X., Cai, Y., Yang, W.: On the mutual information and precoding for spatial modulation with finite alphabet. IEEE Wirel. Commun. Lett. **2**(4), 383–386 (2013)

19. Ding, Z., Ma, Z., Fan, P.: Asymptotic studies for the impact of antenna selection on secure two-way relaying communications with artificial noise. IEEE Trans. Wirel. Commun. **13**(4), 2189–2203 (2014)

20. Huang, Z., Peng, Y., Li, J., Tong, F., Zhu, K., Peng, L.: Secrecy enhancing of SSK systems for IoT applications in smart cities. IEEE Internet Things J. **8**(8), 6385–6392 (2021)

21. Zhu, H., Peng, Y., Xu, H., Tong, F., Jiang, X.Q., Mirza, M.M.: Secrecy enhancement for SSK-based communications in wireless sensing systems. IEEE Sens. J. **22**(18), 18192–18201 (2022)

22. Shang, P., Yu, W., Zhang, K., Jiang, X.Q., Kim, S.: Secrecy enhancing scheme for spatial modulation using antenna selection and artificial noise. Entropy **21**(7), 626 (2019)

23. Aghdam, S.R., Duman, T.M.: Physical layer security for space shift keying transmission with precoding. IEEE Wirel. Commun. Lett. **5**(2), 180–183 (2016)

24. Zhu, H., Peng, Y.: Secrecy enhancing for SSK-based communications in the presence of imperfect CSI estimation. IEEJ Trans. Electr. Electron. Eng. **16**(11), 1544–1546 (2021)

Multi-user Service Placement in LEO Satellite Constellations

Lei Yan$^{(\boxtimes)}$, Chao Wang$^{(\boxtimes)}$, and Qibo Sun$^{(\boxtimes)}$

State Key Laboratory of Networking and Switching Technology, School of Computer Science, Beijing University of Posts and Telecommunications, Beijing 10086, China
{timingup,c-wang,qbsun}@bupt.edu.cn

Abstract. With the rapid development of the research of space-air-ground integrated network, the importance of studying low Earth orbit (LEO) satellite network has become increasingly prominent. One of the important research directions is to cope with the challenges caused by the high-speed movement of LEO satellites for service placement. In this paper, we study how to place the service instances on LEO satellite constellations effectively. First, we model a satellite-ground communication scenario, giving constraints on several service metrics such as communication delay, load, etc. Then, we propose an algorithm based on time-slice, transforming the original problem into a shortest path problem with a weighted directed graph. In accordance with the characteristics of satellite motion, we introduce the concept of the service duration window and propose a polynomial time complexity approximation algorithm. Finally, we construct the LEO48 satellite constellation for simulation. The results show that, compared with other algorithms, the performance of this algorithm is greatly improved.

Keywords: Satellite Edge Computing · Service Placement · Periodicity · Shortest Path · Service Duration Window

1 Introduction

With the rapid development of network communication technologies, a prototype of a space-air-ground integrted network covering natural spaces such as ocean, land, and space has taken shape [1]. As an important extension of space-air-ground integrted network in space, satellite network has the advantages of wide coverage and ignoring terrain limitation compared with traditional terrestrial communication networks [2]. Satellite has completed its metamorphosis from its initial functions of sending broadcasts and positioning. It is now capable of supporting services such as satellite broadband access, satellite mobile data transmission, and environmental awareness [3]. Computing and storage capabilities on satellites are also being enhanced.

Supported by the Fundamental Research Funds for the Central Universities.

Satellite systems can be divided into three types of satellites: high Earth Orbit (HEO), medium Earth Orbit (MEO) and low Earth Orbit (LEO) according to the orbit height from high to low [4]. Among them, LEO has become the first choice for space-air-ground integrted network because of its small communication delay close to the earth, complete and continuous coverage, relatively low cost, and high system persistence capability.

In the edge computing scenario of LEO satellite networks, LEO satellites close to users play the role of edge nodes in this satellite network by placing services from remote cloud centers, which significantly reduce the end-to-end communication latency. However, in the satellite-ground communication link, the inter-satellite link (ISL) propagation delay, as an important component of the end-to-end delay, is greatly influenced by the location of the service placement [5]. Therefore, a reasonable service placement strategy for edge computing in satellite networks needs to be given to significantly improve the user service quality and reduce the energy consumption and other overheads associated with migration.

The edge computing scenario of satellite network brings many problems compared to the different traditional edge computing scenario. High-speed movement of LEO satellites leads to frequent inter-satellite switching. User service latency is affected by the dynamic changes of ISL. We propose a new service placement scenario and model the corresponding algorithm.

The main contributions of this paper are as follows:

- We construct a system model of the LEO satellite edge computing placement scenario. Reasonable evaluation indexes for parameters such as delay and load are given. The service placement optimization problem is proposed.
- We propose a time-slice based algorithm. The original problem is transformed into a shortest path problem with a weighted directed graph. The corresponding solution algorithm is given afterwards.
- The original problem is transformed by using the predictability of satellite motion characteristics. We propose a polynomial-time service placement algorithm based on the service duration window, and give the corresponding theoretical proof.
- A LEO constellation is constructed for simulation, and the effectiveness of our placement algorithm is demonstrated.

The remainder of the paper is organized as follows. In Sect. 2, related work is reviewed. The problem formulation is described in Sect. 3. We describe our algorithm in Sect. 4. The simulation part is in Sect. 5. Finally, Sect. 6 concludes this paper.

2   Related Work

Existing research works on the service placement problem have mainly focused on the terrestrial scenarios. In [6], the article presents the problem of service placement in mobile edge computing scenarios. The corresponding algorithm is given by proposing a Markov chain-based assumption for user mobility behavior. However, the user mobility can be neglected with respect to the high-speed motion of the satellite. Therefore, the algorithmic framework derived from the above study cannot be applied. A dynamic service placement scenario is presented in [7]. The optimization is modeled using the Lyapunov method and a distributed algorithmic framework is given. But it is not generalizable. A genetic algorithm is used in [8] for heuristic search, giving priority to latency sensitivity. However, migration cost is not considered and is not suitable for the satellite environment.

Less work has been done on service placement of LEO satellites. Reference [9] considers satellite collaborative ground centers to place virtual network function (VNF), transforming it into an integer nonlinear programming problem. But the given algorithm is too complex to adapt to the priority resource environment on the satellite. The problem of VNF placement based on routing traffic is proposed in [10], and a resource-aware algorithm is proposed. However, the traffic information of the satellite ground station is not applicable to the future LEO constellation scenario.

3   Problem Formulation

3.1   System Model

Table 1. Notations

Notation	Meaning
S	low orbit satellite collection
U	ground user collection
t	discrete time slices
$\mathbf{x}_s^u(t)$	binary decision variables for user u's service placement on satellite s
C	communication delay
$\mathbf{R}_e$	Earth radius
H	satellite orbit altitude
β	elevation angle between the satellite and the ground
e	number of ISL hops
$\mathbf{r}^u$	service resource overhead for user u
$\mathbf{W}_{ab}^u$	cost of migrating the services of user u from satellite a to satellite b
$\mathbf{X}(t)$	service placement decision variable solution matrix at moment t
$\mathbf{G}(t)$	space of the solution matrix at moment t
$\mathbf{T}^u$	service duration of user u
$\mathbf{Q}^u$	the queue of transiting satellites in time T^u in the order of transit time
E	ISL hop composition sequence between two migrations

In the satellite edge computing scenario, direct communication between ground users and LEO satellites. LEO satellites deploy MEC services to provide to ground users. In general, the functional structures of multiple satellites in a satellite constellation are similar, or even identical. The spacing within orbital planes and the spacing between orbital planes are uniformly distributed. It is assumed that the satellites studied in this paper are all isomorphic. The ensemble of satellites in the LEO satellite constellation is denoted as $S = \{1, 2, 3, \ldots, S\}$, and the set of ground users is denoted as $U = \{1, 2, 3, \ldots, U\}$. If the access satellite covering the user has already placed the service required by the current user, the user can obtain the corresponding service directly. Otherwise, users need to access the service via ISL or migrate the service to the current transit satellite.

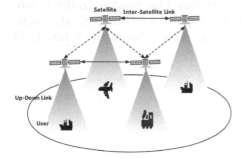

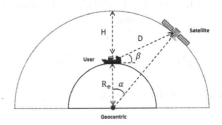

Fig. 1. Satellite edge computing model

Fig. 2. Geometric relationship diagram of UDL

3.2 Placement Model

Decision Variables. Using the binary variable $x_s^u(t)$ to denote the decision variable for service placement. When $x_s^u(t) = 1$, it means that at time t the service of the user node $u \in U$ is placed on the satellite $s \in S$. Thus, we have the following constraints for the decision variable $x_s^u(t)$.

$$\sum_{s=1}^{S} x_s^u(t) = 1, \quad \forall s \in S, t \in T \tag{1}$$

$$x_s^u(t) \in \{0, 1\}, \quad \forall s \in S, u \in U, t \in T \tag{2}$$

Time Delay Constraint. Figure 1 shows the transmission link between the user u and the LEO constellation S serving it at a certain time, and the link is mainly composed of two parts: the up-down link (UDL) and the ISL. The UDL is the communication link between user and the access satellite directly covering the user, which generally operates in the L/S band. The ISL is the communication link between satellites in the constellation, which generally operates in the L/S band. Therefore, the transmission delay can be formulated as

$$C^u(t) = C^u_{UDL}(t) + C^u_{ISL}(t) \tag{3}$$

If the communication transmission rate between the access satellite and the user is τ, Combining with what Fig. 2 shows that we can get

$$C^u_{UDL}(t) = \frac{\sqrt{R_e^2 + (R_e + H)^2 - 2R_e H \cos \alpha^u(t)}}{\tau} \tag{4}$$

For typical LEO constellation (Iridium, Globalstar, LEO48), all satisfy the minimum hop path must be the shortest path, so the number of hops can be used instead of the path to measure the communication delay [5]. Let the communication delay of two adjacent satellites be C_{neb}, and the hop count of user u ISL be $e^u_{ISL}(t)$ and we get

$$C^u_{ISL}(t) = e^u_{ISL}(t) * C_{neb} \tag{5}$$

Load Constraints. The storage and computing resources on an LEO satellite are very limited. Placing too many services on a single satellite can cause it to be overloaded for long periods of time. This drastically shortens the satellite lifetime and destroys the integrity of the satellite constellation. Therefore, it is necessary to constrain the load in the service placement strategy. Let the resource limit of the satellite be R and the service resource overhead of user u be r^u, then we have the following constraint.

$$\sum_{u=1}^{U} r^u * x^u_s(t) \leq R \quad , \forall s \in S \tag{6}$$

Migration Cost Constraints. In order to address the gradual increase in user access service latency due to the high-speed movement of LEO, service migration between satellites is required. However, frequent service migration consumes a large amount of resources, which is unacceptable for the highly resource-constrained on-board environment and needs to be constrained. The source satellite of the migrated service is denoted as a and the target satellite is denoted as b. Using $W^u_{ab}(t)$ to denote the resource overhead of migrating service from satellite a to b, the migration overhead can be expressed as

$$W^u(t) = \sum_{b=1}^{S} \sum_{a=1}^{S} W^u_{ab}(t) * (x^u_a(t-1) \wedge x^u_b(t)) \tag{7}$$

In this paper, we adopt a predefined upper limit of overhead to let the long-term migration cost meet our predefined value and we get

$$\lim_{T \to \infty} \frac{\sum_{t=1}^{T} \sum_{u=1}^{U} W^u(t)}{T} < W_{max} \tag{8}$$

Thus, the optimization problem mentioned above can be get form

$$P_1 : \min \lim_{T \to \infty} \frac{\sum_{t=1}^{T} \sum_{u=1}^{U} C^u(t)}{T} \tag{9}$$
$$s.t.(1) - (9)$$

4   Service Plactment Algorithm

4.1   Time Slice Solving Algorithm Model

At time t, we take the satellite space S as the rows of the matrix and take the user space U as the columns of the matrix. The composed service placement decision variable solution matrix is denoted as

$$X(t) = \begin{pmatrix} x_1^1(t) & \cdots & x_S^1(t) \\ \vdots & \ddots & \vdots \\ x_1^U(t) & \cdots & x_S^U(t) \end{pmatrix} \tag{10}$$

The solution set can be expressed as $G(t) = \{X_1(t), X_2(t), X_3(t), \ldots, X_{h(t)}(t)\}$. Consider each solution in the solution set as a point. Adding an edge for each solution in the solution set at two adjacent moments with the weight of the transition overhead from the feasible solution at the previous moment to the feasible solution at the next moment. We obtain the directed graph with weights shown in Fig. 3.

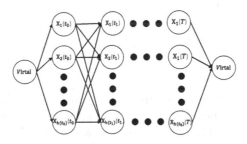

Fig. 3. A weighted directed graph composed of the solution space

The solution set of the optimal solution matrix is the node containing the shortest path of node values between the two virtual nodes in Fig. 3. We can calculate the shortest path in a time-slice by time-slice manner, and the specific steps are shown in Algorithm 1.

There exists an upper bound on the number of nodes in each layer $h(t) \le S^U$, A total of T layers of iterative computation is required, so the complexity of Algorithm 1 is $\mathbf{O}(T * (S^U)^2)$. The complexity of the algorithm grows exponentially with the number of users.

Algorithm 1. TSS algorithm model

Define set X_* to recode the min cost from the virtual node to the previous moment
node. When the iteration is over, it is the optimal solution
for $t = t_0;\ t < T;\ t + +$ **do**
   set $CalculateOverheadperLayer$
   for $i = 1;\ i < h(t);\ i + +$ **do**
      set $tmp \to \infty$
      for each $x\ \in X_*$ **do**
         set $Determinecurrentsolution$
         set $tmp \to min\{tmp, x + weight\}$
      end for
      set Add **tmp** $to\ record$
   end for
   set $X_* \to$ **record**
end for

4.2 Service Duration Window Algorithm Model

The LEO constellation is distinctly periodic, and the trajectory of individual
satellites can be predicted. Therefore, we use the service duration as a window
to the consider the placement problem. Let the ervice duration of each user be
T^u, then the problem P_1 can be reduced to the problem P_2.

$$P_2:\ min\ \lim_{T \to \infty} \frac{\sum_{u=1}^{U} \sum_{t=t_0^u}^{T^u} C^u(t)}{T} \tag{11}$$

$$s.t.(1) - (9)$$

Considering the case of the service of a single user u, the queue of the tran-
siting satellites from the LEO constellation to the end of the service for the
user based on the transit time is denoted as $Q^u = \{s_1, s_2, s_3, \ldots, s_L\}$, $L = |Q^u|$.
The queue of satellites corresponding to the optimal service placement for user u
based on the placement time is denoted as $Q_*^u = \{s_1^*, s_2^*, s_3^*, \ldots, s_{L^*}^*\}$, $L^* = |Q_*^u|$.

Theorem 1. *For the user u, the optimal service placement satellite sequence
Q_*^u is a subsequence of Q^u.*

Proof. Using the converse method, assume that Q_*^u is not a subsequence of Q^u,
then $\exists\ s^* \in Q_*^u$, $s^* \notin Q^u$. Define $s \odot u(t)$ to operate as the satellite s covering
the user u at moment t, then $\forall\ t \in T^u, \exists\ s \in Q^u$, $s \odot u(t)$. Therefore, we can
get

$$s\prime \odot u(t),\ \forall\ s^* \in Q_*^u\ \wedge\ s^* \notin Q^u, \forall\ t \in T_{s^*}^u, \exists\ s\prime \in Q^u \tag{12}$$

Using all satellites $s\prime$ satisfying Eq. (12) to replace the corresponding $s^* \in$
$Q_*^u\ \wedge\ s^* \notin Q^u$, the sequence formed is noted as $Q_\prime^u = \{s_1', s_2', s_3', \ldots, s_{L^*}'\}$.
Let the communication time delay between $s\prime$ and s^* be $C(s', s^*, t)$, and we
have

$$C_*^u(t) = C_\prime^u(t) + C(s', s^*, t) \geq C_\prime^u(t) \tag{13}$$

Therefore, Q_r^u sequence service placement is better than Q_*^u. Contradictory to the conditions of the question, so the original proposition is proved.   □

According to Theorem 1, the service placement target considers only the satellites in Q^u. The service migration among satellites can significantly reduce the delay of users to access the service. Therefore, we take to go for as many service migrations as possible. The sequence of hops between each migrating satellite is denoted as $E = \{e_1, e_2, e_3, \ldots, e_Y\}$, we can get

$$\sum_{i=1}^{Y} e_i = L - 1 \tag{14}$$

Theorem 2. *Finite migration service placement is optimal when the migration hop sequence elements satisfy* $e_1 = e_2 = e_3 = \ldots = e_Y$.

Proof. First, consider the case of migration between two satellites a and b, the services placed on a need to be migrated to b. Suppose that the service migration occurs during the transit of satellite c. Then the ISL delay of segment from a to b can be expressed as

$$C_{ISL-ab}^u = \sum_{t=t_a}^{t_b} C_{ISL}^u(t) = (\sum_{i=0}^{e_{ac}-1} i + \sum_{i=e_{ac}}^{e_{ab}} (e_{ab} - i)) * C_{neb} \tag{15}$$

Simplifying the partial expression in Eq. (15). It is easy to obtain the minimum time delay of the ab segment when $e_{ac} = \frac{e_{ab}+1}{2}$. So the migration delay is minimized when the user is at the midpoint of the migration link between the two satellites. Considering that e_{ac} takes the value of an integer, when e_{ac} is an odd number, the ISL delay of user u can be expressed as

$$C_{ISL}^u \geq C_{neb} * \sum_{i=1}^{Y} ((\frac{e_i+1}{2})^2 - (e_i+1) * (\frac{e_i+1}{2}) + \frac{e_i^2 + e_i}{2}) = C_{neb} * \sum_{i=1}^{Y} \frac{e_i^2 - 2}{4} \tag{16}$$

Combined with Eq. (14), it is easy to obtain from the mean value inequality. The minimum value of Eq. (16) is obtained when $e_1 = e_2 = e_3 = \ldots = e_Y$. The same is true when e_{ab} is an even number. Therefore, the original proposition is proved.   □

So far, we have obtained the optimal placement strategy for a single user service. However, when this strategy is adopted one by one for multiple users, there may be a situation where some of the satellites in the optimal placement sequence are identical, resulting in partial satellite overload. For two services in this situation, we refer to it as two services in conflict. We adopt the strategy of prioritizing the placement for the service with longer service duration. When a conflict occurs, the position of the conflicting satellite in the service with shorter service duration is adjusted to select the satellite in front or behind the original optimal placement satellite in Q^u.

For the migration cost constraint, we agree on a maximum number of migrations. Half of the maximum value is chosen as the initial value of the number of migrations for service placement. Determine whether the long-term constraint on migration cost is satisfied. Adjust the number of migrations using dichotomous lookup until the placement solution with the maximum number of migrations satisfying the migration cost constraint is found.

Algorithm 2. SDW algorithm model

$U \rightarrow$ *Collection of services to be placed*
Sort(U)
for $t = u_0$; $u < u_U$; $u + +$ **do**
    Calculate Q^u
    $r_u \rightarrow Q^u$ *with Theorem 2*
    for each $r \in$ *Result* **do**
        Detecting conflicts between r_u and r
        set $tmp \rightarrow mintmp, x + weight$
    end for
    set Adjust migrations
end for

The outer loop of the algorithm requires U iterations of computation, and both placement and conflict resolution can be given in $\mathbf{O}(1)$ time. There exists an upper bound on the migration cost constraint adjustment $\mathbf{O}(U * \log(K))$, so the complexity of Algorithm 2 is $\mathbf{O}(\log(K) * U^2)$, which is a polynomial complexity approximation algorithm.

5 Performance Evaluation

5.1 Setup

Low Orbit Satellite Constellation Construction. In order to compare and analyze the performance of TSS and SDW algorithms, We use the STK to construct LEO48 constellation for simulation. This satellite constellation is proposed by reference [11]. The constellation consists of a total of 48 satellites scattered on 6 orbital planes as shown in Fig. 4, with 8 satellites evenly distributed on each orbital plane. The angle between orbital planes is 32.6°, the inclination of the orbits is 86°, and the phase factor of adjacent orbits is 22.5°. The rate between the satellite-ground user link is 9.6 kbps (2.4/4.8/9.6 Kbps for the Globalstar constellation system), and the satellite beam coverage radius is 700 km.

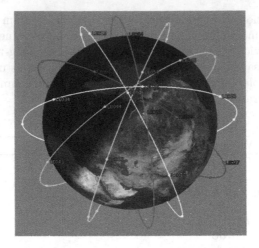

Fig. 4. Satellite orbit setting

Comparison Algorithms. To better verify the performance of the algorithms proposed in this paper, we introduce two algorithm for comparison experiments.

(1) Nearest Service Algorithm (NSA): Place the service on the closest possible satellite to the user (generally this satellite is the access satellite for the user to the satellite constellation). When this satellite is already overloaded, newly received requests will not be immediately responded to. The user's request time will include the lag time of waiting. Service migration will occur when the satellite is no longer able to cover the user.

(2) Weighted Response Time Rule (WRTR): Ribbon, as a effective load balancer in microservices, has seven default load balancing policies. Here we use the WRTR as the comparison algorithm. Specifically, the service instance weight is calculated based on the service time, the shorter the service time, the higher the corresponding weight. Services with high weight will be placed first, and vice versa.

5.2   Analysis of Simulation Results

Delay and Load Experiments. We use ten sets of requests generated by the extracted features to compare the latency and load performance of several algorithms under different request loads, and the results are shown in Fig. 5 and Fig. 6.

As can be seen from Fig. 5, the NSA algorithm results are optimal because it uses a distance greedy based strategy. But it can lead to overload situation. The results of the TSS algorithm and SDW algorithm are not very different, which indicates that the adjustment strategy used by SDW algorithm does not increase the latency too much while reducing the complexity of the algorithm. The worst result for the average request time is the WRTR algorithm because its strategy is to average the load instead of optimizing the latency.

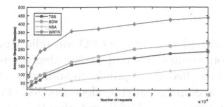
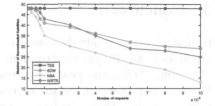

Fig. 5. Comparison of the average request time with the number of user requests

Fig. 6. Comparison results of the number of overloaded satellites with the number of user requests

It can be seen from Fig. 6 that the optimal one is the TSS algorithm because it uses a strong constraint for the overload limit. In the experiments with high requests, the SHW algorithm proposed in this paper is to outperform the WRTR algorithm results, which fully verifies the optimization effect in this aspect of satellite service overload. When the number of user requests increases, the number of unoverloaded satellites in the NSA decreases rapidly, so the plain greedy strategy is not practical.

Migration Cost Experiments. The higher the number of requests, the more likely it is to trigger an overload and cause a service migration to occur. Therefore, we use the dataset with the maximum number of requests from the previous section for this experiment, and dynamically recorded the solution process of several algorithm models on a time-slice by time-slice basis. To be more generalizable, the ratio of migration cost and maximum constraint cost is used to reflect the algorithm effect, and the results are shown in Fig. 7.

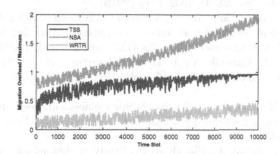

Fig. 7. Results of migration cost experiments

It can be seen intuitively that the TSS algorithm leads to an increasing migration cost due to frequent migrations. The migration cost of the NSA algorithm gradually stabilizes around the maximum constraint range as the iterations proceed. The optimal performance of the WRTR algorithm is mainly due to its lack of concern for delay optimization, which does not lead to an increase in the number of migrations due to delay reduction.

6   Conclusion

In this paper, we study the problem of service placement in a LEO constellation. We model a satellite-ground communication scenario. We propose two algorithms (TSS and SDW), and give the corresponding theoretical proofs. In addition, we build a simulation scenario to experimentally demonstrate the effectiveness of our placement algorithm. The load constraints are satisfied while reducing the user access service latency, and the long-term migration cost constraint is maintained.

References

1. Wang, C., Zhai, L., Xu, X.: Development and prospects of space-terrestrial integrated information network. Radio Commun. Technol. **46**(05), 493–504 (2020)
2. Zhang, Z., Zhang, W., Tseng, F.H.: Satellite mobile edge computing: Improving QoS of high-speed satellite-terrestrial networks using edge computing techniques. IEEE Netw. **33**(1), 70–76 (2019)
3. Xie, R., Tang, Q., Wang, Q., Liu, X., Yu, F.R., Huang, T.: Satellite-terrestrial integrated edge computing networks: architecture, challenges, and open issues. IEEE Netw. **34**(3), 224–231 (2020)
4. Leopold, R.J.: The iridium communications systems. In: [Proceedings] Singapore ICCS/ISITA92, pp. 451–455. IEEE (1992)
5. Jian, Y.: Research on IP routing technology for LEO satellite constellation networks. Tsinghua University, Beijing (2010)
6. Ouyang, T., Zhou, Z., Chen, X.: Follow me at the edge: mobility-aware dynamic service placement for mobile edge computing. IEEE J. Sel. Areas Commun. **36**(10), 2333–2345 (2018)
7. Wang, S., Urgaonkar, R., He, T., Chan, K., Zafer, M., Leung, K.K.: Dynamic service placement for mobile micro-clouds with predicted future costs. IEEE Trans. Parallel Distrib. Syst. **28**(4), 1002–1016 (2016)
8. Maia, A.M., Ghamri-Doudane, Y., Vieira, D., de Castro, M.F.: A multi-objective service placement and load distribution in edge computing. In: 2019 IEEE Global Communications Conference (GLOBECOM), pp. 1–7. IEEE (2019)
9. Gao, X., Liu, R., Kaushik, A.: A distributed virtual network function placement approach in satellite edge and cloud computing. arXiv preprint arXiv:2104.02421 (2021)
10. Gao, X., Liu, R., Kaushik, A.: Service chaining placement based on satellite mission planning in ground station networks. IEEE Trans. Netw. Serv. Manage. **18**(3), 3049–3063 (2021)
11. Guangman, L., Sultan, L., Shaodong, F.: Study of channel assignment scheme for LEO constellation communication system combining switching reserved channels and new call queuing. J. Commun. **27**(9), 135–140 (2006)

Cooperative Computation Offloading in Multi-tier Satellite Terrestrial Network

Zefei Xu$^{(\boxtimes)}$, Hongman Wang, Chao Wang, and Shangguang Wang

State Key Laboratory of Networking and Switching Technology, School of Computer Science, Beijing University of Posts and Telecommunications, Beijing 100876, China
{xuzefei,wanghm,c-wang,sgwang}@bupt.edu.cn

Abstract. Onboard computing has become extremely popular in recent years due to their ability to provide universal Internet connectivity. However, the envisioned computation platform poses numerous new challenges, among which the limited computation resources and the mobility of satellites are critical issues. To address the above issues, we exploit the multi-tier satellite terrestrial computation resources (onboard and cloud resources) to improve quality of service. We formulate the problem as an optimization problem that minimizes the task completion time under the constraint of the limited computational capability of a satellite. Since the optimization problem is NP-hard, a satellite-adaptive earliest completion time first algorithm (SAEFT) is proposed to obtain the optimal solution. The simulation results show that the algorithm can effectively reduce the task completion time compared with other algorithms by 13%.

Keywords: Satellite Terrestrial Networks · Resource Limitation · Mobility of Satellites · Computation Offloading

1 Introduction

1.1 Background and Motivation

Natural disasters can destroy the connectivity of terrestrial networks. Moreover, Internet is an uneven network and some remote rural areas are unreachable by terrestrial networks. It is meaningful to provide uninterrupted and continuous service in underserved regions [4,10]. Satellite communication can provide all-weather stable and reliable service, which becomes a feasible solution to the above problem. Multiple companies have committed to construct satellite constellations, such as OneWeb [9], SpaceX [6], and O3b [20].

Nanosatellites [5] can be equipped with edge computation resources thanks to technical breakthroughs in the space industry. Tasks are allowed to be offloaded to the onboard computation resources, effectively reducing the extra cost incurred by long-distance communication. Further, the combination of

Supported by the Fundamental Research Funds for the Central Universities.

software-defined network (SDN) and satellite communication enables efficient management of the satellite terrestrial network [3,13].

However, task offloading in the satellite terrestrial network also faces some challenges. First, compared with the cloud computing center, the computation resources of a satellite is rather limited [15]. Second, satellites are in high-speed motion, and the network topology changes rapidly. Satellite motion and environmental changes can will lead to link interruptions, rerouting, and additional latency overhead [2]. At present, there are many studies take the latency optimization as the goal of offloading decision-making. In these studies, tasks are usually offloaded to the same server, ignoring idle computing resources in the network. Meanwhile, the link interruption that may occur when offloading is also ignored.

1.2   Our Solution and Contributions

To address the above issues, a multi-tier architecture for cooperative computation offloading is proposed, in which the satellite network can be divided into several control domains, and tasks can be forwarded to other satellites in the same control domain via horizontal cooperation. Furthermore, the vertical cooperation among terminal, satellites, and ground cloud resources can help to relieve the problem of resource limitation. Under this architecture, an optimization problem is formulated to minimize the task completion time with the computation capability constraint of onboard resources. However, the problem is NP-hard [1] and makes it difficult to obtain the optimal offloading strategy. Based on the idea of constructing a priority list of the HEFT [16] algorithm, the SAEFT (Satellite-adaptive Earliest Completion Time First) algorithm is proposed. The main contributions of this paper are summarized as follows:

- We propose a multi-tier architecture for cooperative computation offloading, and formulate the cooperative computation offloading as a optimization problem.
- A novel satellite-adaptive earliest completion time first algorithm is designed to solve the NP-hard problem. The algorithm is based on the table scheduling algorithm, and an adaptive coefficient c is designed to reflect the link change of the satellite network.
- We evaluate the effectiveness of the SAEFT algorithm on reducing average completion time via extensive simulations. The experiment results illustrate that the proposed algorithm can reduce the task completion time by 13% and the average completion time of subtasks by 13%.

The remainder of this paper is organized as follows. The related works are presented in Sect. 2. In Sect. 3, the system model of the multi-tier architecture for cooperative computation offloading is illustrated. Section 4 introduces SAEFT. Section 5 presents the simulation results. Finally, this paper is concluded in Sect. 6.

2   Related Work

In recent years, many studies have investigated computational offloading with the goal of reducing energy consumption or task completion time.

In the framework of satellite MEC, a scheduling algorithm based on dynamic priority queuing was proposed, which can adapt to highly dynamic satellite networks [8]. [14] proposed a three-layer computing architecture that integrates ground users, low-orbit satellites, and cloud servers, and solved the problem of computing offload based on the distributed deep learning to reduce execution latency. [19] proposed a double-edge computing structure and optimized energy consumption through the Hungarian algorithm. Combined with the SDN, a satellite terrestrial edge computing architecture is proposed, which can effectively reduce the delay in [12].

Judging from the current research status, the studies usually omitted idle computing resources in the network. Meanwhile, these studies ignored satellite changes during the task. The interruption of communication links is rarely considered. This paper proposes the SAEFT algorithm to solve the problem of cooperative computing offload in the time-varying satellite terrestrial network environment.

3   System Model and Problem Formulation

3.1   Multi-tier Architecture for Cooperative Computation Offloading

The computing network proposed in this paper includes local terminals, low Earth orbit (LEO) satellites, and cloud computing center. Each LEO satellite holds four inter-satellite links (ISLs): two links in the same orbital plane and two in neighboring planes. Satellites provide access services to terminals within their coverage. MEC servers are deployed on satellites to form a satellite terrestrial network with edge computing capabilities.

This solution considers that the satellite SDN is managed by the dividing control domain. Terminals, access satellites, other satellites in the control domain and the cloud computing center cooperate with each other for tasks. In this solution, the satellite that the terminal communicates directly with is used as the access satellite, which is the control center of the entire offloading process. It can not only undertake offloading tasks, but also exchange status information with the control satellite in the control domain through ISL, and return offloading scheme to the terminal. Therefore, the terminal can perform tasks locally, or offload tasks to the access satellite. Tasks offloaded to the access satellite can also be further offloaded to other satellites in the control domain or cloud computing center. This solution makes full use of idle satellite computing resources and avoids related problems caused by limited resources.

In this paper, a directed acyclic graph (DAG) $G = (V, E)$ is used to represent the task [7]. The task M can be divided into n subtasks, and each vertex in DAG corresponds to a subtask, i.e. $M = \{v_1, v_2...v_n\}$.

These subtasks can be independently selected on which server to perform. Each subtask includes two attributes of input data volume w_{in} and output data volume w_{out}. Meanwhile, each edge $e_{(i,j)}$ represents a dependency between the i_{th} and j_{th} subtasks, the task i needs to be completed before task j. K represents the control domain, which consists of k satellites.

3.2   Communication Model

The communication delay of the task includes three aspects: the transmission delay, the propagation delay, and the delay consumption caused by link interruption.

When the task is calculated locally, no communication consumption is considered in this paper. The visible period of the access satellite is generally much longer than the task completion time. Therefore, it is assumed that the access satellite remains unchanged during the task and the access satellite is represented by S_{ac} [17]. At the same time, this solution is mainly aimed at the scenario where a single user performs offloading, so the mutual influence between multiple channels is not considered. R_1 represents the uplink transmission rate between the ground terminal and the access satellite, and the downlink is represented by R_s. The satellite communicates through ISL, and the communication rate is set to R_{ISL}. The entire task can be divided into a task offloading period and a task feedback period [7]. Taking $w_{i,in}$ and $w_{i,out}$ represents the input and output data volume of the subtask v_m. If the subtask v_m is calculated on server k, where k is a satellite server, the transmission delay during the offloading period $T_{m,k}^{tran}$ and the transmission delay $T_{m,k}^{re}$ during the task feedback period can be expressed as [8],

$$T_{m,k}^{tran} = \frac{w_{m,in}}{R_l} + hop(ac, k) * \frac{w_{m,in}}{R_{ISL}}, \tag{1}$$

$$T_{m,k}^{re} = \frac{w_{m,out}}{R_s} + hop(k, ac) * \frac{w_{m,out}}{R_{ISL}}, \tag{2}$$

where $hop(ac, k)$ and $hop(k, ac)$ respectively represents the number of hops of the link between accessing satellite and calculating satellite in two periods. If k is the access satellite, the value of hop is 0.

Similarly, when the task is calculated on the cloud server, the uplink transmission rate between the satellite and the cloud server is r_l while the downlink transmission rate is r_s. The delays in the two periods can be given by,

$$T_{m,cloud}^{tran} = \frac{w_{m,in}}{R_l} + hop(ac, cloud) * \frac{w_{m,in}}{R_{ISL}} + \frac{w_{m,in}}{r_s}, \tag{3}$$

$$T_{m,cloud}^{re} = \frac{w_{m,out}}{R_s} + hop(cloud, ac) * \frac{w_{m,out}}{R_{ISL}} + \frac{w_{m,out}}{r_l}. \tag{4}$$

The propagation delay is mainly related to the distance. If the subtask v_m is calculated on the server k, we have,

$$T_{l,k}^{prop} = \frac{D_{l,k}}{v}, \tag{5}$$

$$T_{k,l}^{prop} = \frac{D_{k,l}}{v}, \tag{6}$$

where v represents the speed of light and D represents the distance of the communication link.

In addition, LEO satellites are under going rapid changes, and are greatly affected by the load and the atmosphere, rain and other environments. The unstable state of the communication link will cause link interruption [2]. When the ISL of the access satellite and other satellites is interrupted, rerouting is required. T_{route} indicates the delay required for each rerouting, and hop_{loss} indicates the hop change because of the rerouting. If the subtask v_m is calculated on server k, the total delay consumption caused in the two periods are expressed as,

$$T_{ac,k}^{loss} = N_{ac,k}^{loss} * T_{route} + hop_{loss}(ac,k) * \frac{w_{m,in}}{R_{ISL}}, \tag{7}$$

$$T_{k,ac}^{loss} = N_{k,ac}^{loss} * T_{route} + hop_{loss}(k,ac) * \frac{w_{m,out}}{R_{ISL}}, \tag{8}$$

where N represents the number of rerouting times.

To sum up, the total communication delays in the two periods are,

$$T_{m,k}^{off} = T_{m,k}^{tran} + T_{l,k}^{prop} + T_{ac,k}^{loss}, \tag{9}$$

$$T_{m,k}^{back} = T_{m,k}^{re} + T_{k,l}^{prop} + T_{k,ac}^{loss}. \tag{10}$$

In this scenario, a single computing server can only provide computing services for one task at the same time, while each task can only be offloaded once. The binary variable a_m is used to indicate whether the task m is executed in the terminal. Meanwhile, $b_{(m,i)}$ indicates whether the task m is executed in the satellite i. Besides, c_m indicates whether the task is offloaded to the cloud computing center. Therefore, we can get,

$$T_m^{off} = \sum_{i=1}^{K} b_{m,i} * T_{m,i}^{off} + c_m * T_{m,cloud}^{off}, \tag{11}$$

$$T_m^{back} = \sum_{i=1}^{K} b_{m,i} * T_{m,i}^{back} + c_m * T_{m,cloud}^{back}. \tag{12}$$

3.3 Computation Model

In this paper, f_l, f_i, and f_{cloud} are computing capabilities of terminals, LEO satellites, and cloud computing centers, which indicate the number of CPU cycles that a server can provide per unit time. Meanwhile, r is the processing density, which means the quantity of CPU cycles required to process a unit of data. Therefore, the computing time of subtasks on different servers can be calculated from,

$$T_{m,l}^c = \frac{w_{m,in} * r}{f_l}, \tag{13}$$

$$T^c_{m,i} = \frac{w_{m,in} * r}{f_i}, \tag{14}$$

$$T^c_{m,cloud} = \frac{w_{m,in} * r}{f_{cloud}}. \tag{15}$$

To sum up, the computing delay of the task can be expressed as,

$$T^c_m = a_m * T^c_{m,l} + \sum_{i=1}^{K} b_{m,i} * T^c_{m,i} + c_m * T^c_{m,cloud}. \tag{16}$$

3.4 Problem Formulation

First, define the relevant parameters:

Definition 1: $Available(k)$ represents the earliest available time of server k.

$$Available(k) = \max_{map(m)=k} EFT(m, map(m)), \tag{17}$$

where $map(m)$ represents the server assigned to the subtask v_m.

Definition 2: $EST(m, k)$ represents the earliest start time when subtasks are offloaded to k.

$$EST(m, k) = \max(Available(k), \max_{j \in pred(m)} (AFT(j, map(j)) + T^{off}_m)), \tag{18}$$

where $pred(m)$ represents the predecessor subtasks of subtask v_m.

Definition 3: $EFT(m, map(m))$ represents the earliest completion time of the subtask v_m.

$$EFT(m, k) = EST(m, k) + T^c_m. \tag{19}$$

Definition 4: $AFT(m, map(m))$ represents the actual completion time of the subtask v_m.

$$AFT(m, map(m)) = EFT(m, k) + T^{back}_m. \tag{20}$$

Definition 5: $makespan$ represents the overall completion time of task M.

$$makespan = \max_{m \in M} AFT(m, map(m)). \tag{21}$$

The main goal is to minimize the overall completion time of the task under the constraint of limited computing resources. Mathematically, the problem reads,

$$Min \max_{m \in M} AFT(m, map(m)), \tag{22}$$

$$a_m + \sum_{k=1}^{K} b_{m,k} + c_m = 1 \forall m, \tag{23}$$

$$\sum_{m=1}^{M} b_{m,k} * w_{m,in} * r \leq Z_k \forall m, k, \tag{24}$$

$$a_m, b_{m,k}, c_m \in \{0,1\} \forall m, k, \tag{25}$$

where Z_k represents the maximum computing resources that the satellite can provide. (22) is the objective function, which represents the overall completion time of the task. (23) indicates that each task can only be offloaded once. (24) represents the maximum computing capacity constraint of the satellite. (25) means three different offloading decision-making methods.

The optimization problem posed by [14] turned out to be NP-hard. The problem in this paper needs to consider the correlation between subtasks on the basis of the above model, which is also NP-hard. Therefore, we design the SAEFT algorithm to solve the problem.

4 Satellite-Adaptive Earliest Completion Time First Algorithm

---
Algorithm 1. SAEFT

Input: DAG,M,K
Output: Schedule result, $Makespan$
1: Initialize the number of scheduled tasks $N=0$, and c
2: Start from the export task, traverse the DAG tasks to calculate the $rank_{up}$ value of all tasks
3: Start from the entry task, traverse the DAG tasks to calculate the $rank_{down}$ value of all tasks
4: Get the priority of each task, build a priority list
5: **while** $N < |M|$ **do**
6:    Select the task with the highest value in the priority list as v_m
7:    **for** k in local,K,cloud **do**
8:       Calculate the weight W of each server
9:       The task is offloaded to the server with the lowest weight
10:    Update c based on actual completion time and estimated completion time
11:    Save the values of $AFT(i)$, $EFT(i)$, $Available(map(i))$
12: Obtain Schedule result
13: Calculate $Makespan$
14: **return** result

The HEFT algorithm usually solves the static scheduling problem and cannot be applied to the scenario in this paper. This section proposes the SAEFT algorithm for the dynamic nature of the satellite terrestrial network inspired by the idea of constructing a priority list. SAEFT refers to the table scheduling algorithm. An adaptive coefficient c is designed to reflect the link change of the satellite network.

The algorithm flow is shown in Algorithm 1. First, we build a priority list based on the amount of task data and the dependencies between tasks to sort the tasks. Next, we assign servers to subtasks in list order based on server weights. Then, c will be dynamically adjusted according to the actual completion time of the subtask. Finally, we compute the $Makespan$ of the task and output the offloading scheme. The calculation method of the task priority and the server weight will be further described later.

4.1   Task Priority

The task priority is comprehensively calculated based on the task forward ranking and the task reverse ranking. The task forward ranking of subtask v_m refers to the longest path distance starting from v_m and ending with the exit subtask v_{exit}. The recursive expression is given by,

$$rank_{up}(m) = w_{m,in} + \max_{j \in succ(m)} rank_{up}(j). \tag{26}$$

Similarly, the reverse task ranking of subtask v_m refers to the longest path distance starting from v_m and ending with the entry subtask v_{entry}. The recursive expression is,

$$rank_{down}(m) = w_{m,in} + \max_{j \in pred(m)} rank_{down}(j). \tag{27}$$

The ranking of the subtask v_m is determined by the forward ranking and the reverse ranking, which can reflect the relative position of the subtask from different angles. And we have,

$$rank(m) = rank_{up}(m) + rank_{down}(m). \tag{28}$$

4.2   Server Weight

Since the future change of the ISL cannot be known in advance when the offloading decision is made, the completion time of the subtask on the target server is estimated by c. Taking the estimated completion time as the weight, the subtasks are assigned to the server with smallest weight. The weight of subtask v_m in server k can be given by,

$$W_{m,k} = \max(Available(k), \max_{j \in pred(m)}(AFT(j, map(j)))$$
$$+ c * (T_{m,k}^{re} + T_{ac,k}^{prop}))) + T_m^c + c * (T_{m,k}^{re} + T_{k,ac}^{prop}), \tag{29}$$

$$c = (1 - \lambda) * c + \lambda * \frac{T_m^{off} + T_m^{back}}{T_{m,k}^{re} + T_{ac,k}^{prop} + T_{m,k}^{re} + T_{k,ac}^{prop}}, \tag{30}$$

(30) represents the changing trend of the adaptive coefficient, and λ is the step size of each change.

5   Simulation Results

5.1   Experimental Setup

We refer to the Starlink I [11] and use STK to build a satellite constellation. The constellation includes 22 orbital planes, each with 72 orbits. The orbital altitude is 550 km and the inclination is 53∘. Through the simulation of the constellation, the topology changes of the satellite network are obtained for subsequent experiments. Furthermore, the proposed algorithm is implemented in python. For communication and computation parameters set in this paper, we refer to [14,18,19], as shown in Table 1.

Table 1. Parameters setup.

Parameters	Value
computing capabilities of the satellite server	[6 GHz, 10 GHz]
computing capabilities of the terminal	2 GHz
computing capabilities of the cloud computing center	20 GHz
the data processing density	1000cycle/s
uplink transmission rate	20 Mbps
downlink transmission rate	30 Mbps
ISL transmission rate	100 Mbps
input data size	[500 KB, 5000 KB]
output data size	[50 KB, 500 KB]
maximum computing capacity of the satellite	100 G
step size of the SAEFT algorithm	0.1

5.2   Results and Analysis

A random task graph generator is used to generate graphs of relationships between subtasks. The control domain satellite is selected within 4 hops of the access satellite. The number of satellites in the control domain, the number of subtasks, and the ISL interruption rate are changed to analyze the *Makespan* and the average completion time. SAEFT is compared with HEFT [16] and SDPLS [8].

Figure 1 shows *Makespan* and the average completion time for different number of tasks. As the number of offloading tasks increases, both *Makespan* and the average completion time increase. Obviously, the SAEFT algorithm can effectively reduce both *Makespan* and average completion time by 13% compared with other algorithms. In addition, when the number is small, the experimental results change little. It indicates that the satellites in the control domain can meet the parallel requirements of subtasks. With the number of tasks increases, subtasks will consume additional time waiting for the servers to be available, which will significantly affect the results.

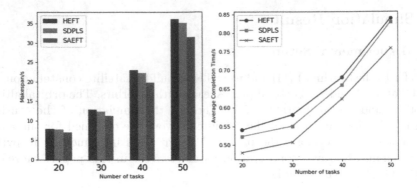

Fig. 1. Makespan and average completion time versus different number of tasks

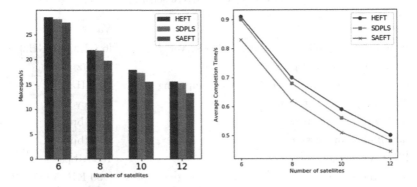

Fig. 2. Makespan and average completion time versus different number of satellites

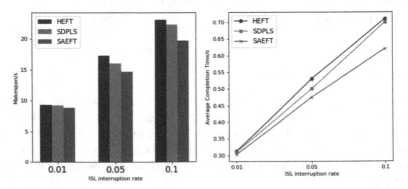

Fig. 3. Makespan and average completion time versus different link interruption rate

Figure 2 shows the experimental conditions under different numbers of satellites in the control domain. Together with the analysis of Fig. 1, the control domain should be reasonably divided according to the task, so as to achieve a balance between the number of satellites and tasks.

Figure 3 shows the situation under different ISL interruption rates. As the ISL interruption rate increases, so does *Makespan* and the average completion time. The SAEFT algorithm performs better than other algorithms when the link interruption rate is high. The generated offloading scheme can adapt to the dynamics of the satellite network. It can reduce *Makespan* by 13% and the average completion time by 13%.

6   Conclusion

In this paper, we studied the cooperative computation offloading problem in multi-tier satellite terrestrial network. Considering the limited computation capability of every satellite, we formulate the problem as an optimization problem towards the goal of minimizing the task completion time. In order to reduce the complexity of the problem, the SAEFT algorithm is proposed to find the optimal solution and generate an offloading scheme. The experimental results show that the SAEFT algorithm has good performance in reducing the task completion time, especially in the scenario of high satellite link interruption rate.

References

1. Chen, B., Quan, G.: Np-hard problems of learning from examples. In: Proceedings of the International Conference on Fuzzy Systems and Knowledge Discovery, vol. 2, pp. 182–186. IEEE (2008)
2. Chen, J., Liang, J., Guo, Z., Xiao, N., Liu, B.: Multi-controller deployment strategy for software-defined satellite network. J. Xidian Univ. **49**(3), 59–67 (2022)
3. Chen, L., Tang, F., Li, X.: Mobility-and load-adaptive controller placement and assignment in LEO satellite networks. In: Proceedings of the IEEE Conference on Computer Communications, pp. 1–10. IEEE (2021)
4. De Cola, T., Bisio, I.: QoS optimisation of eMBB services in converged 5G-satellite networks. IEEE Trans. Veh. Technol. **69**(10), 12098–12110 (2020)
5. Denby, B., Lucia, B.: Orbital edge computing: nanosatellite constellations as a new class of computer system. In: Proceedings of the International Conference on Architectural Support for Programming Languages and Operating Systems, pp. 939–954 (2020)
6. Foreman, V.L., Siddiqi, A., De Weck, O.: Large satellite constellation orbital debris impacts: case studies of oneweb and spacex proposals. In: AIAA SPACE and Astronautics Forum and Exposition, p. 5200 (2017)
7. Gao, J., Wang, J.: A multi-edge cooperative computing offloading scheme based on genetic algorithm. Comput. Sci. **48**(01), 72–80 (2021)
8. Han, J., Wang, H., Wu, S., Wei, J., Yan, L.: Task scheduling of high dynamic edge cluster in satellite edge computing. In: Proceedings of the IEEE World Congress on Services, pp. 287–293. IEEE (2020)
9. Henri, Y.: The oneweb satellite system. Handbook of Small Satellites: Technology, Design, Manufacture, Applications, Economics and Regulation, pp. 1–10 (2020)

10. Kaneko, K., Nishiyama, H., Kato, N., Miura, A., Toyoshima, M.: Construction of a flexibility analysis model for flexible high-throughput satellite communication systems with a digital channelizer. IEEE Trans. Veh. Technol. **67**(3), 2097–2107 (2017)

11. McDowell, J.C.: The low earth orbit satellite population and impacts of the spacex starlink constellation. Astrophys. J. Lett. **892**(2), L36 (2020)

12. Suzhi, C., et al.: Space edge cloud enabling network slicing for 5G satellite network. In: Proceedings of the International Wireless Communications & Mobile Computing Conference, pp. 787–792. IEEE (2019)

13. Tang, F.: Dynamically adaptive cooperation transmission among satellite-ground integrated networks. In: Proceedings of the IEEE Conference on Computer Communications, pp. 1559–1568. IEEE (2020)

14. Tang, Q., Fei, Z., Li, B.: Distributed deep learning for cooperative computation offloading in low earth orbit satellite networks. China Commun. **19**(4), 230–243 (2022)

15. Tang, Q., et al.: MEC enabled satellite-terrestrial network: architecture, key technique and challenge. J. Commun. **41**, 162–181 (2020)

16. Topcuoglu, H., Hariri, S., Wu, M.Y.: Performance-effective and low-complexity task scheduling for heterogeneous computing. IEEE Trans. Parallel Distrib. Syst. **13**(3), 260–274 (2002)

17. Wang, B., Feng, T., Huang, D., Li, X.: Mobile edge computing for LEO satellite: a computation offloading strategy based improved ant colony algorithm. In: Liu, Q., Liu, X., Chen, B., Zhang, Y., Peng, J. (eds.) Proceedings of the 11th International Conference on Computer Engineering and Networks. LNEE, vol. 808, pp. 1664–1676. Springer, Singapore (2022). https://doi.org/10.1007/978-981-16-6554-7_183

18. Wang, X., Wu, J., Shi, Z., Zhao, F., Jin, Z.: Deep reinforcement learning-based autonomous mission planning method for high and low orbit multiple agile earth observing satellites. Adv. Space Res. **70**, 3478–3493 (2022)

19. Wang, Y., Zhang, J., Zhang, X., Wang, P., Liu, L.: A computation offloading strategy in satellite terrestrial networks with double edge computing. In: Proceedings of the IEEE International Conference on Communication Systems, pp. 450–455. IEEE (2018)

20. Wood, L., Lou, Y., Olusola, O.: Revisiting elliptical satellite orbits to enhance the o3b constellation. arXiv preprint arXiv:1407.2521 (2014)

SPath: An Energy-Efficient DAG Task Offloading Scheme with Space-Ground Cooperative Computing

Tianqi Zhao[1,2], Mingyue Zhao[1], Yue Shi[1], and Kuangyu Zheng[1,2(✉)]

[1] Department of Mathematics and Theories, Peng Cheng Laboratory,
Shenzhen, China
{zhaomy,shiyue306}@buaa.edu.cn
[2] School of Electronic and Information Engineering, Beihang University,
Beijing, China
{zy2102522,zhengky}@buaa.edu.cn

Abstract. The fast improvement of satellites in both computation ability and numbers in the network, makes them possible to form as promising edge computing nodes for space-ground cooperative computing. These satellite edges are especially helpful to cover IoT terminals in remote areas (e.g. deserts, forests, and oceans) who have both limited computation and battery resource, as well as short time deadlines. However, the mobility and flexibility of satellites, and the dependence between subtasks of terminal DAG (Directed Acyclic Graph) tasks, pose new challenges to the cooperative offloading scenarios. Moreover, the energy supply for both the ground terminals and the edge satellites are very constrained, and are demanded to be optimized for longer services.

To solve this problem, we propose SPath, an energy-efficient satellite-ground cooperative offloading scheme, which can reduce the energy consumption and latency of DAG tasks. Moreover, it transforms the offload performance optimization problem into a shortest path problem for a more direct solution. The simulation results with real StarLink satellite movement data show that SPath manages to reduce the energy consumption of DAG tasks by 40.1% and the delay by 39.5% over the exited methods.

Keywords: Energy Optimization · Satellite Cooperative Offloading · DAG Task · Shortest Path Algorithm

1 Introduce

Recent years have witnessed the fast developments of both IoT terminal applications on the ground, as well as satellite Internet such StarLink and OneWeb in the space, leading to both space-ground cooperative computing opportunities and challenges. On the ground, the types of tasks that terminal devices handle are becoming more complex that often have a certain dependence relationship,

© The Author(s), under exclusive license to Springer Nature Singapore Pte Ltd. 2023
C.-H. Hsu et al. (Eds.): DataCom 2022, LNCS 13864, pp. 499–510, 2023.
https://doi.org/10.1007/978-981-99-2233-8_36

which usually can be represented as the DAG (Directed Acyclic Graph) model [1], such as common image or terrain recognition, unmanned driving, etc. With the gradual growth of terminal computing technology and the increasing complexity of task requirements, DAG tasks account for an increasing proportion of all terminal tasks.

Energy consumption is an important performance indicator when terminal devices process DAG tasks. Because the energy resources of terminals are often limited. This becomes more critical, when terminals are located in remote areas(e.g., deserts, forests, mountains and oceans). For example, when unmanned aerial vehicles(UAVs) or IoT(internet of things) terminals conduct exploration tasks in the field, their battery capacities are usually limited, so it is more important to efficiently process tasks to extend their service time.

Another important performance metric for DAG tasks in remote areas is processing delay. On one hand, cloud computing centers in remote areas are usually sparse, and terminals are often far away from the cloud center, which leads to a long transmission delay. On the other hand, there could be many terrain obstacles between the terminal and the cloud, which will affect the channel quality and reduce the data transmission speed, resulting in task timeout.

As more satellite networks like Starlink, OneWeb, etc. are deployed, an effective way to solve the above problem is to adopt satellites for space-ground cooperative computing. With the continuous development of satellite technology, satellites will be equipped with high-speed inter-satellite links for data communication [3] and advanced on-board computing systems [4,5], making it possible to transmit data with low delay and high throughput [6–8]. In remote areas, terminals can offload tasks to satellites instead of cloud centers, and the quality of communication can be significantly improved.

To sum up, in remote areas, adding satellites to the cloud edge systems can optimize task offload performance. For example, we can use the satellite ground cooperative system to calculate the tasks such as automatic driving and detection of automatic equipment in the field.

However, the highly dynamic nature of satellites, the limited computing resources, and the dependence on DAG subtasks bring great challenges to the energy consumption optimization of DAG tasks. First, Low Earth Orbit (LEO) has mobility and flexibility, which makes the connection between satellites and ground devices change over time, thus affecting the offloading of tasks to the satellites. Second, the cost of satellite computing and transmission between terminals and clouds is high, but the energy supply of terminals and satellites is limited. Finally, the DAG scheduling problem is NP-hard [2].

The main contributions of this paper are as follows:

- We proposed SPath algorithm and established the satellite-ground cooperative computing system to realize the joint computation of DAG tasks between satellite-ground equipment.
- Reconstruct the structure of DAG tasks, and change the problem of minimum task energy consumption into the problem of the shortest path under the premise of satisfying the interdependence between DAG subtasks.

- Simulation results show that SPath can reduce the energy consumption of DAG task as much as 40.1%, and reduce the delay by 39.5% than current methods.

2 Framework Description and System Model

2.1 SPath Framework Description

We consider building a collaborative communication framework in the air-ground fusion network, as shown in Fig. 1. It consists of three parts: satellite, cloud, and terminal. The satellites are evenly distributed in low-Earth orbit with communication and computing capabilities. Cloud edge devices and terminals on the ground can communicate with each other and with satellites.

Overall collaborative computing steps are described as follows: When a DAG task arrives, SPath treats it as a series of concatenated subtask sets. At the same time, SPath will judge the availability of the satellite at the time of the arrival of the mission, and build the terminal device, cloud, and available satellite at the current moment into a collaborative task offloading system. Next, SPath corresponds the offloading strategy of each task to a path, calculates the corresponding energy consumption and latency, and assigns it as the path weight.

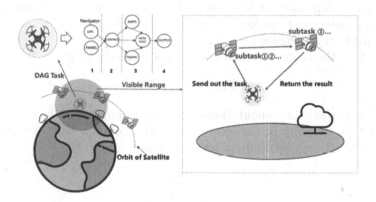

Fig. 1. Structure of satellite cooperative offloading system.

2.2 Task Model

In this paper, we defined the DAG task issued by the terminal as A, and the size, output data size, and deadline of A are respectively $A_{size}, A_{out}, A_{ddl}$:

$$A_{info} = \{A_{size}, A_{out}, A_{ddl}\} \tag{1}$$

A contains m independent atomic-shaped subtasks:

$$A = \{a_1, a_2, ..., a_m\} \tag{2}$$

Each subtask has the corresponding task size $a_{i,size}$ and output $a_{i,out}$:

$$a_i = \{a_{i,size}, a_{i,out}\} \tag{3}$$

Therefore, the size of the entire DAG task can be expressed as follows:

$$A_{size} = \sum_{i=0}^{m} a_{i,size} \tag{4}$$

$i = 1, 2, ..., m$, a_i denotes the ith subtask.

2.3   Calculation Model

For different computing devices, computing resources are highly heterogeneous, so the cost of computing the same task is different for different devices. The latency caused by the task execution is related to the computation amount of the task itself and the computing power of the device. The computation time of a_i is:

$$t_{ai,o}^{com} = a_{i,size}/f_o \tag{5}$$

o can be m,c, and s, which respectively represent terminal equipment, cloud and satellite. Similarly,f_o can take the value of f_m,f_c and f_s, which represent the amount of data that can be calculated per second by terminal devices, cloud computing centers and satellites, respectively. The definition of corner indices o is the same in the following paragraphs.

Therefore, the energy consumption of task a_i on device o is:

$$E_{ai,o}^{com} = t_{ai,o}^{com} P_o^{com} \tag{6}$$

P_o^{com} represents the computational energy consumption of the three devices.

We set the capacity of the computing device to allow only one task to be calculated at a time, the resulting waiting time of task a_i is :

$$t_{ai,o}^{wait} = \frac{N_{o,size}}{f_o}) \tag{7}$$

where $N_{o,size}$ is the number of existing tasks on device o when task a_i reaches.

2.4   Transmission Model

We get the transmission speed from the Shannon formula:

$$r = B_{o1,o2} log_2(1 + \frac{P_{o1,o2}^{tran}}{\delta^2}) \tag{8}$$

$P_{o1,o2}^{tran}$ means the transmission rate from device $o1$ to device $o2$.In the same way, δ^2 is the noise between $o1$ and $o2$.

The time that task a_i sents from device $o1$ to $o2$ can be expressed as:

$$t_{ai,o1,o2}^{tran} = a_{i,size}/r \tag{9}$$

So the transmission energy consumption that task a_i sents from device $o1$ to $o2$ is

$$E_{ai,o1,o2}^{tran} = t_{ai,o1,o2}^{tran} P_{o1,o2}^{tran} \tag{10}$$

2.5 Problem Formulation

The main optimization objective of this paper is to optimize the energy consumption of equipment and satellite under the constraints of task time. Energy consumption is mainly divided into the calculation energy consumption of tasks on different devices and the transmission energy consumption of results transmitted between different devices. The same is true for latency, so the optimization objective can be expressed as follows:

$$min(\omega_E E + \omega_t t) = min(\omega_E \sum_{i=1}^{m}(E_{ai,o1,o2}^{tran} + E_{ai,o}^{com}) + \omega_t \sum_{i=1}^{m}(t_{ai,o1,o2}^{tran} + t_{ai,o}^{com} + t_{ai,o}^{wait})) \tag{11}$$

3 Algorithm

In order to solve the above problems, we propose SPath: An energy consumption shortest path optimization algorithm based on a space-integrated cooperative network. The proposed algorithm is described as follows.

3.1 DAG Task Structure Reconstruction

Due to the limitation of the node path model, only DAG tasks with serial structure can be optimized by path model [9]. In order to extend it to DAG tasks with parallel structure, we need to separate and reconstruct DAG tasks, and finally form a new DAG task consisting of sub-task sets with only serial structure.The principles of separation and reconstruct are as follows:

(1) The node that has a parallel relationship with node N is in the same layer as N;
(2) The number of nodes in each layer should be as small as possible to reduce the algorithm complexity.

The reconstruction diagram is as shown in the Fig. 2.

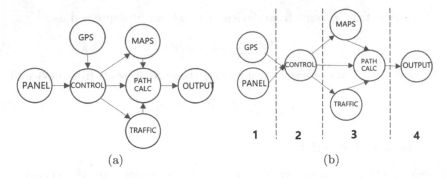

Fig. 2. The structure of the DAG task before and after reconstruction. (*a*)The original DAG task;(*b*)The reorganized DAG task: Consists of four sub-task layers 1, 2, 3, and 4.

3.2 Satellite Availability Judgment

In the model in this paper, we assume that all satellites continuously move around the earth, and only when the satellite communication targets are located within the coverage range of the satellite, communication, and collaborative computing can be carried out with the satellite. Therefore, the visibility of the satellite is mainly divided into two parts:

Satellite and Ground. The traditional way to determine whether a satellite communicates with the ground is to determine whether the ground equipment is within the range of the satellite. However, this method needs to obtain the position of all satellites when the task arrives, then use the visible Angle to judge the coverage range of the satellite, and then judge whether the ground equipment is in the visible range of the satellite.This method requires frequent acquisition of satellite positions and complex calculations, which can lead to high delays.

Therefore, we use the predictability of satellite orbit to calculate the visible period between each satellite and ground equipment and then simplify the problem by judging whether the ground equipment is in the satellite coverage time when the task arrives.

Due to the motion of the satellite, the coverage time of the satellite to the ground is limited. And because of the different trajectories of the satellites, the coverage time of the satellites is also different for the missions that appear at different times. We only select the satellite groups that are covering the ground equipment when the mission appears, and preferentially select the satellite groups with longer coverage time to ensure the stability of mission completion.

Satellite and Satellite. When more than one satellite covers the ground equipment at the same time, it is considered that these satellites can communicate with each other, so as to further increase the optional offloading strategy and optimize the energy consumption of task processing.

3.3 Shortest Path Algorithm

For ease of interpretation, we use the DAG model in the Fig. 3 and set the number of computing devices (which can be clouds, terminals, and visibility-compliant satellites) to two, named c_0, c_1.

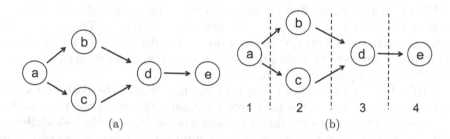

Fig. 3. The structure of the autopilot task.

The path model is shown as Fig. 4:

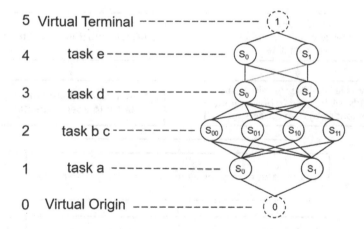

Fig. 4. The path model of DAG task after structural reconstruction.

Each layer in the path model represents the corresponding subtask set and its offloading strategy. The model is divided into two components: nodes and paths.

Node. The bottom node 0 and the top node 1 in the model are virtual starting points created for convenient calculation, and every other node represents an offloading strategy. For example, the node "S_{01}" in the second line indicates that subtask b is unloaded at c_0 and subtask c is unloaded at c_1.

Path. The path weight below the node to represent the weighted sum of the time and energy consumption generated by the node policy. The weighted sum is defined by the formula 11.In the formula, ω_E and ω_T are weighted weights. Since the magnitude of energy consumption and delay is different, ω_E and ω_T are taken as the average of energy consumption and delay of all strategies to strike a balance.

For example, the red line segment represents the weighted sum of task d processed by server c_0, and task e processed by server c_1. The energy consumption includes the energy consumption calculated by d at server c_0 and the transmission energy consumption of d's calculation result from c_0 to c_1, that is $E_{d,1}^{com} + E_{dout,0,1}^{tran}$.The time is the same.

Particularly, a virtual beginning 0 to the first line of the path of the two nodes' weight is equal to the task from terminal equipment send to c_0 and c_1 transmission energy consumption and calculate the sum of the calculation of energy consumption on the corresponding equipment, the fourth row two nodes to the 1 the path of the virtual node weights is equal to the subtasks e results respectively from the processing of c_0 and c_1 back to the end of transmission energy consumption.

The whole algorithm process is as Fig. 5.

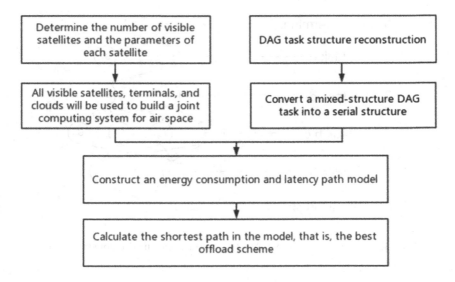

Fig. 5. Flowchart of SPath Algorithm

4 Evaluation

4.1 Experiment Setup

Task Model. Since the difference in DAG structure has a great impact on energy consumption and delay, in order to obtain more intuitive experimental results and rules, we chose a classical navigator task as the simulation object instead of randomly generating a DAG structure, as is shown in Fig. 6.

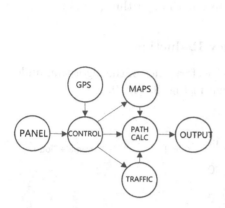

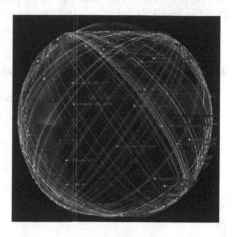

Fig. 6. Navigator Task Structure

Fig. 7. 200 Low-Earth Orbit (LEO) Satellites in Starlink

Simulation Environment. In the experimental setting, we used a terminal device, a cloud computing center, and about 200 low-Earth orbit satellites. The simulation parameters are shown in the Table 1.

Table 1. Simulation Parameters of SPath

parameter	data
terminal device computing power	$50(kW)$
cloud computing power	$0(kW)$
satellite computing power	$[80, 120](kW)$
terminal device computing frequency	$500(kb/s)$
cloud computing frequency	$5000(kb/s)$
satellite computing frequency	$[1000, 2000](kb/s)$
terminal device transmission power	$[1, 1.5(kW)$
cloud transmission power	$[2, 4](kW)$
satellite transmission power	$[3, 10](kW)$
bandwidth	$[3000, 20000](kbps)$
task size Default value	$250KB$
time threshold t_r	$0.8(s)$
deadline	$2(s)$
longitude and latitude of terminal device	$(40, 100)$

Baseline. We chose three baseline algorithms: terminal, cloud, and ground. terminal and cloud represent offloading all DAG tasks to terminal devices and cloud computing centers for computing respectively, while ground represents allocating DAG subtasks to devices on the ground (terminal devices and cloud computing centers, excluding satellites) using the shortest path algorithm (Fig. 7).

4.2 Energy Consumption and Latency Reduction

Through simulation experiments, we get the performance of the algorithm under DAG tasks with different data sizes as shown in Fig. 8, Fig. 9:

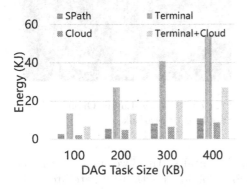

Fig. 8. Energy Consumption.   **Fig. 9.** Latency.

Firstly, it can be seen from the experimental results that SPath has obvious advantages over the other three algorithms, with the energy consumption and delay reduced by 40.1% and 39.5%, respectively. In addition, it can be found that the terminal algorithm consumes a large amount of energy but has a small delay, and the cloud algorithm consumes a small amount of energy but has a large delay, which further reflects that the computing capability of the terminal is insufficient and the distance between the terminal and the cloud computing device is too large.

It can also be found that when the SPath algorithm is used for task offloading of the ground computing system which only has cloud and terminal, and the satellite is not involved, the SPath algorithm can still obtain a relatively balanced task offloading scheme. The simulation results show that our algorithm has better performance of joint optimization.

4.3 Impact of Satellite Numbers

In the above experiments, the satellites are in constant motion, the coverage of each is constantly changing, and the number of satellites that can cooperate with the ground is not fixed. In order to explore the influence of the number of satellites on the performance of SPath, we assume that the satellite position is fixed in this section, that is, $1/2/3$ satellites are fixed for task processing. The simulation results are as Fig. 10:

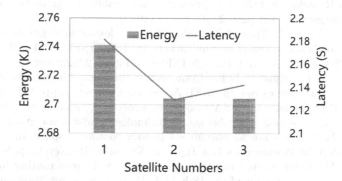

Fig. 10. Impact of the number of satellites on SPath performance.

As can be seen from Fig. 10, when satellites participate in collaborative computing, the performance of the algorithm will be greatly improved, and with the increase of the number of satellites, the comprehensive performance of satellites will also become better.

In addition, we can observe that with the increase in the number of satellites, mission unloading time and energy consumption are not monotonously decreasing. This is because, in the task offloading path model, the weight of the path is the weighted sum of time and energy. Therefore, the optimal strategy finally found is not the optimal one of energy consumption and time, but the optimal comprehensive performance of task offloading. As a result, when one path has a significant energy consumption or time advantage, the algorithm will still choose even if the path has a lower performance in another way.

5   Conclusion

In this paper, we propose SPath algorithm, an energy consumption optimization algorithm for satellite cooperative DAG task processing in remote areas. By reconstructing the structure of the DAG task, SPath can model the DAG task allocation strategy as an path energy consumption model, and by introducing satellite collaborative computing, the optimization problem of DAG task offload is transformed into the shortest path problem. The simulation results with real StarLink movement data show that the SPath can reduce the energy consumption of the DAG tasks by 40.1% and the delay by 39.5% compared with existed methods.

References

1. Yuan, Y., Li, J.X.: Scheduling algorithm based on the cost constraints on the cloud. J. Comput. Res. Dev. **2**, 194–201 (2009)
2. Garey, M.R., Johnson, D.S.: Computer and intractability: a guide to the theory of NP-completeness. SIAM Rev. **24**(1), 90–91 (1979)
3. Lai, Z.F., Liu, S.W.: SpaceRTC: unleashing the low-latency potential of mega-constellations for real-time communications. In: IEEE INFOCOM 2022, pp. 1339–1348 (2022). https://doi.org/10.1109/INFOCOM48880.2022.9796887
4. Gretok, E.W.F., Kain, S.E.T.: Comparative benchmarking analysis of next-generation space processors. In: IEEE Aerospace Conference, pp. 1–16 (2019)
5. Pingree, P.J.: Advancing NASA's on-board processing capabilities with reconfigurable FPGA technologies. In: Aerospace Technologies Advancements, vol. 69 (2010)
6. Handley, M.: Delay is not an option: low latency routing in space. In: Proceedings of the 17th ACM Workshop on Hot Topics in Networks (HotNets), pp. 85–91 (2018)
7. Handley, M.: Using ground relays for low-latency wide-area routing in megaconstellations. In: Proceedings of the 18th ACM Workshop on Hot Topics in Networks (HotNets), pp. 125–132 (2019)
8. Lai, Z.F., Li, S.H.: StarPerf: characterizing network performance for emerging mega-constellations. In: 2020 IEEE 28th International Conference on Network Protocols (ICNP), pp. 1–11 (2020). https://doi.org/10.1109/ICNP49622.2020.9259357
9. Zhang, F.W., Wen, S.Y.: Energy-efficient scheduling policy for collaborative execution in mobile cloud computing. In: 2013 Proceedings IEEE INFOCOM, pp. 190–194 (2013). https://doi.org/10.1109/INFCOM.2013.6566761

Improving Performance of Docker Instance via Image Reconstruction

Qingyuan Jiang[✉]

State Key Laboratory of Networking and Switching Technology,
Beijing University of Posts and Telecommunications, Beijing 100876, China
qingyuan_jiang@bupt.edu.cn

Abstract. Docker has become a key paradigm for application deployment in cloud computing. A running Docker instance need to access its corresponding docker image for searching the required file from time to time. The more layers a docker image has, the longer the search time is. The number of image layers has significant impact on the efficiency of the application. However, reducing the number of image layers via layer merging will reduce the shareability of image layers and increase the storage occupation. To address the above issue, we exploit image reconfiguration to achieve a trade-off between the operation efficiency and storage occupation. We formulate the image reconstruction problem as a knapsack problem, and design a dynamic programming-based offline image reconstruction algorithm named DPOIRA to solve it. We conduct experiments on the busybox and crate, and the experiment results show the effectiveness of our algorithm.

Keywords: Container · Docker · Image Reconstruction

1 Introduction

Due to its rapid deployment and efficient virtualization, Docker [1] has become a key paradigm for application deployment in cloud computing. When Docker is employed, applications run on Docker container instance for isolation. Docker container instance is started from docker image. A Docker container image is a executable package that contains everything needed to run an application. A running Docker instance need to access its corresponding docker image for searching the required file from time to time. Because the container image adopts a hierarchical structure and always consists multiple layers, the system will search the required file from the top layer of the image to bottom layer. The more layers a docker image has, the longer the search time is. The number of docker image layers has significant impact on the efficiency of the application. [2] We find that reducing the number of layers through image reconstruction can solve the above problems. However, reducing the number of layers is obtained by merging two or more layers to one layer, which will reduce the shareability of the image layer and lead to high storage resource occupancy.

C.-H. Hsu et al. (Eds.): DataCom 2022, LNCS 13864, pp. 511–522, 2023.
https://doi.org/10.1007/978-981-99-2233-8_37

Therefore, we investigate how to achieve a trade-off between the operation efficiency and storage resource occupation in this paper. Firstly, we formulate the image reconstruction problem as a knapsack problem. Then, we design a dynamic programming-based offline image reconstruction algorithm named DPOIRA to solve the problem. To show the effectiveness of our algorithm, we conduct experiments on two image storage system: AUFS [3] and overlay2 [4]. The experiment results show that our algorithm can reduce the number of layers while still keep a acceptable storage resource consumption.

2   Background

This section introduces union file system to clarify the docker image layering mechanism. The union file system (UnionFS) [5] is a hierarchical file system that construct the overlaying changes to the file system as a layer. Union file system is the foundation of docker image. A image consists multiple layers. Image is built layer by layer, and the previous layer is the foundation of the next layer. After a layer has been built, it becomes read-only. All changes made to the layer are constructed into a new layer. For example, deleting a file in the previous layer does not actually delete the file in the previous layer. On the contrary, the system constructs a new layer and marks the file as deleted in the new layer. Each layer is identified and referred by hashing the content of the layer using the SHA-256 algorithm [6]. At present, there are several kinds of union file systems supported by docker, including AUFS, overlay, overlay2 and so on (Fig. 1, Fig. 2, Fig. 5).

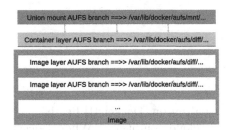

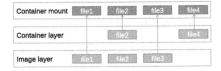

Fig. 1. Structure of image on AUFS   **Fig. 2.** Structure of image on OverlayFS

Advanced Multi-layered unification filesytem (AUFS) is a stackable unification file system, which unifies several directories and provides a merged single directory. AUFS is low efficiency in file searching because it need to traverse all the branches.

The Overlay File System (OverlayFS) is a file system that is very similar to AUFS, but is lighter and faster. OverlayFS refers to the lower-level folder as lowerdir and the high-level folder as upperdir. The multi-layered images is loaded into lower-level folder. Docker provides two types of OverlayFS named overlay and overlay2. Due to high storage efficiency, overlay2 is highly recommended instead of overlay.

3   Performance Analysis

To illustrate the motivation of this paper, we conducted experiments on a six-core Intel 6700HQ processor with 32 GB of RAM. In our experiment, busybox was used as the basic image, and experiments were repeated many times on AUFS and overlay2.

3.1   Performance Analysis of Image Building

We use the command "COPY" in dockerfile to construct image. We study the time to to build images under the following conditions: (1) 100 number of 1 MB files were used to create 100 images; (2) 1,000 number of 1 MB/10,000 number of 1 MB/10,000 number of 1 B files were used to create 11 images respectively.

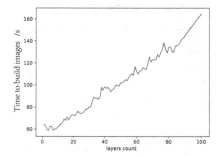

Fig. 3. Time to build 100 images using 100 number of 1 MB files.

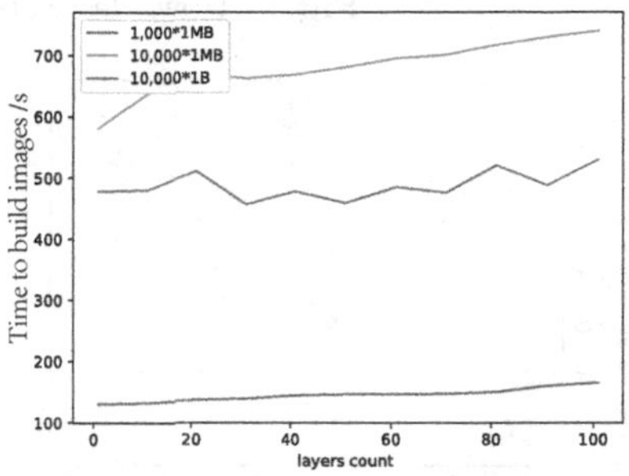

Fig. 4. Time to build 11 images using different size of file.

As shown in Fig. 3, the building time gradually increases with the increase number of image layers. There is a linear correlation between the building time and the number of image layers. Moreover, we observer from Fig. 3 and Fig. 4 that more number of files will result in higher building time. When a small number of small files are used to build an image, distributing the files into few layers or copy the files into one layer almost lead to the same building time. When the size of the files increases to a certain extent, the building time gradually increases with the increase number of image layers.

3.2   Performance Analysis of File Accessing in Container

The impact of file system on performance of container instance is reflected by I/O. First, we use 10,000 number of 1 B files to created 11 images. Figure 7 show how files were distributed in some layers. There is a directory named tempA in each layer, and a directory named tempB in the highest layer. The directory tempA in the lowest layer contains 4,000 files, and the directory tempB contains 5,000 files. Then, we traverse the image using the command "ls -l". If the current layer has no target file, then the next layer is searched until the target file has been found. We experiment on AUFS and overlay2.

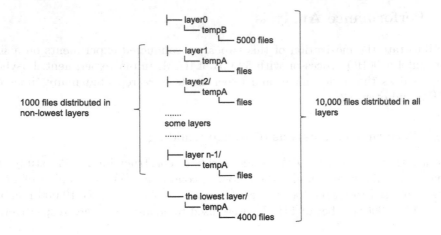

Fig. 5. How files were distributed in some layers.

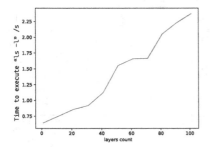

Fig. 6. Time to execute "ls -l" when AUFS is adopted.

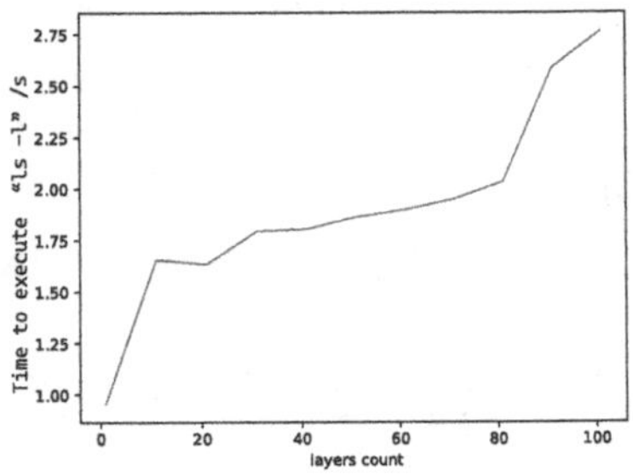

Fig. 7. Time to execute "ls -l" when overlay2 is adopted.

The experiment results on AUFS and overlay2 are illustrated in Fig. 6 and Fig. 7, respectively. We can observe from Fig. 6 that the access time under a 100-layers image is 4 times longer than that under a 1-layer image. The search time is linearly related to the number of layers. And it takes more time to find a file in lower layer. When overlay2 is adopted, the execution time of "ls -l" varies unsteadily with the number of image layers. That's because overlay2 merges image layers into only two layers.

4   System Model

This section models the problem of image reconstruction. The research object is the images in one repository.

4.1   Time Weight

Time to build an image is linearly related to the number of layers. The number of layer is denoted as x. The time cost of building image is denoted as $f(x)$. If files are evenly distributed and the probability of accessing each file is the same, the $f(x)$ can be expressed as:

$$f(x) = a * x + b, \tag{1}$$

where constants a and b are related to the machine. Time to access a file is linearly related to its depth which is denoted as i. The time cost of accessing the file which is denoted as $g(i)$ can be expressed as:

$$g(i) = c * i + d, \tag{2}$$

where constants c and d are related to the machine. Assuming that there are N files evenly distributed in x layers, then time to access N files can be expressed as:

$$\bar{T}(N, x) = N/x * \sum_{i=1}^{x} g(i) = N * c * (x + 1)/2 + N * d \tag{3}$$

Then the average time cost of accessing a file in container can be expressed as Eq. (4), which we use to present the time cost of a container.

$$\bar{T}(1, x) = c * (x + 1)/2 + d \tag{4}$$

We use the time cost of building the image and the sum of the time cost of accessing a file in all the containers spawned from the image as the time weight of the image. The number of containers spawned from an image is denoted as C, and then an image's time weight, which is denoted as $W(C, x)$, is expressed as follows:

$$W(C, x) = C * \bar{T}(1, x) + f(x) = (C * c/2 + a) * x + C * c/2 + C * d + b \tag{5}$$

4.2   Storage Weight

The storage occupied by the repository is the sum of the storage occupied by files in all layers, regardless of the registration information. The set of all layers in the repository is denoted as L. The set of files in all layers is denoted as $F = \{..., f, ...\}$. We use $SD(f)$ to denote the size of file f. Then the storage weight of L repository which is denoted as $S(L)$ can be expressed as:

$$S(L) = \sum_{layer \in L} \sum_{f \in layer} SD(f) \tag{6}$$

4.3   Problem Formulation

We consider trading off time weight against storage weight. The sum of all images' time weight is set as the optimization goal. We set that the number of layers in an image should not exceed the limited value K, and overall storage of repository should not exceed limited value M. The problem is a backpack problem. A union of some layers can be regarded as an image, and the number of layers formed image is image's height. The set of all images is denoted as I, each image in I is a file set. The file set, which can be obtained through union of all images or all layers, is denoted as F. Then the problem is calculated as Eq. (7) and satisfy the condition Eq. (5):

$$Min(\sum_{i \in I} W(C_i, x_i)) \tag{7}$$

$$\begin{cases} F = \cup L \\ S(L) \leq M \\ \forall i \in I, x_i \leq K \end{cases} \tag{8}$$

4.4   Image Reconstruction Algorithm

We proposes a dynamic programming offline image reconstruction algorithm (DPOIRA). As shown in Algorithm 1, it uses Algorithm 2, 3 to reorganize the layers according to the relationship between files and images. The output of Algorithm 1 is a forest. Each node of the forest is a file set that can form a layer. The nodes in path from the root node to another node can form an image.

Algorithm 1: Dynamic Programming Offline Image Reconstruction

Input: I, K, M
Output: $Trees$
1 $Trees, sumOfC \leftarrow TreeAdjustment(LayerTreeBuilding(I, 0, K), M)$;
2 Return $Trees$;

Algorithm 2: Layer Tree Building

Input: $I, nowdepth$ denoted as $Depth, K$
Output: $Trees$
1 $Trees \leftarrow []$;
2 **if** $Depth == K$ or $|I| == 1$ **then**
3 $\quad$ $Trees \leftarrow [each\ image \in I\ is\ formed\ into\ a\ tree\ with\ only\ one\ node]$;
4 $\quad$ Return $Trees$;
5 **while** $I \not\subseteq \emptyset$ **do**
6 $\quad$ $F = \cup image \in I$;
7 $\quad$ $subF \leftarrow \{file|\ file \in F$
     $\quad \wedge file\ is\ owned\ by\ the\ the\ most\ images\ and\ the\ same\ images\}$;
8 $\quad$ $subI \leftarrow \{image|\ image \in I \wedge subF \subset image\}$;
9 $\quad$ $Trees+ = NewTree(subF)$;
10 $\quad$ $I- = subI$;
11 $\quad$ Delete $subF$ from all images in $subI$;
12 $\quad$ Delete images with no files from the $subI$;
13 $\quad$ $Trees[-1].next \leftarrow Layer\ Tree\ Building(subI, Depth + 1, K)$;
14 Return $Trees$;

Algorithm 3: Tree Adjustment

Input: $Tree, M$
Output: $tuple(Trees, sumOfC)$

1   **if** $record[(Tree, M)] \not\subseteq \emptyset$ **then**
2 | **Return** $record[(Tree, M)]$;

3   **if** $Tree$ has only one node **then**
4 | $sumOfC \leftarrow \sum_{image \supset Tree} C_{image}$;
5 | **if** $M < Tree's$ storage weight **then**
6 | | $sumOfC \leftarrow \infty$
7 | $record[(Tree, M)] \leftarrow ([Tree], sumOfC)$;
8 | Return $record[(Tree, M)]$;

9    $Subtrees \leftarrow [size(Tree.next)][M + 1]$;
10   **for** $i \leftarrow 0$ **to** $size(Tree.next) - 1$ **do**
11 | **for** $j \leftarrow M$ **to** 0 **do**
12 | | $Subtrees[i][j] \leftarrow Tree\ Adjustment(tree.next[i], j)$;

13   $dp \leftarrow [size(Tree.next)][M + 1]$;
14   **for** $i \leftarrow 0$ **to** M **do**
15 | $dp[0][i] \leftarrow Subtrees[0][i]$;

16   **for** $i \leftarrow 1$ **to** $size(Tree.next) - 1$ **do**
17 | **for** $j \leftarrow 0$ **to** M **do**
18 | | **for** $k \leftarrow 0$ **to** j **do**
19 | | | $dp[i][j] \leftarrow Selecting\ Trees\ with\ Larger\ SumOfC(dp[i - 1][j],$
                 $dp[i - 1][j - k] + Subtrees[i][k])$;

20   $mergedp \leftarrow [M + 1]$;
21   **for** $j \leftarrow 0$ **to** M **do**
22 | $c \leftarrow j/Tree.root.storageweight$;
23 | **for** $i \leftarrow 0$ **to** c **do**
24 | | $mergedp[j] \leftarrow Selecting\ Trees\ with\ Larger\ SumOfC(mergedp[j],$
                 $Merge(dp[size(Tree.next) - 1][j - i * Tree.root.storageweight],$
                 $i, Tree.root))$;
25 | $record[(Tree, j)] \leftarrow mergedp[j]$;

26   Return $record[(Tree, M)]$;

First of all, we use Algorithm 2 to establish a forest with a height not exceeding K. The inputs of Algorithm 2 are a set of images that each image will be divided into some nodes, the depth of the current node, and the limited depth. The shared times of a file is the number of the images including the file. The shared image of some files is the image including the files. First of all, the files, which have the most shared times and the same shared images, are fetched from the shared images, and put into a new node. Then using the shared images as the input and increasing depth, Algorithm 2 is executed again to get new child nodes recursively. And using the non-shared images as the input, Algorithm 2 is executed again to get new brother nodes iteratively. When the depth reaches the limit, or the image has been processed, Algorithm 2 is finished. The forest return by Algorithm 2 can be regard as a tree with a virtual root.

Then, Algorithm 3 is use to get a forest whose storage weight do not exceed M and time weight is optimal. The inputs of Algorithm 3 are a tree and available storage M. The outputs of Algorithm 3 is a tuple containing the adjusted forest and the $sumOfC$. The $sumOfC$ means the sum of the number of containers spawned from images which have files in trees. The $sumOfC$ is used to decide whether to merge layers to improve time weight. A part of the M is allocated to adjust the sub-trees, and another part of M is allocated to merge the root node into the sub-trees. Algorithm 3 chooses the best method of allocation. We execute the Algorithm 3 on every sub-tree, and find the best combination of adjusted sub-trees under different M. Then consider using extra space to try to merge the root node into some adjusted sub-trees. This means that there may be some more brothers in the current node.

Algorithm 4: Merge

Input: $tuple(Trees, sumOfC), Count, treenode\ P$
Output: $tuple(newTrees, newSumOfC)$

1   $bestTrees \leftarrow topN$ trees with bigest $sumOfC$ in $Trees$;
2   $anoTrees \leftarrow Trees - bestTrees$;
3   **foreach** $tree \in bestTrees$ **do**
4     $\lfloor$ $tree.root+ = P$;
5   **if** $anoTrees \notin \emptyset$ **then**
6     $\lfloor$ $P.next \leftarrow anoTrees$;
7   **if** $anoTrees \notin \emptyset \lor P$ can be formed into the top layer of image **then**
8     $\lfloor$ $anoTrees \leftarrow P$;
9   $newSumOfC \leftarrow \sum_{image \supset P} C_{image}$;
10 Return $(bestTrees + anoTrees, newSumOfC)$;

Algorithm 5: Selecting Trees with Larger SumOfC

Input: $tuple(TreesA, sumOfCA), tuple(TreesB, sumOfCB)$
Output: $tuple(Trees, LargerSumOfC)$

1   **if** $sumOfCA \geq sumOfCB$ **then**
2     $\lfloor$ Return $(TreesA, sumOfCA)$;
3 Return $(TreesB, sumOfCB)$;

The Algorithm 4 is a part of Algorithm 3 and aims to merge a root node into some sub-trees and to get the smallest time weight. The inputs of Algorithm 4 are a tuple of a forest with $sumOfC$, the number of trees that ready to be merged, and the tree node denoted as P ready to be merged. We merge the P's file set into the roots of trees with the largest $sumOfC$. The trees which are merged will not become taller so that their $sumOfC$ will not be changed.

And other trees are P's sub-trees so that P's $sumOfC$ is changed. Then we can get the optimal $newSumOfC$ under these inputs. We assume that there are V images and N valid files. In the worst case, the tree with a height of k and V leaf nodes forms a full $\sqrt[k]{V}$-fork tree. From the up bottom, Algorithm 2 are executed at all $(\sqrt[k]{V}^{k+1} - 1)/(\sqrt[k]{V} - 1)$ nodes so that the order of magnitude of the node is $\mathcal{O}(V)$. In a node, to get $subF$ and $subI$, the time complexity to index files and images is $\mathcal{O}(VN)$ because of iterating through all the files of each image, the time complexity of comparing the corresponding image sets of two files is $O(V)$, so the time complexity of sorting files to get $subF$ is $\mathcal{O}(NlogN*V)$ if using quick sort. Finding a definite layer for each file costs $\mathcal{O}(1)$. To find the corresponding layers for all files of all image costs $\mathcal{O}(VN)$. So the time complexity of Algorithm 2 is $\mathcal{O}(V^2NlogN)$. In the first time executing Algorithm 3 on a node, initializing array $subtrees$ costs $\mathcal{O}(M * \sqrt[k]{V})$, initializing array dp costs $\mathcal{O}(M)$, and getting dp costs $\mathcal{O}(\sqrt[k]{V} * M * (M + 1)/2)$. Then we consider the time complexity of the Algorithm 4. The time complexity of getting $bestTree$ is $\mathcal{O}(c)$. The number of trees handled by Algorithm 4 is no more than V so that handling trees and getting $sumOfC$ cost $\mathcal{O}(V)$. So the time complexity of getting $mergedp$ in Algorithm 3 by executing Algorithm 4 is $\mathcal{O}(c*M) * (\mathcal{O}(c) + \mathcal{O}(V))$. The value of c is related to the number of files. There is at least one file in a node, so the maximum value of c is M. Because the calculation result is recorded, the Algorithm 3's execution on this node again costs $\mathcal{O}(1)$. From the bottom up, Algorithm 3 are executed at all $(\sqrt[k]{V}^{k}-1)/(\sqrt[k]{V}-1)$ non-leaf nodes. The root and leaf nodes of the tree returned by Algorithm 2 do not need to perform Algorithm 4. So the cumulative time complexity of the above operations in Algorithm 3 on all nodes is $\mathcal{O}(V * M^2 + V * M^3 + V^2 * M^2)$. So that the time complexity of DPOIRA is $\mathcal{O}(V^2NlogN + V * M^3 + V^2 * M^2)$.

5   Evaluation

In this section, we evaluate DPOIRA by comparing it with the following schemes:

(1) SOIRA [7]. Only adjust the new image, and share old layers as many as possible
(2) One-File-Per-Layer (OPFL). Each layer contains a file.
(3) Layered Images from Docker Hub (LIDH). Original images created by developers independently

We use 256 different files to randomly build 127 images. The number of files of each image is randomly generated from the range [1], and the number of layers are also randomly generated. The value of C in Eq. (5) is randomly selected from the range $[1, 10]$. For DPOIRA, we set the value of K to 127 and set the value of M to infinity. We first analyze the time cost of all algorithms. The experimental results in Fig. 8 show that the image reconstructed by DPOIRA algorithm can obtain the optimal file access delay. This is because DPOIRA can optimize time by reducing the number of layer. Compared with LIDH, SOIRA reduces 6.6% time cost and DPOIRA reduces 12.3% time cost. Then, we analyze the storage cost of all algorithms. The experimental results in Fig. 9, 10 show that the images reconstructed by DPOIRA algorithm occupy the lest storage space. Compared with LIDH, SOIRA reduces 2.1% storage cost and DPOIRA reduces 12.6% storage cost.

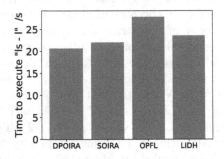

Fig. 8. Time to execute "ls -l" when different algorithms are adopted.

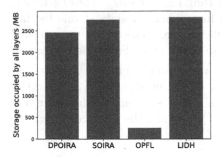

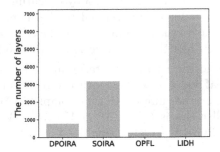

Fig. 9. Storage occupation.   **Fig. 10.** The number of layers.

Then we use the latest 10 images of crateDB from docker-hub, all of which are docker official image. The value of C in Eq. (5) is 1. For DPOIRA, we set the value of K to 4 and set the value of M to infinity. OPFL cannot be used here, because docker image has an upper limit on the number of layers. We first analyze the time cost of all algorithms. The experimental results in Fig. 11 show that the image reconstructed by DPOIRA algorithm can obtain the optimal file access delay. Compared with LIDH, DPOIRA reduces 17.1% time cost, but SOIRA doesn't work. Then, we analyze the storage cost of all algorithms. The experimental results in Fig. 12, 13 show that the images reconstructed by DPOIRA algorithm occupy the lest storage space. Compared with LIDH, DPOIRA reduces 7.4% storage cost, but SOIRA doesn't work.

DPOIRA consumes less storage resources and achieves lower file access time compared with SOIRA and LIDH. That's because SOIRA tries to avoid generating similar layers, but does not make changes to the existing layers. However, DPOIRA reconstructs all layers and merges as many layers as possible to reduce the number of layers.

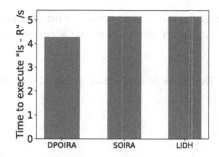

Fig. 11. Time to execute "ls -R" when different algorithms are adopted.

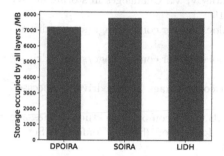

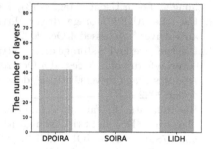

Fig. 12. Storage occupation.   **Fig. 13.** The number of layers.

6   Related Work

Prior works mainly improve performance for docker instance via optimizing image caching, pulling and reconstruction. Anwar et al. [8] analyzed the performance of Docker registry, and reduce the docker startup latency via valid registry cache and image pre-pull. Li et al. [9] introduced a block-based image storage framework, which employs incremental change storage and duplicate files deletion to reduce storage cost. IBM [10] designed a greedy algorithm that organizes files into images to maximize their overlap so that the repository can be compressed. Li et al. [7] exploited layer similarity to reduce the image storage cost. However, the impact of the layer number of an image on docker instance performance is not considered by the prior works.

7   Conclusion

This paper presents an image reconstruction approach to optimize the container instance performance. We first evaluate the image building time and image data access time under different number of image layers. Second, we construct a correlation mode among the number of image layers, storage weight and docker image instance based on the evaluation results. Then, we formulate the the image reconstruction problem as an knapsack problem, and design a dynamic programming-based offline image reconstruction algorithm named DPOIRA to achieve a trade-off between docker image instance time weight and storage weight. The experimental results show that better time weight or storage weight can be obtained by using DPOIRA.

Acknowledgements. This work is supported by the Fundamental Research Funds for the Central Universities.

References

1. Docker. https://www.docker.com/. Accessed 4 Oct 2022
2. Anwar, A., Rupprecht, L., Skourtis, D., Tarasov, V.: Challenges in storing docker images. Login Usenix Mag. **44**(3), 1–6 (2019)
3. Use the AUFS storage driver. https://docs.docker.com/storage/storagedriver/aufs-driver/. Accessed 4 Oct 2022
4. Use the OverlayFS storage driver. https://docs.docker.com/storage/storagedriver/o-verlayfs-driver/. Accessed 4 Oct 2022
5. About storage drivers. https://docs.docker.com/storage/storagedriver/. Accessed 4 Oct 2022
6. Rachmawati, D., Tarigan, J.T., Ginting, A.B.C.: A comparative study of message digest 5 (MD5) and SHA256 algorithm. In: Journal of Physics: Conference Series, vol. 978, p. 012116. IOP Publishing (2018)
7. Li, S., Zhou, A., Ma, X., Xu, M., Wang, S.: Commutativity-guaranteed docker image reconstruction towards effective layer sharing. In: Proceedings of the ACM Web Conference 2022 (WWW 2022), 25–29 April 2022, Virtual Event, Lyon, France. ACM, New York, NY, USA, p. 9 (2022). https://doi.org/10.1145/3485447.3512154
8. Anwar, A., et al.: Improving docker registry design based on production workload analysis. In: Proceedings of the 16th USENIX Conference on File and Storage Technologies (FAST) (2018)
9. Li, Y., An, B., Ma, J., Cao, D.: Comparison between chunk-based and layer-based container image storage approaches: an empirical study. In: 2019 IEEE International Conference on Service-Oriented System Engineering (SOSE), 197–1975. IEEE (2019)
10. Skourtis, D., Rupprecht, L., Tarasov, V., Megiddo, N.: Carving perfect layers out of docker images. In: 11th USENIX Workshop on Hot Topics in Cloud Computing (HotCloud 2019) (2019)

Edge Cloud Selection Strategy for Micro-service Chain Migration in Mobile Edge Computing

Lanqing Xu[✉], Hongman Wang, Jie Huang, and Hongyan Wang

State Key Laboratory of Networking and Switching Technology, School of Computer Science, Beijing University of Posts and Telecommunications, Beijing 100876, China
{xulanqing,wanghm,huangjie,hywang19}@bupt.edu.cn

Abstract. Micro-service, splitting and combining services in a finer granularity, is an emerging service architecture. With the rapid development of 5G and 6G mobile communication network, the migration of micro-services in edge computing has gradually become a hot topic. However, the range of edge cloud is limited, and user movement will increase the service delay. We consider the characteristics of service interdependence and serial parallel relationship in the micro-service chain and put forward an edge cloud selection strategy for micro-service chain migration based on Gibbs Monte Carlo sampling, in order to minimize the total micro-service chain migration delay and the distributed computing resources, and to achieve seamless and realtime response to mobile users' service request. Experimental results show that, compared with other algorithms, the proposed algorithm can guarantee better global performance and reduce the total delay of service migration effectively.

Keywords: Edge Computing · Service Migration · Micro-Service Chain

1 Introduction

Mobile Edge Computing (MEC), sinks computing and storage resources closer to the user [9], so that the data generated on the edge side can be timely and effectively processed. At the same time, MEC makes it possible for the network structure to support delay-sensitive services and mass computing services, laying a good hardware foundation for future intelligent services with low delay, high bandwidth and multi-scenario situational awareness. Research on mobile edge computing has driven the development of virtual machine and Docker technology [3,18]. Driven by container technology [16], IT service providers such as Netflix [6] provide complex services to users with micro-service architecture by traversing a series of micro-services in the service chain in turn. Micro-service architecture can bring flexibility and scalability [14], and it is widely used in

Supported by the Fundamental Research Funds for the Central Universities.

intelligent transportation, video cloud and other scenarios. The combination of mobile edge computing with the new service model of micro-service architecture has attracted wide attention [7] in academic and industry. The combination of micro-services and edge computing provides low latency service for nearby mobile users and it can be dynamically deployed, quickly started, and easily migrated on demand.

Although this new service model has many advantages, it still faces great challenges. First of all, the coverage of a single edge cloud is limited and the mobility of user device is high. When users are far away from the current edge cloud [12], the service delay will be greatly increased. Secondly, compared with the single service migration, micro-service chain migration is more complex. Micro-services are interdependent and have a series-parallel relationship. This dependency pattern puts more restrictions on the order in which micro-services can be executed. The start time of a single micro-service must be after all of its precursors have finished running. However, the majority of existing studies have not considered this situation. In addition, when the micro-service chain selects the edge cloud, the selection of the current edge cloud has an impact on the selection of the subsequent edge cloud and may increase additional migration delay. Therefore, the optimal migration delay of a single service does not mean the optimal migration delay of the whole micro-service chain.

In this paper, we investigate edge cloud selection strategy for micro-service chain migration with the goal of minimizing total latency and total allocated re-sources. The main contributions of this work are summarized below:

1) We studied the structure of the micro-service chain, and combined the structural characteristics of the micro-service in the micro-service chain with the dependency and serialization relationship, and formulated to a mathematical problem by taking the micro-service as the unit.
2) As the number of micro-services increases, the structural complexity among micro-services increases, and the computational complexity of this problem will increase dramatically. Gibbs Monte Carlo sampling is simple to implement and is suitable for situations where direct sampling is difficult but easy to sample from. Therefore, we proposed an edge cloud selection strategy for micro-service chain based on Gibbs Monte Carlo sampling to find the optimal solution to minimize the total delay of micro-service chain and allocate resources, so as to improve the service quality of edge cloud.
3) The simulation results show that, considering the accuracy of the algorithm and the runtime of the algorithm, the Gibbs Monte Carlo sampling algorithm is superior to the Breadth First algorithm and the Greedy algorithm.

The remainder of this article is organized as follows.

Section 2 reviews the related work. Section 3 introduces the system model and problem formulation. Section 4 proposes the micro-service chain migration selection strategy algorithm based on Gibbs Monte Carlo sampling. Section 5 provides the experimental results. Finally, Sect. 6 provides the conclusion.

2   Related Work

In recent years, a series of literatures focused on the migration of edge computing services in order to reduce the migration delay. Jun Li et al. [8] proposed a bandwidth slicing mechanism to dynamically and efficiently allocate bandwidth to migrating and non-migrating traffic to meet their different delay requirements. C. Pu et al. [4] proposed an edge computing service migration method based on environment awareness and dynamic compression to improve the amount of migrated data, service downtime and total service migration time. A. Mukhopadhyay et al. [1] used Markov decision process, learning automata and combinatorial optimization to reduce service downtime. X. Li et al. [17]also expressed the problem as Markov decision process and proposed an intelligent business migration algorithm based on learning. From the perspective of service migration environment. P. Bellavista et al. [10] proposed that edge computing platform architecture supports service migration with different granularity options. However, they all studied the migration problem of single service, but do not consider the migration method of micro-service architecture.

With the development of container technology, the research on micro-service is also developing. Pethuru Raj et al. [5] proposed how to design, develop, deploy and manage event-driven micro-services. V. Bushong et al. [13] provide a method for analyzing microservice grids and using static code analysis to generate communication diagrams, context maps, and finite contexts specific to microservices. Yan Guo et al. [11] considered the problem of resource availability and dynamic changes of service requests related to user mobility, and proposed an online micro-service coordination algorithm based on reinforcement learning to learn the optimal policy, aiming to find the optimal edge cloud sequence to provide micro-services for mobile users. W. Li et al. [15] proposed a heuristic algorithm for micro-services scheduling for dynamically available containers and resource requirements. Aiming at the problems of overhead, resource utilization, long boot time and cost of running mobile applications. A. Ali et al. [2] proposed A dynamic decision task scheduling technology for mobile cloud computing applications based on microservices. However, most of studies do not consider the problem of splitting migration of parallel services.

To sum up, there are numerous researches on the migration technology of mobile edge computing services, but most of them are for the services of single architecture. With the development of container technology and the needs of service providers, micro-service architecture is emerging. The research on micro-service is not comprehensive, and the parallel micro-service problem is rarely considered. In this paper, a service chain migration selection strategy based on Gibbs Monte Carlo sampling is proposed to reduce the total migration time delay and total allocation resources.

3   System Model and Problem Definition

3.1   Definition Model of Micro-service Chain Structure

As shown in Fig. 1, micro-services execute services in the chains. In this paper, directed acyclic graph (DAG) is used to represent the whole micro-service chain.

Therefore, DAG with n vertices is used to represent all micro-services and the line with arrows is used to represent their dependencies. The number of micro-services in whole micro-services chain S is m, and the ith micro-service can be represented by $s_i(1 \le i \le m)$. These microservices can be processed independently. Each micro-service in the micro-service chain has the following properties(A micro-service is represented by six tuple in Fig. 1): p_i represents the input size of a single micro-service (in bits), and ω_i represents the computation intensity (CPU cycles). Each edge represents the dependency relationship between micro-services and the priority constraint between micro-services. Therefore, the service also has the attributes of preorder node sequence pre_i (the fifth term in parentheses) and subsequent node sequence $back_i$ (the sixth term in parentheses), that is, all preorder nodes that need to complete micro-service i before starting micro-service j. At this time, the properties of micro-service i also include τ_i: the service start execution time (in seconds), and de_i represents the completion deadline (in seconds).

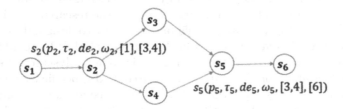

Fig. 1. Micro-service Chain Structure

3.2   Problem Definition

A mobile edge network consists of an Internet cloud, base stations andedge clouds. We assume that the number of base station is n_1 and the number of edge cloud is $n_2(n_2 \le n_1)$. B represents the base station, and C represents the edge cloud. Each edge cloud is implemented on a base station equipped with servers based on an existing network topology. The Internet cloud hosts all microservices. In Fig. 2, there are 9 base stations, 5 edge clouds, and one Internet cloud.

We use the Markov chain prediction algorithm to determine the user's moving trajectory, so as to determine the user's nearby edge cloud at any time. When users move from the coverage of one edge cloud to another, a micro-service chain migration selection strategy is required to determine which edge cloud performs which computing micro-service. The goal of the micro-service chain migration selection strategy is to minimize the overall delay (including computation delay, transmission delay, and migration delay) and the allocated resources.

Computation Delay. Let $f_{i,j}$ denote the computation frequency (per CPU cycle) that edge cloud C_j can allocate to microservice s_i. If edge cloud C_j is chosen to execute micro-service s_i, the execution time of micro-service is denoted by $r^e_{i,j}$. It can be calculated as:

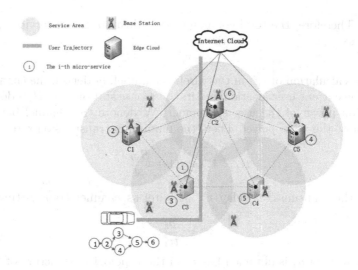

Fig. 2. Micro-service chain migration model

$$r_{i,j}^e = \frac{p_i * \omega_i}{f_{i,j}}. \tag{1}$$

At the same time, each edge cloud can allocate computing resources for multiple micro-services from different users. However, the computing resources of edge cloud are relatively limited, and there may be some unfinished micro-services waiting for processing. Therefore, queue time should be considered. Let p_{jl}^q represent the number lth unfinished data size of a single micro-service in edge cloud C_j. ω_{jl}^q represents the corresponding computational intensity of the micro-service in edge cloud C_j, f_{jl}^q represents the computational intensity assigned to the microservice in edge cloud C_j. Therefore, the queuing delay of microservice s_i on edge cloud C_j should be equal to the sum of computing delays of all incomplete microservices on edge cloud C_j. It can be expressed as:

$$r_{i,j}^q = \sum_{i=1}^{l} \frac{p_{jl}^q * \omega_{jl}^q}{f_{jl}^q}. \tag{2}$$

Therefore, the total computation delay of micro-service s_i executed by edge cloud C_j is:

$$r_{i,j}^c = r_{i,j}^e + r_{i,j}^q. \tag{3}$$

Communication Delay. A single micro-service data transmission can consist of two steps: data transmission from a user to his local base station over a wireless channel; data transmission from its local base station to the selected edge cloud. The data of micro-service s_i transmitted by the user to the local base station through the wireless channel can be denoted as r_i^w. d_j is denoted as the sum of communication delays between the local base station and the selected edge cloud C_j. Therefore, the total communication delay of micro-service s_i can be expressed as:

$$r_{i,j}^t = r_i^w + d_j. \tag{4}$$

For the calculation of r_i^w, in the wireless channel, g_t denote the channel gain between the current user location and its local base station $b_t \subseteq B$, S denote the transmission power of the user equipment, W denote the channel bandwidth, and N denote the noise power. Then, the maximum transmission rate is:

$$tr_t = W log_2(1 + \frac{Sg_t}{N}). \tag{5}$$

Then, the transmission delay r_i^w of wireless channel transmitting micro-service s_i is:

$$r_i^w = \frac{p_i}{tr_t}. \tag{6}$$

The calculation of d_j is obtained based on the topological structure of the base station. $e_{k,j} \subseteq E$ is denoted as the communication delay from base station B_k to base station B_j, and the topology is (if $e_{k,j}$ is finite, then base station B_k is connected to base station B_j, otherwise, they are disconnected).

$$\begin{bmatrix} e_{11} & \cdots & e_{1n_1} \\ \vdots & & \vdots \\ e_{n_1 1} & \cdots & e_{n_1 n_1} \end{bmatrix} \tag{7}$$

Migration Delay. When users move and service edge cloud switches, additional delay is incurred due to service migration and possible deployment of micro-services. In this paper, if the micro-service s_i and its preorder node sequence pre_i in the micro-service chain are not executed on the same edge cloud, migration delay will occur.

$$r_i^p = \lambda \prod x(i) \neq x(pre_i). \tag{8}$$

λ is the downtime of the migration, $\prod(y)$ is the indicator function, and $\prod(y) = 1$ if the event y is true, and $\prod(y) = 0$ otherwise. $x(i) \subseteq C$ represents the edge cloud of the microservice s_i service.

Computing Resources. Due to the limited computing resources of the edge cloud, the computing resource allocation of each micro-service in the micro-service chain by the edge cloud affects the cost demanded by operators from users. Therefore, we considers the computing resource allocation of the micro-service chain, and the computing resource is related to the computing frequency allocated by the edge cloud. $f_{i,j}$ represents the computing frequency that edge cloud C_j can allocate to microservice s_i, then the computing resource allocated to microservice s_i is $u(f_{i,j})$.

3.3   Problem Formulation

The goal is to find the optimal micro-service chain migration selection scheme that minimizes the total delay and total allocated computing resources in a long time. Firstly, the relevant parameters of the problem model are defined as follows:

Definition 1: R_i represents the total execution delay of the ith micro-service:

$$R_i = r^c_{i,j} + r^t_{i,j}. \tag{9}$$

Definition 2: τ_i represents the begin time of the ith micro-service:

$$\tau_i = \max_{j \in pre_i} (\tau_j + R_j) + \sum i = pre_i r^p_i. \tag{10}$$

For micro-service chain $S = s_1, s_2, \ldots, s_m$ total delay:

$$R = \tau_m + R_m. \tag{11}$$

The total computing resource of micro-service chain S is:

$$U(f) = \sum_{i=1}^{m} u(f_{i,j}). \tag{12}$$

The edge cloud selection strategy for micro-service chain migration problem is formulated as:

$$\min_{m \in S} R, U(f).$$
$$s.t. R_i \leq de_i \forall i \in M \tag{13}$$
$$x(i) \in C \forall i \in M$$

4   Gibbs Monte Carlo Sampling Algorithm

The basic idea of the Monte Carlo Simulation and Markov Chain algorithm is to assume that the target randomly samples from a probability distribution or find the mathematical expectation of the function about the probability distribution. Gibbs Monte Carlo sampling algorithm every state transition can be generated to simulate the distribution of a sample, not only improves the random variable sampling acceptance rate, and applies only to the high dimensional situations. This is very suitable for the problem of multi-service selection and multi-edge cloud in the micro-service chain studied in this paper. At the same time, the selection of each preorder service has an impact on the migration delay of subsequent micro-services. Therefore, in order to minimize the overall migration delay and allocate resources, we propose an edge cloud selection strategy for micro-service chain Migration based on Gibbs Monte Carlo sampling. As shown in Algorithm 1.

Algorithm 1. Edge Cloud Selection Strategy for Micro-service Chain Migration

---

Input: $S = s_1, s_2, \ldots, s_m$ and each micro-service chain attribute, E, each edge cloud computing intensity and waiting task

Output: Optimal micro-service chain migration selection strategy

1: Initialize the conditional probability distribution, set the threshold of the number of state transitions p, and the number of samples q

2: Initialize the initial state of the micro-service randomly s_1^0, s_2^0, ..., s_m^0

3: Start from the entry task, traverse the DAG tasks to calculate the $rank_{down}$ value of all tasks

4: **for** state in 0, $p+q-1$ **do**

5:     **for** num in 0,m **do**

6:         Obtain the edge cloud where service 1 resides by sampling from the conditional probability distribution $s_{num}^{state+1}$

7:         The sample set is the one corresponding to the stationary distribution $St = \left(s_1^{sr}, s_2^{sr}, ..., s_m^{sr}\right), ..., \left(s_1^{sr+sp-1} s_1^{sr+sp-1}, ..., s_m^{sr+sp-1}\right)$

8: **while** $kinSt$ **do**

9:     **for** se in M **do**

10:         Calculate the service runtime function

11:         Take the derivative to get the minimum value of allocated resources

12:         Decide whether to migrate the micro-service chain and save the migration time

13: obtain the final migration plan

14: **return** result

---

5   Experiment and Results

In this section, we compare Gibbs Monte Carlo sampling algorithm with Greedy algorithm and Breadth-First Search (BFS) algorithm. We compare the algorithms from the accuracy of whether they approach the minimum delay and the speed of whether they converge quickly. The former corresponds to the total time delay index of service chain migration obtained by the edge cloud selection strategy for micro-service chain migration. The latter corresponds to the index of the running time of the edge cloud selection strategy for micro-service chain migration. We initially set up 10 base stations, 5 edge clouds, and 6 micro-services in the micro-service chain. We compare BFS algorithm, Greedy algorithm and the Gibbs sampling process with iteration number 100 and iteration number 150. The results show the comprehensive superiority of the Gibbs Monte Carlo sampling algorithm.

Firstly, we use the random task graph generator to generate the relationship graph between micro-services. The random number generates the micro-service data volume, edge cloud computing intensity and the waiting time of the service as the input parameters. We analyze the algorithm to predict the completed and total micro-service chain migration delay based on different micro-service number and micro-service size.

Figure 3 and Fig. 4 show the micro-service chain migration calculation delay and algorithm running time under different number of micro-services. The blue

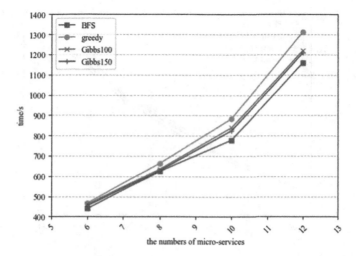

Fig. 3. Relationship between the number of services and the total migration delay

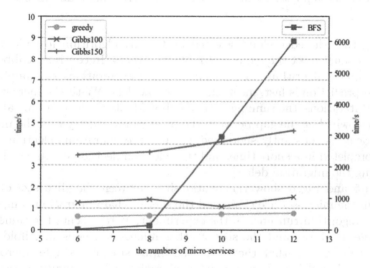

Fig. 4. Relationship between the number of services and algorithm runtime (Color figure online)

line looks at the right scale, the others look at the left scale in Fig. 4. It can be seen that with the increase of the number of micro-services in the micro-service chain, the computing delay of micro-service chain migration and the algorithm prediction time both rise to a certain extent. Although the BFS algorithm has the most accurate prediction, when the prediction time of its algorithm increases exponentially, it cannot meet the needs of fast decision-making in the process of user movement. Although Greedy algorithm has the least prediction time, its prediction accuracy decreases with the increase of the number of micro-services,

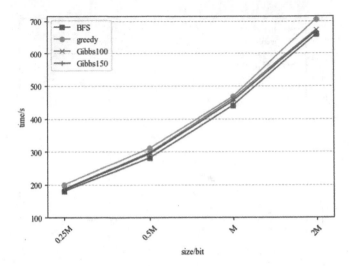

Fig. 5. Relationship between the size of a single service and total migration delay

indicating that the edge cloud selected by Greedy algorithm for micro-service operation cannot meet the requirement of low latency. In contrast, Gibbs Monte Carlo sampling algorithm, we takes 100 and 150 iterations of sampling, the algorithm prediction is fast, meet the goal of low delay. With the increase of the number of iterations, the running time of Gibbs Monte Carlo sampling algorithm increases slowly, but the gap between the total running delay and the minimum running delay is constantly shortened, so that the migration selection decision can be completed in a short time, and the selection decision can meet the needs of reducing the migration delay.

Figure 5 and Fig. 6 show the relationship between the slice size of micro-services in the micro-service chain and the service chain migration computation delay and algorithm runtime. In the experiment, M represents the same micro-service size as above, and the size of other micro-services is multifold related to M. It can be seen that the larger the input size of a single micro-service is, the total time delay of service chain migration will gradually increase. The inclination is also increasing. This indicates that when the calculation intensity is certain, the input size of micro-service should be reasonably slice out, and the overcoupling between micro-services should be avoided, otherwise the total time delay of service migration will be increased. It may be that the size of the micro-service does not change very much and the values of several algorithms are close to each other, but we can also see from Fig. 5 that the Greedy algorithm is increasing the distance from the lowest delay. While Fig. 6 shows that the running time of the BFS is much higher than that of the other two algorithms. Therefore, in a comprehensive view, Gibbs Monte Carlo sampling algorithm is more suitable for service chain migration selection strategy. By comparing the Gibbs sampling process with iteration number 100 and iteration number 150,

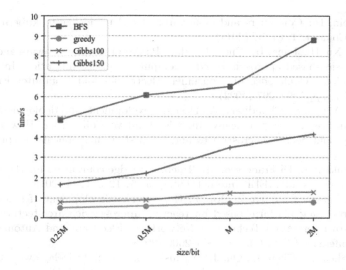

Fig. 6. Relationship between the size of a single service and algorithm runtime

when the total migration delay does not change much, we can choose a smaller iteration number to obtain a better algorithm running time for faster service migration.

6   Conclusion

In this paper, we investigate the problem of service chain migration in a mobile edge computing environment to select the appropriate edge cloud to execute each micro-service as mobile users move. In order to reduce the overall delay and allocated resources, we propose a service chain migration selection strategy based on Gibbs Monte Carlo sampling to find the best migration strategy when the system information is available in the future. In addition, experiments are carried out, and the results show that from the perspective of the accuracy of the minimum delay and the speed of convergence of the algorithm, the proposed algorithm is better in delay and resource allocation, especially for the scenario with long micro-service links. For the future work, the migration decision of service chain in mobile edge computing system will be studied in depth under the condition of multi-user competition for resources.

References

1. Mukhopadhyay, A., Iosifidis, G., Ruffini, M.: Migration-aware network services with edge computing. IEEE Trans. Netw. Serv. Manage. **19**, 1458–1471 (2022)
2. Ali, A., Iqbal, M.M.: A cost and energy efficient task scheduling technique to offload microservices based applications in mobile cloud computing. IEEE Access **10**, 46633–46651 (2022)

3. Bernstein, D.: Containers and cloud: from LXC to docker to kubernetes. EEE Cloud Comput. **1**, 81–84 (2014)
4. Pu, C., Xu, H., Jiang, H., Chen, D., Han, P.: An environment-aware and dynamic compression-based approach for edge computing service migration. In: 2022 2nd International Conference on Consumer Electronics and Computer Engineering (ICCECE), pp. 292–297 (2022)
5. Raj, P., Vanga, S., Chaudhary, A.: Design, development, and deployment of event-driven microservices practically. In: Cloud-native Computing: How to Design, Develop, and Secure Microservices and Event-Driven Applications, pp. 129–142 (2023)
6. Premsankar, G., Di Francesco, M., Taleb, T.: Edge computing for the internet of things: a case study. IEEE Internet Things J. **5**, 1275–1284 (2018)
7. Lv, H., Zhang, T., Zhao, Z., Xu, J., He, T.: The development of real-time large data processing platform based on reactive micro-service architecture. In: 2020 IEEE 4th Information Technology, Networking, Electronic and Automation Control Conference (ITNEC), pp. 2003–2006 (2018)
8. Li, J., Shen, X., Chen, L., Ou, J., Wosinska, L., Chen, J.: Delay-aware bandwidth slicing for service migration in mobile backhaul networks. J. Opt. Commun. Netw. **11**, B1–B9 (2019)
9. M. Patel, Naughton, C.B.: Mobile-edge computing introductory technical white paper. Mob.-Edge Comput. Ind. Initiat. (2014)
10. Bellavista, P., Corradi, A., Foschini, L., Scotece, D.: Differentiated service/data migration for edge services leveraging container characteristics. IEEE Access **7**, 139746–139758 (2019)
11. Wang, S., Guo, Y., Zhang, N., Yang, P., Zhou, A., Shen, X.: Delay-aware microservice coordination in mobile edge computing. A Reinforcement Learning Approach. IEEE Trans. Mob. Comput. **20**, 939–951 (2021)
12. Wang, S., Xu, J., Zhang, N., Liu, Y.: A survey on service migration in mobile edge computing. IEEE Access **6**, 23511–23528 (2018)
13. Bushong, V., Das, D., Al Maruf, A., Cerny, T.: Using static analysis to address microservice architecture reconstruction. In: 2021 36th IEEE/ACM International Conference on Automated Software Engineering (ASE), pp. 1199–1201 (2021)
14. Vassiliou-Gioles, T.: Quality assurance of micro-services - when to trust your microservice test results? In: 2021 IEEE 21st International Conference on Software Quality, Reliability and Security Companion, pp. 01–06 (2021)
15. Li, W., Li, X., Ruiz, R.: Scheduling microservice-based workflows to containers in on-demand cloud resources. In: 2021 IEEE 24th International Conference on Computer Supported Cooperative Work in Design (CSCWD), pp. 61–66 (2021)
16. Li, X., Jiang, Y., Ding, Y., Wei, D., Ma, X., Li, W.: Application research of docker based on Mesos application container cluster. In: 2020 International Conference on Computer Vision, Image and Deep Learning (CVIDL), pp. 476–479 (2020)
17. Li, X., Chen, S., Zhou, Y., Chen, J., Feng, G.: Intelligent service migration based on hidden state inference for mobile edge computing. IEEE Trans. Cogn. Commun. Netw. **8**, 380–393 (2022)
18. Niu, Y., Liu, F., Li, Z.: Load balancing across microservices. In: IEEE INFOCOM 2018 - IEEE Conference on Computer Communications, pp. 198–206 (2018)

Service Migration in Mobile Edge Computing Based on 5G Network User Plane

Liu Hui[(⊠)] and Sun QiBo[(⊠)]

State Key Laboratory of Networking and Switching Technology,
Beijing University of Posts and Telecommunications, Beijing, China
{lh98,qbsun}@bupt.edu.cn

Abstract. The development of mobile edge computing under 5G network provides basic technical support for low latency and high reliability and also poses new challenges to service migration. 5G provides an uplink classifier (UL CL) function in data transmission, which makes it possible to build a new data transmission path. This paper proposes a new service migration decision model based on the 5G network user plane. Based on the new service migration model, this paper uses Markov decision process to construct service migration decision problem, and proposes an online service migration algorithm based on reinforcement learning to learn the optimal migration strategy. Finally, we compare the proposed algorithm with other benchmark algorithms. The results show that the online algorithm is close to the global performance, superior to the existing benchmark algorithm in terms of problem formulation proposed in our paper.

Keywords: 5G · Service Migration · Mobile Edge Computing

1 Introduction

The 5G mobile edge computing (MEC) standard is one of the new network architectures of 5G. 5G MEC mainly provides edge computing capabilities for nearby users by sinking the core network functions to the edge network. 5G MEC can meet the new business requirements of ultra-low latency, ultra-low power consumption, ultra-reliable, and ultra-high-density connections. The sinking and flexible deployment of the 5G user plane function (UPF) realizes local offloading of data traffic. Edge computing nodes are deployed in different locations of the network to meet service requirements that are sensitive to latency and bandwidth.

In 5G transmission, the data transmission distance from the user to the edge computing node can lead to a transmission delay of 80+ms [12]. Moreover, the switching of control surfaces may lead to a transmission delay of 1.9 s [1]. In service migration, the delay is an important factor that affects migration decisions. If the transmission delay in the 5G network is not considered, the migration decision will be greatly affected, thus affecting the quality of service.

© The Author(s), under exclusive license to Springer Nature Singapore Pte Ltd. 2023
C.-H. Hsu et al. (Eds.): DataCom 2022, LNCS 13864, pp. 535–546, 2023.
https://doi.org/10.1007/978-981-99-2233-8_39

With the demand for ultra-low latency and ultra-high reliability of 5G and the development of MEC, service migration research will have to pay attention to network level latency. The technical challenges faced by this paper are as follows:

(1) The delay from the base station to the edge server node has never been considered in the previous service migration model.
(2) The computation of long-term delay and cost is an integer nonlinear programming problem, and it is a NP hard problem.
(3) During user movement, the current service migration decision will affect the next decision. Users can choose to migrate services or dynamically insert the UL CLs.

This paper proposes a new service migration model based on the 5G network user plane. Based on the new migration scenario, we propose the following solutions:

(1) Based on the separation of the control plane and the user plane of the 5G network architecture and the UL CL offload function, a new service migration system model is proposed.
(2) Aiming at the proposed service migration system model, this paper proposes the use of reinforcement learning to solve the problem of minimizing overall delay and cost in the long-term service migration.
(3) For the server selection sequence problem, this paper proposes to use the Q-learning algorithm to solve the server selection problem.

The rest of this paper is organized as follows. Section 2 reviews related work. Section 3 introduces the system model and problem formulation of this paper. Section 4 proposes a service migration algorithm based on the 5G user plane. Section 5 compares the algorithm proposed in this paper with the other three algorithms, and Sect. 6 makes a summary of the full paper.

2   Related Work

The research on service migration mainly lies in two aspects: the first is the decision-making algorithm design of service migration; the second is the optimization of the migration process.

Tao et al. [7] proposed a mobile edge service performance optimization scheme under the constraint of long-term cost budget for service migration caused by user movement, and achieved an ideal balance between user-perceived delay and migration cost in average time. Wang et al. [10] considered the uncertainty of user movement, described the problem of service migration decision as a Markov decision process. Rui et al. [8] proposed to initialize service placement according to the user's initial location and service request for the uncertainty of user movement. Wang et al. [9] used the Markov decision process framework to reconstruct the microservice coordination problem, and then proposed an online microservice coordination algorithm based on reinforcement learning to learn the optimal strategy. Guo et al. [4] proposed a service migration framework using mobile agents. Peng et al. [13] considered the computing load of edge computing servers in the 5G handover algorithm to optimize the handover algorithm in 5G. Chen et al. [2] considered service migration when multiple users moved, and proposed a multi-user server migration strategy based on deep reinforcement learning-based approach. Ge studied the multi-vehicle service migration problem of the vehicle network in MEC [3], and consider the interference between users to accurately describe the service delay and energy consumption.

However, these studies on service migration do not consider the delay caused by UPF transmission. However, according to the research of Xu et al. [12], it can be seen that user mobility will increase the 5G delay, and UPF transmission may cause an 80+ms delay. Therefore, this paper proposes to consider service migration decisions based on the 5G user plane. Different from the previous research points of service migration, this paper considers the optimization of long-term cost and delay from the 5G network architecture.

3 System Model and Problem Definitions

3.1 System Model

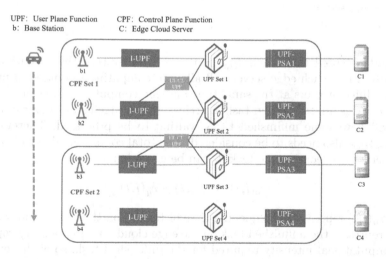

Fig. 1. Service migration scenario based on the 5G user plane.

As shown in Fig. 1, we consider a mobile edge network $G = (B \cup C \cup U \cup CPF)$ consisting of several base stations B, several edge servers C, several UPFs U, and several core network control plane areas CPF. Establishing a session between UPFs in different core network control plane areas will bring about the cost and delay [1], and even lead to the failure of replacing the core network control plane.

In Fig. 1, the user arrives at the destination according to a certain trajectory, which is $l_u = l_u(t)$. $l_u(t)$ represents the user's position at time t. When moving, user's local base station performs seamless automatic handover according to the mobility management protocol. The handover between base stations will cause the transmission path from the base station to the original edge server to change. When $b(t) \neq b(t-1)$, the service migration decision algorithm needs to determine whether to perform service migration or dynamically insert UL CLs to establish a new session connection with the original edge server. In this paper, the goal of our service migration decision algorithm is to minimize the total delay and cost.

3.2   Problem Definition

(1) Computation Delay. The user initiates a service request and transmits the task to the edge cloud server for computing. The task at time t can be represented by $T(d_t, w_t)$ where d_t represents the amount of data of the task (unit: bit), and w_t represents the computational intensity required by the task (unit: CPU Cycles/bit).

During the user movement, each edge server has a limited service time. Let $f_{(i,t)}$ represent the computing intensity that the edge cloud server c_i can allocate to task d_t at time t, i.e. the CPU frequency (CPU Cycles/s). If the edge cloud server c_i is selected to execute the computing task d_t, the execution delay $r_e(i, t)$ can be expressed as,

$$r_e(i, t) = \frac{d_t \cdot w_t}{f_{(i,t)}} \tag{1}$$

It should be noted that when $f_{(i,t)} = 0$, we consider that the execution delay is infinite. Since each edge server will allocate computing resources to multiple tasks of different users at the same time and the computing power of each edge cloud server is limited. When task T arrives at the edge cloud server c_i at time t, c_i will have some unfinished tasks waiting to be processed. Therefore, the queuing time also needs to be considered. The total computing delay of the edge cloud server c_i executing the task d_t can be given by:

$$r_c(i, t) = r_e(i, t) + r_q(i, t) \tag{2}$$

where $r_q(i, t)$ represents the queuing time of task d_t on the edge cloud server c_i. Let d_t^q represent the unfinished task on the edge cloud server c_i, and w_t^q represent the computational intensity required for the unfinished task, so we have:

$$r_q(i, t) = \frac{d_t^q * w_t^q}{f_{(i,t)}} \tag{3}$$

(2) Communication Delay. In this system model, we mainly divide the task data transmission into two parts: the data transmission between the user and the local base station through the wireless channel, and the data transmission from the base station to the target edge server.

In the data transmission of the wireless channel, g_t represents the channel gain of the wireless channel transmission between the user at the position $l_u(t)$ and the local base station $b_t \in B$, S represents the transmit power of the user equipment. While W represents the channel bandwidth, and N represents the noise power. The maximum transmission rate in the wireless channel can be calculated from:

$$tr_t = W \log_2(1 + \frac{Sg_t}{N})$$
(4)

The data transmission delay between the base station and the edge server is determined by the UPF hops between the base station and the edge server.

$$R_U = \begin{bmatrix} u_{(1,1)} & \cdots & u_{(1,n)} \\ u_{(2,1)} & \cdots & u_{(2,n)} \\ \vdots & \ddots & \vdots \\ u_{(m,1)} & \cdots & u_{(m,n)} \end{bmatrix}$$
(5)

$u_{(i,j)}$ represents the number of UPF hops between base station b_i and edge cloud server c_j. The delay consumed by each hop is a fixed constant τ. If b_i and c_j do not belong to the same core domain, the delay of core network control plane replacement needs to be considered,

$$P_t = \omega T_1 + (1 - \omega)T_2$$
(6)

ω is the probability that the core network control plane is successfully replaced, T_1 is the time consumed by the successful replacement of the core network control plane, and T_2 is the time recovering from the failure of the control plane replacement. Therefore, the communication delay of the task T transmitted to the edge cloud server c_i can be expressed as,

$$r_t(i,t) = \frac{d_t}{tr_t} + u_{(i,j)} * \tau + P_t \prod \{CPF_t \neq CPF_{(t-1)}\}$$
(7)

$\prod$ is a sigmod function with a value of 0 or 1. Its value condition mainly depends on whether the communication and transmission at time $t - 1$ and time t cross the core network control plane area,

$$\prod \{CPF_t \neq CPF_{(t-1)}\} = \begin{cases} 1 & CPF(b_i) \neq CPF(c_j) \\ 0 & CPF(b_i) = CPF(c_j) \end{cases}$$
(8)

(3) Migration Delay and Cost. Service migration will result in the delay of service migration and the cost of service migration and recovery. Let $x(t) \in C$ represent the edge cloud server at time slot t. At time slot t + 1, the communication delay from the local base station to x(t) is too long, which affects the user experience. Therefore, the service needs to be migrated to a new edge cloud server x(t + 1). Unfinished computing tasks, the user's file system, and state data will be migrated to the edge cloud server x(t + 1) to synchronize the state.

The computation delay of the task before migration has been given in the previous formula. Meanwhile, the time of service migration is fixed as γ_t, so the remaining tasks that need to be computed after migration can be calculated from,

$$d_t^m = min\left\{d_t, max\left\{0, d_t - \frac{\Delta t - r_t(x(t),t) - r_q(x(t),t)}{r_e(x(t),t)}\right\}\right\} \tag{9}$$

Δt is the service time provided by the base station at t. Therefore, the remaining task data size that needs to be migrated is d_t^m. If only a part of the tasks is completed in Δt, the data size of tasks that need to be migrated is $d_t - \frac{\Delta t - r_t(x(t),t) - r_q(x(t),t)}{r_e(x(t),t)}$, which represented by $\tilde{d}$, and $d_t^m = \tilde{d}$. If the user's task can be completed in Δt, i.e. $\Delta t - r_t(x(t),t) - r_q(x(t),t) > r_e(x(t),t)$, then, $\tilde{d} < 0$, indicating that there is no task data that needs to be migrated. Therefore, after giving the expression of remaining data that needs to be migrated, the service migration delay can be get from:

$$r_m(x(t), x(t+1), t+1) = \left\{\gamma_t + \frac{d_t^m \omega_t}{f(x(t+1),t+1)} - \frac{d_t^m \omega_t}{f(x(t),t)}\right\} \tag{10}$$

γ_t represents the fixed delay of service migration. Service migration occurs only when the edge cloud servers at time t and time t + 1 are inconsistent, resulting in migration delay. After the migration, the unfinished tasks will continue to be executed on the new edge cloud server. Therefore, when the computing power of the new edge cloud server x(t + 1) is stronger than that of the original edge cloud server x(t), $\frac{d_t^m \omega_t}{f(x(t+1),t+1)} - \frac{d_t^m \omega_t}{f(x(t),t)} < 0$, which means that after the service is migrated, the execution delay can be reduced. We set $rm(;,;,1) = 0$, for which we believe that no migration occurred in the first time slot. We assume that the user's state data and system data are migrated together in the process of service migration without distinction, and the service recovery time is not considered separately. The fixed delay of service migration includes the time to migrate and recover.

The cost of migration mainly includes the consumption of system resources and service placement. This article does not do in-depth study on the cost of migration, and simply describes the cost of migration as a monotonically increasing function of the distance between edge cloud servers:

$$u(x(t), x(t+1), t+1) = \mu(x(t), x(t+1), t+1) \tag{11}$$

$\mu(x(t), x(t+1), t+1)$ is a monotonically increasing function of the distance between the edge cloud server x(t) and the edge cloud server x(t + 1). The greater the distance between two edge cloud servers, the higher the cost of migration.

(4) Problem Formulation. The ultimate goal of this paper is to find a sequence combination of edge cloud servers to minimize the long-term total delay and total cost. The total delay in time slot t can be expressed as,

$$r(x(t-1), x(t), t) = r_c(x(t), t) + r_t(x(t), t) + r_m(x(t-1), x(t), t) \tag{12}$$

The total delay of a sequence combination of edge cloud servers can be get from:

$$R(x) = \sum_{t=1}^{\infty} (r_c(x(t), t) + r_t(x(t), t) + r_m(x(t-1), x(t), t)) \tag{13}$$

The total cost can be calculated from:

$$U(x) = \sum_{t=1}^{\infty} u(x(t-1), x(t), t) \tag{14}$$

The sequence combination problem of edge cloud servers can be formulated as follows:

$$P1: \min_{x(1,2,\dots,\infty)} \{R(x), U(x)\} \qquad x(t) \in C, \forall t \tag{15}$$

However, it is not easy to find the best solution for P1, because it requires all edge server information, user task information, and UPF topology information during user movement. In real life, it is unreasonable to know the dynamic information in advance. Therefore, this paper proposes an online learning algorithm based on the current state to learn and solve the P1 problem.

4 Algorithm

4.1 Markov Decision Process Modeling

The state at time slot t is denoted by $s(t) = \{b(t), x(t)\}$, where $b(t)$ is current base station, $x(t)$ is current edge cloud server. Action $a(s(t)) \in C$ represents the action of selecting a new edge cloud server for state $s(t)$. If the selected edge cloud server does not change, service migration will not occur, but UL CL is dynamically inserted to offload sessions. Policy π is a probability distribution on the action set.

$$\pi(a|s) = \begin{cases} \epsilon & \text{if } a = arg\max_a Q(s,a) \text{ and } Q\text{-table is not } 0 \\ 1 - \epsilon & else \end{cases} \tag{16}$$

An action taken in state $s(t)$ according to policy π will cause the system to transmit to a new state $s(t+1) = s'(t) = \{b(t+1), x(t+1), b\_cpf(t+1), c\_cpf(t+1)\} = a(s(t))$. The immediate reward R_s^a of action $a(s(t))$ is a scalar function of delay and cost. When the delay of service migration is longer, the cost is higher, and the reward value fed back to the agent by the environment is smaller.

$$R_s^a = -\left\{ \omega * \frac{r(x(t-1), x(t), t) - r_{min}}{r_{max} - r_{min}} + (1-\omega) * \frac{u(x(t-1), x(t), t) - u_{min}}{u_{max} - u_{min}} \right\} \tag{17}$$

ω is the proportion factor of delay and cost. From the initial state $s(0)$, the long-term cumulative reward value is,

$$G_\pi(0) = \sum_{k=0}^{T} \gamma^k R_{s(k)}^{a_\pi} \tag{18}$$

where $\gamma \in (0,1)$ is the discount factor that rewards received n steps hence are worth less than rewards received now. T can be infinite. $R_{s(k)}^{a_\pi}$ represents the reward value obtained by taking action a according to π policy in $s(k)$ state. The objective of the service migration problem is to find an optimal policy that maximizes cumulative reward. We denote under a policy π, the state-value function can be expressed as,

$$V_\pi(s) = E\left[\sum_{k=0}^{T} \gamma^k R_{s(k)}^{a_\pi} | s(0) = s\right] \tag{19}$$

Moreover, the optimal state-value function obtained by Bellman Optimality Equation is,

$$V^* = \max_\pi V_\pi(s) \tag{20}$$

4.2   RL-Based Online Service Migration Algorithm

To find the optimal policy of the service migration problem based on the Markov decision process framework, we propose a RL-based online service migration algorithm inspired by the Q-learning algorithm, as shown in Algorithm 1.

Algorithm 1. RL-based Online Service Migration Algorithm

Input: uesr path $l_u(t)$, current base station $b(t)$, current user task $T(d(t), w(t))$, the state of current edge cloud server including the computation intensity and the unfinished computing tasks S, the matrix about distance between edge cloud servers D, the matrix of UPF hops between base station and edge cloude server U, the distribution of core network control plane area CPF
Output: optimal service migaration scheme Q-Table
    for episode=1,2,...n **do**
        $s_0 = \{b(0), x(0), b\_cpf(0), c\_cpf(0)\}, Q = \{0\}$
        while s is not the termination state **do**
            Select a edge cloud server based on ϵ-policy
            Observe s', Predict R
            $Q(s,a) = Q(s,a) + \alpha(R + \gamma \max_{a'} Q(s',a') - Q(s,a)$
            $s = s'$
        end while
    end for

---

5   Experiments and Results

In this section, we will use three benchmark algorithms to make some comparisons with our algorithm. At first, we will introduce the three benchmark algorithms, and then give the comparison results of the algorithms and analyze the results.

5.1 Dataset Description

The user's vehicle travels along a certain path, passing through different base stations and edge servers. In this simulation experiment, we assume that there are 14 base stations and 14 edge servers. Other simulation parameters are as follows,

Simulation parameter	Simulation value
$u_{(i,j)}$	[5, 160]
τ	[0.36, 0.5] ms
d_t	600 MB
w_t	1000 CPU Cycles/bit
$f_{(i,t)}$	600 MB
d_t^q	[50, 100] bits
w_t^q	50 CPU Cycles/bit
tr	300 Mbps
ω	0.5
T_1	[0.5, 1] s
T_2	[1, 2] s
γ_t	5 ms

We compare our algorithm with the other three algorithms:

1) **1-step Look-ahead:** In this algorithm, we consider both delay and cost, and the user always selects the edge server with the minimum delay and cost at the time.
2) **Nearest Edge Server First:** In this algorithm, the user always selects the nearby edge server, ignoring the cost and delay caused by service migration.
3) **Non-UPF Online Algorithm:** The difference between this algorithm and the algorithm proposed in this paper is that UPF delay is not considered.

5.2 Effect of the Computing Intensity of Servers on Reward

In order to study the impact of edge server computing intensity on the online algorithm proposed in this paper, we doubled the computing intensity of the edge server every time.

Figure 2(a) shows that with the increase of edge server computing intensity, the reward value of the algorithm will approach. Because the server's computing power is far greater than the user's needs, the delay has less impact on the algorithm. It can be seen from the figure that the Online algorithm we propose always achieves a better reward.

Figure 2(b) shows that with the increase of UPF transmission delay, the reward value tends to decrease except for the static algorithm Nearest Edge

Server First. The increase of UPF transmission delay will lead to the increase of total delay, thus affecting the value function of delay and cost to influence the service decision. The Online algorithm proposed by us can still obtain better reward value. Obviously, the reward value obtained by the Non-UPF Online algorithm without considering UPF transmission delay will become worse with the increase of UPF transmission delay.

5.3   Effect of UPF Transmission Delay

In order to study the impact of UPF transmission delay on the online algorithm proposed in this paper, we increase the delay of each UPF hop from 4.8 ms to 5 ms, with an increase of 0.02 ms every time. Figure 3(a) shows that with the increase of UPF transmission delay, the algorithm proposed in this paper can effectively reduce the impact of delay, and even select the edge server with greater computing power to reduce the computing delay so as to reduce the total delay. However, the total delay of the Non-UPF algorithm is always larger than that of the algorithm proposed in this paper, because it does not consider the UPF transmission delay in the training process. The delay of Nearest algorithm is always small because it is an algorithm that only considers the delay. The delay of 1-step algorithm is very high because it only considers the delay and cost of each step, and does not consider the optimization of long-term total delay and cost.

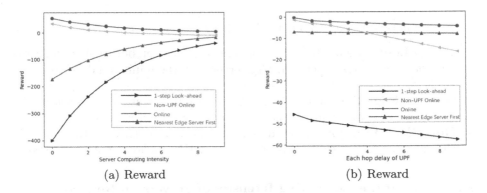

(a) Reward   (b) Reward

Fig. 2. Performance of different algorithms

Figure 3(b) shows that with the increase of each hop delay of UPF, the algorithm proposed in this paper also effectively reduces the impact of cost. The reason why the cost of online algorithm increases when the delay of each hop of UPF increases to 4.9 ms is that the reward model we set up in the training process is a singular function with respect to cost and delay. When the proportion of delay components is large, it is necessary to sacrifice cost to reduce delay. The Non-UPF algorithm is trained without considering the UPF delay, so the factors affecting the delay are small and cost can be smaller. Nearest algorithm only considers the delay, while the assumed UPF hop matrix is a symmetric matrix, and the distance between adjacent servers is equal. Therefore, the cost of Nearest algorithm is almost unchanged with the increase of UPF delay.

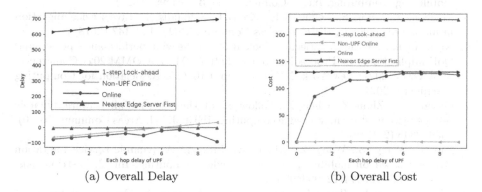

(a) Overall Delay   (b) Overall Cost

Fig. 3. Performance of different algorithms with respect to UPF transmission delay

6   Conclusion

In this paper, we study the service migration decision problem based on the user plane of 5G network, and the purpose is to solve how to select edge cloud servers to execute services during user movement. To reduce the long-term total time delay and total cost in the future, we propose an online algorithm based on reinforcement learning to obtain the optimal strategy for service migration.

The algorithm proposed in this paper takes the transmission delay of 5G user plane and the delay of core domain transformation into account. The simulation results show that the migration decision after considering the UPF transmission delay for training has a certain effect compared with the corresponding migration algorithm in reducing the delay and cost.

In the future, we can further study how the 5G network affects the delay and cost of service migration. Meanwhile, we can consider how to deploy UPF to achieve the best effect of service migration in the 5G MEC application scenarios.

References

1. - Ahmad, M., et al.: A low latency and consistent cellular control plane. In: Proceedings of the Annual Conference of the ACM Special Interest Group on Data Communication on the Applications, Technologies, Architectures, and Protocols for Computer Communication, SIGCOMM 2020, New York, NY, USA, pp. 648–661. Association for Computing Machinery (2020)
2. Chen, W., Chen, Y., Jiaxing, W., Tang, Z.: A multi-user service migration scheme based on deep reinforcement learning and SDN in mobile edge computing. Phys. Commun. **47**, 101397 (2021)

3. Ge, S., Wang, W., Zhang, C., Zhou, X., Zhao, Q.: Multi-user service migration for mobile edge computing empowered connected and autonomous vehicles. In: Qiu, M. (ed.) ICA3PP 2020. LNCS, vol. 12453, pp. 306–320. Springer, Cham (2020). https://doi.org/10.1007/978-3-030-60239-0_21

4. Guo, Y., Jiang, C., Wu, T.Y., Wang, A.: Mobile agent-based service migration in mobile edge computing. Int. J. Commun Syst **34**, e4699 (2021)

5. Machen, A., Wang, S., Leung, K.K., Ko, B.J., Salonidis, T.: Live service migration in mobile edge clouds. IEEE Wireless Commun. **25**(1), 140–147 (2018)

6. Narayanan, A., et al.: A variegated look at 5G in the wild: performance, power, and QoE implications. In: Proceedings of the 2021 ACM SIGCOMM 2021 Conference, SIGCOMM 2021, New York, NY, USA, pp. 610–625. Association for Computing Machinery (2021)

7. Ouyang, T., Zhou, Z., Chen, X.: Follow me at the edge: mobility-aware dynamic service placement for mobile edge computing. IEEE J. Sel. Areas Commun. **36**(10), 2333–2345 (2018)

8. Rui, L., Wang, S., Wang, Z., Xiong, A., Liu, H.: A dynamic service migration strategy based on mobility prediction in edge computing. Int. J. Distrib. Sens. Netw. **17**(2), 1550147721993403 (2021)

9. Wang, S., Guo, Y., Zhang, N., Yang, P., Zhou, A., Shen, X.: Delay-aware microservice coordination in mobile edge computing: a reinforcement learning approach. IEEE Trans. Mob. Comput. **20**(3), 939–951 (2021)

10. Wang, S., Urgaonkar, R., Zafer, M., He, T., Chan, K., Leung, K.K.: Dynamic service migration in mobile edge computing based on Markov decision process. IEEE/ACM Trans. Netw. **27**(3), 1272–1288 (2019)

11. Watkins, C.J.C.H., Dayan, P.: Q-learning. Mach. Learn. **8**, 279–292 (2004). https://doi.org/10.1007/BF00992698

12. Xu, D., et al.: Understanding operational 5G: a first measurement study on its coverage, performance and energy consumption. In: Proceedings of the Annual Conference of the ACM Special Interest Group on Data Communication on the Applications, Technologies, Architectures, and Protocols for Computer Communication, SIGCOMM 2020, New York, NY, USA, pp. 479–494. Association for Computing Machinery (2020)

13. Zhou, P., et al.: 5G MEC computation handoff for mobile augmented reality. ArXiv, abs/2101.00256 (2021)

An Overview of the Internet of Things (IoT) Applications in the Health Sector in Saudi Arabi

Feisal Hadi Masmali[1,2](✉), Shah Jahan Miah[3](✉), and Nasimul Noman[4](✉)

[1] School of Electrical Engineering and Computing, The University of Newcastle, Newcastle, NSW, Australia
feisal.masmali@uon.edu.au
[2] College of Business Administration, Jazan University, Jazan, Saudi Arabia
[3] Newcastle Business School, The University of Newcastle, Newcastle City Campus, Newcastle, NSW, Australia
shah.miah@newcastle.edu.au
[4] School of Information and Physical Sciences, University of Newcastle, Newcastle, NSW, Australia
nasimul.noman@newcastle.edu.au

Abstract. The Internet of Things (IoT) makes it possible for integrating medical information services with multiple sources. Government's information technology solutions often include sensing devices that measure health information in real time. IoT has a significant impact on the healthcare industries by helping to manage medical operations and healthcare such as for reducing effects of chronic diseases. Effective information dissemination could save lives by offering real time information to take certain precautions or by letting doctors know when something alarming happens. Internet of Things (IoT) mobile apps for medical treatment were just released in Saudi Arabia. During the COVID-19 pandemic, people in the country used IoT a lot because it helped doctors keep an eye on patients from far away. A reliable IoT platform makes it easy to connect devices, manage them in bulk through cloud services, and use analytics to make changes. The vast majority of healthcare data is kept in separate places called "silos." It is hoped that one day, Saudi Arabia's new healthcare system will be able to connect patients in different parts of the country. Giving this background, it is important to conduct research to outline a overview of the IoT applications in healthcare for early-career researchers and students who may have benefits of understanding the body of the knowledge trends.

Keywords: IoT · Internet of Things · Healthcare services · Saudi Arabia · Mobile Application · Healthcare innovation

1 Introduction

Most business sectors have profited from the advent of new technologies. The innovation has benefited the health industry. Because technology has become more accessible in various settings, the use of technology in the health sector has become more accessible,

© The Author(s), under exclusive license to Springer Nature Singapore Pte Ltd. 2023
C.-H. Hsu et al. (Eds.): DataCom 2022, LNCS 13864, pp. 547–557, 2023.
https://doi.org/10.1007/978-981-99-2233-8_40

and they may connect. The Internet of Things (IoT) has evolved through time. It has become something that can be implemented in an organization since it can assist with the manner that they help reach particular business objectives. IoT is a relatively new ICT breakthrough that has the potential to improve many areas of business. Many technologies benefit the health care and medical sectors, and the Internet of Things is employed in many different aspects of healthcare service. Consequently, organizations and industries must now adhere to the IoT as one of the essential technological developments to efficiently offer their services.

The Internet of Things has exhibited the trending technology in the information revolution over the past couple of years, and this has occurred over time. The usage of IoT provides the element of a more extensive intelligence network that would guarantee that they link several items and therefore help deploy a number of things on the various platforms. The increased usage of IoT in healthcare has meant that they can plan and offer highly effective approaches that are also entirely sustainable. Most hospitals utilize a variety of healthcare resources that are capable of delivering a variety of services to locations where they are most needed.

The usage of data in IoT is critical. Data is essential for developing IoT systems for the technology to be effective in its application. Big data and data analytics are critical for developing a successful IoT solution in the healthcare industry. This research aims to identify operational areas in the healthcare industry where IoT growth may boost the sector's long-term sustainability. The kind of healthcare services the community offers influences people's economic success and quality of life.

2   Healthcare System Use of IoT

The primary focus of this research is the present level of IoT deployment in Saudi Arabia. Because they may bridge the communication gap between healthcare practitioners and patients, most Internet of Things (IoT) healthcare systems are designed to illustrate and emphasize aspects employed in the nation. As a result, the study focuses heavily on the already accessible technologies in the nation and their applications, advantages, obstacles, and possibilities as they evolve through time. Devices that measure real-time health information are a frequent component of governments' technology solutions.

Today, a broad range of technologies are in use. As a result, this includes a means for tracking patients' information and providing individualized treatment. People and objects can communicate easily to provide a wide variety of services. The computer's administration of the items through the created authentication mechanisms provides the gadgets with a realistic way of providing different types of communication between themselves and humans.

Whereas today's internet links people, IoT connects items. Apps, which are often loaded on mobile devices such as smartphones, act as an interface between the user and the objects, enabling them to effectively perform a range of services [1]. IoT enables the transmission of data and other types of information through a network.

Big data is quickly becoming a valuable tool in the healthcare industry. Because of the wealth of data, health care experts can properly diagnose patients and propose appropriate therapies. The technology for smart gadgets that can provide patient data is already available on the market. Wearable technologies, which measure users' health conditions, are critical for addressing various healthcare challenges.

A comprehensive physical examination is required to detect issues early and tell the appropriate authorities that these individuals need medical assistance. This has considerably assisted healthcare supply to individuals who could not afford it. The extensive deployment of technology in the healthcare industry has become a vital resource for administrative reasons [2]. As a consequence of the Internet of Things, there is a significant likelihood that the availability of these services to the community shall rise.

Healthcare technology integration has grown into a critical component that provides a solid approach to many problems. The Internet of Things has been a game changer wherever there is a demand for highly effective service delivery [3]. Without the assistance of technology, the healthcare business would not have developed to its present position. Healthcare leaders must push for IoT solutions to address various concerns.

The Internet of Things (IoT) is critical for solving various healthcare challenges since it allows medical equipment to connect and conduct multiple analyses. These advancements have made it much simpler to develop treatments. It is critical to have highly efficient strategies for delivering healthcare services using effective technology. IoT significantly influences the healthcare industry by assisting in operations management and lowering chronic disorders. It keeps track of a patient's health and warns medical workers of any unexpected variations by using radio frequency identification tags and the technology of an actual locating system [4]. They benefit from the use of IoT-enabled devices like as glucometers, skin sensors, and health trackers such as wristbands to monitor vitals such as heart rate, blood sugar levels, and oxygen saturation levels. It has the potential to save lives by prescribing particular safeguards or notifying physicians and guardians of any alarming developments. It also supports using "smart shirts" with various sensors to monitor the patient's health and communicate that information to medical personnel.

3 Saudi Healthcare System and IoT Systems

In the 1950s, Saudi Arabia began implementing a hybrid public, private, and government-run healthcare system. The Saudi Arabian Ministry of Health campaigned to change the country's healthcare system that focuses on primary care. Many primary care networks are now connected to regional hospitals around the Kingdom [5]. A referral from a primary care physician is necessary to access high-acuity services at a Ministry of Health facility. More recently, this feature has been severely enforced, increasing service consumption and decreasing total costs.

Primary care in Saudi Arabia has improved dramatically since its start. Indicators of its success include access to vaccines, maternal health, and the control of endemic illnesses. The trade-off includes longer wait times for care, more visits to the emergency department, and more people opting for private healthcare [5]. Patients seeking elective surgeries at a public hospital may have to wait many months, if not an entire year, to be seen. The public often has a negative impression of the Ministry of Health MOH services, ranking them far lower in quality than those offered by private companies or other government healthcare providers.

Conventionally, the Saudi Ministry of Health (MOH) has been the government agency responsible for overseeing all aspects of health care. The breadth of authority granted to the MOH for regulatory purposes is extensive [4]. Pricing and quality controls for medical goods and services are among them. In addition, it distributes national funding for healthcare facilities via state and provincial health departments. But there is a critical distinction in the absence of absolute power. The Saudi Ministry of Health (MOH) does not have control over two major public sector health systems. This contrasts with many other nations where the healthcare ministry is responsible for all aspects of the healthcare system. They don't cover medical centers like those at universities or the military. Not only that, but the Ministry of Health has little influence over the expanding private sector.

College medical centers report directly to the Department of Higher Education and get budgetary support from the Treasury Department. The MOH has competition from the National Guard, the Armed Forces, and the hospitals in the Interior, all of which are directly administered and financed via their ministry budgets. This opens the door for resource diversity and hiring practices [4]. Non-MOH hospitals have far larger budgets per bed, and doctors working at the National Guard Hospital may be paid twice as much as their MOH counterparts. As a result of these factors, patients often assume that non-MOH hospitals offer superior care in terms of medical expertise, convenience, and cutting-edge medical equipment.

The Ministry of Health has the right to determine the price by creating price tiers that are most relevant for private services. Hospitals might have a single fee structure that uses three categories according to the quality of care they provide. Based on this, they can be compensated for private services at the set rates. The MOH also caps maximum medicine prices.

There are many challenges that come to the ministry of health in the country; therefore, the introduction and the use of IoT have helped in several ways. The increasing demand for healthcare services underscores the need to encourage sustainable development within the business. With the assistance of the Internet of Things, which shall be deployed to ensure effective service delivery, a range of issues prevalent in the healthcare sector may be resolved. The quality of life that individuals already lead is an essential factor to consider while attempting to improve their quality of life [6]. Utilizing technology in healthcare is essential to attaining a highly sustainable healthcare sector. This is because using technology in healthcare shall minimize the burden on healthcare facilities and increase the efficiency of different healthcare service providers. If the healthcare business is going to advance in the long term, just like any other industry, it must use technology. Because it is abundantly evident that embracing technology has benefited the medical industry, this sector needs to emphasize doing so.

Due to the quick pace at which the country has industrialized itself over the last four decades, it has not been able to create a sufficient number of medical professionals such as physicians, nurses, and technicians [6]. Even though there has been a considerable increase in educational possibilities available, most of Saudi Arabia's medical professionals and nurses are still not Saudi natives. Despite the most significant efforts of the government, only roughly 17% of Saudi Arabia's overall population is comprised of people who are qualified to work in the healthcare industry.

As a result of this staff turnover, many problems have arisen, the most obvious of which is the expensive equipment that frequently remains unused after departing foreign experts, particularly doctors, because they are required by contract to have it. This is one of the many issues arising from this staff turnover. The workers receiving this kind of salary also get generous time off for vacation and holidays [7]. To recruit and retain skilled medical personnel, hospitals often provide extensive paid leave policies of up to 58 days a year. It is fascinating to learn that many Saudi physicians work for the Ministry of Health and other government institutions. In 2005, the MOH was responsible for the employment of 3,541 Saudi doctors, representing 19% of the country's total medical workforce. In contrast, the private sector was only responsible for employing 5,077 physicians.

The healthcare business is more motivated to acquire and maintain capital equipment on the cutting edge of technological advancement as competition for patients rises. Investing a lot of money into a company's infrastructure may elevate its standing to a higher level [7]. Global budgets for operations and specific equipment allocations may give individual facilities an advantage over the competition by enabling them to acquire high-end items of apparatus without giving any incentive to put them to good use. This may give individual facilities an edge over the competition. There is a possibility that the operational expenses of the service might be lowered, with the savings being put to use in another area.

This is particularly true with institutions with a limited capacity, such as the hospitals run by the Ministry of Health. There is no financial incentive for medical institutions under the Ministry of Health that have access to cutting-edge technology to compete financially with other facilities for patients. The potential for sharing equipment across facilities and industries is hampered significantly by a lack of planning and financial incentives to split the costs of purchasing and maintaining the equipment. Consequently, essential pieces of capital equipment are collecting dust around the Kingdom [8]. The failure of people to pool their resources contributes to the already existing challenges, which are made worse by the lack of educated healthcare workers. Around the world, there is a severe shortage of trained professionals who can operate contemporary machinery. At some places, there may be an excessive number of workers but not enough work for them, while at other locations, there may not be enough staff to run the essential equipment.

The yearly rate of population increase is 3.6%, which is the primary factor contributing to the rise in the cost of medical care. A relatively small percentage of persons over 65 live in the population. Another factor contributing to growing costs is the government's policy of providing free medical care to all Saudi nationals [9] (TechSci Research, 2019). It is expected that both the volume and the intensity of use shall drastically grow due to the absence of any financial risk on the provider's part in providing these services for free.

Nonetheless, consumers' desire for specialist medical services and cutting-edge technology has increased among consumers and their level of understanding of these areas. The dissemination of knowledge and an increase in the demand for specialist medical care have both been facilitated, as they have been in other industrialized countries, by the media and the internet [8, 10]. Despite the significant financial burden it places on providers, consumers continue to prioritize receiving the highest possible level of treatment.

As a result of the growing demand and the slow installation of extra capacity, there are now long lineups for various services and facilities. As a result, the nation has developed beneficial solutions for patients thanks to IoT technologies. Apps for medical treatment developed on the Internet of Things were recently launched in Saudi Arabia in partnership with several clinics and hospitals. Technologies can potentially reduce the costs associated with the prevention and treatment of chronic diseases.

This category includes a wide range of technologies, some examples of which include devices that monitor a patient's health data in real-time as the patient administers their therapy on their own. Smartphone applications are becoming more popular as a means for individuals to monitor their health since an increasing number of individuals now have access to the internet and mobile devices [11]. These mobile applications and devices may be smoothly coupled with telemedicine thanks to the medical Internet of Things (IoT) architecture.

The great majority of the digital breakthroughs in the medical area are included in the IoT. Additionally, it paves the way for developing innovative business models, which, in turn, allow for the introduction of modifications to the medical diagnostic, treatment, and reimbursement processes. These modifications raise the health care providers' productivity and improve patients' quality of care.

It is anticipated that the integration of consumer electronics and mobile applications shall push the digital revolution in healthcare, increasing the interpretations of relevant data in analytics and, as a result, reducing the time required to make decisions. The expected need for personalized health monitoring and preventive treatment has increased due to the expanding population of elderly people worldwide [12]. Wearable technology, made possible by the Internet of Things, might play an essential role in reducing the expensive cost of monitoring patients' health. On the other hand, IoT is used to integrate mobile applications and wearable devices employed in telemedicine.

4   Expenditure of IoT in Healthcare in Saudi Arabia

There is a great increase in the health expenditure that the country has spent, and it has a positive relationship with the country's economy. A country's GDP isn't the only health statistic that rises with time spent in good health, such as life expectancy. Health is vital, but many other non-monetary measures of economic success must also be considered. Society places a premium on longevity and health, and those who work toward these goals are held to very high standards. Second, the likelihood of achieving this goal of living a long and healthy life differs considerably between nations [5]. The Human Development Index not only suggests a link between financial resources and health but also provides concrete evidence of a correlation between an individual's place in income distribution and health outcomes across countries.

This connection between individuals inside each emerging country is the strongest. When comparing the results of growing prosperity and improved health, it is common practice to account for the potential of simultaneous causation [13]. Good health may be a precursor to increased economic development because, for instance, healthy people are more likely to be able to concentrate and get things done at school and work. Organizations and governments can invest more in health improvement programs with more money in the bank. Finally, the cyclical nature of health and wealth is influenced by differences in human capital, technological advancement, and educational and administrative quality among countries [6]. It is also essential to evaluate the dynamic effects included in many potential causal pathways. Investments in public health, for instance, may not see any returns on their production costs for decades. Similarly, a rise in life expectancy may cause a temporary drop in per capita income.

Money well spent may improve people's health. When this happens, people shall begin to see human capital accumulation as a critical factor in fostering economic growth. Increases in healthcare expenditure are likely to have a positive effect on GDP. In the second scenario, rising healthcare prices may lead to an increase in preventive medical care use (such as check-ups, screenings, and other diagnostic procedures), which in turn may increase output in the economy via increased labour and productivity. Both approaches show that healthcare expenditure follows the business cycle of GDP. Nonetheless, research on the fixed effects of the link is necessary.

5   Benefits of the Uses of IoT in Saudi Arabia

During the covid-19 pandemic, the use of IoT in the country became rampant as it could help doctors monitor patients from a distance. Overcrowding in hospitals, threats to the well-being of healthcare professionals, and a general lack of necessary supplies are just some of the severe problems plaguing the healthcare industry. Most of these issues arose from ineffective patient communication, but IoT technology may make it easier to keep tabs on patients. The Internet of Things (IoT) can monitor and gather real-time data and information from sick patients, ensuring that all contaminated patients are isolated and monitored through an online network. The benefits of IoT for the COVID-19 epidemic shall be significantly enhanced if its implementation is effective [3]. The "probability of errors," "provide better therapy," "lower expenditures," "effective control," and "improve patient diagnosis" shall all decrease thanks to this. Not only may infected individuals benefit from this technology, but so can the elderly and those at high risk of acquiring the disease more seriously.

Costs may be reduced, the patient can return to his "regular surroundings," and healthcare providers in different countries and periods can take on less work thanks to remote health and monitoring [14]. It's an annual tragedy in certain nations that they don't have enough money to hire enough doctors and nurses, especially during and following peak sickness seasons. One solution to the increase in chronic illnesses, mainly attributable to the aging population, is telehealth tracking, which is reasonably practical owing to the Internet of Things [15]. Patients in outlying places can benefit significantly from remote health monitoring.

Healthcare stakeholders may benefit from remote health monitoring by analyzing the data collected from these devices and other gadgets [16, 17]. Integrating (extensive) information and analytics, the Internet of Things provides new insight and representations of patterns. Other benefits, therefore, are centered on the fact that it helps increase patient satisfaction. The system also helps reduce the cost f the time and effort put in place in that the quality and services of the number of products increase.

6 Challenges of IoT

This advanced technology should ensure that they enable aspects of it in the following areas.

- A reliable IoT platform makes it easy to connect devices, manage them in bulk via cloud services, and use analytics to get insight and implement change across a whole enterprise.
- Careful device management may increase asset availability, boost productivity, reduce unplanned downtime, and save maintenance costs.
- Data collected by sensors connected to the Internet of Things must be processed and stored intelligently. Cloud data may be accessible using APIs, which serve as the connecting mechanism. All sorts of data from all sorts of data platforms are taken in, and then the most crucial details are extracted using complex analytics.
- Improve your decision-making and the efficacy of your operations with the help of insightful analytics gleaned from vast volumes of data generated by the Internet of Things (IoT). Keep tabs on the present by using real-time analytics and reacting as needed. Use cognitive analytics by integrating it with structured and unstructured data to enhance your ability to understand context, make informed decisions, and respond to changing conditions. Everything is conveniently displayed on an easy-to-read dashboard.
- Administrators can react to alarms and contain incidents happening everywhere in the company from a single place, significantly reducing the potential for damage.

7 The Challenges, Therefore, Fall Under These Two Categories

Difficulties in both the legal and economic systems It's possible that physicians and other medical professionals won't be paid until they actually see patients under the fee-for-service model of reimbursement. This has resulted in a significant bias against the tools that favor online rather than in-person ways of engagement, and this bias has led to significant problems. As we transition away from this paradigm and toward value-based care, a system in which delivery businesses are paid based on their worldwide risk, new technologies that eliminate the need for needless office visits become more economically viable [15]. In this kind of system, face-to-face interactions are seen more as an expense than a potential source of revenue, and the emphasis is shifted toward commending the favourable health results of whole populations.

The Following Are Some Consequences of The Advancement of Technology: The current condition of health data is, however, the most major technological impediment that stands in the way of reaching this aim. Sadly, the vast majority of data pertaining to healthcare is stored in silos. These structures, regardless of how massive they are, are still silos in their core. Communication formats are now the focus of a significant amount of work that is being done in order to facilitate the migration of individual data from one silo to another. However, this does not provide much assistance in solving the issue of data. Those who research and operate in the field of health information exchange are starting to realize that the next generation of health technology shall focus on aggregating data rather than just exchanging copies of patients' individual medical records [6]. It is not possible to fully understand the potential usefulness of the data until it has been collected from a variety of sources, standardized into a common format, and resolved around the identity of specific patients and providers.

8 Conclusion

The growth of the Internet of Things technology has a substantial impact on healthcare infrastructure and contributes to the expansion of healthcare information technology. In spite of this, the Internet of Things (IoT) healthcare systems is one of the most pressing and important difficulties that every nation and its healthcare professionals are progressively facing in the context of the need to develop creative techniques to enhance care protocols and practices. There is a great deal of concern over the impact that the growing expense of medical care shall have on the overall quality of life of individuals, particularly among those who are afflicted with chronic conditions. The Internet of Things is mostly used by the country of Saudi Arabia's healthcare sector. As a result of the broad use of these services, patients are receiving improved care, and they have access to an increased variety of treatment options. The broad availability of wearable sensors and applications that gather data like temperature and blood pressure may greatly help patients. However, this problem might be solved by constructing an Internet of Things platform that allows sensors to transmit data to a centralized server. This shall allow the problem to be sidestepped. In addition, the process of swiftly evaluating a significant quantity of data and the need to expand the amount of equipment are two of the key challenges that arise when conventional applications and IoT systems are combined in the health care field. However, the low cost of the analytics platform, the ever-increasing number of connected devices, and the consistency of the data obtained from the devices might all be factors in increasing the chance of adoption. Cloud computing is a crucial instrument for these kinds of activities because it is the only technology that can store the massive volumes of data that are generated by sensors and other types of equipment in a secure and confidential manner. It is hoped that the Internet of Things (IoT) healthcare system being developed in Saudi Arabia shall one day be able to connect patients who are located in various geographic areas. To effectively coordinate patient care, hospitals and medical practices need to collaborate. A variety of challenges, such as managing data, system capacity, connectivity, standardization, security, and privacy, must be surmounted prior to the broad application of IoT health care.

Because it shall more reliably improve patient health and the quality of treatment that is provided, Internet of Things (IoT) healthcare has a good chance of thriving and doing well in the future in Saudi Arabia. This gives it a reasonable likelihood of succeeding and doing well. The transition to internet-based healthcare shall be managed by the Ministry of Health in conjunction with the administrative leadership of information systems and health informatics departments inside hospitals. It is true that Saudi Arabia's traditional method of providing patient care and a shortage of IoT specialists shall be obstacles to the growth of IoT health care in that country. The majority of people are also not very knowledgeable about the internet of things (IoT) health care or whether or not their data would be secure if it were transferred over the internet. Before medical cities can fully embrace IoT healthcare integration, they shall need to overcome a number of problems first. The subsequent step is to provide the essential services and infrastructure that shall make it possible for IoT to be used in clinical environments. Concerns about the privacy and security of patient data must be taken into consideration, and a backup strategy in case the Internet of Things healthcare system fails must also be developed.

Further research in terms of new IoT oriented solution design can be conduced through adopting design science research methodologies [18–22] in the public healthcare sector in Saudi Arabia. In this case, the impact analysis of IoT application design [23, 24] in other domain can be applicable for initial analysis for articulating case background to setup design research context.

References

1. Qaffas, A.A., Hoque, R., Almazmomi, N.: The Internet of Things and big data analytics for chronic disease monitoring in Saudi Arabia. Telemedicine E-Health (2020). https://doi.org/10.1089/tmj.2019.0289
2. Kruse, C.S., Kothman, K., Anerobi, K., Abanaka, L.: Adoption factors of the electronic health record: a systematic review. JMIR Med. Inform. 4(2), e19 (2016). https://doi.org/10.2196/medinform.5525
3. Radwan, N., Farouk, M.: The growth of Internet of Things (IoT) in the management of healthcare issues and healthcare policy development. Int. J. Technol. Innov. Manag. (IJTIM) 1(1), 69–84 (2021). https://doi.org/10.54489/ijtim.v1i1.8
4. Almalki, M., Fitzgerald, G., Clark, M.: Health care system in Saudi Arabia: an overview. EMHJ - Eastern Mediterr. Health J. 17(10), 784–793 (2011). https://apps.who.int/iris/handle/10665/118216
5. Flores, M., Glusman, G., Brogaard, K., Price, N.D., Hood, L.: P4 medicine: how systems medicine shall transform the healthcare sector and society. Pers. Med. 10(6), 565–576 (2013). https://doi.org/10.2217/pme.13.57
6. Khan, M.A., Quasim, M.T., Algarni, F., Alharthi, A.: Internet of Things: on the opportunities, applications and open challenges in Saudi Arabia. IEEE Xplore, 1 February 2020. https://doi.org/10.1109/AECT47998.2020.9194213
7. Mufti, M.H.: Healthcare Development Strategies in the Kingdom of Saudi Arabia. Springer, New York (2000). https://doi.org/10.1007/b112322. https://books.google.co.ke/books?hl=en&lr=&id=8h-YENxCRYUC&oi=fnd&pg=PA1&dq=+HEALTH+SECTOR+IN+SAUDI+ARABIA&ots=YD_2ELu2eQ&sig=XU0WqETO_VwpO1jnEJbaaRvs_Bs&redir_esc=y#v=onepage&q=HEALTH%20SECTOR%20IN%20SAUDI%20ARABIA&f=false
8. Alonazi, W.B., Altuwaijri, E.A.: Health policy development during COVID-19 in Saudi Arabia: mixed methods analysis. Front. Public Health 9 (2022). https://doi.org/10.3389/fpubh.2021.801273
9. TechSci Research: Saudi Arabia Internet of Things (IoT) Market Size, Share, Growth & Forecast 2027. TechSci Research (2019). www.techsciresearch.com. https://www.techsciresearch.com/report/saudi-arabia-internet-of-things-iot-market/7663.html
10. Aghdam, A.R., Watson, J., Cliff, C., Miah, S.J.: Improving theoretical understanding towards patient-driven healthcare innovation: online value co-creation perspective: a systematic review. J. Med. Internet Res. 22(4), e16324 (2020). https://doi.org/10.2196/16324
11. Said, O., Masud, M.: Towards Internet of Things: survey and future vision. Int. J. Comput. Netw. (IJCN) 5(1), 1–17 (2013). https://cs.brown.edu/courses/csci2270/archives/2017/papers/Towards_Internet_of_Things_Survey_and_Fu.pdf

12. Ru, L., et al.: A detailed research on human health monitoring system based on Internet of Things. Wirel. Commun. Mob. Comput. **2021**, e5592454 (2021). https://doi.org/10.1155/2021/5592454

13. Otaibi, M.N.A.: Internet of Things (IoT) Saudi Arabia healthcare systems: state-of-the-art, future opportunities and open challenges. J. Health Inform. Dev. Countries **13**(1) (2019). https://jhidc.org/index.php/jhidc/article/view/234

14. Ashton, K.: That "Internet of Things" thing in the real world, things matter more than ideas (2002). http://www.itrco.jp/libraries/RFIDjournal-That%20Internet%20of%20Things%20Thing.pdf

15. Zanella, A., Bui, N., Castellani, A., Vangelista, L., Zorzi, M.: Internet of Things for smart cities. IEEE Internet Things J. **1**(1), 22–32 (2014). https://doi.org/10.1109/jiot.2014.2306328

16. Fadlullah, Z.M., Pathan, A.-S., Singh, K.: Smart grid Internet of Things. Mob. Netw. Appl. **23**(4), 879–880 (2017). https://doi.org/10.1007/s11036-017-0954-2

17. Masmali, F., Miah, S.J.: Internet of Things adoption for Saudi healthcare services. Pac. Asia J. Assoc. Inf. Syst. **13**(3), 6 (2021)

18. Fahd, K., Miah, S.J., Ahmed, K.: Predicting student performance in a blended learning environment using learning management system interaction data. Appl. Comput. Inform. (2021). https://doi.org/10.1108/ACI-06-2021-0150

19. Fahd, K., Miah, S.J., Ahmed, K., Venkatraman, S., Miao, Y.: Integrating design science research and design based research frameworks for developing education support systems. Educ. Inf. Technol. **26**(4), 4027–4048 (2021). https://doi.org/10.1007/s10639-021-10442-1

20. Miah, S.J.: An ontology based design environment for rural decision support. Unpublished Ph.D. thesis, Griffith Business School, Griffith University, Brisbane, QLD, Australia (2008)

21. Miah, S.J.: A new semantic knowledge sharing approach for e-government systems. In: The Proceedings of the 4th IEEE International Conference on Digital Ecosystems and Technologies, Duabi, UAE (2010)

22. Miah, S.J., McKay, J.: A new conceptualisation of design science research for DSS development. In: The Proceedings of the 20th Pacific Asia Conference on Information Systems (PACIS 2016), Taiwan (2016)

23. Shee, S., Miah, S.J., de Vass, T.: Impact of smart logistics on smart city sustainable performance: an empirical investigation. Int. J. Logist. Manag. **32**(3), 821–845 (2021)

24. de Vass, T., Shee, H., Miah, S.J.: IoT in supply chain management: opportunities and challenges for businesses in early industry 4.0 context. Oper. Supply Chain Manag. Int. J. **14**(2), 148–161 (2021)

Author Index

C.-H. Hsu et al. (Eds.): DataCom 2022, LNCS 13864, pp. 559–560, 2023.
https://doi.org/10.1007/978-981-99-2233-8